THE LONG EIGHTH CENTURY

THE TRANSFORMATION OF THE ROMAN WORLD

A SCIENTIFIC PROGRAMME OF THE EUROPEAN SCIENCE FOUNDATION

Coordinators

JAVIER ARCE · EVANGELOS CHRYSOS · IAN WOOD

Series Editor

IAN WOOD

VOLUME 11

THE LONG EIGHTH CENTURY

THE LONG EIGHTH CENTURY

BY

INGE LYSE HANSEN

AND

CHRIS WICKHAM

BRILL

LEIDEN · BOSTON · KÖLN

2000

This book is printed on acid-free paper.

Library of Congress Cataloging-in-Publication Data

The Long eighth century : production, distribution and demand / edited by
Inge Lyse Hansen and Chris Wickham.
    p. cm. — (Transformation of the Roman world, ISSN 1386–4165
  ; v. 11)
  Includes index.
  ISBN 9004117237 (alk. paper)
  1. Europe—Economic conditions—To 1492- 2. Cities and towns—Europe-
—History—To 1500. 3. Commerce—History—To 1500. I. Title: Long 8th century.
II. Hansen, Inge Lyse. III. Wickham, Chris, 1950- IV. Series.
HC240 .L597 2000
330.94'01—dc21
                                             00–064167
                                             CIP

Die Deutsche Bibliothek - CIP-Einheitsaufnahme
The long eighth century / by Inge Lyse Hansen and Chris Wickham. –
Leiden ; Boston ; Köln : Brill, 2000
  (The transformation of the Roman world ; Vol. 11)
  ISBN 90–04–11723–7

ISSN 1386–4165
ISBN 90 04 11723 7

PRINTED IN THE NETHERLANDS

CONTENTS

LIST OF ILLUSTRATIONS

INTRODUCTION

Chris Wickham

The sixth century, edited by Richard Hodges and William Bowden (Leiden, 1998) was the first product of the collective work of Group 3 of the 1993-8 European Science Foundation project, The Transformation of the Roman World. We initially intended it to be the first of three volumes on "Production, distribution and demand" with a second on the seventh century and a third on the eighth-ninth. In the end, however, we opted for a single volume as our post-Roman reference point, focussed on the eighth century, or, rather, the "long" eighth century of 680-830, a period which seemed to us to have both a general homogeneity and a long enough span to allow for the pinning down of differences. The memory of the intermediate period, 600-80, has not entirely left us: Simon Loseby, in particular, has written his article in this volume as a sequel to his sixth-century article, which enforces consideration of the seventh century; and of course several others have used that century as a starting-point for their analyses. All the same, the eighth century is in the foreground in this book. After an introductory chapter by John Moreland on current problems in the theory of exchange, we move roughly from North to South, beginning in Denmark and ending in Syria-Palestine. Our aim throughout has been to illustrate the problems of eighth-century production, distribution and demand in each region as a separate entity, which has to be seen in its own terms, not those of other regions and centuries. Comparative issues are, however, picked up in the conclusion. We intended, when planning this book, to use the eighth century as the focus for a discussion of what one might call the "post-transformation" period, so that we could see what had actually changed, in production, distribution and demand, after the definitive end of the Roman world-system. We think and hope that some of this aim has been achieved.

We have pursued this theme for five years of our lives, in (roughly) twice-yearly meetings located all across Europe and the Mediterranean, in Birka, Tunis, Mérida, Lausanne, S. Vincenzo al Volturno, Strasbourg, Ribe, Isernia, Istanbul and, finally, Utrecht. Until Isernia in 1997, our group leader was Richard Hodges; when he had to bow out, I took over, with the remit of guiding the present book to completion. The group itself gradually changed composition, and in fact only four of the contributors to this volume were there at the start; furthermore, our two eastern Mediterranean contributors, John Haldon and Alan Walmsley, were invited at a late stage and did not come to group meetings at all. But it has to be said that the slow evolution of the membership of the group did not upset the unity and cumulative nature of its deliberations; like George Washington's axe, it maintained its identity throughout. Much of the credit for this is due to the charisma of Richard Hodges' leadership, and the quality and intensity of his *Problemstellung*; I feel that my role has simply been to routinise Richard's charisma in the two years following. The rest of the credit is due to the group members themselves, who kept their eye on the main issues throughout, and whose collective discussions never failed to leave each of us feeling enthusiastic about returning to work on the project as we caught the flights home. The ESF project indeed fully succeeded in one of its primary tasks, to create an international community of scholars, which has continued to exchange ideas, and will—I hope and expect—go on doing so.

Participators in this book also included four scholars who had to withdraw at the final stages, for various reasons, Sonia Gutiérrez, Federico Marazzi, Paolo Delogu and Leslie Brubaker. Their contributions will be greatly missed by readers. It must be said, nonetheless, that the drafts they presented to the group sessions, and their active contributions to group discussions, inform the intellectual framing of the book quite as much as do the contributions that made it to press. We owe much of the group's cohesion to them too.

I would also like to thank Vuokko Lepistö-Kirsilä for her calm and constructive direction at the ESF end when I began my tenure of Group 3 leadership, Julian Deahl of Brill for his similar calm and helpfulness at the editorial end, Marios Costambeys for his able translations of two articles, and my co-editor Inge Lyse Hansen for picking up *all* the slack.

Birmingham
November 1999

CONCEPTS OF THE EARLY MEDIEVAL ECONOMY

John Moreland

economic wants are . . . culturally determined, and it is only some form
of anthropology which holds out the hope of providing that sociological explanation of economic life which the economic interpretation of
social life has come to require.[1]

Introduction

The title of working group 3—*Production, Distribution and Demand*—of
the European Science Foundation's *Transformation of the Roman World*
Project, highlights those "processes" which most archaeologists and
historians would agree are central to the economy of societies, past
and present.[2] Study of the precise ways in which these processes
functioned, and of the specific nature of the interactions between
them, should *in theory* provide an understanding of specific economies.
Comparison of such moments should, *in theory*, enable us to construct
an overview of infrastructural transformation across time.[3] However,
several factors, apart from the problem of recovering the relevant
data, have prevented historians and archaeologists from reaching a
real understanding of how specific economies functioned in the
past, and from appreciating the significance of their transformation.

---

[1] K. Thomas, "History and anthropology", *Past and Present* 24 (1963), pp. 3-27,
at p. 7.
[2] Several members of the group (myself included) believed that the theme title
should have been "Production, Distribution and Consumption", both to reflect past
reality, and to avoid the "economistic" implications of the word "demand".
[3] This is leaving aside the question of whether the "economy" can ever be understood apart from the other structures of society. This matter has been much debated
within archaeology – see for example, I. Hodder, *Reading the Past. Current Approaches
to Interpretation in Archaeology* (Cambridge, 1986), pp. 18-33 – but here I would like
to summarise the feelings of many by continuing the quotation from Sir Keith
Thomas with which this chapter opens – "One of the great anthropological lessons
is that the study of economics cannot be isolated from the study of society. 'In a
primitive society there is no relationship which is of a purely economic character'"
("History and Anthropology", p. 7).

Of these, I would argue, one of the most debilitating has been our tendency to see the past as Same (a primitive version of our present, which teleologically evolves into it) or as Other (as a remote, alien, fundamentally *different*, world).[4] Both "visions", as monolithic perceptions, impose uniformity on a variegated past and thereby obscure rather than reveal.[5]

When we write histories of the Same, wittingly or unwittingly we transpose the values and *mores* of our world onto theirs, we write our world into theirs, and thereby destroy them. When we write of the past as Other, the qualities of that Otherness are frequently simply the antitheses of the Same emphasised to construct the *difference* of the past.[6] The Same (Us, Our world) is thus implicit in its absence. In constructing and emphasising that difference, we run the risk of simplifying and romanticising the past and of losing track of those elements which *do* link it to the present. Further, as Mayke de Jong points out, the construction of radical difference leads to a "self-defeating epistemological stance". For if past modes of thinking are entirely different from our own, we no longer have a basis for understanding "what the hell they thought they were up to".[7] I would

---

[4] Although now in common usage, I derive the terms Same and Other from P. Ricoeur, *The Reality of the Historical Past* (Milwaukee, 1984); see J. Moreland, *Archaeology, History and Theory: Settlement Patterns and Social Relations in Central Italy A.D. 700-1000*, unpublished Ph.D. thesis, University of Sheffield 1988. The essence of the problem, as Nicholas Thomas notes, is that "on one side we fail to recognize what is different in other social regimes; on the other we tend to make radical alterity out of partial or contingent difference" – *Entangled Objects. Exchange, Material Culture and Colonialism in the Pacific* (Cambridge, MA., 1991), p. 34.

[5] For a general consideration of the middle ages as Same and Other, see M. de Jong, "The foreign past. Medieval historians and cultural anthropology", *Tijdschrift voor Geschiedenis* 109 (1996), pp. 326-42. R. Balzaretti, "Reply 1 to J.R. Maddicott's "Trade, industry and the wealth of king Alfred", *Past and Present* 135 (1992), p. 142, is in no doubt about the Otherness of the early middle ages – "In the course of their work all historians . . . have to engage in the struggle to express the essential strangeness of the past. For those who study the early medieval West the task is especially hard, for this strangeness *Otherness* is to be found wherever one looks. . . . Statistics and graphs have to be left behind, and instead we have to imagine, as Karl Polanyi did, an economy (or rather economies) which operated in ways very different from those we in the modern West are most familiar with". For contemporary (medieval) constructions of the Other, see P. Freedman, *Images of the Medieval Peasant* (Stanford, 1999).

[6] Ricoeur, *Reality of the Historical Past*, pp. 14-24; J. Moreland, "Through the looking glass of possibilities: understanding the middle ages", in H. Hundsblicher, G. Jaritz and T. Kühtreiber eds., *Die Vielfalt der Dinge. Neue Wege zur Analyse mittelalterlicher Sachkultur* (Vienna, 1998), pp. 85-116, at pp. 105-109; Thomas, *Entangled Objects*, pp. 10, 34; de Jong, "The foreign past", pp. 335, 341.

[7] de Jong, "The foreign past", p. 335.

argue that it is only when we recognise that conceptions of the early medieval economy have veered from one extreme to the other, and have thereby overwritten the past, that we can begin to sail between this Scylla and Charybdis and begin the construction of something which approaches "the reality of the historical past".

A brief historiography of the Early Medieval economy[8]

Autarky and the market

One hundred years ago, Patrick Geary tells us, the early middle ages were characterised as having a "'natural economy', in which barter and payment in kind were the normal means of exchange".[9] This was a radically "different" world from that of the late nineteenth century. This Otherness was largely supplanted, in the course of the first sixty years of the twentieth century, by the construction of societies in which the early medieval peasant bought and sold land, paid tolls and dues and participated in markets—all through the use of coinage. This change in perception was not just a product of historical and archaeological research, although documents did provide examples of the many contexts in which coins were used,[10] while archaeology uncovered "coin hoards . . . that contain moneys minted at places thousands of kilometres distant".[11] As important in this construction of the medieval economy as Same was the desire to provide a precocious early development for present national economies. Thus

> a generation of historians . . . began to revise the image of the commercial world of the early Middle Ages and to present a picture of a rudimentary but nonetheless important commercial structure tying

---

[8] In what follows, many of the examples will be drawn from Anglo-Saxon England, since this is the area I am currently researching. However, as the examples quoted from other areas of Europe should make clear, the patterns I outline have a wider relevance.

[9] P. Geary, "Sacred commodities: the circulation of medieval relics", in P. Geary, *Living with the Dead in the Middle Ages* (Ithaca, 1994), pp. 194-218 at p. 195. The concept of the "natural economy" was first formulated by Bruno Hildebrand in 1864 – M. Bloch, "Natural economy or money economy? A false dilemma", in S. Thrupp ed., *Early Medieval Society* (New York, 1967), p. 196 (originally published as "Economie de nature ou économie d'argent . . .", *Annales d'Histoire Sociale* 11 (1939).

[10] See, for example, Bloch, "Natural economy", p. 200.

[11] Geary, "Sacred Commodities", p. 197.

together the lands between the Mediterranean and the North Sea, a structure that differed from that of later medieval trade *more in organisation than in volume or nature*.[12]

Until very recently, the underlying belief that essentially the Same patterns of economic behaviour link the modern world with the middle ages permeated most histories. Thus in Henry Loyn's 1962 discussion of the Anglo-Saxon economy he maintains that the significant processes were indigenous, with overseas trade presented as an "exotic"; the origins of towns too, by and large, had their source in internal developments.[13] Central to economic development was the appearance in the late seventh century of the *sceatta* silver coinage which was used to mediate the limited overseas trade (in slaves, textiles and wine), principally with the Frisians.[14] Internally, the rural economy was largely, but not completely, self-sufficient. Whatever exchange there was—in metals, salt, textiles, and ordinary agricultural surplus—was mediated through coinage, especially after Offa's late eighth century coin reforms.[15] Despite the preponderance of production for use, Loyn rejects the idea that the Anglo-Saxon economy should be seen as an autarkic or "natural economy"—"it is certain that money was *in general use* for the last four centuries of Anglo-Saxon England".[16] The existence of the *sceattas* and the later silver pennies "implies a steady demand throughout the small local markets of England. They were markets in a community whose *chief medium of exchange was minted money*".[17]

Robert Latouche provides a very similar picture of a ninth century European economy articulated through coinage and markets.[18] His is an image of a world dominated by Charlemagne "the economic planner", reforming the monetary system through the imposition of a new, universal silver coinage; a currency which allowed people to buy basic commodities (bread, meat, salt) in the local markets; markets which were both profuse and weekly; had been "cleaned

---

[12] Geary, "Sacred Commodities", p. 197; emphasis added.
[13] H.R. Loyn, *Anglo-Saxon England and the Norman Conquest* (London, 1962), pp. 66, 92, 100.
[14] Loyn, *Anglo-Saxon England*, pp. 82-89; 119.
[15] Loyn, *Anglo-Saxon England*, pp. 114-20.
[16] Loyn, *Anglo-Saxon England*, pp. 116-17, emphasis added.
[17] Loyn, *Anglo-Saxon England*, p. 120, emphasis added.
[18] R. Latouche, *The Rebirth of Western Economy. Economic Aspects of the Dark Ages* (London, 1981), (originally published as *Les Origines de l'Economie Occidentale* (Paris, 1956)).

up" by Charlemagne's energetic standardisation of weights and measures; and in them "goods from distant parts" were sold alongside local products.[19] Latouche is adamant that this was not a capitalist economy, but one organised on "sound Christian morals", and "made in a vast Empire, which could be entirely self-sufficient".[20] It is interesting to note that the concept of self-sufficiency is here transferred from household to empire, but the abiding image is of buying, selling and markets.

Here we have constructions of the early medieval economy in which money and markets mediate the flow from production to consumption. In these economies of the Same any possibility of Other ways of organising production, distribution and consumption is firmly denied through the outright rejection of the "natural economy", and through Loyn's polite dismissal of Philip Grierson's attempt to focus our attention on "gift-exchanges, tribute, and even plunder rather than . . . free trade".[21]

Grierson and the Gift

For Geary, Grierson's 1959 article constituted "an important warning" of the possibility that historians and archaeologists were being misled by the "commercial histories" of the middle ages.[22] Grierson explicitly rejected the notion that early medieval commerce was simply a less highly organised version of that found in later periods, and argued that the evidence perceived as indicative of *trade* might in fact have been the product of Other mechanisms for the movement of goods, Other forces integrating and articulating the economy.[23]

At the most basic level Grierson's image of the early medieval economy is similar to Loyn's—production for use with the localised

---

[19] Latouche, *Rebirth of Western Economy*, pp. 148-51; 152; 158-59; 160. J.R. Maddicott, "Trade, industry and the wealth of King Alfred", *Past and Present* 123 (1989), pp. 3-51, has attributed similar economic foresight and intentionality to the West Saxon king. See the comments on Maddicott's thesis by R. Balzaretti, *Past and Present* 135 (1992), pp. 142-50; J. Nelson, *Past and Present* 135 (1992), pp. 151-63; and Maddicott's "Reply", *Past and Present* 135 (1992), pp. 164-88.

[20] Latouche, *Rebirth of Western Economy*, p. 173.

[21] Loyn, *Anglo-Saxon England*, p. 79. For Grierson's arguments, see below pp. 5–8 and note 31.

[22] Geary, "Sacred Commodities", p. 197; P. Grierson, "Commerce in the Dark Ages: a critique of the evidence", *Transactions of the Royal Historical Society* (5th series) 9 (1959), pp. 123-40.

[23] Grierson, "Commerce in the Dark Ages", p. 124.

exchange of subsistence products "when all else failed", when the "natural, and "universal" goal of self-sufficiency was thwarted.[24] Above, and largely divorced from this, goods circulated through gift-exchange and, its inverse, theft, with "a varied series of payments, such as ransoms, compensations, . . . fines, . . . dowries, the wages of mercenaries, property carried to and fro by political exiles" being seen in the same light.[25]

The advocacy of an essential autarky and of a higher level system of gift-exchange certainly renders Grierson's early medieval economy as Other than that presented by Loyn; the minimisation of money and the market as the principal media for structuring exchange effectively removes those economic forces which, in the work of the latter, teleologically connect past and present. However, in at least one crucial respect Grierson and Loyn share a common understanding—that the forces for change in the early medieval economy are to be found at the level of exchange. I have already noted Loyn's emphasis on the transformational effects of the *sceattas* and Offan pennies (above p. 4). Grierson appears to attribute a similar efficacy to gift-exchange. Thus he argues that the exchange of luxury goods, "the taste for spices and the charm of luxuries", by the *mercatores* "injected the element of a profit motive into a society so organized as to exclude it from many aspects of its daily life".[26] In this context, the apparent belief in the transformational power of gift-exchange between elites is reinforced by Grierson's appreciative quotation from Richard Southern's *The Making of the Middle Ages* (London, 1953)—"the activities and organization [of exchange] which existed to satisfy the demands of the relatively few coloured the whole history of the Middle Ages".[27]

What is also noteworthy about Grierson's account of "commerce in the Dark Ages" is that there is no attempt to articulate the proposed systems of exchange with those of production. As I have already noted, he bracketed production for use with localised exchange; but within his model this production and this exchange are almost epiphenomenal. No connection is made with the circulation of goods via

---

[24] Grierson, "Commerce in the Dark Ages", p. 128.
[25] Grierson, "Commerce in the Dark Ages", p. 131. In the light of later discussion (see below, p. 9 and note 38) it is interesting to note that Grierson believed these to be *survivals* into the early middle ages of a "primitive Germanic pattern" (pp. 137, 133).
[26] Grierson, "Commerce in the Dark Ages", p. 126.
[27] Grierson, "Commerce in the Dark Ages", p. 126.

gift-exchange, either in terms of the impact of the latter on these more localised systems; or in terms of the transformation of systems of production to meet the "needs" of gift-exchange. Indeed he explicitly argues that there are good reasons for keeping the two spheres separate.[28]

It is also significant that Grierson pays little or no attention, at an analytical level, to the gifts themselves, to the objects exchanged. Despite his work with coins and his reputation as "England's leading numismatist",[29] it may be that Grierson did not share the archaeologist's predilection for reading meaning from material culture. His infamous comment on the vocality of archaeological evidence would suggest that this was the case—"the archaeological evidence . . . in its very nature substitutes inference for explanation. It has been said that the spade cannot lie, but it owes this merit to the fact that it cannot even speak".[30] Perhaps it was felt that the materiality of such objects renders interpretation unnecessary—they just are, their meaning and "function" are self-evident. As we shall see, the absence of detailed consideration of the kinds of objects exchanged is not unique to Grierson's short paper, and others have less excuse than he for the omission (see below). Like others, Grierson appears to have been more interested in the (undoubtedly important) social and political consequences of gift-exchange, but as I will suggest later the *kinds* of gifts exchanged played an important part in the construction and reproduction of such relationships.[31] Finally, Grierson pays no attention to the *production* of gifts.

The above critique is unfair but necessary. It is unfair since Grierson's short paper was devoted to a particular theme—warning of the dangers of "commercial histories". He was not in a position to address many of themes which I have outlined above, especially since many of them only became of critical concern to archaeologists

---

[28] Grierson, "Commerce in the Dark Ages", p. 127. He does not actually tell us what these "good reasons" are. We should also note that in the quote from Southern, the latter does appear to recognise some of the effects of "the taste for spices and the charm of luxuries" on systems of production – "it was to satisfy this taste . . . that peasants raised the numbers of their sheep".

[29] Geary, "Sacred Commodities", p. 197.

[30] Grierson, "Commerce in the Dark Ages", p. 129.

[31] Grierson's interest can perhaps be summed up in the following – "[the] mutual exchange of gifts at first sight resembles commerce, but its objects and ethos are entirely different. Its object is not that of material and tangible 'profit' . . . rather it is the social prestige attached to generosity, to one's ability and readiness to lavish one's wealth on one's neighbours and dependents. The profit consists in placing other people morally in one's debt" ("Commerce in the Dark Ages", p. 137).

and anthropologists in the years after 1959. The critique is, however, necessary, since Grierson's paper has been influential in steering perceptions of early medieval economies from Same to Other. As such its concerns, and its omissions, played a significant role in creating the kind of Other early medieval economy which, for many, now exists. Before outlining the latter, however, we should consider a text which, both directly and indirectly (via Grierson amongst others), contributed to the construction of this alterity.

Marcel Mauss

In writing his seminal paper, Philip Grierson was quite clearly influenced by Marcel Mauss' classic anthropological study of gift-exchange, produced more than thirty years previously.[32] One of Mauss' primary objectives in this work was to deny the existence, anywhere, of "natural economy", and the universality of impersonal and "economically rational" market exchange.[33] He had detected in the contemporary social welfare programmes of England and France the beginnings of a return to anOther society, to an "old and elemental" world structured through the social relationships which were consequential upon the "total prestations" of gift-exchange.[34] Mauss took as his point of departure the contention that Man had only recently become "an economic animal . . . a machine, a calculating machine". In the past, before the transformation into *homo œconomicus*, Man was "something quite different".[35] Then exchanges involved

> not exclusively . . . things of economic value. They exchange rather courtesies, entertainments, ritual, military assistance, women, children, dances, and feasts; and fairs in which the market is but one element and the circulation of wealth but one part of a wide and enduring contract.[36]

---

[32] M. Mauss, *The Gift. Forms and Functions of Exchange in Archaic Societies* (New York, 1967, orig. publ. 1925). For the influence, see Grierson, "Commerce in the Dark Ages", p. 137, n. 1; G. Astill, "Archaeology, economics, and early medieval Europe", *Oxford Journal of Archaeology* 4 (1985), pp. 215-31 at p. 220.

[33] Mauss, *The Gift*, p. 3.

[34] Mauss, *The Gift*, pp. 66-68. For the contemporary social context in which Mauss developed his ideas, see M. Godelier, *The Enigma of the Gift* (Cambridge, 1999), pp. 4-5, 62-64, 75.

[35] Mauss, *The Gift*, p. 74.

[36] Mauss, *The Gift*, p. 3.

Then the exchange of goods was "not a mechanical but a *moral* transaction, bringing about and maintaining human, personal, relationships between individuals and groups".[37] Many such "embedded" exchanges took place through the medium of *the gift*.

Mauss constructed his concept of gift-exchange from readings on the anthropology of the *potlatch* of north-west America and the *kula* exchange systems of the Trobriand Islands, and from the history of the early Germans, Romans and Hindus.[38] In essence, he argued that gift-exchange was characterised by three obligations—the obligation to give; the obligation to receive; and the obligation to repay. The *giving* of gifts to others demonstrates the power of the donor; a chief can only maintain his authority if he can show that he is favoured by the spirits, and this can only be done by being seen to be able to give lavishly.[39] The *receiving* of gifts puts the recipient in the "moral debt" of the donor. It creates a relationship of subordination. Unwillingness to receive, like the inability to give, results in loss of dignity.[40] Hence the obligation to *repay*. Failure to repay, at the appropriate time and in an appropriate manner, reproduces the social relationship of subordination. It was impossible to avoid getting into "social debt" by refusing a gift, since "face is lost for ever if . . . *"worthy return"* is not made".[41]

---

[37] E. Evans-Pritchard, "Introduction", in M. Mauss, *The Gift: Forms and Functions of Exchange in Archaic Societies* (New York: 1967), p. ix.

[38] See Godelier, *Enigma of the Gift*, p. 73; Thomas, *Entangled Objects*, p. 17. Given the role of Germanic "peoples" in the construction of the kingdoms of the early middle ages, and Grierson's belief that early medieval gift-exchange was a relic of a "primitive Germanic pattern", Mauss' observations on the "economy" of early Germanic society assume a particular relevance here – "Germanic societies . . . had . . . a clearly developed system of exchange with gifts voluntarily and obligatorily given, received and repaid. *Few systems were so typical.*" – "Germanic civilization, too, was a long time without markets. It remained essentially feudal and peasant; the notion and even the terms of price, purchase and sale seem to be of recent origin. In earlier times it had developed the potlatch and more particularly the system of gift exchange to an extreme degree. Clans within tribes, great extended families within clans, tribes within themselves, chiefs and even kings, were not confined morally and economically to the closed circles of their own groups; and links, alliances and mutual assistance came into being by means of the pledge, the hostage and the feast or other acts of generosity" (Mauss, *The Gift*, p. 59, emphasis added; also pp. 24-25).

[39] Mauss, *The Gift*, p. 37.

[40] Mauss, *The Gift*, p. 40.

[41] Mauss, *The Gift*, p. 41. This very brief summary of Mauss' arguments on gift-exchange can be supplemented by the discussion of C. Gosden, "Debt, production, and prehistory", *Journal of Anthropological Archaeology* 8 (1989), pp. 355-87. For an

The essential point about this process of giving, receiving and repaying is that through it a series of *personal* social relationships are created; relationships which anthropologists and archaeologists usually contrast with the impersonality of monetary exchange (see below). However, the "intimacy" of the relationships does not imply any necessary egalitarianism. Through the creation of "social debt", this process structured and reproduced social hierarchies. Nor was the process consensual. Mauss makes frequent reference to the fact that although gifts are theoretically given voluntarily, in reality the process is obligatory.[42] Lying behind this obligation is the sanction of "private or open warfare". Refusal to give or receive a gift is "the equivalent of a declaration of war"; not returning a gift can by avenged through the invocation of magic, by invoking the power of the gift to destroy the person who has received it. The "war of property" which is the potlatch is coupled with "armed hostilities" in the reproduction of social hierarchy.[43] More positively, gifts (to men and gods) buy peace, and through this form of intercourse people substitute "alliance, gift and commerce for war, isolation and stagnation. . . . In order to trade, man must first lay down his spear".[44] As Marshall Sahlins notes, for Mauss "the gift is Reason. It is the triumph of human rationality over the folly of war".[45]

This system, although fundamentally *different* from ours, was seen to provide the logic for some of the most extensive movements of products in the non-capitalist world—e.g. the Trobriand Island system. Mauss, and later Karl Polanyi and George Dalton, emphasised the essential *Otherness* of these forms of exchange, *not their inferiority* to some supposedly rational economic standard.[46] In fact, as we shall see, their Otherness was created in and through their antithesis to this "rationality".

---

elaboration on Mauss' suggestion that gift-exchange takes various forms, see Godelier, *Enigma of the Gift*. See also, C. Gregory, *Gifts and Commodities* (Cambridge, 1982).

[42] Mauss sums it us as follows – "prestations . . . are in theory voluntary, disinterested and spontaneous, but are in fact obligatory and interested. The form usually taken is that of the gift generously offered; but the accompanying behaviour is formal pretence and social deception" (*The Gift*, p. 1).

[43] Mauss, *The Gift*, pp. 3, 24, 8, 35.

[44] Mauss, *The Gift*, pp. 14, 80.

[45] M. Sahlins, *Stone Age Economics* (London, 1974), p. 175.

[46] K. Polanyi, "The economy as instituted process", in K. Polanyi, C. Arensberg, and H. Pearson eds., *Trade and Market in Early Empires* (Glencoe, Illinois, 1957), pp. 243-69; G. Dalton, "Aboriginal economies in stateless societies", in T. Earle and J. Ericson eds., *Exchange Systems in Prehistory* (New York, 1977), pp. 191-212.

Mauss and the Middle Ages

At the conclusion of his discussion of the mechanisms through which objects were moved over distance, Philip Grierson asserted that "much evidence alleged to 'prove' the existence of trade proves nothing of the kind". Instead he suggests that "in any picture we might make of exchange in the early Middle Ages, the phenomenon of gift and counter-gift must be allowed a conspicuous place".[47] Georges Duby too was indebted to Mauss for his understanding of the early medieval economy. In the specific context of gift-exchange, he refers to Mauss as "one of the great masters of ethnology",[48] and while, like Grierson, he detects a leaning towards self-sufficiency",[49] he also argues that

> a considerable proportion of what was produced was drawn into *the heavy traffic of necessary generosity*. Many of the payments and offerings that peasants would have no option but to deliver to their lords' homes were for long referred to in contemporary parlance as 'presents' (*eulogiae*).[50]

Despite the rejection by Henry Loyn and many like-minded scholars, the insights of Mauss, Malinowski, and other anthropologists infected the historical mind and diverted its gaze from the present in the past to the Otherness of the past.[51] Among archaeologists, Grierson's (and Mauss') paper had a delayed impact, and the later advocacy of the structuring effects of gift-exchange within archaeology had as much to do with the anthropological leanings of the New Archaeology and the discovery of "Annales" history as they did with *The Gift* or *Commerce in the Dark Ages*.[52] The net result, however, was a conceptual

---

[47] Grierson, "Commerce in the Dark Ages", p. 140, 139.

[48] G. Duby, *The Early Growth of the European Economy* (Ithaca, 1974), p. 50; generally, see pp. 48-57.

[49] Duby, *Early Growth of the European Economy*, p. 56. In fact, compared to Grierson, Duby appears to place more emphasis on "gifts to the gods", and to downplay slightly more the autarky of the age. See also R. Hodges, *The Anglo-Saxon Achievement* (London, 1989), p. 41.

[50] Duby, *Early Growth of the European Economy*, p. 51, emphasis added.

[51] Thomas, "History and anthropology"; B. Cohn, "Anthropology and history in the 1980's", *Journal of Interdisciplinary History* 12 (1981), pp. 253-65, at pp. 232-36; for the influence of Malinowski on Huizinga's Other Middle Ages, see de Jong, "The foreign past", pp. 332-34. See also A. Gurevich, "Wealth and gift-bestowal among the ancient Scandinavians", in A. Gurevich, *Historical Anthropology of the Middle Ages* (Cambridge, 1992), pp. 177-89; originally published in *Scandinavica* 7 (1968).

[52] J. Moreland, "Method and theory in medieval archaeology in the 1990's", *Archeologia Medievale* 18 (1991), pp. 7-42; L. Binford, "Archaeology as anthropology", in L. Binford, *An Archaeological Perspective* (New York, 1972), pp. 20-32; Thomas, "History and anthropology". For archaeologists' discovery of the *Annales* tradition

move towards the Other in images of the early medieval economy.
For an increasing number of archaeologists and historians, the early
medieval economy is no longer seen as a primitive version of our
own, but, essentially, as anOther world.[53]

As a brief, but necessary, aside to the main argument, I should
make it clear that the concept of the early medieval economy as
structured upon Other principles has not gained universal acceptance.
There are still those who, for example, see the *sceatta* and *styca*
coinages of eighth- and ninth-century England as hard evidence for
the use of money as the structuring mechanism of the middle Saxon
economy, operating across all social levels. Michael Metcalf is the
prime exponent of this view, and in the course of almost forty years
has countered Grierson's (and others) concept of the principles around
which the Anglo-Saxon economy was structured. The terminology
of his argument is unambiguously modernist. Thus he writes that
the study of late seventh and early eighth century Continental coinage
in Britain is

> of particular interest as showing the principal directions of cross chan-
> nel trade, or more precisely as showing those regions on the Continent
> with which England had *a balance of trade surplus*.[54]

Regarding the earliest English *sceattas*, generally found in the south
east of England, he argues that

> these scarce early coins seem to be relatively more plentiful as con-
> tinental finds than their output in relation to the succeeding primary
> series would have led us to expect. In monetary terms the pattern is
> one of contacts between Kent and the Thames estuary and the Rhine
> mouths, and quite possibly a net drift of coin from south eastern
> England to the Continent; that is to say, *England may have run a small
> balance-of-payments deficit*, which was inimical to a net drift of coin in
> the other direction, namely towards the English midlands.[55]

---

within which Duby worked, see J. Moreland, "Restoring the dialectic: settlement
patterns and social relations in medieval central Italy", in B. Knapp ed., *Archaeology,
Annales and Ethnohistory* (Cambridge, 1992), pp. 112-29, at pp. 112-18.

[53] In general see R. Hodges, *Dark Age Economics* (London, 1982); R. Hodges,
"Method and theory in medieval archaeology", *Archeologia Medievale* 8 (1982), pp.
7-37; Astill, "Archaeology, economics, and early medieval Europe"; P. Rahtz, "New
approaches to medieval archaeology, part 1", in D. Hinton, ed., *Twenty Five Years
of Medieval Archaeology* (Sheffield, 1983), pp. 12-23.

[54] D.M. Metcalf, "Monetary circulation in southern England in the first half of
the eighth century, in D. Hill and D.M. Metcalf eds., *Sceattas in England and on the
Continent* (Oxford, 1984), pp. 27-69 at p. 28, emphasis added.

[55] Metcalf, "Monetary circulation", p. 30, emphasis added.

Metcalf's construction of an Anglo-Saxon monetary economy is reinforced, he contends, by the numbers of coins he believes were in existence. Thus he estimates that some 2-3 million coins were produced in some of the *sceatta* series, while the coinage of Offa should be numbered in tens of millions.[56] The total penetration of the Anglo-Saxon economy by coins, and their use in everyday exchanges is suggested, he argues, by "the detailed topographical pattern of the finds, namely their widespread occurrence in villages and in the open countryside, with no obvious patterns or concentrations such as could be interpreted in terms of privileged or restricted access to the use of money".[57]

Metcalf's image of the Anglo-Saxon economy as Same should be rejected for reasons which I, and others, have outlined elsewhere.[58] There is no need to repeat these arguments in this context beyond noting that the "maximalist" calculation of the number of coins produced and in circulation must be doubted, and by remembering that this monetary system apparently operated with relatively few, single denomination, high value coins.[59] What is interesting, however, is that he does acknowledge that not all of the economy was monetised—"a self-contained, non-monetized economy of agricultural estates, royal manors, and so on existed, of course, and will have left virtually no trace on the numismatic evidence".[60] However, the examples of places not reached by coins and the monetary economy, while they speak of an Otherness, this would appear to be the Otherness of autarky rather than anything else. In this sense Metcalf's concept of the Anglo-Saxon economy is simply a more developed

[56] D.M. Metcalf. "How large was the Anglo-Saxon currency?", *English History Review* 18 (1965), pp. 475-82.

[57] D.M. Metcalf, "The monetary economy of ninth-century England south of the Humber: a topographical analysis", in M. Blackburn and D. Dumville eds., *Kings, Currency and Alliances. History and Coinage of Southern England in the Ninth Century* (Woodbridge, 1998), pp. 167-97, at 171. In this paper (at p. 182) Metcalf also argues that "millions of coins" circulated within the economy.

[58] J. Moreland, "Production and exchange in historical archaeology", in G. Barker, ed., *Companion Encyclopedia of Archaeology* (London, 1999), pp. 637-71 at pp. 656-67; Hodges, *Dark Age Economics*, p. 115.

[59] Metcalf himself ("Monetary economy", p. 171), notes (but does not accept) this line of argument – "the average number of coins struck from each die may have been far below the technical capacity of the die. The volume of the mint-output may therefore . . . have been much smaller than has been claimed . . . and the uses of money may . . . have been restricted to the higher levels of society and even to purposes which served to reinforce their status".

[60] Metcalf, "Monetary economy", p. 197.

and sophisticated version of that proposed by Loyn almost forty years previously, and one which equally vehemently, if not so politely, rejects the insights offered by *The Gift*.[61]

For many others in the last twenty years, the economy and society of the sixth-, seventh- and, to a certain extent, eighth-centuries came to be seen as having been structured through gift-exchange, at the local, regional and international scales. Thus we have images of the emerging elites of the post-Roman world creating networks of alliances, and generating relations of power and dominance, through the medium of gift-exchange.[62] The coins which were once taken as signs of the existence of our mentality, are no longer seen (by many) as a pure index of the monetisation of the economy, and of the structuring power of the market, and have either been assigned roles within the realms of long-distance trade and "the social", or placed at the lower end of an evolutionary typology of "money-like" things.[63]

---

[61] Michael Metcalf is fairly explicit about his concept of the early medieval economy. For others, in fact for most others, the problems which beset us in attempting to reconstruct this aspect of past life do not exist – the facts (the bones, the pots, the texts) speak for themselves and "common sense" puts them together to tell us about historical economies. In fact this common sense almost always results in the construction of history as Same, for, as Marc Bloch (*The Historian's Craft* (New York, 1953), p. 80) tells us, "the worst of common sense is that it exalts to the level of the eternal observations necessarily borrowed from our brief moment of time".

[62] I will consider this in the context of eighth century England in more detail in a later chapter. Examples of the adoption of gift-exchange as a significant element in the structuring of economic and social relationships in early medieval archaeology are too numerous to mention, but see Hodges, *Dark Age Economics*; Hodges, *Anglo-Saxon Achievement*, p. 41, 53-58; R. Hodges, "Peer polity interaction and socio-political change in Anglo-Saxon England", in C. Renfrew and J. Cherry eds., *Peer Polity Interaction and Socio-Political Change* (Cambridge, 1986), pp. 69-78, especially pp. 71-75, 77; R. Hodges and J. Moreland, "Power and exchange in middle Saxon England", in S. Driscoll and M. Nieke eds., *Power and Politics in Early Medieval Britain and Ireland* (Edinburgh, 1988), p. 84; A. Hauken, "Gift-exchange in early Iron Age Norse society", in R. Samson ed., *Social Approaches to Viking Studies* (Glasgow, 1991), pp. 105-12; D. Peacock, "Charlemagne's black stones: the re-use of Roman columns in early medieval Europe", *Antiquity* 71 (1997), pp. 709-715 at pp. 712-13; J. Bazelmans, "De representatie van het geschenk in het Oud-Engelse epos 'Beowulf'. Het 'cultuurlijke' van het prestigegoed", (paper presented in Leiden, May 1992); J. Staecker, "Brutal Vikings and gentle traders", *Lund Archaeological Review* 3 (1997), pp. 89-103; M. Bäck, "No island is a society. Regional and interregional interactions in central Sweden during the Viking Age", in H. Anderson, P. Carelli and L. Ersgård eds.), *Visions of the Past. Trends and Traditions in Swedish Medieval Archaeology* (Lund, 1997), pp. 129-161.

[63] Thus R. Hodges, "Trade and urban origins in Dark Age England: an archaeological critique of the evidence", *Berichten van de Rijksdienst voor het Oudheidkundig Bodemonderzoek* 27 (1977), pp. 191-215 at p. 200, following Dalton, "Aboriginal economies" (and consciously emulating the title of Grierson's article) suggests that –

The Gift and war

Some historians and (it seems) more archaeologists comment on the bellicosity of the early sections of many early medieval documentary sources and seek to account for the discrepancy between their more general cohesive image of the period and this apparent willingness to let blood.[64] However, as we shall see, many now acknowledge the intimacy of the relationship between war and "the gift"—I have already referred to Marshall Sahlins' suggestion that, for Mauss, "the gift is Reason. It is the triumph of human rationality over the folly of war".[65] As Mauss himself says

> it is by opposing reason to emotion and setting up the will for peace against rash follies of this kind that peoples succeed in substituting alliance, gift and commerce for war, isolation and stagnation.[66]

"the sceattas may be seen to develop from *primitive valuables*, copies of finely decorated Continental objects, in the seventh century Kentish cemeteries, to *primitive coinage* controlled by kings and ecclesiastics in the early eighth century and beyond. Early cash or *early coinage* in Dalton's terms was . . . certainly present in Anglo-Saxon England" (emphasis added to highlight the use of Dalton's typology). See also R. Hodges, *Primitive and Peasant Markets* (Oxford, 1988), pp. 102-24; Hodges, *Dark Age Economics*, pp. 107-108.

However, we should note that the location of coins within such evolutionary schemes retains elements of history as Same, since the endpoint of such schemes is normally Us. See Thomas, *Entangled Objects*, pp. 9-10; de Jong, "The foreign past", p. 335. In this case, the money-like things acquire, over the course of time, more and more of the qualities of Our money. The status of coins as a marker of "Sameness" can be seen from the fact that the great French historian Fernand Braudel wrote that "the operation of the money supply can be seen as an instrument, a fundamental and regular phenomenon of any moderately developed commercial life" (*The Structures of Everyday Life. The Limits of the Possible* (London, 1981), p. 436), and the great English archaeologist Colin Renfrew argued that "the presence of coins in a civilisation is a crucial one" ("Trade as action at distance: questions of integration and communication", in J. Sabloff and C. Lamberg-Karlovsky eds., *Ancient Civilization and Trade* (Albuquerque, 1975), pp. 3-59 at p. 53).

[64] See, for example, Hodges, *Anglo-Saxon Achievement*, pp. 34-42; Also H. Härke, "'Warrior graves'? The background of the Anglo-Saxon weapon burial rite", *Past and Present* 126 (1990), pp. 22-43.

[65] Sahlins, *Stone Age Economics*, p. 175. The essence of my argument here, and in the pages that follow, is that Mauss' concept of gift-exchange has profoundly influenced recent concepts of the early medieval economy as Other. However, we should also be aware of the fact that much of Mauss' own image of the operation of gift-exchange was based on "Germanic" texts. He constructed a generalised Otherness from a variety of sources, and historians and archaeologists have used his general vision, and some of the texts he worked from, to impose that vision back onto early medieval economies. In other words, the Otherness of the early middle ages comes both from Mauss and from readings of contemporary texts.

[66] Mauss, *The Gift*, p. 80.

However, Reason does not always prevail, as the battles and assassinations recounted on the pages of the *Anglo-Saxon Chronicle* (and other sources) graphically illustrate. While we cannot know how frequently these were the consequence of appropriate or inappropriate responses within a "gift-economy",[67] it is clear that this "failure of Reason" had direct consequences for the systems of gift-exchange which are postulated for early medieval Europe since the taking of plunder was one of the activities intimately associated with such wars. This plunder not only provided a material reflection of regnal splendour; it also helped fuel the cycle of gift-exchange by being distributed among the noble retinue, both as a reward for service and to bind them more closely to the king.[68] However, the taking of plunder (as theft) and of life, which were the inevitable consequences of warfare, necessitated retaliation. As Ross Samson has argued, such "negative reciprocity" "as much as the giving of gifts, creates a binding social relationship, one of feud and vendetta".[69]

---

[67] But see R. Samson, "Economic anthropology and Vikings", in R. Samson ed., *Social Approaches to Viking Studies* (Glasgow, 1991), pp. 87-96, at pp. 91-93; Gurevich, "Wealth and gift-bestowal", pp. 179-80.

[68] Grierson, "Commerce in the Dark Ages", p. 131; Gurevich, "Wealth and gift-bestowal", pp. 182-84; Hodges, *Anglo-Saxon Achievement*, p. 57. Duby, *Early Growth of the European Economy*, p. 105, echoing Mauss, argues that "trade was simply a substitute for pillage. It supplied what war could only supply irregularly. Like war, it brought into the homes of the overlords . . . things to be worn, to amuse, to embellish and to be given away as presents". The inspiration for the underlying logic of this system of acquisition, distribution, and consumption derives not only from medieval texts, but also from Roman perceptions of the barbarian "other". Tacitus (b. c. 56 A.D.) describes the Germanic relationship between gift, war, and lordship as follows – "one [a chieftain] would not maintain a large retinue except by violence and war. For they [young nobles] claim from the generosity of their chieftain that glorious war horse, that renowned *framea* which will be bloodied and victorious; for banquets and provisions, not luxurious yet abundant, serve as pay. The wherewithal for generosity is obtained through wars and plunder" *Germania* 14 (trans H. Benario, *Tacitus' Agricola, Germany and Dialogue on Orators* (Oklahoma, 1991), p. 70).

For the impact of readings of Tacitus on early modern perceptions of Germanic society see J. Bazelmans, "Conceptualising early Germanic political structure: a review of the use of the concept of Gefolgschaft", in N. Roymans and F. Theuws eds., *Images of the Past. Studies on Ancient Societies in Northwestern Europe* (Amsterdam, 1991), pp. 91-130. See also L. Hedeager, "Warrior economy and trading economy in Viking-Age Scandinavia", *Journal of European Archaeology* 2 (1994), pp. 130-48; T. Reuter, "Plunder and Tribute in the Carolingian Empire", *Transactions of the Royal Historical Society* (5th series) 35 (1985), pp. 75-94.

[69] Samson, "Economic anthropology", p. 91. In fact Samson goes on to argue that Mauss overemphasised the harmonious, "'stabilising" effects of gift-exchange, and underplayed the "violence [which] like a heavy cloud, hung over transactions" (pp. 92-93). As we have seen, however (above p. 10), Mauss was only to well aware of the "sanction" which lay behind the obligations to give, receive, and repay.

The relevance of all this for my argument is that this "necessary inverse" of gift-exchange adds to the construction of a certain "aristocratic" image of early medieval economy and society. Whereas the giving of gifts provides the objects which lie behind the imagery of feasting and "ring-giving", its inverse provides the rationale for the warfare and plunder which seep through the historical accounts, and for the "heroic" ethos which is felt by many (implicitly or explicitly) to dominate the age. The following from Lotte Hedeager in many ways encapsulates the image—

> no chieftain gained influence—or kept what influence he already had—just by sitting on large tracts of land or great heaps of treasure. On the contrary his wealth had to circulate. Military power depended upon a chieftains' ability to bind warriors to himself by ties of loyalty. And this he could best achieve by liberally sharing out his wealth, thus committing those who accepted it to make some repayment, be that in the form of reciprocal gifts, military service or something else.
>
> The surplus which was essential for keeping this flow of gifts going was not only gained from the products of the soil. *War, plundering and theft were . . . necessary to keep the system intact. It is the warlord whom we meet again and again* in the Germanic . . . legendary and saga literature; *he is the lord of land, horses, ships and gold who freely shares out his wealth and who provides great feasts. . . .* The warrior aristocracy and gift-giving were thus inseparably linked.[70]

---

[70] L. Hedeager, "The creation of Germanic identity. A European origin-myth", in P. Brun, S. van der Leeuw, and C.R. Whittaker eds., *Frontières d'Empire. Nature et Signification des Frontières Romaines* (Nemours, 1993), pp. 121-31, at p. 122, emphases added. Frans Theuws envisages the survival of elements of this "tribal warrior ideology in which martiality and generosity play an important part" well into the Middle Ages – see, F. Theuws, "Landed property and manorial organisation in northern Austrasia: some considerations and a case study", in N. Roymans and F. Theuws eds., *Images of the Past: Studies of Ancient Societies in Northwestern Europe* (Amsterdam, 1991), pp. 299-407 at p. 303. Barbara Yorke tells us that "a large military following was necessary to prevent conquest from other kingdoms, but had to be held together by constant war and the giving of gifts, the former being necessary to acquire the means of providing the latter", *Kings and Kingdoms of Early Anglo-Saxon England* (London, 1990), pp. 166-67. See also Duby, *Early Growth of the European Economy*, pp. 48-52; D. Gerrets, "Evidence of political centralization in Westergo: the excavations at Wijnaldum in a (supra-) regional perspective", in T. Dickinson and D. Griffiths eds., *The Making of Kingdoms*, Anglo-Saxon Studies in Archaeology and History 10 (Oxford 1999), pp. 119-26 at p. 121; L. Hedeager, "Kingdoms, ethnicity and material culture: Denmark in European perspective", in M. Carver ed., *The Age of Sutton Hoo* (Woodbridge, 1992), pp. 279-300; Gurevich, "Wealth and gift-bestowal".

John Hines, in his "Ritual hoarding in Migration-period Scandinavia: a review of recent interpretations", *Proceedings of the Prehistoric Society* 55 (1989), pp. 193-205, at p. 195 places considerable emphasis on the importance of giving the "gifts of war" for the creation and reproduction of social relationships at the upper levels

An Economy without Production

As I outlined in note 65, the main point of the last few pages has
been to argue that the general image of the early medieval economy as Other has been profoundly influenced by Maussian concepts
of gift-exchange. However, the world which has been constructed is
one of exchange and consumption—feasting was an essential feature
of gift-exchange—divorced from production.[71] Much as Philip Grierson
(and, as we shall see, Mauss himself) envisioned, this is an aristocratic world far removed from the simplicity of the closed, autarkic
system of self sufficiency which previously (and to some still does)
characterised the Dark Ages.[72] However, it is also a world where
production *per se* has little place.[73]

As I have already pointed out, Grierson saw "good reason" for
keeping gift-exchange separate from the production and circulation
of goods at the local level (see above, pp. 6-7). In essence he postulated the existence of ranked spheres of exchange. This concept,
reinforced by other anthropological parallels, has also played its part
in the construction of this early medieval economy. A classic anthropological example is that of the pre-colonial Tiv of the lower Benue
river, Nigeria where, before the introduction of European money
undermined the whole system, there were three separate spheres of

---

of society – "It is tolerably clear that gift-exchange, particularly of the spoils and
rewards of warfare, was perceived as one of the fundamental bonds of the relevant
warrior societies both before and after, and therefore plausibly through this period
[4th to 7th century]. In early medieval literature the practice is presented as being
elevated by and into an ideology, as a practice laudable in itself and not simply a
socially functional device. The primary axis of exchange is between the *comitatus*
and lord/chief, the mutual giving and receiving of gifts placing an obligation upon
the receiver of *future* loyalty and support to the giver".

[71] On feasting and gift-exchange in the early middle ages, see Gurevich, "Wealth
and gift-bestowal", pp. 185-87. It is noteworthy that production is not mentioned
in this account of "*wealth* and gift-bestowal" in the early Scandinavian world.

[72] A characteristic also noted by Astill, "Archaeology, economics, and early
medieval Europe", p. 216; and Samson, "Economic anthropology", p. 96. Mauss
in fact refers to the agonistic gift-exchanges of the north-west American potlatch as
"an *aristocratic* type of commerce characterised by etiquette and generosity", and tells
us that the Trobriand "Kula trade is *aristocratic*. It seems to be reserved for the
chiefs" (*The Gift*, p. 36; 20; emphases added).

[73] I should point out that Richard Hodges (*Dark Age Economics*, pp. 130-50) does
consider the nature of agricultural production and its relationship with long-distance
trade. However, he does so in a rather descriptive manner, and in a way which
tends to envisage the two operating in largely discrete spheres, see pp. 148-49.

exchange.[74] In the most prestigious sphere, rights over women were controlled by lineage heads, and were used by them to create and reproduce a network of alliances. In the next sphere, objects such as cloth, slaves, guns, and metal rods circulated. Significantly (given the discussion on pp. 15-17), these goods were obtained "by war or trade". Young men used the acquisition of these goods, and their contribution to the "lineage treasury", to gain the good reputation necessary to secure a marriage alliance. Domestic goods circulated in the lowest ranking sphere. At this level, chickens, baskets, pots and grain could be exchanged for each other. Within this system, exchange in "the domestic sphere was high frequency, low status in its normal activities, and the other was low frequency, high status"; here "luxuries were used as weapons of exclusion".[75]

The idea of such exclusive and ranked spheres of exchange has been used by some to construct their particular image of the early medieval economy. Thus Grenville Astill, in his critique of Hodges' *Dark Age Economics*, and in a direct echo of the Tiv system, argues that

> recent anthropological work on exchange in pre-market societies ... [shows] that several levels of exchange existed and *did not mix*. The most important distinction is between luxury goods and products connected with subsistence. Thus prestige goods were given as gifts and were reciprocated by other luxuries that were regarded as equivalent to, or having the same rank as, the original gift.[76]

I suggest here that the appropriation of the concept of ranked spheres of exchange further enhances the separation of production and exchange (and the lack of consideration given to the former) within this vision of early medieval economies. Here the fruits of agrarian production are generally held to circulate at the lowest levels of

---

[74] See M. Douglas and B. Isherwood, *The World of Goods. Towards an Anthropology of Consumption* (London, 1979), 138-41 for this and the following discussion.

[75] Douglas and Isherwood, *The World of Goods*, pp. 138; 131.

[76] Astill, "Archaeology, economics, and early medieval Europe", p. 223, emphasis added. See also p. 221, 222 – "While there is evidence in medieval Europe for the exchange of jewellery and slaves, these widely differing commodities may not have had an equivalence, and it may be necessary to propose that goods were exchanged in various ways according to different standards". See also Hodges, "Trade and urban origins", p. 200; Hodges, *Dark Age Economics*, pp. 104-105; Bäck, "No island is a society", p. 138; M. Gaimster, "Money and media in Viking Age Scandinavia", in R. Samson, ed., *Social Approaches to Viking Studies* (Glasgow, 1991), pp. 113-22, at pp. 118-20.

exchange, totally divorced from the objects of prestige exchange which move at the higher, and more determining, levels.

Strangely, even some accounts of early medieval economic processes written from an explicitly Marxist perspective, in which one might expect production to be brought to the fore, still ascribe the same determinacy to elite exchange. Thus in Tom Saunders' discussion of parallel developments in England and Norway in the early middle ages, gift-exchange is seen as a "closed and regulated" system, in which prestige goods not only "played a vital role in the interaction of the king and his military following", but also served as "an essential means of mediation in the potentially antagonistic relationship between tributary king and feudal lord".[77] As with Mauss and Grierson, here gift-exchange is an essentially elite activity, serving to reproduce social relations amongst those who wielded greatest power in early medieval society. The dependence of kings on prestige goods for the reproduction of these elite-level social relationships induced the former to restrict access to such objects—

> the Anglo-Saxon *wics* were the instrument of royal constraint upon trade. The establishment of *emporia* secured the royal monopoly of the production and exchange of prestige goods, and maintained the value of the gift as a symbol of royal authority.[78]

Mirroring the social exclusivity of gift-exchange, these sites are seen as "dependent settlements cut off from the rural economy"; as "divorced from the economy as a whole, detached and isolated on the periphery of kingdoms".[79] That economy presumably operated on different principles, and we find out what these are when Saunders discusses the development of towns and market centres across the landscape of England in the late ninth and early tenth centuries. Saunders sees the burhs of Alfredian England as "centres of petty commodity production",[80] and argues that "the demands exerted by feudal exploitation *reduced the peasantry's self-sufficiency* and forced them to enter the urban market in order to acquire basic commodities such as salt, cloth, tools, household utensils etc.".[81] From this we can

---

[77] T. Saunders, "Trade, towns and states: a reconsideration of early medieval economics", *Norwegian Archaeological Review* 28 (1995), pp. 31-53, at p. 37.

[78] Saunders, "Trade, towns and states", p. 37. I will discuss the *wics/emporia* in more detail in a later chapter.

[79] Saunders, "Trade, towns and states", p. 37.

[80] Saunders, "Trade, towns and states", pp. 40-41.

[81] Saunders, "Trade, towns and states", p. 41, emphasis added.

conclude that Saunders sees the middle Saxon economy as bipolar—trade/gift-exchange among the elite; self-sufficiency amongst the peasantry. The inherently conservative, autarkic and closed nature of the kind of economic system proposed for the vast majority of the population implies that any historical directionality which stemmed from "economic forces" must be sought in the more dynamic system attributed to the elite, and this despite the fact that Saunders explicitly argues that "the expansion of a prestige goods system in early medieval England, and the founding of large *emporia* such as at Southampton, London, Ipswich, and York, need not be seen as the driving force behind social development".[82]

The efforts of archaeologists to distance themselves from the Other of autarky and the Same of "the market", through the adoption and imposition of insights from anthropology, and in particular of Maussian concepts of gift-exchange, has thus resulted only in the construction of anOther concept of the early medieval economy. This is an economy in which aristocratic exchange and consumption are placed at some remove from production; and in which the emphasis on "generosity and martiality" link the archaeological and historical accounts in the construction and reproduction of an heroic age. This approach is one which fails to consider the totality of economic activity in the early middle ages.

To the extent that the emphasis on gift-exchange has helped undermine the Sameness and universality of "market exchange", and to erode belief in the Otherness of early medieval economic autarky, it has been valuable. However, in its emphasis on elite exchange and consumption as the driving forces in structuring and transforming society, it has simply perpetuated anOther, but equally stereotypical image of the early middle ages as a world of "mead halls" and "ring-givers".[83] This conception is in fact a mirror in which the other great images of the period—warfare and heroes—are reflected.

Through its construction of anOther early medieval economy, this is also an account which does little justice to the (archaeological *and* anthropological) evidence. For while the ethos of a "gift-economy" clearly does find expression in the written sources (and we have seen how Mauss drew inspiration from these), and some of the

---

[82] Saunders, "Trade, towns and states", p. 37.
[83] Perhaps exemplified in Gurevich, "Wealth and gift-bestowal"; and Hedeager, "Germanic identity".

archaeological evidence can be explained in terms of the mechanisms outlined by Grierson and others, there are also abundant indicators that production, distribution and consumption in early medieval
Europe were linked in much more complex and variegated ways. I
will consider this below, but first we should consider the impact on
the concept of an economy dominated by *The Gift* of recent critiques
of Mauss' great work.

Rethinking Mauss

It is perhaps symptomatic of the perceived role of theory in what
we might call "medieval studies" that while Maussian (and other
anthropological) insights were being used in the construction of the
Other, as outlined above, anthropologists were taking a cold, hard
look at themselves and their relationship with their subject.[84] The
recognition that "anthropology is a discourse of alterity, a way of
writing in which us/them distinctions are central, and which necessarily distances the people studied from ourselves",[85] and the dawn-
ing of the realisation that these peoples were not relics of the past
at once existing in, yet untouched by, the modern world, but had
in fact been (at least partially) constructed through their "entangle-
ment" with capitalism, forced anthropologists to consider the validity of the worlds they had constructed for the Others.[86]

Anthropologists also came to understand (as did scholars in many
other disciplines) that their location in the Western present, and their
perception of the morality or immorality of that present, coloured
the images of social and economic relations which they constructed

---

[84] This is not the place to outline the reasons behind, or the conclusions of, this
introspection, but see J. Clifford, *The Predicament of Culture. Twentieth-Century Ethnography,
Literature, and Art* (Cambridge, MA., 1988); G. Marcus and M. Fischer, *Anthropology
as Cultural Critique. An Experimental Moment in the Human Sciences* (Chicago, 1986);
Thomas, *Entangled Objects*.

[85] Thomas, *Entangled Objects*, p. 3. On the same page, Thomas writes that "modern anthropology has been, in a fundamental sense, about 'other cultures'. The fact
of difference is thus anterior to any contingent similarities between ourselves and
other peoples".

[86] As Thomas, *Entangled Objects*, p. xi writes – "nearly all the societies which anthropologists made into case studies for exchange theory were or still are colonized, but
this context of illiberal domination entered into these accounts, if it was mentioned
at all, only as external contingency, never as a fact that needed to be central to
analysis".

for their subjects. For many in the West, anthropologists included, the modern world came to be seen as one of social, moral and environmental impoverishment. The nature of relations of production and exchange in twentieth century capitalism were held to dehumanise the subject and to destroy the "traditional" bonds of family and community, while the effects of industrial production polluted and contaminated the natural world in which they lived. The consequence, argues Nicholas Thomas, is that the past, and the small scale, isolated societies studied by anthropologists, is celebrated, "because they display what has been lost and provide a model for a more wholesome way of living".[87]

The problem with this "ideology of primitivism" is that the societies which are constructed through it are "celebrated" not for what they are or were, but for what they mean to Us. This is a "romantic counter-modernism in which selected features of their world serve to relativize and destabilize cherished features or cultural tenets of

---

The older perspective, and the one in which many of the current generation of archaeologists were bought up, is perhaps exemplified in (exaggerated by?) this early quote from Marshall Sahlins ("Poor man, rich man, Big Man, Chief: political types in Melanesia and Polynesia", *Comparative Studies in Society and History* 5 (1963), pp. 285-303 at p. 285) – "the native peoples of the Pacific islands present . . . to anthropologists a generous scientific gift; an extended series of experiments in cultural adaptation and evolutionary development . . . From Australian aborigines, whose hunting and gathering activities duplicate in outline the cultural life of the upper palaeolithic, to the great chiefdoms of Hawaii, where society approached the formative levels of the old Fertile Crescent civilizations, almost every phase in the progress of primitive culture is exemplified"; (see also Moreland, "Production and exchange", pp. 640-42).

[87] Thomas, *Entangled Objects*, p. 10. In the same vein, and writing specifically of concepts of the middle ages, Paul Zumthor, *Speaking of the Middle Ages* (Lincoln, Nebraska, 1986), p. 9, 11 writes that – "whatever perspective . . . people may adopt, they implicitly acknowledge a difference between their own time and the Middle Ages. Perhaps their curiosity is based in part on a vague desire to escape the oppressiveness of the civilization they have created: in that case their 'Middle Ages' takes on more or less the same qualities as their ecological myths" – "More than other past eras, the Middle Ages appear to this audience as the soil from which spring its deep biological and psychic roots. . . . In the Middle Ages it senses a 'before' that is nearer at hand, less orderly, more primitive, one in which modern regional cultural movements hope to discover a vein that antedates the great standardization".

For other perceptions of the Middle Ages as Other, see C. Frayling, *Strange Landscape. A Journey through the Middle Ages* (London, 1995), pp. 7-36; U. Eco, *Travels in Hyper-reality* (London, 1986), pp. 61-72. For the "ideology of primitivism" in the middle ages, see G. Boas, *Essays on Primitivism and Related Ideas in the Middle Ages* (New York, 1966). For an alternative evaluation of the relationship between our world and the Otherness of the Middle Ages, see Freedman, *Images of the Medieval Peasant*, pp. 299-303.

our own".[88] One of the features central to the modern world which
was relativised, and its universality, its naturalism, thereby undermined, was the process of exchange. Thomas shows how Bronislaw
Malinowski, in his famous work on the kula of Melanesia, had a
strategic interest in differentiating this particular exchange system
from concepts of "primitive commerce". He thus argued that the
necklaces and armshells which circulated within the system were not
at all equivalent to money. They were valuables which could only
be exchanged for each other within systems of *ranked spheres of exchange*.
They could not be used to "buy", they could not be exchanged for,
other goods and services. They were fundamentally different.[89]

The same "romanticism", the same strategic interest, can be found
in the Maussian conception of gift-exchange as central to the structuring of social relationships in the past and "distant" present, and
inevitably therefore in the Middle Ages constructed around this principle.[90] One of the underlying themes of Mauss' work is that there
is a simple equation of gift = traditional society, commodity = modern society, and the qualities ascribed to these two forms of exchange
are such that the former is simply the inverse of the latter. The gift
is constructed as that which the commodity is not—it is personal, it
is not alienable, it cannot be exchanged for other things, it creates
relationships between people.[91] In the past it was not only different,
it was also better.

---

[88] Thomas, *Entangled Objects*, p. 13; de Jong, "The foreign past", pp. 335-36;
J. Adams, "Anthropology and history in the 1980's", *Journal of Interdisciplinary History*
12 (1981), pp. 253-65, at pp. 257, 265.

[89] Thomas, *Entangled Objects*, p. 12. As Thomas notes, in this Malinowski "misled
his readers. Like shell valuables elsewhere in Melanesia, kula items could be used
in a great variety of ways – in payment for food, canoes, assassinations etc.".

[90] For some of the many anthropological works which have begun the process
of "rethinking Mauss", see M. Bloch and J. Parry, "Introduction: money and the
morality of exchange", in M. Bloch and J. Parry eds., *Money and the Morality of
Exchange* (Cambridge, 1989), pp. 1-32; M. Godelier "'Salt money' and the circulation of commodities among the Baruya of New Guinea", in M. Godelier, *Perspectives
in Marxist Anthropology* (Cambridge, 1977), pp. 127-51; Godelier, *Enigma of the Gift*,
pp. 10-107; Sahlins, *Stone Age Economics*, pp. 149-83; Samson, "Economic anthropology", pp. 87-96; Thomas, *Entangled Objects*; A Weiner, *Inalienable Possessions. The
Paradox of Keeping-while-Giving* (Berkeley, 1992).

[91] Thomas, *Entangled Objects*, p. 15; Moreland, "Production and exchange", p. 644.
A. Appadurai, "Introduction: commodities and the politics of value", in A. Appadurai
ed., *The Social Life of Things. Commodities in Cultural Perspective* (Cambridge, 1986),
p. 11 – "the exaggeration and reification of the contrast between gift and commodity
in anthropological writing has many sources. Among them are the tendency to
romanticize small-scale societies; [and] the proclivity to marginalise and underplay

In a sense, Mauss himself admitted the "presentist" nature of his argument. I have already noted the connection he made between his project and the contemporary social welfare programmes of England and France. At the beginning of his essay he suggests that from his work "we may draw conclusions of a *moral* nature about some of the problems confronting us in *our present economic crisis*".[92] In the more organic world of *The Gift*, the problems of the modern world could be resolved.

The essential problem with *The Gift* is that, although it was constructed from the ethnographies and histories of particular societies, the romantic lens through which this information was filtered resulted in an emphasis on similarities and in the creation of a rhetorical type—"what counts theoretically is always 'the' gift".[93] Once the ideal type had been created, subsequent work, including that in archaeology and history, was conducted within its premises. The particulars of historical economies were reduced to the overall form of *The Gift*.[94] The antidote to this ahistoricism, Thomas argues, could be found in "a movement of perspective from economic abstractions to historical forms"; in the fracturing of the general concept of gift-exchange "through the nuances of practice and history".[95] The consequence of this re-focussing would be the recognition of

---

the calculative, impersonal and self aggrandizing features of non-capitalist societies".

[92] Mauss, *The Gift*, p. 2, emphasis added; see also pp. 64-68, and Godelier, *Enigma of the Gift*, pp. 63-64.

[93] Thomas, *Entangled Objects*, p. 26.

[94] Thomas, *Entangled Objects*, p. 26. It may be that Thomas and others are, in fact, overly critical of Mauss. While his essay has clearly acquired iconic status, and while the rhetorical (or ideal) type which is "the" gift has clearly determined the ways in which anthropologists and archaeologists construct their subjects, Mauss himself (*The Gift*, p. 76) made it clear that his essay was a provisional statement of work in progress – "we do not set this work up as a model; it simply proffers one or two suggestions. It is incomplete: the analysis could be pushed farther. We are really posing questions for historians and anthropologists and offering possible lines of research for them rather than resolving a problem and laying down definite answers".

Although focusing on the gift and its obligations, Mauss did recognise the essentially arbitrary nature of the oppositions which could flow from his work. Thus he informs us (The *Gift*, p. 70) that – "our terms 'present' and 'gift' do not have precise meanings, but we could find no others. Concepts which we like to put in opposition – freedom and obligation; generosity, liberality, luxury on the one hand and saving, interest, austerity on the other – are not exact and it would be well to put them to the test".

[95] Thomas, *Entangled Objects*, pp. 15-16; 27.

a multiplicity of other economies and forms of sociality [which] also permits difference to be envisaged among a plurality of others, rather than confined to a gulf between us and them.[96]

The important point for us is that when we turn to the ethnographies of gift-exchange we find much that contradicts, or is not included within, the Maussian model.

As we have seen, one of the essential elements in this model is the construction of social debt through the obligations to give, receive and repay. While this may be the case in some of the societies which Mauss studied, it is not true of all societies which practice forms of gift-exchange.[97] Just as significantly, a return to the field, and a re-reading of older ethnographies does not uphold the rigid dichotomy between gift and commodity, between a traditional world before the penetration of capitalism, and an alienated one afterwards. Rather there exist a broad range of social and economic forms between those in which quasi-Maussian principles apply and others in which

> forms of alienation and what are virtually commodity transactions occur. The general view that Melanesian, Polynesian, or any other tribal societies can be regarded as communal or 'gift' economies is thus rejected.[98]

Tackling the same issue (gifts = tribal, commodities = modern) from a different direction, Maurice Godelier argues that "the world of gifts and that of commodities are in fact comparable", in the sense that in both the relationship between people and objects is "mystified".[99]

---

[96] Thomas, *Entangled Objects*, p. 33.

[97] Thomas, *Entangled Objects*, pp. 15, 17, 22.

[98] Thomas, *Entangled Objects*, p. 4. Again, however, Thomas' critique, while valid of the "rhetorical type", is perhaps overstretched. Thus when Mauss speaks of 'the gift' he makes it clear that, while this is his research focus, it co-existed with other forms of exchange, with other ways of linking production and consumption; and it still does today (Mauss, *The Gift*, pp. 2, 74). The Trobriand *kula* is "the gathering point of many other institutions"; the exchange of *vaygu'a* (armshells and necklaces) is – "set amidst a series of *different kinds of exchange*, ranging from barter to wage-payment . . . all *kula* transactions are an opportunity for ordinary exchange, *gimwali*, which does not necessarily take place between established partners. Alongside the established partnerships there is an open market between persons of allied tribes" (*The Gift*, p. 25 emphasis added).

[99] Godelier, *Enigma of the Gift*, pp. 70-71 – "the two worlds, the world of gifts and that of commodities, are in fact comparable. To the fetishism of the objects given corresponds that of commodities, and to the fetishism of sacred objects corresponds that of money functioning as capital, as value endowed with its own power to engender value, as money capable of engendering money. This is the mythology

Just as significant in terms of breaking down the polarity between gifts and commodities, Godelier develops the idea that "the gift" operated alongside other means of exchange, other economies. Generally, he suggests that "commercial" relations have co-existed with gift-exchange for centuries, and sees no essential opposition between "Melanesian societies as 'gift-based' societies and Western society as a 'commodity-based' society".[100] As a specific instance of this he refers to the co-existence of European influenced trade and *moka* gift-exchange systems in New Guinea—"after the arrival of Europeans, *two parallel economies grew up*, one based on gift-exchange, the other on trade".[101]

Godelier also points out that, contrary to the Maussian "type", on islands other than Kiriwina,[102] *vaygu'a* (armshells and necklaces) were *not* restricted to *kula* exchanges. Elsewhere, the necklaces and arm-rings could be withdrawn from the *kula* and used in other types of exchanges.[103] The notion that gifts always operate in ranked spheres of exchange, can only be exchanged for goods which circulate within the same rank, and cannot articulate with other levels of exchange (and production) is thus not universal.

In an earlier section, I noted that the emphasis on gift-exchange and its operation in ranked spheres of exchange in the middle ages

---

of capital. . . . In both instances . . . an identical process has been at work: in each case the real relations people entertain with the objects they produce, exchange (or keep) have vanished, disappeared from their consciousness, and other forces, other, this time imaginary, actors have replaced the human beings who originally pro-duced them. . . . We are in either case in the presence of man-made worlds, but ones which have become detached from man and are peopled by phantasmic doubles, duplicates: these are often benevolent and succor man, often they crush him, but in all events they dominate him".

[100] Godelier, *Enigma of the Gift*, p. 229, note 146; Godelier, "Salt money", pp. 128, 151. I have already pointed out that this fact is acknowledged, but under-played, by Mauss (see note 98). From a reading of his work, it would seem clear that while Godelier acknowledges the co-existence of gift and commodity exchange, and would agree on the impossibility of "speaking generally of gift or commodity economies", he would not wish to totally abolish the concepts since that would remove the possibility of capturing alterity in whatever form. See also Thomas, *Entangled Objects*, pp. 33-34.

[101] Godelier, *Enigma of the Gift*, p. 99; emphasis added. We should also note the impact of European trading systems on the north-west American potlatch, and the Melanesian *kula*, pp. 75-78; 85. For another example, see M. Rowlands, "Local and long distance trade and incipient state formation on the Bamenda Plateau", *Paideuma* 25 (1979), pp. 1-19.

[102] The location of Malinowski's original research in the kula system.

[103] Godelier, *Enigma of the Gift*, p. 85. See note 98 above.

has its concomitant in a distinct lack of concern with production (either agrarian or of gifts).[104] In some ways this is not at all surprising since the concepts are largely drawn from Mauss (and Grierson), and a similar lack of concern is apparent in their essays.[105] Thus Godelier points out that "as a rule Mauss does not concern himself with the relations men entertain in the course of producing things, only with those formed between men by the circulation of the things they produce".[106] This is despite the fact that all of the objects which circulate in the kula, for example, are man-made.[107] As he noted in an earlier essay,

> we generally forget that all these precious objects, whether fabricated or obtained at the price of great labour or large payments, were rare products, which when bartered had exchange value. From the barrier reefs, one person could not collect, polish or pierce more than two armbands of pearls (at most) per month. . . . The Yap millstones came from far distant islands and veritable sea expeditions were undertaken to extract them, hew them and bring them back.[108]

Anthropologists', and Mauss', overwhelming interest in exchange at the expense of production may be a product of the fact that for them "exchange relations seem to be substance of *social* life";[109] to this I would counter that people also enter into and construct social relations in the process of production; that the realm of production is not isolated from ideological and cosmological concerns (see note 121). It may also stem from the fact that anthropologists have long seen exchange systems as the basis for classifying societies on an evolutionary scale from primitive to modern.[110] Be that as it may. The

---

[104] Although we should note that some archaeologists do think about it some of the time. Thus Hodges, "Trade and urban origins", p. 200 does note that "we know surprisingly little about the production of the goods which were traded, and imported as prestige objects. . . . The production of most utilitarian goods also remains obscure". See also Hodges, *Anglo-Saxon Achievement*, p. 70.

[105] For Grierson, see above p. 7.

[106] Godelier, *Enigma of the Gift*, p. 61; also pp. 74-75.

[107] Godelier, *Enigma of the Gift*, p. 88.

[108] Godelier, "Salt money", p. 128.

[109] Thomas, *Entangled Objects*, p. 7. For an exception, see Gosden, "Debt, production and prehistory"; but then Gosden is an archaeologist.

[110] Thomas, *Entangled Objects*, p. 10. This focus on exchange "as a marker in these evolutionary narratives" is itself probably a product of the valorisation of exchange relations in the early capitalist societies from which the principal anthropological research was carried out. This research was in fact intimately connected with the globalisation which was the consequence of the expansion of these exchange systems.

point is that if we are to understand past societies, in all their similarity and difference, if we are to understand the complexity and uniqueness of particular economic systems, if we are to appreciate the different webs of association and dominance which connect and articulate production, distribution and consumption, then we cannot allow the appeal of a "rhetorical type" to fix our attention on only one aspect of that triad.

It is the case that in Maussian gift-exchange, a gift is both a object and an action. However, the anthropologist's (and archaeologist's) focus has often been on the social relationship created by the action rather than on the nature of the object.[111] This situation has changed in the last decade as archaeologists and anthropologists have become aware not only of the role of artifacts in the structuring of social relationships, but also of the significance of the contextual meanings ascribed to objects in the construction of their "social value".[112] Artifacts are no longer seen simply as the physical manifestation of (but somehow epiphenomenal to) a social act, but as objects with biographies, as fully implicated in the construction and transformation of human social life. What recent anthropological research has shown is that the "social value" of an object—a value derived from its intrinsic and attributed qualities—plays a significant role in the ways in which it may be exchanged. As we shall see, this understanding not only further undermines the gift/commodity, Other/Same polarity, but also weakens the case of those who see the economic "laws" of scarcity, supply and demand as the governing factors in the construction of value in exchange.

Thomas illustrates this point through a consideration of what he calls "the sentiment-burdened gift in the modern industrial situation"—a wedding ring.[113] The meanings ascribed to this object in particular social and cultural contexts determine the ways in which it can be exchanged. Originally produced as a *commodity*, of some intrinsic value, in a workshop, the object is offered for sale as such. It is purchased with cash in the context of a money economy. It is then given as a *gift* in a wedding ceremony, where it becomes emblematic of the social relationship entered into. Continual wearing of the

---

[111] M. Helms, *Craft and the Kingly Ideal. Art, Trade and Power* (Austin, Texas, 1993), p. 92; Samson, "Economic anthropology", p. 92. Thomas, *Entangled Objects*, p. 17.
[112] Moreland, "Through the looking glass", pp. 95-103.
[113] Thomas, *Entangled Objects*, p. 18. For what follows see Thomas, pp. 18-20.

ring (or its rejection) is "an index of the extent to which those relations are sustained or disfigured". On the death of the original female
bearer, the ring may be bequeathed by a mother to a daughter or
granddaughter and as such serves as a physical bond linking the
female generations "in a context in which patriliny is dominant".
This female generational linkage makes the object *inalienable*—it cannot normally be given outside this context—not because of any intrinsic value it might have but because of the personal histories and
memories which it carries. However, there are contexts in which the
ring might lose this quality and enter other forms of exchange.[114]
The breakage of the female generational link, and/or poverty might
mean that it is sold, in which case it once again becomes a detached
commodity. As Maurice Godelier argues in an entirely different situation

> objects do not need to be different in order to operate in different
> areas, ... sometimes the same object can be first sold, then given,
> and finally stashed away in a family or clan treasure. It is not the
> object which creates the differences, it is the different logics govern-
> ing the areas of social life as it moves from one domain to the other,
> changing functions and uses as it goes.[115]

The lessons to be drawn from the above are simple—that the intrinsic and attributed qualities of an object can determine the ways
in which it is exchanged; that the value of an object lies not just
(or even) in its scarcity or utility but also in the historical, senti-
mental and cosmological qualities with which it is felt to be imbued;[116]
that the capacity of the same article to be gift, commodity, inalienable object in particular circumstances disables the basic gift = traditional, commodity = modern polarity. Gifts are not invariably gifts,
and commodities are not invariably commodities.[117] The shift from
gift to commodity (or vice versa) can be achieved either in the move-

---

[114] Weiner, *Inalienable Possessions*, p. 6.

[115] Godelier, *Enigma of the Gift*, p. 108. Elsewhere ("Salt Money", pp. 128-9) Godelier
writes that – "we must perforce conclude that *very often* the precious objects we
encounter in primitive societies have a *dual nature*: they are both goods and non-
goods, 'money' and gifts, according to whether they are bartered between groups
or circulate within the group" – "They function primarily as commodities if they
have been imported or produced for export. Subsequently they function as prestige
objects, as objects of social exchange when circulated within a group through the
mechanism of gifts and other forms of distribution. The same object, therefore
changes its function".

[116] Thomas, *Entangled Objects*, p. 21.

[117] Thomas, *Entangled Objects*, p. 39.

ment of the object from one social and economic system to another (from the heart of the Roman empire to "barbarian" Denmark, say) or by its recontextualisation within a particular social formation (as in the case of the ring, above). The point is that gifts and commodities are not mutually exclusive, and need not be seen as successive stages in an evolutionary developmental cycle. As I will show in another chapter in this volume, this is a crucial insight for appreciating what is truly distinctive (as opposed to Same/Other) about the economy of eighth century England (and other early medieval European "economies").

Conclusion

There can be little doubt that the Maussian ideal, or rhetorical, type of "the Gift" has had a profound impact upon anthropological studies of present, and archaeological studies of past, economies. Viewed as an ideal type in the Weberian sense, we should not expect every attribute of the Maussian Gift to accord with observed reality in particular social formations. However, problems arise when, over time, the characteristics of the ideal type become reified and yet conflict dramatically with the practices encountered by anthropologists and archaeologists. This, I would argue, is now the case with *The Gift*. While it would be going too far to conclude that the whole concept of the Gift must now be rejected,[118] specific analogies and categorical oppositions drawn from the "type" must give way to a deeper appreciation of the intricacies of real historical social and economic formations. In this way we can use the "spirit" of The Gift, combined with the "body" of observed fact, to construct an early medieval economy which does indeed avoid the Scylla and Charybdis of Same and Other to which I referred at the beginning.[119]

The first, and most essential lesson we have learned from "rethinking

---

[118] Thus while Thomas notes that "there seems to be a distinct cleavage between generalized discussion of 'the' gift and a vast world of ethnographic intricacies", this does not force him (nor need it force us) to "reject his theory in the categorical manner that its empirical inadequacy might demand" (*Entangled Objects*, pp. 33-34).

[119] It must be obvious that we can never know how successfully we have charted these waters. Subsequent generations, or even current reviewers, may conclude that our attempts have been in vain. The only defense we can offer in the light of these possibilities is the recognition of the problem and a willingness to resolve it.

Mauss", is that there are no such thing as gift economies and commodity economies, and even where gift-exchange is practised the
social relationships constructed are not always those envisaged within
the Maussian model. Within all historical economies there were a
range of exchange mechanisms. The task of the archaeologist and
historian is to discover what these were and to reconstruct the particular way in which they articulated. Following on from this is the
recognition that the objects are not inherently gifts or commodities.
The ways in which objects are exchanged depends (to some extent
at least), on the social and cultural meanings attributed to them.
Thus an object can be produced and circulate as a commodity in
one cultural context but becomes a gift when it moves into another.
Thomas refers to this as the "mutability of things in recontextual-
ization".[120] As I suggested earlier this is an important insight when
we are dealing with economic systems which encompass a range of
social and economic forms.

It is also clear from the work of Godelier and others that we have
grossly neglected consideration of the realm of production. Many of
the precious objects which functioned within the gift-exchange systems of Melanesia were *manufactured*, and, as Mary Helms reminds
us, both craft production and craft producers were linked to notions
of ancestral and cosmological origins.[121] The value attributed to such
objects, and their function within systems of exchange, stems from
the connections they make with identity and the Beginning, rather
than from the logic of *the Gift* or from scarcity.[122] Control over the
production, distribution and consumption of these objects can thus
be intimately associated with the creation and transformation of relationships of power and domination.

What is rather less well developed within the work of anthropologists is the relationship between these concepts of exchange and
agricultural production.[123] This may be, as I have already remarked,
because of anthropology's traditional focus on exchange, but the
point is that we should not expect the kind of exchange relationships envisaged by Godelier, Helms and Thomas to have had no

---

[120] Thomas, *Entangled Objects*, p. 28.
[121] Helms, *Craft and the Kingly Ideal*.
[122] See also Godelier, *Enigma of the Gift*, p. 121.
[123] Though see M. Godelier, "The concept of 'social and economic formation':
the Inca example", in M. Godelier, *Perspectives in Marxist Anthropology* (Cambridge,
1977), pp. 63-69, and Godelier, "Salt money", for some thoughts.

connection with, and impact upon, systems of agrarian production. At the most basic level, many of the non-exotic (and indeed some of the exotic) materials used in craft production will have been acquired locally and this must have had an effect on existing economic relationships. Further, if objects acquired from a distance, and the products of craftsmen, really do have a connection with ancestral origins (as Mary Helms argues), then control over the acquisition and distribution of such products may play a significant part in the reproduction and/or intensification of existing social relationships—including those which involved the payment of tribute, tax or rent.

Anthropologists' emphasis on the classificatory possibilities of exchange, and archaeologists, focus on the provenancing of the exotic may, at least partially, account for the seemingly recurrent belief that exchange, and the objects of exchange, lie at the heart of power relations in early medieval Europe. Further, it seems to be commonly accepted that the driving forces for change within the early medieval economy have to be sought within transformations in the means of distribution. As we have seen this understanding is common even to those who differ in seeing this aspect of the past as Same or Other.[124] However, this belief seems dramatically at variance with the images gleaned from the early medieval texts with their persistent emphasis on the land. Even if this were not the case, one must question the theoretical adequacy of focusing on one aspect of past economies without considering the recursive relationship it must have enjoyed with others. The point here is that historians and (especially) archaeologists have been guilty of neglecting empirical analysis of production in early medieval Europe and of failing adequately to consider the intricacies of the dynamic relationships which must have existed between all three elements of the economic triad—production, distribution and consumption. This being the case, those histories written under the sign of the Same or the Other are doubly flawed.

Just as Marcel Mauss and Philip Grierson alerted us to the dangers of the Sameness of commercial histories, so Nicholas Thomas and the current generation of anthropologists have warned us of the simplistic construction and imposition of the Other. However, towards

---

[124] It is, perhaps, most difficult to understand when propounded (at least implicitly) by those who write from an orthodox Marxist perspective – see pp. 20-21.

the beginning of *Entangled Objects*, Thomas admits that his book is only a partial insight into the impact of the West on the economic regimes of the Pacific. For a complete analysis, he argues, he should have considered "divisions of labor, production processes, and articulations of daily or mundane transactions, larger-scale ceremonial exchange, and external trade".[125] I would argue that it is precisely this kind of integrated analysis, written with the voices of Mauss and Thomas in our ears, that will eventually allow us to approach the reality of early medieval economic relations.

---

[125] Thomas, *Entangled Objects*, p. 36. I would add processes of consumption to the list.

EXCHANGE AND POLITICS:
THE EIGHTH-EARLY NINTH CENTURY IN DENMARK

Ulf Näsman

The peripheral geographical as well as economic position of the regions of Scandinavia makes them, I believe, very sensitive to changes in the European economic exchange systems. Studies of Scandinavian external contacts are thus important contributions to the understanding of the distribution of goods and the economic as well as political network that in the Early Middle Ages connected European realms with one another as well as with Byzantium. One important aspect of the problem of production, distribution, and demand is the prelude of urbanism outside the former Roman empire, and here Scandinavian archaeology has much to offer. The long eighth century saw the establishment of the first proto-urban sites in South Scandinavia and their subsequent growth into early towns.[1]

In the sixth century, Scandinavia was a periphery outside the Merovingian sphere of interest, and consequently very seldom mentioned in the written sources; in the seventh century all is silence.[2] As a result of a growing Frankish interests in northern Europe, especially after the northerly expansion of the Carolingians, South Scandinavia appears again in the eighth century. Early in the century, Angantyr is the second Danish *rex* to be mentioned in a Frankish source.[3] The conquests of Charlemagne in the late eighth century made the realm of the Danes into a Frankish border land, and as

---

[1] For the concept proto-towns, see H. Clarke and A. Simms "Towards a comparative history of urban origin", in H. Clarke and A. Simms eds., *The comparative history of urban origins in non-Roman Europe*, BAR International Series 255/1-2 (Oxford, 1985), pp. 669-714.

[2] I. Wood, *The Merovingian North Sea* (Alingsås, 1983); U. Näsman, "The Justinianic era of South Scaninavia: an archaeological view", in R. Hodges and W. Bowden eds., *The sixth century. Production, distribution and demand*, The Transformation of the Roman World 3 (Leiden, 1998), pp. 255-78.

[3] Appears as Ongendus in Alcuin: *Vita Sancti Willibrordi*, ed. W. Levinson, *Monumenta Germaniae Historica. Scriptaes rerum merovingicarum* 7 (Hannover, 1920), pp. 81-141; quoted in I. Skovgaard-Petersen, "The written sources", in B. Bencard ed., *Ribe excavations 1970-76*, vol. 1 (Esbjerg, 1981), pp. 21-62.

such it frequently appears in the Frankish annals.[4] The improved knowledge about Scandinavian geography is of course a result of closer trade relations between Scandinavia and western Europe. Certainly the growing political and military importance of the Danish kingdom necessitated better understanding of the political situation in the North as well; the Frankish annals indicate at many occasions that diplomacy was disguised undercover activity.

The economic setting of the development that moved the Danish realm from a remote position at the Merovingian periphery to a dangerous situation at the Carolingian margin will be the theme of this paper.

Long distance trade

In the sixth century volume, I argued that the north-south trade routes through central and eastern Europe broke down in that century with significant consequences for the Scandinavian polities, which for the next centuries were directed towards the western parts of Europe.[5] In the present eighth century context, the key position that the new trade network gave to South Scandinavia still deserves special attention. The position enabled a strong power in the region to control traffic between Scandinavia proper and the Continent as well as a between the Baltic and the North Sea.[6] In the Viking Age it is obvious that the pressure on the regions at the channels between the Baltic and the North Sea, the Belts and the Sound, was a factor of great stress on the Danish kingdom, but also one of great profit.[7] In the sixth century, the Merovingians were the main external force that shaped Scandinavian societies by an *imitatio regni Francorum* as the late Hayo Vierck expressed it.[8] The material culture of the

---

[4] *Annales Regni Francorum*, ed. F. Kurze, *Monumenta Germaniae Historica. Scriptaes rerum germanicarum* 6 (Hannover, 1895).

[5] Näsman, "The Justinianic era".

[6] U. Näsman, "The ethnogenesis of the Danes and the making of a Danish kingdom", in T. Dickinson and D. Griffiths eds., *The making of kingdoms*, Anglo-Saxon Studies in Archaeology and History 10 (Oxford, 1999), pp. 1-10.

[7] O. Olsen, "Royal power in Viking Age Denmark", in H. Galinié ed., *Les mondes normands* (Caen, 1989), pp. 27-32; O. Olsen, "Royal power in Viking Age Denmark", in H. Bekker-Nielsen and H.F. Nielsen eds., *Beretning fra syvende tværfaglige vikingesymposium 1988* (Højbjerg, 1989), pp. 7-20.

[8] H. Vierck, "Imitatio imperii und Interpretatio Germanica vor der Wikinger-

Scandinavian elite evinces that the leading families longed for and tried hard to obtain the life-style of the Franks. So still during the decline of Merovingian power, Francia remained a dominating European power with considerable influence on South Scandinavia by stimulating the demand of the elite for luxuries, weapons, etc., and thus the development of production and distribution. Under the Carolingians and their successors in Austrasia, the German Ottonians, the continental impact on Danish society grew rapidly.[9] This political development had of course an economic aspect also to be studied in the archaeological record. The material is rich but a couple of examples are sufficient.

Glass vessels

In the sixth century volume, the glass vessels imported into Scandinavia were used as a good source for the study of long-distance trade, and they still are in the eighth century. The claw beakers, mainly of a sixth and seventh century date, showed a market area including Anglo-Saxon England, the northern parts of the Merovingian realm, Saxony as well as Scandinavia. In this period grave finds still constitute a large number of the finds, including some almost complete vessels. In contrast, the finds of the eighth century rarely represent graves and mainly consist of shards from settlements, often proto-urban and early urban sites. Because of the fragmentary character of the glass material scholars have refrained from closer study, and thus only few easily identified glass types have been thoroughly studied, among them vessels decorated with *reticella* cables.

Shards or vessels with *reticella* decoration are found at nineteen sites in Scandinavia, and date from the seventh century (Eketorp, Valsgärde) to the Viking Age, the ninth (Birka) and tenth centuries (Århus).[10] Shards or vessels are found in graves at five sites; shards

zeit", in R. Zeitler ed., *Les Pays du Nord et Byzance* (Uppsala, 1981), pp. 64-113, cf. H. Steuer, "Helm und Ringschwert", *Studien zur Sachsenforschung* 6 (1987), pp. 189-236.

[9] H. Vierck, "Mittel- und westeuropäischer Einwirkungen auf die Sachkultur von Haithabu/Schleswig", in H. Jankuhn *et al.* eds., *Archäologische und naturwissenschaftliche Untersuchungen an Siedlungen im deutschen Küstengebiet, 2 Handelsplätze des frühen und hohen Mittelalters* (Weinheim, 1984), pp. 366-422; E. Wamers, "Zwischen Salzburg und Oseberg. Zu Ursprung und Ikonographie des nordischen Greiftierstils", in U. von Freeden *et al.* eds., *Völker an Nord- und Ostsee und die Franken. Akten des 48. Sachsensymposium in Mannheim 1997* (Bonn, 1999), pp. 195-228.

[10] U. Näsman, "Vendel period glass from Eketorp-II, Öland, Sweden", *Acta*

come from fifteen settlements. It is unclear what kind of site some of the grave finds represent. Three sites with graves seem to represent normal rural settlements, but the glass could indicate the presence of an elite settlement.[11] Six sites are magnate manors or central places or central places of a rural character,[12] one is a fortified village and rural centre,[13] and many shards come from nine central-places/trading sites, proto-towns and early towns.[14] Note that the many finds from central-places and towns represent something new and that the *reticella* vessels thus reflect both a different source situation (the rich finds from excavations at proto-urban and urban sites) and a change in exchange and trade (a increasing part of the total economy is passing through proto-towns). The widely dispersed European distribution reveals that considerable lacuna disturb our picture, but indicates also that we have to reckon with a number of production areas (Fig. 1). The *reticella*-decorated beads support the guess that many of the Scandinavian vessels were made in England.[15]

In addition to *reticella* vessels, a number of West European glass types are to be expected in the shard finds of Scandinavia. Bell-tumblers, funnel-beakers, squat jars, pouch bottles, bottles, vessels with metal-foil decoration, mould-blown vessels, and others will probably be found when the shard assemblages from for instance Ribe and Åhus are published in due time.[16]

Our knowledge about Viking Age glass is limited, due to very few grave finds and few publications of settlement shards. The lack

Archaeologica 55 (1984 [1986]), pp. 55-116; V.I. Evison, "Some Vendel, Viking and Saxon glass", in B. Hårdh *et al.* eds., *Trade and exchange in prehistory. Studies in honour of Berta Stjernquist*, Acta Archaeologica Lundensia, Ser. in 8° 16 (Lund, 1988), pp. 237-45.

[11] Hopperstad in Sogn og Fjordane; Slagsta in Södermanland, Salum in Ångermanland.

[12] Borg in Lofoten, Valsgärde in Uppland, Slöinge in Halland, Uppåkra in Scania, Strøby in Zealand, and Sorte Muld on Bornholm.

[13] Eketorp on Öland.

[14] Kaupang in Vestfold, Birka and Helgö in Lake Mälaren, Paviken on Gotland, Åhus and Trelleborg in Scania, Århus, Ribe, and Hedeby in Jutland.

[15] Näsman "Vendel period glass"; Evison "Some Vendel, Viking and Saxon glass".

[16] The types are presented by D.B. Harden, "Glass vessels in Britain A.D. 400-1000", in D.B. Harden ed., *Dark Age Britain. Studies presented to E.T. Leeds* (London, 1956), pp. 132-67; cf. E. Baumgartner and I. Krueger, *Phönix aus Sand und Asche. Glas des Mittelalters* (München/Basel/Bonn, 1988). See also the types represented at Birka: G. Arwidsson, "Glas", in G. Arwidsson ed., *Birka* II.1, *Systematische Analysen der Gräberfunde* (Stockholm, 1984), pp. 203-12; and at Hedeby: P. Steppuhn, *Die Glasfunde von Haithabu*, Berichte über die Ausgrabungen in Haithabu 32 (Neumünster, 1998).

Fig. 1. The North-European distribution of glass vessels and shards decorated with *reticella* cables. New excavations are producing new finds, so the map is by no means complete. Dots indicate certain identifications, clover uncertain identifications. For references, see appendix.

of continental and insular material is problematic and the many
Scandinavian finds are very unevenly distributed, Birka—where a
rich burial custom was still practised—being the richest find spot in
northern Europe,[17] but this is of course a distorted impression. In
her study of the material from Birka, the late Greta Arwidsson dis-
tinguished nine different types, two of which unfortunately only known
as shards and further three types are only represented by one vessel
each. Her type 3, the *reticella* vessels, was presented above, and here
will only her type 1, funnel beakers, be treated as the most numerous of the late eighth-ninth century vessel glass.

A systematic study of the glass funnel beaker is not available and
for instance the virtual lack of this vessel type in central and eastern Europe is plausibly erroneous. Grave finds are only known in
Frisia and Scandinavia and, regrettably the few settlement finds from
the Continent and the British Isles makes it difficult to discuss production areas and trade routes. A problem is of course that funnel
beakers have few characteristic traits, so that shards consequently
will be difficult to identify with certainty.

Funnel beakers cannot be considered a new vessel type so much as
a development of the palm cups, already frequent in the sixth century.[18]
The true funnel beaker was probably developed already in the eighth
century. However, the new studies based on the Birka material enables
us to date the main period of the funnel beaker to the early Viking
Age; a vessel firmly dated to the first half of the ninth century is
found in the rich royal ship burial at Hedeby.[19] Most scholars suggest that funnel beakers are the produce of Frankish glassworks, plausibly in the region around Trier and Namur, but on the basis of the
Hamwic finds a production also in England cannot be ruled out. As
observed by energy dispersive X-ray fluorescence analysis, the
Scandinavian funnel beakers from Helgö are similar in composition
to shards from Dorestad but distinct from the glass from Hamwic.[20]

The distribution map (Fig. 2) is evidently very incomplete but

---

[17] H. Arbman, *Schweden und das Karolingische Reich* (Stockholm, 1937); cf. Arwidsson,
"Glas".

[18] J. Ypey, "Die Funde aus dem frühmittelalterlichen Gräberfeld Huinerfeld bei
Putten", *Berichten van de Rijksdienst voor het Oudheidkundig Bodemonderzoek* 12-13 (1962-
63 [1964]), pp. 99-152; Näsman "Vendel period glass", n. 227.

[19] Chronological table fig. 110 in I. Jansson, *Ovala spännbucklor* (Uppsala, 1985),
summary; cf. Arbman, *Schweden und das Karolingische Reich*, p. 83; for the Hedeby
ship grave, see E. Wamers, "König im Grenzland. Neue Analyse des Bootkammer-
grabes von Haiäaby", *Acta archaeologica* 65 (1994), pp. 1-56.

[20] J. Hunter, "The glass", in Ph. Holdsworth ed., *Excavations at Melbourne Street,*

Fig. 2. The North-European distribution of vessels and shards of funnel beakers in northern Europe. New excavations are producing new finds, so the map is by no means complete. Dots indicate certain identifications, clover uncertain identifications. For references, see appendix.

resembles nevertheless the map of the *reticella*-decorated vessels above. In Scandinavia funnel beakers are found in graves at eight sites and shard finds are made at fifteen settlements. The type occur at four sites that seem to be quite normal rural settlements,[21] five sites are magnate manors or central places of a rural character,[22] one site represents a beach market of a rural central-place[23] and many shards come from seven central-places/trading sites, proto-towns and early towns.[24]

It is questionable whether the coastal trading sites and early towns really had the dominating position in the consumption of imported goods as is indicated by the two samples of glass vessels. It seems less likely that the luxury import stopped there and was not distributed to the rural settlements where we in fact find most of the residences of the military and political leaders, including those of the members of the royal family. The bias is easily explained by the fact that we in trading sites and proto-towns find thick occupation layers with numerous small finds preserved, while the thinner occupation layer on many rural sites, also those of the elite, has been ploughed away since long. In my opinion, the few finds from sites in the countryside that do exist indicate that the use of glass was in fact more widespread than the archaeological record is able to reveal. I do not find it unreasonable to expect that a wealthy farmer at a hamlet like Omgård and Vorbasse in Jutland drank his ale from a glass vessel, like his predecessors in the Migration period.[25]

Glass vessels are typical luxury goods and as such their distribution into Scandinavia represents ancient systems of exchange in Europe. The glass vessels themselves do not indicate any change in this, but the new find contexts reveal a development between the Late Roman Iron Age (third-fourth centuries) and the late Merovingian-Carolingian/early Viking Age (the long eighth century). The

---

Southampton, 1971-76, Council for British Archaeology. Research report 33 (London, 1980), pp. 59-72; D. Sanderson, J.R. Hunter and S.E. Warren, "Energy dispersive X-ray fluorescence analysis of 1st millenium A.D. glass from Britain", *Journal of Archaeological Science* 11 (1984), pp. 53-69.

[21] Hadsel in Nordland, Andersminde, Darum and Elisenhof in Jutland.

[22] Borg in Lofoten, Ås-Husby in Uppland, Aggersborg in Jutland, Strøby on Zealand, and Sorte Muld on Bornholm.

[23] Lundeborg on Funen.

[24] Kaupang in Vestfold, Birka and Helgö in Lake Mälaren, Åhus and Trelleborg in Scania, Ribe and Hedeby in Jutland.

[25] U. Näsman, *Glas och handel i senromersk tid och folkvandringstid* (Uppsala, 1984), summary.

obvious difference is that the bulk of the luxuries in the late Merovingian and Carolingian periods were distributed via specialised trading places, some of which can be classified as proto-towns or early towns. The question is now, whether this change can be observed in other parts of the archaeological record.

Glass beads

Glass beads have received greater attention during the last decades and a growing number of scholars realises that bead assemblages contain important information concerning distribution of goods, be it beads stringed as jewellery in a grave, stray beads lost on at dwelling site, or defect beads discarded at a trading place or in a workshop.[26] But still we lack a comprehensive Scandinavian study of both bead import and domestic bead production in the long time perspective from the Roman period till glass beads lost their position as dress ornament in the High Middle Ages. However, there exist fortunately a number of studies of glass beads of the "long eighth century".[27]

In Ribe careful excavations at different sites in the market and craft area have produced an excellent stratigraphic bead chronology.[28] Workshop debris proves the production of blue glass beads, mostly of simple rounded shapes but also polyhedral or melon-shaped. Many have a trail decoration in red-and-white. They were produced here mainly in the years 705–760, and the blue beads are so common and characteristic that the excavators call them "Ribe beads". In other parts of Scandinavia they are so frequent in women's graves that the era is named "the blue period". The glass metal was imported via western Europe as blue glass cakes for the body and coloured

---

[26] See papers in two recent bead books: U. von Freeden and A. Wieczorek eds., *Perlen* (Frankfurt a.M./Bonn, 1997); and M. Rasmussen *et al.* eds., *Glass Beads*, Historical-archaeological experimental centre. Studies in technology and culture 2 (Lejre, 1995).

[27] For references, see J. Callmer, "Beads and bead production in Scandinavia and the Baltic region c. A.D. 600-1100", in *Perlen*, pp. 197-202 and pl. 15-18; the following is based on this paper and my own studies of the import and manufacture of glass beads at Ribe, see the prelim. note "Die Herstellung von Glasperlen" in M. Bencard, "Wikingerzeitliche Handwerk in Ribe", *Acta Archaeologica* 49 (1978 [1979]), pp. 124-33.

[28] My own studies of Ribe bead making debris, cf. note 27; and studies by C. Feveile and S. Jensen, "Ribe in the eighth and ninth centuries a contribution to the chronology in north-western Europe", *Acta Archaeologica* 17 (2000), in press.

tesserae for the trailed decoration, but the production was certainly Nordic. Rich evidence from workshops at Ribe and Åhus reveals a large output.[29] In fact, the workshop debris is so similar at the two sites that it must represent bead makers with the same training, the same group of bead makers, or indeed, the same itinerant craftsmen.

In this early period also another bead type was produced in large numbers at Ribe. Made from blue and white *reticella* cables and with a red equator it has an evidently Celtic insular origin.[30] The evidence of Ribe and Åhus suggests that *reticella* rods were made on the site, but an import from the British Isles is another possibility. In any case, identical beads in Scandinavia and the British Isles demonstrate very close links. Furthermore, so-called *millefiori* beads were also made at both Ribe and Åhus; a bead type certainly based on imported technology. Probably most of the *millefiori*-rods were imported as well, but in Ribe strong indications of local manufacture are present.

In the second half of the eighth and the first of the ninth century the bead spectrum changed, and the import of beads increased and the domestic production seemingly decreased correspondingly; the "Ribe" beads and the *reticella* beads disappeared almost totally. Typical imports are segmented beads made from glass tubes, often with a clear or "golden" overlay covering a metal foil, small beads cut from a drawn cane, stratified eye beads, and the so-called *Mosaikaugenperlen* (mosaic eye beads).[31] These beads seem to be produced in the eastern Mediterranean, Byzantium, and the Caliphate. The bulk of the eastern beads found in West and South Scandinavia were probably imported via trade routes through central Europe (Hungary-Moravia-Thuringia-Saxony), while most of the oriental beads found in the northern Baltic area probably followed the newly opened routes along the east European rivers.

This shift is clearly seen in the Ribe stratigraphy, in which the blue "Ribe" types are rare or lacking after c. 760 A.D. and their place

---

[29] J. Callmer and J. Henderson, "Glassworking at Åhus, S. Sweden", *Laborativ arkeologi* 5 (1991), pp. 143-54.

[30] Näsman, "Vendel period glass".

[31] R. Andrae, "Mosaikaugenperlen", *Acta praehistorica et archaeologica* 4 (1973), pp. 101-98; Callmer, "Beads and bead production"; Callmer, "The influx of oriental beads into Europe during the 8th century A.D.", in *Glass Beads*, pp. 49-54; M. Jönsson and P. Hunner, "Gold-foil beads", in *Glass Beads*, pp. 113-16.

taken by new types. Among these are the imported eastern beads, many of which are misshapen and discarded, appearing in large numbers after c. 790 A.D. Domestic production of simple wound monochrome beads did not stop, however, but the types changed. A new Scandinavian type is the so-called wasp bead, black with yellow trails; debris indicates that many were made at Ribe in the decades before and around 800.

Perhaps the most interesting observation enabled by the bead studies is the enormous amount of evidence at Ribe and Åhus for frequent visits by both specialised craftsmen and traders. In contrast, the evidence is much smaller and more sporadic at central places and landing places of earlier centuries. Now in the eighth century, we certainly see that the economic development has passed the threshold to urbanisation. Furthermore, it is—as Callmer has pointed out—characteristic that the competition from the imported oriental beads obviously became a serious threat to the domestic bead-makers at the end of the century, an observation that allows us to suggest that the treaty trade of the Migration period and the early Merovingian period is now changing towards a market economy.

Other important observations made possible by the bead studies in Ribe are the precise dating of the opening of the oriental import into west Denmark to not before 780 and not after 800, and that the beads probably went along a trade route through central Europe. In the northern Baltic, the import may have started somewhat earlier as indicated by Callmer's studies (at Staraja Ladoga they appear already in layers of the 760s),[32] but here the trade route followed the Russian rivers. This means that in the first eight decades of the eighth century the economic basis of the first Scandinavian *emporia* at Ribe, Hedeby, and Åhus, was based on the exchange with West Europe. The early bead technology certainly demonstrates the strong western impact on Scandinavian craftsmen.

The links to the growing eastern economy of Russia and the east Baltic zone did not become significant until well into the ninth century.[33] It is important to note that oriental imports into Scandinavia are extremely rare in the seventh century, so the oriental beads mark

[32] E.A. Rjabinin and V.A. Galibin, "New data concerning early glass making in Ladoga", in *Glass Beads*, pp. 109-12.
[33] I. Jansson, "Wikingerzeitlicher orientalischer Import in Skandinavien", *Bericht der Römisch-Germanischen Kommission* 69 (1988 [1989]), pp. 565-647.

the exchange and trade with the east that characterised the Viking Age. After the break in the late Migration period (discussed in the sixth century volume), expanding economic activities of the Slavs in central and eastern Europe now involved their realms in a network including both Byzantium and the Caliphate. Eventually, in the late eighth century these contacts reached also Scandinavia.

Pottery

An import to South Scandinavian of pottery of West-European provenance began in the eighth century, and shards occurring at Danish settlements represent vessel types produced at potteries along the Rhine, so-called Badorf, Reliefband, and Tating ware, as well as in Frisia, the so-called Muschelgrus ware.[34] These wares were certainly traded in large quantities within the Carolingian realm. A fraction found its way to the Nordic regions but the character of the distribution is far from clear. In Ribe the earliest finds of Muschelgrus ware date to the 780s, Badorf ware to the 790s, Reliefband ware to the 810s and Tating shards are common from c. 800. Some believe the vessels were not proper trade goods but simply came as containers—for instance the Reliefband amphora that presumably held wine—or as part of the personal equipment of merchants and seamen, an interpretation based on the fact that imported pottery is mainly found at urban sites and trading places. As Heiko Steuer has pointed out, the finds seem to be companions of western civilisation and mark the routes of foreign merchants. However, the Tating jugs with their tin-foil decoration are in contexts frequently associated with glass funnel beakers, for instance in graves, and thus certainly represent traditional luxury exchange. Compared to the number of shards of domestic wares on sites of the eighth century, the small

---

[34] H. Steuer, "Der Handel der Wikingerzeit zwischen Nord- und Westeuropa aufgrund archäologischer Zeugnisse", in K. Düwel *et al.* eds., *Untersuchungen zu Handel und Verkehr der vor- und frühgeschichtlichen Zeit in Mittel- und Nordeuropa,* IV *Der Handel der Karolinger- und Wikingerzeit,* Abhandlungen d.Akad.d. Wissenschaften, Phil.-Hist. Kl. III 156 (Göttingen, 1987), pp. 113-97; S. Jensen, "Handel med dagligvarer i vikingetiden", *Hikuin* 16 (1990), pp. 119-38, 156 (abstract); H.J. Madsen, "Vikingetidens keramik som historisk kilde", in P. Mortensen and B. Rasmussen eds., *Fra Stamme til Stat i Danmark,* 2 *Høvdingesamfund og kongemagt,* Jysk arkæologisk selskabs skrifter 22/2 (Højbjerg/Aarhus, 1991), pp. 217-34 (summary); Feveile and Jensen, "Ribe in the eighth and ninth centuries".

quantity of imported vessels (5-7% of the ceramic finds at both Hedeby and Ribe) indicates that pottery must not be considered to be important trade goods.[35] Nevertheless, the few shards found in the rural hamlets and farmsteads of southern Jutland indicate nevertheless that in the region of Hedeby and Ribe, ceramic vessels were exchanged between *emporia* and countryside, but due to uncertain datings it is at present uncertain when this exchange started.[36]

A further indication of a strong western influence on the economy of south-western Denmark is the recent discovery that a wheel-turned ware of hitherto unknown provenance is, in fact, domestic.[37] Using magnetic susceptibility and thermoluminescence analyses it has been established that at least two distinct potteries produced turned and decorated vessels in the Ribe region, at Ribe itself and at Okholm, an adjacent rural centre settlement at the coast at which also glass beads were made and bronze objects cast. Up to now a Scandinavian production of wheel-turned pottery was not expected to date earlier than around 1200 A.D., so it is remarkable that this technology now is found in south Jutland as early as the early eighth century. In Ribe the turned ware disappeared again after c. 750. Obviously it could not stand the double competition with the hand-made semispherical vessel type, which with its probable origin in northern Jutland became the dominating ware during the ninth and tenth centuries, and an increasing import from western Europe that gave south-western Jutland its own character as ceramic province of Denmark. It seems obvious that the unsuccessful introduction of new technology was based on the know-how of the potters along the Rhine valley.

Hone stones, quern stones and soapstone vessels

Another important new element in the eighth century exchange is the appearance in South Scandinavia of imported household utensils like hone stones, quern stones, and soapstone vessels. The earliest import of lava quern stones from Mayen in the Rhineland is dated

---

[35] Madsen, "Vikingetidens keramik".

[36] M. Müller-Wille, "Hedeby und sein Umland", in B. Hårdh *et al.* eds., *Trade and exchange in prehistory. Studies in honour of Berta Stjernquist*, Acta Archaeologica Lundensia, Ser. in 8° 16 (Lund, 1988), pp. 271-78.

[37] C. Feveile, S. Jensen and K.L. Rasmussen, "Produktion af drejet keramik i Ribeområdet i sen yngre germansk jernalder", *Kuml* 1997-98, pp. 143-59 (summary).

to the Late Roman Iron Age and restricted to southernmost Jutland.[38]
In the eighth century the import grew considerably as indicated by
the excavations in Ribe and at Omgård.[39] Fragments of lava quern
stones are common on Viking Age settlements in the southern part
of Jutland, with a rapidly falling frequency on Funen, Zealand, and
further into the Baltic (Fig. 3).[40] The earliest finds in Ribe date to
the beginning of the eighth century. In Viking Age contexts imported
quern stones of mica schist with garnets are common but so far not
frequent before the tenth century.[41]

Hone stones belong to a common and overlooked find type in
settlements. A violet type that presumably is imported from the
Continent is in Ribe present from c. 800, while the well-known
Eidsborg-hones from south Norway do not appear in Ribe before
c. 850. At present we do not know whether it was traded to northern Jutland earlier. Fragments of soapstone vessels are also common
on Viking Age settlements in Jutland. In Ribe they do not occur
before the ninth century, but in northern Jutland the import probably started already in the eighth century, but proof is lacking.

Equipment made of stone is regularly well preserved in archaeological contexts, and it is assumed that the increasing import of stone
goods parallels an increasing trade in perishable goods.

Sceattas

After the end of the *solidus* import in the mid-sixth century, there is
no use of imported coins in Scandinavia during from the late sixth
to the early eighth century. Neither do we know finds of cut silver
or gold used as unminted means of payment. The use of minted as
well as unminted money in the Late Roman and Migration periods
seems thus to have been a superficial phenomenon above and outside the basic production economy of rural Scandinavian polities.

But in the early eighth century things changed, a small light silver
coin, the *sceat*, was introduced as trade coinage in South Scan-

---

[38] L. Christensen and N. Hardt, "Kværnsten af basaltlava – en overset romersk
oldsag?" *Arkeologi i Slesvig* 5 (1996), pp. 61-68.
[39] L.C. Nielsen, "Omgård. The Viking Age water-mill complex", *Acta Archaeologica*
57 (1986), pp. 177-204; Jensen, "Handel med dagligvarer".
[40] Näsman, "Vendel period glass", pp. 94ff.; Steuer, "Der Handel der Wikingerzeit"; L.C. Nielsen, "Trelleborg", Aarbøger for nordisk oldkyndighed og historie
(1990), pp. 105-78 (Zusammenfassung).
[41] Nielsen, "Omgård", p. 195.

dinavia.[42] The distribution of *sceattas* in Scandinavia is with few exceptions restricted to proto-urban and early urban sites, the largest and best stratified material coming from Ribe. The suggestion that the Woden/monster type might have been struck in Ribe is tempting but in lack of a die-find still very uncertain. At Ribe the *sceattas* occur in occupation layers deposited from c. 725 to c. 800. In layers dated from c. 800 to c. 850 a number of coins of so-called Hedeby types are present, some of which have the Woden/monster sceat as prototype. The Hedeby types are the first certain domestic mintage,[43] and dating to the early ninth century they demonstrate the maturing economy of the southern province of the Danish kingdom. But already the contexts of the many *sceattas* reveal that coins were used in the commerce in Ribe and probably also other ports-of-trade in South Scandinavia. So far, very few *sceattas* are found on rural sites, so evidently their use is connected to the commerce of the specialised trading sites, which obviously could be labelled "pools of currency" as well.[44]

In the course of the ninth century, the silver from the west was replaced by silver from the east, the Arabic silver that came to dominate the economic transactions for the next hundred years. The silver stream from the east resulted in a widespread use of hack silver as means of payment, which made the Danish attempt to introduce a domestic monetary system unsuccessful or, as Steuer puts it, a western *Münzgeldwirtschaft* was replaced by an eastern *Gewichtsgeldwirtschaft*, Jutland being placed in the border zone between the two systems.[45]

---

[42] K. Bendixen, "Finds of sceattas from Scandinavia" and D.M. Metcalf, "A note on sceattas as a measure of international trade, and on the earliest Danish coinage", in D. Hill and D.M. Metcalf eds., *Sceattas in England and on the Continent*, BAR British Series 128 (Oxford, 1984), pp. 151-57 and 159-64; J. Callmer, *Sceatta problems in the light of the finds from Åhus* (Lund, Scripta Minora 1983-1984/2). B. Malmer and K. Jonsson, "Sceattas och den äldsta nordiska utmyntingen", *Nordisk numismatisk unions medlemsblad* 1986/4, pp. 66-71; D.M. Metcalf, "Nyt om sceattas af typen Wodan/monster", *Nordisk numismatisk unions medlemsblad* 1986/6, pp. 110-20; K. Bendixen, "The coins from the oldest Ribe", *Nordisk numismatisk Årsskrift* 1989-90 [1994], pp. 27-44.

[43] B. Malmer, *Nordiska mynt före år 1000*, Acta Archaeologica Lundensia, ser. in 8° 4 (Lund, 1966).

[44] B. Malmer, "Om vikingatidens betalningsmedel", in *Fra stamme til stat i Danmark*, 2 *Høvdingesamfund og kongemagt*, pp. 209-15 (summary).

[45] H. Steuer, "Gewichtsgeldwirtschaften in frühgeschichtlichen Europa", in K. Düwel et al. eds., *Untersuchungen zu Handel und Verkehr der vor- und frühgeschichtlichen Zeit in Mittel- und Nordeuropa*, IV *Der Handel der Karolinger- und Wikingerzeit*, Abhandlungen d.Akad.d. Wissenschaften, Phil.-Hist. Kl. III 156 (Göttingen, 1987), pp. 405-527; B. Hårdh, *Silver in the Viking Age. A Regional-Economic Study*, Acta Archaeologica Lundensia. Ser. in 8° 25 (Lund, 1996).

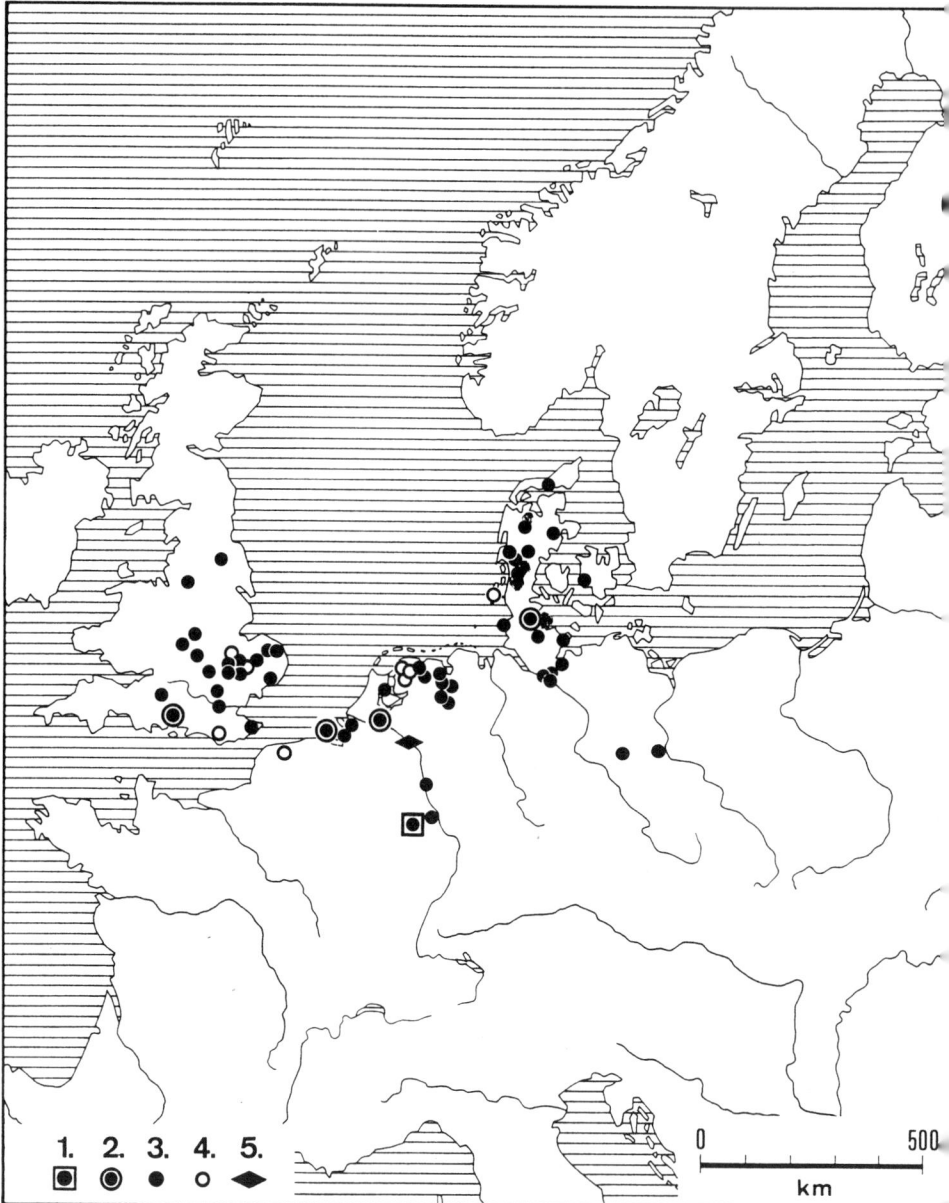

Fig. 3a. The distribution of Mayen lava quern stones in northwestern Europe. 1: the quarrie
2: several finds, 3: finds, 4: uncertain context, 5: shipload.

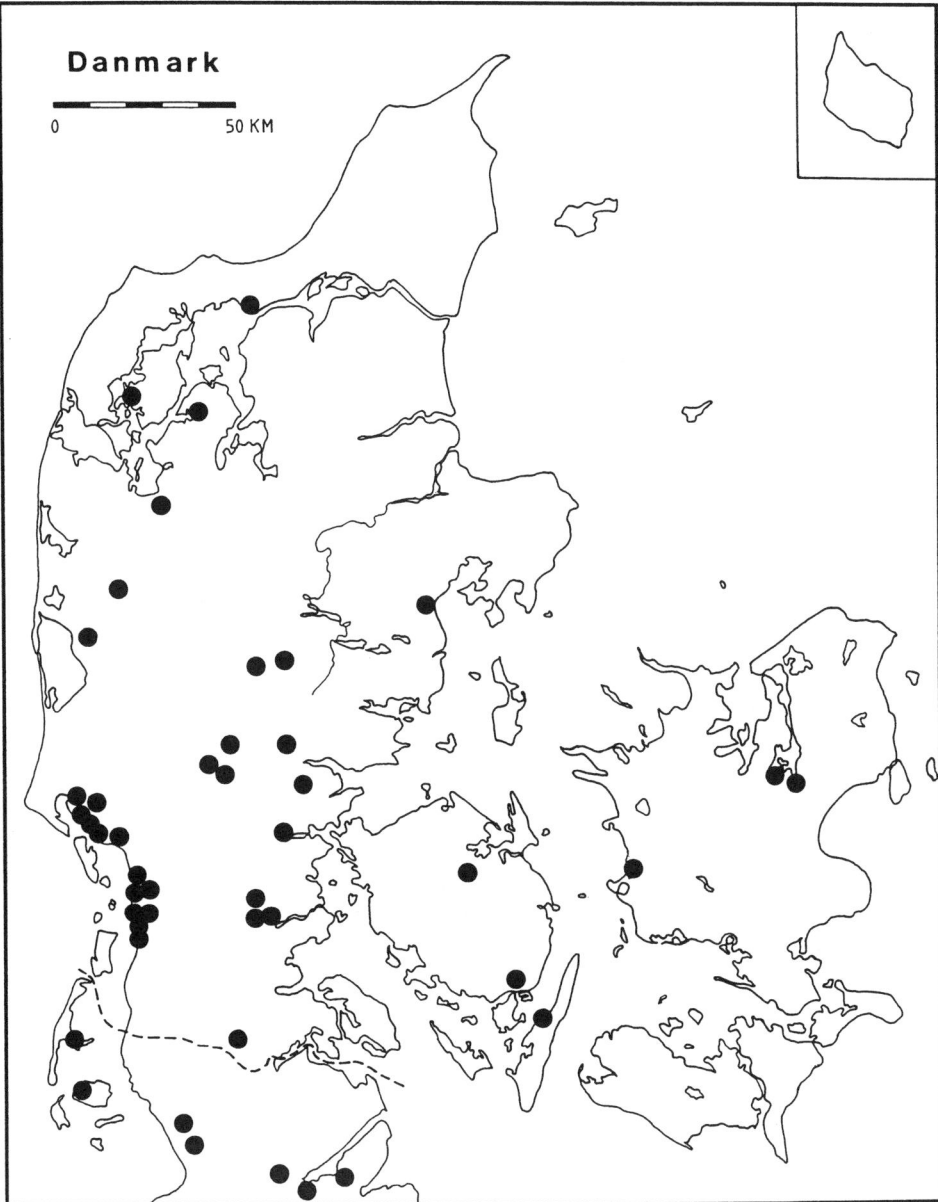

Fig. 3b. The distribution of Mayen lava quern stones in Denmark and Schleswig. Settlement excavations in this part of Europe are produ   many new finds, so the maps are by no means complete.

To sum up: The advanced ceramic and glass bead technologies introduced in the eighth century support one another in demonstrating
that the south-western part of the Danish realm was in rapid technological as well as economic development. The monetary evidence
indicates that the economic system at the trading places and early
towns was heading towards an integration in the West-European economic system. The distribution of finds related to the increasing trade
in basic commodities and bulk cargo reveals that frequent and varied
exchange between rural settlements and proto-urban sites began
already in the eighth century in the economically most developed
part of the Danish realm, i.e. south Jutland.

Early urbanisation

A traditional view on Scandinavian urbanisation has as its central
assumption that urbanisation was a slow gradual process. Towns are
considered to grow organically out of rural landing sites or ham-
lets/villages near coasts or navigable streams via simple trading sites,
temporary markets or manorial estates. The progress of urbanisation
is usually believed to be simply a linear result of increasing trade.
The interests of the elite and the kings in towns were consequently
regarded as a secondary phenomenon, kings using existing trading
sites to increase their incomes by taking "protection money" in various
forms. A seminal paper by Erik Cinthio[46] opened a new perspective,
rejecting trade as the main explanation and placing the initiative of
urbanisation in the hands of early medieval kingship. Cinthio also
sketched a sequence of stages in Scandinavian urbanisation, ideas subsequently developed by others.[47]

Archaeological discoveries during the last years have again changed
our perspective. It is the identification of proto-urban centres in a

---

[46] E. Cinthio, "Variationsmuster in dem mittelalterlichen Städtewesen Schones"
in H. Hinz ed., *Frühe Städte im westlichen Ostseeraum* (Neumünster, Kiel Papers 1972).
[47] The discussion is summarised by *i.a.* A. Christophersen, "Royal authority and
early urbanization in Trondheim," *Archaeology and the urban economy. Festschrift to Åsbjørn
Herteig*, Historisk Museum, Arkeologiske skrifter 5 (Bergen, 1989), pp. 91-135; and
A. Andrén, "Comments on Trade, towns, and states: a reconsideration of early
Medieval economics", *Norwegian archaeological review* 28/2 (1995), pp. 123-26.

rural setting that has set the agenda of the discussion. An increasing number of these so-called central-places have prolonged the proto-urban phase from the early Viking Age back into the Late Roman period, the earliest site dating to the third century.[48] One may today assume that the central-places represent a new economic and political organisation, which started to develop already in the Late Roman Iron Age, i.e. before a Danish kingdom had appeared on the historical scene. From the fifth century onwards the number of centres and landing places increased rapidly in South Scandinavia.[49] These centres were not urban communities, but give evidence of a new type of centralised economy. They were places where the agrarian surplus was mobilised for use in the construction of a more complex social system. Presumably, a significant amount of the resources of the incipient Danish kingdom was created at these centres. Certainly, they also fulfilled important religious and political functions. They can be regarded as South Scandinavian non-urban centres, and the small finds give rich evidence of their links to continental centres.

Later, in the early eighth century, a new development seems to begin with the establishment of the first Scandinavian proto-towns. Ribe in Jutland, the earliest so far, was established as a market and craft centre in the first decades of the eighth century. The economic system behind the Scandinavian proto-towns was created in economic and political interaction with western Europe, and here we find their proto-types: Quentovic, Dorestad, Hamwic, etc. Certainly the inclusion of Ribe among the *emporia* of the eighth century is justified.[50]

---

[48] On South Scandinavian central-places and early urbanisation, see U. Näsman, "Some comments on the symposium "Social organization and regional variation", Sandbjerg Manor, April 1989", in Ch. Fabech and J. Ringtved eds., *Samfundsfundsorganisation og regional variation*, Jysk Arkælogisk Selskabs skrifter 27 (Højbjerg/Aarhus, 1991), pp. 328-33; J. Callmer, "Urbanization in Scandinavia and the Baltic region c. A.D. 700-1100", in B. Ambrosiani and H. Clarke eds., *Developments around the Baltic and the North Sea in the Viking Age. The Twelfth Viking Congress*, Birka studies 3 (Stockholm, 1994), pp. 50-90; P.O. Nielsen, K. Randsborg and H. Thrane eds., *The archaeology of Gudme and Lundeborg*, Arkæologiske studier 10 (Copenhagen, 1994); Ch. Fabech, "Centrality in Sites and Landscapes", in Ch. Fabech and J. Ringtved eds., *Settlement and Landscape* (Højbjerg/Aarhus, 1999): pp. 455-74.

[49] J. Ulriksen, "Danish sites and settlements with a maritime context A.D. 200-1200", *Antiquity* 68 (1994), pp. 797-811; J. Ulriksen, Anløbspladser, Besejling og bebyggelse i Danmark mellem 200 og 1100 e.Kr. (Roskilde, 1997), p. 182 (summary).

[50] See e.g. R. Hodges, *Dark Age Economics* (London, 1982) and A. Verhulst in this volume.

Ribe

Near the west coast of south Jutland, c. six km upstream a small east-west navigable river and at the ford of a north-south road, Ribe appeared around 705 A.D. as a trading and craft centre.[51] A short prelude is characterised by irregular ditches and a thin occupation layer with few finds representing craft and trade. It was replaced by a system of tenement plots for craftsmen and traders along more than two hundred meters of the northern riverbank, marked out by ditches and alleys perpendicular to a road that probably ran parallel to the river (Fig. 4). A well-preserved stratigraphy allows the archaeologist to study the development of the workshops through decades from c. 705 to c. 850 (younger debris was plausibly used as fill in a milldam during the High Middle Ages). The stratigraphic chronology is based on dendrodated wood samples, many so-called Woden/monster *sceattas*, and small find typologies (jewellery, beads, pottery, etc.).

The market area was probably used only seasonally, but remains of the residential quarters are found a short distance behind the market area. Very little dating evidence is available, unfortunately, but according to the excavator the beginning of permanent occupation is not later than the mid-eighth century. Eventually, permanent buildings were erected also on the plots of the market area and not later than the end of the eighth century. Parts of cremation cemeteries at the urban perimeter have been excavated as well, dating to eighth and early ninth centuries. The richest archaeological material comes from the thick occupation layers of the market area, while the residential areas have thin layers and like the graves are relatively poor in finds. Thus the obvious importance of early eighth century Ribe rests almost entirely on the excavations in the narrow zone of riparian activities, an observation of significance when evaluating the evidence of early Hedeby (see below).

---

[51] M. Bencard ed., *Ribe excavations 1970-76*, 1 (Esbjerg, 1981); *Ribe excavations 1970-76*, 2 (Esbjerg, 1984); M. Bencard *et al.* eds., *Ribe excavations 1970-76*, 3 (Esbjerg, 1991); *Ribe excavations 1970-76*, 4 (Esbjerg, 1990); L.B. Frandsen and S. Jensen "Pre-Viking and early Viking Age Ribe", *Journal of Danish Archaeology* 6 (1987 [1988]): pp. 175-89; S. Jensen, *The Vikings of Ribe* (Ribe, 1992); C. Feveile, "The latest news from Viking Age Ribe", in B. Ambrosiani and H. Clarke eds., *Developments around the Baltic and the North Sea in the Viking Age. The Twelfth Viking Congress*, Birka studies 3 (Stockholm, 1994): pp. 91-99; Feveile and Jensen, "Ribe in the eighth and ninth centuries"; thanks for unpublished information given by Claus Feveile, Ribe.

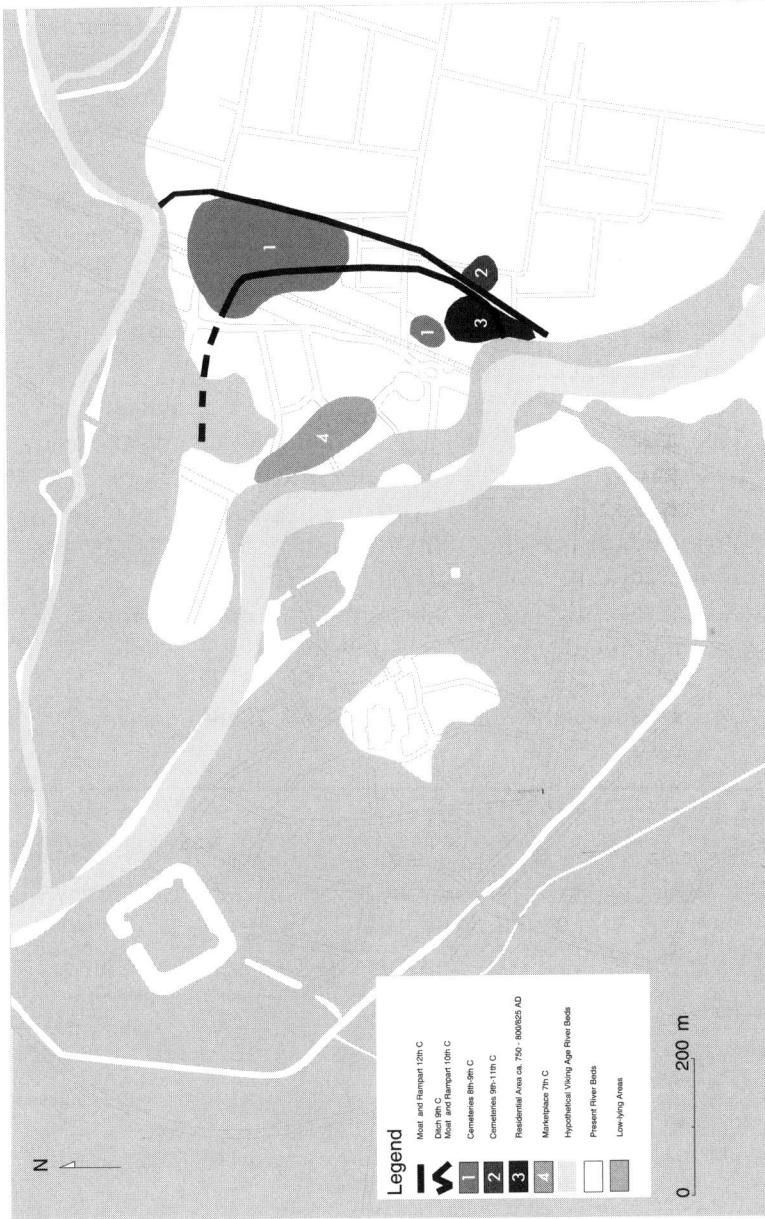

Fig. 4. Map of early urban Ribe, Jutland, situated between Ribe and Tved River. Though settlement remains have been revealed in a number of small trenched within the perimeter dith, these are often of uncertain date and have not been marked on the map. In the twelfth century the cathedral was built on the west side of Ribe River and here the high and late medieval town developed. Data produced by Claus Feveile, Den Antikvariske Samling, Ribe; map edited by Peter Steen Nielsen, Dept. of Prehistoric Archaeology, University of Aarhus.

In the first half of the ninth century Ribe got a shallow perimeter ditch that marked a boundary between the surroundings and the town itself, and indeed, the ditch indicates that Ribe now had left its status as proto-urban. It is not yet established whether the ditch delimited a half-circular area like at many other sites or whether it simply cut across the peninsula between Ribe River and the smaller Tved River. Anyhow, the few traces of permanent settlement seem to be restricted to the area within the perimeter ditch and the graves are placed outside. Later in the tenth century a real defence consisting of moat and rampart replaced the ditch. The enclosed area is c. 10 ha; Hedeby grew in the ninth century to c. 24 ha, and Hamwic covered c. 42 ha, Ipswich c. 100 ha, and Dorestad was even larger, so Ribe was not a large site and comparable to Swedish Birka with c. 11 ha.[52]

Nevertheless, Ribe is the oldest town of the Danish kingdom that we know today. The planned lay-out of tenements in the market area, the boundary ditch, the urban defences, and King Horik the younger's obviously important role when the missionary bishop of Hamburg-Bremen Anskar had a church built here in the 850s,[53] all indicate a strong royal presence in Ribe from its foundation in the early eighth century till the High Middle Ages.[54] But it has to be admitted that archaeology cannot prove whether Ribe was founded by a king or grew up following an initiative of the local elite, the presence of which is testified by the magnate manor Dankirke nearby.[55]

Hedeby

The largest Scandinavian town of the early ninth centuries was Hedeby, situated at the bottom of the Schlei Fjord at the east coast of southern Jutland, in the present German federal state of Schleswig-Holstein.[56] In the seventh and eighth centuries the nearby dyke

---

[52] Hodges, *Dark Age Economics*.

[53] *Vita Ansgarii* by Rimbert; English translation: C.H. Robinson, *Anskar, the apostle of the North* (London, 1921).

[54] Jensen, *The Vikings of Ribe*; O. Olsen, "Nogle tanker i anledning af Ribes uventet høje alder", *Fra Ribe amt* (Ribe, 1975), pp. 225-58.

[55] H. Jarl Hansen, "Dankirke: affluence in late Iron Age Denmark", in K. Randsborg ed., *The birth of Europe: Archaeology and social development in the first millennium A.D.*, Analecta Romana Instituti Danici. Suppl. 16 (Rome,1989), pp. 123-28; H. Jarl Hansen, "Dankirke", *Kuml* 1988-89 (1990), pp. 201-24 (summary).

[56] H. Jankuhn, *Haithabu. Ein Handelsplatz der Wikingerzeit* 8th ed. (Neumünster,

Danevirke barred the main watershed of Jutland just north of Hedeby and near the southern limit of Danish settlement.[57] In fact, Hedeby is placed in a danger zone created by the interaction between Germanic speaking Danes, Frisians and Saxons, and the Slavic speaking Obodrites. So besides a position at an economically favourable junction between land and water routes, one can guess that the site quickly came to serve as a political and military stronghold of the Danish kingdom. Traditionally, scholars have focused on Hedeby as a transit station in long-distance trade, but recent investigations reveal that a hinterland existed.[58]

The earliest settlement is dating to the eighth century, but only small parts have been excavated. Remains of houses and the small finds of the occupation layers resemble the Ribe find. The material is much smaller, however, since it is only the residential quarters that have been excavated while a presumed market and craft area has not been found. As in Ribe, it should probably be looked for at the shore. So whether the early Hedeby was an as thriving centre as contemporary Ribe is at present uncertain. As the evidence stands, Ribe must have been the more important centre of the eighth century.

Later in the early ninth century, a new and larger settlement core developed just north of the early southern settlement. Water-logged occupation layers near the shore have enabled archaeologists to unveil the town plan in details, and well-preserved wood have given dates covering the time span 811 to 1020. This Hedeby is mentioned a number of times in the Frankish annals, the first time in 804. The annals reveal that the Danish King Godfred was in power here and had great influence on the urban development. Later the missionary Anskar got a permission by King Horik the elder around year 850 to build the first church in the Danish realm, and after the first church had been torn down during a pagan reaction, a new permission was given by his successor King Horik the younger.[59]

Rich finds have been made both in the settlement and in the harbour, where a number of wrecked ships are among the finds.

1986); K. Schietzel ed., *Berichte über die Ausgrabungen in Haithabu* 1 – continued (Neumünster, 1969 – continued); O. Crumlin-Pedersen, "The rise and decline of Hedeby/Schleswig as a major port of the Baltic trade", in *Beretning fra det ellevte tværfaglige vikingesymposium* (Højbjerg, 1992), pp. 27-34.

[57] H.H. Andersen, *Danevirke og Kovirke: arkæologiske undersøgelser 1861-1993* (Aarhus, 1998), in Danish and German.

[58] Müller-Wille, "Hedeby und sein Umland".

[59] *Annales Regni Francorum; Vita Ansgarii.*

Thousands of small finds reveal the wide trade relations of Hedeby in the ninth century and its function as a port between Western Europe and the North Sea, and Eastern Europe and the Baltic is evident. The first Danish mintage was located here in the early ninth century, the so-called Hedeby coins.[60]

It seems as if Hedeby had passed Ribe in importance by the early ninth century, and now the town was not only an economic centre at the Baltic, in both archaeological and historical sources the site appears as a main centre of the Danes. The later history of the town falls outside the scope of this paper. The impressive rampart now surrounding the 24 ha large town area belong to this later phase, the earliest rampart is dated to the mid-tenth century, i.e. more or less contemporary with the urban defence of Ribe. It soon became an integrated part of the extended Danevirke complex. It has to be emphasised that in the eighth-ninth century both Ribe and Hedeby were open settlements. At Hedeby, however, a hill fort just north of the town could possibly offer some protection as a refuge in danger. Whether Hedeby in the ninth century had a perimeter ditch like the one identified in Ribe is unfortunately not known, but the presence of a *comes*, Hovi, who obviously was the king's authority in Hedeby, strongly indicate that its administrative function differed from a normal rural settlement.[61]

Åhus

The important investigations at Åhus in east Scania are so far only described in preliminary papers.[62] Three different sites are located, representing three different phases of urbanisation. Situated near the mouth of Helgeå ("Holy River"), which drains the rich plain of Vä, they were certainly riverine ports serving this more or less independent polity.[63] No written evidence exists. The earliest site dates to

---

[60] Malmer, *Nordiska mynt.*

[61] *Vita Ansgarii,* chs. 30-31.

[62] J. Callmer, "Platser med anknytning till handel och hantverk i yngre järnålder", in *Fra stamme til stat i Danmark,* 2 *Høvdingesamfund og kongemagt,* pp. 29-47, summary; J. Callmer, "Hantverksproduktion, samhällsförändringar och bebyggelse", in H.G. Resi ed., *Produksjon og samfunn. Om erverv, spesialisering og bosetning i Norden i 1. Årtusind e.Kr.,* Universitetets Oldsaksamling. Varia 30 (Oslo, 1995), pp. 39-72 (summary); thanks to Johan Callmer for unpublished information.

[63] Opinions differ: Ch. Fabech, "Skåne – et kulturelt og geografisk grænseland i

the eighth century, and a rich material of trade and craft production has been found, but the building remains indicate that it was
used only seasonally. The small finds demonstrate very close similarities to contemporary Ribe, but the structure of the site is different
and seemingly less well organised. The early market place at Åhus
fits into a pattern of seasonal market sites along the coasts of the
Baltic during the eighth century,[64] and these coastal sites were probably attached to a regional system of magnate manors and central-
places.[65] Thus the first phase at Åhus can be a constituent of a
settlement hierarchy and a regional lordship. Ribe was undoubtedly
a proto-town that rapidly developed into an early town, while Åhus
rather seems to have been a shore-market attached to a wealthy
inland and its centre at Vä.

The seasonal market place at Åhus seems to be deserted in the
late eighth century for an obviously more permanent trading site,
placed closer to the coast. Evidence of crafts and trade is rich, but
the limited excavations give only vague answers to the question
whether the settlement was permanent or seasonal. Nevertheless a
regularity of settlement layout could indicate that this second phase
at Åhus had a semi-permanent and proto-urban character. This second site was possibly abandoned already in the mid-ninth century.
Unfortunately it is unclear whether a lacuna in the tenth century
reflects a real stop in the trading activities at the Helgeå, or whether
there was a continuity till the beginning of the medieval town Åhus
in the eleventh century, a royal town that became a main port in
the eastern part of medieval Denmark.

The second permanent/semi-permanent site at Åhus has by Callmer
been related to a phase of spontaneous urbanisation at the Baltic and
explained as the result of an increase of trade that the Baltic experienced during the second half of the eighth century and the early
ninth century. However, the great similarities in small finds and craft
debris at Ribe and the first settlement at Åhus certainly indicate that

---

yngre jernalder og i nutiden", *Tor* 25 (1993), pp. 201-45 (summary), dates the sub-
mission to Danish power to the eleventh century; Callmer, "Urbanization in
Scandinavia", dates the event to the late tenth century.

[64] D. Carlsson, "Harbours and trading places on Gotland A.D. 600-1000", in
O. Crumlin-Pedersen ed., *Aspects of maritime Scandinavia* (Roskilde, 1991). pp. 145-58;
Callmer, "Urbanization in Scandinavia"; Ulriksen, "Danish sites and settlements
with a maritime context A.D. 200-1200".

[65] See Näsman, "The Justinianic era", p. 269.

the eastern part of the North Sea region and the western area of
the Baltic were closely linked to one another. The second proto-
urban phase at Åhus may thus rather indicate that more permanent
trade and craft centres as at Ribe now appeared, almost a century
later, also at the Baltic. More evidence elucidating the settlement
pattern is needed, however, before the second site at Åhus can without doubt be paralleled with the early towns Ribe and Hedeby.

The hinterland

In order to understand the rural production basis that carried the
demand of the elite, a short summary of Danish settlement and landscape archaeology is necessary. Nucleated settlements (hamlets, villages) appeared already in the pre-Roman Iron Age. Manors, that
is magnate estates, existed probably long before the Viking Age.[66]
The economy was a mixture of cereal cultivation and stock raising.
Probably the extension of the arable land increased, especially from
the eighth century onwards, and as evidenced by pollen diagrams a
rural expansion started in the Merovingian period and continued
through the Viking Age to end in the well-known fourteenth century setback.[67]

Based on changes in the well-studied settlement pattern of Jutland,
archaeologists can point to two periods of settlement change in the
first millennium A.D.: the period around 200 A.D., and another change
took place around 700 A.D. Both seem to represent a rural expansion, while the Migration period is considered to be a period of sta-

---

[66] S. Hvass, "The status of the Iron Age settlement in Denmark", in M. Bierma
et al. eds., Arheologie en landschap, Festschrift to H.T. Waterbolk (Groningen,1988), pp.
97-132; S. Hvass, "The Iron Age and the Viking Period: Settlement", in S. Hvass
and B. Storgaard eds., Digging into the past. 25 years of archaeology in Denmark (Copenhagen/
Højbjerg, 1993), pp. 187-94; J. Callmer, "A contribution to the prehistory and early
history of the south Scandinavian manor", in L. Larsson et al. eds., The archaeology
of the cultural landscape. Fieldwork and research in a south Swedish rural region, Acta
Archaeologica Lundensia Ser. in 4° 19 (Stockholm, 1992), pp. 411-57; Ch. Fabech
and J. Ringtved, "Magtens geografi i Sydskandinavien", and L. Jørgensen "The
warrior aristocracy of Gudme? The emergence of landed aristocracy in Late Iron
Age Denmark", in H.G. Resi ed., Produksjon og samfunn. Om erverv, spesialisering og bosetning i Norden i 1. Årtusind e.Kr., Universitetets Oldsaksamling, Varia 30 (Oslo, 1995),
pp. 11-37, 205-20 respectively (summaries); L. Jørgensen, "Stormandssæder og skat-
tefund i 3.-12. århundrede", Fortid og nutid 1995/2, pp. 83-110.
[67] B. Berglund ed., The cultural landscape during 6000 years in southern Sweden – the
Ystad Project, Ecological bulletins 41 (Lund/Copenhagen, 1991).

bilisation or stagnation. The changes around 200 A.D. led to larger farms, each with a large fenced-off yard with more buildings, including a long dwelling-cum-byre house. The change around 700 A.D. entailed much larger farmyards, more buildings and a new house construction, all set in the well-planned setting of seemingly regulated hamlets.

In general settlements had developed:

• from an economy dominated by subsistence production to a more centralised system aiming at the production of a large surplus,
• from farms within a common fence to individual farmsteads in hamlets and villages, each with their own fence, an individualisation of production is surmised,
• from small household farms to large farmsteads and manors.

The pattern of church villages, hamlets, and single farms known from High Medieval written sources as well as later enclosure maps has its roots as far back as in the Migration period or the Late Roman period.[68] The study of building tradition and inter-site organisation demonstrates long continuity and a conservative tradition and it has to be emphasised that the development by and large follows that of the north-western continental plain area down to the Rhine.[69] For instance, the lay-out of a hamlet of seven farms at Vorbasse from the eighth and ninth centuries shows a regulated, well planned settlement that it is fairly similar to hamlets in the northern parts of the Carolingian empire, for instance at Kootwijk just north of the Rhine.[70] The evidence of farm buildings and settlement patterns do not support any idea that Danish farmers were more barbaric than the Franks, Frisians, or Anglo-Saxons, nor that their agriculture was less productive.

---

[68] J. Callmer, "To stay or to move", *Meddelanden från Lunds universitets historiska museum* n.s. 6 (1985-1986), pp. 167-208.

[69] W.H. Zimmermann, "Die früh- bis hochmittelalterliche Wüstung Dalem", in H.W. Bökme ed., *Siedlungen und Landesausbau zur Salierzeit, 1 In den nördlichen Landschaften des Reiches* (Sigmaringen, 1991), pp. 37-46; W.H. Zimmermann, *Die Siedlungen des 1. bis 6. Jahrhunderts nach Christus von Flögeln-Eekhöltjen, Niedersachsen. Die Bauformen und ihre Funktionen*, Probleme der Küstenforschung im südlichen Nordseegebiet 19 (Hildesheim, 1992); H.T. Waterbolk, "Patterns of the peasant landscape", *Proceedings of the Prehistoric Society* 61 (1995), pp. 1-36.

[70] H.A. Heidinga, *Medieval settlement and economy north of the Lower Rhine. Archaeology and history of Kootwijk and the Veluwe* (Assens, Cingula 9, 1987).

So it seems certain that the elite of Denmark could base its social and military position on a surplus, and that this surplus was growing. Technology improved and the rural produce increased, especially from the eighth century onwards, and this expansion continued through the Viking Age. It is this surplus that was turned into other commodities at the new economic centres, the *emporia*. It was this surplus that enabled the early Danish kingdom with its administration, military power, church, towns, etc.

Danes between the North Sea and at the Baltic

As described in the sixth century volume, a relatively homogeneous South Scandinavian culture had developed by the seventh century. It seems probable that the Danes had won a more or less pronounced hegemony in the south-western Baltic.[71] After the strong Merovingian impact on Scandinavia during the formative period of the sixth and seventh centuries, it seems as if Scandinavia during the eighth century had chosen to manifest a Scandinavian identity. Scandinavian arts and crafts were certainly not uninfluenced by contemporary developments on the Continent or in England, but nevertheless the adherence to the traditional shapes and styles of the pagan past gave Scandinavian culture of the Carolingian and Viking periods its own face.[72] In the eighth century Scandinavian material culture continued the development of the old "pagan" animal art that earlier had been popular also among some of the Germanic-speaking peoples on the Continent and in England, but now it had become obsolete in the wake of the expanding ideals of the Mediterranean Christian civilisation. Most Scandinavian women also stuck to the old "pagan" dress customs for another three hundred years, while a more Mediterranean dress was adopted in western Europe; only among the elite families in western Denmark do we see that a

---

[71] M. Ørsnes, *Form og stil i Sydskandinaviens yngre germanske jernalder* (Copenhagen, 1966), summary; K. Høilund Nielsen, "Centrum og periferi i 6.-8. Årh.", in *Fra stamme til stat i Danmark, 2 Høvdingesamfund og kongemagt*, pp. 127-54 (summary); Näsman, "The ethnogenesis of the Danes".

[72] M. Ørsnes, "Südskandinavische Ornamentik in der jüngeren Germanischen Eisenzeit", *Acta Archaeologica* 40 (1969 [1970]), pp. 1-121; K. Høilund Nielsen, "Zur Chronologie der jüngeren Germanischen Eisenzeit auf Bornholm", *Acta Archaeologica* 57 (1986 [1987]), pp. 47-86; D. Wilson and O. Klindt-Jensen *Viking art* (London, 1966, 2nd ed. 1980).

"Christian" dress was accepted before the conversion in the mid-ninth century.[73] The Scandinavians thus signalled cultural self-consciousness and independence.

So it is indeed a paradox that the Danish realm in the eighth century turned its attention away from both the Baltic scene and Scandinavia proper. In stead its political and economic efforts seem to be concentrated in continental affairs and as a result we can see an increasing South Scandinavian adaptation to western norms and standards. Thus a domestic scene dominated by old values based on the warrior elite and its pagan cosmology came in conflict with new ideas, inspired first by contacts to the Merovingians, later to the Carolingians and the Anglo-Saxons, ideas that ultimately were Mediterranean, Roman-Byzantine, and Christian.

The coincident expansion of the Danish economy and the increasing activity of the West Slavs led, however, at the turn to the ninth century to the opening of old but since long rarely used routes from the Baltic through east-central Europe to the eastern Mediterranean. The import of oriental beads along these routes forebodes in a way the beginning of the Viking Age in the southern Baltic.

At the very end of the eighth century and in the early ninth, the Danish raids on western Europe burst out, plausibly controlled by the king and his men.[74] The internal conflicts in Scandinavian attitudes reached a climax in the 830s when things seemingly went out of royal control and in 836 the Danish King Horik denied responsibility for the recent raids in Frisia and the repeated plundering of Dorestad.[75]

Already in the early eighth century and particularly in the second half of the century the importance of west Denmark, i.e. Jutland grow rapidly as a result of the increasing economic activity around the North Sea basin, not least caused by the Frisians.[76] The military

---

[73] H. Vierck, "Religion, Rang und Herrschaft im Spiegel der Tracht", in C. Ahrens ed., *Sachsen und Angelsachsen* (Hamburg-Harburg, 1978), pp. 271-83; Vierck, "Mittel- und westeuropäischer Einwirkungen"; A. Hedeager Krag, "Fränkisch-Byzantinische Trachteinflüsse in drei dänischen Grabfunden des 10. Jahrhundersts", *Archäologisches Korrespondenzblatt* 29 (1999), pp. 425-44.

[74] P. Hernæs, "Storpolitikk og vikingetog pÂ slutten av 700-tallet", in I. Fuglestvedt and B. Myhre eds., *Konflikt i forhistorien* (Stavanger, 1997), pp. 57-67; U. Näsman "Raids, migrations, and kingdoms – the Danish case", in S. Stummann Hansen ed., *Vikings in the West* (Copenhagen, in press).

[75] *Annales Regni Francorum* A.D. 836.

[76] D. Ellmers, "Die Bedeutung der Friesen für die Handelsverbindungen der

expansion of the Carolingian empire and the fights of the Frisians, Saxons, and Obodrites to preserve their independence of the Franks were other significant geopolitical factors. It seems obvious that the Jutish provinces enjoyed considerable stimulus both economically and politically, and south Jutland certainly appears to be the main province of Viking Denmark during the ninth and early tenth centuries. The eastern provinces served merely as a back up of the kingdom. Not until Norwegian, Swedish and West Slav pressure once more forced Danish kings to turn their attention towards the Kattegat and the Baltic, the eastern provinces did again become of economic and political interest in the late tenth and eleventh century.[77]

Conclusion: trade and power

The development of chiefdoms and kingdoms means the mobilisation of resources into a centralised political system. Power is accumulation and use of resources. Thus the study of production, distribution and demand cannot be separated from the study of political organisation. As the evidence stands, I believe that an urbanised economy of west European "medieval" character was first implemented in the south-western part of Denmark. Due to the strategic position in relation to the political, economic, and military pressure from the south, the king had probably taken more or less total control over this part of the Danish realm, as indicated by both the Frankish annals and the archaeological record. However, old structures of a system of tribal confederation prevailed in large parts of the Danish area. Local chieftains resident at the by now old and traditional central places were thus still in control of the economy of the northern and eastern provinces, which nevertheless were more or less well-integrated constituents of the kingdom. In southern Jutland, the ports at Hedeby and Ribe were developed both as royal strongholds and as gateways open to the more advanced monetary eco-

---

Ostseeraumes bis zur Wikingerzeit", in S.-O. Lindquist ed., *Society and trade in the Baltic during the Viking Age*, Acta Visbyensia 7 (Visby, 1985), pp. 7-54; Näsman, "Vendel period glass".

[77] A. Andrén, "Städer och kungamakt – en studie i Danmarks politiska geografi före 1230", *Scandia* 49/1 (1983), pp. 31-76, 159f. (summary); P.H. Sawyer, "Da Danmark blev Danmark", in O. Olsen ed., *Gyldendals og Politikens Danmarkshistorie* 3 (Copenhagen, 1988).

nomies of western Europe, while the contacts with the non-monetary barter-markets at the Kattegat and the Baltic were still fulfilled by the central-place system. Thus I see the first proto-towns as developed in the interest of a Danish kingdom and an aristocracy *in spe* which grew stronger in the course of the seventh and eighth centuries. With their support to the early towns, kings aimed at the creation of alternative power bases, I suggest.

Still in the ninth century Ribe and Hedeby are the only known urban communities in South Scandinavia. In his *Vita Ansgarii* Rimbert did not mention any other urban-like sites in Denmark, and archaeology has not yet been able to establish other proto-towns and early towns belonging to the ninth century, except perhaps at Åhus (east Scania) in its second phase. In both Ribe and Hedeby a considerable development took place in the ninth century, but in the rest of the South Scandinavia nothing similar can be observed. The royal influence on the affairs of the two towns is evident in the written sources, and of course significant. In fact, both must have been very important instruments in the royal control of south Jutland, strategically important from both an economic and a military perspective, an aspect supported by the story about King Godfred and his actions against Obodrites, Franks, and Saxons in 808.[78]

In the rest of South Scandinavia the regional functions seem for another one to two centuries to have been fulfilled by central-places and ports with roots far back into the Migration-Merovingian periods or earlier. Plausibly another proto-town had begun to grew at Åhus, but the site obviously functioned only less than 100 years, and it seems possible that it ended without direct contact to the hundred years later evidence of an urban development at the present town of Åhus.[79]

Thus, south-west Denmark seems for about two centuries to have been economically and politically more developed than the northern and eastern provinces. A new phase in the urbanisation of Denmark started in the tenth century, but it falls outside the scope of this paper.[80] Years ago it was believed that the economy of early

---

[78] *Annales Regni Francorum* A.D. 808.
[79] Callmer, "Platser med anknytning till handel och hantverk"; "Urbanization in Scandinavia".
[80] For overviews, see A. Andrén, "State and towns in the Middle Ages. The Scandinavian experience", *Theory and society* 18 (1989), pp. 585-609; and Callmer, "Urbanization in Scandinavia".

Viking towns were based on "external exploitation", i.e. plunder and tributes, and that the towns should be considered mere junctions where resources of Viking raids were turned over. This gives of course a wrongful impression of Scandinavian economy, as we know it today. In fact, the initial urbanisation of South Scandinavia has little relation to raids and plunder. Both Ribe and Hedeby started long before we have reports of Viking raids. The economy of Ribe was certainly based on the produce of local and itinerant craftsmen, and the import is characterised by goods that were acquired through exchange, not plunder. Wealth consisting of plunder and tribute was certainly important for the reproduction of the political superstructure since long, but the early towns are a new phenomenon, and their strength is that they in one place combined the functions of the traditional magnate centres with the functions of the early market sites and landing places.

In the long eighth century, the old "pagan" or "barbarian" social system prevailed in large parts of the Danish realm and here the chieftains' residences at the central-places were still the foci of power and economy, for instance at Stentinget (North Jutland), Lejre (Zealand), and Uppåkra (Scania).[81] Only in south-west Jutland do we find early towns, and here they are in reality a remarkable indication of the growing influence exercised by Christian societies on South Scandinavia. The early towns could thus be considered a kind of "pseudo-Christian" element in Danish society, reflecting the introduction of a west European economy and new royal ambitions as they are. The rapid urbanisation of the northern and eastern provinces from the tenth century went hand in hand with the conversion and the spread of direct royal rule.

In the process of building the kingdom, the surmised transformation of Jutish, Anglian and other petty kingdoms into integrated provinces of a growing Danish kingdom could be compared to the roughly contemporary development in England. There traditional local leaders were replaced by royal servants in the eighth century and earlier subkingdoms became ealdormanries.[82] In south Jutland

---

[81] T. Nilsson, "Stentinget", *Kuml* 1990 (1992), pp. 119-32 (summary); T. Christensen, "Lejre beyond legend – the archaeological evidence", *Journal of Danish Archaeology* 10 (1991 [1993]), pp. 163-85; B. Stjernquist, "Uppåkra, a central place in Skåne during the Iron Age", *Lund archaeological reports* 1 (1995), pp. 89-120.

[82] B. Yorke, *Kings and kingdoms of early Anglo-Saxon England* (London, 1990; 2nd ed. 1992).

the existence of royal agents and direct royal rule are recorded in the early ninth century: a *comes* called Hovi was obviously the king's authority in Hedeby, and in 817 a royal *custos*, Gluomi, commanded the border forces based at Danevirke.[83] One has to assume that similar positions by necessity were created already in the eighth century to organise the growing proto-towns Ribe and Hedeby, and when the dyke Danevirke was built, repaired, and manned.[84] But in many regions the local magnates had still control over local affairs, and thus kings needed their support.

Perhaps the reasons for the localisation of the Danish centre to south Jutland is found in these archaeological and historical observations: the military and political pressure from the south made the presence of the king necessary. The economic possibilities of an integration into the growing North Sea market must have been an obvious option to finance the military and political expenditure. The islands were still important, however, since they served as a stronghold and a refuge as during the Frankish attack in 815.[85]

It is not easy to disentangle the cause and effect of the processes that are behind the changes in production, distribution and demand, observable in the archaeological record of South Scandinavia during the second half of the first millennium A.D. However, to me it seems evident that the interaction between the Mediterranean civilisation and the European barbarians during the late Roman period and especially during the Migration period rapidly increased the social complexity north of the *limes*.[86] This process is one of the most important elements in the transformation of the Roman world. In Scandinavia, it included the ethnogenesis of the Danes and eventually the making of a Danish kingdom. The formation of complex polities—as the surmised tribal confederacies—stimulated a growth in rural production, not least to support the increasing demand of the warrior elite. Eventually the size of the territory under dominance of one lord grew and consequently it became necessary to

---

[83] *Vita Ansgarii*, ch. 30-31; *Annales Regni Francorum* A.D. 871.
[84] Andersen, *Danevirke og Kovirke*.
[85] *Annales Regni Francorum* A.D. 815.
[86] U. Näsman, "The Scandinavians' View of Europe in the Migration Period", in L. Larsson and B. Stjernquist eds., *The World-View of Prehistoric Man*, Kungl. Vitterhets Historie och Antikvitets Akademien, Konferenser 40, Festskrift till Gad Rausing (Stockholm, 1998), pp. 103-21.

improve the distribution of resources and wealth. At first these factors triggered the appearance of the many central places and landing sites. Later on the north-west European *emporia* became the basis of the proto-towns and early towns that fulfilled the demand of the early Danish kingdom. Certainly, the final integration of pagan Scandinavia into the transformed Roman-Christian West Europe began in the long eighth century.

Appendix

References for the finds on the maps Figs. 1-3

Fig. 1 references for the finds on the map may be found in:
Näsman, "Vendel period glass", and U. Näsman, "Om fjärrhandel i Sydskandinaviens yngre järnålder", *Hikuin* 16 (1990), pp. 89-118, summary p. 155f. The finds from Saint Denis are now published – N. Meyer and M. Wyss in D. Foy and G. Sennequier, *À travers le verre du moyen âge à la renaissance* (Rouen, 1989), no. 60. New finds are Paviken, Uppåkra, and Trelleborg – B. Stjernquist, "Glass from Uppåkra", in B. Hårdh ed., *Fynden i centrum* (Lund, 1999), pp. 67-94; Slöinge – L. Lundqvist, "Central places and central areas in the Late Iron Age", in H. Andersson *et al.* eds., *Visions of the past, Trends and traditions in Swedish medieval archaeology* (Stockholm/Lund, 1997), pp. 179-97; Strøby – S.Å. Tornbjerg, "Fra gubbernes verden", *Skalk* 1997/3, pp. 6-10.

Fig. 2 references for the finds on the map may be found in:
Näsman, "Om fjärrhandel", above. New finds are Borg – J. Henderson and I. Holand, "The glass from Borg", *Medieval archaeology* 36 (1992), pp. 29-58, Trelleborg – Stjernquist, "Glass from Uppåkra", above; Lundeborg – unpublished information from P.O. Thomsen, Svendborg og Omegns Museum; and Strøby – Tornbjerg, "Fra gubbernes verden", above.

Fig. 3a-b references for the finds on the maps may be found in:
J. Parkhouse, "The Dorestad quernstones", *Berichten van de Rijksdienst voor het Oudheidkundig Bodemonderzoek* 26 (1976), pp. 181-88; Näsman, "Vendel period glass"; Steuer "Der Handel der Wikingerzeit" and L.C. Nielsen, "Trelleborg". New finds from e.g. Birka in central Sweden are not included.

THE SIGNIFICANCE OF PRODUCTION
IN EIGHTH-CENTURY ENGLAND*

John Moreland

Introduction

In the course of this paper, I want to make four simple points which I believe are crucial to our understanding of the economies of eighth-century England.

- we cannot understand these (or any early medieval economies) if we continue to isolate exchange from the other economic processes (consumption and production), and to assign it causal primacy;
- the economies of eighth-century England cannot be understood in terms of a series of active cores (the *emporia*), surrounded by conservative, autarkic peripheries;
- we destroy the distinctiveness of economic processes in the eighth century by the imposition of evolutionary and developmental models;
- the significance of production in the regions of England has been massively underestimated, and that an argument can be made for seeing transformations in this element of the economic triad as the providing the force for economic development in the early middle ages.

In many ways the necessity to emphasise these points flow from some of the observations I made in an earlier chapter in this book about archaeologists' predilection for exchange,[1] and from the almost total

* I am grateful to the other members of the Transformation of the Roman World working group 3 for their intellectual stimulation and friendship. I am especially grateful to the editors of this volume for their forbearance, and to Paul Blinkhorn, Mark Pluciennik and Richard Hodges for invaluable conversations. Much of the research (and some of the writing) for this paper was done while I was Guest Professor in the Department of Prehistoric Archaeology, University of Århus. My special thanks go to Henrik Thrane, Ulf Näsman, Charlotte Fabech and Anita Laursen for creating the conditions for a very enjoyable and productive visit. As in the rest of this volume, the title refers to the "long eighth century", from c. 680-830. However, for reasons that I hope will become clear, I focus on the earlier part of that period c. 670-750.

[1] J. Moreland, "Concepts of the early medieval economy", (this volume).

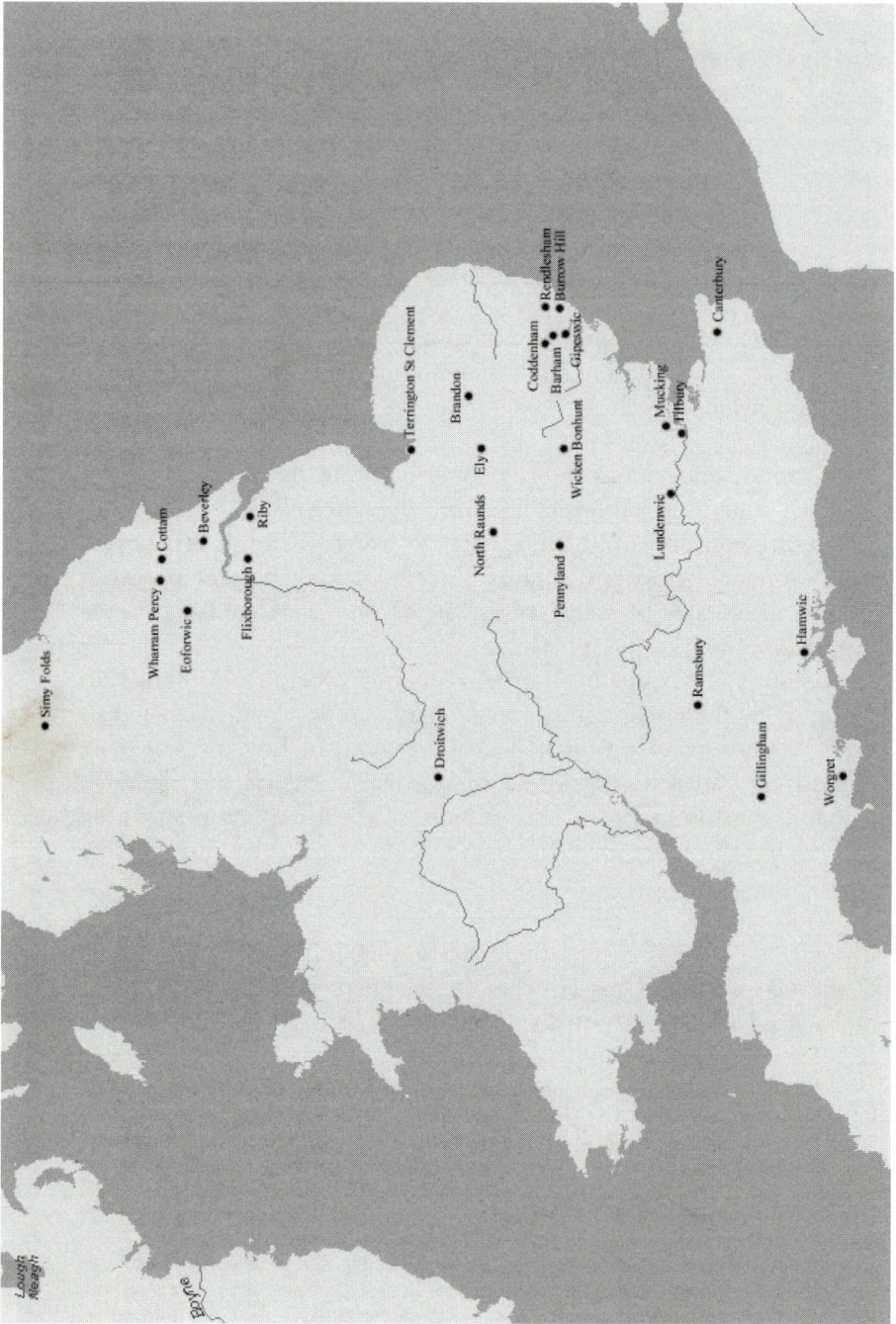

Fig. 1. England. Sites mentioned in the text.

dominance that studies of *emporia* have exercised over our research into the economies of the early middle ages.

For many, the eighth century in England (and in much of NW Europe) is "the age of the *emporia*".[2] The emergence of these large and clearly specialised sites at the beginning of the "long eighth century" is held to distinguish it from what went before, and from what followed. Not only are these settlements thought to mark a chronological rupture; they are also seen as largely divorced from their hinterlands. For many, the *emporia* were not "organically" embedded in the economies of their regions; they are seen as centres of exchange existing at some remove from (low-level) production in the countryside.[3] The emphasis placed on the *emporia* as centres of long-distance trade has only served further to divorce these communities from their environs. Further, it can be argued that the time and resources spent on these sites has led us to exaggerate their separation from the wider economic currents of the eighth century.[4]

The apparent exceptionality of the *emporia* is enhanced by a belief that they emerged abruptly from a society in which economic activity (apart from some high-status gift-exchange) operated at a near-subsistence level. In such a scenario, the scale of the evidence for long-distance trade and craft production on the *emporia* does seem to signal radical developments and a new age. However, the production and distribution systems of the seventh century were not as autarkic as once assumed, and the *emporia* were not the only locales in which significant transformations were taking place in the eighth.

It is important to stress here that perceptions of the *emporia* have changed somewhat in the last decade—in particular as a shift to focus on the craft activities practised there has led to a questioning of the importance of long distance trade as the rationale for these

[2] See R. Hodges, *The Anglo-Saxon Achievement* (London, 1989), chapter 4.

[3] Tom Saunders, for example, sees the *emporia* as "dependent settlements cut off from the rural economy"; as "divorced from the economy as a whole, detached and isolated on the periphery of kingdoms" – T. Saunders, "Trade, towns and states: a reconsideration of early medieval economics", *Norwegian Archaeological Review* 28 (1995), pp. 31-53, at p. 37. In the same vein, Julian Richards, "Anglo-Saxon settlements of the Golden Age", in J. Hawkes and S. Mills eds., *Northumbria's Golden Age* (Stroud, 1999), pp. 44-54, at p. 44, asserts that there was "limited contact" between the *emporia* and their hinterlands. See also Moreland, "Concepts".

[4] J. Newman, "Wics, trade and the hinterlands – the Ipswich region", in M. Anderton ed., *Anglo-Saxon Trading Centres and their Hinterlands. Beyond the Emporia* (Glasgow, 1999), pp. 32-47, at p. 34.

settlements. Further, consideration of the provisioning of the *emporia* with the raw materials for production and for sustenance has, to a certain extent, "grounded" them in their more immediate context.[5] However, despite this emerging understanding, what we might call the "classic model" of the *emporia* still dominates much archaeological (and, to a lesser extent, historical) thought on the eighth century. In the following sections I will outline what we might call the "classic model" for the emergence and functioning of the *emporia*. I will also discuss one "variant" of this model which purports to detect a shift in the economic logic, not only of the *emporia* but also of the Anglo-Saxon economy in general. I will then present evidence to show that significant transformations were taking place in the regions of England at the same time as (or even earlier) than the emergence of the *emporia* in attempt to embed these sites in regional production, and to undermine the causal primacy usually assigned to "exchange".

Emporia—*the classic model (and a variant)*

In England, Hamwic (Southampton), Lundenwic (London), Gipeswic (Ipswich) and Eoforwic (York) are seen as the "classic" *emporia* of the eighth century.[6] It is generally argued that the major kingdoms in England each created, and monopolised, an *emporium*. This makes the apparent absence of one in Kent seem strange, especially given that kingdom's long-standing trading and social relationships with Continental Europe, and should encourage further consideration of the archaeological evidence from sites like Canterbury, Fordwich and Sarre.[7] Be that as it may, one of the fundamental assumptions about

[5] For now see, C. Scull, "Urban centres in pre-Viking England?", in J. Hines ed., *The Anglo-Saxons from the Migration Period to the Eighth Century* (Woodbridge, 1997), pp. 269-98, at pp. 286-88; and the papers in M. Anderton ed. *Anglo-Saxon Trading Centres: Beyond the Emporia* (Glasgow, 1999).

[6] These *emporia* (or *wics*) have been categorised as a single *type* but there are significant differences between them. See H. Clarke and B. Ambrosiani, *Towns in the Viking Age* (Leicester, 1991), p. 36. Hamwic is the name universally applied to Anglo-Saxon Southampton. I therefore see no reason why we should refer to the other *wics* by the names of their modern "descendents".

[7] For Kent generally, see C. Arnold, *An Archaeology of the Early Anglo-Saxon Kingdoms*, 2nd ed. (London, 1997), pp. 114-25; J. Huggett, "Imported grave-goods and the Anglo-Saxon economy," *Medieval Archaeology* 32 (1988), pp. 63-96; T. Tatton-Brown, "The Anglo-Saxon towns of Kent", in D. Hooke ed., *Anglo-Saxon Settlements* (Oxford, 1988), pp. 213-32, at pp. 213-21; A. Vince, "Saxon urban economies: an archaeological

the appearance and operation of the "classic" *emporia* is that of a direct connection with *kingship*, and most scholars seem to accept that the principal *raison d'être* of these sites was to funnel prestige goods and other products of far-away lands to the court of the king. In the "classic model", *emporia* are all about royal control over long-distance trade.[8]

This "classic model" owes almost everything to the work of Richard Hodges, and especially his *Dark Age Economics*. What Hodges, and now others, have argued is that by the end of the seventh century the distribution of overseas exotica as gifts to peers and subordinates had become an essential element in the reproduction of elite power relationships. The position of the king at the head of a noble ret-inue was, in part, guaranteed by his ability to act as chief "ring-giver", or giver of gifts. His status vis-à-vis other kings was also partially dependent on the gifts he could acquire. Whilst the ability of the king to dispense largesse was to some extent derived from

---

perspective", in J. Rackham ed., *Environment and Economy in Anglo-Saxon England* (York, 1994), pp. 108-19, at pp. 109-10; B. Yorke, *Kings and Kingdoms of Early Anglo-Saxon England* (London, 1990), pp. 39-41, 166; also C. Wickham, "Overview: production, distribution and demand, II" (this volume). For Canterbury, see N. Brookes, *The Early History of the Church of Canterbury* (Leicester, 1984), pp. 22-30; for the coins from Canterbury, see D. Metcalf, "The monetary economy of ninth-century England south of the Humber: a topographical analysis", in M. Blackburn and D. Dumville eds., *Kings, Currency and Alliances. History and Coinage of Southern England in the Ninth Century* (Woodbridge, 1998), pp. 167-97, at pp. 183-88; for Sarre, see R. Hodges, *Dark Age Economics* (London, 1982), p. 69. See also S. Kelly, "Trading privileges from eighth-century England", *Early Medieval Europe* 1 (1992), pp. 2-28.

[8] Hodges, *Dark Age Economics*, p. 55 asserts that "the historical evidence for royal control of long-distance trade either directly or through agents is widely confirmed in the early medieval period". Martin Welch essentially agrees that Hamwic was a "specialised royal site established by Ine to provide access to the luxury goods shipped across the Channel from the Frankish kingdoms", "Rural settlement patterns in the early and middle Anglo-Saxon periods", *Landscape History* 7 (1985), pp. 13-25, at p. 16. Barbara Yorke (*Kings and Kingdoms*, p. 166) also makes the connection between *wics*, kings and trade – "In the seventh and eighth century, trade with the Continent seems to have become increasingly important to Anglo-Saxon kings, as can be seen from . . . the rise of the specialized trading base (*wic*)". Writing of Eoforwic, Terry O'Connor hypothesises that "a *wic* was a highly-developed port-of-trade, maintained by a ruling elite in order to control the movement and possession of prestige goods", "8th-11th century economy and environment in York", in J. Rackham ed., *Environment and Economy in Anglo-Saxon England* (York, 1994), pp. 136-47, at p. 141; Ailsa Mainman suggests that "the *wic* [at York] may have been established by, and designed to serve, the possible royal, administrative and ecclesiastical centre thought to have been based on the nearby area of the Roman legionary fortress", *Pottery from 46-54 Fishergate* (York, 1993), p. 547.

war and plunder,[9] traded objects played an increasingly important role in these social transfers. Direct exchange between alien traders and subordinate nobles would undermine the position of the king at the apex of the intra-societal hierarchy, while the diminution of exotica coming directly to the king would reduce his inter-societal standing. It was for this reason, it is argued, that kings established centres such as Hamwic, Lundenwic, Gipeswic, and Eoforwic, where men-from-afar, and their goods, could be monitored and controlled.[10]

This model for the functioning of the ideal-type *emporium* was largely written through a reading of (some of) the then available evidence, especially from Hamwic, while under the influence of contemporary thinking in anthropology. However, we can now see that this anthropological influence has not always been conducive to clear focus.[11] At the same time, new archaeological evidence has come to light, and aspects of the old have been brought into sharper perspective. The "classic model", the ideal-type, has become a hindrance to a clear understanding of "production, distribution and consumption" in eighth-century England, and is in urgent need of re-evaluation. However, one recent attempt to do this only further clouds our view of the "reality" of the eighth-century past.

In a radical departure from the "classic model", Richard Hodges now argues that

> Hamwic was a centre of intensive craft production . . . showing that previous interpretations of Hamwic solely as a settlement for trading with the Franks are questionable. . . . [Hamwic represents] a new stage in the evolution of the Anglo-Saxon town, being a planned centre in which craft production plays a great part.[12]

---

[9] See Moreland, "Concepts", p. 16. Also L. Hedeager, "Warrior economy and trading economy in Viking-Age Scandinavia", *Journal of European Archaeology* 2 (1994), pp. 130-48; T. Reuter, "Plunder and tribute in the Carolingian Empire", *Transactions of the Royal Historical Society*, 5th series 35 (1985), pp. 75-94.

[10] For reservations about the postulated extent of royal control over *emporia* see I. Wood, *The Merovingian Kingdoms 450-751* (London, 1994) p. 302; and D. Hinton *Archaeology, Economy and Society: England from the Fifth to the Fifteenth Century* (London, 1990), p. 39; "The archaeology of eighth- to eleventh-century Wessex", in M. Aston and C. Lewis eds., *The Medieval Landscape of Wessex* (Oxford, 1994), pp. 33-36, at p. 34; *The Gold, Silver and other Non-ferrous Alloy Objects from Hamwic* (Stroud, 1996), pp. 97, 100. Also Scull, "Urban centres", pp. 287-88.

[11] See Moreland, "Concepts", pp. 22-34.

[12] Hodges, *Anglo-Saxon Achievement*, pp. 84-85.

As such, it is, he argues, a manifestation of the shift from a "prim-itive" gift-economy to a more "developed" commodity economy.[13] One of the reasons for this proposed shift from gifts to commodities was a change in strategy by King Ine of Wessex (688-726), caused by a postulated decline in the availability of goods from overseas. This resulted in a new emphasis on the *production* of commodities from the second decade of the eighth century.[14] As a consequence of the development of craft production, it is argued, Hamwic became a town manufacturing *commodities* on a massive scale, and since they were not manufactured on a large scale elsewhere in the kingdom, "it is reasonable to suppose that they were commodities which had their own regional value"; implying that the commodities produced at Hamwic circulated within the "region" of Wessex.[15] With the demise of the system of prestige goods exchange, and the development of an incipient trade in commodities, administered from the *emporia*, the "pre-conditions for an economic take-off" were set, in place.[16]

I have already pointed to the theoretical flaws in this kind of argu-ment. It is clear from recent anthropological research that gift exchange and commodity exchange can, and frequently do, operate within the same social formations—"gifts and commodities are not mutually exclusive, and need not be seen as successive stages in an evolu-tionary developmental cycle".[17] The postulation of a transition from a gift economy to a commodity economy, beginning in the eighth cen-tury and reaching its conclusion in the reign of Alfred, is an exer-cise in unreality. As in the evolutionary anthropologist's dreams, there appears to be a distinct and sudden shift from simple to complex, from Other to Same, from Them to Us. It is to squeeze the evi-dence for a complex and diverse set of social and economic rela-tionships into a set of reified, evolutionary categories which have themselves largely been dismissed by the anthropologists who cre-ated them.

Hodges' variant on the classic model presupposes two phases of

---

[13] Hodges, *Anglo-Saxon Achievement*, p. 104.
[14] Hodges, *Anglo-Saxon Achievement*, pp. 90-91.
[15] Hodges, *Anglo-Saxon Achievement*, pp. 88, 104. See also R. Hodges, "Society, power and the first English industrial revolution", in *Il secolo di ferro: mito e realtà del secolo X*, Settimane di studio del Centro italiano di studi sull'alto Medioevo 38 (Spoleto, 1991), pp. 121-50, at p. 132.
[16] Hodges, "Industrial revolution", p. 132.
[17] Moreland, "Concepts", p. 31.

economic activity on the *emporia*, an early "gift exchange phase", and
a later "production phase". I will present the evidence for this, and
(crucially) for the dating of the change, as the prelude to a more
general argument that patterns of production had dramatically altered
long before the production phase of the *emporia*. The result will not
only provide an empirical counterpart to the theoretical arguments
against such teleological models, but will also (and more importantly)
situate the emergence of the *emporia* within the context of a transformation in production in the late seventh and early eighth centuries. The aim is to "re-embed" exchange within the economic triad
of which it should be an indissoluble part.

"Production phase" emporia[18]

Hamwic was established at the beginning of the eighth century, and
craft production was practised there from the beginning.[19] Three
early nuclei have been identified within the overall settlement—at
Six Dials, around St Mary's church, and on the waterfront.[20] All the
crucibles used for melting silver were found in and around these
areas;[21] the evidence for gold comes from the Six Dials area, and the
same site has produced the only crucible used for melting brass;[22]
moulds for the manufacture of more decorative items came from

---

[18] I should point out here that I will not discuss other aspects of the evidence
from the *emporia*. Restrictions of space, and the need to maintain a focussed argument, preclude such discussion. However, details can be found in many of the publications cited.

[19] For details of the Hamwic excavations, see P. Holdsworth, *Excavations at Melbourne
Street, Southampton, 1971-76* (London, 1980); A. Morton ed., *Excavations at Hamwic:
Volume 1* (London, 1992); P. Andrews ed., *Excavations at Hamwic: Volume 2* (York,
1997); M. Garner, "Middle Saxon evidence at Cook Street, Southampton (SOU254),
Proceedings of the Hampshire Field Club and Archaeological Society 49 (1993), pp. 77-127.
The material culture from the excavations is being published in a steady stream
of specialist reports and synthetic articles, including – P. Andrews ed., *The Coins
and Pottery from Hamwic* (Southampton, 1988); Hinton, *Gold, Silver*; J. Hunter and
M. Heyworth eds., *The Hamwic Glass* (York, 1998); J. Bourdillon, "Countryside and
town: the animal resources of Saxon Southampton", *Anglo-Saxon Settlements* (Oxford,
1988), pp. 176-95; J. Bourdillon, "The animal provisioning of Saxon Southampton",
Environment and Economy in Anglo-Saxon England (York, 1994), pp. 120-25. Specialist
reports on the material from the crucial excavations in the Six Dials region of
Hamwic are included in Andrews, *Excavations at Hamwic 2*.

[20] Morton, *Excavations at Hamwic 1*, pp. 36-40.

[21] J. Bayley, "Crucibles and cupels", in Hinton, *Gold, Silver*, pp. 86-92, at p. 88.

[22] Bayley, "Crucibles and cupels", pp. 88-89. "Brass was a relatively uncommon
copper alloy at this period – possibly new metal imported from Germany", p. 89.

Cook Street and from the waterfront. We should also remember that *sceattas*—silver coins which have very strong royal and high ecclesiastical connections—were minted at Hamwic.[23] This all looks like small-scale, prestige craft production.

The details of the excavation reports, however, show that "Industrial debris is found most often in the *late, upper* layers of pits"; that the most ubiquitous of all signs of craft-production—smithing slag—was "generally absent from early pits".[24] Textile production appears to "take-off" in the middle of the eighth century.[25] Significantly, at the same time a decreasing proportion of the ceramic assemblage is formed from Continental imported pottery.[26] This pattern is clearest at Six Dials, the waterfront and (perhaps) the area around St Mary's church—the proposed early nuclei of the settlement.[27]

Lundenwic existed from the mid-late seventh to the mid-late ninth centuries.[28] This early origin suggests an immediate contrast with Hamwic, but we know almost nothing about the functions and status of the mid-late seventh-century phases.[29] However, it is clear from

---

[23] For the possible connection between the *sceattas* and the evidence for silver working at Hamwic, see Bayley, "Crucibles and cupels", p. 88; Hinton, *Gold, Silver*, pp. 97-98. For the royal and ecclesiastical associations with *sceattas*, see D. Metcalf, *Thrymsas and Sceattas in the Ashmolean Museum Oxford, Volume 3* (London, 1994), pp. 308-309.

[24] Morton, *Excavations at Hamwic 1*, p. 57, emphasis added; Andrews, *Excavations at Hamwic 2*, p. 225.

[25] Andrews, *Excavations at Hamwic 2*, p. 238.

[26] J. Timby (with P. Andrews), "The pottery", in Andrews, *Excavations at Hamwic 2*, p. 208.

[27] For Six Dials, see Timby "The Pottery", pp. 207-209; for the waterfront, J. Timby, "The Middle Saxon pottery", in P. Andrews ed., *Southampton Finds, Volume 1: The Coins and Pottery from Hamwic* (Southampton, 1988), pp. 1116-118; for the zone around St Mary's, see E. Pieksma, "Pottery", in M. Garner, "Middle Saxon evidence at Cook Street, Southampton (SOU 254), *Proceedings of the Hampshire Field Club and Archaeological Society* 49 (1993), pp. 103-04.

[28] For recent work on Lundenwic, see R. Cowie and R. Whytehead, "Lundenwic: the archaeological evidence for middle Saxon London", *Antiquity* 63 (1989), pp. 706-18; L. Blackmore *et al.* "Royal Opera House", *Current Archaeology* 158 (1998), pp. 60-63; R. Cowie, "A gazetteer of middle Saxon sites and finds in the Strand/Westminster area", *Transactions of the London and Middlesex Archaeological Society* 39 (1988), pp. 37-46; R. Cowie *et al.* 1988 "Two middle Saxon occupation sites: excavations at Jubilee Hall and 21-22 Maiden Lane", *Transactions of the London and Middlesex Archaeological Society* 39 (1988), pp. 47-163; R. Whytehead, R. Cowie, and L. Blackmore, "Excavations at the Peabody site, Chandos Place, and the National Gallery", *Transactions of the London and Middlesex Archaeological Society* 40 (1989), pp. 35-175; B. Hobley, "Lundenwic and Lundenburh: two cities rediscovered", in R. Hodges and B. Hobley eds., *The Rebirth of Towns in the West, A.D. 750-1050* (London, 1988), pp. 69-82.

[29] Although we do have early seventh-century coins, issued by the king of Kent,

the archaeology that the settlement expanded in the late seventh and early eighth centuries, and the ceramic evidence suggests "that the settlement's heyday began in the 720s".[30] Although we do not have the detailed evidence to examine chronological differences at Lundenwic, it would seem that here too we see a major expansion of production—probably in the early eighth century.

The same pattern can be seen at Gipeswic.[31] Imported pottery of the early to mid-seventh century, and early seventh-century gravegoods from the Buttermarket cemetery, provide the evidence for the earliest phase of occupation. It used to be thought that Gipeswic had good evidence for production—in the form of Ipswich ware—in the mid-seventh century, but Paul Blinkhorn's comprehensive study of Ipswich ware now demonstrates that "all the seventh-century artefactual associations are somewhat questionable", and that a date of c. 720 is to be preferred.[32] Ipswich ware represents an major development in craft production. The use of the slow wheel and the kiln in its production contrasts with the hand made, bonfire fired tradition of other early and middle Saxon pottery.[33] The scale of distribution is unprecedented for Anglo-Saxon England.[34] The ware is found on sites as far north as York, Beverley and Flixborough and as far south as London and Kent.[35] It is found on all classes of sites

---

which bear a London mint-mark – see A. Vince, "The economic basis of Anglo-Saxon London", in R. Hodges and B. Hobley eds., *The Rebirth of Towns in the West, A.D. 750-1050* (London, 1988), pp. 83-92, at pp. 86, 90; Hobley, "Lundenwic and Lundenburh", p. 70.

[30] Blackmore, "Royal Opera House", p. 62; Vince, "Economic basis", p. 83; Whytehead, Cowie and Blackmore, "National Gallery", p. 107.

[31] K. Wade, "Ipswich", in R. Hodges and B. Hobley eds., *The Rebirth of Towns in the West, A.D. 750-1050* (London, 1988), pp. 93-100; Newman, "Wics".

[32] P. Blinkhorn, "Of cabbages and kings: production, trade and consumption in middle-Saxon England", in M. Anderton ed., *Anglo-Saxon Trading Centres: Beyond the Emporia* (Glasgow, 1999), pp. 4-23, at p. 9; P. Blinkhorn, *The Ipswich Ware Project. Ceramics, Trade and Society in Middle Saxon England* (London, forthcoming). I am very grateful to Paul for letting me see a draft of this important publication.

[33] Blinkhorn, "Cabbages and kings", pp. 4-5; Hodges, *Anglo-Saxon Achievement*, pp. 134-35.

[34] The contrast between the scale of Ipswich ware distribution and that of earlier Anglo-Saxon pottery traditions has been reduced by a growing awareness that some of the latter covered extensive areas. See, for example, D. Williams and A. Vince, "The characterization and interpretation of early to middle Saxon granitic tempered pottery in England", *Medieval Archaeology* 41 (1997), pp. 214-20; Mainman, *Pottery from Fishergate*, pp. 580-81, and below, p. 101. Nevertheless the scale of Ipswich ware production and distribution remains exceptional.

[35] Generally, see Blinkhorn, "Cabbages and kings", pp. 9-10. For London, see Blackmore, "Royal Opera House", p. 62; Cowie *et al.*, "Middle Saxon occupation", pp. 103-106; Whytehead, Cowie and Blackmore, "National Gallery", p. 106. For

in East Anglia, and was the local pottery for the region.[36] Within the wider distribution pattern, however, it occurs more commonly on sites with strong elite connections. Further, what might be seen as storage vessels (jars and pitchers) are much more common on sites outside East Anglia.[37]

The Fishergate excavations provide the best archaeological evidence for the significance of craft production at Eoforwic. The finds show that the site was established in the late seventh or early eighth centuries.[38] Around 740 the settlement was systematically dismantled and the area covered by a charcoal-rich deposit, almost certainly derived from the middens and debris of the earlier settlement. Re-occupation took place in the early ninth century, but the area was abandoned again in the middle of the ninth century.[39] This sequence makes it very difficult to detect changes in the scale and character of production, since occupation effectively ends at the point when we see such transformations at the other *emporia*. However, there does appear to have been a quite dramatic decline in the availability of imports in the second phase of the settlement, and Ailsa Mainman suggests that the "network of international contacts was less important by the second half of the 8th century".[40]

York, see B. Kemp, "The archaeology of 46-54 Fishergate", in A. Mainman (ed.), *Pottery from 46-54 Fishergate* (York, 1993), pp. 543-56, at pp. 546-50; A. Mainman, *Anglo-Scandinavian Pottery from Coppergate* (York, 1990), pp. 510-11; Mainman, *Pottery from Fishergate*, pp. 560, 595-600. For Beverley, see G. Watkins, "The pottery", in P. Armstrong, D. Tomlinson, and D. Evans, *Excavations at Lurk Lane Beverley 1979-82* (Sheffield, 1991), pp. 61-103, at pp. 71, 102. For Wharram Percy, see J. Richards, "What's so special about 'productive sites'? Middle Saxon settlements in Northumbria", in T. Dickinson and D. Griffiths eds., *The Making of Kingdoms*, Anglo-Saxon Studies in Archaeology and History 10 (Oxford 1999), pp. 71-80, at p. 76. For Flixborough, see K. Leahy, "The middle saxon site at Flixborough, North Lincolnshire", in J. Hawkes and S. Mills eds., *Northumbria's Golden Age* (Stroud, 1999), pp. 87-94, at p. 90; C. Loveluck, "A high-status Anglo-Saxon settlement at Flixborough, Lincolnshire", *Antiquity* 72 (1998), pp. 146-61, at pp. 154, 157.

[36] Blinkhorn, "Cabbages and kings", p. 5; *Ipswich Ware Project*.
[37] Blinkhorn, *Ipswich Ware Project*. See, for example, Mainman, *Anglo-Scandinavian Pottery*, pp. 510-11.
[38] R. Kemp, *Anglian Settlement at 46-54 Fishergate* (York, 1996), p. 66. The *sceattas* from the site begin in the 710's – Metcalf, *Thrymsas and Sceattas*, p. 366.
[39] Kemp, *Anglian Settlement*, pp. 34, 54-59; "Archaeology of Fishergate", pp. 547-50; Mainman, *Pottery from Fishergate*, pp. 607, 611-12.
[40] Mainman, *Pottery from Fishergate*, pp. 582, 570; Kemp, *Anglian Settlement*, p. 63. This is actually much too strong a reading of the evidence. The decline in imports at Fishergate may have been caused by the focussing of activity on another part of Eoforwic, and not by the demise of that settlement's interest in, or ability to obtain, the products of long-distance trade.

At first sight, the pattern which emerges would appear to support Hodges' argument for a switch in focus from long-distance trade to craft production, from a gift-economy to a commodity economy, c. 720/730.[41] However, the archaeological and documentary evidence make it clear (as we would now expect from the anthropology) that long-distance trade and gift exchange did not die out with the emergence of large-scale iron smithing, textile and ceramic production on the *emporia*. More importantly, we now have evidence for an intensification of agrarian and rural *production* (whether of "commodities" is another matter) from the very beginning of the "long eighth century"; pre-dating the "production phase" of the *emporia* and casting considerable doubt on the continued validity of the "classic model".

Regional production and the emporia

The notion of *emporia* as somehow cut off from the rural economy has been undermined in recent years, and especially by studies of the animal bones from these sites.[42] One of the implications of this research is of a well-managed and "productive" countryside. Jennifer Bourdillon concludes that the quantity and quality of the beasts supplied to Hamwic are "a testimony to the effective richness of its hinterland at a time when such rural prosperity has been in doubt".[43] However, it is no longer enough to say that the *emporia* were supplied from well-managed and productive regions. To all (except those who take the most primitivist view of the Anglo-Saxon economy), this is pretty much what one would expect. The questions now are to what extent was the scale of regional production a product of the demands placed on it by the *emporia*; or did the latter in fact emerge from earlier transformations in regional economies. In other words, were the *emporia* the cause or consequence of "economic growth" in eighth-century England?

For most of those who have even considered the matter, the former is the obvious position to take—the relatively sudden appearance of

---

[41] Hodges, *Anglo-Saxon Achievement*, p. 104.

[42] "One has a sense of *considerable integration*, of animals that had been reared and used in the countryside coming to the end of their lives in the town" – Bourdillon, "Countryside and town", p. 184, emphasis added.

[43] Bourdillon, "Countryside and town", p. 193. See also "Animal provisioning", pp. 122-23; and Scull, "Urban centres", pp. 277, 287.

these large sites is held to be the catalyst for structural transformation. David Hinton, for example, suggests that the *emporia* "contributed to that rearrangement of much of the rural settlement pattern . . . so that production of an agricultural surplus could be more vigorously pursued, and new land brought into cultivation".[44] Richard Hodges, characteristically, goes one step further and argues that the creation of Hamwic "set in motion the pre-conditions for an economic take-off".[45] He also suggests that *specialised production* was developed in an attempt to "fully mobilise" the economy to meet the needs of the new centres.[46] This link between the *emporia* and the emergence of specialised production in the countryside is one to which I shall return, but here it is a argument which assumes the primacy of the *emporia* in social and economic transformation.

What is not often considered, however, is the possibility that the *emporia* may have emerged from transformations in the structure and organisation of production which were already taking place. This may or may not be what Philip Holdsworth had in mind when he stated that "the organisation which would have been necessary to supply 'Hamwih' with its needs *already existed* in southern England",[47] but it is an argument I want to consider further. As we shall see, chronological imprecision makes it very difficult to provide a definitive answer, but in the light of the new dating possibilities offered by refined C^{14} techniques I believe that enough evidence exists to raise it as a serious possibility for further research. In putting this suggestion forward I do not wish to suggest that the *emporia* did not *in any way* affect the structure of production in the countryside—they clearly did, and in much the way proposed by some of the authors cited above. What I will try to do in the sections which follow is firstly to demonstrate the significance of production "beyond the *emporia*", and secondly to suggest that these were elements in a set of structural transformations whose origins may pre-date the *emporia*.

---

[44] Hinton, *Archaeology, Economy and Society*, p. 58. This "rearrangement of the rural settlement pattern" is commonly known as the "middle Saxon shift", or "shuffle". I will discuss it in more detail in the next section.

[45] Hodges, "Industrial revolution", p. 132.

[46] Hodges, *Dark Age Economics*, p. 130. It is strange that his later works contain little investigation of the evidence for this predicted specialisation, and in one case it is suggested that there is, in fact, no evidence for "intensification" in production in the "age of *emporia*" – "Peer polity interaction and socio-political change in Anglo-Saxon England", in C. Renfrew and J. Cherry eds., *Peer Polity Interaction and Socio-Political Change* (Cambridge, 1986), pp. 69-78, at p. 78.

[47] Holdsworth, *Melbourne Street*, p. 133, emphasis added.

Settlements and settlement patterns

In a seminal, but brief, paper in 1981, Arnold and Wardle presented the case for a major transformation in settlement patterns before c. 700, with the early sites on light, well drained soils being abandoned for new ones on more fertile (but more difficult to work) land.[48] They further propose that this "middle Saxon shuffle" or "middle Saxon shift", as it has become known,[49] was one element in a series of transformations which saw the development of new territorial and land-holding arrangements and, perhaps, the emergence of systems of open-field cultivation the remains of which still surround many Midland villages.[50] The model implies that settlements were being relocated in an effort to "intensify" production in a period *preceding*, or coincident with (and here the dating is crucial), at least the "production phase" of the *emporia*.

The model has, however, come in for sustained critique in recent years. In particular, it has been suggested that the proposed settlement shift is simply one moment in the life history of early medieval "wandering settlements"—*Wandersiedlung*.[51] Thus Helena Hamerow shows that between the fifth and late seventh centuries the focus of settlement at Mucking, in Essex, shifted from the south-west to the north-east of the gravel terrace on which it was situated.[52] The crucial point, she argues, is that had only the northern sector of Mucking been excavated then it would have been taken as one of the "new sites" founded as part of the Arnold and Wardle's settlement shift.

However, in the few cases where such "wandering" has been identified,[53] there is no evidence that this process continued beyond the eighth century. As Chris Arnold notes, "stability appears to have

[48] C. Arnold and P. Wardle, "Early medieval settlement patterns in England", *Medieval Archaeology* 25 (1981), pp. 145-49, at pp. 145-47; Arnold, *Early Anglo-Saxon Kingdoms*, p. 63.

[49] Hodges, *Anglo-Saxon Achievement*, p. 62; H. Hamerow, "Settlement mobility and the "middle Saxon shift": rural settlement and settlement patterns in Anglo-Saxon England", *Anglo-Saxon England* 20 (1991), p. 1.

[50] Arnold and Wardle, "Settlement patterns", p. 148; Arnold, *Early Anglo-Saxon Kingdoms*, p. 65.

[51] Hamerow, "Settlement mobility", p. 13. Hamerow provides some of the Continental background in her "The archaeology of rural settlement in early medieval Europe", *Early Medieval Europe* 3 (1994), pp. 167-78.

[52] See Hamerow, "Settlement mobility", fig. 1, p. 4; H. Hamerow, *Excavations at Mucking Volume 2: The Anglo-Saxon Settlement* (London, 1993), pp. 86, 97.

[53] For other examples, see Hamerow, "Settlement mobility", p. 5; *Excavations at Mucking*, p. 97.

occurred from the eighth century onwards".[54] In fact, most recent fieldwork has confirmed not only the date, but also the presumed "rationale" for the settlement shift.[55] Thus systematic fieldwalking in Suffolk has charted the abandonment of early sites on the light soils of the Sandlings, and the occupation (for the first time since the end of the Roman period) of the claylands, by the beginning of the eighth century.[56] One site which did not conform to this pattern was the presumed royal centre at Rendlesham, where field survey located a scatter of Ipswich ware covering c. 15 hectares.[57] The settlement, "goes against the trend for a settlement shift in the seventh century... Continuity through the seventh century is naturally of particular interest given Rendlesham's close royal connections over this period".[58] The fact that the royal site remained in the same place while the settlement pattern around it changed might suggest that its royal occupants had a role to play in encouraging/directing that change. More generally, it would seem that, despite the efforts of critics to undermine its distinctiveness, the rupture in settlement patterns by the end of the seventh century is real.[59]

Explanations for this phenomenon have generally focussed on eco-logical and functional variables. While denying the general validity of settlement change by the eighth century, Martin Welch argues that any abandonment of the lighter soils which did take place was the consequence of soil erosion.[60] Tim Unwin (and others) have preferred to seek their reasons in that perennial favourite of

---

[54] Arnold, *Early Anglo-Saxon Kingdoms*, p. 59.

[55] See below (p. 88) for some examples from East Anglia.

[56] J. Newman, "The late-Roman and Anglo-Saxon settlement pattern in the Sandlings of Suffolk", in M. Carver ed., *The Age of Sutton Hoo* (Woodbridge, 1992), pp. 25-38, at pp. 32-34.

[57] Newman, "Anglo-Saxon settlement pattern", pp. 36-38; *HE* 3.22.

[58] Newman, "Anglo-Saxon settlement pattern", p. 37.

[59] Interestingly, Hamerow herself notes similar developments in Continental Europe at roughly the same time – "By the eighth century in Drenthe, the mostly small, unstructured hamlets of the fourth and fifth centuries were replaced in many cases by villages. ... More clearly significant [in the development of European settle-ment patterns] were the seventh and eighth centuries, which saw widespread archi-tectural developments and a formalization of settlement layout" – "Archaeology of rural settlement", pp. 173, 178. See also H. Waterbolk, "Patterns of the peasant landscape", *Proceedings of the Prehistoric* ʳ ·ety 61 (1995), pp. 1-36, at pp. 17-21; and T. Unwin, "Towards a model of Anᵧ ᵤndinavian rural settlement in England", in D. Hooke *Anglo-Saxon Settlements* (1988), pp. 77-98, at p. 89.

[60] Welch, "Rural settlement patterns", pp. 21-22.

functionalist explanations—population growth.[61] More recently, John
Maddicott has argued precisely the opposite—the settlement shift was
a consequence of population decline caused by the rapid spread of
bubonic plague in the mid- and late seventh century.[62] In a truly
millennial twist, Chris Arnold has recently asserted that "extreme
fluctuations in climate are more likely to have a detectable effect on
settlement patterns than gradual changes", and finds the cause of
this presumed climatic change (and dislocation of settlement) in a
collision between the Earth and an asteroid or comet.[63] More pro-
saically, others have supposed that technological advances must have
encouraged farmers to abandon less fertile zones and take up the
challenge (and reap the rewards) of cultivating the heavier clays.[64]

These kind of explanations lack real explanatory depth. They do
not tell us why, for example, population should grow, or technological developments take place. Just as importantly, however, I would
argue that, framed as they are within "practical" concerns, they have
failed to grasp the truly dramatic nature of the "middle Saxon shuffle".

The change in location was not the only significant transformation in late seventh- and early eighth-century settlement. An extensive study of Anglo-Saxon building types reveals that the eighth
century witnessed "a breakdown in the coherent building tradition
that had survived from the fifth century".[65] We have to appreciate
that this is not just about variations in the mechanics of how one
builds a house. Transformations in the vehicles in and through which
people live their lives generally bespeak more fundamental alterations
in their perception of themselves and their relationship with the world
and the cosmos. In other contexts, this kind of breakdown in long-
standing building traditions has been used as evidence for such
significant moments as "the birth of capitalism" or the "emergence

---

[61] Unwin, "Anglo-Scandinavian rural settlement", pp. 93-94. On p. 96 he slightly
qualifies the argument by stating that "population growth by itself would not guarantee the changes observed, but it can nevertheless be considered as a catalyst".

[62] J. Maddicott, "Plague in seventh-century England", *Past and Present* 156 (1997),
pp. 7-54, at pp. 37-45.

[63] Arnold, *Early Anglo-Saxon Kingdoms*, p. 65. For the "full story", see M. Baillie,
Exodus to Arthur. Catastrophic Encounters with Comets (London, 1999), and D. Keys,
Catastrophe. An Investigation into the Origins of the Modern World (London, 1999) – books
whose tone and argument are heavily influenced by their publication date.

[64] Hamerow, "Settlement mobility", pp. 10-11.

[65] A. Marshall and G. Marshall, "Differentiation, change and continuity in Anglo-
Saxon buildings", *The Archaeological Journal* 150 (1993), pp. 366-402, at p. 400.

of the modern world".[66] The transformations in the location, and in the use of, lived space in the English countryside in the eighth century may not be the product of changes on the scale inferred by Matthew Johnson for the sixteen, but they do suggest that something other than/as well as purely economic forces were at work.

This is also illustrated by the fact that the beginning of the "long eighth century" also seems to witness the "death of the ancestors". The "wandering" of settlements like Mucking was pivoted around cemeteries which remained in the same location.[67] This observation has been linked to a "Germanic" conception of the cemetery as a sacred zone, as the point in the landscape connecting the world of the living and that of the dead, the ancestors. The dead were those who connected Anglo-Saxons with their Beginnings, and whose presence in the land legitimised its possession and use by the community of the living. As Chapelot and Fossier argue, the

> abandonment of this custom [of linked cemetery and settlement] and the regrouping of all subsequent interments around the church, or even within it, is an indication of much more than the victory of Christianity: it signifies the breaking of the religious link between the land belonging to the dead and that of the living.[68]

A concomitant of the settlement shift was the end of burial in the old cemeteries.[69] Their abandonment did not necessarily mean, as

---

[66] M. Johnson, *Housing Culture. Traditional Architecture in an English Landscape* (London, 1993); and his *An Archaeology of Capitalism* (Oxford, 1996). While not wishing to draw direct parallels between Johnson's conclusions about the sixteenth century and the above observations about the eighth, it is nevertheless interesting that the process of "closure" which he sees as lying behind the changes in the structure of houses also fundamentally altered (though the process of enclosure) patterns of land-holding and agricultural exploitation – *Archaeology of Capitalism*, pp. 70-96.

[67] Hamerow, "Settlement mobility", pp. 9-10; for examples of the association of cemetery and settlement, see Hamerow, *Excavations at Mucking*, p. 89, note 4. For some new examples in East Anglia, see J. Newman, "Metal detector finds and fieldwork on Anglo-Saxon sites in Suffolk", *Anglo-Saxon Studies in Archaeology and History* 8 (1995), pp. 87-93, at pp. 89-91; "Anglo-Saxon settlement pattern", at pp. 32-34.

[68] J. Chapelot and R. Fossier, *The Village and House in the Middle Ages* (London, 1985), p. 41. In the same vein, Thomas Charles-Edwards sums up as follows the consequences of a similar process in early historic Ireland, "Relegated to the graveyards of churches the dead lost their power to defend the land which they left to their heirs" – "Boundaries in early Irish law", in P. Sawyer ed., *Medieval Settlement: Continuity and Change* (London, 1976), pp. 83-87, at p. 86.

[69] In her study of so-called "conversion-period" (c. 600-c. 850) cemeteries in England, Helen Geake points out that "none of the sites with migration-period origins outlasted the early eighth century" – H. Geake, *The Use of Grave-Goods in Conversion Period England, c. 600-c. 850* (Oxford, 1997), p. 18.

we once thought, that all burial now took place in churchyards. Donald Bullough has shown that "the early Church showed itself surprisingly indifferent to where Christians were laid to rest"; while John Blair argues that "It mattered little that rural Christians were . . . buried where their ancestors had been buried".[70] However, it does seem that churches did become the focal point for burial (and for settlement) from the eighth century onwards.[71] The "shifting" settlement at Mucking just overlaps chronologically with the monastery founded by St Cedd c. 653 at "*Tilaburg*" (Tilbury, c. 3km away). As Hamerow herself notes, the "foundation of a monastery at Tilbury must have had an effect on the community at Mucking"[72]—we can suggest that the "effect" would have been the demise of the community and the death of the ancestors.

To sum up, it would seem that there was a major dislocation in settlement patterns in England by the end of the seventh century. The move was to heavier and more productive soils, with obvious implications for at least part of the rationale for the change. However, the dramatic nature of this rupture has been diminished by a tendency to focus on its purely practical/secular implications (although, these were undoubtedly important). As the ultimate liminal act, burial is perhaps more expressive of deep-seated human attitudes and beliefs than any other; as the place where they live their lives, houses are a repository of accumulated meaning. The transformations in the houses of the living and in the tombs of the dead speak volumes for the importance of the changes we are witnessing in the countryside of eighth-century England.[73]

In terms of economic development, I want to emphasise once again that, on the available evidence, the process of transformation

---

[70] D. Bullough, "Burial, community and belief in the early medieval West", in P. Wormald ed., *Ideal and Reality in Frankish and Anglo-Saxon Society* (Oxford, 1983), p. 186; see also p. 192; J. Blair, "Minster churches in the landscape", in D. Hooke ed., *Anglo-Saxon Settlements* (Oxford, 1988) p. 55. For some examples of other burial places, see S. Lucy, "Changing burial rites in Northumbria A.D. 500-750", in J. Hawkes and S. Mills eds., *Northumbria's Golden Age* (Stroud, 1999), pp. 12-43, at p. 20.

[71] It is from the eighth century that we have (admittedly Carolingian) liturgies for the dead; see R. Samson, "The church lends a hand", in J. Downes and T. Pollard eds., *The Loved Body's Corruption. Archaeological Contributions to the Study of Human Mortality* (Glasgow, 1999), pp. 120-44, at pp. 138-39. See below (pp. 104-105) for church and settlement.

[72] Hamerow, *Excavations at Mucking*, pp. 86-89; "Settlement mobility", p. 10.

[73] The final move towards burial without grave-goods was another element in this change; for a recent discussion, see Samson, "Church lends a hand".

may have begun before the emergence of the *emporia*, and certainly before they themselves shifted to a "production mode". As we shall see in the conclusion, the fact that the Church can be linked to this process is immensely significant.

New Beginnings in the eighth century

A central element in the "settlement shift" model is the foundation of new sites before c. 700, and one of the most important developments in Anglo-Saxon studies in recent years has been the discovery of numerous such settlements. Many have been located by metal detecting, and are characterised by large quantities of (often quite fine) metal work. These "productive" or "prolific" sites are now fairly common in East Anglia, Lincolnshire, Yorkshire and Humberside, precisely those areas, as Julian Richards notes, "where archaeologists have been prepared to collaborate with 'treasure hunters'".[74]

In East Anglia, as part of the recent Sutton Hoo project, selected areas of the landscape were field-walked by archaeologists and metal detected by local enthusiasts.[75] The new sites of the middle Saxon period (not all of them "productive sites") usually manifested themselves as scatters of Ipswich ware close to churches.[76] This pottery links the sites directly to the "economic" activities of the *emporium* at Gipeswic. Further connections with the *emporium* are the large numbers of *sceattas* found on "productive sites". Of the fifty or so from a site at Barham (to the north-west of Ipswich) more than 20% were series R, probably minted at Gipeswic.[77] At Coddenham, more than 50 *sceattas* formed part of a much larger assemblage of coins and other metal objects of the late seventh and eighth centuries. The material culture from these sites suggests that they were "economic central places" within the kingdom of East Anglia, and that they

---

[74] Richards, "Anglo-Saxon settlements", p. 45. As we shall see later in this section, there is also evidence from some of the more westerly parts of England that similar sites and similar processes are to be found there too.

[75] For recent publications, see Newman, "Anglo-Saxon settlement pattern"; "Metal-detector finds"; "Wics", pp. 37-44. For the Sutton Hoo project generally, see M. Carver, *Sutton Hoo. Burial Ground of Kings?* (London, 1998).

[76] Newman, "Anglo-Saxon settlement pattern", p. 34; "Wics", p. 39. I have already noted the potential significance of the church as a central structuring force in the new pattern of settlement in the earlier discussion of the characteristics of the middle Saxon shift, and I will return to it again later.

[77] Newman, "Metal-detector finds", p. 92; "Wics", p. 43. For series R production at Gipeswic, see Metcalf, *Thrymsas and Sceattas*, p. 315.

functioned within an integrated economic system which included Gipeswic. Documentary evidence and archaeological excavation allows us to add some flesh to these bare bones.

In the late Saxon period, Barham was part of a major estate of the monastery at Ely, and these ecclesiastical connections may have originated earlier.[78] Ely also had an estate at Brandon and here excavations have shown that in the late seventh century a settlement was established on a sand ridge in the flood plain of the river Ouse.[79] Thirty-five buildings set within enclosures, a church, and a cemetery were identified within the excavated area. High-quality silver and glass, and copper alloy pins, inscribed tweezers, window and vessel glass, and styli, are among the objects which can be dated to the eighth century.[80] The styli are especially significant as they are undoubted signs of the practice of literacy at Brandon. It is well known that this was a socially-restricted skill in the early middle ages, and it is commonly believed to have been largely confined to the ecclesiastical elite.[81] A symbol of St John the Evangelist, set in niello on a gold plaque, and surrounded by an inscription, adds to the impression of a high-status, literate and ecclesiastical community.[82]

This was, however, a community with very worldly concerns. *Sceattas*, including "locally" produced Series Q types, and 17,000 sherds of Ipswich ware provide immediate connections with the region, while imported ceramics link the ecclesiastical community (even indirectly) with Continental Europe.[83] It seems that the site's occupants

---

[78] Newman, "Wics", pp. 39, 43. It should be noted that Newman has proposed Ely as the mint for the series Q *sceattas*, pp. 43-44; see also Metcalf, *Thrymsas and Sceattas*, pp. 483-87.

[79] For this and the following, see R. Carr, A. Tester, and P. Murphy, "The middle Saxon settlement at Staunch Meadow, Brandon", *Antiquity* 62 (1988), pp. 371-7; P. Murphy, "The Anglo-Saxon landscape and rural economy: some results from sites in East Anglia", in J. Rackham ed., *Environment and Economy in Anglo-Saxon England* (York, 1994), pp. 23-39, at pp. 31-35. The dating is provided by a C^{14} date from the surface on which the settlement was established – see Murphy, "Anglo-Saxon landscape", p. 31; Blinkhorn, *Ipswich Ware Project*.

[80] These are illustrated in L. Webster and J. Backhouse, *The Making of England. Anglo-Saxon Art and Culture A.D. 600-900* (London, 1992), pp. 81-88.

[81] See, however, S. Kelly, "Anglo-Saxon lay society and the written word", in R. McKitterick ed., *The Uses of Literacy in Early Medieval Europe* (Cambridge, 1990), pp. 36-63, for lay literacy.

[82] It should be noted, however, that this (and some of the styli) probably date to the early ninth century – Webster and Backhouse, *Making of England*, pp. 82-93.

[83] For the *sceattas*, see Metcalf, *Thrymsas and Sceattas*, p. 483; for the Ipswich ware, see Blinkhorn, *Ipswich Ware Project*.

received grain in a semi-cleaned state from the surrounding region, and there is good evidence that it was the focus for specialised, large-scale cloth (probably linen) production.[84] The importance of the cereals and cloth-production lie in the fact that they make a connection between these high-status sites, Ipswich ware, imported pottery, *sceattas* and *production*. In fact, this connection is repeated on other sites that would be called "productive" had they been located by field survey alone.

At Burrow Hill, Suffolk, a cemetery, a stylus, imported northern French pottery, imported quernstones, Ipswich wares and early eighth-century *sceattas* were found in association with evidence of craft production—including metal and leather-working.[85] At Terrington St Clement, Norfolk, imported continental pottery, Ipswich wares, and evidence (in the form of brine pits) for specialised meat production have been found on a site which may cover seven hectares.[86] Michael Metcalf has tentatively suggested that this may have been a mint for Series Q *sceattas*.[87] At Wicken Bonhunt, Essex, twenty-five buildings (including workshops and storage facilities), evidence for craft production, and Ipswich ware were found in association with evidence for the specialised meat production.[88] Pig bones comprised 68% of the faunal assemblage,[89] but the dearth of juveniles and an imbalance in the proportions of body parts with an "overabundance" of heads, suggests that the animals were supplied from sites in the surrounding territory, processed at Wicken Bonhunt, and the (headless) carcasses passed on to other/another centre in the region.[90] Like Terrington St Clement and Brandon, Wicken Bonhunt appears to have received the yield of regional agrarian production.

Similar patterns can be seen on sites outside the kingdom of East Anglia. At North Raunds, Northamptonshire, the quantity of wheat present has led to the suggestion it may have been at the heart of

---

[84] Murphy, "Anglo-Saxon landscape", pp. 34-35.

[85] V. Fenwick, "Insula de Burgh: excavations at Burrow Hill, Butley, Suffolk", *Anglo-Saxon Studies in Archaeology and History* 3 (1984), pp. 35-54.

[86] Blinkhorn, *Ipswich Ware Project*. The site itself is currently unpublished.

[87] Metcalf, *Thrymsas and Sceattas*, pp. 485-86. As he notes, however, metal detecting of the site failed to uncover any *sceattas*.

[88] The site is unpublished, but see K. Wade, "A settlement site at Bonhunt Farm, Wicken Bonhunt, Essex", in R. Buckley ed., *Archaeology in Essex to A.D. 1500* (London, 1980), pp. 96-102.

[89] P. Crabtree, "Animal exploitation in East Anglian villages", in J. Rackham ed., *Environment and Economy in Anglo-Saxon England* (York, 1994), p. 41, table 5.1.

[90] Crabtree, "Animal exploitation", p. 47.

a system specialising in the production of grain.[91] Quantities of Ipswich ware were also present, and residue analysis on these, and on the locally produced Maxey wares, revealed the presence of significant traces of honey and beeswax—both attested as valuable products in the early eighth century.[92] Paul Blinkhorn argues that North Raunds was merely "a farmstead",[93] but the evidence for specialisation, for Ipswich ware outside East Anglia, and for products like honey surely point to a higher-status settlement, if not as "high" as sites like Brandon.

Pennyland, Buckinghamshire, does not entirely conform to the picture I have been sketching, but in this case the exception does seem to prove the rule. Some time between the seventh and early eighth centuries, a small, dispersed settlement was transformed through the construction of a series of halls and sunken-featured-buildings set within a "well-defined and regulated" network of enclosures and trackways.[94] Ipswich wares arrived here c. 750, by which time the enclosures had been abandoned, and there is some evidence that occupation commenced near the church at Great Limford, less than 1km to the northwest.[95] At first sight this is an almost classic example of middle Saxon settlement shift. However, my particular interest in this site stems from the fact that the enclosures and the faunal evidence imply some specialisation in livestock production.[96] The presence of grain storage facilities, and evidence that "deep cultivation was practised . . . [on] a wide range of soil types", reinforces the impression of the beginnings of agricultural intensification in the seventh century.[97] As such, Pennyland may provide some evidence

---

[91] Blinkhorn, "Cabbages and kings", p. 16. The assemblage is distinctive in that it consists almost entirely of hexaploid free-threshing wheat, with little or no sign of the broad range of cereals found on "normal" sites of the period. Either the inhabitants specialised in the production of this one crop – perhaps for delivery elsewhere; or they were in a position to make demands that it be delivered to them from outlying sites.

[92] Blinkhorn, *Ipswich Ware Project*; "Cabbages and kings", p. 16. Hodges, *Dark Age Economics*, p. 127 suggests that "their [bee-keepers] products were traded in controlled circumstances".

[93] Blinkhorn, "Cabbages and kings", p. 8.

[94] R. Williams, *Pennyland and Hartigans. Two Iron Age and Saxon Sites in Milton Keynes* (Aylesbury, 1993), p. 54. The date given here is later than that proposed by the excavator and depends of the re-dating of Ipswich ware – see Blinkhorn, "Cabbages and kings", p. 14.

[95] Williams, *Pennyland*, p. 95; Blinkhorn, "Cabbages and kings", p. 14.

[96] Williams, *Pennyland*, p. 148; Blinkhorn, "Cabbages and kings", p. 14.

[97] Williams, *Pennyland*, p. 96. It should be noted that my interpretation differs somewhat from that presented in Blinkhorn, "Cabbages and kings", p. 14.

for the transformation of the Anglo-Saxon economy in the period immediately preceding the emergence of the *emporia*.

The sites I have been discussing are all connected by the fact that they have evidence for high-status occupation and/or signs of economic intensification at the beginning of the "long eighth century". Sites like Pennyland may have been further down the socio-economic scale than Brandon, or some of the "productive sites", but they are clearly integrated within the same system. However, the precise function of the latter within this system is unclear. They share some of the characteristics of *emporia*—the presence of *sceattas*, evidence for regional and long-distance trade, and for craft production, and John Newman has taken these similarities and tried to fit the "productive sites" (including the excavated ones) into the "classic" *emporia* model. In this model, Hodges saw an evolutionary development from small, seasonally occupied, "type A" *emporia* to the planned, permanent "type B" settlements like Hamwic, Gipeswic, Lundenwic and Eoforwic.[98] What Newman proposes is that these two categories co-existed and that sites like Barham were seasonal trading places, often centred on churches, tied into the exchange patterns of the coastal *emporia*.[99] It is noteworthy that "exchange" lies at the core of the model and provides the stimulus for "economic growth". As is so often the case, the realm of production is ignored. Some recent work in the Yorkshire Wolds allows us to rethink the model.

Since 1987 the "productive site" at Cottam, Humberside, has produced numerous finds of gilt, silver plated and copper alloy pins, and three early eighth-century *sceattas*. Knives, sharpening stones, a scythe and lead spindle whorls illuminate the role of production in the economy of the settlement.[100] Excavations uncovered the remains of *permanent structures* and settlement debris of the eighth and ninth centuries, along with evidence for non-ferrous metalworking.[101] The finds were confined with a sub-rectangular enclosure beside a track-

---

[98] Hodges, *Dark Age Economics*, pp. 50-52.

[99] Newman, "Wics", pp. 37-39; "Metal detector finds", p. 92.

[100] The discovery and finds were promptly published. See D. Haldenby, "An Anglian site on the Yorkshire Wolds", *The Yorkshire Archaeological Journal* 62 (1990), pp. 51-63; D. Haldenby, "An Anglian site on the Yorkshire Wolds – continued", *The Yorkshire Archaeological Journal* 64 (1992), pp. 25-39; D. Haldenby, "Further Saxon finds from the Yorkshire Wolds", *The Yorkshire Archaeological Journal* 66 (1994), pp. 51-56. The earliest closely dated find is the primary sceatta of c. 690-725 – Haldenby, "An Anglian site – continued", pp. 27, 37.

[101] For the excavations, see Richards, "Anglo-Saxon settlements"; "Productive sites".

way which was linked to network of fields and tracks of probable Romano-British origins.[102] The strong resemblance between this enclosure and several other (undated) examples in the region may indicate a previously unsuspected expansion of settlement and economy in a region commonly regarded as marginal.[103]

Cottam clearly shares many of the characteristics of the East Anglian "productive sites" (although it seems to have been beyond the distribution of Ipswich ware), and a similar function would seem to be implied. However, as Julian Richards argues, the presence there of permanent structures and "normal" settlement debris does not support the idea that it (and by implication sites like it) was a periodic market or trading community—in other words one of Newman's rural *emporia*.[104] He also reminds us that the "productive site" category may in fact mask a variety of site types.[105] One of the distinctive features of Cottam is the combination of coins, dress fittings, tools of production, and a large number of knives. The "productive site" at South Newbald, East Yorkshire, by contrast, produced 126 coins (72 of them from the eighth century) and many dress fittings, but no knives, "animal bone, loom weights or other evidence for human occupation".[106] It would seem that these sites, while sharing elements of a "rich" material culture and participation in exchange systems mediated (at least partially) through the *sceatta* coinage, functioned in different ways, with Cottam being perhaps closer to the basic systems of production. Again, excavations at sites

---

[102] Richards, "Productive sites", p. 72. For aerial photography, see C. Stoertz, *Ancient Landscapes of the Yorkshire Worlds* (Swindon, 1997), pp. 53-55, figure 27, and map 1.

[103] Richards, "Anglo-Saxon settlements", p. 49. Also Stoertz, *Ancient Landscapes*, pp. 55-59, 67; figure 30, p. 58. See also, A. Fleming, *Swaledale. Valley of the Wild River* (Edinburgh, 1998), pp. 18-30. A similar looking set of enclosures at Riby Cross Roads, Lincolnshire, dated to the eighth century, has produced evidence for an intensification of livestock rearing, regional and long-distance trade (including Ipswich wares and a *sceat*), and craft production; see K. Stedman *et al.* "Excavation of a Saxon site at Riby Cross Roads, Lincolnshire", *The Archaeological Journal* 151 (1994), pp. 212-306.

In terms of settlement expansion, it is worth noting the sites at Simy Folds in a remote part of Upper Teesdale, which contained extensive traces of iron smelting and smithing, and dated to the mid seventh century by thermoluminesence – D. Coggins, K. Fairless and C. Batey, "Simy Folds: an early medieval settlement site in Upper Teesdale, Co. Durham", *Medieval Archaeology* 27 (1983), pp. 1-26, especially pp. 18-20.

[104] Richards, "Anglo-Saxon settlements", p. 49.

[105] Richards, "Productive sites", p. 79.

[106] Leahy, "Flixborough", p. 93; Richards, "Productive sites", pp. 76, 79.

that would have been classified as "productive" had they been discovered by detectorists provide more nuanced insights into the economic systems within which they were integrated.

Wharram Percy is well known as the site of the deserted medieval village, but recent work has demonstrated high status middle Saxon occupation, perhaps focussed on the hall excavated on the site of the later "South Manor".[107] A single *sceatta* of c. 700-710 provides the earliest firm dating for this phase of occupation. Imported hone stones, querns, northern French wares, and Ipswich ware confirm participation in long-distance exchange systems, while quartz sand-tempered wares of a type noted at Eoforwic point to regional level systems.[108] The significance of production is attested by evidence for the first post-Roman "enclosure" of the landscape.[109] The smithy, and evidence for textile manufacture indicate craft production, while crucibles and clay moulds for making copper-alloy objects with interlace decoration suggest that at least some of this was fairly high-status.[110] Two sword pommels and a hilt guard are further testimony to an elite presence, while the fragment of an eighth-century cross-head and some disturbed burials imply that at least some of this was ecclesiastical.[111]

Once again, the pattern is of high-status occupation from early in the "long eighth century", linked with evidence for the intensification of production, craft production and participation in regional and long-distance trade systems. The permanent structures and the evidence for agrarian production means that we cannot consider this, or other productive sites, as rural *emporia*—the term is too loaded to adequately encompass their "economic" functions. Nor, however, are they "normal settlements", as Richards argues.[112] His assertions that Wharram Percy functioned within a "self-sufficient economy", and that there "appears to have been little trickle-down from the thriving *wic* site at York" fly in the face of the numismatic and ceramic evidence.[113] These overtly negative judgements serve to reinforce

---

[107] M. Beresford and J. Hurst, *Wharram Percy Deserted Medieval Village* (London, 1990), pp. 82-84.

[108] Beresford and Hurst, *Wharram Percy*, pp. 77-78, 82-83; Richards, "Productive sites", p. 76; Mainman, *Pottery from Fishergate*, p. 580.

[109] Richards, "Anglo-Saxon settlements", p. 51.

[110] Richards, "Anglo-Saxon settlements", p. 52; "Productive sites", p. 76; Beresford and Hurst, *Wharram Percy*, pp. 82-83.

[111] Richards, "Productive sites", p. 76; Beresford and Hurst, *Wharram Percy*, p. 83.

[112] Richards, "Productive sites", p. 73.

[113] Richards, "Anglo-Saxon settlements", p. 52.

orthodox impressions of both the dynamism and "uniqueness" of the
emporia, and the conservatism and autarky of the countryside. The
material culture from sites like Wharram (and perhaps Cottam) suggests that these were centres in and through which elites controlled
the production and distribution of goods at the regional level, and
which were integrated into wider-scale economic systems through
their links with the *emporia*. We might even call them estate centres!
As I have already noted, however, there are signs of hierarchy within
this category—the imported wares at Wharram perhaps signalling
that this was a more "important" central place that say Cottam.[114]
Excavations at Flixborough, north Lincolnshire, provide us with a
glimpse of life at its upper end.[115]

The ceramic evidence, and a series D *sceat* of c. 700-715, suggest
that Flixborough was founded in the late seventh century.[116] In this
early phase the settlement showed signs of planning and consisted
of at least six buildings set within a ditched enclosure.[117] The graves
cut into the floor of building 1 suggest that it was a church, and we
can probably associate finds of window glass and lead cames with
it.[118] Further indicators of an ecclesiastical presence are the eleven
bodies which were excavated at an early stage in the evaluation of
the site,[119] and (most critically) the discovery of twenty-seven styli—
at least one of which was silver.[120] As at Brandon, these styli are a
sure sign that writing played a very significant part in the life of the
community, a conclusion supported by a lead plaque inscribed with
seven or eight personal names, and a ring decorated with the first
eleven letters of the alphabet.[121] Everything points to high-status ecclesiastical occupation, with evidence for participation in both regional

---

[114] Blinkhorn, "Cabbages and kings", p. 10.

[115] Loveluck, "Flixborough"; Leahy, "Flixborough".

[116] Leahy, "Flixborough", p. 90. See, however, Loveluck, "Flixborough", p. 159
note 1 where unspecified evidence for earlier seventh- and tenth/eleventh-century
occupation is cited.

[117] Loveluck, "Flixborough", p. 151, figure 5, phase 3.20.

[118] Loveluck, "Flixborough", p. 152; Webster and Backhouse, *Making of England*,
p. 95.

[119] Leahy, "Flixborough", p. 88.

[120] Leahy, "Flixborough", p. 93. Some of these, and other finds, are illustrated
in Webster and Backhouse, *Making of England*, pp. 94-101.

[121] For comparison we should note that six styli are known from the monastery
at Whitby, and two from that at Jarrow – Leahy, "Flixborough", p. 93. The plaque
is illustrated and discussed in Webster and Backhouse, *Making of England*, p. 95. See
also Loveluck, "Flixborough", p. 155. figure 9.

level and long-distance trading systems, from the start of the "long eighth century".

The significant quantities of lead which must have come from production centres in the Peak District to the west, and the shell-tempered pottery with a distribution pattern covering much of the east Midlands, Lincolnshire and Humberside, illustrate regional level production and exchange.[122] Ipswich ware storage vessels, exported as containers for other goods, probably started arriving by the middle of the eighth century.[123] As at Eoforwic, the imported pottery came primarily from northern France and the Low Countries.[124] Tools and production debris show the manufacture of objects from bone, leather, iron, lead and other non-ferrous metals,[125] and it has been suggested that the quantities of carding-combs, spindle whorls, loom weights, needles and thimbles demonstrate "the production of cloth on an industrial scale".[126] Direct participation by at least some of the inhabitants in agrarian production is suggested by an iron plough coulter and hoe-sheath. Cattle, sheep and pigs (as usual) dominated the faunal assemblage, although marine and riverine fish, wildfowl, deer, hare and woodcock are all present in the faunal assemblage, as are significant numbers of skeletal elements from cetaceans.[127] The variety evident in the diet is indicative of a site occupied by people who commanded the resources of the region.

While it seems clear (to me, at any rate) that the late seventh and early eighth century focus of Flixborough was ecclesiastical, it is worth noting Chris Loveluck's point that many of the characteristics commonly taken to be indicative of early medieval monasteries— a planned layout within an enclosure, specialist craft-working and evidence for long-distance trade, and signs of the practice of literacy—can be found on secular sites of the period.[128] Loveluck is here making a case for a change in the character of occupation in the early ninth century. For me, however, the point is that the characteristics which he sees as linking the estate centres of secular and

---

[122] For the lead, see Loveluck, "Flixborough", p. 157, also p. 154, figure 8b. For the pottery, see Mainman, *Pottery from Fishergate*, p. 580; Leahy, "Flixborough", p. 90; Loveluck, "Flixborough", p. 157.

[123] Blinkhorn, "Cabbages and kings", p. 9; *Ipswich Ware Project*.

[124] Loveluck, "Flixborough", pp. 154, 157.

[125] Loveluck, "Flixborough", pp. 154, 156-57; Leahy, "Flixborough", p. 91.

[126] Leahy, "Flixborough", p. 91.

[127] Loveluck, "Flixborough", pp. 155-56.

[128] Loveluck, "Flixborough", p. 159.

ecclesiastical elites can be seen as the product of fact that both were
heavily implicated in the intensified management of resources which
lies at the heart of the economic transformations of the late seventh
and early eighth centuries. What makes Flixborough an ecclesiastical elite centre is the (probable) church and (especially) the extensive evidence for literacy. What we have to remember, however, is
that the styli wielded by the clerics there could just as easily have
been used in recording the product of the land and the renders due
to the brothers (or sisters), as in the transcription of the Holy Word.
Literacy was a powerful economic weapon and, as I will argue later,
it is no coincidence that it begins to become more prevalent at the
same time as the other transformations I have been charting.

In terms of understanding the relationship between the "place" of
the *emporia* in the economies of the "long eighth century", several
significant conclusions flow from this detailed consideration of settlements from the Thames to the Tees. Firstly, the presence of *sceattas*, Continental pottery and Ipswich ware demonstrates the existence
of a set of integrated regional economies, which also encompassed
the *emporia*. There is no sign here of an autarkic and self-sufficient
countryside, or of isolated and divorced trading centres. Secondly,
there are clear indications that these economies were integrated at
the regional level through a hierarchy of settlements. To initiate discussion we might propose a system of at least four levels—

- major ecclesiastical (and secular) sites like Flixborough and Brandon,
  characterised by coinage, imports, craft production, evidence that
  they were regional central places, and (for me, crucially) literacy;
- settlements such as Barham and Wharram Percy, which share some
  of the features of the above, but which seem materially less well
  endowed;
- sites (Pennyland and Riby Cross Roads)[129] which have some evidence for participation in the exchange networks, but which appear
  more deeply embedded in the structures of rural production;
- the numerous sites across the region which must have serviced the
  above centres, but which are currently archaeologically invisible
  because they did not receive the fruits of the economic transformations which they ultimately drove.

---

[129] See note 103.

One of the most significant features of all the sites in this proposed hierarchy (apart, obviously, for those in the last) is the evidence for the significance of production at the beginning of the "long eighth century". This can take the form of intensified livestock or cereal production/processing, or of craft activities such as the textile manufacture at Brandon, but the crucial point is that it can now be seen as a reality in the English countryside at a time coincident with or, more probably, antedating the "emergence of production" on the *emporia*.

This leads directly to the question of the origins of the phenomenon. The settlement shift model, with the move to more "productive" soils implies a date before the end of the seventh century. This is confirmed by much of the evidence cited above. Many of the sites are dated by the *sceattas* and Ipswich ware to the early eighth century. However, where other dating methods are available there are good signs that the settlements owe their origins to a systemic change by the late seventh century. Thus C^{14} dates and ceramic evidence provide late seventh-century foundation dates for Brandon and Flixborough, while there are signs of intensified production at Pennyland before the "settlement shift". It would be foolish to push this evidence too far at this stage, but we can certainly dismiss the argument that the intensification of craft production on the *emporia* in the third decade of the eighth century represents a shift from a "primitive" gift economy to a more "advanced" commodity economy. Further we can show that the emergence of the *emporia* was intimately connected with intensified production in the English countryside. More precise dating of both rural sites and *emporia*, and a better understanding of the "character" of early occupation on the latter, might allow us to go further and argue that the *emporia* were in fact a product of this transformation in production.

I do not believe that it is any coincidence that we find styli and other evidence for writing on the most "productive" sites of the period. This evidence has to be situated within a context which saw what we might call the "secularisation of literacy",[130] and (as I noted above) while the writing implements at Flixborough and Brandon could have been used in the service of God, they could also have recorded the material wealth of His earthly representatives. While I would not

---

[130] Kelly, "Anglo-Saxon lay society", pp. 40-46.

suggest that writing was the cause of the economic transformations
I have been describing, it certainly could have been used to record
them, thereby enhancing their effectiveness.[131]

It will have been noted that the evidence for the above argument
comes only from the eastern half of England. It may be, as Chris
Wickham suggests in his concluding comments on this volume, that
this is a product of an early medieval reality; that proximity to
Francia stimulated the development of integrated and hierarchical
economic systems only in this half of the country.[132] Before accept-
ing this argument, however, we should note that there are some
signs of economic "development" in western parts of the Anglo-
Saxon lands at the beginning of the "long eighth century".

Ramsbury, Wiltshire, was a specialised iron production centre in
the eighth century. Excavations have uncovered the remains of several iron smelting furnaces and smithing hearths of eighth- and ninth-
century date, which seem to have produced on a large scale and to
a high quality.[133] This production has to be situated within an integrated pattern of procurement and distribution since the ore used
must have come from sources about 30 kms away from the site;[134]
and some of the iron may have been supplied to Hamwic.[135] While
the generally accepted late eighth-century date for the site does not
fully accord with the pattern I have been trying to construct, it
should be noted that the C^{14} dates (which are the principal chronological markers) have ranges which encompass the late seventh and
early eighth centuries.[136]

It is possible to accommodate this production within the "classic
model" since Ramsbury appears to have been the centre of a royal
estate, and the movement of iron to Hamwic could be seen as an
interestate transfer of resources. However, the development of this
specialised production can also be seen as "an attempt to meet the
demand for iron artefacts by a large and probably fully working

---

[131] For some thoughts on the economic impact of literacy, see J. Moreland,
"Production and exchange in historical archaeology", in G. Barker ed., *Companion
Encyclopedia of Archaeology* (London, 1999), pp. 637-71, at pp. 647-50.
[132] Wickham, "Overview II", p. 359.
[133] J. Haslam, "A middle Saxon iron smelting site at Ramsbury, Wiltshire", *Medieval
Archaeology* 24 (1980), pp. 9-30. For the quality, see pp. 41, 53.
[134] Haslam, "Ramsbury", p. 56.
[135] Haslam, "Ramsbury", p. 56.
[136] Haslam, "Ramsbury", pp. 54-55.

estate", and as such it represents "an exercise . . . in efficient estate management" rather than a reaction to the demands of the *emporium*.[137]

Some support for the possibility that Ramsbury could have been producing iron from beginning of our "long eighth century" comes in the form of evidence that it was happening elsewhere in the region at this time. At Worgret, near Wareham in Dorset, the timbers of a possible watermill have been dated to the late seventh century. The structure had been filled with iron-slag and furnace lining residues—suggesting that smelting had been taking place nearby. Viewed separately these are important indicators of an intensification of production; their significance is magnified by the suggestion that the mill may have been used in the iron production process. Interestingly, "the metallurgy does not preclude the use of a mechanically-powered bellows in the production of the Worgret slag".[138] This combination would represent a truly dramatic development in the scale and technologies of production. Given the close relationship we have already seen between elites and this kind of intensification, it is important to note that Worgret has ecclesiastical and (possible) royal connections—it was almost certainly part of the *parochia* of the Anglo-Saxon minster of Wareham.[139]

At Gillingham, near Shaftsbury in Dorset, excavations uncovered the remains of two large stone and clay ovens, archaeomagnetically and C^{14} dated to the late seventh and early eighth centuries.[140] The structures were associated with considerable deposits of iron smelting slag (attesting to local iron production), but there is no evidence that they were used in this process. Rather, it seems that they were connected with the processing of grain, and that the size and arrangement of the facilities precludes their use for purely domestic purposes.[141] The ovens were clearly an important centralised facility, and represent an attempt to intensify production within the region.

There are some indications "of a pre-Conquest royal presence by the ninth century" and, as the excavator argues, while

---

[137] Haslam, "Ramsbury", p. 64.

[138] D. Hinton, "Revised dating of the Worgret structure", *Proceedings of the Dorset Natural History and Archaeological Society* 114 (1992), pp. 258-59, at p. 259.

[139] Hinton, "Worgret", p. 259.

[140] M. Heaton, "Two mid-Saxon grain driers and later medieval features at Chantry Fields, Gillingham, Dorset", *Proceedings of the Dorset Natural History and Archaeological Society* 114 (1992), pp. 97-126, at p. 114.

[141] Heaton, "Chantry Fields", p. 125.

it would be foolish to suggest that the ovens are evidence for any direct aristocratic or ecclesiastical influence, . . . they cannot be seen as having performed a simply domestic function . . . They could be seen as providing evidence for the existence of a social hierarchy supported by an established exchange network based on either trade and/or tribute, and not necessarily based around the established hinterlands of entrepôts like Hamwih.[142]

As at Ramsbury, we have to recognise that the role of production in the eighth century was not just to supply the needs of *emporia* like Hamwic.

Salt was one of the most important resources in pre-modern societies, and we can expect elites to have attempted to control its production and/or distribution. It is therefore significant for our understanding of the eighth century that such attempts have recently been charted at Droitwich, one of the major production sources in England. Salt production from the Upwich brine springs is known from the Roman period, but for our purposes the first notable phase of activity is in the sixth and seventh centuries. Ten brine-boiling hearths of this period have been excavated, associated with considerable quantities of lead (from the pans in which the brine was boiled).[143] Production on this scale in a period of supposed economic autarky is certainly worth noting, as are the regional connections implied by the lead and the "non-local" pottery.[144] This period of production was ended as alluvium washed over the site in the late seventh century, but such was the significance of the source, and its product, that in the eighth century attempts were made to control the course of the river "by revetting its banks and dumping so that the river was moved southwards and away from the brine springs".[145]

Importantly, it is from this period that we get documentary references to the springs at Upwich, and to an elite interest in them.[146] The brine wells are mentioned in the late seventh century, and by the eighth the settlement is referred to as *Saltwich* and as *vicus emptorium salis*—illustrating the importance of trade in the product by

[142] Heaton, "Chantry Fields", pp. 97, 125.

[143] J. Hurst, ed. *A Multi-Period Salt Production Site at Droitwich: Excavations at Upwich* (York, 1997), pp. 17-27.

[144] Hurst, *Droitwich*, pp. 31, 23.

[145] Hurst, *Droitwich*, pp. 54, 30.

[146] J. Moreland, "Review of P. Andrews, ed. *Excavations at Hamwic, Volume 2* and of J. Hurst ed. *A Multi-Period Salt Production Site at Droitwich*", *Urban History* 26 (1999), pp. 129-32, at p. 132.

this date. Records for the "reorganisation of properties associated with salt-making, which were owned by the Mercian king and the Church of Worcester, in A.D. 716-717" show (once again) the active involvement of elites in production (and presumably in trade).[147]

The quality and quantity of the evidence for economic transformations in the "west" is clearly not as good as in the "east", but we do have to remind ourselves that the "visibility" of the eastern pattern of productive sites is to some extent a product of the distribution of Ipswich ware and the preoccupation which archaeologists currently have with it. It is true that there is no sign of ceramic production and distribution on this scale in the west, but we have to measure the significance of this absence against that for the reality of parallel developments in the east and west—in particular the intensification of production and elite involvement in the process. We also have to remember that the number of sites now known, surveyed and excavated is to a large extent the product of the close relationships which have developed between archaeologists and metal detectorists in East Anglia, Lincolnshire and East Yorkshire/Humberside (see above). As David Hinton laments—

> it is one of the major frustrations of the archaeology of this period [in Wessex] that there are so few sites that produce any pottery at all.... [The result is that] a more precise pattern of abandonment and foundation of sites cannot yet be established in Wessex as it can further east.[148]

In the light of all this, we have to consider the possibility that the few signs we do have for "the significance of production" in the western half of England are indeed manifestations of more widespread changes; but changes which remain as masked as they once were in the east.

The hidden hand(s)

In the "classic model" the hidden hand behind the operation and functioning of the *emporia* was that of the king. It was he who conceived of the idea, executed it, supplied the settlement with provisions and resources, and directly profited from it—not least by denying

---

[147] Hurst, *Droitwich*, pp. 30-31.
[148] Hinton, "Eighth- to eleventh-century Wessex", p. 35.

subordinates access to exotic imports. Control over exchange, and the products of exchange, not only provided the rationale for the settlement but also the stimulus for economic and social transformation. The realm of production has little place in this account.

In the course of this chapter I have sought to demonstrate that this emphasis on exchange has fundamentally distorted our understanding of the reality of eighth-century economic processes. The radical shift in the pattern of settlement, the emergence of new, integrated structures and the intensification of agrarian and craft production at the beginning of the long eighth century forces us to abandon the idea that the *emporia* were *the* foci of economic development. By the beginning of the eighth century (at the latest) central places had emerged in the English countryside in and through which secular and ecclesiastical elites channelled the fruits of regional production *and* long-distance trade. Most of these elites must have been non-royal, and their possession of long-distance trade products should make us reconsider how successful our "classic model" king really was in monopolising exchange via the *emporia*. It is possible, of course that the imported wares at, for example, Wharram Percy were the product of royal redistribution, but we do know from charters concerning the remission of royal tolls at Lundenwic that some ecclesiastical elites were actively involved in long-distance trade in their own right.[149] We have similar indications, from a rather different source, that the same may have been true at Eoforwic.

In his recent discussion of the date and provenance of Series J *sceattas*, Michael Metcalf not only argued that they were minted in Eoforwic in the 720's, but also suggested that some (type 85) were issued by the king, and others (type 37) jointly by the king and the bishop of York. The two sets of coins were issued at the same time, the former decorated with a single head, the latter with the image of "two facing diademed heads, separated by a cross on a stand".[150]

---

[149] Kelly, "Trading privileges". The fact that the king was in a position to issue these remissions, and on occasion exercised his right to preferential access to the cargo of the ship concerned, shows that ultimately some royal control was still exercised in these cases.

[150] Metcalf, *Thrymsas and Sceattas*, pp. 343, 365. In support of this argument, Metcalf (p. 366) points out that "twenty years later there was a dual series of coins [Series Y] which without any doubt were struck respectively for the king [Eadberht] and jointly for the king and the archbishop [his brother, Ecgberht]. What could be more obvious than the possibility that Series J reflects an earlier but similar sharing?". See also pp. 576-93.

Metcalf is certain that they were minted at the *wic*.[151] The implications of the coins, vis-à-vis the *wic*, would be that the king exercised ultimate power (hence only he issued by himself, only he was shown alone on the coins) but that he also delegated some of that secular power to the bishop. Thus Metcalf suggests that the king may have "laid secular tasks on the bishop in York, to oversee the king's peace and justice in his *wic*, and rewarded him with the right of coinage".[152] Thus the situation might be something like that deduced from the Lundenwic charters in which the church, through the aegis of the king, enjoyed the right of using and benefiting from the *wic*. The difference might be that, in actually issuing coins (albeit jointly) the church of York had more control over, and benefited more directly from Eoforwic.

The point I am trying to make here is that there is evidence for non-royal involvement in long-distance trade (although this is conveniently ignored in the "classic model"), and we might combine this with the evidence for elite control over rural production and distribution to suggest that the products of the former were used to ensure participation in the latter. Although, the king ultimately remained the real "hidden hand" behind the system, this hand had a power which was nowhere near as singular and as unbridled as is assumed in the "classic model", nor was it the only one which profited directly.

Ecclesiastical elites are particularly prominent in the archaeology of late seventh- and early eighth-century rural settlement. This may be because of their use of a distinctive, and particularly lavish, material culture, but we should consider the possibility that they had a special role to play in the transformations of the beginning of the long eighth century. John Blair has recently proposed that the late seventh century saw the creation of a system of minster churches, with an attendant territorial structure.[153] He has also shown that these minsters quickly became the focus for "commercial activity"—markets were established at their gates.[154] Might it not be in the creation and structuring of this system that we can find an explanation for the "significance of production" in the late seventh- and early

---

[151] Metcalf, *Thrymsas and Sceattas*, p. 359.
[152] Metcalf, *Thrymsas and Sceattas*, p. 344.
[153] Blair, "Minster churches", p. 38; "Ecclesiastical organisation and pastoral care in Anglo-Saxon England", *Early Medieval Europe* 4 (1995), pp. 193-212, at p. 199.
[154] Blair, "Minster churches", pp. 47-48.

eighth-century countryside, much as Jeremy Haslam argued for the intensification of production at Ramsbury? This would not preclude the development of production as a means of gaining access to the products of long-distance trade, but this would not be its necessary or only logic. The late seventh-century date would also account more satisfactorily for the timing of the transformation, and the "'ideological/cosmological" foundations of the minster-based structure might begin to provide insights into the reasons for those other, non-economic, changes which were part of the transformations of the (long) year 700.

ROMAN CITIES, *EMPORIA* AND NEW TOWNS (SIXTH-NINTH CENTURIES)

Adriaan Verhulst

The aim of this chapter is to present the stages which in our opinion mark the evolution of urban settlements in north-west Europe from the late Roman period to the end of the ninth century. Each of these stages are characterised by the pre-dominance of specific urban types: late Roman towns from the fourth to the seventh century; the new, so-called *emporia* from the seventh to the middle of the ninth century; and new, commercial settlements, most often called *portus*, from the ninth century onwards. This succession of urban types can be found in the Low Countries, northern France and the Rhineland, more particularly in the valleys of the rivers Scheldt, Meuse and Rhine and on the continental southern shores of the North Sea.

The aspects of particular interest here will be some of the specific problems concerning the second stage—broadly coinciding with the "long" eighth century—during which the so-called *emporia* had their ephemeral existence.

After having been militarised in the fourth century, mainly by the building of walls, several towns of Roman origin in this area (called *civitates, castella* or *vici*) remained centres of political, military and ecclesiastical power and of administration, as the residences of kings, bishops, counts and aristocratic families. Their commercial and manufacturing functions were only secondary. From the fourth century onwards the towns were less densely occupied than before, though by no means deserted. Kings, bishops, counts and aristocratic families took residence in more or less well preserved Roman buildings (*praetoria, aulae, basilicae, horrea*) or in urban or semi-rural fortifications, and churches were built in them or upon their ruins.[1]

---

[1] F. Vercauteren, *Etude sur les civitates de la Belgique seconde* (Brussels, 1934); E.M. Wightman, *Gallia Belgica* (London, 1985), pp. 75-100, 222-27; W.A. van Es, "Dorestad centred", in J.C. Besteman, J.M. Bos and H.A. Heidinga eds., *Medieval Archaeology in the Netherlands* (Assen, 1990), pp. 163-65.

After a deep fifth-century decline, a revival is found in most of
these places from shortly before the middle of the sixth to some time
after the middle of the seventh century. This is marked by new or
restored buildings, mainly churches, built through the ecclesiastical
initiatives of bishops and missionaries: Nicetius (c. 525-566) in Trier,
Sidonius (mid sixth century) in Mainz, Monulfus (second half of the
sixth century) in Maastricht, Géry (590-624/27) in Cambrai, Cunibert
(c. 626-648) in Cologne, Amandus (c. 630) in Ghent, and Audebertus
(c. 650/60) in Arras.[2] Some of these churches were built *intra muros*,
but others, like those in Maastricht and Cologne, were situated on
the outskirts of the Roman town, which developed during the seventh century into large suburban settlements around the originally
cemeterial church, now transformed into a monastery. In some towns
the revival was effectuated by lay rulers, like the Merovingian kings
of Austrasia who chose Metz as their capital in the second half of
the sixth century.[3]

About the same time, minting activity started in most of these
towns and in some other places of Roman origin, mostly former
castella or *castra* like Huy, Namur and Dinant on the river Meuse
and Dorestat on the Rhine. This trend continued for almost a century, from c. 580 to c. 670. Gold pieces worth a third of a *solidus*, *tremisses*, were struck by moneyers whose position guaranteed the quality
of the gold pieces, although their exact position as private and rich
persons working for the king is still not clear. In the region under
consideration no less than 12 moneyers are known to have been
working at Maastricht between c. 590 and c. 670, 8 at Huy from
c. 580 to c. 660, 4 at Namur and 6 at Dinant, 5 at Mainz, 3 at

---

[2] Trier, Mainz: E. Ewig, *Frühes Mittelalter*, Rheinische Geschichte I.2 (Düsseldorf,
1980), pp. 37-39; Maastricht: T. Panhuysen and P.H. Leupen, "Maastricht in het
eerste millennium", in *La genèse et les premiers siècles des villes médiévales dans les Pays-
Bas méridionaux*, Crédit Communal, Collection Histoire in-8°, no. 83 (Brussels, 1990),
pp. 429-33; Cambrai: Vercauteren, *Civitates*, pp. 208-09; Cologne: O. Doppelfeld,
"Kölner Wirtschaft von den Anfängen bis zur Karolingerzeit", in H. Kellenbenz
ed., *Zwei Jahrtausende Kölner Wirtschaft* I (Cologne, 1975), p. 82; and the bibliography cited below in note 9; Ghent: A. Verhulst and G. Declercq, "Early medieval
Ghent", in J. Decavele ed., *Ghent. In Defence of a Rebellious City* (Antwerp, 1989), pp.
9-10, 15 (reprinted in A. Verhulst, *Rural and Urban Aspects of Early Medieval Northwest
Europe*, Variorum. Collected Studies CS 385 (Aldershot, 1992); Arras: Vercauteren,
Civitates, p. 188.
[3] G. Halsall, "Towns, Societies and Ideas: the Not-so-strange Case of Late Roman
and Early Merovingian Metz", in N. Christie and S.T. Loseby eds., *Towns in Transition. Urban Evolution in Late Antiquity and the Early Middle Ages* (Aldershot, 1996), pp.
235-61.

Cologne and only two in Dorestat (probably in the Roman fort—the antique *Levefanum?*—south of the Carolingian *emporium*).[4] One of the Dorestat moneyers was Madelinus who had been working in Maastricht since c. 625 and who moved to Dorestat about 640. The general opinion at present is that this minting activity did not necessarily have an economic significance and ought not to be interpreted straightforwardly as a proof of trading activities. The small *tremisses* had too high a value for small commercial transactions and may rather have been used for the acquisition of luxury goods obtained via international trade. But there are many other possibilities, such as their use for bribing political allies, as gifts (particularly to the dead), for treasure, for jewellery making, etc.[5] The importance of Maastricht during the first half of the seventh century, as revealed by the large number of moneyers, ought therefore not to be interpreted simply as an indication of the economic role of this place. Certainly such a role cannot be presumed for the Meuse valley as a whole—from Huy, some 60 kilometres upstream from Maastricht, to Namur and Dinant. Although an economic influence of Dorestat on Maastricht and Huy, the most important and most northerly of the minting places on the Meuse, cannot be totally excluded, Dorestat at the beginning of the seventh century was most probably still a rich Chamavian elite settlement, partly rural in character, situated beside a Roman fort (the antique *Levefanum?*), and cannot yet be described as an *emporium* since the development of its harbour on the river (Kromme) Rhine had not yet been initiated.[6] The explanation for the important minting activity in the middle Meuse region might therefore be linked to the fact that it was the heartland of the landed possessions of the Pippinid family. In fact, these forefathers of the Carolingians began their struggle for power against other elite groups in the seventh century.[7] During the first half of the seventh century they rapidly, but temporarily, gained

---

[4] A. Pol, "Les monétaires à Huy et Maastricht. Production et distribution des monnaies mérovingiennes mosanes", *Bulletin de l'Institut Archéologique Liégeois*, 107 (1995), pp. 185-200; van Es, "Dorestad centred", p. 166.

[5] Pol, "Monétaires", pp. 190-92; J.-P. Devroey and Ch. Zoller, "Villes, campagnes, croissance agraire dans le pays mosan avant l'an mil vingt ans après", in J.-M. Duvosquel and A. Dierkens, *Villes et campagnes au moyen âge. Mélanges Georges Despy* (Liège, 1991), pp. 241-46.

[6] Van Es, "Dorestad centred", pp. 164-65; H.A. Heidinga, *Frisia in the First Millenium* (Utrecht 1997), p. 44.

[7] F.C.W.J. Theuws, "Centre and Periphery in Northern Austrasia (6th-8th Centuries)", in Besteman, Bos and Heidinga, *Medieval Archaeology*, pp. 45-46.

control over large parts of northern Austrasia, as far as Dorestat itself, before it was reconquered by the Frisians c. 650, then temporarily recaptured by Pippin II in 690 but re-occupied soon afterwards by the Frisians until the death of their "king" Radbod in 719. Perhaps these struggles around 700 may be held responsible for the decline shown by the histogram of the Dorestat coins between 690 and 725, although there is no reason to think that minting was only possible in a Frankish context.[8]

The contrast between the amount of evidence, not only monetary, which is available for the middle Meuse region in the seventh century, and the scarcity, or complete lack, of information regarding the towns on the middle Rhine, especially Cologne, during the same century is striking. The situation in Cologne may have changed somewhat after Bishop Cunibert of Cologne about 629 took over the position of Arnulf of Metz as counsellor, first of young King Dagobert at the side of Pippin I and, after Dagobert's death in 638 or 639, of his eight years old son Sigebert III, the head of a small kingdom centred around Cologne. Foundations of a big, seventh-century building have recently been discovered by Sven Schütte at the Heumarkt, and Nico Aten in the same area has uncovered traces of six sunken huts (*Grübenhäuser*) belonging to an artisanal quarter, further there are strong archaeological indications that Roman buildings either continued to be used or were not destroyed by the Franks. These (not yet completely published) findings contrast strongly with the hitherto prevailing views of Heiko Steuer. They suggest a continuity of settlement in Cologne during the Merovingian period rather than the so-called "continuity of ruins".[9] Some of the glass ware, ceramics and goldsmith's art, found in Merovingian cemeteries in the region of Cologne, may indeed have been manufactured in the town of Cologne itself.[10] However, Mainz still appears to have been more important than Cologne and to have remained so for the following two cen-

---

[8] R. Hodges, *Dark Age Economics. The Origins of Towns and Trade A.D. 600-1000* (London, 1982), pp. 40-41; van Es, "Dorestad centred", pp. 166-167; A. Pol, "Remmerden 1988: een vondst van vroegmiddeleeuwse munten bij Rhenen", *De Beeldenaar. Munt- en Penningkundig Nieuws* 13 (1989), pp. 44-45.

[9] Ewig, *Frühes Mittelalter*, pp. 26-29, 70-71; M. Gechter and S. Schütte, "Zwischen St. Alban und Judenviertel in Köln", *Rheinische Heimatpflege* 35 (1998), pp. 37-56, esp. pp. 40-43; S. Schütte, "Continuity Problems and Authority Structures in Cologne", in G. Ausenda ed., *After Empire. Towards an Ethnology of Europe's Barbarians* (San Marino, 1995), pp. 163-75; H. Steuer, *Die Franken in Köln* (Cologne, 1980).

[10] Doppelfeld, "Kölner Wirtschaft", pp. 75-79.

turies.[11] There was a sixth- to seventh-century cemetery near the former Roman commercial quarter of Mainz, though no traces of craft production itself have been found.

Compared to this scanty and uncertain evidence, the archaeological finds from Maastricht and Huy may be interpreted as signs of a much more active urban life. In the centre of present-day Maastricht, south-west of the Roman *castellum*, the stone structures of sixth- and seventh-century houses were uncovered. Some five hundred metres north of the *castellum*, parts of narrow paved streets and ditches demarcating the border of parcels of land were discovered. Numerous traces of sixth- and seventh-century artisanal activity were also found: bone workshops, a foundry producing bronze buckles and ornaments, a pottery and the remains left behind by a sixth-century glass-bead maker. Most of these artisanal workshops were situated in the then still partly rural but densely populated settlements close to the Roman *castellum*.[12] In Huy, some sixty kilometres upstream from Maastricht, bone and metal workshops, and kilns dating from the second half of the sixth century, were discovered on both banks of the Meuse and throughout the area on the right bank of the Hoyoux close to its confluence with the Meuse.[13] Huy had been a Roman *castrum* and was probably the centre of a Merovingian crown estate where Bishop Domitian of Tongeren-Maastricht was buried in the second half of the seventh century. It may therefore be considered to have been a base which would have offered support for episcopal power and influence. Its urban character may be deduced from the famous will of Adalgisel Grimo, deacon of Verdun, A.D. 634, in which he left a manor on the river Ourthe to the poor, registered in the *matricula* of the Notre-Dame church at Huy.[14]

---

[11] Ewig, *Frühes Mittelalter*, p. 45; P. Berghaus, "Wirtschaft, Handel und Verkehr der Merowingerzeit im Licht numismatischer Quellen", in K. Düwel, H. Jankuhn, *et al.* eds.,*Untersuchungen zu Handel und Verkehr der vor- und frühgeschichtlichen Zeit* III. *Der Handel des frühen Mittelalters*, Abhandlungen der Akademie der Wissenschaften in Göttingen, Philologisch-Historische Klasse, 3d Series, no. 150 (Göttingen, 1985), pp. 209-212; Doppelfeld, "Kölner Wirtschaft", pp. 75-79. See in this book also the chapter by Ian Wood.

[12] Panhuysen and Leupen, "Maastricht in het eerste millenium", p. 446.

[13] A. Dierkens, "La ville de Huy avant l'an mil", in *La genèse et les premiers siècles*, pp. 391-409.

[14] W. Levison, "Das Testament des Diakens Adalgisel Grimo (634)", *Trierer Zeitschrift* 7 (1932), pp. 69-85; F. Irsigler, "Gesellschaft, Wirtschaft und religiöses Leben im Obermosel-Saar-Raum zur Zeit des Diakons Adalgisel Grimo", *Hochwälder Geschichtsblätter* 1 (1989), pp. 5-18.

The lead with respect to urban life which the middle Meuse valley held over the valley of the middle Rhine in the late sixth and the seventh century had its counterpart in a similar lead over the Scheldt valley and the interior of the Flemish North Sea and Channel coast. From the Roman *civitates* of Cambrai and Tournai, both on the river Scheldt, and from the *civitas* of Arras more to the West, only respectively four, two and two seventh-century moneyers are known. Their production, judging from the number of preserved pieces, must have been equally low.[15] No traces are left of the famous Roman textile manufacture in these three towns, although the start of textile manufacturing in Arras as early as the ninth century has inspired the hypothesis of some continuity through the preceding centuries.[16] These episcopal cities, like some minor *municipia* of Roman origin more to the north, for example Kortrijk, Ghent and Bruges in western present-day Belgium, probably continued to function as ecclesiastical and administrative centres in the seventh century, but their economic and political role must have been minimal.[17] No emerging political powers comparable to the Pippinid family in eastern Belgium had their seat in any of these towns. Members of the Merovingian royal family resided in Cambrai and Tournai for the last time in the second half of the sixth century. The only seventh-century element worth mentioning here, because of its significance for the revival of economic life in this part of the Frankish kingdom in the eighth and ninth centuries, is the founding of abbeys or of churches soon developing into abbeys, in Cambrai, Arras and Ghent.[18]

*   *   *

However, before turning to this revival, we have to examine the question of a new urban phenomenon which manifested itself from the end of the sixth or the beginning of the seventh century through to the middle of the ninth century. The so-called *emporia* on the

---

[15] J. Lafaurie, "Les monnaies émises à Cambrai aux VIᵉ-IXᵉ siècles", *Revue du Nord* 69 (1986), pp. 393-404.

[16] L. Kéry, *Die Errichtung des Bistums Arras 1093/1094* (Sigmaringen, 1994), p. 276.

[17] A. Verhulst, "An Aspect of the Continuity between Antiquity and Middle Ages: The Origin of the Flemish Cities between the North Sea and the Scheldt", *Journal of Medieval History* 3 (1977), pp. 175-205, (reprinted in Verhulst, *Rural and Urban Aspects*).

[18] Vercauteren, *Civitates*, pp. 188, 208-09; Verhulst and Declercq, "Early Medieval Ghent", pp. 6-17.

southern coast of the North Sea, both on the continent and in England and on both sides of the Channel coast,[19] played a role in the general revival of economic and urban life of north-west Europe from the ninth century onwards. Of particular interest is their possible role in assuring a continuity of urban life during the transition from the very early to the high Middle Ages, compared to that played by the towns of Roman origin considered so far.

This question is, however, a particularly difficult one because of the very specific nature of these *emporia*, which is well known from the many studies devoted to them. The *emporia* share several common characteristics. Geographically they were all located at a protected estuarine site not far from the coastline, which served as a territorial frontier for a kingdom. Some of them, like Dorestat or Quentovic, were for that reason important toll stations, administered by a special royal agent, *praefectus* or *comes*, who also controlled other *emporia* along the same coast.[20] The function of these places was mainly to be "gateways" through which luxury products (such as wine, textiles, arms, amber, skins, furs and even slaves) were brought from great distances. These goods were destined for the king and his court, for members of aristocratic families and for rich episcopal churches and abbeys. It is difficult to say to what extent these goods entered into regional or local trade. Such trade did exist and was provided by products, for example pottery, tools in metal or in bone and other goods of daily use, manufactured in the *emporia* themselves or in workshops located on large rural estates in their neighbourhood.[21] The merchants implicated in this regional or long-distance trade were mainly free men, trading for their own profit and on their own initiative but at the same time also for the king and his court, to whom they stood in a special relationship, apparent from their yearly accounting to him. But many others were bound to a bishop's church or to an abbey in a relation of bondage and traded under their command.[22]

---

[19] Hodges, *Dark Age Economics*, pp. 47-86; H. Clarke and B. Ambrosiani, *Towns in the Viking Age*, 2nd ed. (Leicester, 1995), pp. 11-45.

[20] S. Lebecq, "Pour une histoire parallèle de Quentovic et Dorestad", in Duvosquel and Dierkens, *Mélanges Despy*, pp. 415-28; S. Lebecq, "Quentovic: un état de la question", *Studien zur Sachsenforschung* 8 (Hildesheim, 1993), pp. 73-82.

[21] Van Es, "Dorestad centred", pp. 168-75.

[22] J.-P. Devroey, "Courants et réseaux d'échange dans l'économie franque entre Loire et Rhin", in *Mercati e Mercanti nell'alto medioevo*, Settimane di studio del Centro italiano di studi sull'alto Medioevo, 40 (Spoleto, 1993), pp. 368-84.

In some, or possibly in the majority, of the *emporia* these merchants, whatever their juridical status, enjoyed royal protection and
privileges, preserved occasionally in written documents. From this
fact the hypothesis has been made that many, if not all, of these
emporia owed their existence to a royal or at least a seigneurial foundation.[23] Such an origin is inferred also from the regular ground-
plan of some of these *emporia*, the most striking example being
Hamwic.[24] Generalisations in this respect, however, are dangerous
since clear differences do exist between the various *emporia* around
the North Sea. Striking differences can be found to appear not only
in physical structure but also in chronology. Quentovic, Ipswich and
Domburg-*Walichrum* started as commercial and/or manufacturing
centres at the end of the sixth or the beginning of the seventh century,[25] whereas, with the exception of Lundunwic (mid seventh century),[26] Dorestat, Hamwic, Ribe and Haithabu started at the end of
the seventh or the beginning of the eighth century.[27] This second
group is precisely composed of places in which a royal foundation
or at least royal influence on their emergence as trading centres is
most likely.[28] In the first, and older group, on the other hand, the
emergence of Quentovic may have been not unrelated to the foundation of several important abbeys in its neighbourhood some fifty
years before, about the middle of the seventh century. Most of these,
like St Vaast, St Bertin, St Riquier and St Wandrille obtained a
foothold in Quentovic. In its immediate surroundings the *cella* of St
Josse (founded 668) functioned as a kind of transit home for voy-
agers to and from England and as a store for goods shipped through

---

[23] Hodges, *Dark Age Economics*, pp. 53-55; van Es, "Dorestad centred", pp. 171-
72; Clarke and Ambrosiani, *Towns in the Viking Age*, pp. 22-23.

[24] R. Hodges, *The Anglo-Saxon Achievement* (London, 1989), pp. 80-92.

[25] Clarke and Ambrosiani, *Towns in the Viking Age*, pp. 17 (Quentovic), 21 (Ipswich);
Domburg: S. Lebecq, "L'*emporium* proto-médiéval de Walcheren-Domburg", in
J.-M. Duvosquel and E. Thoen eds., *Peasants and Townsmen in Medieval Europe. Studia
in honorem Adriaan Verhulst* (Ghent, 1995), pp. 73-89.

[26] L. Blackmore, "From beach to burh: new clues to entity and identity in 7th-
to 9th-century London", in G. De Boe and F. Verhaeghe eds., *Urbanism in Medieval
Europe*, Papers of the 'Medieval Europe Brugge 1997' Conference, vol. 1 (Zellik,
1997), pp. 123-32.

[27] Van Es, "Dorestad centred", p. 163 (Dorestat); Hodges, *Anglo-Saxon Achievement*,
p. 80 (Hamwic); Clarke and Ambrosiani, *Towns of the Viking Age*, pp. 53-54 (Ribe),
56-58 (Haithabu).

[28] Hodges, *Anglo-Saxon Achievement*, pp. 88, 104; Clarke and Ambrosiani, *Towns in
the Viking Age*, p. 23.

Quentovic.[29] Royal interference, and the eventual establishment of royal authority over the *emporia* may have been the consequence of political and even military expansion, for example from Wessex to Hamwic, from Neustria to Quentovic and from Austrasia to Dorestat.[30] It was followed, once these towns were firmly established, by their commercial expansion from the coast where they were situated, into the interior, as can be seen from the appearance from the beginning of the eighth century onwards, first of Anglo-Saxon and later of mainly Frisian merchants on the continent. The presence of a Frisian (merchant?) in London as early as 678 is an isolated case.

This Frisian expansion has been studied by many scholars for a long time, in recent years most thoroughly by Stéphane Lebecq.[31] He explains the expansion as the effect of several factors: the geographical condition of their homeland with its numerous waterways, the advantage of their ship building and sailing technique, the importance and influence of Dorestat, etc. However, Lebecq's studies do not explain one specific aspect of the Frisian expansion, namely the fact that though their colonies are well attested in several towns on the river Rhine at a date already well advanced into the ninth century, there is a complete absence of any mention of Frisians in the Meuse valley in the same period.[32] Some may explain this in terms of an economic decline of the Meuse valley in favour of the Rhine route. This may have been the case; although about 830 Maastricht, according to Einhard, was still a thriving city full of merchants, and Huy is called a *portus* in 862, while on the other hand, we hear nothing of Namur and Dinant at that time.[33] Neither is there, in fact, much written information on urban life in the two main cities on the Rhine, Cologne and Mainz, during the first three quarters of the ninth century;[34] nonetheless, Frisian merchants, though apparently

---

[29] Lebecq, "Quentovic:un état de la question", pp. 80-81; "Histoire parallèle", p. 426.

[30] Lebecq, "Histoire parallèle", pp. 421-423; S. Lebecq, "La Neustrie et la Mer", in H. Atsma ed., *La Neustrie*, Beihefte der Francia 16.2 (Sigmaringen, 1989), pp. 405-40.

[31] S. Lebecq, *Marchands et Navigateurs frisons du haut moyen âge* (Lille, 1983).

[32] Lebecq, *Marchands et Navigateurs*, pp. 93-94; Devroey and Zoller, "Villes, campagnes", p. 229.

[33] Devroey and Zoller, "Villes, campagnes", pp. 234-41.

[34] E. Ennen, "Kölner Wirtschaft im Früh- und Hochmittelalter", in Kellenbenz, *Zwei Jahrtausende Kölner Wirtschaft*, pp. 95-96, 116; Ewig, *Frühes Mittelalter*, pp. 144-153. There is however new strong archaeological evidence for building activity in Cologne in the Carolingian period: Gechter and Schütte, "Zwischen St Alban", pp. 43-50; Schütte, "Continuity Problems", p. 168.

not yet settled in colonies, were travelling on the Rhine, passing the
Lorelei (St Goar, 839), trading in Worms (829) and shipping as far
as Alsace,[35] earlier in the ninth century. That the date of their settling in colonies along the Rhine appears later, especially in Mainz,
may be due to the above mentioned lack of sources.[36] The phenomenon of Frisian colonies on the Rhine and its date is, however,
paralleled by the shift of Frisian trading activity from Dorestat to
Tiel and Deventer about the same time (second half of the ninth
century). This meant a movement farther into the interior and away
from the Vikings, who in 834 had attacked Dorestat for the first
time, in 836 had destroyed the *emporium* of *Witla* in the estuary of
the Meuse[37] and to whom in 841 was given in fief by Lothar I the
isle of Walcheren with its *emporium* at Domburg.[38] Perhaps the great
inundation which in 838 struck the delta of Rhine, Meuse and
Scheldt[39] may also have played a role in the move of the Frisians
eastward, and determined the settlement in colonies on the Rhine.

The end of Dorestat was, however, not an isolated event, although
the specific causes mentioned may have contributed to it and determined its date. It is, indeed, a characteristic common to nearly all
the *emporia* around the North Sea that they declined from the second quarter of the ninth century onwards and finally disappeared
from the face of the earth at the latest in the middle of the tenth
century. Here again the chronology is not identical for all the places:
Hamwic, Ribe and Haithabu continued into the tenth century, probably thanks to the continuing royal protection in England and
Denmark, contrasting with the collapse of royal power on the north-
west European continent.[40] More important, however, are the causes
of the final decline and the fact that none of these *emporia* generated a town of some importance in their very location. There were
of course shifts in the local topography of these towns from the
moment of their decline well into the tenth century. The present-
day small Dutch town of Wijk-bij-Duurstede—note the name!—still

---

[35] Lebecq, *Marchands et navigateurs*, pp. 26-27.
[36] Lebecq, *Marchands et navigateurs*, pp. 27-29.
[37] Lebecq, *Marchands et navigateurs*, pp. 145-47; van Es, "Dorestad centred",
p. 163.
[38] Lebecq, "Walcheren-Domburg", pp. 84-85.
[39] M.K.E. Gottschalk, *Stormvloeden en rivieroverstromingen in Nederland* I (Assen, 1971),
pp. 17-30.
[40] Hodges, *Dark Age Economics*, pp. 151-61.

covers a large part of Carolingian Dorestat that has not been excavated.[41] The population of Quentovic—perhaps dislodged by the rising water level—found a shelter on the elevated and fortified site of the small, tenth-century town of Montreuil, a few kilometres upstream on the river Canche.[42] Hamwic shifted to medieval Southampton, Haithabu to the town of Schleswig and Carolingian Ribe moved south along the river Ribe to the present town of the same name.[43] But almost none of these smaller successors, although they have remained in the same location to the present day, developed into an important medieval city; the only exceptions were London and, to a lesser extent, Southampton. This suggests that the cause of their weakness and lack of dynamism was the same which had caused the decline of the *emporia*: firstly, the collapse of the political—and hence the economic—power that had helped them to emerge and to develop into important trading centres, without however making them administrative or ecclesiastical centres controlling a surrounding district; and secondly, the weakness of the political powers and structures that succeeded the Carolingian empire, powers which, furthermore, were based on different places than the *emporia*.

*   *   *

What was left after the disappearance of the Carolingian *emporia* were, indeed, the old political and ecclesiastical centres which had existed since Roman times; even if some of them, like Rouen and Amiens, beside their role as central places had also temporarily functioned as *emporia*—some of them even being partly under their authority, as was the case of Rouen vis-à-vis Quentovic.[44]

In most of these pre-Carolingian towns, mainly in those situated on the waterways of the rivers Scheldt, Meuse and Rhine in the interior, though also in formerly minor towns, a revival of urban and economic life can be observed from the middle of the ninth century onwards.[45] In most cases it is only revealed by the qualification

---

[41] Van Es, "Dorestad centred", p. 163.
[42] Lebecq, "Quentovic: état de la question", pp. 81-82; "Histoire parallèle", p. 427.
[43] H. Steuer, "Die Handelsstätten des frühen Mittelalters", in *La genèse et les premiers siècles*, pp. 86, 94-95, 101-04.
[44] Lebecq, "Quentovic: un état de   question", p. 79; "Histoire parallèle", p. 423.
[45] A. Verhulst, *The Rise of Cities in Northwest Europe* (Cambridge, 1999), pp. 44-67.

portus, that is given to them in written sources and on coins. But other indications, like archaeological data, point in the same direction. Since the seventh century important abbeys, episcopal churches and royal estates were situated or had developed in or next to them. They must have played a role in the revival of these places and in their development into ports. The latter were centres of local and regional trade, with strong links to the surrounding countryside from where the well organised estates of the churches brought their surplus of agricultural and industrial products to be stocked and sold on the local market. But there are also traces of industrial activity in these towns, as the case of Arras makes clear shortly after the middle of the ninth century. Before looking at this case in detail, we must ask how far, generally speaking, the *emporia* had been responsible for this revival. This question has already partly and implicitly been answered by what has just been said about the disappearance of the *emporia*, but the answer must be illustrated by some concrete data.

The *emporia* were certainly not responsible for the revival of the towns in the Scheldt valley, to whom Domburg-*Walichrum* and Quentovic had been the nearest *emporia*. Not a single one of the not very numerous Carolingian silver *denarii* found in Domburg dating from the time of Charlemagne and Louis the Pious, come from the Scheldt valley. Instead there are a few from the Rhineland and from Dorestat. On the other hand the *denarii* from the middle and the third quarter of the ninth century found in Domburg derive almost exclusively from mints along the Scheldt and the Flemish coastal region (Bruges).[46] It was during this later period, which also coincides with Domburg's period of decline, that commercial settlements emerged along the Scheldt in Valenciennes, Tournai and Ghent and perhaps also on the coast at Bruges. These numismatic data are sufficient to argue that the influence of Domburg-*Walichrum* at the height of its prosperity (last quarter of the seventh/first half of the eighth century) was not directed at its immediate hinterland, the Scheldt

---

[46] H. Jankuhn, "Die frühmittelalterlichen Seehandelsplätze im Nord- und Ostseeraum", in *Studien zu den Anfängen des europäischen Städtewesens*, Vorträge und Forschungen 4 (Lindau/Konstanz, 1958), pp. 464-72, of which the chapter on Domburg "Der Handelsplatz am Strand von Domburg" is reprinted in A. Verhulst ed., *Anfänge des Städtewesens an Schelde, Maas und Rhein*, Städteforschung. Veröffentlichungen des Instituts für vergleichende Städtegeschichte in Münster, vol. 40 (Cologne, 1996), pp. 137-44; R.M. van Heeringen, P.A. Henderikx and A. Mars, *Vroeg-Middeleeuwse ringwalburgen in Zeeland* (Amersfoort, 1995), pp. 44-47 (numismatic aspects by A. Pol).

valley. Quentovic on the other hand lay somewhat apart from the Scheldt valley and the traffic from England which passed through this port was directed southwards to Amiens and Paris.

The question of the economic impact of the coastal *emporia* on the towns of the interior may probably be answered differently for the valleys of the Meuse and the Rhine. As far as the latter is concerned we pointed earlier to the Frisian trade on the Rhine, visible during the first half of the ninth century, and to the Frisian colonies in several towns of that area at a later date, namely in the last quarter of the ninth century, after the decline of Dorestat. Both phenomena are certainly linked to the standing of Dorestat, although the influence of the Frisians on the activity of autochthonous traders and craftsmen in the towns on the Rhine as a whole remains questionable before the last quarter of the ninth century.

As for the towns in the Meuse valley, only Maastricht (and possibly also Huy) would have felt the impact of Dorestat as early as the eighth century. Rather, the revival of the whole middle Meuse valley in the ninth century, particularly in its second half, was due, as Georges Despy demonstrated in 1968, to the agricultural and even industrial expansion of the countryside, for which the towns on the Meuse functioned as regional markets well into the tenth century.[47] Liège, as a new purely ecclesiastical town, is the only major exception to this. The explanation of Despy may be valid for towns in other regions as well, for example Mainz and Worms on the Rhine, with their rich agricultural hinterland of grain and wine production. It holds good also for the towns situated in, or with links to, the Scheldt Valley, as demonstrated for Ghent and for Arras.[48]

Arras had been a Roman *civitas* and Ghent a small *municipium* possibly also of Roman origin, and in each of these towns a fairly rich and important abbey had been founded or had developed between the seventh and the ninth century. St Bavo's abbey in Ghent had developed during the seventh and eighth centuries from a church founded c. 630 by Amandus, within the most densely populated centre of the area where the traces of Roman habitation are numerous. This urban settlement, called "Ganda" with its Celtic name, in other words existed long before the foundation of the church and

---

[47] G. Despy, "Villes et campagnes aux IXe et Xe siècles: l'exemple du pays mosan", *Revue du Nord*, 50 (1968), pp. 145-68.
[48] Verhulst, *The Rise of Cities*, pp. 59-62.

abbey, as the centre of a *pagus*, an administrative district headed by
a count. In c. 865 it was qualified as a *portus*, which meant that it
was not a small town subordinate to the abbey like many others in
the ninth century—a "*vicus monasterii*", but rather a trade centre in
its own right, though probably with strong links to St Bavo's abbey.
These links were not only geographical, both being situated on the
left bank of the river Scheldt, but probably also economic, since the
radiation and richness of St Bavo's abbey had attracted merchants
who settled next to it. Hence the qualification *portus*. This *portus*,
however, was destroyed together with the abbey by the Vikings in
879, when they pitched their camp there for a year. It was then
relocated some 500 metres upstream before the end of the ninth
century. A semicircular D-shaped moat, whose two extremities ter-
minated in the Scheldt, was constructed around the settlement, which
was probably of an older date and possibly already inhabited by
merchants. In the tenth century it gradually extended beyond the
earlier moat to incorporate the whole area between the rivers Leie
and Scheldt, an area which henceforth was called "Gandavum", the
name of the medieval city of Ghent.

   The abbey of St Vaast in Arras was founded in the seventh century outside the fortified Roman *civitas*. Next to the abbey, in the
centre of the actual city, a charter of Charles the Bald from 867
mentions a *vicus monasterii* and distinct from the latter, but still next
to the abbey, an apparently new *vicus*, called "*Nova Villa*" ("*vicus qui
vocatur Nova Villa juxta monasterium ipsum situm*"). The former, like many
other *vici monasterii* in the ninth century, like those near the abbey
of St Riquier and the abbey of Corbie,[49] was probably inhabited by
people in the service of the abbey employed in various crafts and
trades, ranging from bakers, brewers, smiths, etc., to merchants. This
was not necessarily the case for the whole of the population in the
other, later *vicus*. In one or both of the two *vici* may also have lived
the workers who had to process the large quantities of flax and wool
which according to Charles the Bald's same charter had to be supplied to the abbey's *camera* by seven manors of St Vaast. Three of
these manors lay in the immediate vicinity of Arras and the others
within a 25 to 60 kilometres radius. According to the same charter

---

[49] E. Lesne, *Histoire de la propriété ecclésiastique en France* VI (Lille, 1943), pp. 389-
97.

the provost of the abbey could dispose as he thought fit of the wool that was in excess of the quantity of 400 pounds which had to be supplied.[50] We may imagine that he sold part of it at the market whose toll belonged to the abbey's infirmary, and which may have been situated in the immediate vicinity of the abbey. The wool may have been bought there by free, independent workers, whom we would expect to live in the "*Nova Villa*" *vicus*.

Both examples of Ghent and Arras enable us to determine a momentum in early medieval urban development that looks more important for the birth of the medieval city in north-west Europe than was the rise and fall of the Carolingian *emporia*. This momentum consisted in a transition from a limited "manorial" phase of trade and industry, carried out in a small town adjoining a large abbey and on its behalf, mainly by people in the service of the abbey, to a wider and free phase of commerce conducted by independent merchants and workers who acted for their own profit.[51] They still lived in the vicinity of the abbey but a little further away than the monastic *vicus*. Clearly the Viking raids and, in the case of Ghent, the destruction and eventual disappearance of the abbey over a longer period, accelerated the evolution from one stage to another. A result of this was the emancipation of the earlier abbey merchants who could now conduct trade for their own benefit.

This evolution was not restricted to the ecclesiastical sphere. The role which can be attributed to large abbeys, like those in Arras and in Ghent, can be ascribed also to royal manors, whether or not they were royal residences. Within the area between the Scheldt and the North Sea this was the case in ninth-century Valenciennes and Tournai, both on the Scheldt. We will not develop these examples here.[52] It may be sufficient to add that unlike several *emporia*, the towns in the valleys of the Scheldt, Meuse and Rhine, whose development into trading and manufacturing centres during the ninth century we have tried to explain as a third stage in the urban history of north-west Europe, survived the Viking raids of the late ninth century. Most of these towns had roots older than the *emporia* and

---

[50] Verhulst, *Rise of Cities*, pp. 53-54.
[51] P. Toubert, "La part du grand domaine dans le décollage économique de l'Occident (VIIIᵉ-Xᵉ siècles)", in *La croissance agricole du Haut Moyen Age*, Flaran 10 (Auch, 1990), pp. 81-84; Devroey, "Courants et réseaux", pp. 367-84.
[52] Verhulst, *Rise of Cities*, pp. 56-58.

were implanted more solidly than the latter in their geographical, economic and social environment. Starting their commercial activities in the ninth century on the more modest scale of local and regional trade, mainly apart from the *emporia*, they slowly developed into centres of international trade towards the end of the tenth century by favour of the general revival of the Western world. The explanation for this, however, was not the aim of the present chapter.

THE ROLE OF THE MONASTERIES IN THE SYSTEMS OF PRODUCTION AND EXCHANGE OF THE FRANKISH WORLD BETWEEN THE SEVENTH AND THE BEGINNING OF THE NINTH CENTURIES*

Stéphane Lebecq

The eighth century casts a relatively pale reflection in the monastic history of the Frankish kingdoms: it was in the seventh century that, largely under the impulse of Columbanus and his disciples, monastic foundations and the transformation of old churches into monasteries proliferated, and in the ninth century that, under the authority of Benedict of Aniane, Benedictine reform and standardisation were imposed. Much the same can be said of the documentation and its contribution to the economic history of the monastic movement. It is the seventh century that has left us the greatest number of charters of foundation or of the donation of landed property, and it is in the ninth century that such normative or normalised documents as Adalard's *Statuta* or the so-called Plan of St Gall were drawn up. In the latter century too the first great polyptychs were redacted, reflecting a concern for a more rational administration of temporal goods in accordance with the enterprise of reform.

Fortunately a few written sources—cartularies, *Gesta abbatum* or well-informed monastic chronicles—partly make up for the documentary hiatus, particularly for northern Gaul: this is the case for the archive of St Denis, especially rich in original documents from the eighth century, but also for those of St-Germain-des-Prés, of Fontenelle, of Corbie and of some others.[1] It is thanks to these that we can sketch an

* I would like to thank Marios Costambeys for translating this paper.

[1] I cite here the collections of sources and fundamental studies of the documents which are used in the pages that follow: *Chartae Latinae Antiquiores*, vols. 13-19, eds. H. Atsma and J. Vezin (Dietikon/Zurich, 1981-1987); *Das Polyptychon von Saint-Germain-des-Prés. Studienausgabe*, ed. D. Hägermann, with K. Elmshäuser and A. Hedwig (Cologne/Weimar/Vienna, 1993); L. Levillain, *Examen critique des chartes mérovingiennes et carolingiennes de l'abbaye de Corbie* (Paris, 1902); *Hariulf (1060-1143). Chronique de l'abbaye de Saint-Riquier (Ve siècle-1104)*, ed. F. Lot (Paris, 1894); F. Lot, *Etudes critiques sur l'abbaye de Saint-Wandrille* (Paris, 1913).

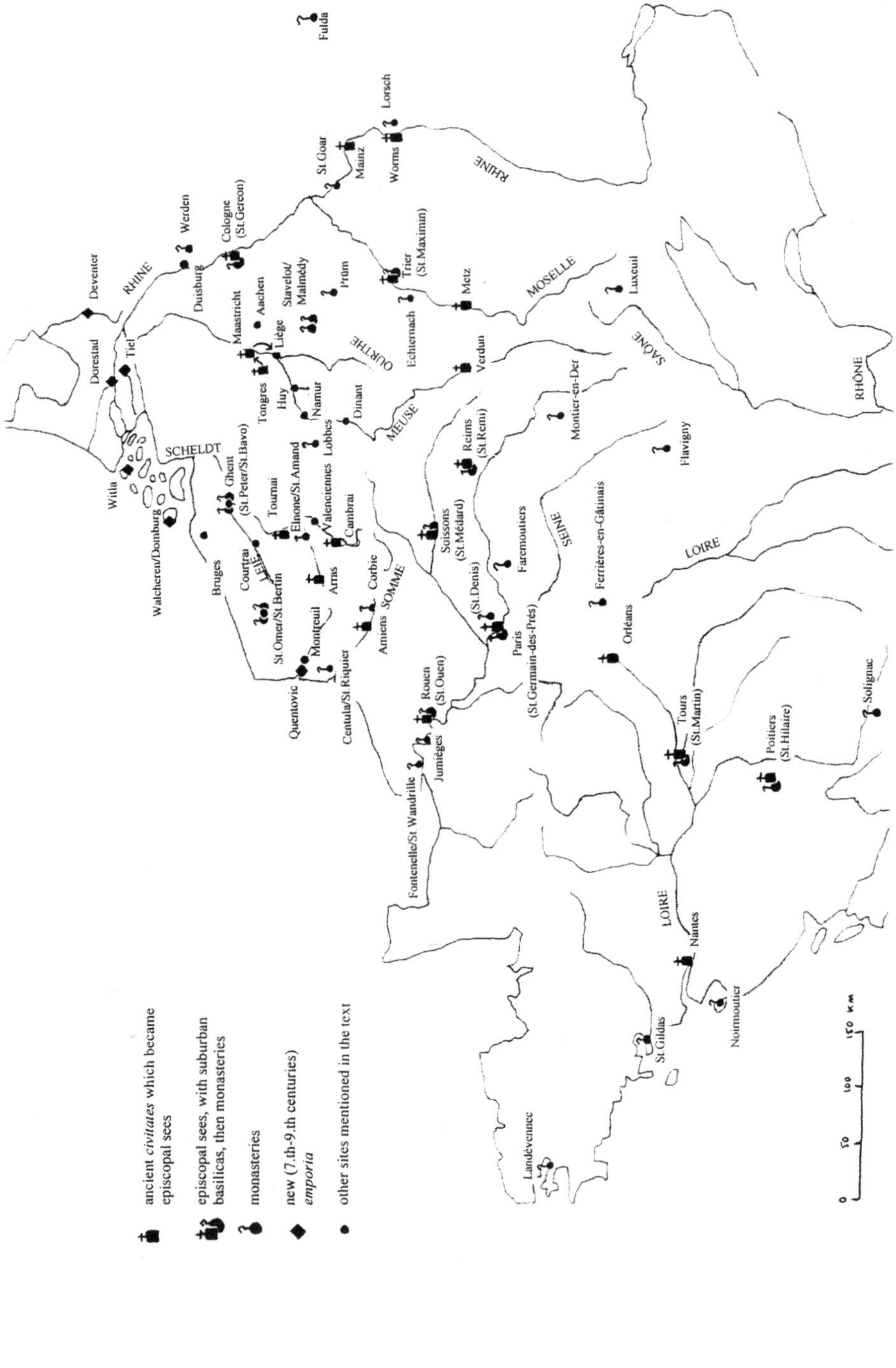

Fig. 1. Francia. Sites mentioned in the text.

economic history for the monastic movement in the eighth-century Frankish world, even if economy is not possible when writing history on the basis of the documentation which proliferates from the beginning of the ninth century.

If we want to understand the establishment of the monastic patrimonies from an economic angle, however, it is clear that we have to go back to the state of affairs revealed in the seventh-century sources. At first sight it seems that in the majority of cases, the "desert" evoked by the monastic movement is more an internalised than an external wilderness.

1. *The monastic patrimonies: a desert within*

The monastic countryside of Frankish Gaul at the turn of the seventh and eighth centuries seems to have grown from three roots and progressed along three paths:[2]

- There are, first, the oldest foundations, of the fourth to sixth centuries, of very various traditions (Martin, John Cassian, Lérins etc.).[3]
- There are then the foundations of the seventh century, of which the majority followed in the wake, or at least came under the influence, of the Columbanan movement. Columbanus, his disciples and successors certainly increased the number of foundations: it has been estimated that in the seventh century the number of monasteries throughout the whole of the Frankish kingdoms, admittedly themselves constantly in expansion, rose from about 215 to nearly 550.[4] Following the example of Luxeuil, around the middle of the seventh century the Columbanan monasteries exchanged the Irish model for a "mixed" model which, though long consid-

---

[2] See the fundamental book by F. Prinz, *Frühes Mönchtum im Frankenreich. Kultur und Gesellschaft in Gallien, den Rheinlanden und Bayern am Beispiel der monastischen Entwicklung (4. bis 8. Jahrhundert)* (Munich/Vienna, 1965); or the synthesis by A. Angenendt, *Das Frühmittelalter. Die abendländische Christenheit von 400 bis 900*, 2nd ed. (Stuttgart/Berlin/Cologne, 1995), esp. pp. 97-111 and 213-22.

[3] C. Courtois, "L'évolution du monachisme en Gaule de saint Martin à saint Colomban", in *Il monachesimo nell'alto medioevo e la formazione della civiltà occidentale*, Settimane di studio del Centro italiano di studi sull'alto Medioevo 4 (Spoleto, 1957), pp. 47-72.

[4] H. Atsma, "Les monastères urbains du nord de la Gaule", *Revue d'histoire de l'Eglise de France* 62 (1976), pp. 163-87, esp. p. 168.

ered Iro-Benedictine or Iro-Frankish, in reality conceals an almost
complete acceptance of the Benedictine model.[5]
• Finally, we can put in their own category the old basilicas, most
  often funerary and nearly always suburban, which until the seventh century had been controlled by colleges of clergy under the
  more or less close supervision of the bishop, and had then nearly
  all adopted a monastic way of life, generally in its Benedictine
  form. The best-studied example is perhaps that of the basilica of
  St Denis, founded by St Genevieve at the end of the fifth century
  and transformed into an abbey around 655.[6]

The economic and/or environmental compromise

As is well known, by definition the monastic vocation implies a radical rupture with the world, which in principle ought to mean that
monks have to choose to live "in the desert" and consequently to
work with their hands. Indeed, whereas Irish practice, in particular
in the west of the island, had a certain penchant for establishing
monasteries isolated from areas of human habitation,[7] the Benedictine
tradition insisted on what chapter 48 of the Rule calls in its title
"everyday manual labour".
    Yet it is interesting to read this chapter again:

> (ch. 48.1). Idleness (*otiositas*) is the enemy of the soul. The brethren,
> therefore, must be occupied at stated hours in manual labour (*labore
> manuum*) . . . (ch. 48.7). But if the circumstances of the place or their
> poverty (*necessitas loci aut paupertas*) require them to gather the harvest
> themselves (*ad fruges recolligendas*), let them not be discontented; (ch. 48.8)
> for then are they truly monks (*tunc vere monachi sunt*) when they live by

[5] A. Dierkens, "Prolégomènes à une histoire des relations culturelles entre les Îles
Britanniques et le continent pendant le haut Moyen Age. La diffusion du monachisme
dit colombanien ou iro-franc dans quelques monastères de la région parisienne au
VIIᵉ siècle et la politique religieuse de la reine Balthilde", in H. Atsma ed., *La
Neustrie. Les pays au nord de la Loire de 650 à 850*, Actes du colloque de Rouen, Beihefte der Francia 16, 2 vols. (Sigmaringen, 1989), vol. 2, pp. 371-94.
[6] J. Semmler, "Saint-Denis: von der bischöflichen Coemeterialbasilika zur königli-
chen Benedikterabtei", in *La Neustrie. Les pays au nord de la Loire de 650 à 850*, vol. 2,
pp. 75-123.
[7] Although this is not necessarily the case for the large monasteries founded in
the sixth century, such as Clonard, Clonmacnoise, Bangor or Durrow, it is true of
the smaller units founded, often later (in the seventh or eighth centuries), in the
extreme west: see N. Edwards, *The Archaeology of Early Medieval Ireland* (London, 1990),
esp. pp. 104-05 and 114-21.

the labour of their hands (*labore manuum suarum*), like our fathers and the apostles (*sicut et patres nostri et apostoli*). (ch. 48.9) Yet let all things be done in moderation, on account of the faint-hearted.[8]

If, therefore, it seemed clear that for St Benedict the true monk was the one who lived by the work of his hands and who himself harvested the fruits of the earth, all monks could, if local conditions allowed them, elude the heaviest field-work: in other words, reading between the lines, they could live by the work of others. We can therefore see that the economic compromise, which brought the monastery into the economy and society of its time, was as integral a part of Benedictine monasticism as refusal of the world. The desert of our texts (*desertum, solitudo* or *vasta*) was above all an internalised desert;[9] it would scarcely be exaggerating to say that it was more metaphorical than real.

This can immediately be seen from a glance at the sites where monasteries were founded, beginning, naturally, with those used for the transformation of suburban basilicas. Located near cities, from the outset these were part of a fairly dense web of habitation. They were close to urban markets that must have remained active to a certain extent, and they benefited from a system of land and river communication that since antiquity had served each *caput civitatis*. One example is provided by one of the oldest monasteries in Gaul, founded around 416 at the tomb of the martyr Victor in the immediate *suburbium* of Marseille, then the most important port of Mediterranean Gaul.[10] It was followed by other funerary basilicas that were transformed into monasteries: St Martin at Tours, St Hilary at Poitiers, St Denis, the Holy Apostles at Paris (later St Genevieve), the Holy Cross/St Vincent at Paris (later St Germain-des-Prés), St Médard at Soissons, St Vaast at Arras, St Maximin at Trier, St

---

[8] *Benedicti Regula*, ed. R. Hanslik, Corpus Scriptorum Ecclesiasticorum Latinorum 75 (Vienna, 1960), p. 114; translated by J. McCann, *The Rule of Saint Benedict* (London, 1952), pp. 53-54.

[9] C. Wickham, "European forests in the early middle ages: landscape and clearance", *L'ambiente vegetale nell'alto medioevo*, Settimane di studio del Centro italiano di studi sull'alto Medioevo 37 (Spoleto, 1990), pp. 479-545, esp. pp. 483-84.

[10] See S.T. Loseby, *Marseille in Late Antiquity and the early Middle Ages* (Oxford, forthcoming); and in addition "Marseille: a late antique success story?", *Journal of Roman Studies* 82 (1992), pp. 165-85; "Marseille and the Pirenne thesis, I", in R. Hodges and W. Bowden eds., *The Sixth Century. Production, Distribution and Demand* (Leiden, 1998), pp. 203-29. I am grateful to Simon Loseby for having pointed out to me that no direct line can be established between the activity of John Cassian and the foundation of Saint-Victor.

Gereon at Cologne and many others; all were established in the
shadows of the walls of important cities.

Foundations of the seventh and eighth centuries between saltus and ager

As for the foundations of the seventh and eighth centuries, often the
result of the initiative of the royal family or their closest courtiers,
they were frequently located on a portion of fiscal land, sometimes
of considerable size. Admittedly, the bulk of the property donated
might have been *saltus*, and have consisted of still largely uncultivated areas. This was the case, probably, with the Atlantic island of
Heriou where Philibert, wanting to find "the solitude of the desert",
founded the monastery of Noirmoutier around 675-7.[11] It was surely
also the case with the fiscal land that Sigebert III gave around 648
to Remaclus *in foreste nostra nuncupante Arduinna* in order to found the
double monastery of Stavelot-Malmédy. Here the most recent paly-
nological research echoes the use of the word *forestis* (which here
means a normally uncultivated royal reserve) and confirms that the
place was a wilderness, predominantly covered with trees, shrubs,
briars and bracken in the first half of the seventh century.[12]

As is well known, however, we can trust the rhetoric neither of
charters nor, especially, of hagiographical discourse, which always
tends to exaggerate the desolate character of these settlements. Thus
the *lenta palus Elnoni* evoked by Jonas of Bobbio, in which Amandus
founded the monastery of Elnone-St Amand just before 639, was
most likely in reality a fiscal domain of nearly 10,000 hectares,
received thanks to a grant by Dagobert and very largely already
occupied.[13] Equally, even in distant Germany, then in the process

---

[11] "Cum . . . sanctus Philibertus semper desideraret heremi vastitatem . . .": this was
the circumstance of the foundation of Noirmoutier according to ch. 21 of the eighth-
century *Vita Filiberti*: see R. Poupardin, *Monuments de l'histoire des abbayes de Saint-
Philibert (Noirmoutier, Grandlieu, Tournus)* (Paris, 1905), p. 13; and pp. XX-XXII for
the date of the monastery's foundation.

[12] R. Noel, "Moines et nature sauvage dans l'Ardenne du haut Moyen Age", in
J.-M. Duvosquel and A. Dierkens eds., *Villes et campagnes au Moyen Age. Mélanges
Georges Despy* (Liège, 1991), pp. 563-97, esp. p. 577; S. Lebecq, "Entre Antiquité
tardive et très haut Moyen Age: permanence et mutations des systèmes de communication dans la Gaule et ses marges", *Morfologie sociali e culturali in Europa fra
Tarda Antichità e Alto Medioevo*, Settimane di studio del Centro italiano di studi sull'
alto Medioevo 45 (Spoleto, 1998), pp. 461-502, esp. pp. 490-92.

[13] H. Platelle, *Le temporel de l'abbaye de Saint-Amand des origines à 1340* (Paris, 1962),
pp. 36 and 47-48.

of being integrated into the Frankish world, the *horrendum desertum* in which, according to his biographer Eigil, Sturm founded the abbey of Fulda in 743 actually referred to a fiscal estate, the centre of which was occupied by a monumental Merovingian complex based on the model of a Roman *villa*.[14]

In fact nearly all these pieces of fiscal land already possessed estate centres, productive organisation and above all the men who cultivated them. The fiscal estate of Solignac, which was given by Dagobert to Eligius in 632 for the foundation of a monastery, already comprised *aedificia, adiacentia, servi,* and *acolani*.[15] At the moment of its foundation in 659, the abbey of Corbie received from Queen Balthild and her son Chlothar III the fisc and villa of the same name, as well as several nearby *villae, cum adiacentias* [sic] *vel appendiciis suis*, to a total of some 20,000 hectares: the whole was offered to the monastery *cum terris, domibus, mancipiis, edificiis, vineis, silvis, pratis, pascuis, farinariis...* Admittedly, this list resembles a ready-made formula, but it is clear that we are dealing here with a densely populated region, where even traces of Roman centuriation may have persisted.[16]

Monasteries and communications

According to the foundation charter of Corbie, one of the *villae* offered to the monks, that of *Templum Martis* (Talmas, in the *pagus* of Amiens), of which the toponym is itself enough to suggest the presence of an ancient cult site, was bounded by a *via publica*, that is, a Roman road, doubtless that which ran from Amiens to Arras.[17] The need to communicate with the outside world played an often essential role in foundation strategies, to the extent that even the monastery that was truly founded in the desert, for example in the remotest part of a *forestis*, still had to be connected to the regional system of communication. It is in this way that we can explain the

[14] Wickham, "European forests", pp. 481-82.

[15] According to the foundation charter of Solignac, added by B. Krusch to his edition of the *Vita Eligii episcopi Noviomagensis*, MGH Scriptores Rerum Merowingicarum 4 (Hannover, 1902), pp. 634-761, esp. p. 746.

[16] Levillain, *Examen critique*, pp. 212-17. On possible traces of Roman centuriation, see M. Rouche, "La dotation foncière de l'abbaye de Corbie (657-661) d'après l'acte de fondation", *Revue du Nord* 55 (1973), pp. 219-26.

[17] M. Rouche, "La dotation foncière"; see also R. Agache, "L'archéologie aérienne et la découverte des voies", *Histoire et archéologie. Les dossiers* 67 (1982), pp. 20-31.

origin of the roadway that bounded the monastic estate of Stavelot-Malmédy to the east, and that allowed it to be linked to the neighbouring towns of Trier to the south and Maastricht to the north. Recent investigations and analyses have in fact shown that this road, the features of which (its route, adjustment to local topography, materials) were of such a kind that for a long time it had been considered Roman, have been built during the early middle ages, perhaps around 700.[18]

Monastic sites were also linked to the outside world by waterways: it was often by boat that founders—especially if they belonged to the Columbanan tradition—had arrived at the place where they finally chose to settle, as, tradition tells us, Amandus did at Elnone and at Ghent.[19] Moreover, a number of monasteries had been founded by the sea, at the mouths of estuaries or on the lower reaches of rivers. Besides the Breton monasteries, the origins of which are often obscure, founded on the coasts or at the end of Armorican inlets (from Alet/Saint-Malo to St-Gildas de Rhuys, including Landévennec and the Trieux islands around Bréhat)[20] we can cite Centula/St-Riquier (founded around 625) near the estuary of the Somme, St Peter and St Bavo at Ghent (the first founded c.630-9, the second probably a little before 676) at the confluence of the Escaut and the Lys, Fontenelle/St-Wandrille (649) and Jumièges (654) in the lower valley of the Seine, St-Bertin (towards 650) at the end of the gulf of the Aa, Heriou/Noirmoutier (towards 660) on an island in the Atlantic, and many more besides.[21]

It is not only because these damp and, maybe, repugnant environments encouraged asceticism that they were chosen by founders. It is also because communications by water offered them opportunities for development. At any rate, this is what the authors of the

---

[18] M.-H. Corbiau, La 'Via Mansuerica'. Etude archéologique du tracé et des structures, Archaeologica Belgica 235 (Brussels, 1981); and Noel, "Moines et nature sauvage", pp. 588-91.

[19] For Elnone-Saint-Amand, see Platelle, Le temporel de l'abbaye de Saint-Amand, p. 36; for the Ghent abbeys, see A. Verhulst, De Sint-Baafsabdij te Gent en haar grondbezit (VIIᵉ-XIVᵉ eeuw) (Brussels, 1958); A. Verhulst and B. Declercq, "Du VIIᵉ au XIᵉ siècle, Gand entre les abbayes et la fortification comtale", in J. Decavelle ed., Gand. Apologie d'une ville rebelle (Antwerp, 1989), pp. 37-59, esp. p. 37.

[20] See J.-C. Cassard, Les Bretons et la mer au Moyen Age (Rennes, 1998), pp. 98-105; on the pitfalls of Breton hagiography, B. Merdrignac, Les Vies de saints bretons durant le haut Moyen Age (Rennes, 1993), passim.

[21] Summarized in S. Lebecq, "La Neustrie et la mer", in La Neustrie. Les pays au nord de la Loire de 650 à 850, vol. 1, pp. 405-40, esp. pp. 409-10.

Gesta of Fontenelle and of the *Vita Filiberti* claimed in relation to the, almost twin, abbeys of Fontenelle and Jumièges—located only a few kilometres from each other:

> to the east flows the greatest of rivers, equal to the Geon [one of the rivers of Paradise, Genesis 2:13], the Seine, famous for its traffic of vessels, excelling in its abundance of fish, and only 800 yards distant from the monastery . . .[22]

> Channel for vessels, means of trade in many goods, (the Seine) provides sea fish fifty feet in length, which complement the diet (of the brothers) and are used to banish the darkness because the liquid they contain feeds with its oil the lamp's flame . . . Royal largesse and the generosity of the faithful gave (Philibert) a good deal of money . . . He could send his monks across the sea with vessels full of merchandise . . .[23]

If therefore we are to believe the monastic redactors of origin tales, intended principally to exalt their founders' heroism, the monasteries were devoted to developing their own prosperity. They had a landed patrimony that, from the moment of their foundation, was usually endowed with production centres and already exploited by those peasants, often, though not necessarily, slaves, who had been given with it. Moreover, they were already connected to the external world—or were to be so before long—thanks to the road, river or sea communication network, not only with the aim of accomplishing their evangelising mission, but also with that of opening themselves to the market.

2. *The monasteries as economic centres*

We have just seen that, in its foundation charter of 659, numerous *villae* and several *farinaria* (mills) had been given to the monastery of Corbie. On a more reduced scale, this also happened at Faremoutiers in the Brie, when in 633 Burgundofara bequeathed by testament to the monastery that she had just founded there "the entirety of the goods that she possessed in the world", that is, her portions of the *villae* at Champeaux, at Chelles, at Augers-en-Brie and in the *suburbium*

---

[22] *Gesta* of the abbots of Fontenelle, I.5: see *Gesta Sanctorum Patrum Fontanellensis Coenobii*, ed. F. Lohier and J. Laporte (Rouen/Paris, 1936), pp. 6-7.
[23] *Vita Filiberti*, chs. 8, 9 and 23: see Poupardin, *Monuments de l'histoire des abbayes de Saint-Philibert*, pp. 6-7 and 14.

of Meaux—each time *cum terris, domibus, vineis, silvis, pratis, pascuis, aquis et mancipiis*—together with two *farinaria* located on the rivers Marne and Aubetin.[24] In both cases, we glimpse how, from the moment of their foundation, the monasteries could become economic centres:

- A domain comprising several centres of exploitation, the fragmented character of which later donations often only exacerbated, and which made of the monastery itself a centre of administration linked with its different components by the continuous movement of men and goods;
- A rich set of those productive elements (for example, in the cited cases, *farinaria* or mills) which served to make of the monastery itself or of some of its dependencies places for the processing of agricultural produce.

The patterning of estates

At first sight, the geographical pattern of each foundation's estates seems to have been the result of accidents of gift-giving. This is especially true in the cases of monasteries based on funerary basilicas, the lands of which had often been enriched by the offerings of pilgrims hailing from various and distant geographical horizons. But in fact numerous donations were deliberately sought, in order to endow the institution with places with particular specialisations (pastures, or forest areas rich in wood or minerals, for instance), with primary produce (wine, salt, fish), or with connections to the communications network.

Setting aside the concern of monasteries in northern Frankish Gaul to find vineyards in more southerly zones of production—the subject many years ago of a classic investigation[25]—the reasons for and modalities of the foundation of great abbeys in the coastal regions can be explored. Whether they were situated directly on the coast, or away from the sea shore, or in a still more distant hinterland, all, or nearly all, felt the desire to acquire property by the sea, either:

---

[24] J. Guerout, "Le testament de sainte Fare. Matériaux pour l'étude et l'édition critique de ce document", *Revue d'Historie Ecclésiastique* 60 (1965), pp. 761-821.

[25] H. Van Werveke, "Comment les établissements religieux belges se procuraient-ils du vin au haut Moyen Age?", *Revue Belge de Philologie et d'Histoire* 2 (1923), pp. 643-62.

- Salt-flats favourable for extensive stock-raising: such as those acquired by St Bravo's in the islands of Zeeland.[26]
- Coastlands specifically for the production of salt, made either by artificial combustion—such as those of Jumièges at Honfleur, Fontenelle in the Talou,[27] or Lorsch in Zeeland, which in 776 acquired there *culinas ad sal faciendam*;[28] or by evaporation—such as the property of St Denis in the bays of Guérande and Bourgneuf, according to documents in the late *Gesta Dagoberti*.[29]
- *Piscationes*, indispensable for the monastic table—such as those belonging to Elnone in coastal Flanders, Ferrières in the lower valley of the Canche, Jumièges and Fontenelle in the coastal properties mentioned above.[30] And, more precisely, of embarkation points suitable for hunting marine mammals, which were much sought-after for their meat, for their bones, and especially for their blubber—examples include Noirmoutier or Jumièges in the waters neighbouring the monastery, the properties of St Vaast on the coast of the Pas-de-Calais, or those of St Denis in the Cotentin.[31] If we can generalise from an example included in the *Miracula sancti Vedasti* redacted at Arras in the ninth century,[32] these everywhere provided the necessary infrastructure, men and boats.

In fact, it was not only favourable natural conditions, but also the presence of workshops and a skilled workforce which determined the economic specialisation of one or other monastic property. Thus we know, thanks to the charter that founded the conventual *mensa* of St

---

[26] See Verhulst, *De Sint-Baafsabdij te Gent*; A. Verhulst, "Das Besitzverzeichnis der Genter Sankt-Bavo-Abtei von ca. 800. Ein Beitrag zur Geschichte und Kritik der karolingischen Urbarialaufzeichnungen", *Frühmittelalterliche Studien* 5 (1971), pp. 193-234; C. Dekker, "Saint-Bavon en Zélande", in J.-M. Duvosquel and E. Thoen eds., *Peasants and Townsmen in Medieval Europe. Studia in honorem Adriaan Verhulst* (Gent, 1995), pp. 379-98.

[27] Lebecq, "La Neustrie et la mer", p. 410.

[28] B.C. Besteman, "Frisian salt and the problem of salt-making in north Holland in the Carolingian period", *Berichten van de Rijksdienst voor het Oudheidkundig Bodemonderzoek* 24 (1974), pp. 171-74.

[29] *Gesta Dagoberti*, ed. B. Krusch, MGH Scriptores Rerum Merowingicarum 4 (Hannover, 1902), pp. 413-14.

[30] Lebecq, "La Neustrie et la mer", pp. 410-11.

[31] S. Lebecq, "Scènes de chasse aux mammifères marins (mers du Nord, VIᵉ-XIIᵉ siècles)", in E. Mornet and F. Morenzoni eds., *Milieux naturels, espaces sociaux. Etudes offertes à Robert Delort* (Paris, 1997), pp. 241-54, esp. pp. 243-46.

[32] *Miracula sancti Vedasti*, ed. O. Holder-Egger, MGH Scriptores 15.2 (Hannover, 1888), p. 400. See Lebecq, "Scènes de chasse aux mammifères marins", pp. 251-52.

Denis (22 January 832), that some of its *villae*, including those of Villiers-le-Sec and Baillet-en-France, had to provide the monastery with clothes of all sorts. Recent excavation of these villages has shown, thanks to the discovery of an abundant material record (forceps, combs, spindles, awls, needles, brooches, whetstones, stones for carding), that sunken huts or *Grubenhäuser* were used for the production of threads and cloth, both woollen and linen, which shows the extent to which the data in our written sources must be taken seriously.[33]

A very interesting fact should be noted at this point: after the burials of Boniface (martyred in Frisia) at Fulda in 754 and Liudger (a Frisian by birth) at Werden in 809, these monasteries were given abundant donations by pious Frisians. Only a few of these consisted of land, the extent of which was always expressed in the number of heads of livestock that could be pastured there—thus, as we read in the archives of Fulda, *pascua XIIII pecodum* (pasture for fourteen sheep) or *terrae X boum* (land for ten cattle). Instead, since private ownership of the land was not very widespread in the coastal districts of medieval Frisia, where the salt-meadow was most often the common property of village communities, the majority of donations consisted of annual rents expressed as a certain quantity of cloth.[34]

Be that as it may, we must acknowledge a distinction between two types of monastic property:-

• The estate centre, around the monastic buildings, was created by the initial donation but was extended by the acquisition of adjoining or nearby lands. This centre (which very often retained a significant area of woodland) was usually given over to mixed farming, at least within the limits allowed by the local environment. It was there that were situated orchards and gardens specialising in the production of rare plants, for the kitchen garden or for medicinal uses, which allowed the monks to fulfil their charitable mission, and which are represented on the famous plan of St Gall.[35]

---

[33] See R. Guadagnin ed., *Un village au temps de Charlemagne. Moines et paysans de l'abbaye de Saint-Denis du VII* siècle à l'an mil*, Catalogue d'exposition (Paris, 1988), esp. pp. 275-76.

[34] See S. Lebecq, *Marchands et navigateurs frisons du haut Moyen Age*, 2 vols. (Lille, 1983), vol. 1, pp. 132-33 and vol. 2, pp. 381-87. See also S. Lebecq, "Entre terre et mer: la mise en valeur des contrées littorales de l'ancienne Frise", *Histoire. Economie et Société* 16 (1997), pp. 361-76, esp. p. 367.

[35] See W. Horn and E. Born, *The Plan of St Gall. A study of the architecture and economy of, and life in, a paradigmatic Carolingian monastery*, 3 vols. (Berkeley/Los

- Further afield, dispersed estates were created by chance gifts or by a deliberate policy of acquisition. These were often organised into *villae* managed by a monk, and sometimes provided with a church that was to become the centre of a future parish. They could have the same profile of mixed farming as the monastic centre itself, but were sometimes required to specialise to a certain extent (for example in textiles or metal-working), according to the aptitude of their environment or inhabitants. In certain cases their task was to provide the monastery with a particular type of product, for example land given over to vineyards on south-facing hillsides or salt flats beside the sea.[36]

Monasteries and large manorial facilities

It is therefore clear that, both far from monastic centres and at their heart, an entire labour force worked to turn the produce of the soil to the advantage of the abbeys, often with the help of those sophisticated workshops that we have noticed in passing and in which only the greatest producers had the means to invest.[37] These included salt ovens in the most northerly lands where the sunlight was insufficient to exploit salt marshes, spinning and weaving looms perhaps attached to those *genicia* mentioned in the capitulary *De Villis*, which offers a model of management to the monasteries,[38] forges (excavations have

---

Angeles/London, 1979); W. Vogler ed., *L'abbaye de Saint-Gall. Rayonnement spirituel et culturel* (Lausanne, 1991), or, with copious detail, M. Rey-Delque ed., *Un plan modèle d'architecture monastique*, Catalogue d'exposition (Toulouse, 1994), esp. p. 13; also C. Heitz, *L'architecture religieuse carolingienne. Les formes et leurs fonctions* (Paris, 1980).

[36] In this connection see E. Lesne, *Histoire de la propriété ecclésiastique en France*, vol. 6, *Les églises et les monastères, centres d'accueil, d'exploitation et de peuplement* (Lille, 1943), passim.; L. Musset, "Signification et destinée des domaines excentriques pour les abbayes de la moitié septentrionale de la Gaule jusqu'au XIe siècle", in *Sous la règle de saint Benoît. Structures monastiques et sociétés en France du Moyen Age à l'époque moderne* (Geneva/Paris, 1982), pp. 167-82; and P. Toubert, "La part du grand domaine dans le décollage économique de l'Occident (VIIIe-Xe siècles)", in *La croissance agricole du haut Moyen Age. Chronologie, modalités, géographie*, Actes du 10e colloque de Flaran (Auch, 1990), pp. 53-86, esp. pp. 76-80.

[37] On the monasteries as centres of artisanal activity, see the important study of F. Schwind, "Zu karolingischerzeitlichen Klöstern als Wirtschaftsorganismen und Stätten handwerklicher Tätigkeit", in *Institutionen, Kultur und Gesellschaft im Mittelalter. Festschrift für Josef Fleckenstein* (Sigmaringen, 1984), pp. 101-23.

[38] *Capitulare de villis vel curtis imperialibus*, chs. 31 and 43, ed. A. Boretius, MGH Legum, Sectio II, Capitularia Regum Francorum (Hannover, 1883); translated by H.R. Loyn and J. Percival, *The Reign of Charlemagne* (London, 1975), pp. 64-73.

revealed the specialisation in metal-working of St Denis's village of Belloy-en-France), and above all, universally widespread, mills, presses and breweries.

The *molendina*, or rather (since this word tends to predominate in the sources for the early middle ages) the several *farinaria* attested in the seventh century unquestionably increased in number on monastic estates in the course of the long eighth century: every valley in Neustria had by then been provided with them, sometimes at considerable trouble, which might include altering the courses of rivers and underwater construction (*de fabrica in aqua*, as certain eighth-century manuscripts say). This technical prowess was sometimes such that we might wonder if the monks used the works of Vitruvius, which at any rate we know were copied in the scriptoria of Corbie and St-Médard at Soissons.[39] It is consequently not surprising that by the beginning of the ninth century Corbie possessed at least 15 mills,[40] Fontenelle 39,[41] St-Germain-des-Prés 84,[42] and that, later in the century, the Austrasian abbeys of Wissembourg, Montierender and Prüm possessed respectively 12, 18 and 45.[43] In fact the polyptych of Irminon's precision about the age of some of them makes it is clear that their construction dates back to around the middle of the eighth century.

In vine-growing regions, there were increasing numbers of wine-presses (*torcularia*), in which mechanical presses began to replace the ancient practice of grape-treading. Here again, from the very end of the eighth century, the capitulary *De Villis* provides an echo of this progressive replacement: "that the *torcularia* of our *villae* are to be in good repair; and that our stewards are to make sure that our grape harvest is not trodden with feet, but that everything is done honestly and properly".[44] The polyptychs of the beginning of the

---

[39] D. Lohrmann, "Le moulin à eau dans le cadre de l'économie rurale de la Neustrie (VIIe-IXe siècles)", in *La Neustrie. Les pays au nord de la Loire de 650 à 850*, vol. 1, pp. 367-404, esp. pp. 397-8.

[40] In addition to Lohrmann, "Le moulin à eau", pp. 386-89, see A. Verhulst and J. Semmler, "Les statuts d'Adalhard de Corbie de l'an 822", *Le Moyen Age* 68 (1962), pp. 91-123 and 233-69, esp. p. 122.

[41] Lohrmann, "Le moulin à eau", p. 373.

[42] Lohrmann, "Le moulin à eau", p. 373; K. Elmshäuser and A. Hedwig, *Studien zum Polyptychon von Saint-Germain-des-Prés* (Cologne, Weimar, Vienna, 1993), esp. pp. 436-53.

[43] E. Champion, *Moulins et meuniers carolingiens dans les polyptyques entre Loire et Rhin* (Paris, 1996), p. 32.

[44] *Capitulare de Villis*, chs. 41 and 48 (whence quotation).

ninth century suggest that certain great monastic institutions, especially northern ones, had followed, and perhaps even anticipated, royal example: thus the *villae* that St-Remi at Reims possessed at Aigny, Muizon, Petit-Fleury and Aubilly each had its own press around the years 810-820.[45] According to the 832 act establishing the conventual *mensa*, some *carpentarii* were requisitioned by the abbey of St Denis on the occasion of the grape harvest (*vindemiae*); this raises the possibility that it used them for the construction or repair of its presses.[46]

More typical of northern regions, however, were breweries (*cambae* or *cammae*), to which the statutes of Adalard pay particular attention, devoting an entire chapter *de cambis quoque et bracibus* ("on breweries and malts").[47] But reports transmitted through the great polyptychs and inventories of the ninth century—of St-Germain-des-Prés, St-Bertin, St-Remi at Reims (2 mentions), Montierender (7 mentions), Lobbes, Prüm, Lorsch, Fulda—which, taken together, indicate a close association between breweries and mills, do not suggest that the former had existed in any number for long.[48]

The great workshops, which had been established in the shadows of the monasteries themselves—even where they did not necessarily constitute demesne centres[49]—as well as in the more important of their *villae* or *curtes*, would become not only centres for the production of goods for the open market, but also what Pierre Toubert has

---

[45] See J.-P. Devroey ed., *Le Polyptyque et les listes de cens de l'abbaye de Saint-Remi de Reims (IXe-XIe siècles)* (Reims, 1984), pp. 3, 5, 6 and 7.

[46] Archives Nationale de Paris (K9 n° 5). Unless these carpenters were only needed to make barrels, as proposed by J.-P. Brunterc'h, in R. Guadagnin ed., *Un village*, pp. 125-28, esp. p. 128.

[47] Adalhard, *Statuta*, II, ch. 15. See Verhulst and Semmler, "Les statuts", p. 237.

[48] J. Deckers, "Recherches sur l'histoire des brasseries dans la région mosane au Moyen Age", *Le Moyen Age* 76 (1970), pp. 445-91, and Toubert, "La part du grand domaine", esp. pp. 68-69. For mentions of Saint-Remi see Devroey, *Le Polyptyque*, p. 16 (Courtisols); for Montierender, to which was added a camba deserta, see C. Droste, "Die Grundherrschaft Montiérender im 9. Jahrhundert", in A. Verhulst ed., *Le Grand Domaine aux époques mérovingienne et carolingienne* (Gent, 1985), pp. 101-11, esp. p. 105.

[49] See J.-P. Devroey, "Ad utilitatem monasterii. Mobiles et préoccupations de gestion dans l'économie monastique du monde fanc", in *Le monachisme à Byzance et en Occident du VIIIe au Xe siècle. Aspects internes et relations avec la société*, Actes du colloque de Bruxelles, Revue Bénédictine 103 (1993), pp. 224-40; and J.-P. Devroey, "Courants et réseaux d'échange dans l'économie franque entre Loire et Rhin", in *Mercati et Mercanti nell'alto Medioevo: l'area euroasiatica e l'area mditerranea*, Settimane di studio del Centro italiano di Studi sull'Alto Medioevo 40 (Spoleto, 1993), pp. 327-89, esp. p. 337.

called "strategic points of seigneurial exaction",[50] meeting points for the dependent peasant population and points of anchorage for the economic domination that the great abbeys exercised over them.

The logistics of transport and the concentration of economic activity in monastic centres

Transport services were required from these same peasant populations to ensure communications not only between the centres of primary and secondary production, but also between outlying estates and monastic centres. In fact, the great quest for profitability undertaken by abbots with the encouragement of the Carolingian authorities came to impose an increasingly rigorous system of transport charges.[51] More than administrative texts like the *Statuta* of Adalard of Corbie, it is the great polyptychs which convey the character and periodicity of requisitions of labour service—that of Prüm in particular, with its *scarae* (modes of transport of all kinds), *angariae* (cartage) and *navigia* (river transport),[52] and, especially interesting for its relatively early date, that of St-Germain-des-Prés.

Here, the polyptych of Irminon tells us,[53] all sorts of *angariae* and *carropera* (literally, cartloads) were exacted from the tenants. But among these services, numerous distinctions were made depending on the transported product (*vinericia*, cartloads of wine), the date of the exaction (*magisca*, in May, specifically for the battens necessary for vinegrowing), the destination (*wichariae*, destined for the port of Quentovic), or varying according to the mode of transport (*portatura* with the help of *parafredi* or palfreys, for light transport by horse, or *navigia* for transportation by boat to the *villa* that the abbey possessed *supra mare*, doubtless Quillebeuf on the Seine estuary).[54]

For long-distance journeys, in particular those which transported

---

[50] P. Toubert, "La part du grand domaine", esp. p. 69.

[51] To Toubert, "La part du grand domaine", esp. pp. 80-84, and Schwind, "Zu karolingischerzeitlichen Klöstern", we can add those of D. Hägerman, "Der Abt als Grundherr. Kloster und Wirtschaft im frühen Mittelalter", in F. Prinz ed., *Herrschaft und Kirche. Beiträge zur Entstehung und Wirkungsweise episkopaler und monstischer Organisationsformen* (Stuttgart, 1988), pp. 345-85.

[52] J.-P. Devroey, "Les services de transport à l'abbaye de Prüm au IXᵉ siècle', *Revue du Nord* 61 (1979), pp. 543-69.

[53] See the edition of D. Hägermann, with the collaboration of K. Elmshäuser and A. Hedwig, cited at note 1.

[54] See J.-P. Devroey, "Un monastère dans l'économie d'échanges: les services de transport à l'abbaye de Saint-Germain-des-Prés au IXᵉ siècle", in *Annales. Économies.*

the produce of outlying estates or that acquired from distant markets, the monasteries obtained from the public power facilities which ranged from the possibility of using the logistics of public transport to all forms of exemption from tolls. Already in 716, the monks of Corbie had acquired from Chilperic II a confirmation of their right to the free hire (*absque dispendio monasterii*) of fifteen carts that were parked *pro loca consuetudinaria* in the lodges at the regular stops between the fiscal warehouse of Fos-sur-Mer (near Marseille) and the monastery itself.[55] For their part, the monks of St Denis obtained from Theuderic III in 680-688 an exemption from toll throughout the Frankish kingdoms for their transportation *tam carrale quam navigale*;[56] those of St-Germain-des-Prés obtained from Charlemagne in 779 the concession that their *negociantes* were freed from payment of all toll *nec de saumas nec de carrigine neque de navigio* ("neither on their beasts of burden, nor on their carts, nor on their vessels").[57]

The result of this transport activity was that the monastic centres became places in which a huge mass of products concentrated. Furthermore, to the profits from their own demesnes or from seigneurial exaction on dependent peasant plots, could be added the revenue from renders which had been granted to them. These could be of private origin, like the Frisian *pallia* given to Fulda and Werden, as mentioned above.[58] But they could also be public in origin, like the income offered in 691-716 to St Denis and that in 716 to Corbie on the customs revenue of Marseille or Fos-sur-Mer.[59] The revenue

Sociétés. Civilisations 39 (1984), pp. 570-89; and Elmshäuser and Hedwig, *Studien*, esp. pp. 406-20.

[55] Edited by L. Levillain, *Examen critique*, pp. 235-37 (no. 15); commentary by Lebecq, "Entre Antiquité tardive et très haut Moyen Age", p. 466.

[56] *Chartae Latinae Antiquiores*, ed. H. Atsma and J. Vezin, vol. 13, pp. 78-79 (no. 568). Commentary by Devroey, "Courants et réseaux d'échange", esp. pp. 359, 362 and 367.

[57] Edited by E. Mühlbacher, MGH, Diplomata Karolinorum, vol. 1, pp. 170-71 (no. 122).

[58] See above, n. 34. To the cases of Fulda and Werden, we can add that of Saint Bavo in Ghent, which had men installed in Zeeland who in the years around 800 had to hand over to the monastery one cloak every year: see Verhulst, "Das Besitzverzeichnis der Genter Sankt-Bavo-Abtei von ca. 800".

[59] For Corbie, see the diploma of 716 edited by L. Levillain, *Examen critique*; for Saint-Denis, see for example the diplomas of 691 and 716 studied by H. Atsma and J. Vezin, *Chartae Latinae Antiquiores*, vol. 14, pp. 6-8 (no. 574) and pp. 63-65 (no. 589). Commentary by D. Claude, "Der Handel im westlichen Mittelmeer während des Frühmittelalter", in K. Düwel, H. Jankuhn, H. Siems and D. Timpe eds., *Untersuchungen zu Handel und Verkehr der vor- und frühgeschichtlichen Zeit in Mittel- und Nordeuropa*, vol. 2 (Göttingen, 1985), esp. pp. 75-77.

from some tolls conceded on a seasonal basis—such as to St Denis
on the occasion of its annual fair[60]—from others on a permanent
basis—such as the revenue from the tolls of the lower Loire offered
by Sigebert III to Stavelot-Malmédy around 652-3.[61] Soon, in addition, these many renders were augmented by tithes, the payment of
which eighth-century Carolingian legislation, especially that of Pippin
III in 765 and Charlemagne in 779, imposed on all the subjects of
their kingdom. This was to become very profitable to those promoters
of rural evangelisation that were the monasteries.[62]

These products were either processed at their place of production,
or else at the monastic centres, or in their immediate neighbourhood; these latter locations had the greatest concentration of large
workshops and a specialised workforce. This, at least, is suggested
by normative and/or normalised documents such as the so-called
plan of St Gall, an ideal expression (made around 825) of a monastery
inspired by Benedict of Aniane and the decisions of the Council of
Aachen of 816, and such as the documentary evidence of the *Chronicon
Centulense* or *Chronicle of Centula/St-Riquier* by Hariulf, notably the
Institutio de diversitate officiorum that Abbot Angilbert wrote for that
abbey, which Charlemagne had wanted to make a laboratory for his
monastic reform. The plan of St Gall locates mills, breweries, bak-
eries, presses, cooperages, forges, tanneries and cobblers close to the
abbatial church.[63] In the monastic town developed around the Picard
abbey, the documents from St-Riquier, too, reveal the presence of
artisan quarters, notably blacksmiths, fullers, leather-workers, cobblers
and bakers.[64]

---

[60] See L. Levillain, "Etudes sur l'abbaye de Saint-Denis à l'époque mérovingienne. Les documents d'histoire economique", *Bibliothèque de l'Ecole des Chartes* 91
(1930), pp. 5-65; or Lebecq, "La Neustrie et la mer", esp p. 423.

[61] See F.-L. Ganshof, "A propos du tonlieu sous les Mérovingiens", in *Studi in
onore di Amintore Fanfani*, vol. 1 (Milan, 1962), pp. 293-315, esp. p. 311; and D. Claude,
"Aspekte des Binnenhandels im Merowingerreich auf Grund der Schriftquellen", in
K. Düwel, H. Jankuhn, H. Siems and D. Timpe eds., *Untersuchungen zu Handel und
Verkehr der vor- und frühgeschichtlichen Zeit in Mittel- und Nordeuropa*, vol. 3, *Der Handel
des frühen Mittelalters* (Göttingen, 1985), pp. 9-99, esp. p. 41.

[62] On the tithe, Lesne, *Histoire de la propriété ecclésiastique en France*, passim; or, more
recently, J. Paul, *L'Eglise et la culture en Occident*, vol. 1, *La sanctification de l'ordre temporel
et spirituel* (Paris, 1986), p. 82.

[63] See the works of W. Horn and E. Born and of M. Rey-Delque cited above,
n. 35.

[64] See the edition of F. Lot cited above, n. 1. See also the comments by J. Hubert,
"Saint-Riquier et le monachisme bénédictin en Gaule à l'époque carolingienne", in
Il monachesimo nell'alto medioevo e la formazione della civiltà occidentale, Settimane di stu-
dio del Centro Italiano di Studi sull'Alto Medioevo 4 (Spoleto, 1957), pp. 293-390;

The example of St Riquier, where a census of 831 counts some 2500 houses and some 7000 inhabitants (!), shows how the monasteries, even the relatively isolated ones, could become foci of new towns, thanks to their numerous peripheral activities. Also notable are the cases of the towns of Ghent and St-Omer, each born of the juxtaposition of two almost contiguous abbeys in the seventh century (St-Bravo's and St-Peter's at Mont Blandin in the former case, Sithiu/St-Bertin and Notre-Dame in the latter), which were also influential in the urban developments to come.[65]

3. *The monasteries in the great economic cycle*

In all cases, the amount of produce thus accumulated and eventually processed in monastic centres was much too great to be destined only for the use of the communities and the satisfaction of their social obligations.[66] There is no doubt that an important part of this produce was consequently sent to market. In the ninth century there was a forum, that is, a market, in the town around St Riquier; Sithiu/St Bertin obtained its own in 873; and it is probable that the *portus Ganda*, recorded around 865 at the very foot of the abbey of St Bavo, consisted not only of a landing stage, but also of a merchant settlement.[67] These three examples are monasteries

---

J. Hubert, in J. Hubert, J. Porcher and W.-F. Volbach, *L'empire carolingien, L'Univers des Formes* (Paris, 1968), pp. 1-4; J. Decarreaux, *Moines et monastères à l'époque de Charlemagne* (Paris, 1980), esp. pp. 238-44; and C. Heitz, "Saint-Riquier en 800", *Revue du Nord* 69 (1986), pp. 335-42.

[65] For Saint-Omer, see A. Derville, *Saint-Omer des origines au XIVᵉ siècle* (Lille, 1995), esp. pp. 17-28; for Ghent, in addition to the works of A. Verhulst and of A. Verhulst and G. Declercq cited above, n. 19, see other research by A. Verhulst: "Neue Ansichten über die Entstehung der Flämischen Städte am Beispiel von Gent und Antwerpen", in *Niederlande und Nordwestdeutschland. Festschrift F. Petri, Städteforschung* A 15 (Cologne, Vienna 1983), pp. 1-17; "Saint Bavon et les origines de Gand", *Revue du Nord* 69 (1986), pp. 455-69; and "Les origines et l'histoire ancienne de la ville de Gand", in *La Genèse et les premiers siècles des villes médiévales dans les Pays-Bas méridionaux. Un problème archéologique et historique*, Actes du colloque de Spa (Brussels, 1990), pp. 293-97.

[66] Thus, nearly a thousand *pallia* were transported each year from Frisia to Fulda and Werden in the ninth century, much more than was needed for monastic consumption: see Lebecq, *Marchands et navigateurs frisons*, vol. 1, pp. 132-33.

[67] For Saint-Riquier (*Chronicon Centulense*), see the works cited at n. 64, esp. Hubert, Porcher and Volbach, *L'empire carolingien*, p. 3; for Sithiu/Saint-Bertin/Saint-Omer, see Derville, *Saint-Omer*, p. 55; and for Ghent/Saint Bavo (the Martyrology of Usuard), see Verhulst and Declercq in *Gand. Apologie d'une ville rebelle*, esp. p. 49.

situated on the northern, virtually coastal, fringe of the Frankish world. That they had at their disposal ports and markets should not surprise us, because it was the northern seas that became the principal vehicles of long-distance exchange in the course of the seventh century. It is towards these that, in the eighth century, the monastic economy of Gaul and Germany would turn to find outlets and markets.

Markets and monastic fairs

The history of the origins of medieval monastic markets is still only in its infancy.[68] It should be remembered that the Carolingians declared a royal monopoly on the establishment of markets and that consequently only a royal concession could allow an abbey to open one. We know that in the eighth century St Denis was authorised to establish rural markets in some of its *villae*, beginning with Faverolles and Néron, in the Beauce towards Maintenon, where a diploma of 774—three years after their acquisition—says explicitly that they were endowed with *mercata* open to those who would come there to trade (*sive mercandi gratia convenientibus*).[69] But it was not until the ninth century that other markets were created on St Denis's estates, in particular at Cormeilles-en-Vexin, Pontoise, Saclas (near Etampes), Chaourse (near Laon), and even Esslingen (near Stuttgart).[70] Beyond St Denis, the earlier period is very badly documented: the forged diploma of 786 which attributes to St-Germain-des-Prés a market at

---

[68] Despite T. Endemann, *Markturkunde und Markt in Frankreich und Burgund vom 9. bis 11. Jahrhundert* (Konstanz, Stuttgart, 1964), M. Mitterauer, *Markt und Stadt im Mittelalter. Beiträge zur historischen Zentralitätsforschung* (Stuttgart, 1980), and P. Johanek, "Der Aussenhandel des Frankenreiches der Merowingerzeit nach Norden und Osten im Spiegel der Schriftquellen", in K. Düwel, H. Jankuhn, H. Siems and D. Timpe eds., *Untersuchungen zu Handel und Verkehr der vor- und frühgeschichtlichen Zeit in Mittel- und Nordeuropa*, vol. 4, *Der Handel der Karolinger- und Wikingerzeit* (Göttingen, 1987), pp. 7-68, esp. pp. 23-26 and 50-51 (on "the markets of the monasteries"). There is a list of recent historiography on the issue in A. Verhulst, "Marchés, marchands et commerce au haut Moyen Age dans l'hisoriogaphie récente', in *Mercati e Mercanti nell'alto Medioevo*, Settimane di studio del centro italiano di studi sull'alto Medioevo 40 (1993), pp. 23-42.

[69] Edited by E. Mühlbacher, MGH, Diplomata Karolinorum, vol. 1, pp. 125-27 (no. 87). See Devroey, "Courants et réseaux d'échange", p. 386.

[70] According to the survey conducted by Endemann, *Markturkunde und Markt in Frankreich und Burgund*. See also Johanek, "Der Aussenhandel", esp. p. 51, and S. Tange, "Production et circulation dans un domaine monastique à l'époque carolingienne: l'exemple de l'abbaye de Saint-Denis", *Revue Belge de Philologie et d'Histoire* 75 (1997), pp. 943-55, esp. p. 951.

Marolles-sur-Seine (near Montereau) is evidence only for the date of its fabrication, around the middle of the ninth century.[71] Royal concession of what German historians call *Markturkunden*, that is, of diplomas conceding the right to a market, numerous for Germany east of the Rhine but exceptional to its west (examples are the estates that Prüm possessed at Romersheim and Münstereifel), only really emerged in the second half of the ninth century.[72]

What is certain, however, is that the development of these rural markets, midpoints between the units of agricultural production and urban markets, allowed access to a lucrative market, and the opportunity to acquire cash, to peasants who had a surplus or specific produce to sell. They found this indispensable for acquiring rare goods for themselves. Cash makes its appearance in the great polyptychs of the ninth century, though still in only a small way at the beginning of the century: in that of St-Germain-des-Prés, for example, the administrator of Palaiseau owed to the abbey, among other renders in kind, four *denarii* for the right to use the wood.[73] But it appears in a much more systematic way at the end of the century, for example in the polyptych of Prüm, where the free tenants of Villance owed the abbey between fourteen and seventeen *denarii*.[74] At the same time, the development of rural markets allowed monastic institutions to disseminate not only the produce amassed in their granaries, cellars and other storehouses, but also their own coins, the right to mint which had been conceded at the same time as the right to hold markets.[75]

We are best informed about the existence of the great seasonal or annual monastic fairs. Some of these may have been very old, of ultimately Gaulish origin, control of which had been recently granted to a monastery. This was the case with the fair on 1 August at Alise-Sainte-Reine in Burgundy, conceded in 775 to the abbey of Flavigny two kilometres away.[76] Others had an apparently more

---

[71] Devroey, "Un monastère dans l'économie d'échanges", p. 581.

[72] Endemann, *Markturkunde und Markt in Frankreich und Burgund*, passim, Devroey, "Les services de transport", p. 553; and Verhulst, "Marchés, marchands", pp. 33-34.

[73] See the edition by Hägermann, Elmshäuser and Hedwig cited above, n. 1, and the comments by Elmshäuser and Hedwig, *Studien*, pp. 41-47.

[74] G. Despy, "Villes et campagnes aux IXe et Xe siècles. L'exemple du pays mosan", *Revue du Nord* 50 (1968), pp. 145-68.

[75] Devroey, "Les services de transport", p. 553, Toubert, "La part du grand domaine", p. 83, and Tange, "Production et circulation", pp. 952-53.

[76] Devroey, "Courants et réseaux d'échange", p. 379, following Mitterauer, *Markt und Stadt im Mittelalter*, pp. 87-93.

recent origin, such as, notwithstanding some statements to the contrary,[77] the fair at St Denis. A forged charter generally dated to the end of the ninth century attributes its creation to Dagobert, and Léon Levillain, who has made an erudite analysis of it, thinks that it was indeed set up in 634-5.[78] The St Denis fair opened each year on 9 October (the feast day of the abbey's patron saint) between the monastery and the banks of the Seine, its date coinciding with the end of the grape harvest in the Ile-de-France. It was primarily a wine fair, even if, as an authentic diploma of 753 attests, other products were sold there (*ad negociandum vel necocia plurima exercendum et vina conparandum*). Among these may have figured those explicitly mentioned in the forgery, such as honey and madder, a red plant dye highly-prized by textile workers.[79]

Since the kings had granted to the monks the collection of tolls from the fair for its entire duration and in the whole jurisdiction of the counts of Paris—an extraordinary privilege, the first of its kind in the history of Merovingian kingship—the counts considered themselves damaged and contested the concession of toll to the abbey. Royal judgements of 710 and 753—the first authentic documents concerning the St Denis fairs that have survived[80]—confirmed the rights of the monastery, and, in doing so, show us the extent of the fairs' success in the first half of the eighth century, as well as the attractive force they exerted on a numerous and varied clientele—formed partly of other producers from the Paris region, partly of buyers from further afield, sometimes from the far north.

---

[77] A. Lombard-Jourdan, "Les foires de l'abbaye de Saint-Denis. Revue des données et révision des opinions admises", *Bibliothèque de l'Ecole des Chartes* 145 (1987), pp. 273-336. I am unconvinced by this study, which sustains the notion of a Gaulish origin for the Saint-Denis fair.

[78] Levillain, "Etudes", esp. p. 14, Lebecq, "La Neustrie et la mer", p. 423. The forged charter of Dagobert can be found in G. Pertz ed., MGH, Diplomata regum Francorum, vol. 1, pp. 140-41 (no. 23), or in Lebecq, *Marchands et navigateurs frisons*, vol. 2, pp. 404-05.

[79] The 753 diploma has been edited by Mühlbacher, MGH, Diplomata Karolinorum, vol. 1, pp. 9-11 (no. 6), and by Lebecq, *Marchands et navigateurs frisons*, vol. 2, pp. 401-02.

[80] See previous note for the 753 diploma; for that of 710, see Pertz ed., MGH, Diplomata regum Francorum, vol. 1, pp. 68-9 (no. 77), or Lebecq, *Marchands et navigateurs frisons*, vol. 2, pp. 401-02.

The opening of monastic markets to northern commerce

In 710, in fact, the St Denis fair was already frequented by *omnes neguciantes aut Saxonis vel quascumquelibit nacionis*, and in 753 there were *omnes necuciantes, tam Saxsones quam Frisiones vel alias naciones promiscuas*.[81] In other words, around the beginning of the eighth century Saxon merchants had established themselves in the great Parisian market; and in the middle of the century the Frisians, who had perhaps been hidden among the other, anonymous, nations present in 710, had certainly joined them.

It is clear, taking account of the terminology of the period, that the Saxons of St Denis were in fact Anglo-Saxons, and we can even add that most of them were West Saxons. Indeed, they appear both in texts and in archaeological sources as the initiators of a regular connection between Wessex, via Hamwic, and the Seine. On the one hand, the *Vita Willibaldi* by Hugeburc shows the existence around 720 of a regular shipping route between the *mercimonium que dicitur Hamwih* (Hamwic, in modern Southampton, Wessex's outlet to the sea) and the *urbs que vocatur Rotum* ("the city which is called Rouen").[82] On the other hand, investigations of the wooded site of La Londe near Rouen have unearthed the eighth-century potters' kilns from which came the majority of the Neustrian ceramics discovered at the site of Hamwic.[83]

The formulae of the St Denis diplomas suggest that these West Saxons were among the foreigners who held a dominant position at the St Denis fair throughout the eighth century (and still in the ninth century, if we can believe the forged diploma of Dagobert, which also mentions them specifically), and that the Frisians came in their wake to some extent (perhaps partly because they had got into the

---

[81] See the references in the two previous notes.

[82] Hugeburc, *Vita Willibaldi* (third quarter of the eighth century), ch. 3, ed. O. Holder-Egger, MGH Scriptores XV.1, p. 91; also Lebecq, *Marchands et navigateurs frisons*, vol. 1, pp. 88-90.

[83] See R. Hodges, *The Hamwih Pottery: the local and imported wares from 30 years' excavations at Middle Saxon Southampton and their European context* (London, 1981), R. Hodges, "The eighth-century pottery industry at La Londe, near Rouen, and its implications for cross-Channel trade with Hamwic, Anglo-Saxon Southampton", *Antiquity* 65 (1991), and N. Roy, "Un atelier de poterie du haut Moyen Age en forêt de La Londe, près de Rouen (Seine-Maritime). Etat de la recherche", in D. Piton ed., *La céramique du IVe au Xe siècle dans l'Europe du Nord-Ouest*, Actes du colloque d'Outreau, Nord-Ouest Archéologie, n° hors-série (1993), pp. 341-54.

habit of visiting the market at Hamwic),[84] even though the sources suggest the existence of an independent connection between the lower Seine and Frisia,[85] and even though Frisians were probably responsible for bringing to the monastic town at St Denis the sherds of the beautiful Rhenish ceramic called Tating ware that have been discovered there.[86]

It is known, in fact, that the Frisians preferred to explore the route in their immediate hinterland, that is, the route up the Rhine, punctuated by important industrial and wine-selling markets, monastic ones among them. Our knowledge begins with the story told in the *Vita*, or rather the *Miracula*, of St Maximin of Trier of the Frisian Ibbo who, in the course of the eighth century, gave himself to the monastery of St Maximin with what the *Vita prima* calls *omnibus quae habebat*, and what the *Vita secunda* calls *sua substantia*, meaning all his fortune: in other words his capital, his boat or boats, and perhaps his slaves. Thenceforth he conducted for the monastery merchant voyages across the sea that until then he had made for his own benefit.[87] Doubtless he had already had business dealings with the monastery before his self-dedication, and it was these dealings which led him to put his person and his goods at the disposal of Trier's patron saint.

Perhaps this anecdote helps to illuminate the development, attested later in the Middle Ages thanks to urban microtoponymy, but which might date back to an earlier era, of the Frisian quarter of Cologne, which developed in the immediate neighbourhood of the suburban monastery of St Gereon, known as having been an important wine market.[88] Perhaps it also helps to explain the mention in the polyptych

---

[84] On the presence of Frisians at Hamwic, see Lebecq, *Marchands et navigateurs frisons*, vol. 1, pp. 90-91.

[85] See Pseudo-Jonas, *Vita Vulframni*, ed., W. Levison, MGH Scriptores rerum merowingicarum V (Hannover, 1910), pp. 657-73. See S. Lebecq, "Vulfran, Willibrord et la mission de Frise; pour une relecture de la Vita Vulframni", in *L'Évangélisation des régions entre Meuse et Moselle et la fondation de l'abbaye d'Echternach (5ᵉ-9ᵉ siècle)*, Actes du colloque de Luxembourg/Echternach, Oct. 1998 (Luxembourg, forthcoming).

[86] N. Meyer-Rodrigues, "Tessons de céramique dite de Tating découverts à Saint-Denis", in *La céramique du IVᵉ au Xᵉ siècle dans l'Europe du Nord-Ouest*, pp. 267-74.

[87] *Vita prima Maximini*, ch. 14, AASS Boll. May VII, p. 24; Lupus of Ferrières, *Vita secunda*, ed. B. Krusch, MGH Scriptores rerum merowingicarum III (Hannover, 1893), pp. 80-1; also in Lebecq, *Marchands et navigateurs frisons*, vol. 2, pp. 142-45, and see the comments in vol. 1, pp. 28-29.

[88] Lebecq, *Marchands et navigateurs frisons*, vol. 1, pp. 39-41.

of Prüm, at the entry for *Dusburhg* (Duisburg, at the confluence of the Ruhr and the Rhine), of Frisians who, in contrast to the majority of other tenants, owed renders in money to the monastery, payable partly at Martinmas, partly at Easter.[89]

Thus it seems that at the dawn of the eighth century the seafaring peoples of the North were drawn by monastic markets and fairs into the heart of Neustria and Austrasia, and that, if some only came there seasonally (such as the Anglo-Saxons at St Denis), others settled for longer periods (as did the Frisians at Trier and Cologne). In order to buy the wine and other produce of which they had ultimately come in search they needed a means of exchange. This was most likely a silver coin, and more specifically the so-called *sceattas* that were disseminated through the heart of the Continent: their proliferation helped to precipitate the monetary conversion of the Continent to the minting of silver *denarii*.[90]

It is not therefore surprising that archaeologists have discovered a presumed English *sceatta* in the excavations at Villiers-le-Sec, in the middle of the land of St Denis, which arrived there at precisely the moment when the abbey began to issue its own *denarii*, minted with the legend "SCI DIONVSII".[91] As a result, the historian might be led to speculate: perhaps the St Denis fair that year had been the occasion of a meeting between an Anglo-Saxon merchant and a dependant of the monastery who had a comfortable surplus; perhaps, with the levy accrued from that transaction and a thousand others, the powerful abbey had recycled the silver as its own *denarii*.

The monasteries in distant markets

Not only did the greatest monasteries of Neustria and Austrasia attract merchants from distant horizons, but they also came to put on the road their own men, sometimes even their own merchants.

---

[89] Lebecq, *Marchands et navigateurs frisons*, vol. 2, pp. 388-90, with comments in vol. 1, p. 29.

[90] See D. Hill and D.M. Metcalf eds., *Sceattas in England and on the continent*, BAR British Series 128 (Oxford, 1984), and P. Grierson and M. Blackburn, *Medieval European Coinage*, vol. 1, *The Early Middle Ages (5th-10th centuries)* (Cambridge, 1986), esp. pp. 149-89.

[91] See Guadagnin, *Un village au temps de Charlemagne*, pp. 307-8 (for the *sceatta* of Villiers-le-Sec) and pp. 310-12 (for the Merovingian and Carolingian *denarii* of Saint-Denis).

I will not discuss in detail those envoys of the monasteries (*missi*, as they were called at Corbie in 716), who collected renders in scarce produce, for example from the *cellaria fisci* of the Midi—privileges normally reserved for the exclusive use of the monastery, like the oil that St Denis fetched from Marseille, and which was used to provide lighting for the monastery, or like the many exotic products that Corbie received from Fos-sur-Mer.[92] The effect of these advantages was anyway progressively reduced, because the eighth century saw a gradual weakening of Mediterranean commerce.[93] On the other hand, according to Charlemagne's diploma of 779 for St-Germain-des-Prés, it was the *negociantes ipsius sancti loci* who plied the routes *ubicumque in regna nostra*, with their pack animals, their carts or their boats. They were exempted from all tolls, not only on the land routes and internal waterways, but also at Rouen, Quentovic, Amiens, Maastricht and Dorestad.[94] It was these sites—old ones like Rouen, Amiens and, to a lesser extent, Maastricht, or new ones like Quentovic and Dorestad[95]—that were in the process of becoming the principal ports of northern Gaul. It was from them that the men of St-Germain got the goods that other sources record in the markets for products from the north and north-east: metals, fabrics, furs, amber and other precious materials, perhaps coming from the far east via the Russian rivers.[96] Nor should we forget the books produced by insular scriptoria, increasingly active from the end of the seventh century, some of which were expressly intended for Continental monasteries.[97]

The case of Quentovic, a *vicus* on the Canche and Neustria's window on the sea, is particularly instructive: a number of monasteries were endowed with lands there that gave ready access to the sea and its traffic. These were not only nearby houses, such as Centula/St Riquier, which in the first half of the ninth century possessed two plots of land in the *vicus* itself, or St Bertin and St Vaast, which

---

[92] See the references above, n. 59.

[93] See Claude, "Der Handel im westlichen Mittelmeer", passim.

[94] See the reference above, n. 57.

[95] See S. Lebecq, "Pour une histoire parallèle de Quentovic et Dorestad", in J.-M. Duvosquel and A. Dierkens eds., *Villes et campagnes au Moyen Age. Mélanges Georges Despy* (Liège, 1991), pp. 415-28.

[96] See Lebecq, *Marchands et navigateurs frisons*, vol. 1, e.g. p. 269.

[97] An obvious example is the Echternach Gospels, an evangeliary made, apparently, at Lindisfarne about 700 and intended for the continental monastery of Echternach: see M.P. Brown, *Anglo-Saxon Manuscripts* (London, 1991), p. 63.

acquired property in the surrounding countryside, but also much more distant foundations, like Ferrières-en-Gâtinais and Fontenelle.[98] The latter case is noteworthy: Fontenelle, which already had its *portus* on the Seine, possessed, according to ninth-century sources, both the church of St Peter *quae vicina est emporio Quentouico* and several farms (*mansi*) *in portu Wiscus*.[99] The establishment of this branch of Fontenelle at Quentovic explains two points in our evidence: the designation by Charlemagne in 787 of its abbot Geroald as procurator at Quentovic and other ports in the vicinity,[100] and the itinerary followed by the monks during the translation of the relics of St Wandrille in 858 because of the Viking threat, which led them to end up very naturally in the aforesaid church of St Peter.[101]

St-Germain-des-Prés, which had no property at Quentovic, seems to have profited rather from a grant by the king of exemption from toll at that port, since, according to the polyptych of Irminon, the peasants of two of its *villae*, Villemeult and Combs-la-Ville, owed it regular *wichariae*, which has been correctly interpreted as obligations of transport service at Quentovic.[102] The demand thus imposed on the peasants suggests that the monks were not seeking solely to acquire imported goods for themselves, but also to sell part of their agricultural surplus there.

*   *   *

Following the example of St-Germain-des-Prés, therefore, the largest monasteries of the Frankish world had unquestionably become components of the new commercial economy that was emerging in northern Europe. Through the intermediary of their monks, their merchants and more simply their "men", they had become active agents of exchange, even of large-scale trade.

---

[98] See Lebecq, "La Neustrie et la mer", esp. pp. 426-28; and S. Lebecq, "Quentovic: un état de la question", *Studien zur Sachsenforschung* 8 (1993), pp. 73-82.

[99] Lebecq, "Quentovic", p. 77 (church of Saint Peter, known from the *Miracula sancti Wandregisili*, ed. O. Holder-Egger, MGH Scriptores XV/1, p. 408) and p. 80 (manses *in portu Wiscus*, cited in a diploma of 854, ed. F. Lot, *Etudes critiques*, p. XIV and p. 34).

[100] Lebecq, "Quentovic", p. 79 (according to the *Gesta sanctum patrum Fontanellensium*, s.a. 787, ed. F. Lohier and J. Laporte (Paris-Rouen, 1936), p. 86).

[101] Lebecq, "Quentovic", esp. pp.   ̄ ?0.

[102] See the edition of D. Hägerı   , K. Elmshäuser and A. Hedwig, cited at note 1, pp. 58 and 139, and the comments of Devroey, "Un monastère dans l'économie d'échanges", pp. 573 and 577.

The seventh-century sources show us the environmental conditions for the foundation of monasteries and their necessary opening to the secular world. Those of the ninth century allow us to glimpse their economic flowering, attained thanks to an increasingly normalised model of administration and to a political environment temporarily made peaceful by Carolingian government. Those of the eighth century, although not very numerous and hardly prolix, have nevertheless allowed us to see, firstly, the first attempts by the Frankish monasteries to turn their principal landed bases into economic centres provided with the necessary capacity for processing their produce and able to exert their influence on the surrounding countryside and peasantry. Secondly, they indicate the monasteries' concern to take advantage of the communication systems and the political and fiscal protection necessary to transport their produce between their more outlying estates and these centres, and between these centres and the markets—transport for which they mobilised the service of their men, some of whom were considered to be specialised merchants. Thirdly, they demonstrate the monasteries' openness to the routes and markets of interregional and international commerce, which increasingly turned its back on the Mediterranean and grafted itself onto the by then fully-developed maritime routes of northern Europe, where they encountered (or from where they attracted) the free merchants of the British Isles and Frisia.

Perhaps it is this openness to the markets and to the outlets of the far north which most characterises the political economy of the Frankish monasteries of the eighth century, or at least those that were closest to the emerging, and later established, centres of power of the Pippinid house. It is surely no accident that the most prominent of them in our sources are those of St Denis, St-Germain-des-Prés, or even St Maximin at Trier, that is, suburban monasteries, next door to substantial cities that, at the same time, were important markets for wine.

[Translated by Marios Costambeys]

BEFORE OR AFTER MISSION
SOCIAL RELATIONS ACROSS THE MIDDLE AND LOWER RHINE IN THE SEVENTH AND EIGHTH CENTURIES

Ian Wood

Central to any reading of the economy of the eighth century is the history of the *emporia* of the Rhineland, Dorestad and Domburg,[1] to which one should add other mercantile centres including the city of Cologne.[2] Dorestad, in particular, is known from archaeological and numismatic evidence to have had trading links over a vast area, stretching from Mainz and the Middle Rhine, to London, York, Haithabu, Kaupang and Birka.[3] The obvious arteries for this trading network are the coastlines of the North Sea and the waters of the lower Rhine. At the same time cemetery archaeology suggests that this riverine pattern was crossed by links from the Frankish heartlands, across the Rhine into Saxony. The majority of this material comes, admittedly, from the Migration period proper,[4] but the evidence for the sixth and seventh centuries has also prompted questions on the extent of Frankish settlement in Westfalia.[5] A subsequent decline in supposedly Frankish material has been linked to a Saxon victory over the Frankish *Bructeri* in the 690s, recorded by Bede.[6] Archaeology might suggest a hiatus in connections in Frankish

---

[1] R. Hodges, *Dark Age Economics* (London, 1982), pp. 47-65.

[2] S. Schütte, "Continuity problems and authority structures in Cologne", in G. Ausenda ed., *After Empire: towards an ethnology of Europe's barbarians* (Woodbridge, 1995), pp. 163-69.

[3] See the map in W.A. van Es and W.A.M. Hessing eds., *Romeinen, Friezen en Franken in het hart van Nederland* (Bodemonderzoek, 1994), p. 95.

[4] H.W. Böhme, "Ethnos und Religion der Bewohner Westfalens", in C. Stiegemann and M. Wemhoff eds., *Kunst und Kultur der Karolingerzeit, Karl der Große und Papst Leo in Paderborn, Beiträge zum Katalog der Austellung Paderborn 1999* (Mainz, 1999), pp. 237-45.

[5] F. Siegmund, "Frühmittelalterliche Gräberfelder in Ostwestfalen", *Kunst und Kultur der Karolingerzeit, Karl der Große und Papst Leo in Paderborn, Beiträge zum Katalog der Austellung Paderborn 1999*, pp. 256-62.

[6] Bede, *Historia Ecclesiastica*, V 11, eds. B. Colgrave and R.A.B. Mynors, *Bede: Ecclesiastical History of the English People* (Oxford, 1969); C. Grünewald, "Frühmittelalterliche Gräbfelder im Münsterland", *Kunst und Kultur der Karolingerzeit, Karl der Große und Papst Leo in Paderborn, Beiträge zum Katalog der Austellung Paderborn 1999*, p. 252.

influence. On the other hand, if there was any disruption, it was soon ended by the expansion of Carolingian power, which also prompted a period of economic expansion in the course of the eighth century.[7] The eastern ports of the Frankish trade-routes—Bardowick, Scheessel, Magdeburg, Erfurt, Hallstadt, Forchheim, Pfreimd, Regensburg, and Lorch—are listed in Charlemagne's Thionville capitulary of 806.[8]

The archaeological picture for the eighth century has not often been set against what the written evidence implies about the aristocracy of the Middle and Lower Rhine, and of the regions directly to the east, in the preCarolingian period. Yet the upper classes of eastern Francia, Thuringia, Hesse, Frisia and Saxony must have formed part of the market for the merchants of the Rhineland. The evidence for these aristocracies is certainly fragmentary, but, arguably, it has been underused, except by proponents of the science of *Namenforschung*.[9] My intention is to look at what can be established of the aristocracies of Thuringia, Hesse, Frisia and Saxony and at their connections with the Rhineland before the Carolingian take-over. As far as possible I will draw on material that predates that expansion, but more often than not I will have to infer information from late eighth century material. The cut-off point of my investigation, however, will be the Saxon wars of Charlemagne.

Bavaria might also have been included in this survey—and indeed Bavarians had a large part to play in the history of the monastery of Fulda, which provides some of my evidence—but historians have been more ready to acknowledge the connections of the Agilolfings with the Merovingian world,[10] than they have those of the Hedenen, of Widukind, Hessi or even, perhaps, Radbod: indeed the Agilolfing family is better known than its northern counterparts. Further, Agilolfing links with Italy mean that parts of Bavaria, at least, had a different orientation than Thuringia and places north.

---

[7] For new gravefields, T. Capelle, *Die Sachsen des frühen Mittelalters* (Darmstadt, 1998), pp. 125-26. For Carolingian trade in the region: H. Steuer, "Handel und Wirtschaft in der Karolingerzeit", *Kunst und Kultur der Karolingerzeit, Karl der Große und Papst Leo in Paderborn, Beiträge zum Katalog der Austellung Paderborn 1999*, pp. 406-16.

[8] *Capitulare* 44, ed. A. Boretius, *Capitularia Regum Francorum* 1, *Monumenta Germaniae Historica, Leges*, sectio 2 (Hannover, 1883).

[9] E.g. W. Metz, "Austrasische Adelsherrschaft des 8. Jahrhunderts. Mittelrheinische Grundherren in Ostfranken, Thüringen und Hessen", *Historisches Jahrbuch* 87 (1967), pp. 257-304.

[10] E. Zöllner, "Die Herrkunft der Agilolfinger", *Mitteilungen des Instituts für Österreichische Geschichtsforschung* 59 (1951), pp. 245-64.

The Carolingian expansion east of the Rhine can, in a sense, be seen as drawing what had once been a group of peripheral duchies into the mainstream of European history. Certainly, one result of that expansion was the multiplication of sources for a region which had hitherto featured only rarely in written evidence. This is not to say that the peripheral duchies of the Merovingian period, Thuringia, Alemannia and Bavaria, had been of no significance in the seventh century, nor that there have been no attempts to write a history of those duchies.[11] Further, there has been considerable study of specific aspects of the archaeology of these eastern territories over recent years. In addition to the finds from cemetery excavations, time and again preCarolingian archaeological layers have been discovered on Carolingian sites—including Eichstätt, Fulda and Solnhofen[12]—providing further insights into this peripheral world. Many of these sites, however, were reused as a result of the "Anglo-Saxon mission", and are, as a consequence, dealt with in the context of a historiographical model which draws a sharp distinction between the so-called "missionary" era and what came before. And just as the sources relating to Anglo-Saxon saints on the continent prompt historians to distinguish between a pagan Merovingian era in the peripheral duchies and a Christian Carolingian era that followed it, so too the sources for Carolingian politics lead modern interpreters to make a distinction between a somewhat haphazard Merovingian hegemony east of the Rhine which failed in the seventh century, and a Carolingian empire which led directly to the creation of the kingdom of Germany.

It is not my concern here to deal directly with these divisions of period—although an implicit aspect of my argument is that the divisions have been radically overstated, or perhaps misrepresented. This is a point to which I shall return in the closing section of this paper.

I will begin with a brief discussion of some early Fulda charters, although these can only shed light retrospectively on the situation in Thuringia and Hesse before the rule of Pippin III. I will then turn to a small number of early charters from the Echternach *Liber Aureus*, to consider the significance of some contacts east and west of the Rhine in the early years of the eighth century. This will raise questions

---

[11] K.F. Werner, "Les principautés périphériques dans le monde franc du VIIIe siècle", *I problemi dell'occidente nel secolo VIII*, Settimane di studio del Centro italiano di studi sull'alto Medioevo 20 (Spoleto, 1973), pp. 483-514; I.N. Wood, *The Merovingian Kingdoms 450-751* (London, 1994), pp. 160-64.

[12] D. Parsons, "Some Churches of the Anglo-Saxon missionaries in southern Germany: a review", *Early Medieval Europe* 8 (1999), pp. 41, 46, 66.

of connections with the peripheral zones of both Thuringia and Frisia. For Frisia it will be necessary to look beyond the charter evidence to the hagiography, most notably to the mid-ninth-century *Life of Liudger* by Altfrid, and this text in turn will raise questions about the extent to which Saxony was connected to the territories to the West. Armed with an awareness of social contacts between the peripheral duchies and Frankish Austrasia, it will be possible to conclude with some observations on the actual, as opposed to perceived, importance of Carolingian expansion and Anglo-Saxon activity to the east of the Rhine in the eighth century.

Boniface founded the monastery of Fulda in 744 in the forest of Bochonia, in what is portrayed in the late-eighth-century *Life of Sturm* as wilderness.[13] Archaeology has shown that the site of the monastery was anything but the desert represented by the hagiographer,[14] and the obvious conclusion to be drawn is that the description of the site provided by Eigil is essentially a *topos*: since the fourth century monasteries had been founded in metaphorical deserts.[15] On the other hand the land round Fulda was territory that had only recently fallen into the jurisdiction of the Carolingians. There might, therefore, be a case for arguing that, while the area round the site of the monastery, *Eihloha* in the *Silva Bochonia*, and more generally the Grapfeld, may not have been wilderness, it could have been an area isolated from the world of the Franks: the foundation of the monastery might suddenly have opened the region up to Carolingian influence. This, indeed, is another way of reading Eigil's account of the foundation of Fulda in the *Life of Sturm*. According to Eigil, once Sturm had identified the site of the future monastery Boniface approached Carlomann, asking him for the land—this may, perhaps, indicate that at least part of it was public, and belonged to the fisc.[16] The *maior* granted what was asked of him, and in addition he instructed the local population to hand over the property in the immediate

---

[13] Eigil, *Vita Sturmi*, 8, ed. P. Engelbert, *Die Vita Sturmi des Eigil von Fulda* (Marburg, 1968).

[14] C.J. Wickham, "European forests in the Early Middle Ages: landscape and land clearance", *L'ambiente vegetale nell'alto medioevo*, Settimane di studio del Centro italiano di studi sull'alto Medioevo 37 (Spoleto, 1990), pp. 482-83.

[15] Wickham, "European forests in the Early Middle Ages: landscape and land clearance", pp. 483-84.

[16] Wickham, "European forests in the Early Middle Ages: landscape and land clearance", p. 484.

vicinity, for the new foundation.[17] Neither of the readings of Eigil presented so far, however, are confirmed by the surviving charters of Fulda. Admittedly we do not have a complete collection of charters, especially from the monastery's earliest years, and it may be that there is a particularly misleading lacuna over the initial endowments, but what survives is substantial enough to be suggestive.

Taking the archive of the monastery for its first thirty years what stands out is the relative absence of land donated by anyone other than the Carolingians in the Grapfeld.[18] Instead there is a predominance of charters for the *pagi* of Mainz[19] (not surprising since that was the cathedral city of Boniface and Lull) and Worms.[20] Indeed so numerous are the charters for these two *pagi*, and so full is the evidence contained in them, that one can reconstruct detailed patterns of property holding. The charters for Mainz and Worms, as well as such other leading settlements in their *pagi* as Bingen, are careful to describe boundaries, and in doing so talk of roads, and of neighbours and their properties. The early Fulda archive is a remarkable source for the urban geography of the middle Rhine.

It is not until 758 that there is an authentic charter donating land in the Grapfeld itself.[21] In that year a man called Manoltus gave property in the district of Meiningen to Fulda. The earlier silence of the charters does not indicate much local enthusiasm for the new foundation—and it may suggest that Eigil was at best referring to very local landowners, perhaps tenants of the royal fisc, when he wrote that Carlomann told the local landowners to give their property to the new monastery, and that they did as he suggested *cum omni diligentia*.[22] Certainly, the evidence as it stands suggests that the population of the Grapfeld in general did not instantly take to supporting Boniface's foundation. After Manoltus' grant there was another gap before more land in the region was granted to Fulda. Then in 770 Egi and Sigihilt gave Münnerstadt in the Grapfeld and Halsheim

---

[17] Eigil, *Vita Sturmi*, 12.

[18] For the Carolingian donations the documentation has to be reconstructed from the hagiography or from forgeries: see the Fulda charters, 4-9, ed. E.E. Stengel, *Urkundenbuch des Klosters Fulda* 1 (Marburg, 1956), (henceforth Stengel). See also Wickham, "European forests in the Early Middle Ages: landscape and land clearance", p. 483.

[19] E.g. Stengel, 11, 18, 29-33, 37, 41, 48, 64.

[20] E.g. Stengel, 22-8, 40, 42, 44, 49, 55, 58, 59, 61.

[21] Stengel, 32.

[22] Eigil, *Vita Sturmi*, 12.

in the Werngau.[23] Two years later Alwalah endowed Fulda with land at Rannungen in the Grapfeld, together with property in a large number of other places, including Bergtheim near Würzburg and Gorsleban and Görsbach *in regione Thuringorum*.[24] The next year, 773, Neriperaht and his wife Ratburg donated land at Nordheim in the Grapfeld.[25] Slowly but surely thereafter property-holders in the Grapfeld came to endow their local monastery.

What, one might ask, do these grants show us about the landowners of the Grapfeld in the eighth century? The land in the *Silva Bochonia* granted by Carlomann may well have been fiscal,[26] which is to say that it will have been under the Hedenen dukes of Thuringia until shortly before the foundation of Fulda—a point that is probably worth bearing in mind,[27] and one to which I shall come back. Turning to other donors, however, it is important to ask, initially, whether they were locals or Frankish incomers. Here it is only possible to say that Manoltus gave an estate which he had inherited from his father,[28] which indicates that his family had longstanding links with the Grapfeld, but since it is the only estate mentioned in the charter it is impossible to tell whether the donor also had lands elsewhere. The grant given by Neriperaht and Ratburg was also of hereditary land,[29] but again the charter only concerns one estate. The best one can say is that neither of these grants are likely to have been made by Frankish incomers. Some of Awalah's vast estates were certainly hereditary—Wolfgang Metz remarked that "*(a)uf ältere Wurzeln dürfte Alawahs thüringischer Besitz in der Tat zurückgehen*" ("Alawah's Thuringian property must in fact have had older roots"),[30] but the charter is not explicit about the estate in the Grapfeld.[31] It is not, therefore, possible to work out to what extent his grant can be used

---

[23] Stengel, 51.

[24] Stengel, 57; Metz, "Austrasische Adelsherrschaft des 8. Jahrhunderts. Mittelrheinische Grundherren in Ostfranken, Thüringen und Hessen", p. 298.

[25] Stengel, 65.

[26] Wickham, "European forests in the Early Middle Ages: landscape and land clearance", p. 484.

[27] One might note here the description of the site as "a somewhat isolated strategic centre": Wickham, "European forests in the Early Middle Ages: landscape and land clearance", p. 483.

[28] Stengel, 32.

[29] Stengel, 65.

[30] Metz, "Austrasische Adelsherrschaft des 8. Jahrhunderts. Mittelrheinische Grundherren in Ostfranken, Thüringen und Hessen", p. 298.

[31] Stengel, 57.

to determine normal patterns of landholding in Hesse and Thuringia in the preCarolingian period—although at face value the Awalah charter does suggest that Thuringian notables could hold widely scattered estates: and here it is worth listing the full extent of his gift: Essleben (Unterfranken, Bezirksamt Schweinfurt), Bergtheim (Mittelfranken, Bezirksamt Würzburg?), Pleichfeld (Bezirksamt Würzburg and Kitzingen), Schwanfeld (Bezirksamt Schweinfurt), Eisenheim (Alsace, Bezirkamt Gerolzhofen?), Gramschatz (Bezirksamt Karlstadt), Schwebenried (Unterfranken, Bezirksamt Schweinfurt?), Rannungen (Bezirksamt Kissingen), Üttingen (Bezirksamt Markheidenfeld), Adalhalmastat (?), Tutinga (?), Gorsleben (Sachsen, Kreis Eckartsberga), Görsbach (Sachsen, Kreis Sangerhausen), Tricusti (Sachsen, Sonderhausen, Schwartzburg), Tennstädt (Sachsen, Kreis Langensalza), Grunaha (Gruna bei Schernberg, Schwarzburg, Landratsamt Sonderhausen?), Auuenheimstetin (Auenheim, Sachsen-Weimar), Sussra (Schwarzburg, Landratsamt Sonderhausen), Hiltigeristetin (Sachsen-Gotha), Ehrich (Schwarzburg, Landratsamt Sonderhausen), and Geisenheim (Hessen-Nassau).[32] However Alwalah acquired this land, it does not represent the property of a purely backwoods family of the Grapfeld. One might wish to compare this case with that of a later charter of 780/1, in which members of the Rhineland Rupertiner clan gave land, held *ab antiquis*, to Fulda,[33] and to see Alwalah likewise as a member of a family, perhaps originally of Frankish extraction, which had long held property over a wide range of territory.

To try to look further into aristocratic landholding, at least in the Würzburg region, where some of Alwalah's property is to be found, it is necessary to turn back in time to the charters of Echternach, which, although fewer in number, begin a generation earlier. The earliest benefactors of Willibrord and his monastery of Echternach are led by Plectrudis, the wife of Pippin II, and her mother, Irmina.[34] There is, however, a small group of charters which are of particular interest for the present enquiry. It is made up of two donations,

---

[32] Stengel, 57: the identifications are given pp. 93-94.
[33] Stengel, 145 a.b.; Metz, "Austrasische Adelsherrschaft des 8. Jahrhunderts. Mittelrheinische Grundherren in Ostfranken, Thüringen und Hessen", p. 288.
[34] C. Wampach, *Geschichte der Grundherrschaft Echternach im Frühmittelalter* 1, 2, Quellenband (Luxembourg, 1930), (henceforth Wampach) 2-4, 6, 9-10, 12, 14-15. It is necessary to note that the majority of the early grants were made to Willibrord personally, rather than to Echternach: M. Costambeys, "An aristocratic community on the northern Frankish frontier 690-726", *Early Medieval Europe* 3 (1994), p. 40.

both of them given by *dux* Heden II of Thuringia (c. 704-c. 717). In
704 he and his wife Theodora gave Willibrord land in the region
of Erfurt (Arnstadt and der Weisse and Mühlberg) and Weimar
(Monra).[35] Thirteen years later, in 717, Heden endowed the saint
with Hammelburg on the Saale, between Würzburg and Fulda.[36]
These grants are of particular importance, because they serve to
highlight the extent to which we have to overcome Carolingian propaganda in order to understand the peripheral duchies of the Frankish
world. In Willibald's *Life of Boniface*, written in the third quarter of
the eighth century, Heden appears alongside Theobald as one of the
rulers who allowed Thuringia to lapse into paganism.[37] Yet he was
one of the earliest benefactors of Willibrord: indeed, if one distin-
guishes, as seems necessary, between grants made to Echternach by
Irmina and Plectrudis and those made by Pippin and Plectrudis, as
well as between benefactions made to the monastery and those made
to Willibrord himself, it becomes clear that Heden was actually
involved in supporting Willibrord, and indirectly his monastery, earlier
than any male Pippinid.[38] The image of Heden as a lacklustre
Christian must derive from the ensuing conflict between Heden and
the Austrasians (presumably Charles Martel), noted in the *Passio
Kiliani*.[39] One might envisage a similar reason for Willibald's dismissal

---

[35] Wampach, 8. On the Heden charters see also Costambeys, "An aristocratic
community on the northern Frankish frontier 690-726", pp. 61-62. See also Metz,
"Austrasische Adelsherrschaft des 8. Jahrhunderts. Mittelrheinische Grundherren in
Ostfranken, Thüringen und Hessen", pp. 259, 277, 280, 283-85, 303-04.

[36] Wampach, 26. For other gifts in the region see Metz, "Austrasische Adelsherrschaft
des 8. Jahrhunderts. Mittelrheinische Grundherren in Ostfranken, Thüringen und
Hessen", p. 283.

[37] Willibald, *Vita Bonifatii*, 6, ed. W. Levison, *Vitae sancti Bonifatii* (Hannover/Leipzig,
1905).

[38] Metz, "Austrasische Adelsherrschaft des 8. Jahrhunderts. Mittelrheinische Grundherren in Ostfranken, Thüringen und Hessen", p. 277, also argued for a seventh-
century connection between the Würzburg *duces* and the monastery of Wießenburg,
citing *Codex Edilini* n. 31, 36, 37, in Zeuß's edition, which was reproduced in J.M.
Pardessus, *Diplomata, Chartae, Epistolae, Leges ad res Gallo-Francicas spectantia*, 2 (Paris,
1849). This does not appear to be supported, however, by the new edition of
C. Dette, *Liber Possessionum Wizenburgensis* (Mainz, 1987), where the properties in
the Saalegau, at Aschach near Bad Kissingen and Fuchsstadt, south of Würzburg,
listed in entries 31, 36, 37, are seen as later acquisitions.

[39] *Passio Kiliani*, 14, ed. W. Levison, *Monumenta Germaniae Historica, Scriptores Rerum
Merovingicarum* 5 (Hannover, 1910); the passage is discussed by H. Mordek, "Die
Hedenen als politische Kraft im austrasischen Frankenreich", in J. Jarnut, U. Nonn
and M. Richter eds., *Karl Martell in seiner Zeit* (Sigmaringen, 1994), pp. 346-48.

of Dettic and Deorulf,[40] two Hessan leaders who may have had connections with Mainz.[41]

It is, in fact, reasonably clear that the family of the Hedenen was
closely tied in to the Merovingian political scene, and that members
of the family played a significant role in the incorporation of Thuringia
into the Frankish world in the late seventh century.[42] Heden I (c. 643–
c. 676) may even have been the ruler who issued the ostentatiously
Christian *Lex Ribvaria*, since the Modena manuscript of the law—a
manuscript of a collection of texts made by Lupus of Ferrières in
836—has a depiction of one Eddanan as a law-giver.[43] If, on the
other hand, the illustration represents Heden II, that serves yet further to undermine the Carolingian image of the man as a lukewarm
Christian.

What is known of the Hedenen may, of course, mean that Heden's
charters for Willibrord are in no sense representative of local Thuringian landholding: they are more strictly evidence for ducal property
in the region, and the ducal family may originally have come from
Francia.[44] They might usefully be juxtaposed with the possibly fiscal
land on which Fulda was established: neither the Hedenen nor the
Silva Bochonia need be representative of the Thuringian aristocracy,
their lands and their contacts. But it is worth emphasizing the point
that Würzburg under the Hedenen, far from being a semi-pagan
cul-de-sac, was a regional centre of some note, and while its rulers
may well not have followed orthodox practices with regard to marriage,[45] neither did the Pippinids in the time of Pippin II.[46]

Conflict between the Hedenen and Charles Martel may well explain
the grim picture of the Thuringian leadership in the Carolingian

[40] Willibald, *Vita Bonifatii*, 6.
[41] Metz, "Austrasische Adelsherrschaft des 8. Jahrhunderts. Mittelrheinische
Grundherren in Ostfranken, Thüringen und Hessen", pp. 289-90.
[42] Costambeys, "An aristocratic community on the northern Frankish frontier
690-726", pp. 61-62 underestimates the extent to which the Hedenen belonged to
the Frankish world before the arrival of Boniface.
[43] Mordek, "Die Hedenen als politische Kraft im austrasischen Frankenreich",
pp. 345-66, esp at pp. 356-58, with n. 72. It is not clear whether the manuscript
is that made by Lupus, or a mid-ninth-century copy.
[44] Metz, "Austrasische Adelsherrschaft des 8. Jahrhunderts. Mittelrheinische
Grundherren in Ostfranken, Thüringen und Hessen", pp. 277-78.
[45] *Passio Kiliani*, 8-10.
[46] Pippin II was either bigamous or had a concubine whose status was effectively
the same as that of his wife. For Alpaida as wife rather than concubine, R.A. Gerberding, "716: a crucial year for Charles Martel", *Karl Martell in seiner Zeit*, p. 207.

sources. Equally this same conflict may go some way to explain the apparent indifference of the inhabitants of the Grapfeld to the foundation of Fulda. The absence of local donations among the early charters is just as likely to reflect hostility to a Pippinid foundation—in other words a monastery founded by an authority newly established in the region—as it is to represent antagonism towards Christianity. Such antipathy to the Carolingians would be particularly likely if those who held land in the Grapfeld had originally been tenants of the Hedenen. On the other hand, when benefactions in the Grapfeld do begin, from what we have seen, there is no reason to suspect that the image of society and landholding implied by the charters reflects social change caused by recent integration into the Frankish world. Thuringia seems to have belonged to the cultural orbit of the Merovingians, and if it needed reintegrating in the eighth century, in all probability that was because of the disruption caused by the Pippinid seizure of power.

Heden's donation to Willibrord is of importance in understanding relations between Thuringia and Francia. Other charters in the *Liber Aureus Epternacensis* help towards an understanding of landholding in another peripheral area—although for the most part that area lay within Francia rather than across its boundaries. Among the grants made to Willibrord himself, a large number are concerned with property in Toxandria (essentially modern North Brabant)[47]—as well as Kleve[48] and the district round Antwerp.[49] Willibrord's "will" (which is actually a transfer to Echternach of lands given to the saint) also mentions an estate situated at the mouth of the Meuse, granted to him by the priest Heribald.[50] In his "will" Willibrord describes the estates listed as having been given to him by *ingenui Franci*. These, then, are estates of Franks on the Frankish side of the border with Frisia—though it should be noted that that they were apparently the indigenous aristocracy of a region that may well have been under

---

[47] Wampach, 11, 16, 17, 20, 21, 28, 36. On these see F.C.W.J. Theuws, "Centre and periphery in Northern Austrasia (6th-8th centuries). An archaeological perspective", in J.C. Besteman, J.M. Bos, H.A. Heidinga eds., *Medieval Archaeology in the Netherlands, Studies presented to H.H. van Regteren Altena* (Assen, 1990), p. 64. For a historical assessment see Costambeys, "An aristocratic community on the northern Frankish frontier 690-726", pp. 39-62.

[48] Wampach, 31, 32: see also 44.

[49] Wampach, 34, 35.

[50] Wampach, 39: see also 38.

Frisian control until c. 690.[51] In the early years the one grant that obviously strays across this boundary is that of the church of Velzen in Kinheim, Kennemerland, given by Charles Martel—no doubt after the annexation of Radbod's Frisian kingdom.[52] But while, with this single exception, the evidence of the earliest charters of the Echternach *Codex Aureus* does not help us to understand social structures in Frisia to the east of the Rhine, the documentation can be set alongside what we can see in the hagiography.

To take the earliest relevant text first: the *Life of Gregory of Utrecht*, written by his pupil, the missionary Bishop Liudger at the the very beginning of the ninth century. This describes (admittedly in a probably fraudulent manner)[53] the work carried out by Boniface when he worked with Willibrord. In that time (which in reality lasted a mere three years) he is supposed to have spent seven years at Woerden, three at Achtienhoven and a further three at Velzen, a site that we have already encountered in the charter of Charles Martel, and which is described by Liudger as being "nearer the pagans".[54] This was land that Liudger knew personally, for he himself was of Frisian extraction and trained at Utrecht.

Fortunately Liudger's own family is well documented in the *Vita Liudgeri*, which was written in the second quarter of the ninth century by the saint's nephew, Altfrid, who was, like Liudger himself, to become bishop of Münster. This is not the place to deal with the long family history which preface's Altfrid's account of his saintly uncle, although it is worth noting that, when Liudger's grandfather Wrssing fell foul of Radbod, he fled across the border to seek refuge with Pippin II's son Grimoald.[55] There he and members of his family were baptised, and he himself received benefices from unnamed Frankish *duces*. Radbod, meanwhile, having fallen ill, started to try to regain support from those he had previously alienated. He asked Wrssing to return, and, when he refused, offered to restore the family property to one of Wrssing's sons, which is what happened.[56] Wrssing

---

[51] Costambeys, "An aristocratic community on the northern Frankish frontier 690-726", pp. 56-60, 61-2.

[52] Wampach, 41.

[53] See I.N. Wood, "The missionary life" (forthcoming).

[54] Liudger, *Vita Gregorii*, 2, ed., O. Holder-Egger, *Monumenta Germaniae Historica, Scriptores* 15 (Hannover, 1887).

[55] Altfrid, *Vita Liudgeri*, I 2, ed. W. Diekamp, *Die Vitae Sancti Liudgeri* (Münster, 1881).

[56] Altfrid, *Vita Liudgeri*, I 3.

and the rest of his family remained in Francia until Radbod's death.

Fortunately Altfrid also sheds some precise light on the family's property holdings. Wrssing held land at *Suabsna*, currently identified as Loenen, immediately to the north Utrecht,[57] territory which in Radbod's day was clearly in Frisia.[58] This, however, is not our only indication of the family's Frisian property, for Liudger built a church on land inherited from his father at *Werthina*,[59] now identified as Muiderberg, near the mouth of the Vecht.[60] The estates at Loenen and Muiderberg were relatively close together, but a third hereditary estate owned by Liudger is more surprising: it was on family land that he built his monastery of Werden.[61] Although the boundary between Frisia and Saxony was ill-defined in this period—even the emperor Lothar found it difficult to distinguish between Frisians and Saxons in 850[62]—Werden must have been within Saxony. The estates of Liudger's family, therefore, stretched from the region between the Rhine and the Ijsselmeer to the edge of Westfalia. They bridge the gap between the world of Toxandria, as evidenced in the *Liber Aureus Epternacensis*, and that of Saxony—and there is nothing to suggest that such patterns of landholding had been upset by Saxon expansion in the 690s, despite the archaeological evidence.[63]

There is one further, and very slight, indication of early property holdings which can be added to this information. One of the saints of the previous generation much revered by Liudger was the Anglo-Saxon Lebuin. According to the earliest *Vita* of Lebuin, which is of the mid to late ninth century, he was supported in his attempt to evangelise Saxony by the Saxon family of Folcbraht, whose power base seems to have lain in the Südergau, the region in which Münster

---

[57] B. Senger, *Liudger in seinem Zeit* (Münster, 1982), p. 24; see also the maps and commentaries in B. Senger, *Liudger, Leben und Werk* (Münster, 1984), pp. 100-08; Diekamp, *Die Vitae Sancti Liudgeri*, p. 9, n. 3, identified the site as Zuilen an der Vecht.

[58] Altfrid, *Vita Liudgeri*, I 4.

[59] Altfrid, *Vita Liudgeri*, I 27.

[60] Senger, *Liudger in seiner Zeit*, p. 41; see also the maps and commentaries in Senger, *Liudger, Leben und Werk*, pp. 100-08.

[61] Altfrid, *Vita Liudgeri*, I 21, 32.

[62] B. Krusch, "Die Übertragung des H. Alexander von Rom mach Wildeshausen durch den Enkel Widukinds 851: Das älteste niedersächsische Geschichtsdenkmal", *Nachrichten von der Gesellschaft der Wissenschaften zu Göttingen aus dem Jahre 1933*, Philologisch-Historische Klasse (Berlin, Weidmann, 1933), p. 413.

[63] Bede, *Historia Ecclesiastica*, V 11; Grünewald, "Frühmittelalterliche Gräbfelder im Münsterland", p. 252.

is to be found.[64] It may be sheer coincidence, but another man called Folcbraht sold Liudger an estate in the Werden region in 799.[65] If we were to envisage a family connection between the two Folcbrahts we would be able to argue for overlapping family estates stretching from the Rhineland to Münster in the early Carolingian period.

Although the last step in this argument is unquestionably tenuous, it is fairly clear that patterns of property-holding to the north and east of Utrecht allowed for families to hold estates over large areas of land, even in the preCarolingian period. In this respect the Liudgeriden present a picture which is not dissimilar from that which can be inferred from Awalah's charter for some members of the Thuringian aristocracy.[66] The evidence of the *Vita Liudgeri*, however, takes us one stage further, for it takes us across what was regarded as the boundary between the Frisians and Saxons, which is explicitly named by Altfrid as being the river Ijssel.[67] Although, as we have seen, this was a somewhat fluid boundary, the fact that it appears to have been possible to hold land in the territory of more than one major tribal group in the region, even before those groups had been incorporated into the Frankish empire by the Carolingians, is significant. We should beware of assuming that integration into the Frankish world radically altered, as opposed to merely expanded, patterns of landholding and communication. Even in Frisia and Saxony the preCarolingian aristocracy was already "international", to some extent. And here the hagiography and the archaeology can usefully be compared. The well-known presence of "Frankish" graves in Saxony may or may not indicate "Frankish" colonisation in the sixth or seventh century,[68] but they can certainly be taken to indicate strong cultural and social links with the Frankish world, which is exactly what the "international" landholdings of a family like the Liudgeriden would have fostered.

The Liudgeriden are indicative of the connections of notable rather than ruling families—and these connections were already in place when the family was still pagan. In the case of the Hedenen in Thuringia we have already seen that leading families of the peripheral

[64] *Vita Lebuini Antiqua*, 3, 5, ed. A. Hofmeister, *Monumenta Germaniae Historica, Scriptores* 30 (Hannover, 1934).

[65] Hofmeister, *Monumenta Germaniae Historica, Scriptores* 30, p. 792, n. 12.

[66] Stengel, 57.

[67] Altfrid, *Vita Liudgeri*, I 13.

[68] Siegmund, "Frühmittelalterliche Gräberfelder in Ostwestfalen", pp. 256-62.

duchies could be closely bound to the centre of Merovingian political society. The same is, of course, true of Radbod in Frisia. Although he received a bad press from most sources which supported Charles Martel and his descendents,[69] his daughter had married Grimoald, the son of Pippin II by Plectrudis.[70] Like Heden, Radbod can be seen as a man who was happy to work with the Pippinids when Plectrudis was a dominant force, but who was less happy when Charles Martel, Pippin II's son by Alpaida, seized power. Indeed it is only with Charles' uprising and Willibrord subsequent desertion of Plectrudis for her stepson, that Radbod abandoned an alliance with the Pippinids: and even then he continued to work with the legitimist Merovingian party in Neustria.[71]

Nevertheless, unlike Heden, Radbod could genuinely be accused of paganism. The same is true of Widukind, the leader of the West-falian Saxons, who was largely responsible for Saxon opposition to Charlemagne between 775 and 785, when he submitted and was baptised.[72] It is interesting to note how quickly Widukind's family were integrated into Frankish court society following the *volte face* of his conversion—the process of integration can be seen clearly in the *De Miraculis sancti Alexandri, sanctae Felicitatis filii*, written by Rudolf and Meginhart of Fulda in the second half of the ninth century.[73] The same can be seen for the family of Hessi, the leader of the *Austreleudi* in 775,[74] who has also been linked to Frankish aristocratic circles by *Namenforschung*.[75] The family was honoured by Charlemagne and his successors, and played a leading role in the subsequent christianisation of Saxony, as is apparent in the late ninth-century *Vita Liutbirgae*.[76]

---

[69] E.g. *Annales Mettenses Priores*, s.a. 692, 697, ed. B. von Simson, *Monumenta Germaniae Historica, Scriptores Rerum Germanicarum in usum scholarum* ((Hannover, 1905).

[70] Fredegar, continuations 7, ed. J.M. Wallace-Hadrill, *The Fourth Book of the Chronicle of Fredegar* (London, 1960).

[71] *Annales Mettenses Priores*, s.a. 714, 715; Wood, *The Merovingian Kingdoms, 450-751*, pp. 269-70.

[72] *Annales Regni Francorum/Annales qui dicuntur Einhardi*, s.a. 777, 778, 782, 785, ed. F. Kurze, *Monumenta Germaniae Historica, Scriptores Rerum Germanicarum in usum scholarum* (Hannover, 1895). Compare Altfrid, *Vita Liudgeri*, I 21.

[73] Krusch, "Die Übertragung des H. Alexander von Rom mach Wildeshausen durch den Enkel Widukinds 851", pp. 405-36, especially *De Miraculis sancti Alexandri, sanctae Felicitatis filii*, 3-4; K. Schmid, "Die Nachfahren Widukinds", *Deutsches Archiv* 20 (1964), pp. 1-47.

[74] *Annales qui dicuntur Einhardi*, s.a. 775.

[75] Metz, "Austrasische Adelsherrschaft des 8. Jahrhunderts. Mittelrheinische Grundherren in Ostfranken, Thüringen und Hessen", p. 280.

[76] *Vita Liutbirgae*, 1-2, ed. O. Menzel, *Das Leben der Liutbirg, Deutsches Mittelalter*,

The Austrasian frontier was, therefore, permeable, and once across the frontier it appears that patterns of aristocratic landholding ensured a network of contact and communication which stretched towards the Slav frontier. It goes without saying that this must have provided a context for the distribution of goods such as Mayen ware and other types of pottery,[77] as well as metalwork, although there is, curiously, a remarkable lack of pre-Ottonian coin-finds in Saxony, despite the significance of the *sceatta* economy for the Rhineland *emporia*.[78] The northern landowners, particularly those known from Toxandria, evident in the charter record and in the hagiography must also provide part of the context for the flourishing of the *emporia*, most notably that of Dorestad, but also of Walcheren. The estates of the Liudgeriden, close as some of them were to Utrecht, are likely to have received goods which had passed through Dorestad, and it is probable that the villa at Walcheren which interested Willibrord was in some way connected to the *emporium* of Domburg.[79] Of course the contacts of the Frisian merchants stretched far beyond those of the aristocracy we have been considering, and, even reasonably close to home, in the Frisian islands and the coastal strip of Saxony, they touched regions which were probably beyond the purview of the landowners of the lower Rhine. Nevertheless, what can be learnt of the landholdings of such families as the Liudgeriden and the Toxandrian supporters of Willibrord need to be set alongside the evidence for the economy of the *emporia*.

Yet if the frontier between Austrasia and the territories to the east of the Rhine was so obviously permeable, it is necessary to ask why the narrative sources suggest that the Carolingian integration of the territories east of the Rhine marked such a change. Undoubtedly, of course, there was change, particularly at governmental and organisational levels, especially in Saxony. Part of the impression we have of developments in these eastern regions, however, is determined not

Kritische Studientexte des Reichsinstituts für ältere deutsche Geschichtskunde, Monumenta Germaniae Historica, 3, (Leipzig, 1937).

[77] See the map in U. Gross, "Die Töpferware der Franken: Herleitung – Formen – Produktion", *Die Franken: Wegbereiter Europas* 2 (Mainz, 1996), p. 592; and W. van Es, "Handel in Karolingische potten", *Romeinen, Friezen en Franken in het hart van Nederland*, pp. 184-88.

[78] H. Steuer, "The beginnings of urban economies among the Saxons", in D. Green and F. Siegmund eds., *The Old Saxons* (forthcoming).

[79] Alcuin, *Vita Willibrordi*, 14, ed. H.-J. Reischmann, *Willibrord, Apostel der Friesen* (Darmstadt, 1989).

by factual detail, but by the very nature of our sources. As we have already seen, the portrayal of Heden was partly determined by some conflict between him and the Austrasians after 717. The same is true of Radbod. In a sense the leader of the Westfalian Saxons, Widukind, did rather better, since his descendants were able to reestablish the family's secular importance, as we have seen in the *De Miraculis sancti Alexandri, sanctae Felicitatis filii*.[80] The *Vita Liutbirgae* shows that the Ostfalian family of Hessi was equally adaptable.[81] In this it might well be compared with what we can glean of the Toxandrian aristocracy.[82] Far to the south the Agilulfings in Bavaria and the Etichonen in Alamannia suffered rather worse fates.[83]

The problem is, thus, partly, the result of the influence of political bias in our Carolingian sources—a bias which is most clearly stated in Einhard's categorisation of the Saxons as alien.[84] It is also related to the question of the evidence for the christianisation of the lands east of the Rhine. The standard interpretation is one which follows the implications of a set of saint's *Lives* concerned with Boniface and his followers. This interpretation sees Boniface as the prime figure in the christianisation of Hesse and Thuringia, his disciples as achieving the christianisation of Frisia, and then as creating a church organisation in Saxony in the wake of Charlemagne's *Schwertmission*. This picture is certainly one which can be extracted from the hagiography of the eighth and ninth centuries. It is, however, doubtful whether the impression given should be taken at face value, especially in the case of Thuringia and Hesse.

That Boniface expected to evangelise the peoples east of the Rhine is very clear from his letters.[85] On the other hand in Hesse and Thuringia his encounters with dyed-in-the-wool pagans seem to have been few and far between. The actual process of mission seems, from linguistic evidence at least, to have been largely achieved by Franks

---

[80] *De Miraculis sancti Alexandri, sanctae Felicitatis filii*, 3-4.

[81] *Vita Liutbirgae*.

[82] Costambeys, "An aristocratic community on the northern Frankish frontier 690-726", p. 61.

[83] R. McKitterick, *The Frankish Kingdoms under the Carolingians 751-987* (London, 1983), pp. 43, 65-67.

[84] Einhard, *Vita Caroli Magni*, 7, ed. O. Holder-Egger, *Monumenta Germaniae Historica, Scriptores Rerum Germanicarum in usum scholarum* (Hannover, 1911).

[85] Boniface, *epp.* 12, 15, 17, 21, 23, 28, 30, 46, 47, ed. M. Tangl, *Monumenta Germaniae Historica, Epistolae Selectae* I (Berlin, 1916).

working before Boniface's arrival.[86] Further, as we have seen, the Hedenen in Würzburg were Christian rulers of Thuringia, who seem to have been responsible for the promulgation of a distinctly Christian law-code. Yet the church that existed in their time left room for the organisational work of Boniface. In Thuringia, as in Bavaria, Boniface's achievement was to organise a Church, rather than found one[87]— this achievement involved creating a system of bishoprics and also introducing a significant monastic tradition to the area.

Frisia and Saxony were somewhat different from Thuringia. They were both led by pagans immediately before the Carolingian take-over, although in southern Frisia, at least, it is easy to underestimate the extent to which Christianity was present already in Radbod's day. Even before Willibrord's arrival significant missionary work had been undertaken by Wulfram of Sens.[88] Willibrord seems to have had *carte blanche* to evangelise up until 716. As we have noted, it appears to have been his decision to team up with Charles Martel, rather than with Plectrudis and her grandson, who was, it should be remembered, also the grandson of Radbod, that made Willibrord *persona non grata*.[89] On the other hand, Liudger's grandfather, Wrssing, was still a pagan at the time he was driven out of Frisia by Radbod for political reasons.[90] Further, his daughter-in-law, Liafburg, very nearly fell victim to her pagan grandmother, who ordered the child to be drowned.[91] Altfrid also reveals that it was only Liafburg's generation which saw the beginnings of a Frisian indigenous clergy.[92] Paganism was, therefore, still normal in southern Frisia in and after Radbod's day—not that this seems to have been much of an issue at those moments when Christian Franks found it useful to ally with or support pagan Frisians. Northern Frisia, of course, remained pagan until the time of Boniface's martyrdom.

---

[86] D.H. Green, *Language and History in the early Germanic World* (Cambridge, 1998), pp. 325-40, esp. pp. 355-56.

[87] Wood, *The Merovingian Kingdoms, 450-751*, pp. 304-10.

[88] S. Lebecq, "Le baptême manqué du roi Radbod", in O. Redon and B. Rosenberger eds., *Les Assises du Pouvoir: temps médiévaux, territoires africains* (St-Denis, 1994), pp. 141-50.

[89] On Willibrord's change of allegiance to Charles Martel, R. Gerberding, *The Rise of the Carolingians and the Liber Historiae Francorum* (Oxford, 1987), pp. 134-6. For Willibrord's earlier work in Frisia, under Radbod, Alcuin, *Vita Willibrordi*, 9-11.

[90] Altfrid, *Vita Liudgeri*, I 2.

[91] Altfrid, *Vita Liudgeri*, I 6-7.

[92] Altfrid, *Vita Liudgeri*, I 5.

Paganism was, therefore, a factor in Frisia, as indeed it was in Saxony, where the Carolingian conquest does indeed seem to have enabled the establishment of Christianity. Further, the coming of Christianity to these areas meant not just the establishment of a new religion, but also the introduction of the written word, with all the implications that has for the existence of documentation. These new developments, however, should not be allowed to obscure the extent to which Thuringia, Hesse, Frisia and Saxony were already part of the Frankish world, before the Carolingian take-over. As we have seen family connections and landholdings imply a world without sharp frontiers, and this same picture is one that is entirely compatible with the distribution maps of eighth-century finds. Against this background the Frankish take-over is easy to overestimate, but it suited the Carolingians to portray their eastern neighbours in as black a light as possible, while the hagiographers, like the monks of Fulda, were concerned to elevate the martyred Boniface, and thus came to downgrade the extent to which Christianity was established in Thuringia and Hesse before his arrival.

The changes caused by the Carolingian expansion east of the Rhine may have been considerable in various ways, but they did not mark a complete rupture with the past, for the Merovingian periphery was something more than a world of isolated backwoodsmen. On the other hand there was one major change, and it is one that is so obvious that it is easy to take for granted. The charters of Fulda, like those of Echternach, are the records of the vast accumulation of land by a monastery. When we consider social developments east of the Rhine as reflected in the charter evidence, we are observing a process of monasticisation—with all the implications that that would have for landholding and social organisation. The equivalent—although not necessarily similar—development in England has long been seen as marking a revolution in land-tenure.[93] The hagiography makes it only too easy to mistake this process for christianisation. The secular narratives, on the other hand, lead us to confuse it with the expansion of the Franks. It is Echternach and Fulda (and one might add a host of other monastic houses stretching from Werden in the north to Freising in the south) that are the novelties, not Frankish contacts or Christianity.

---

[93] E. John, *Land Tenure in early England* (Leicester, 1960).

MARSEILLE AND THE PIRENNE THESIS, II:
"VILLE MORTE"

S.T. Loseby

Introduction

This paper is the sequel to my contribution to the first volume of articles arising out of the meetings of this working group.[1] There it was argued that the considerable use which Henri Pirenne made of evidence from Marseille in constructing the first part of his famous thesis was justified, both in the emphasis which he laid upon the city in his evaluation of post-Roman Mediterranean trade, and in his assessment of it as a "great port" under the Merovingians. For the meagre written sources which were available to Pirenne can be combined with archaeological and numismatic evidence to show that at the end of the sixth century Marseille was able to function effectively as an *emporium*, the primary intention behind its original foundation over a thousand years earlier, and the role which it has always played during its periods of greatest prosperity. The particular significance of Marseille in this period is further reflected in the determination of the Frankish kings to control the port and the development of specific mechanisms through which they strove to maximise their exploitation of its trade.

This paper aims to pursue the economic history of Marseille through the seventh and on into the eighth century, as far as Pirenne's contention that "*la rupture de la tradition antique a eu pour instrument l'avance rapide et imprévue de l'Islam. Elle a eu pour conséquence de séparer définitivement l'Orient de l'Occident, en mettant fin à la unité méditerrannéenne*".[2] Just as Marseille had been crucial to Pirenne's convictions about the

---

[1] S.T. Loseby, "Marseille and the Pirenne thesis, I: Gregory of Tours, the Merovingian kings, and 'un grand port'", in R. Hodges and W. Bowden eds., *The Sixth Century. Production, Distribution and Demand* (Leiden, 1998), pp. 203-29.

[2] H. Pirenne, *Mahomet et Charlemagne*, 3rd ed. (Brussels, 1937), p. 260: "the break with the tradition of antiquity was caused by the rapid and unexpected advance of Islam. Its consequence was the definitive separation of the east from the west, putting an end to the unity of the Mediterranean".

enduring vitality of Mediterranean trade, so did he again make significant reference to the port as epitomising the devastating impact upon it of the Arab conquests: *"au IXe siècle . . . le vide se fait dans le grand port de Marseille qui avait été jadis la principale étape de l'Occident avec le Levant"*.[3] "[The Corbie diploma of 716 is] *la dernière et ultime mention que nous ayons de produits orientaux entreposés dans les ports de Provence. Quatre ans après d'ailleurs, les Musulmans débarquent sur ces côtes et pillent le pays."* This was the end for Marseille as far as Pirenne was concerned: *"Marseille est mort à cette époque"*.[4] Until that point, however, he believed that the port had been very much alive.

Few scholars today would accept the straightforward causal relationship between the rise of Islam and the end of Mediterranean trade which dominated Pirenne's perception of the exchange-networks of the later seventh and early eighth century. The archaeological evidence in particular provides increasing confirmation of a much more gradual deterioration from the fifth century onwards of the international Mediterranean exchange-network inherited from Antiquity; the supposedly decisive impact of the Arab conquests upon this general pattern, at least in the West, is archaeologically more or less invisible.[5] Pirenne's perception of the changing fortunes of Marseille, and his conclusions concerning the decisive reorientation of Frankish economic geography away from the Mediterranean and towards the north in this period may nevertheless retain more validity than his monocausal explanation of the decline of Mediterranean trade. This can be tested by reconsidering the seventh- and early eighth-century evidence from Marseille, both as an index of the persistence or otherwise of the trading-system which had previously sustained it as an *emporium*, and as a barometer of Frankish royal interest in the Mediterranean; we might suspect that the two will be connected. The evidence for the fortunes of Marseille in the later Merovingian

---

[3] Pirenne, *Mahomet et Charlemagne*, p. 145: "in the ninth century . . . the great port of Marseille, which had once been the principal western centre of trade with the Levant, was empty".

[4] Pirenne, *Mahomet et Charlemagne*, p. 148: "[716 is] the latest and final reference which we have to eastern products stored up in the Provençal ports. Four years later, moreover, the Muslims land on these coasts and plunder the region. Marseille is then dead".

[5] C. Panella, "Merci e scambi nel Mediterraneo tardoantico", in A. Carandini, L. Cracco Ruggini and A. Giardina eds., *Storia di Roma* 3.ii (Turin, 1993), pp. 613-97, is a fine concise synthesis of the archaeological data.

period is not as rich as in the second half of the sixth century, which is illuminated by a combination of the anecdotal prolixity of Gregory of Tours, new numismatic developments and a considerable range of excavated data. Nevertheless, the same three types of evidence can again be used, even if, as one might expect in attempting to prove a negative, increasing weight has to be attached to arguments from silence.

Archaeology

The problem of how to interpret an absence of data is most intractable in the case of the archaeological evidence. Although a plethora of sites featuring late antique material have been excavated at Marseille over the last two decades, the latest (generally desultory and materially unimpressive) traces of occupation or deposition at the vast majority of them do not extend beyond the middle of the seventh century at the latest.[6] The re-occupation of some of these sites is not perceptible until as late as the thirteenth century, although when it does resume it is notable that there are some marked survivals of orientations and terracing of antique origin. The most that can safely be said about this prolonged hiatus is that many areas of the city feature an absence of recognisable traces of human activity, which may or may not be indicative of the abandonment of any given site. This increasing lack of evidence might nevertheless reasonably be taken to imply a change for the worse in material culture, whether in the use of perishable materials for building, or the absence of manufactured goods. Such material impoverishment is suggested in another sense, for example, by the steady deterioration of the regional DSP (*dérivées-des-sigillées paléochrétiennes*) fine ware both in its range of forms and in the quality of its manufacture and decoration. The seventh-century specimens of this ware found and, in all probability, produced at Marseille have, as elsewhere in southern Gaul, become so debased

---

[6] The evidence is summarised in L.-F. Gantès and M. Moliner eds., *Marseille, itinéraire d'une mémoire: cinq années d'archéologie municipale* (Marseille, 1990) and Musées de Marseille, *Le temps des découvertes: Marseille, de Protis à la reine Jeanne* (Marseille, 1993). The material from some of these sites has now been published in detail: M. Bonifay, M.-B. Carre and Y. Rigoir eds., *Fouilles à Marseille. Les mobiliers (Ier-VIIe siècles ap. J.-C.)* Études massaliètes, 5 (Paris/Lattes, 1998), pp. 197-291.

that it becomes progressively more difficult, and arguably inappropriate, to continue to distinguish them from local common wares.[7]

Even so, the archaeological hiatus which afflicts the whole of Provence between the mid-seventh and the tenth century, caused by a combination of the shortage of diagnostic material and, at least at cities like Marseille, the potential destruction of the intervening strata by later medieval buildings, is gradually being both filled and narrowed. The continuing refinement of a typology of local common ware production offers hope that it will eventually be possible to distinguish deposits of the intervening period more precisely, even if close dating on ceramic grounds alone is likely to remain elusive.[8] Meanwhile, both at Marseille, and at sites elsewhere in the region, an increasing number of contexts have now been identified which appear on the basis of the associated finds to date from the second half of the seventh century or early in the eighth. These begin to flesh out what is still a very fragmentary picture.

On the Bourse site at Marseille the archaeological sequence from the inner harbour (the Corne) and the suburb which had developed beside it at the rear of the Vieux-Port in Late Antiquity persisted through to the end of the seventh century.[9] Attempts to maintain the Corne as a functioning part of the harbour by the repeated dredging of silt and the building of rudimentary quays had finally been abandoned at around the end of the sixth century.[10] The zone of intense suburban settlement between the Corne and the walls of the city thereafter continued to expand onto the accumulated build-up of silt (it is tempting to imagine that this was in the direction of an area of the harbour which continued in operation).[11] The suburb as a whole appears to have been predominantly industrial or

---

[7] For DSP at Marseille see most recently M. Bonifay and Y. Rigoir, "Les dérivées-de-sigillées gauloises", *Fouilles à Marseille*, pp. 366-70.

[8] J.-P. Pelletier, "Les céramiques communes grises en Provence de l'Antiquité tardive au XIIIe siècle", in *La céramique médiévale en Méditerranée* (Aix-en-Provence, 1997), pp. 111-24.

[9] M. Bonifay, "Éléments d'évolution des céramiques de l'Antiquité tardive à Marseille d'après les fouilles de la Bourse", *Revue archéologique de Narbonnaise* 16 (1983), pp. 285-346, esp. at pp. 290-97, 303-26, modified in M. Bonifay, "Observations sur les amphores de Marseille d'après les fouilles de la Bourse (1980-1984)", *Revue archéologique de Narbonnaise* 19 (1986), pp. 269-305, at pp. 270-71. See also now *Fouilles à Marseille*, pp. 102-96, for the welcome publication of the results from other sondages at the Bourse, with only minor modifications to the chronology.

[10] For the dating, most recently *Fouilles à Marseille*, p. 196.

[11] R. Guéry, "Le port antique de Marseille", in M. Bats, G. Bertucchi, G. Congès,

artisanal in function, featuring signs of iron, bone, leather and wood-working and, especially, glass manufacture.[12] The seventh-century occupation levels from the former area of the Corne were extremely fragmentary, but it appears that this final phase of suburban expansion south-westwards was short-lived.[13] A layer containing African amphora sherds was deposited after occupation had ceased, and immediately before the walls were robbed-out; one destruction level contained a silver coin of Childeric II minted, interestingly enough, as far away as Bayeux, and providing a *terminus post quem* in the 670s for the associated deposit.[14] There is no indication here of any persistence of occupation into the eighth century. The first archaeological traces of a resumption of activity in this area take the form of secondary features such as silos, ditches and wells; these are hard to date, but the polished grey wares and odd sherd of imported *vetrina pesante* recovered from them point to the tenth century.[15]

This exceptional sequence has now been complemented by the recent excavations in the place Jules-Verne, within the walled area of the city on the northern shore of the Vieux-Port, only a short distance west of the Bourse. The site included what had once been the shoreline, and is renowned principally for the remarkable wrecks of earlier periods which were excavated there. By the sixth century, however, deposition had pushed the quayside further southwards,

---

and H. Tréziny eds., *Marseille grecque et la Gaule*, Études massaliètes 3 (Lattes/Aix-en-Provence, 1992), pp. 109-21; Gantès and Moliner, *Marseille, itinéraire d'une mémoire*, pp. 53-58. For the northern extension of the suburb, H. Marchesi, L. Vallauri *et al.*, "L'antiquité tardive", in H. Marchesi, J. Thiriot and L. Vallauri eds., *Marseille, les ateliers de potiers du XIIIe s. et le quartier Sainte-Barbe (Ve-XVIIe siècle)*, Documents d'Archéologie Française 65 (Paris, 1997), pp. 21-40.

[12] This data remains for the most part unpublished, but see the comments in M. Bonifay, "Marseille aux temps barbares (V^e-VIIe siècles)", *Marseille* 160 (1991), pp. 64-69, esp. pp. 67-68, and for the glass, D. Foy and M. Bonifay, "Éléments d'évolution des verreries de l'antiquité tardive à Marseille d'après les fouilles de la Bourse", *Revue archéologique de Narbonnaise* 17 (1984), pp. 289-308; D. Foy, "Les verres", *Marseille, les ateliers de potiers*, pp. 35-37; D. Foy, "Le verre", *Fouilles à Marseille*, pp. 372-75. It seems likely that glass manufacture at Marseille continued into the seventh century. For the possibility of silver production, see below n. 52.

[13] Bonifay, "Éléments d'évolution des céramiques de l'Antiquité tardive à Marseille", pp. 295-97.

[14] J. Lafaurie, "Monnaie mérovingienne de Bayeux trouvée à Marseille", *Bulletin de la société française de numismatique* 41 (1986), pp. 49-51.

[15] Bonifay, "Éléments d'évolution des céramiques de l'Antiquité tardive à Marseille", pp. 297-99; M. Bonifay, L. Paroli and M. Picon, "Ceramiche a vetrina pesante scoperte a Roma e a Marsiglia; risultati delle prime analisi fisico-chimiche", *Archeologia Medievale* 13 (1986), pp. 79-95, esp. pp. 85-86.

beyond the perimeter of the excavated area; occupation now extended onto this reclaimed land for the first time. Few structural features of this period have survived the subsequent installation of cellars, but there is a relative abundance of material in their associated ditches which, although as yet largely unpublished, shows that activity continued here into the later seventh century or even the early eighth.[16] Evidence of similar date from slightly further afield is now provided by the welcome publication of the finds from the wreck known as Saint-Gervais 2, which went down in shallow water off Fos-sur-Mer, only a short distance around the coast to the west of Marseille, and, as will become apparent, an important later Merovingian harbour.[17] This wreck had been dated to the early seventh century on the basis of a coin of Heraclius minted at Carthage in 611/2, but the association between this find and the wreck is not watertight, and would in any case provide only a *terminus post quem*; the small ceramic assemblage is more suggestive of a date in the second half of the seventh century. The principal cargo of the ship appears to have been grain, which is interesting in its own right, but unfortunate for dating purposes, as is the fact that the vessel sank close enough to shore for much of its contents to have been retrieved. Finally, one recent discovery from across the Rhône in Languedoc is particularly worthy of note. It comes from Bouquet/San Peyre (Gard), one of a cluster of hilltops between Alès and Uzès, some forty kilometres north of Nîmes. A fire in a building of at least five or six rooms had sealed a remarkable archaeological deposit, containing, among other things, clear indications of a series of connections with the Mediterranean world. The function of the building is unclear, but the finds make it extremely tempting to identify it as an aristocratic residence of some description. These included a stock of six or seven African amphorae of large cylindrical type, a specimen of the latest African lamp type, *Atlante* X, and four sherds akin to the eastern Mediterranean Carthage Late Roman Amphora

---

[16] A. Hesnard, "Les ports antiques de Marseille, Place Jules-Verne", *Journal of Roman Archaeology* 8 (1995), pp. 65-77, esp. p. 77 for a brief account of the late antique phase; *Fouilles à Marseille*, p. 358 and p. 419, provides a summary of the latest material; M. Bonifay and D. Pieri, "Amphores du Ve au VIIe siècle à Marseille: nouvelles données sur la typologie et le contenu", *Journal of Roman Archaeology* 8 (1995), 94-120, incorporates some discussion of the amphorae from Jules-Verne.

[17] M.-P. Jézégou, "Le mobilier de l'épave Saint-Gervais 2 (VIIe s.) à Fos-sur-Mer (B.-du-Rh.)", *Fouilles à Marseille*, pp. 343-51.

(LRA) type 1, as well as a number of bone objects and evidence of iron-working. On the basis of the ceramic material the deposit could be dated typologically to the period between the sixth and the early eighth centuries; the singular discovery within the deposit of a seal bearing characters in Kufic script suggests it belongs towards the end of that period.[18]

These enticing fragments of information have not all been fully published, and they remain difficult to contextualise. The finds from the Bourse site in particular had already suggested that Marseille continued to be linked in to a Mediterranean-wide exchange-network in the late sixth and the first half of the seventh century. The fine ware assemblage in that period continues to be dominated by the latest forms of African Red Slip ware (Hayes 91D, 105, 108 and 109A, together with another *Atlante* X lamp),[19] indeed its domination is if anything accentuated by the deterioration in both quantity and quality of the locally-produced DSP fine ware, to the extent that the latter scarcely continues to merit classification in this category at all.[20] African imports are similarly dominant among the amphorae, but the analysis of further assemblages from the Bourse now suggests that amphorae continued to be imported to Marseille from diverse regions of the eastern Mediterranean (as represented by LRA types 1b, 4b, 5/6, 7, and to a lesser extent 2), in rather greater numbers than had been thought.[21] Specimens of all these types of container of eastern origin continue to figure in one or more of the few available contexts of later seventh-century date outlined above, alongside a new form of globular amphora which appears to originate in this period, and may also derive from the eastern Mediterranean. The latest known forms of African ceramic production are

---

[18] C. Pellecuer and J.-M. Pène, "Bouquet/San Peyre, Suzon (Gard)", in CATHMA, "Céramiques languedociennes du haut moyen age (VIIe-XIe s.): études micro-régionales et essai de synthèse", *Archéologie du Midi Médiéval* 11 (1993), at pp. 150-51. C. Citter *et al.*, "Commerci nel Mediteraneo occidentale nell'alto medioevo", in G.P. Brogiolo ed., *Early medieval towns in the western Mediterranean* (Mantua, 1996), pp. 121-42.

[19] Bonifay, "Éléments d'évolution des céramiques de l'Antiquité tardive à Marseille", conveniently updated in *Fouilles à Marseille* at pp. 361-6, with summaries by period at pp. 357-58.

[20] *Fouilles à Marseille*, p. 370.

[21] Bonifay, "Observations sur les amphores de Marseille d'après les fouilles de la Bourse" is fundamental, but now updated by M. Bonifay and D. Pieri, "Amphores du Ve au VIIe siècle à Marseille", pp. 94-120 and *Fouilles à Marseille*, pp. 371-72, with summaries by period at pp. 357-58.

also present (in particular ARS Hayes 109B, *Atlante* X lamps of very debased type, and, among the amphorae, Keay LXI and VIIIA and miniature *spatheia*).[22]

At Marseille, therefore, the Bourse site and, especially, the place Jules-Verne can be added, together with Bouquet/San Peyre and probably the Saint-Gervais 2 wreck, to the select but growing number of Mediterranean archaeological contexts of later seventh and early eighth century date, dominated in the west by the Crypta Balbi at Rome, and in the east by Saraçhane at Constantinople.[23] The material from southern Gaul has features in common with the ceramic assemblages from both of these sites (including, most strikingly, a fragment of Saraçhane cooking ware type 3, found at the place Jules-Verne), and, somewhat closer to hand, with the early seventh-century deposit at the *castrum* of Sant'Antonino di Perti along the coast in Liguria.[24] Given the incomplete publication of the southern Gallic sites and the preliminary nature of much of the available data, any interpretation of these deposits is clearly somewhat premature, while the shortage of comparative contexts makes close dating and contextualisation difficult enough in any case. Nevertheless, one might hazard one or two general observations. The contexts of late sixth and early seventh century date had already shown that the *emporium* at Marseille continued to be closely tied in to what remained of the declining Mediterranean exchange-network, receiving imports from both Africa and the East on a scale unusual for western sites in this

---

[22] *Fouilles à Marseille*, p. 358 and p. 419; Bonifay and Pieri, "Amphores du Ve au VIIe siècle à Marseille", esp. p. 116.

[23] L. Saguì, M. Ricci and D. Romei, "Nuovi dati ceramologici per la storia economica di Roma tra VII et VIII secolo", *La céramique médiévale en Méditerranée* (Aix-en-Provence, 1997), 35-48; L. Sagui, "Il deposito della Crypta Balbi: una testimonianza imprevedibile sulla Roma del VII secolo?" and M. Ricci, "La ceramica comune dal contesto di VII secolo della Crypta Balbi", in L. Saguì ed., *Ceramica in Italia: VI-VII secolo* (Florence, 1998), 305-33, 351-82; A. Rovelli, "Some considerations on the coinage of Lombard and Carolingian Italy", (this volume), pp. 202, 208; J.W. Hayes, *Excavations at Saraçhane in Istanbul, ii: The pottery* (Princeton, 1992).

[24] E. Bonora *et al.*, "Il 'castrum' tardo-antico di S. Antonino di Perti, Finale Ligure (Savona): fasi stratigrafiche e reperti dell'area D. Seconde notizie preliminari sulle campagne di scavo 1982-1987", *Archeologia Medievale* 15 (1988), pp. 335-96; E. Castiglioni *et al.*, "Il 'castrum' tardo-antico di S. Antonino di Perti, Finale Ligure (Savona): terze notizie preliminari sulle campagne di scavo 1982-1991", *Archeologia Medievale* 19 (1992), pp. 279-362; G. Murialdo *et al.*, "La ceramica comune in Liguria nel VIe VII secolo", in Saguì, *Ceramica in Italia*, pp. 209-26; A. Gardini and G. Murialdo, "La Liguria", in R. Francovich and G. Noyé eds., *La storia dell'alto medioevo italiano (VI-X secolo) alla luce dell'archeologia* (Florence, 1994), pp. 159-82, for the wider regional context.

period, and especially for those lying outside imperial territory. The subsequent deposits from Marseille and elsewhere in the region suggest that these connections persisted into the later seventh and perhaps even the early eighth century, and so beyond the Arab conquest of at least some of the regions in which these imported ceramics were manufactured. The exchange-network in which Marseille was involved thus continued to span the Mediterranean throughout this period. Although it is tempting to imagine that the port's commercial connections were becoming increasingly attenuated, the variety of form and origin, if not the quantity, of the later seventh century material is exceptional for the north-western Mediterranean, and perhaps indicative of the enduring attraction of the lucrative Frankish market for whatever long-distance trade continued to take place.[25] It seems increasingly likely that Marseille, and by extension the southern coast of Francia, remained integrated into the ancient Mediterranean exchange-network for as long as its archaeologically-visible manifestations, the latest forms of African fine ware, amphorae, and lamps, but also the various eastern LRA types, continued in production. Beyond the early eighth century, however, imported ceramics cease to arrive, and the archaeological void is punctuated only by locally-produced common wares. Any continuing commercial connections between the region and the rest of the Mediterranean are archaeologically imperceptible.

It would be unwise, however, to allow the arrival of imported ceramics at Marseille throughout the seventh century to negate the overall impression of decline suggested by the collapse of the regional fine-ware pottery industry, the abandonment of what had previously been a remarkably dynamic zone of extra-mural settlement at the rear of the Vieux-Port, and the apparent desertion of many of the excavated intra-mural sites within the walls. The new evidence from the place Jules-Verne will perhaps modify this gloomy picture somewhat, but it seems unlikely to redraw it entirely. And if we compare the archaeological material with the other categories of evidence at our disposal, this impression of a decline in the fortunes of Marseille in the course of the seventh century can be brought into sharper focus.

---

[25] For some suggestions that the absolute volume of African amphora imports to Marseille may have been declining in the seventh century, S.T. Loseby, "Marseille: a late antique success story?", *Journal of Roman Studies* 82 (1992), pp. 165-85, at pp. 184-85.

Texts and coins

The documentary and numismatic evidence offers two ways of considering the question of how far Marseille remained a significant commercial centre in the seventh and early eighth centuries. The first of these lies in the persistence of direct indications of the role of the port in exchange- and communications-networks. The second, more indirect approach is to examine how far the Frankish kings maintained their political interest in Marseille and, in particular, the specific mechanisms which they had established in order to profit from its trade.[26]

The direct evidence for exchange via Marseille in this period has often been discussed, and can be swiftly summarised. Two commodities stand out in the written sources: oil and slaves. In so far as Gregory of Tours troubles to be specific about the trade of Marseille, his thinking is dominated by oil imports.[27] This emphasis is reflected in the Merovingian formulary of c. 700 which names Marseille as the principal port of purchase of oil for lighting purposes.[28] Dagobert I (629-39) granted the monastery which he had founded at St-Denis an annual rent of 100 solidi from the royal customs-dues at Marseille. The monastery's agents were to use this to purchase oil from the *cellarium fisci* at the port, again for the purpose of lighting, which they could then convey north on six carts, free from toll. All this was subject, however, to the arrival of cargoes (*secundum quod ordo cataboli esset*), which tends to confirm that this concerns imported rather than local oil production; it also gives the impression that the availability of oil could not be guaranteed.[29] Two of the several later confirmations of this original grant survive, those of Clovis III in

---

[26] For which see Loseby, "Marseille and the Pirenne thesis, I", pp. 221-27.

[27] Gregory of Tours, *Historiae* V.5 and IV.43, ed. B. Krusch and W. Levison, *Monumenta Germaniae Historica, Scriptores Rerum Merovingicarum* I.1 (Hannover, 1937); Loseby, "Marseille and the Pirenne thesis, I", pp. 218-21.

[28] *ad Massilia vel per relicos portos infra regna nostro*: Marculf, *Formulae, Supplementum*, 1, ed. K. Zeumer, *Monumenta Germaniae Historica, Formulae* I (Hannover, 1886), pp. 107-12. It is important to bear in mind, however, that this need not be indicative of circumstances at the time when the formula was written down.

[29] *Gesta Dagoberti I regis Francorum*, 18, ed. B. Krusch, *Monumenta Germaniae Historica, Scriptores Rerum Merovingicarum* II (Hannover, 1888), pp. 401-25. For the significance of *cataplus*, F. Vercauteren, "*Cataplus* et *catabolus*", *Bulletin du Cange* 2 (1926), 98-101. It is generally accepted that the oil discussed in these documents was imported, not least because neither Marseille nor Fos are well-placed to act as collection or storage-centres for surplus Provençal oil-production.

691 and Chilperic II in 716; I will return to it in due course.[30] But the potential scale of oil imports into Francia via Provence emerges more clearly in another royal grant originally drawn up under Chlothar III (657-73) for his monastic foundation at Corbie, which has come down to us only in the form of the confirmation issued by Chilperic II in 716. This remarkable document concerns the rights of the monastery to an annual rent from the customs-post at Fos, immediately off which the wreck Saint-Gervais 2 had sunk, perhaps around the date of the original concession. The list of commodities to which the monastery was entitled is quoted in full below; it is headed by 10,000 pounds of oil.[31]

Marseille was the great slave-market of the age as far as Pirenne was concerned;[32] we have no quantitative evidence for the slave-trade to set alongside the figures for oil, of course, but it does appear to have been significant in the seventh century. During his period of office in Provence in the 630s, the *patricius* Eligius is said to have redeemed Romans, Gauls, Britons, Moors, and especially Saxons from slavery; some of these unfortunates—*utriusque sexus ex diversis gentibus*—had arrived by ship in cargoes of up to a hundred at a time.[33] Bonitus engaged in similar activity when *patricius* in Marseille at the end of the seventh century.[34] And it was of course in Provence that Pope Gregory had sought to acquire Anglo-Saxon slaves for missionary training a century earlier.[35] This evidence is thoroughly anecdotal, and substantially hagiographical. However, it seems sufficient to suggest thriving and, if the *Vita Eligii* can be trusted, two-way traffic in slaves via Provence and, in particular, Marseille until at least the end of the seventh century.

---

[30] *Chartae Latinae Antiquiores* XIV, *France II*, nos. 574, 589, eds. H. Atsma and J. Vezin (Dietikon/Zurich, 1982); S. Lebecq, "The role of the monasteries in the systems of production and exchange of the Frankish world between the seventh and the beginning of the ninth centuries", (this volume), pp. 137, 146.

[31] L. Levillain, *Examen critique des chartes mérovingiennes et carolingiennes de l'abbaye de Corbie* (Paris, 1902), no. 15, pp. 236-37.

[32] Pirenne, *Mahomet et Charlemagne*, p. 81.

[33] *Vita Eligii episcopi Noviomagensis*, I.10, ed. B. Krusch, *Monumenta Germaniae Historica, Scriptores Rerum Merovingicarum* IV (Hannover, 1902), pp. 634-741. Krusch concluded that this episode took place at Marseille, an opinion which has since been widely adopted. It could nevertheless conceivably have occurred at Arles, where Eligius was also active.

[34] *Vita Boniti episcopi Arverni*, 3, ed. B. Krusch, *Monumenta Germaniae Historica, Scriptores Rerum Merovingicarum* VI (Hannover, 1913), pp. 110-39.

[35] Pope Gregory I, *Registrum epistularum*, VI.10, ed. D. Norberg (*Corpus Christianorum series latina* 140 and 140A), 2 vols. (Turnhout, 1982).

Virtually the only other direct documentary reference to Provençal trade in this period is provided by the celebrated cornucopia of commodities listed in the afore-mentioned *tractorium* issued by Chilperic II in favour of Corbie on 29 April 716. Its interest is such that Pirenne saw fit to quote in full the terms of the concessions to the representatives of the monastery to be made each year from the toll-station at Fos;[36] it seems worth doing likewise here:

> 10000 pounds of oil; thirty modii of *garum* (fish-sauce); thirty pounds of pepper; 150 pounds of cumin; two pounds of cloves; one pound of cinnamon; two pounds of spikenard; thirty pounds of *costum*; fifty pounds of dates; 100 pounds of figs; 100 pounds of almonds; thirty pounds of pistachios; 100 pounds of olives; fifty pounds of *hidrio* [not certainly identified]; 150 pounds of chick-peas; twenty pounds of rice; ten pounds of orpiment [for making yellow dyes]; ten oilskins; ten skins of Cordoba leather; fifty quires [*tomi*] of papyrus.

The diploma goes on to specify the supplies to be given to the abbey's agents on their journey, not to mention the provision of a strong escort and the fifteen carts required to convey such a transport of delights over the long journey up into north-eastern Francia. Although one or two of the commodities mentioned could have been cultivated in Provence, the vast majority can only have been imported, some from around the shores of the Mediterranean from Spain (the Cordoban skins) to Egypt (the papyrus), others, such as the orpiment, pepper, cloves and cinnamon, from even farther afield via the Red Sea or the Persian Gulf. It is worth bearing in mind that this is supposedly an *annual* render, throwing into sharp relief Gregory of Tours' passing comment on the partiality of ascetics for Egyptian herb-roots.[37] The quantity of pepper is perhaps a particularly astonishing illustration of the scale of the traffic in commodities of this nature, the ramifications of which reached beyond Corbie to the further reaches of the northern world, where Bede, for example, kept

---

[36] Pirenne, *Mahomet et Charlemagne*, pp. 71-72; Lebecq, "The role of the monasteries", pp. 137, 146.

[37] Gregory of Tours, *Historiae* VI.6. For further references to the availability of a wide range of oriental herbs and spices in Merovingian Francia, cf. esp. Marculf, *Form.* I.11 and Anthimus, *De observatione ciborum ad Theodericum regem Francorum epistula*, ed. E. Liechtenhan, *Corpus medicorum latinorum* VIII.1 (Berlin, 1963). These commodities are usefully discussed by item in D. Claude, *Untersuchungen zu Handel und Verkehr der vor- und frühgeschichtlichen Zeit in Mittel- und Nordeuropa, II, Der Handel im westlichen Mittelmeer während des Frühmittelalters* (Göttingen, 1985), pp. 71-92.

pepper and incense in his box in the monastery at Jarrow.[38] Taken
as a whole, the list offers a fascinating and unparalleled insight into
the range of commodities which were shipped from the Mediterranean
to Francia via Provence in the post-Roman period, and, in theory,
on into the early eighth century. As such it can be set alongside the
diversity and complexity of commercial relationships which is implied
archaeologically by the several varieties of amphorae excavated at
the Bourse and elsewhere. The problem to which we will have to
return is whether all the items listed in the Corbie diploma really
were still available at the Provençal ports on such a scale as late as
716, when the archaeological evidence suggests that the long-distance
Mediterranean exchange-network was in crisis.

These few but significant pieces of evidence for the trade of the
Provençal ports and the transport of commodities through them into
the Frankish heartlands via the Rhône valley are indirectly corrob-
orated in several respects. Those venturing between the northern
world and the Mediterranean had from the 570s onwards preferred
to travel via the Rhône valley and the Tyrrhenian Sea rather than
over the Alpine passes. This preference persists, as far as our anecdotal evidence permits us to tell, for much of the seventh century.[39]
The unfortunate Bishop Romanus of Rochester sank off Provence
when en route to Rome in the late 620s, while Archbishop Theodore
and Abbot Hadrian took the same course in reverse, but with better luck, when travelling from Rome to Canterbury via Marseille in
668.[40] Similarly, Bishop Ansoald of Poitiers returned to his see from
Sicily by ship in 638.[41] From the last quarter of the seventh century
onwards, however, the land-route over the Alpine passes resumes its
former dominance in international communications. Travel by ship
to or from Provence never ceased altogether, of course, but it seems
thereafter to be preferred primarily in those periods when the problematic relations of the Franks and the Lombards dictated that it
was expedient to bypass northern Italy, notably in the third quarter

---

[38] Cuthbert, *Epistola de obitu Bedae*, eds. B. Colgrave and R.A.B. Mynors, *Bede's Ecclesiastical History of the English People* (Oxford, 1969), p. 584.
[39] Claude, *Untersuchungen zu Handel und Verkehr*, pp. 134-44; Loseby, "Marseille and the Pirenne thesis, I", pp. 220-1; R. Buchner, *Die Provence in merowingischer Zeit. Verfassung-Wirtschaft-Kultur* (Berlin, 1933), pp. 37-39.
[40] Bede, *Historia ecclesiastica gentis A⸱ ᵗ ᵐum*, eds. B. Colgrave and R.A.B. Mynors (Oxford, 1969), II.20; IV.1.
[41] *Gesta Dagoberti I*, 44.

of the eighth century.[42] If it is reasonable to regard the movement
of persons as a secondary indicator of dominant exchange-routes,
then it is tempting to associate this change in the major axis of travel
between Francia and the Mediterranean world at least in part with
the transformations taking place at around this time in the commercial sphere.

Two mechanisms were identified in my previous article which it
was suggested had been developed by the Frankish kings with the
specific intention of reaping maximum benefit from traffic on the
lower Rhône valley trade route: a distinct and carefully managed
coinage, and the royal warehouses at the Provençal ports standing
at the head of a chain of toll-stations extending inland up the Rhône
corridor. It was further argued that the references to Marseille in
the works of Gregory of Tours are best interpreted as indications of
its exceptional political significance within the Frankish polity, a
significance which is explicable only in terms of its successful operation as an *emporium*, the Merovingian gateway onto the Mediterranean.[43] None of this changes in the seventh century; indeed, if
anything the peculiar political and economic importance of Marseille
becomes more explicit.[44] First and foremost, the status of Marseille
as a centre of political power seems to have been formalised in this
period. In the late sixth century authority over Provence had been
divided between different Merovingian *regna*, whose principal representatives in the region were based, respectively, at Arles and Marseille.[45]
Although there were intermittently periods of partition in the seventh century as well, the prefecture or patriciate of Provence is now
invariably attached to Marseille in the sources, and never to Arles.[46]

---

[42] F.L. Ganshof, "Notes sur les ports de Provence du VIIIe au Xe siècle", *Revue
historique* 183 (1938), pp. 28-37; Claude, *Untersuchungen zu Handel und Verkehr*, p. 144.

[43] Loseby, "Marseille and the Pirenne thesis, I", pp. 221-27.

[44] For example, in the overtly royal nature of the coinage and the emergence of
the first direct references to the *cellaria fisci*, although there are reasons for suspecting
that they antedate their earliest appearance in the written record under Dagobert I.

[45] R. Buchner, *Die Provence in merowingischer Zeit*, esp. pp. 10-13. For some observations on the political situation of the region in the late sixth century, Loseby,
"Marseille and the Pirenne thesis, I", pp. 224-27, and in general for the Merovingian
period, S.T. Loseby, *Marseille in Late Antiquity and the early Middle Ages* (Oxford, forthcoming), ch. 5.

[46] E.g. *Vita Desiderii Cadurcae urbis episcopi*, 1, 2, 7, ed. B. Krusch, *Monumenta Germaniae
Historica, Scriptores Rerum Merovingicarum* IV (Hannover, 1902), pp. 547-602; *Passio
sancti Leudegarii episcopi et martyris*, I.9, ed. B. Krusch, *Monumenta Germaniae Historica,
Scriptores Rerum Merovingicarum* V (Hannover, 1910), pp. 282-322; *Passio Praiecti et martyris Arverni*, 23, ed. B. Krusch, *Monumenta Germaniae Historica, Scriptores Rerum Merovingicarum* V (Hannover, 1910), pp. 225-48; *Vita Boniti*, 3. The political divisions of the

Under the Roman empire, Arles had replaced Marseille as the principal focus of power in the lower Rhône area. In the seventh century the reversion to the pre-Roman situation, already long achieved in the commercial sphere, was formally acknowledged with the resumption by Marseille of regional political hegemony.[47]

There is, moreover, a significant difference between the backgrounds of those who held office in Marseille in the time of Gregory of Tours, and their seventh-century successors. In the earlier period they were drawn from the ranks of the local Gallo-Roman aristocracy, whose machinations were not always easy to control.[48] These families disappear permanently from view, for whatever reason, in the generation after Gregory. Five individuals are known to have exercised authority in Marseille in the seventh century: Syagrius, Desiderius, Hector, and Bonitus as patricians or prefects, and the minter Eligius, whose significance in contemporary politics is clear, even if the formal position which he held at Marseille is unrecorded.[49] Four of these men, Syagrius, Desiderius and Eligius in the 620s and 630s, and Bonitus in the 680s, have several characteristics in common.[50] Like the late sixth-century patricians, they are well-born Gallo-Romans; but they are also outsiders, all of whom had served their political apprenticeships at the royal court. Our knowledge of the seventh-century patricians is perhaps too partial to push this evidence too far, especially since it can be objected that we know about these men precisely because they were court placemen whose fidelity and high birth assisted their elevation to bishoprics, sainthood and finally, via their *Vitae*, to a place in the history books. Even so, it seems reasonable to regard the presence of such up-and-coming men in Marseille as indicative of the enduring interest in the administration

---

seventh century probably help to explain the existence of *cellaria* at both Marseille and Fos, connected with their role as Mediterranean gateways for different *regna*. I intend to discuss this hypothesis in more detail elsewhere.

[47] E. Ewig, "Die fränkischen Teilreiche im 7. Jahrhundert (613-714)", in *Spätantikes und Fränkisches Gallien*, I (Zurich/Munich, 1976), pp. 212-13, suggests that Arles remained the basis of a Burgundian patriciate, but there is no evidence to connect the holders of this office with Arles, and it is much more likely to have been based on the middle Rhône. For Arles and Marseille, Loseby, "Marseille: a late antique success story?", pp. 179-82.

[48] Loseby, "Marseille and the Pirenne thesis, I", p. 225, and more fully, Loseby, *Marseille*, ch. 5.

[49] Buchner, *Die Provence*, pp. 96-101, for a full list of Provençal *patricii*. For Eligius, J. Lafaurie, "Eligius monetarius", *Revue numismatique*, 6th ser. 19 (1977), pp. 111-51.

[50] The exception is the obscure Hector, for whom see H. Ebling, *Prosopographie der Amtsträger des Merowingerreiches von Chlothar II (613) bis Karl Martell (741)* (Munich, 1974), p. 172 (no. 207).

of the port taken by the Merovingian kings, who had perhaps come to regard it as too valuable to be entrusted to a local aristocracy whose loyalties had proved somewhat flexible in the time of Gregory of Tours. What it indubitably shows, meanwhile, is that close central control continued to be exercised over Marseille throughout the seventh century.

One isolated indication of this control is probably provided by a pair of silver dishes found in 1900 at Valdonne, some twenty-five kilometres north-east of Marseille, one of Byzantine, the other of Frankish manufacture. The latter is unique in offering a Merovingian version of the five control-stamps common on Byzantine silver-plate of this period; two of these feature crosses, two depict Frankish royal busts closely comparable to those found on the Marseille royal coinage of the early seventh century, and the fifth the name *Arbaldo*, who by analogy with Byzantine practice should very probably be seen as an official who was charged with guaranteeing the fineness of local silver production. The Merovingian plate duly matches its Byzantine counterpart in having a silver content of just over 90%.[51] The location of the discovery, the similarity with the royal coinage of Marseille, and the existence there of the *cellarium fisci*, another mechanism concerned with control over the distribution of goods, make it tempting to associate the organisation of this hallmarking with the port. There exists, moreover, an isolated documentary reference which implies the production of precious-metal plate at Marseille in the Merovingian period.[52] The affinities with contemporary Byzantine practice, already implicit in the minting of the quasi-imperial coinage and the similarities between the *cellaria fisci* and the *apotheke*, are particularly evident in this case, but the precise workings of the Byzantine system of control-stamps are once again scarcely any less obscure than those of its Merovingian counterpart.[53] Even so, the Valdonne dish would seem to represent a seventh-century manifestation of

---

[51] J. Werner, "Arbaldo (Haribaldus). Ein merowingischer *vir inluster* aus der Provence? (Bemerkungen zu den Silbertellern von Valdonne, Dép. Bouches-du-Rhône)", in P. Bastien *et al.* eds., *Mélanges de numismatique, d'archéologie et d'histoire offerts à Jean Lafaurie* (Paris, 1980), pp. 257-63.

[52] The will of Leudebod (651), *Recueil des chartes de l'abbaye de Saint-Benoît-sur-Loire*, I.1, eds. M. Prou and A. Vidier (Paris, 1900), p. 9: *idemque et scutellas II minores massilienses deauratas quae habent in medio cruces niellatas.*

[53] It is also worth noting that while the Valdonne dish falls into the familiar general category of *imitatio imperii*, the imitation in this case is knowing rather than slavish.

Frankish interest in the production and distribution of manufactured goods, influenced by contemporary Mediterranean models, which is particular to Provence, and probably centred upon Marseille.

The particular interest of the Merovingian kings in Marseille and its trade is more fully exhibited by the output of its mint. The early years of the sole reign of Chlothar II (613-29) saw the transformation into a royal coinage of the quasi-imperial gold coinage which had been minted in Provence since the 570s.[54] The switch from emperor to king notwithstanding, the royal coinage is identical with its predecessor, is issued from the same four principal mints—Marseille, Arles, Uzès and Viviers—and continues to represent a centrally-inspired attempt to profit from trade on the Rhône-valley axis.[55] It also remains unique in several respects. It is the only royal coinage to be issued on a regular basis in seventh-century Francia, the only one in which the *solidus* continues to be struck alongside the *tremissis*, and, with rare exceptions, the only one not to feature moneyers' names. One such exception is of particular importance, since it concerns no ordinary minter. The legend *Eligius monet(arius)* appears on coins struck at Marseille between c. 625 and c. 638 and, after the partition which followed Dagobert's death, on those issued at Arles between c. 638 and 641, before Eligius returned north to be consecrated bishop of Noyon. Eligius has persuasively been identified as some sort of royal master-minter, who endeavoured to preside over a controlled debasement of the gold coinage in Marseille, Arles and, notably, Paris.[56] While most coins minted in Francia were by this time falling below 50% fineness, the gold content of those struck by Eligius remains significantly higher: 72%-80% at Paris, 83%-91% at Marseille, and 54-71% at Arles.[57] As in the case of the name of Arbaldus on the Valdonne dish, so the stamping of Eligius' name on the royal coinage may have been intended as a further certification

[54] P. Grierson and M.A.S. Blackburn, *Medieval European Coinage, I: the Early Middle Ages (5th-10th centuries)* (Cambridge, 1986), pp. 128-31; E. Felder, "Zur Münzprägung der merowingischen Könige in Marseille", in P. Bastien *et al.* eds., *Mélanges de numismatique, d'archéologie et d'histoire offerts à Jean Lafaurie* (Paris, 1980), pp. 223-29.

[55] Loseby, "Marseille and the Pirenne thesis, I", pp. 223-7, for discussion of the quasi-imperial gold coinage of Marseille and associated bibliography.

[56] Lafaurie, "Eligius monetarius"; J.P.C. Kent, "Gold standards of the Merovingian coinage, A.D. 580-700", in E.T. Hall and D.M. Metcalf eds., *Methods of chemical and metallurgical investigation of ancient coinage* (London, 1972), pp. 69-74.

[57] One might suspect that the single surviving coin issued from Marseille by Eligius in the name of Sigibert III of being a later imitation, since its fineness of

of its quality.[58] The very presence of Eligius in the south, coupled with the exceptional standard of his coinage, suggests a desire to keep the royal issues as fine as possible despite difficulties which may be connected with a growing shortage of bullion. It also provides further confirmation of the particular interest of the state in the production of the Rhône-corridor royal coinage, and, indeed, is a further hint at the existence of a Merovingian economic policy of some description. But whatever Eligius was trying to achieve, the problems with the royal coinage of the lower Rhône valley ultimately proved insuperable. After his departure the fineness of the Marseille gold issues drops markedly, while at the other three main mints production appears to have ceased altogether between the 630s and the 650s. Only at Marseille, which had probably always been the dominant mint, does a gold coinage continue to be struck in the names of all the Austrasian kings down to Dagobert II (676-9), but it is increasingly debased and poorly-executed, and now bears additional initials, whether those of moneyers or patricians.[59]

The Marseille mint follows the rest of Francia over to a silver coinage thereafter, but its issues retain a peculiarity all of their own, and much about them remains equally obscure or controversial.[60] For present purposes I will confine myself to two basic points. First, the silver coinages struck in Provence in this period (the overwhelming majority of the surviving examples of which derive from the Cimiez hoard of c. 720 and were minted at Marseille) are consistently of lighter weight than those issued elsewhere in Francia in this period. Secondly, the names and monograms on the Marseille coinage can, at least in some cases, be identified with patricians of Provence named in the written sources of the late seventh and early eighth centuries.[61] The presence of a political authority on the Marseille issues is once again exceptional among contemporary coinages, and it is tempting to speculate that this anomaly is not unconnected with their short-weight, which could represent a cut taken by the patricians in con-

---

only 36% is consistent with other issues from the port in the name of that king, but not with those of Eligius.

[58] Werner, "Arbaldo (Haribaldus). Ein merowingischer *vir inluster* aus der Provence?", p. 261.

[59] Lafaurie, "Eligius monetarius", esp. pp. 136-39 and 128-29, slightly modified by Grierson and Blackburn, *Medieval European Coinage, I*, p. 130.

[60] Grierson and Blackburn, *Medieval European Coinage, I*, pp. 142-49.

[61] *Ibid*. The two identifiable patricians are Nemfidius and Antenor. However, the status of other named individuals cannot be verified, and the large M on some of the coins may simply indicate minting in the name of the city or its church.

verting silver bullion into coin. If so, this would be the last in the series of distinctive attempts to profit from control of the Provençal money-supply. But in this period the deterioration in central political authority over Provence makes it unclear whether any such profits from authority over minting were still being forwarded to the crown, or were being diverted into the patricians' own pockets.

Although many ambiguities in the workings of the various Marseille coinages persist (and speculation about them lies beyond the scope of this paper), the interest of the central authority in their production is assured until at least the middle of the seventh century, and there are vestigial traces of distinct management in the subsequent history of the silver coinage. Meanwhile, the findspot distribution of the Marseille gold and silver coinages up the Rhône and Saône, and thence along the Seine, Meuse, Moselle and Rhine valleys into the Frankish heartlands and across the Channel to Britain, continues to confirm the association of Marseille with the dominant axes of the burgeoning northern exchange network.[62] The links between the Marseille mint and the emerging poles of economic activity on the rivers feeding into the North Sea are also perceptible typologically, first in the influence of the quasi-imperial gold coinage of Provence upon late sixth-century northern Frankish issues from *castellum* Nijmegen and elsewhere, and, over a century later, in the connections between Frisian and Kentish issues and coins in the Cimiez hoard which were probably struck at Marseille.[63] Finds of Marseille silver issues in the North are admittedly few, but typological links such as these are at least suggestive of a continuing connection between Marseille and the exchange-network of the northern seas at the beginning of the eighth century.

A further mechanism which was established with a view to the exercise of some sort of control over Mediterranean imports into Francia is the *cellaria fisci*. These managed royal warehouses are only directly attested in the seventh and early eighth-century grants to the monasteries of St-Denis and Corbie mentioned above, and are seemingly peculiar to the ports of Marseille and Fos.[64] Taken at face

---

[62] J. Lafaurie, "Les monnaies de Marseille du VIᵉ au VIIIᵉ siècle", *Bulletin de la société française de numismatique* 36 (1981), p. 72.

[63] Lafaurie, "Les monnaies de Marseille", p. 70; Grierson and Blackburn, *Medieval European Coinage, I*, pp. 136-7, 149, 153-54, 170; A. Verhulst, "Roman cities, *emporia*, and new towns (sixth-ninth centuries)", (this volume).

[64] F.-L. Ganshof, "Les bureaux de tonlieu de Marseille et de Fos: contribution

value, the surviving references to the operations of these *cellaria* might be thought to indicate that Mediterranean imports were still arriving in some volume as late as 716, the date of the latest confirmations both of the rights of St-Denis at Marseille, and of those of Corbie at Fos, in the document which includes the extraordinary list of imports quoted above.[65] This would further suggest that the Merovingian kings had retained their close and controlling interest in the commerce of the Provençal ports. However, even the normally positivistic Pirenne was sceptical about the Corbie grant in particular, since his opinion of the devastating impact of the Arab conquests forced him to regard it as "merely an archaism".[66] In fact, it is not necessary to follow Pirenne's *a priori* assumptions in order to question the relevance of this and the contemporary grant in favour of St-Denis to the realities of Mediterranean trade at this time.

The history of the grant to St-Denis of privileges at Marseille is rather curious. It will be remembered that this originated with Dagobert in the 630s. Although this diploma is lost, along with four subsequent confirmations by Dagobert's successors, its terms are recorded by the author of the *Gesta Dagoberti*, and recur with minor modifications in the two extant *tractoria* issued by Clovis III in 691 and Chilperic II in 716.[67] These differ from the terms of the *Gesta* as described above in two particulars; they cease to specify oil as the commodity to be purchased, and omit the limitation on exemption from toll to six carts, observing simply that no toll or tax should be exacted on the goods acquired by the monastery. The omission of the specific reference to oil can be explained in a number of ways, whether as a simple accident, a streamlining of the grant, or a generous attempt to give the monastery's representatives more discre-

à l'histoire des institutions de la monarchie franque", *Études historiques à la mémoire de N. Didier* (Paris, 1960), pp. 125-33 is to be preferred to H. Pirenne, "Le *cellarium fisci*: une institution économique des temps mérovingiens", reprinted in his *Histoire économique de l'occident médiéval* (Paris, 1951), pp. 104-12. For a summary discussion of their possible operations, see also Loseby, "Marseille and the Pirenne thesis, I", pp. 222-23.

[65] Levillain, *Examen critique des chartes*, no. 15, pp. 236-37.

[66] Pirenne, *Mahomet et Charlemagne*, p. 147: "*je crois pourtant qu'il n'y a là qu'un archaïsme*". Pirenne nevertheless also tries to resolve the problem by hypothesising that the *cellarium* may have been drawing upon its stocks, conjuring up the unsavoury image of huge mounds of spices, slowly mouldering away in the Provençal ports until the *cellarium* was finally empty or, as he thinks very likely, was finally burnt down by the Arabs: *ibid.*, p. 151.

[67] *Gesta Dagoberti I*, 18; *Chartae Latinae Antiquiores* XIV, nos. 574, 589.

tion over their acquisitions. In a sense, it could even be thought to enhance the credibility of these documents, given that the archaeological evidence for the shipment of oil amphorae around the Mediterranean is in increasingly short supply by around 700. These minor changes notwithstanding, the determination of the monastery to secure the regular renewal of this grant is suggestive of its continuing value in the second half of the seventh century. Its history is rendered more complicated, however, by the survival of a precept of 694 which reveals that Childebert III had given St-Denis the royal villa of Nassigny, in the Berry, in exchange for the monastery yielding up an annual rent of 200 solidi given to it by the fisc and its rent of 100 solidi from the *cellarium* at Marseille.[68] The last recorded renewal of the monastery's rights at Marseille in 716 cannot therefore be quite as straightforward an act as it superficially appears.

The Corbie diploma of 716 gives more obvious grounds for suspicion, simply by virtue of the variety and volume of the imports listed therein. The stipulation of substantial quantities of oil sits uncomfortably with both the disappearance of any reference to this commodity in the surviving *tractorium* concerning St-Denis, and with the archaeological record, even if, as we have seen, it may now be possible to push the latest arrivals in Provence of the imported amphorae in which much of this oil must have been transported to the period around 700. The availability of the voluminous fifty *tomi* of papyrus, even if it is taken to refer to rolls rather than *tomi* proper (which would amount to 25000 sheets), seems equally improbable.[69] The last surviving document to be issued on papyrus from the Merovingian chancery rather than parchment dates from between 658/9 and 678/9, the latest private charter from 691.[70] The Corbie diploma itself exists only in a tenth-century copy, but the original documents from 691, 694 and 716 concerning the rights of St-Denis at Marseille do survive and are all, for example, written on parchment. As for the many other listed items, we have no means of assessing how far they were still available in the Provençal ports. But it is perhaps worth pointing out that although the Alpine passes

---

[68] *Chartae Latinae Antiquiores* XIV, no. 577.

[69] E. Sabbé, "Papyrus et parchemin au haut moyen âge", *Miscellanea historica in honoris Leonis van Essen* (Brussels/Paris, 1947), pp. 95-103, at p. 98; for a general summary of the availability of papyrus in the western Mediterranean in this period, Claude, *Untersuchungen zu Handel und Verkehr*, pp. 89-92.

[70] *Chartae Latinae Antiquiores* XIV, nos. 557, 563.

would generally have been less convenient for long-distance trade than river- and sea-transport, any continuation of the international trade in spices could, given their high value but low volume, have readily been carried on via these newly-revived land routes.

There is in fact a political context for the final confirmations of these grants to St-Denis and Corbie which helps to explain their existence without requiring them to be representative of the contemporary commercial context. When they were issued in 716, Chilperic II, known until recently as Daniel, a monk of St-Denis, had just been taken out of the monastery to serve as a Merovingian figurehead for the Neustrian opponents of Arnulfing domination. Whatever one thinks of the effectiveness of Chilperic's regime, it is undeniable that an unusual number of grants, especially in favour of the Neustrian monasteries, survive from the opening years of his reign, suggestive of a charm-offensive by a ruler of questionable legitimacy.[71] Chilperic's obvious affinities with the community from which he had just emerged could help to explain the confirmation of a grant in favour of St-Denis which the monastery had previously surrendered. Furthermore, Chilperic's ability to command the operations of the distant Provençal toll-stations, particularly so early on in his reign, is highly questionable. The revolt of Provence in the early eighth century is recorded only in two confused documents dating from the time of Charlemagne, and remains desperately difficult to disentangle, especially since it has often been considered in the light of the resistance of the region to Charles Martel in the 730s, the precise political context of which may have been very different.[72] Although it has sometimes been assumed that the Provençal aristocracy would have been sympathetic to Chilperic's regime, there is no explicit evidence to number its members among his active supporters; the two *tractoria*, which have been used in support of this

---

[71] The author of the *Liber Historiae Francorum*, writing in the next decade, appears despite his Neustrian sympathies to have taken a very sceptical view of Chilperic and his legitimacy: P. Fouracre and R.A. Gerberding, *Late Merovingian France. History and hagiography, 640-720* (Manchester, 1996), pp. 85-6; I.N. Wood, *The Merovingian kingdoms, 450-751* (London, 1994), pp. 267-70, sees Chilperic II in a more positive light.

[72] Buchner, *Die Provence in merowingischer Zeit*, pp. 98-100; F.-L. Ganshof, "Les avatars d'un domaine de l'église de Marseille à la fin du VIIe et au VIIIe siècle", in *Studi in onore di Gino Luzzatto*, vol. 1 (Milan, 1950), pp. 55-66. P.J. Geary, *Aristocracy in Provence. The Rhône basin at the dawn of the Carolingian age* (Stuttgart, 1985), pp. 126-43, for an interpretation of the revolts against the broader Frankish political background.

view, are as likely to be expressions of hope or statements of intent as manifestations of effective political power, particularly given the novelty of Chilperic's rule and the distance separating the new king from the Provençal ports.[73] The reception of these *tractoria* in Provence is thus far from guaranteed, but they were in any case aimed at an audience closer to home. They make most sense as acts of political opportunism, propaganda ploys to conciliate support, assert authority, and associate the so-called Chilperic with the enactments of his supposed Merovingian forebears. The Neustrian monasteries, meanwhile, have nothing to lose from the reassertion of their rights, or in the case of St-Denis from perhaps exploiting the situation to lay claim to privileges to which they were no longer entitled. But the letter of the grants may have been doubly meaningless. The ability of Chilperic's court to direct the operations of the Provençal ports is in doubt in the light of ill-documented rebellions by the local patricians and the novelty and fragility of his regime. More to the point, however, it is debatable how far those operations were still worth directing in any case.

Conclusions

The emergence of archaeological contexts of later seventh- and perhaps early eighth-century date in southern Gaul cannot conceal the likelihood that the protracted decline of the interregional Mediterranean exchange-network had finally reached crisis point. The closely-datable assemblages recovered from two deposits of later seventh and early eighth century date in the Crypta Balbi at Rome demonstrate this with exceptional sharpness. The former features a diversity of ceramic material, especially amphorae, indicative of continuing contacts with various regions of the Mediterranean; the latter consists almost entirely of more local material, exhibiting no obvious trace of contacts further afield than southern Italy.[74] The few archaeological deposits of this period in southern Gaul do not at present offer such a well-defined break, not least because no deposits have yet been

---

[73] Geary, *Aristocracy in Provence*, p. 141, sees the *tractoria* as proof of Chilperic's power in Provence.

[74] Saguì, Ricci and Romei, "Nuovi dati ceramologici per la storia economica di Roma tra VII et VIII secolo".

identified which are unequivocally of eighth-century date. Although it is now certain that imported ceramics were continuing to arrive in southern Gaul in the second half of the seventh century, it is not yet clear how far they went on doing so into or beyond that period. Nevertheless, the evidence generally converges to suggest a steady deterioration in the vitality of the region's principal trading-centre, Marseille, from the third quarter of the seventh century. The once-thriving artisanal suburb at the rear of the Vieux-Port enters its final abandonment phase. The switch by long-distance travellers from the Rhône valley route to the Alpine passes from the 670s may be indic-ative of a parallel transformation in patterns of exchange, such that any traffic in low-volume luxury items began to bypass Marseille. The determined efforts to maintain the fineness of the region's anom-alous royal gold coinage fail, suggesting a diminishing availability of gold and, much more hypothetically, a possible decline in traffic; meanwhile, the coinage itself begins to go out of production, finally ceasing to be struck at Marseille in the 670s. Even if the silver coinage struck at the Marseille mint retains some idiosyncracies of its own, the change from gold to silver appears to mark a change in the manner (and perhaps the value) of exploitation of the lower Rhône money-supply, and the end of any overt central interest in the minting of coin in the region.

A hypothetical context for the decline of Marseille as an *emporium* might therefore be thought to lie between the dates of the initial grants to St-Denis and Corbie, in the 630s and the 660s respect-ively, and the final reassertions of these concessions in 716. If there are various reasons for suspecting that the latter were not worth the parchment they were written on, it seems excessively cynical to doubt that the privileges were originally conferred upon these royally-spon-sored monastic foundations (very probably to match those granted to other communities besides) in good faith. The availability of such imports at the Provençal ports was perhaps becoming increasingly sporadic by around the middle of the seventh century, but, as the archaeological evidence now begins to confirm, it was far from out of the question. Furthermore, the royal court took the trouble to retain close control over Marseille until at least as late as the 680s, when Bonitus held the patrician office. While the meaningful exer-cise of royal authority in Provence becomes much more uncertain at the beginning of the eighth century, it remains debatable whether this is indicative of the growing insignificance of Marseille and its region or whether it merely represents another facet of the emerging weakness of the Merovingian centre in relation to the peripheral areas of the Frankish kingdom in this period. But the disappearance of documents written on papyrus, the likely decline of oil imports, and the decision of St-Denis to cash in its rights at Marseille against an estate in the Berry suggests that these privileges were declining in value, and casts doubt on the credibility of their latest confirmations in 716. The decline in Marseille's fortunes was gradual and complex, but by then it had reached a critical stage. It is ironic that our fullest documentary account of the scale and variety of Mediterranean imports to Francia in the post-Roman period, the Corbie diploma, almost certainly dates from a time when those imports were at long last petering out.

The demise of Marseille was brought about by the familiar historical combination of a long-term trend finally brought to a head in a short-term crisis. Its weaknesses were essentially structural. The port has always been dependent upon Mediterranean trade to fulfil its time-honoured role as a gateway community, and as such it can, as Pirenne saw, serve as a useful barometer of the general vitality of such exchange. In the late sixth and seventh centuries the late antique exchange-system was progressively contracting, but Marseille appears to some extent to have been insulated from this trend, probably by virtue of its function as the main gateway for the vast and wealthy Frankish market. The consistent Merovingian interest in the port is inexplicable unless its trade remained of sufficient quantity or value to be worth fighting over or exploiting. There are indeed signs that Marseille may have remained a preferred western Mediterranean market for interregional trade for much of the seventh century, even if the limited ceramic evidence from this period necessitates caution. Such trade was not therefore confined to those areas of the western Mediterranean which remained under direct imperial control.

The collapse of Marseille as an *emporium* is more likely to be caused by a failure of production and distribution-networks in the Mediterranean than by a failure of demand on the Frankish market. There is no reason to think that the secular and ecclesiastical élites of the northern world had ceased to seek supplies of oil and papyrus, indeed the St-Denis and Corbie charters imply they were as eager to guarantee their access to such commodities as the Merovingian kings were to control the redistribution of prestige items. But as they became progressively harder for even the well-connected to acquire, so recourse was increasingly had to more readily available alternatives, whether, like wax and parchment, for practical purposes, or for reasons of status-display. In truth, the Merovingian elite seem remarkably wedded to the material culture of late antiquity in lighting their churches, writing their charters, and, for the privileged few, in drinking their wine, and to give it up only with surprising reluctance. Marseille survived as an *emporium* for as long as Mediterranean trade persisted; it was the final extinction of the exchange-network inherited from Late Antiquity rather than any failure of demand which brought about its downfall.

Finally, the chronology advanced by Pirenne for the final collapse of that exchange-network has increased in credibility over the last few years, even though it should be emphasised that the archaeological evidence gives every reason to think that this was a much more gradual process than he had envisaged; the Arab conquests are still unlikely to be more than a contributory factor to a longer-term transformation of patterns of exchange. His identification of a fundamental shift in the economic geography of Francia, though excessively simplistic, also stands up well to scrutiny. While a dynamic new generation of *emporia* emerges from the seventh century onwards around the coasts of the North Sea, Marseille dwindles away into Carolingian obscurity. It is true that the rumours of its death put about by Pirenne were somewhat exaggerated. Documentary evidence has been assembled to show the continued use of the ports on the Provençal coast in the eighth and ninth centuries;[75] to give just one example, the maintenance of commercial connections with the northern world is epitomised by one Botto, an Anglo-Saxon merchant who lived at Marseille in around 750.[76] Even so, indications that Marseille continued to matter in the wider scheme of things are conspicuously lacking. Instead, the greatest Merovingian port had been relegated to the margins of the Carolingian empire. The late antique Mediterranean *koine*, its international ramifications represented above all by thousands upon thousands of sherds of amphorae

---

[75] Ganshof, "Notes sur les ports de Provence du VIIIᵉ au Xᵉ siècle".

[76] *Annales Petaviani*, s.a. 790, ed. G.M. Pertz, *Monumenta Germaniae Historica, Scriptores* 1, (Hannover, 1885), 7-19. For a more optimistic view than mine of continuing Mediterranean 'connectivity' see now the excellent P. Horden and N. Purcell, *The Corrupting Sea. A Study of Mediterranean history*, (Oxford, 2000), esp. pp. 160-72.

and fine pottery, had slowly but inexorably dissolved, leaving only the host of regional and local economies lurking beneath it. By comparison with other areas, such as southern Italy, the regional economy of Provence does not seem especially sophisticated in this period; it could not, for example, sustain a fine-ware pottery industry. In any event, Marseille has always been ill-placed to fulfil the role of regional economic centre. Its hinterland is not the *arrière-pays* of Provence, from which it is geographically isolated, but the wider vistas of the Mediterranean. Unfortunately for the port, this meant that it had relied for its special significance upon the more elevated tiers of the economy which all the evidence suggests had virtually ceased to exist. This did not have to imply the death of Marseille; institutions such as the monastery of St-Victor helped to ensure that it retained a role as a central place within Provence, amply revealed in one of the very few sources to survive from the region in this period, the abbey's polyptych, until recently interpreted with excessive pessimism.[77] But it is no coincidence that in the Carolingian period political power within Provence gravitated back towards Arles. Marseille had been founded as an *emporium*; the tides of Mediterranean trade would have to come in again before the life of the port could properly be revived, and this would not occur before the tenth century at the earliest. The Carolingian *renovatio* would encompass many things; a revival of Mediterranean trade was not among them.

---

[77] M. Zerner, "Sur la croissance agricole en Provence", *La croissance agricole du Haut Moyen Age* (Auch, 1990), pp. 153-67.

Fig. 1. Italy. Sites and monasteries mentioned in the text.

SOME CONSIDERATIONS ON THE COINAGE
OF LOMBARD AND CAROLINGIAN ITALY*

Alessia Rovelli

Among the provinces which constituted the western Roman empire, Italy had a particular destiny, and not just because of its centrality in the Mediterranean region: the kingdom of Theoderic, far from representing a break, explicitly described itself as a restoration of the ancient Roman order; the Justinianic conquest further reinforced connections with the Roman-Byzantine tradition. Italy's "Mediterranean vocation" decisively influenced the process of its transformation from the late antique to the medieval era. Nor was this vocation eradicated by the Lombard invasion, however violent it might have been; and it probably explains, at least in part, the marginal character that Italian Carolingian coin issues seem to have had, when compared with those of other more central regions of the Frankish empire.

The weight of Roman-Byzantine tradition is particularly evident in the evolution of the monetary systems adopted in Italy, which, as we shall see, followed different paths from the coinages of the other Roman-barbarian kingdoms, except, in part, in the use of bronze coinage.[1] In northern Italy, conquered by the Lombards in 568, the

---

* In writing this article I have been able to benefit from many friendly discussions with Ermanno Arslan, whom I thank for also having provided me with vital information from unpublished material. I am grateful to Marios Costambeys for translating this article.
[1] On monetary production and circulation in the Ostrogthic era, which lies outside the chronological limits of this study, see E.A. Arslan, "La monetazione dei Goti", *XXXVI Corso di cultura sull'arte ravennate e bizantina* (Ravenna, 1989), pp. 17-72; E.A. Arslan, "La struttura delle emissioni monetarie dei Goti in Italia", *Teodorico e i Goti d'Italia. Atti del XIII Congresso internazionale di studi sull'alto Medioevo* (Spoleto, 1993), pp. 517-53. For regional studies: E. Ercolani Cocchi, "La circolazione monetale fra tardo antico e alto medioevo: dagli scavi di Villa Clelia", *Studi romagnoli* 29 (1978), pp. 367-99; E. Ercolani Cocchi, "Il circolante divisionale a Ravenna, fra la fine del V e gli inizi del VI sec. d.C.", in P. Kos and Z. Demo eds., *Studia Numismatica Labacensia Alexandro Jeločnik oblata* (Ljubljana, 1988), pp. 43-52; G. Gorini, "Moneta e scambi nel Veneto altomedievale", in A. Castagnetti and G.M. Varanini eds., *Il Veneto nel Medioevo. Dalla "Venetia" alla Marca Veronese* (Verona, 1989), pp. 167-97.

contraction of the bronze coinage and the resultant simplification of the currency is evident in the second half of the sixth century.[2] While it is possible, if not probable, that the abundant late Roman and Ostrogothic bronze issues had a prolonged life, no issues of Lombard coinage in this metal have come to light up to now, with the single exception of the *folles* of Aistulf at Ravenna in the 750s.[3]

As far as the circulation of Mediterranean goods is concerned, the Lombard conquest in its initial phase seems to have exacerbated the isolation of the regions around the Po, already perceptible in the late Roman era. These goods ceased to flow in, yet still arrived in other parts of northern Italy—in Liguria and Romagna, for example—which, besides being on the coast, remained Byzantine. At the same time, typical products of the Lombard Po valley, such as stamped ceramics, were not diffused elsewhere.[4] However, the "negative" impact of the Lombards must be carefully analysed and circumscribed in time. It remains to be established how far *Langobardia*'s isolation depended on its conquerors and how far on a collection of other causes.

From the point of view of currency, Luni on the Ligurian coast presents an interesting case, even though the small size of the areas excavated makes it premature to draw general conclusions. At any rate, Byzantine coins from the mints of Constantinople, Carthage, Syracuse and Rome continued to arrive there even after the Lombard occupation, which took place in 641-2. These therefore circulated in

---

[2] E.A. Arslan, "La circolazione monetaria (secoli V-VIII)", in R. Francovich and G. Noyé eds., *La storia dell'Alto Medioevo italiano (VI-X secolo) alla luce dell'archeologia*, Atti del Convegno internazionale, Siena, 2-6 dicembre 1992 (Florence, 1994), pp. 497-519, with a complex synthesis on the different regions and a review of coin finds; there are further important clarifications in E.A. Arslan, "Problemi di circolazione monetaria in Piemonte dal V all'VIII secolo", in L. Mercando and E. Micheletto eds., *Archeologia in Piemonte 3, Il Medioevo* (Torino, 1998), pp. 289-307.

[3] Ercolani Cocchi, "La circolazione monetale fra tardo antico e alto medioevo: dagli scavi di Villa Clelia", p. 381; Arslan, "Problemi di circolazione monetaria in Piemonte dal V all'VIII secolo", p. 301; on Aistulf's *folles* see note 11; for some general points relating to the long-lasting circulation of late Roman bronze coinage: L. Saguì and A. Rovelli, "Residualità, non residualità, continuità di circolazione. Alcuni esempi dalla Crypta Balbi", in F. Guidobaldi, C. Pavolini and Ph. Pergola eds., *I materiali residui nello scavo archeologico*, Collection de l'Ecole française de Rome 249 (Rome, 1998), pp. 173-95.

[4] P. Delogu, "La fine del mondo antico e l'inizio del medioevo: nuovi dati per un vecchio problema", in *La storia dell'Alto Medioevo italiano (VI-X secolo)*, pp. 7-29; on the pottery, see G.P. Brogiolo, S. Gelichi and S. Massa in L. Saguì ed., *Ceramica in Italia: VI-VII secolo*, Atti del Colloquio in onore di John W. Hayes, Roma, 11-13 maggio 1995 (Florence, 1998), pp. 209-26, 591-97.

parallel to gold *tremisses* from the Lombard mints, especially Lucca.[5] In spite of the clear archaeological evidence of the decline of the city, these discoveries indicate the persistence of exchange across the Mediterranean.[6] Peculiar to Luni also is the production of lead coins in the seventh and eighth centuries, probably issued in order to supplement the bronze currency.[7] We can see that the currency was therefore articulated, combining gold coins with lower value issues, whether bronze or lead.

If bronze or lead currency in the Lombard kingdom appears at the moment to be attested at coastal sites—which, like Luni, are probably atypical—and is very sporadic elsewhere, in Byzantine Italy the situation was more complex.[8] In the Byzantine provinces of southern Italy the currency seems to have been numerous and varied, in both urban and rural contexts, from the time of the Justinianic reconquest. It was in fact the troop movements of Belisarius and Narses that brought about the first imports of eastern coin, to which were joined, between 538 and 552, Byzantine issues at Rome and Ravenna.[9]

---

[5] A. Bertino, "Monete attestate a Luni dal IV al IX secolo", *Rivista di studi liguri* 49 (1983), pp. 265-300. There are reports of ships landing at Luni until the twelfth century. Among the coin finds note the presence of a *follis* of Manso III, duke of Amalfi, lord of Salerno (981-983) and of Roger Borsa, duke of Apulia (1085-1111): A. Frova ed., *Luni, guida archeologica* (Sarzana, 1985), p. 326; A. Bertino, "Soprintendenza alle Antichità della Liguria", *Annali dell'Istituto italiano di Numismatica* 14 (1965-1967), pp. 171-210. For the early medieval contexts at Luni, see B. Ward Perkins, "Two Byzantine Houses at Luni", *Papers of the British School at Rome* 49 (1981), pp. 91-98; S. Lusuardi Siena, "Lo scavo nella cattedrale di Luni (SP). Notizie preliminari sulle campagne 1976-1984", *Archeologia Medievale* 12 (1985), pp. 303-11.

[6] See also the case of Marseille: S.T. Loseby, "Marseille and the Pirenne Thesis, I: Gregory of Tours, the Merovingians kings and 'un grand port'", in R. Hodges and W. Bowden eds., *The Sixth Century. Production, Distribution and Demand* (Leiden, 1998), pp. 203-29; M. Bonifay *et al.* eds., *Fouilles à Marseille. Les mobiliers (Ier-VII siècles ap. J.-C.)* (Paris, 1998). On the finds at San Peyre, a rural site in the hinterland of the Languedoc, see C. Citter, L. Paroli, Ch. Pellecuer and J.M. Péne, "Commerci nel Mediterraneo occidentale nell'alto medioevo", in G.P. Brogiolo ed., *Early medieval towns in the Western Medieterranean* (Mantua, 1996), pp. 121-42.

[7] R. Ricci, "Le coniazioni altomedievali dei vescovi di Luni", *Giornale storico della Lunigiana e del Territorio Lucense* n.s. 39 (1988), pp. 45-63.

[8] E.A. Arslan, "Le monete", in G.P. Brogiolo ed., *Santa Giulia di Brescia: gli scavi dal 1980 al 1992. Reperti pre-romani, romani e altomedievali* (Florence, 1999), pp. 347-99.

[9] G. Guzzetta, "Per la Calabria bizantina: primo censimento dei dati numismatici", *Calabria bizantina. Istituzioni civili e topografia storica* (Rome/Reggio Calabria, 1986), pp. 251-80. On the circulation of Byzantine coins struck in Sicily, see C. Morrisson, "La Sicile byzantine: une lueur dans les siècles obscurs", *Numismatica e Antichità classiche, Quaderni ticinesi* 27 (1998), pp. 307-334; G. Guzzetta, "La circolazione monetaria in Sicilia dal IV al VII secolo d.C.", *Bollettino di Numismatica* 25 (1995), pp. 7-30.

Moreover, from sources written a little after 732, we can see that in the theme of Sicily, composed roughly of Sicily and modern Calabria, the Byzantine state received a tax of at least 25,000 *solidi*.[10] Information for the other parts of Byzantine Italy is more dispersed. With the possible exception of the Exarchate, where the entirely tri-metallic (i.e. gold, silver and bronze) currency seems to have been fairly homogeneous, elsewhere the available evidence shows the coin-age, especially the bronze coinage, concentrated in urban centres with a strong Byzantine presence, generally those in which there was an active mint.[11] Otherwise, it appears at sites that were important for their economic or institutional role, such as episcopal sees or milit-ary garrisons. Rome and Lazio, where excavations are in progress in sample areas, provide some interesting examples. At Rome, it is possible now to posit the full circulation of a bronze currency up to the first decades of the eighth century.[12] In extra-urban contexts,

---

[10] F. Marazzi, "Roma, il Lazio, il Mediterraneo: relazioni fra economia e polit-ica dal VII al IX secolo", in L. Paroli and P. Delogu eds., *La storia economica di Roma nell'alto Medioevo alla luce dei recenti scavi archeologici*, Atti del Seminario, Roma, 2-3 aprile 1992 (Florence, 1993), pp. 267-85, esp. 283-84, which proposes a new reading of the estimates put forward by A. Guillou, "La Sicile byzantine. Etat de recherches", *Byzantinische Forschungen* 5 (1977), pp. 95-145, esp. 105-107 where a tax of 373,332 *solidi* is calculated.

[11] At Ravenna, the issues of *folles* effected by the Lombard king Aistulf (751-756), on the day after his conquest of the city, are proof that bronze still played an important part in the currency. According to Arslan this would confirm the remark-able sophistication of Ravenna's economy and currency on the eve of the closure of its mint: Arslan, "La circolazione monetaria (secoli V-VIII)", pp. 502-03.

[12] A. Rovelli, "Monetary circulation in Byzantine and Carolingian Rome: a recon-sideration in the light of recent archaeological data", in T.S. Brown and J.M.H. Smith eds., *Early Mediaeval Rome and the Christian West*, University of St Andrews, 11-14 June, 1998 (Leiden, forthcoming). The opening of the mint at Naples during the reign of Constans II should be noted. At Naples, the emperors coined *solidi, tremis-ses* and, until about 695, bronze coins of 20 nummi. The attribution to Constantine V of a *follis* that carries the busts of the emperor and of Leo IV on the obverse is uncertain. This evidence, however fragmentary, suggests a situation analogous to that at Rome, with a currency that remained multifaceted. The *folles* issued in the course of the ninth century by some Neapolitan dukes and by Bishop Athanasius II help to confirm this impression, especially in urban contexts. There is no evidence, partly due to an absence of excavation, for the surrounding area. On the issues from Byzantine Naples, see P. Grierson, *Catalogue of the Byzantine Coins in the Dumbarton Oaks Collection and in the Whittemore Collection* vol. II (Washington, 1968), pp. 48-49, vol. III (Washington, 1973), pp. 84-87; see further P. Grierson and L. Travaini, *Medieval European Coinage 14, Italy (III) (South Italy, Sicily, Sardinia)* (Cambridge, 1998), pp. 43-49. On early medieval Naples, see P. Arthur, "Naples: a case of urban sur-vival in the early Middle Ages?" *Mélanges de l'Ecole française de Rome, Moyen âge* 103.2 (1991), pp. 759-84.

however, the bronze currency seems to have been maintained at appreciable levels throughout the sixth century, but not beyond. As far as the seventh century is concerned, in fact, the more or less systematic excavations undertaken near Orte (Viterbo) and at some sites in the Sabina have recovered ceramics, all of very local manufacture, but no coins. One exception is Santa Rufina (Rome), which was an episcopal see and, significantly, is the only site in the *suburbium* apart from the abbey of Farfa to have produced seventh-century African Red Slip ware hitherto. The importance of the two sites—one an episcopal see, the other abbatial—probably explains the quality of the ceramic and numismatic finds.[13] The overall conclusion that can be drawn from this recently-acquired data relating to the Byzantine territories of north-central Italy is that the circulation of a bronze currency is now more tangible than it previously was. Yet its use seems to be attested largely in urban environments, and it should probably be connected to the presence of a social stratum composed of soldiers and officials of the Byzantine bureaucracy.[14]

The disappearance from the scene of the bronze currency was compensated for by the production, in both Lombard and Byzantine areas, of a silver coinage of very low fineness. Such silver issues themselves emphasise the uniqueness of the currency and, quite possibly, of the economic structure of Italy in comparison to the situation developing beyond the Alps. Let us first look briefly at the Lombard issues, which have not yet been entirely systematised into an organic corpus.[15] Generally considered to have been produced in Lombard northern Italy are the different fractions of *siliquae* (probably quarters and eighths) that imitate Ravennate types of Justinian and Justin II. There are also rare imitations of half-*siliquae* of Tiberius II (578-82) and Maurice (582-602).[16] The dating of these imitations,

---

[13] H. Patterson and A. Rovelli, "Ceramics and coins in the Middle Tiber Valley from the late Imperial period to the early Middle Ages", in H. Patterson ed., *Further Approaches to Regional Archaeology in the Middle Tiber Valley*, Rome, 27-28 February 1998 (forthcoming).

[14] On the nature and functioning of the currency in the late Roman and Byzantine world, see M.F. Hendy, "East and West: Divergent Models of Coinage and its Use", *Il secolo di ferro: mito e realtà del secolo X*, Settimane di studio del Centro italiano di studi sull'alto Medioevo 38 (Spoleto, 1991), pp. 637-74.

[15] For Byzantine issues, see W. Hahn, *Moneta imperii byzantini* vol. 1 (Wien, 1973), vol. 2 (Wien, 1975), vol. 3 (Wien, 1981); for those after 720, not included in Hahn's work, see Grierson, *Catalogue of the Byzantine Coins*, III.

[16] P. Grierson and M. Blackburn, *Medieval European Coinage 1, The Early Middle Ages (5th-10th centuries)* (Cambridge, 1986), p. 63.

which are generally held to begin in the years immediately following the conquest, is uncertain, because these types could have been
fossilised.[17] Another important nucleus of silver issues is that attributed to Perctarit (661-2, 672-88) and Cunincpert (679-700), known
principally from the Biella hoard (of around 1600 coins), although
examples of this type have also been found in Corsica and Sardinia.[18]
In contrast to previous silver issues, that are imitations, these carry
monograms on the obverse that, although not easily legible, may be
interpreted as the names Perctarit and Cunincpert. It is thought that
the issue of these fractions of *siliquae* continued up to 720-30, again
with a probable fossilisation of the type, since the Biella hoard also
contained gold tremisses of Liutprand (712-44).[19]

The difficulty of classification, added to the scarce number of
examples preserved in collections (they are very light coins, weigh-
ing between 0.15 and 0.4 gram, and therefore very fragile), probably explains why these coins are often held to have performed only
a secondary role in the currency of the period. It was for this reason
that G.P. Bognetti, underestimating the role of silver, but at the
same time conscious that the economic and monetary landscape of
Lombard society must have been more varied than is often supposed, hypothesised the use in small transactions of substitutes for
coins, such as the *panis* and *scutella de cambio*, bread used as a medium
of small-scale exchange.[20] Bognetti's analysis, as well as earlier solutions that had been put forward, reflects the scholarly debate of the
time, which was strongly influenced by arguments about the Carolingian silver coinage and, more generally, about the contrast between
two different models: the natural economy and the monetary economy.

---

[17] P. Grierson, "The silver coinage of the Lombards", *Archivio storico lombardo* 8a
serie, 6 (1956), pp. 130-47.
[18] J. Lafaurie, "Trésor de monnaies lombardes trouvé à Linguizzetta (Corse)",
Bullettin de la société française de numismatique 22 (1967), pp. 123-25; on the circulation
of Lombard coinage in Sardinia, see Arslan, "La circolazione monetaria (secoli
V-VIII)", p. 504, n. 62.
[19] E. Bernareggi, *Moneta Langobardorum* (Milano, 1983), pp. 130-49; Grierson and
Blackburn, *Medieval European Coinage* 1, p. 66; J. Lafaurie, "Les monnaies lombardes
de Bravone", *Les églises piévanes de Corse de l'époque romaine au Moyen-Age* 14, *Cahiers
Corsica* 134-35 (1990), pp. 93-96.
[20] G.P. Bognetti, "Il problema monetario dell'economia monetaria", in C.M.
Cipolla ed., *Storia dell'economia italiana* I (Torino, 1959), pp. 51-60. The problem has
also been dealt with several times by E. Bernareggi, see "Struttura economica e
monetazione del Regno longobardo", *Numismatica e Antichità classiche. Quaderni ticinesi*
5 (1976), pp. 331-76.

Bognetti, however, did have the important intuition that the Lombard monetary system was not based solely on gold *tremisses*. The most innovative aspect of recent archaeological and numismatic research is to have given greater prominence to the distribution of these tiny silver coins.[21]

Next to the imitations of Byzantine coins and the royal types with the monograms of Perctarit and Cunincpert, the existence of probable ducal silver issues should be noted. Examples of these are the fragments of *siliquae* found in Austria, in Slovenia, and also at Luni that W. Hahn has attributed, on the basis of monograms, to Ago and Vectari, dukes of Friuli, the former around 650, the latter 670.[22] The duchy of Benevento too, in addition to its important and well-known gold coinage (dealt with below), produced 1/8 fractions of *siliquae*. On the basis of numerous local finds, the anonymous imitations of Ravennate types of Heraclius have been definitively attributed to the Beneventan mint (there are about twenty just in the cemetery of Campochiaro, and every coin seems to have been struck with a different pair of die stamps). The very close correlation between their weight and those of the fractions in the names of Perctarit, Cunincpert and others, has led E. Arslan to suggest a dating between the middle of the seventh century and the end of the reign of Duke Romuald (662-77).[23]

---

[21] Arslan, "Problemi di circolazione monetaria in Piemonte dal V all'VIII secolo" pp. 295-98. The excavations at the baptistery of San Giovanni in Fonte and Santa Tecla at Milan have thrown up two (?) fragments of a 1/8 *siliqua*, from a Lombard mint, perhaps imitations in the name of Justin II (565-578); the same excavation has also revealed a Lombard *tremissis* in the name of Maurice (582-602): see E.A. Arslan, "La testimonianza delle monete", in S. Lusuardi Siena ed., *La città e la sua memoria: Milano e la tradizione di sant'Ambrogio*, Catalogo della mostra, Milano, 3 aprile-8 giugno 1997 (Milan, 1997), pp. 63-67, 134-35, 175-77. Fragments with monograms of Perctarit and Cunincpert have been found at Rovereto (Trento), Pecetto di Valenza Po (Alessandria), Brescia, and Campione d'Italia (Como): Arslan, "Le monete", in *Santa Giulia di Brescia*.

[22] W. Hahn, "Die Kleinsilbermünzen der langobardischen Herzöge von Friaul", in P. Kos and Z. Demo eds., *Studia Numismatica Labacensia Alexandro Jelocnik oblata* (Ljubljana, 1988), pp. 317-20; on the area of circulation, see P. Kos, "The monetary circulation in the south-eastern Alpine region c. 300 B.C.-A.D. 1000", *Situla* 24 (1984-5 [1986]), pp. 229, 232.

[23] Inital information on the necropolis of Campochiaro, near Vicenne and Morione, (Campobasso) can be found in S. Capini and A. Di Niro eds., *Samnium. Archeologia del Molise* (Rome, 1991), pp. 325-65. At Vicenne the excavation of 167 tombs from the Lombard period has revealed 21 grave deposits with coins (10 gold, 13 silver and 4 bronze); at the excavation at Morione, still in progress, 143 tombs have been found, 21 of them with coins (17 gold, 7 silver and 2 bronze); this material is being

Thanks to the progress in excavation techniques, analogous examples in silver from Byzantine mints are being found with greater frequency. At Rome, in the excavations of the Crypta Balbi, it has been possible to recover a hoard of around 50 fractions of *siliquae* of Constans II (641-668), and 16 single finds from the reigns of Heraclius (610-41), Constans II and Justinian II (second reign 705-11).[24] Also in Rome, attention should be drawn to finds on the Via Amba Aradam, in the Roman Forum near the Basilica Julia and, finally, to the famous hoard with papal monograms.[25] Also notable are the finds at Sant'Antonino di Perti at Finale Ligure (Savona), Luni (La Spezia) and Lomello (Pavia), each with a fraction of a 1/8 *siliqua* of Maurice. From Ostiglia (near Mantua) comes another fraction of a coin of Leontius (695-8).[26] The above find of a Byzantine specimen in Lombard territory, like that of another one of the latter emperor in the already-mentioned cemetery at Campochiaro are indications of a circulation "without frontiers" between the Byzantine and Lombard

studied by E.A. Arslan. Others come from Altavilla Silentina (Salerno): M.T. Volpe, "Le monete di Eraclio", in P. Peduto ed., *Villaggi fluviali nella pianura pestana del secolo VII* (Altavilla Silentina, 1984), pp. 143-48; from Pratola Serra (Salerno): A. Rovelli, "Monete e problemi di monetazione tardo antica e longobarda", in P. Peduto ed., *S. Giovanni di Pratola Serra* (Salerno, 1992), pp. 367-76; from Grumento (Potenza): P. Bottini, "L'altomedioevo nell'area grumentina", *Mélanges de l'Ecole française de Rome, Moyen âge* 103.2 (1991), pp. 859-64 (interpreted as Byzantine); and from Cagnano Varano (Foggia): G. Guzzetta, "Le monete", *Gli scavi del 1953 nel Piano del Carpino (Foggia). Le terme e la necropoli altomedievale della villa romana di Avicenna* (Taranto, 1988), pp. 73-86.

[24] The writer is in the course of cataloguing the numismatic finds from the exedra of the Crypta Balbi. A partial description of the sequence of finds can be found in Saguì and Rovelli, "Residualità, non residualità, continuità di circolazione. Alcuni esempi dalla Crypta Balbi", pp. 186-95.

[25] L. Travaini, "Monete medievali in area romana: nuovi e vecchi materiali", *Rivista italiana di Numismatica* 94 (1992), pp. 163-82; G. Maetzke, "La struttura stratigrafica dell'area nord-occidentale del Foro Romano come appare dai recenti interventi di scavo", *Archeologia Medievale* 18 (1991), pp. 43-200, esp. p. 85, n. 39; C. Morrisson and J.N. Barrandon, "La trouvaille de monnaies d'argent byzantines de Rome (VII-VIII siècle): analyses et chronologie", *Revue numismatique* ser. 6, 30 (1988), pp. 149-65.

[26] The material from around Sant'Antonino di Perti at Finale Ligure is of particular interest, not only from a quantitive point of view. We can note there specimens from unknown mints (perhaps Lombard or Byzantine), in the names of Justinian I, Justin II, Phokas and Heraclius; the finds will be published by E. Arslan in the publication of the excavation, edited by G. Murialdo; there is a preliminary report in G. Murialdo, "Alcune considerazioni sulle anfore africane di VII secolo dal "Castrum" di S. Antonino nel Finale", *Archeologia Medievale* 22 (1995), pp. 433-53. For the other sites, see Arslan, "La circolazione monetaria (secoli V-VIII)", pp. 509-17 and the bibliography cited above in n. 2.

areas or, at least, of the fact that these frontiers were fairly permeable.

There is therefore no break in the sequence including the Ravennate issues of Justinian I and Justin II, the Lombard imitations in the names of the same emperors—probably fossilised types which can therefore be dated across a *longue durée*, the Beneventan eighth-*siliquae* with monograms of Heraclius, and the royal ones with monograms of Perctarit and Cunincpert, which were perhaps coined until the reign of Liutprand. In Byzantine areas, specifically at Rome, this tiny silver coinage, which seems to have decreased in number over time, ends only during the pontificate of Stephen II (772). In contrast to the Merovingian coinage, which became increasingly monometallic from the end of the sixth century—slipping from gold *tremissis* to silver *denarius*, with the two never circulating side by side—or to the Visigothic—consistently made of a single metal, gold—the Lombard coinage was therefore solidly bimetallic.

The difference of the Lombard coinage from the Merovingian experience, which moved towards the creation of the silver *denarius*, is also evident in the evolution of fineness and weight. In Gaul, issues of fractions of *siliquae* in the late imperial tradition, the so-called *minuti argentei*, disappeared around 570/80 at the latest. From that point, only gold *tremisses* were issued. The weight, in comparison to Byzantine *tremisses*, fell from 1.5 to 1.3 gram (equivalent to about 20 Troy grains in the Germanic imperial system, and no longer to 8 *siliquae*).[27] About a century later, around 670, the Merovingian coinage changed definitively. Gold issues, characterised for some decades by a very low fineness, were abandoned in favour of silver.[28] When this metal was re-coined in Merovingian Gaul, however, after about a century of exclusively gold coinage, weights had entirely changed. In place of the so-called *minuti argentei* (0.15-0.40 gram), we are confronted with a heavier coinage, which had inherited the weight of the 20-grain *tremissis*. The new silver coinage—the *denarius*—was

---

[27] On Merovingian coinage, see Grierson and Blackburn, *Medieval European Coinage*, pp. 81-154.

[28] Between 625 and about 640, the gold content of the *tremissis* decreased rapidly, from 95-85% to a maximum of 45%, by about 650/660 it was about 40% and decreased further until it did not exceed 10% in the *tremisses* of Avitus II, bishop of Clermont (674-689): M. Hendy, "From Public to Private: The Western Barbarian Coinages as a Mirror of the Disintegration of Late Roman State Structures", *Viator* 19 (1988), pp. 62-68; M. Bompaire, "Du solidus d'or au denier d'argent: genèse de la monnaie médiévale", in Ph. Contamine, M. Bompaire, S. Lebecq and J.-L. Sarrazin eds., *L'économie médiévale* (Paris, 1993), p. 116.

therefore a "heavy" coinage. The Lombards, on the contrary, preserved the system of *siliquae*, of which they coined very small fractions (probably eighths, if not sixteenths), which in the course of the
seventh century tended towards a medium weight of about 0.20
gram. This remained a "small" coinage.

Moreover, even the Lombard gold coinage had a rhythm of evolution that was tangibly different from the Merovingian. Above all,
during the seventh century the gold content of the Lombard *tremissis*
was still rather high, rarely falling below 75% fineness. Furthermore,
the process of alteration and impoverishment of this value was far
from linear and gradual. Even in the years in which the Merovingian
tremissis—now of very poor intrinsic value (10%)—disappeared to be
replaced by the silver *denarius*, the Lombard King Cunincpert, by
raising the fineness to average between 94% and 99%, adjusted his
tremissis to the hegemonic Byzantine coinage. It was only from the
reign of Liutprand that the Lombard gold coinage would see its
value fall steadily, in a process that should be read alongside that
of the Byzantine mints of Ravenna and Rome, on which, in fact, it
depended.[29] Although it is highly likely that Cunincpert's issues were
not particularly abundant, they demonstrate that Byzantium remained
the main monetary influence on the Lombards, not only in Benevento
but also in the kingdom.[30]

The Lombard gold coinage—which until the end paralleled issues
of the Byzantine mints in peninsular Italy—and the silver both attest
to a certain homogeneity between the remaining Byzantine areas
and the Lombard realms. A homogeneity and a specificity, in comparison with the rest of the West, which was based on the persistence of plurimetallic currencies and was connected to the complex
political and, probably, economic reality of the peninsula.

---

[29] In its turn, the gold content of the issues from Rome and Ravenna is closely
connected with the fate of the Byzantine possessions on the Italian mainland. It is
not accidental that Sicily and the mint at Syracuse have a different history: Rovelli,
"Monetary circulation in Byzantine and Carolingian Rome: a reconsideration in
the light of recent archaeological data"; on the intrinsic content of gold coinages,
see W. Hahn and W.E. Metcalf eds., *Studies in Early Byzantine Gold Coinage*, Numismatic
Studies 17 (New York, 1988).

[30] On the similarities between the Beneventan coinage and that of the Italian
kingdom, see E.A. Arslan, "Il ripostiglio di monete auree beneventane e bizantine
'da Napoli 1896' nella Collezione di re Vittorio Emanuele III", *Festschrift für Katalin
Bíró-Sey und István Gedai zum 65. Geburtstag* (Budapest, 1999), pp. 237-53.

As far as silver is concerned, we should note the choice of a small denomination, that is, the eighth (if not the sixteenth) *siliqua*, over heavier ones. In Lombard and Byzantine Italy, therefore, for part of the eighth century a small silver coinage was maintained, attested both in an urban setting and in rural contexts. Consequently, we must assume that the economic sectors which made use of small coinage, even if they were in growing crisis (the numismatic record for the second half of the eighth century is almost entirely a blank), also remained alive in some way.[31]

It is into the context just described that Charlemagne's monetary reform was introduced. Some observations should first be made before describing the Italian situation in the Carolingian era.

Above all, as we have seen, the adoption of the silver *denarius* in the *Regnum Langobardorum* was in no way the end point of a long evolution, as happened in Merovingian Francia. In fact, silver monometallism was introduced by a new sovereign authority—Charlemagne—following a series of political and military events of which the most important were the decline of Byzantine power in northern and central Italy (which was accompanied by the collapse of the administration and, therefore, a decrease in gold coinage, part of which, flowing from the Exarchate to the Lombards, was reminted), and by the head-on confrontation between the Franks and the Lombards.

It was in 781, when Charlemagne issued the capitulary of Mantua, that Italy, with the exception of the Lombard and Byzantine south, entered the Carolingian monetary system.[32] The success and effectiveness of this change must now be assessed. The disappearance of gold coinage from the scene is an incontestable fact; and it is true, moreover, that the effects of the aforementioned capitulary are quickly perceptible in documents, which record prices calculated in the new

---

[31] Similar conclusions can be found in Arslan, "Problemi di circolazione monetaria in Piemonte dal V all'VIII secolo", p. 297.

[32] The hypothesis of M. Bompaire, for whom "... il peut être significatif que ce soit sur le monnayage d'argent de Rome que les papes impriment la marque de leur autorité, à partir du pontificat de Serge (687-701), en attendant d'adopter le modèle franc à l'époque de Charlemagne" seems to me to place too much significance to the arrival of the Carolingian silver *denarius*. In reality, as we have already seen, the issues in question are fractions of *siliquae*, entirely consistent with Byzantine coinage. If anything, they ought to be considered as heirs of the fractions of Ostrogthic *siliquae* that bore the royal monogram.

currency from the years immediately following 781. But to what extent, and at what levels of exchange, was a currency of silver *denarii* maintained in Charlemagne's Italian dominions?

As is well known, the problem of the role of commerce and of the monetisation of the economy in the Carolingian era is at the centre of a historiographical debate that, constantly reinvigorated by responses to the "Pirenne thesis", has seen the lively defence of "minimalist" and "maximalist" positions.[33] Scholars are in agreement only on one point: the passage to a silver coinage ought not to be regarded as symptom and effect of an economic crisis in the West, but rather the base from which recovery began. Having adopted a silver system, the Carolingian empire was in a position to use its own metallic resources. Mints could therefore count, at least in theory, on a strikable metal that was more easily accessible.[34] The reduction of the monetary system to a single metal, however, makes it difficult to evaluate either its buying power or its capacity to deal with the full variety of economic transactions.[35] Equally controversial are assessments of the volume of issues and the productivity of mines and mints.[36]

In the particular case of Italy, research that has hitherto been conducted predominantly on the written sources has come, as with

---

[33] The terms are those of M. Blackburn, "Money and Coinage", in R. McKitterick ed., *The New Cambridge Medieval History, Volume II, c. 700-c. 900* (Cambridge, 1995), p. 539. On the debate in Italy, see B. Ward-Perkins, "Continuitists, catastrophists, and the towns of post-Roman Northern Italy", *Papers of the British School at Rome* 65 (1997), pp. 157-75.

[34] P. Grierson, "Problemi monetari dell'alto medioevo", *Bollettino della Società pavese di storia patria* 54 (1954), pp. 67-82; P. Grierson, "Money and coinage under Charlemagne", in W. Braunfels ed., *Karl der Grosse* I (Düsseldorf, 1965), pp. 501-36, both now in P. Grierson, *Dark Age Numismatics* (London, 1979).

[35] By way of an example, see the judgement of R. Doehaerd, *Le haut Moyen Age occidental. Économies et sociétés* (Paris, 1982), p. 317: "La nouveauté du système monétaire des Carolingiens consiste dans le fait qu'ils lui ont donné pour base une monnaie de valeur faible". However, Guy Bois has expressed the opposite opinion, in a recent contribution to a Spoleto conference: "Le denier de Charlemagne est encore trop lourd et cher pour être un instrument commode dans les échanges", *Il secolo di ferro*, p. 678.

[36] Some estimates for medieval mintings calculate that a pair of dies could strike between 10,000 and 30,000 coins: see F. Dumas, "La monnaie au Xe siècle", in *Il secolo di ferro*, p. 566. On the problem, see G.F. Carter, "Numismatic Calculations from Die-link Statistics", in M. Gomes Marques ed., *Problems of Medieval Coinage in the Iberian Area* (Santarém, 1984), pp. 91-104; T.V. Buttrey, "The President's Address. Calculating Ancient Coin Production: Facts and Fantasies", *Numismatic Chronicle* 153 (1993), pp. 335-51; T.V. Buttrey, "The President's Address. Calculating Ancient Coin Production II: Why it Cannot be Done", *Numismatic Chronicle* 154 (1994), pp. 341-52.

other regions of the Carolingian empire, to contradictory conclusions. The introduction of the silver *denarius* in place of the Lombard gold *tremissis* allowed the Carolingian monetary system, according to P. Toubert, "to eliminate that great blind corner of early medieval currency that was the everyday economy, with its need for cash with low purchasing power". The possible role played by fractions of *siliquae* was not considered here, but, as has been said, this lightweight silver coinage has attracted attention only very recently. Toubert's hypothesis is opposed to the more cautious assessments of G.P. Bognetti, R.S. Lopez and C.M. Cipolla, according to whom the Carolingian silver *denarius* retained a high value and so would not have been able to solve the problem of the lack of small change.[37]

Tackling the question anew, in some recent works I have undertaken a re-examination of the documentary sources and archaeological data.[38] In what follows I will repeat some of the assessments that I have already made, beginning with the archaeological material. To my mind, the latter poses a question which tends to remain unanswered: in contrast to the written sources that suggest a wide diffusion of coinage, the archaeological data present a picture in which monetary circulation would seem to have been reduced to insignificant levels. In fact, Carolingian *denarii* are notably rare in archaeological contexts. We are therefore faced with the problem of hypothesising different levels of exchange and different uses of money. At the same time, we need to frame correctly the questions that we want to ask of two different sources: the written and the archaeological one. It is probable, in fact, that the contrasting results obtained up to now depend in part on the fact that generalisations have been made on the basis of indications offered by the written documents, on the assumption that they offer us a comprehensive picture of monetary circulation.

---

[37] G.P. Bognetti, "Il problema monetario dell'economia longobarda e il 'panis' e la 'scutella de cambio'", in C.M. Cipolla ed., *Storia dell'economia italiana* (Turin, 1959), p. 56, published earlier in *Archivio storico lombardo* n.s. 9 (1944), pp. 112-20; R.S. Lopez, "Moneta e monetieri nell'Italia barbarica", *Moneta e scambi nell'alto medioevo*, Settimane di studio del Centro italiano di studi sull'alto Medioevo 8 (Spoleto, 1961), p. 81; C.M. Cipolla, *Money, Prices, and Civilisation in the Mediterranean World* (Princeton, 1956), p. 12.

[38] A. Rovelli, "La moneta nella documentazione altomedievale di Roma e del Lazio", in *La storia economica di Roma nell'alto Medioevo*, pp. 333-52; A. Rovelli, "La funzione della moneta tra l'VIII e il X secolo. Un'analisi della documentazione archeologica", *La storia dell'Alto Medioevo italiano (VI-X secolo)*, pp. 521-37.

As has been mentioned, Italian archaeological sites are characterised by the almost complete absence of *denarii* of the Carolingian type in contemporary strata. This is evident in different types of settlement. Urban excavations, those of incastellated sites, of monastic centres, and of *curtes* have all proliferated, and certainly now provide a meaningful sample of evidence. A few examples suffice to give a picture of the situation, beginning with some of the great urban excavations. Although 500 coins have been unearthed at Milan, in the course of numerous archaeological operations occasioned by the enlargement of the underground system, not one of them is Carolingian. The situation is the same at Brescia, where there are no silver *denarii* among the 1191 coins found in the excavations at the Santa Giulia complex. In fact we have at present only a single example of Carolingian coinage from the entire city: a denarius of Charlemagne, issued at Milan and found on the stage of the Roman theatre.[39]

As far as Rome is concerned, I shall not dwell on the often-discussed material from the Crypta Balbi, except to underline the contrast between the rarity of silver *denarii* (a single *denarius* of the *antiquiores* type out of a total of about 2000 coins discovered) and the remarkable quantity of Carolingian ceramic finds, which amount to tens of thousands of fragments. Consequently, the absence of coins cannot be explained by the nature of the archaeological deposit, which is of considerable size, but must indicate the meagre daily circulation of silver *denarii*. The excavations in progress in the area of the Forum of Nerva, where a Carolingian monumental phase has been identified, have thus far served to confirm these numismatic observations.[40]

This situation appears to be general, without distinction between urban and rural centres, be they *curtes, castella* or monastic sites. A typical case is Scarlino, an incastellated centre on the Tuscan coast, which experienced various phases of habitation from the late Bronze Age onwards. An undoubtedly early medieval settlement has been identified here, that was of some importance to judge from the ninth-century frescoes that decorated the church and the buildings of a

---

[39] Arslan, "Le monete", in *Santa Giulia di Brescia*.

[40] A. Rovelli, "La Crypta Balbi. I reperti numismatici. Appunti sulla circolazione a Roma nel Medioevo", *La moneta nei contesti archeologici. Esempi dagli scavi di Roma*, Atti dell'incontro di studio, Roma 1986 (Rome, 1989) pp. 49-95; A. Rovelli, "Monete, tessere e gettoni", in L. Saguì and L. Paroli eds., *Archeologia urbana a Roma; il progetto della Crypta Balbi. 5. L'esedra della Crypta Balbi nel Medioevo (XI-XV secolo)* (Florence, 1990), pp. 169-94; A. Rovelli, "Monetary circulation in Byzantine and Carolingian Rome: a reconsideration in the light of recent archaeological data".

curtis that were fortified in the late tenth century.[41] The numismatic record, however, begins only with a *denarius* of Otto II. This is followed by a Henrician *denarius*, but we see a real increase only in the twelfth, and above all in the thirteenth and fourteenth centuries.[42]

To conclude this brief but representative review, we can refer to two emblematic cases: the excavations at the great abbeys of Farfa and San Vincenzo al Volturno. Not a single Carolingian issue appears among the 178 coins found at Farfa. At San Vincenzo al Volturno, the silver *denarii* number only a few pieces: two, perhaps three, examples.[43]

Everywhere—at Rome, as at Milan, Brescia, Scarlino and Farfa (to list only the aforementioned examples) the gap in Carolingian issues begins to be filled by *denarii* of the Ottonian dynasty and then, in ever growing numbers, by *denarii* from the end of the twelfth century. The latter, with a silver content that hardly reached 0.2 gram, are very different from their Carolingian antecedents, which were of good weight and fineness.[44]

Based on these considerations, Toubert's conclusions on the use of the Carolingian *denarius* in the *Regnum Italiae* seem to be formulated too closely on a Frankish model: "The problem of low-value coinage was reformulated by the introduction of the silver *denarius*. As long as that *denarius* was assured a relatively strong and stable value, that is, up to the reign of Louis II, the contemporaneous coining, with the same types and in the same mints, of clearly lighter coins called 'oboli' or half-*denarii* certainly responded to this sector of monetary demand".[45]

In reality, we know that the mints of the Italian *Regnum* did not strike "oboli".[46] Nor, we might add, have excavations uncovered

---

[41] R. Francovich ed., *Scarlino I. Storia e territorio* (Florence, 1985).

[42] A. Rovelli, "Le monete del castello di Scarlino. Materiali per lo studio della circolazione monetaria nella Toscana meridionale", *Annali dell'Istituto italiano di Numismatica* 43 (1996), pp. 225-54.

[43] I am grateful to Richard Hodges, who directed the excavations, for this information.

[44] D.M. Metcalf and J.P. Northover, "Coinage Alloys from the Time of Offa and Charlemagne to c. 864", *The Numismatic Chronicle* ser. VII, 149 pp. 101-120.

[45] P. Toubert, "Il sistema curtense: la produzione e lo scambio interno in Italia nei secoli VIII, IX e X", in R. Romano and U. Tucci eds., *Economia naturale, economia monetaria. Storia d'Italia*, Annali 6 (Turin, 1983), p. 54.

[46] O. Murari, "I presunti mezzi denari veronesi dell'imperatore Ottone I", *Rivista italiana di Numismatica* 60 (1958), pp. 37-44; Grierson and Blackburn, *Medieval European Coinage*, pp. 194 and 250.

examples of *denarii* cut in two, as occurs with some frequency in England.[47] The concept of "silver bi-metallism" that Toubert himself introduced to explain, very appropriately, the mechanisms for the alternation of various types of coin in twelfth-century Lazio, according to the principles of "Gresham's law", cannot be applied to Carolingian issues in Italy, which were limited only to *denarii*.[48]

As a comparison, it is useful to examine the archaeological finds in those regions of southern Italy that remained Byzantine, where, as has been said, a plurimetallic currency was maintained and the Byzantine empire received taxes in coin. The excavations at Otranto, for example, have recovered over 300 coins, all copper or mixed alloy dating form the Roman era to the thirteenth century. There are 45 coins minted between the ninth and the first half of the tenth century. The total of all the finds of *denarii* issued up to the middle of the tenth century, in archaeological excavations in northern and central Italy, in the territories of the old *Regnum Italiae*, probably does

---

[47] D.M. Metcalf, "A Sketch of the Currency in the Time of Charles the Bald", in M.T. Gibson and J.L. Nelson eds., *Charles the Bald: court and kingdom* (Aldershot, 1990²), pp. 73-75.

[48] P. Toubert, *Les structures du Latium médiéval*, Bibliothèque des Écoles Françaises d'Athènes et de Rome 221 (Rome, 1973), pp. 584-601; P. Toubert, "Une des premières vérifications de la loi de Gresham: la circulation monétaire dans l'Etat pontifical vers 1200", *Revue Numismatique* ser. 6, 15 (1973), pp. 180-89, now in P. Toubert, *Etudes sur l'Italie médiévale (IXe-XIVe s.)* (London, 1976). Recently, along the same lines, L. Feller, "Les conditions de la circulation monétaire dans la périphérie du royaume d'Italie (Sabine et Abruzzes, IXe-XIIe siècle)", in *L'argent au Moyen Age* (Paris, 1998), pp. 61-75; I should like to correct L. Feller's reference to my work on p. 68 n. 18: "A. Rovelli cherche à démontrer qu'une monnaie d'or appelée *mancus*, frappée par les Francs a effectivement circulé en Italie centrale. . . ."; I have never written that the *mancus* was a coin struck by the Franks! Rather, I analyzed some aspects of the circulation of Arab coins in Italy; and I hypothesized that the silver *mancus*, frequently cited in charters from Lazio as a money of account with a value of 30 *denarii*, constituted the monetary representation of a ratio between gold and silver of 1:12 when it first appeared (in the first decades of the ninth century). In fact, a *dinar*, that is a gold *mancus* of 4.25 grams of gold, was equal to 30 silver *denarii* of 1.7 grams, or 51 grams in total (51/4.25 = 12). A silver *mancus*, as a money of account, meaning 30 Carolingian *denarii*, was therefore equivalent in metallic value to a gold *mancus*. Exchange between the gold *mancus*, *dinar*, and the Carolingian denairius was possible by means of the silver *mancus*: A. Rovelli, "Circolazione monetaria e formulari notarili nell'Italia altomedievale", *Bullettino dell'Istituto storico italiano per il Medio evo e Archivio muratoriano* 98 (1992), pp. 109-144; on the problem of the *mancus* and its identification with the *dinar*, see C. Cahen "Quelques problèmes concernant l'expansion économique musulmane au haut Moyen Age", *L'Occidente e l'Islam*, Settimane di studio del Centro italiano di studi sull'alto Medioevo 12 (Spoleto, 1965), pp. 391-432.

not amount to the same number.[49] Furthermore, we should also note that the rarity of isolated finds is matched by that of hoards: less than ten in all.[50] Nor does the danger of the Magyar invasions seem to have increased the number. The number eventually rises in the twelfth century, in tandem with the growth in isolated finds. We are therefore dealing with an increase made possible by the development of the supply of coinage, independent of the hazards of war or general insecurity.

Analysis of archaeological contexts therefore provides a starting point for answering one of the questions posed earlier, of the value to be assigned to the silver *denarius*. The numismatic evidence suggests that the Carolingian silver *denarius* had a high purchasing power that limited casual losses.[51] Like all "heavy" coins, it is found rarely in stratigraphic contexts. As with every coin of high weight and fineness, we should therefore reject the notion that the *denarius* was used for small transactions.

---

[49] On the evidence from the excavations at Otranto, see A. Travaglini, "Le monete", in F. D'Andria and D. Whitehouse eds., *Excavations at Otranto. Volume II: The Finds* (Galatina, 1992), pp. 243-73.

[50] For the hoards of Sarzana, Vercelli and Bondeno (Ferrara) see the bibliography cited in K.F. Morrison and H. Grunthal, *Carolingian Coinage* (New York, 1967), pp. 342-44; and, further, J. Lafaurie, "Le trésor carolingien de Sarzana-Luni", *Le zecche minori toscane fino al XIV secolo*, Atti del 3° Convegno Internazionale di studi, Pistoia, 16-19 settembre 1967 (Pistoia, 1974), pp. 43-55; and M.T. Gulinelli, "Un rinvenimento di età carolingia", in F. Berti, S. Gelichi and G. Steffà eds., *Bondeno e il suo territorio dalle origini al Rinascimento* (Bondeno, 1988), pp. 375-79. On the hoard from Pavia (240 denarii of Charlemagne, Berengar and Guy of Spoleto), see L. Cremaschi, "Circa il ritrovamento monetale in Pavia, 1934", *Bollettino della Società pavese di Storia patria* 55 (1955) pp. 91-92. For the treasure from Briosco (Milano), (an imprecise number of *denarii* of Berengar I, Guy of Spoleto, Lambert and Arnul), see L. Deschamps "Quelques monnaies des empereurs de la race Carolingienne frappées en Italie", *Revue numismatique* (1839), pp. 371-91. On the very recent find at Larino (Campobasso), (of 20 *denarii*), see G. De Benedittis and J. Lafaurie, "Trésor de monnaies carolingiennes du VIIIe siècle trouvé à Larino (Italie, Molise). Les monnaies de Louis, roi d'Aquitaine (781-794)", *Revue numismatique* 153 (1998), pp. 217-43. On the hoards of Anglo-Saxon coins, which, as is well known, constitute a problem of their own, see C.E. Blunt, "Anglo-Saxon coins found in Italy", in M.A.S. Blackburn ed., *Essays in memory of Michael Dolley* (Leicester, 1986), pp. 159-69.

[51] Italy provides no data from finds by metal detectors. These have revealed much new information in countries where their use is regulated by law. In Great Britain, for example, the British Numismatic Journal has counted over 3000 coins from the period between 550 and 1180 discovered by metal detectors. However, the limited increase in the number of "official" finds in Italy has a positive side of its own: the evidence is almost en   made up of finds from excavations. The uniformity of the methods of source-gathering produces samples that are not

The written sources, moreover, provide evidence for the use of the silver *denarius* in very specific transactions, that took place on a medium-to-high level of exchange—such as property sales, concessions of various legal types, fines, tolls etc.—and that, it is clear, cannot be used arbitrarily as evidence of a generalised use of monetary means of exchange.[52]

Having described the level of use of the *denarius* in Carolingian Italy, it remains to assess the level of its circulation. The documentary sources, in particular private charters, bring to light important differences in the circulation of coinage in various regions that have generally been considered as united by their common membership of the silver *denarius* zone.

In the Po plain, for example, the coinage introduced by Charlemagne would seem to have been successfully imposed. The silver *denarius* is the only coin cited by the sources. The provision of coinage, especially for transactions of some importance, was adequate. The cases that attest recourse to substitute coinage or uncoined metal are few.[53] In

---

"contaminated" by the antiquarian curiosity of amateurs who might direct their investigations towards particular types of coin. In a sample collected largely from pluristratificated sites, with a long continuity of life, the repetition of gaps that interrupt the series of finds acquires historical significance. This is not merely a case of a simple and chance lack of evidence, but of genuinely negative evidence that has proved useful, for example, in determining the level of use of the *denarius*. It is equally important to be able to verify situations which reveal clear increases in currency. Part of the recent, and optimistic, evaluations of the monetarisation of the early medieval economy have included metal detector finds, but it ought not to be forgotten that "after 1180 coin finds in England become too plentiful and the currency was too uniform to make comprehensive recording of single-finds a practical proposition" (information on Great Britain is provided by M. Blackburn, "Coin Circulation in Germany during the Early Middle Ages. The Evidence of Single-Finds", in B. Kluge ed., *Fernhandel und Geldwirtschaft. Beiträge zum deutschen Münzwesen in sächsischer und salischer Zeit* (Sigmaringen, 1993), p. 37.

[52] The progressive prevalence of rents in coin over those in kind is generally considered as an indication of the "monetarisation" of the manorial economy. Yet rents are not the best indicators of the rate of diffusion of coinage, above all small coin. We just have to note that during the twelfth to fourteenth centuries rents would return to being predominantly in kind, amounting to almost 90% of renders in some places, such as Lucca (L.A. Kotel'nikova, "Rendita in natura e rendita in denaro nell'Italia medievale (secoli IX-XV)", in *Economia naturale, economia monetaria*, pp. 93-112). The return to payments in kind, however, corresponds to a period of great expansion in the amount of currency, then notably more fully evolved. Small *denarii* were minted (found abundantly in archaeological levels), silver *grossi* and, from about the middle of the thirteenth century, gold coins.

[53] Only the written sources reveal the extent to which, in a given region, the silver *denarius* was available, at least for middle- to high-level transactions. Archaeological sources (which are those that best reflect the use of coin in everyday exchanges)

charters, the prices are always given in units of coined money, worded thus: *argentum denarios bonos solidos and argenti denarios bonos libras*.[54]

In Lazio and central Italy, on the other hand, the silver *denarius*, even if the charters quickly attest its introduction, was generally slow to impose itself as a means of exchange. In comparison with the Po region, the charters of Lazio, in particular those for Farfa, reveal a variegated situation. A recourse to uncoined metal, suggested by generic references to *argenti unciae* and *argenti librae*, should not be excluded. The use, not to say necessity, of making payments in monetary substitutes (in *res valentes*), seems to have been very common.[55] We can hypothesise an analogous situation for the Abruzzo. The documents for the abbey of Casauria frequently give price indications that imply a possible recourse to goods as substitutes for coin.[56] Significantly, coinage begins to be attested in the archaeological record only from the end of the twelfth century.[57] Moreover, it is in this period that mints begin to proliferate in Italy and, at the same time, prices expressed in coin substitutes disappear.[58]

---

can only be associated with the already-mentioned "negative evidence" in which Carolingian *denarii*, coins not suitable for everyday transactions, are absent, both in the excavations at Milan and in those at Rome, for example.

[54] Rovelli, "Circolazione monetaria e formulari notarili nell'Italia altomedievale", 133-37.

[55] Rovelli, "La moneta nella documentazione altomedievale di Roma e del Lazio", pp. 333-52. Contra P. Toubert, who judges such use irrelevant (Toubert, *Les structures du Latium médiéval* I, pp. 603-04). He calculates that out of the over 3000 charters collected in the Regestum Farfense only a few dozen include payments in money substitutes. To give this evidence its correct weight, however, we should consider the Regestum Farfense in its entirety and should furthermore bear in mind that sales represent a small part of the collected charters, in comparison with the diplomas, *placita*, *chartae refutationis*, exchanges and donations. If we focus on the eleventh century, the period from which comes the greatest number of charters of sale, we can see that payments in money substitute comprise 2/3 of payments for sales of land. Out of a total of 62 sales, only 19 were carried out by means of coin, while the others make reference to payments in *res valentes*. We can add that, throughout the whole of the eleventh century, donations to the abbey were preponderant in comparison to every other form of exchange of landed property. The cartulary registers 416 donations, 49 exchanges and 62 sales. Out of a total of 512 transactions which, under different titles, effected the transfer of landed property, coinage played a part in only 19.

[56] Feller, "Les conditions de la circulation monétaire dans la périphérie du royaume d'Italie (Sabine et Abruzzes, IXe-XIIe siècle)", pp. 61-75.

[57] A. Rovelli, "La circolazione monetaria in Sabina e nel Lazio settentrionale nel Medio Evo. Materiali dagli scavi di alcuni siti incastellati", in E. Hubert ed., *Une région frontalière au Moyen Âge. Les vallées du Turano et del Salto entre Sabine et Abruzzes*, Actes du Colloque, Collalto Sabino, 5-7 luglio 1996 (Rome, 2000), pp. 407-22.

[58] On the problem of mints, see below notes 81-82.

Obviously, these observations refer to the availability of coinage rather than to the level of prices. On the latter it is worth citing the work of C. Wickham who, analysing Tuscany, has shown how social relationships, which were established between two parties as a result of the transfer of land, played a decisive role in determining the prices of land. This phenomenon is found not only in relatively isolated areas but also in the plain of Lucca where no consistency in the prices of land can be noted before the twelfth century, in spite of the general homogeneity of the landscape.[59] When this factor, which we might call "political" or "social", influenced the fixing of a price in a transaction, it is clear that the economic aspect would have notably less impact. As a consequence, the role of money in an exchange perceptibly diminishes, as also does our ability to calculate purchasing power.

In the light of the nature of the Italian data (negative evidence, even if significant because drawn from homogeneous sampling, based in large part on archaeological investigations) it is therefore appropriate to reconsider finds of Italian coins beyond the Alps. Here, particular emphasis has been given to a few hoards: Apremont-Veuillin, Bélvezet and, to a lesser degree, Ibersheim (Kreis Worms, Rheinland-Pfalz, Germany) and Biebrich (Wiesbaden-Biebrich, Hessen, Germany).[60] At present 27% of the coins from Biebrich (deposited c. 790-814) and Ibersheim (deposited c. 814) comprise coins from Italian mints.[61] But we should note that, having been mostly dispersed, their value as evidence is greatly reduced. Forty-eight examples out of 4000 remain from Biebrich, fifteen out of 30 from Ibersheim. Furthermore, the two hoards are difficult to compare because of their differing sizes. The French hoards are more useful. The hoards of Apremont-Veuillin (cant. La Guerche-sur-L'Aubois, arr. Saint-Amand-Mont-Rond, dép. Cher, France) and Bélvezet (cant. Lussan, arr. Nîmes, Dép. Gard, France) were buried, according to the most recent hypothesis, in about 820, and chiefly comprise *denarii* of Louis

---

[59] C. Wickham, "Vendite di terra e mercato della terra in Toscana nel secolo XI", *Quaderni storici* 65 (1987), pp. 355-77.

[60] D.M. Metcalf, "North Italian Coinage Carried across the Alps. The Ostrogothic and Carolingian Evidence Compared", *Rivista italiana di Numismatica* 90 (1988), pp. 448-56; S. Coupland, "Money and Coinage under Louis the Pious", *Francia* 17.1 (1990), pp. 23-54.

[61] H.H. Völckers, *Karolingische Münzfunde der Frühzeit (751-800)* (Göttingen, 1965), pp. 104, 182 and 110, 186; Morrison and Grunthal, *Carolingian Coinage*, pp. 343-44.

the Pious, (Class 2, with mint name in field).[62] More precisely, in
the Apremont-Veuillin hoard there are 195 *denarii* from Venice, 47
from Milan, 26 from Pavia and 6 from Treviso out of a total of
755 silver coins. In that of Bélvezet there are 293 coins, of which
41 are from Pavia, 34 from Venice and 17 from Milan. Taking both
together, the percentage of Italian coins is therefore about the same
at around 36%, and for this reason they have been taken as showing the importance of Italy in the Carolingian economy.[63] Apart from
these two cases, however, in the roughly 70 hoards found in France
(counting, from J. Duplessy's catalogue, those buried between 781—
the year of the capitulary of Mantua—and the end of the ninth century) the presence of Italian coins looks marginal: only four or five
coins in total.[64]

Certainly, the important question of the *denarii* with a temple and
the legend *Christiana religio* on the reverse (Class 3), still not attrib-
utable to the various mints of the Empire, remains firmly open.[65] It
will obviously be easier to define the production of individual mints,
including Italian ones, once this problem is resolved. However, on
the basis of the evidence currently available, the *Christiana religio* issues
of probable Italian provenance are especially numerous in the hoards
from Hermenches (cant. Vaud, Switzerland) and Chaumaux-Marcilly
(cant. Sancergues, arr. Bourges, Dép. Cher, France).[66] In fact, we

---

[62] J. Duplessy, *Les trésors monétaires médiévaux et modernes découverts en France* I (Paris,
1985), p. 27 n. 17; p. 35 n. 40; C.M. Haertle, *Karolingische Münzfunde aus dem 9.
Jahrhundert* (Cologne, Weimar, Vienna, 1997), pp. 27-30, 239-49 and 31-33, 250-55.

[63] Coupland, "Money and Coinage under Louis the Pious", p. 32.

[64] A *denarius* of Charlemagne from an unknown mint forms part of the hoard
from the Jura comprising 7 coins. A *denarius* of Louis the Pious from Pavia comes
from the hoard found at Angers in 1919 (29 coins), but no Italian coin appears in
another hoard, of 33 coins, discovered at Angers around 1812. There is a Pavese
denarius of Louis the Pious in the hoard from Brioux (composed of at least 145
coins). Finally, there is at least one *denarius* of Charles the Bald and Pope John VIII
in a hoard from Avignon (of about 800 coins): Duplessy, *Les trésors monétaires*, p. 137
n. 389; p. 26 nn. 11 and 12; p. 41 n. 59; p. 31 n. 27.

[65] For the classification, refer to Grierson and Blackburn, *Medieval European Coinage*,
pp. 212-17.

[66] For the hoard from Hermenches: Coupland, "Money and Coinage under Louis
the Pious", p. 43, who believes that about 130 pieces were issued at Milan; Haertle,
Karolingische Münzfunde aus dem 9. Jahrhundert, pp. 38-41 and 262-89 attributes, doubt-
fully, 103 *denarii* to Milan, 73 to Pavia, 26 to Venice, and 38 to Milan or Pavia,
out of a total of about 320 coins. The hoard of Chaumoux-Marcilly was composed
of 303 *denarii* of which 178 may have been from Milan (Coupland, "Money and
Coinage under Louis the Pious", p. 43). The attribution was first advanced by
P. Chenu, "Notes de numismatique et de sigillographie. Un depôt de monnaies

are again dealing with two fairly isolated cases, that need to be eval-
uated in the context of the scarce presence of Italian coins in other
great hoards: Pilligerheck (15 *Christiana religio denarii* of Louis the
Pious, perhaps from the Milan mint, and one of Lothar, from a total
of 1500 coins), Roermond (3 *Christiana religio denarii* of Louis the Pious,
perhaps from the Milan mint, and 21 of Lothar, out of 1081 coins),
and Wagenbogen (a few items out of about 500 pieces), and no
Italian *denarii* at all in the hoards of Emmen and Ide.[67] The list could
be extended. The same pattern, if not "negative" then certainly modest, predominates among occasional finds.

These latter pieces reflect an international commerce that had
clearly never entirely vanished, and indeed had one of its principal
routes in the Po valley. International commerce also explains the relatively substantial number of Carolingian *denarii* at Luni, the *denarius*
of Charlemagne found at Torcello (Venezia), and especially those
from the Valle d'Aosta.[68] The case of Aosta is worth examining,
since the *denarii* came to light in an urban context, and together with
those found along the main transit points of the valley represent the
most notable group of Carolingian coins recovered in Italy. At Aosta,
there are seven Carolingian *denarii* out of a total of over 3000 discovered, mostly imperial Roman or late medieval issues.[69] Among

---

carolingiennes dans le département du Cher", *Memoires de la Société historique, littéraire
du Cher* 39 (1931-1932), pp. 103-30. Accepted by Grierson and Blackburn, *Medieval
European Coinage*, p. 530 n. 791; it is not mentioned by Duplessy, *Les trésors moné-
taires*, p. 49 n. 94, nor addressed by Haertle, *Karolingische Münzfunde aus dem 9.
Jahrhundert*, pp. 406-24. The hoard has been dispersed: Morrison and Grunthal,
Carolingian Coinage, p. 357 n. 54.

[67] The observation is that of Coupland, "Money and Coinage under Louis the
Pious", p. 43. For the hoards of Roermond (prov. Limbourg, Netherlands), Wagen-
bogen (prov. Groningen, Netherlands) and of Ide (prov. Drenthe, gem. der Vries,
Netherlands) see Haertle, *Karolingische Münzfunde aus dem 9. Jahrhundert*, pp. 102-12.

[68] A. Bertino, "Monete attestate a Luni dal IV al IX secolo", *Rivista di studi
liguri* 49 (1983), pp. 265-300; S. Tabaczynski, "Monete e scambi", in L. Leciejewicz
et al., *Torcello. Scavi 1961-1962* (Rome, 1977), pp. 271-86; M. Orlandoni, *Antiche
monete in Val d'Aosta* (Aosta, 1983); M. Orlandoni, "La via commerciale della Valle
d'Aosta nella documentazione numismatica", *Rivista italiana di Numismatica* 90 (1988),
pp. 433-48.

[69] A *denarius* of Pippin III struck at Antrain, and two of Charlemeagne struck at
Milan and Pavia, come from the church of San Lorenzo. A fragment of a *denarius*
from the mint at Dorestad, associated with a *denarius* of Charles the Bald from that
at Rheims, and one of Louis II, perhaps from Milan, were found in the excavations of the so-called insulae 51/52. A *denarius* of Pope Hadrian I has been found
in the area of the Forum. We can date to the tenth century five Pavese *denarii* of
which one is in the name of Berengar I of Italy (915-924) and four are of the

the later coins of Italian provenance there are *denarii* of Genoa, Pavia, Milan, Como, Brescia, Venice, Mantua, Parma and Piacenza. From France there are royal *denarii, denarii* of the dukes of Normandy (eleventh to twelfth centuries) coined at Rouen, *denarii* from Chartres, Le Mans, Blois, Viviers, Dombes, Lyons, Chateau-Renaud, papal issues from Avignon and those of the dukes of Lorraine. From Switzerland, there are coins of Lausanne, Fribourg, Luzern, Basel, the abbey of St Maurice d'Agaune and of the bishops of Valais. At the Great St Bernard Pass the situation is very similar. The material is copious and heterogeneous: about 500 Gaulish coins, over 1300 Roman, various late medieval issues.[70] Yet, although the pass remained an important route in the Carolingian age (the monastery of Bourg-St-Pierre enjoyed imperial protection; and in 784 Pope Hadrian I appealed to Charlemagne for the defence of the hostels situated on the higher Alpine routes), there are only nine Carolingian *denarii*.[71]

The finds associated with the great commercial roads do not therefore belie a broader picture characterised, as we have seen, by a generalised shortage of coinage, that becomes particularly evident in the regions along the Appennine ridge. Nor is this surprising, since the factors that lead to a wide diffusion of coinage were absent.[72] One basic problem remains that of evaluating how much coinage was available in a given area. In this regard attention should be focused on monetary production: that is, on mints.

It is known that in Italy, after an initial phase under Charlemagne in which Lombard mints (of which sixteen are known) remained active, the number of issuing centres decreased, becoming confined to Pavia, Milan, Lucca, and Treviso, later replaced by Verona.[73] To

Ottonians (962-1002), and two *denarii* from the mint at Langres struck for Louis IV d'Outremer (936-954). There are also two *sceattas*: a piece of Eadberht, king of Northumbria (737-758) and an anonymous coin struck in south Wessex in the same period (Orlandoni, *Antiche monete in Val d'Aosta*).

[70] To underline the importance that the Aostan routes had, from antiquity, in international commerce, Orlandoni notes the repeated finds of Greek, Punic and Ptolemaic coins ("La via commerciale della Valle d'Aosta nella documentazione numismatica"), pp. 435-37.

[71] Orlandoni "La via commerciale della Valle d'Aosta nella documentazione numismatica", pp. 435-37: a *denarius* of Carloman, from an unknown mint, two *denarii* of Charlemagne from the mints of Verdun and Milan, two *denarii* of Lothar, from the mints of Verdun and Dorestad, a *denarius* of Charles the Bald from the mint of Melle, a *denarius* and obol of Louis the Pious.

[72] See Hendy, "East and West: Divergent Models of Coinage and its Use", and the bibliography cited there.

[73] Strangely Metcalf, "North Italian Coinage Carried across the Alps. The

these we can add those of Venice and Rome which, though they operate under different jurisdictions, also struck *denarii* of a Carolingian type. We have at present little information with which to assess the production of individual mints, with the exception of Benevento. Even this was not strictly a Carolingian mint, but Charlemagne and Louis II managed to impose the coining of silver *denarii* there.[74] This is an opportune moment to discuss the Beneventan situation which, although atypical, offers some concrete information on the scale of coinage of a Carolingian type in Italy.

The first issue of *denarii* from the Beneventan mint date from the reign of Grimoald III (788-806). The introduction of the *denarius* into Beneventan territory therefore followed soon after the first silver issues from mints of the Italian kingdom, decreed by the capitulary of Mantua of 781. Yet in contrast to the *Regnum*, where gold coins were no longer struck, at Benevento the coining of *solidi* and *tremisses* was not immediately interrupted. This continued, despite progressive reductions in fineness, up to the end of the reign of Radelchis I (839-52). Following that, until the point around 900 when the mint was closed, Radelchis's successors struck only silver *denarii*.

The charters of the abbey of Cava dei Tirreni allow us to identify the phases of this passage from gold to silver. The first isolated reference to a payment in *denarii* dates from 816, so about thirty years after the first silver issues.[75] Until about 870, moreover, sums continue to be expressed in terms of gold coin. From about 880, however, gold gives way to the silver *denarius*. But, it is right to ask, for how long? This change has generally been interpreted as a sign of the adjustment of most of southern Italy to the western model.[76] In reality the "supremacy" of silver coinage was only a brief parenthesis, as the evidence from Cava itself demonstrates. In the abbey's charters the silver *denarius* dominates only for the period between

---

Ostrogothic and Carolingian Evidence Compared", p. 450 states that after the reform of 781 "very soon the number of mint-places began to multiply".

[74] On the Beneventan and Salernitan *denarii*, see E.A. Arslan, "La monetazione", in G. Pugliese Carratelli ed., *Magistra barbaritas* (Milan, 1984), pp. 430-43; Grierson and Blackburn, *Medieval European Coinage*, pp. 66-73.

[75] *Codex Diplomaticus Cavensis* I, eds. M. Morcaldi, M. Schiani and S. De Stephano (Naples, 1873), doc. VI, p. 7.

[76] J.M. Martin, "Economia naturale ed economia monetaria nell'Italia meridionale longobarda e bizantina (secoli VI-XI)", in *Economia naturale, economia monetaria*, pp. 179-219; J.M. Martin, *La Pouille du VIe au XIIe siècle*, Collection de l'École française de Rome 179 (Rome, 1993), pp. 189-93.

880 and the very first years of the tenth century, when gold coinage returns in considerable quantity, this time comprising essentially Arab *tarì* and, to a lesser extent, Byzantine *solidi*.[77]

Calculations recently made by E. Arslan of the volume of gold and silver issues from the mint at Benevento help to confirm the picture drawn from the written sources. From the die-stamps it can be shown that gold coinage was in fact decidedly more abundant than silver.[78] For example, Arslan has put the number of die-stamps drawn from the obverse of tremisses of Arechis II with a ducal title (758-74) at 245, and at 78 and 119 respectively those from *solidi* and tremisses with the title of prince (774-87). For Grimoald III and Charlemagne, he has calculated about 54 dies for *solidi*, 112 for *tremisses* and 4 for *denarii*. In the second half of the ninth century, when only *denarii* were struck, the single issues of any quantity, albeit limited, are those of Adelchis (853-78) (63 dies) and of Louis and Engelberga (around 870) (73 dies). For most of their successors only a single coin has survived. Although this makes any calculation impossible, it does explicitly confirm how small the number of issues was.[79]

The considerable size of the *tremissis*-issues of Arechis II, verified by calculating the number of dies, is mirrored very clearly by written sources, which also underline their persistence as a currency. Around 865/70, when gold coinage, though still preferred to silver,

---

[77] A. Rovelli, "Il denaro carolingio nel Meridione d'Italia: una discussione da riaprire", *Annali dell'Istituto italiano di Numismatica* 42 (1995), pp. 255-62; W.R. Day Jr., "The monetary reforms of Charlemagne and the circulation of money in early medieval Campania", *Early Medieval Europe* 6.1 (1997), pp. 25-45.

[78] E.A. Arslan, "Sequenze dei conii e valutazioni quantitative delle monetazioni argentea e aurea di Benevento longobarda", in G. Depeyrot, T. Hackens and G. Moucharte eds., *Rythmes de la production monétaire de l'Antiquité à nos jours*, Actes du Colloque international, Paris, 10-12 Jan 1986 (Louvain-la-Neuve, 1987), pp. 387-409.

[79] On the basis of this evidence, I cannot share the opinion of J.M. Martin, who believes that the "Franks thus provided the Lombards of the South with a system adapted to their new monetary situation". The Beneventan denarius of Frankish origin would, he holds, have been able "to satisfy the demand of most of southern Italy for a century and a half". "Southern Italy", continues Martin, "rejoins the common model of the rest of the west at the end of the ninth century, with a delay of one or two centuries and following a different path. Bimetallism is only a transitory phase in this development", Martin, "Economia naturale ed economia monetaria nell'Italia meridionale longobarda e bizantina (secoli VI-XI)", p. 188. On the scarcity of currency in the Beneventan lands during the Carolingian era, M. Del Treppo's analysis remains valid: "La vita economica e sociale di una grande abbazia del Mezzogiorno: San Vincenzo al Volturno nell'alto medioevo" *Archivio storico per le Province napoletane* n.s. 35 (1955), pp. 31-110, esp. pp. 62-63.

probably began to become scarce, contracts specify that payment
ought to be made in gold coin and, more precisely, in *tremisses* of
Arechis which evidently constituted the majority of the available stock
of gold, having been struck in the greatest quantity.[80] The information relating to Beneventan issues cannot be generalised for obvious
reasons, given the different political situation of the duchy-principate
of Benevento, but it is in some ways emblematic of the limited production of silver *denarii* throughout ninth-century Italy.

Returning to the north after this digression, we can focus on Rome
and Lucca. In these cases, and in those that follow, we cannot make
use of such precise data as that from Benevento. It would seem,
however, that Lucca and Rome struck little, and in alternate phases.
Lucca was inactive for an undetermined period in the ninth and
tenth centuries. The papal mint at Rome seems to have struck few
coins, and was closed completely around 980, a little after the return
to activity of the imperial mint at Lucca.[81] The limited production
of these two mints, the only ones in central Italy, seems to fit with
the considerable dearth of coinage in Tuscany, Lazio, the Abruzzo
and Marche. The paucity of coins in circulation in these regions is
apparent even in the specific and elevated part of the economy—so
different from that usually attested by numismatic finds—documented
by the charters, in which coinage appears in various cases as a measure of value, rather than an effective means of payment.

It remains to examine the northern mints: Milan, Pavia and Treviso
(later replaced by Verona).[82] The imperial mints, together with that
of Venice, are concentrated in the Po valley, the area that, as we
have seen, seems to have been the only one in which the quantity
of coin was sufficient not to have to resort to alternative methods
of payment, at least for large-scale transactions. The development of
commerce along the Po and its tributaries explains, at least in part,
the concentration of mints in this fairly small area. The scarcity of

---

[80] For example, *Codex Diplomaticus Cavensis*, docc. LXIII, LXV, LXVI, LXIX, LXXIII.

[81] L. Travaini, "La moneta milanese tra X e XII secolo" *Atti dell' 11° Congresso
Internazionale di Studi sull'alto Medioevo*, Milano, 26-30 Oct. 1987 (Spoleto, 1989), p. 226.

[82] Travaini, "La moneta milanese tra X e XII secolo": Italy did not witness the
sharp increase in the number of mints that occurred in Francia thanks to the efforts
of counts and abbots from the end of the ninth century. In the *Regnum Italiae*,
in the period between the ninth and the twelfth centuries before the appearance
of mints in the communes, they remained limited to those of Milan, Pavia, Verona
and Lucca.

archaeological finds, to which reference has already been made, suggests however that the silver *denarius* was used essentially for transactions of a relatively high value. Commerce on the Po also probably explains the modest incidence of transalpine Italian coinage. The Po seems, however, to have been the only commercial route of any prominence in Italy. Elsewhere currency circulated only at a reduced level: there was only a marginal flow of coinage in the kingdom's marches in central Italy.

The truth is that this shortage of coin did not only affect Italy. The phenomenon is noticeable, to differing degrees, elsewhere in the Empire.[83] It has been encountered in the Spanish March and it appears increasingly strongly the further away one goes from the heartlands of the Frankish monarchy: 625 isolated finds of Carolingian coins are known at present from the Low Countries, but from Germany, for the whole period between 751 and 936, there are only 106.[84] This fact is not surprising if we note that nine tenths of mints were located in the area where finds are concentrated. The scarce monetisation of some newly-conquered regions, like those to the east of the Rhine (where only two mints were in operation: Regensburg under Louis the Pious and later, occasionally, Würzburg), is well-known and not surprising.[85] The Italian situation is perhaps more unexpected. But it seems to be in tune with recent research in other fields that has emphasised the need to overcome the traditional tendency to generalise from Francia north of the Loire, and the Rhineland, to the entire Carolingian empire.[86]

As far as coinage is concerned, it is undeniable that, with the restoration of royal control over the issue of coin, the Frankish monarchy meant to use it as a tangible expression of imperial—and, therefore, supranational—sovereignty. The issues of the *Christiana*

---

[83] P. Spufford, *Money and its use in medieval Europe* (Cambridge, 1988), pp. 27-54.

[84] On Spain, see D.M. Metcalf "Some Geographical Aspects of Early Medieval Monetary Circulation in the Iberian Peninsula", in M. Gomes Marques and M. Crusafont I Sabater eds., *Problems of Medieval Coinage in the Iberian Area* 2 (Aviles, 1986), pp. 307-24; Metcalf himself notes the rarity of Carolingian coins, stating: "This argument throws us into the thick of the debate about the Pirenne thesis, the continuity of economic activity through the early middle ages, and the balance between a natural economy and a money economy" (p. 324); O. Jeanne-Rose, "Trouvailles isolées de monnaies carolingiennes en Poitou: inventaire provisoire", *Revue numismatique* 151 (1996), pp. 241-83, at p. 251.

[85] Grierson and Blackburn, *Medieval European Coinage*, p. 196.

[86] S. Gasparri, "Presentazione", in C. Azzara and P. Moro eds., *I capitolari italici* (Rome, 1998), pp. 9-12.

religio type are the most mature and sophisticated manifestation of this conception. But the argument about the effective level of monetisation of Carolingian society is a different one. The capacities and, especially, the weak points of the monetary system imposed by Charlemagne throughout his empire have been fully and convincingly discussed in general terms by M. Hendy in various studies comparing the monetary system of antiquity with that of the Carolingians.[87]

Putting aside those aspects that involve the Carolingian empire in its entirety, some factors associated solely with the political and economic evolution of Italy could have exacerbated the problem of the availability of coinage. The problem of a scarcity of currency was felt less keenly in the area of the Po, thanks to the distinctive development of commerce along the river and its tributaries.

The situation in central Italy, which does not seem to have been organically linked to the trade flowing along the Po, was very different. The most recent studies of artisan production—in particular of ceramics—have highlighted the absence of any meaningful medium- or long-range commerce between the northern and central zones of the peninsula, and between the centre and the south.[88] We should also not forget that the power exercised in Italy by the Frankish aristocracy settled there after the conquest often had a predatory character, with serious repercussions both for the social order and for economic structures.[89] Nor, in what appears to have been a peri-

---

[87] In the Roman-Byzantine world, the production of coinage was closely linked to the needs of public finance. In this complex mechanism, the stipends paid to the army and to imperial officials on the one hand, and fiscal exactions on the other, constituted the greatest forces propelling the currency. The Carolingian *denarius*, lacking the predominantly fiscal features of the Roman-Byzantine coinage, had the potential to become a coinage for commercial use. But the process was slow and fragmented. When it appeared, the Carolingian *denarius* lacked the "motors" that had driven the circulation of ancient coin, without adequately replacing these with commercial activity: Hendy, "From Public to Private: The Western Barbarian Coinages as a Mirror of the Disintegration of Late Roman State Structures"; "East and West: Divergent Models of Coinage and its Use".

[88] G.P. Brogiolo and S. Gelichi eds., *Le ceramiche altomedievali (VI-X secolo) in Italia settentrionale: produzioni e commerci*, Atti del 6° seminario sul tardoantico e l'altomedioevo in Italia centrosettentrionale, Monte Barro, 1995 (Mantua, 1995).

[89] P. Delogu, "Lombard and Carolingian Italy", in R. McKitterick ed., *The New Cambridge Medieval History, Volume II, c. 700-c. 900* (Cambridge, 1995), pp. 290-319, esp. 308-309. On the general crisis in Italian material culture see, for the pottery: R. Francovich and M. Valenti, "La ceramica d'uso comune in Toscana tra V-X secolo. Il passaggio tra età tardoantica ed altomedioevo", in G. Démians d'Archimbaud ed., *La céramique médiévale en Méditerranée*, Aix-en-Provence 1995 (Aix-en-Provence, 1997), pp. 129-37, which emphasises the progressive passage from an industrial to

pheral area of the Frankish domain, and not only in a political sense, were the rulers ever really in a position (perhaps even through lack of interest) to assure an adequate supply of coinage. As we have seen, the mint at Lucca was inactive for a long time. The probable difficulty of providing mints with the necessary metal perhaps helped to aggravate the situation. The Poitou silver-mines at Melle were far away, after all, and research in progress on local areas of silver extraction seems to rule out the possibility of any significant activity earlier than the tenth or eleventh centuries.[90] In this way a process of deflation (aggravated by the lack of production of "oboli") must have been primed. This lay at the root of the monetary void in whole regions of Carolingian and post-Carolingian Italy, which explains why the number of coin finds is remarkably small and also why the silver *denarius* acquired higher purchasing power there than elsewhere.

In a context which witnessed a weak and inefficient issuing authority, sparse production of coin (aggravated by the striking of only one denomination), and a commerce still far from capable of impelling monetary circulation on its own (except in a few specific instances), the interpretation put forward by C.M. Cipolla remains one of the most convincing: ". . . the degree of liquidity of coinage", he maintains, "depends in large part on the degree of efficiency of the market. If . . . the imperfect functioning of the market creates in the consumer a high degree of uncertainty about the supply of the desired commodity, the 'utility' of coinage is strongly diminished. The liquidity of the coinage and the demand for it is proportionately reduced. . . . Institutions like that of the gift flourish, acquiring great economic importance".[91]

[Translated by Marios Costambeys]

---

a local production from the seventh century, and the "rebirth" of a wider market from the end of the tenth century.

[90] I should like to thank R. Francovich, who is studying this problem, for the information.

[91] C.M. Cipolla, "Appunti per una nuova storia della moneta nell'alto medioevo", *Moneta e scambi nell'alto medioevo*, Settimane di studio del Centro italiano di studi sull'alto Medioevo 8 (Spoleto, 1961), p. 623.

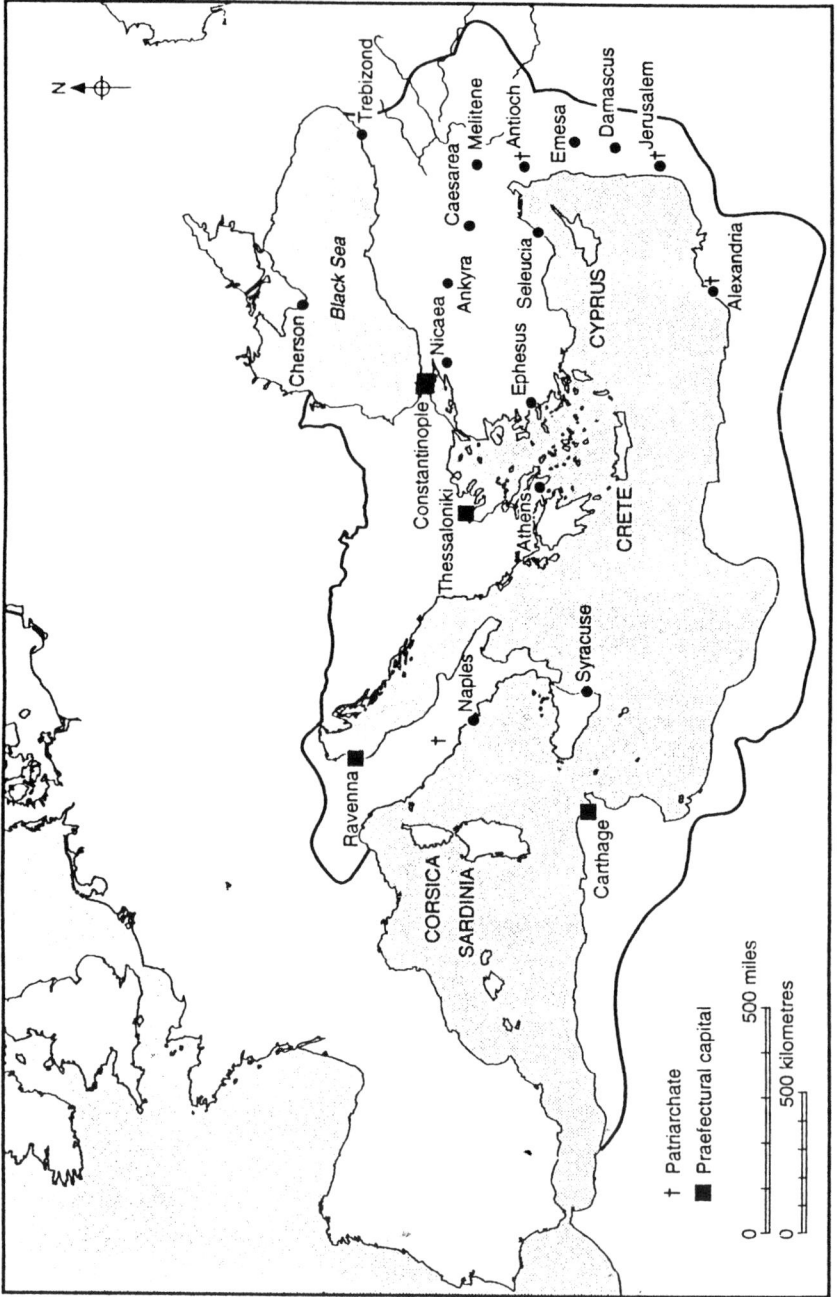

Fig. 1. The Empire in 565 AD: approximate extent.

PRODUCTION, DISTRIBUTION AND DEMAND
IN THE BYZANTINE WORLD, c. 660-840

John Haldon

Production, distribution and demand represent three key features of medieval East Roman economic and social relations, and in a short contribution such as this it will be possible to highlight only some of the more salient features for the period in question. More importantly, perhaps, it should be emphasised at the outset that an analysis of these features of the economic and social life of the East Roman empire is hindered from the outset by the current state of the archaeological, and more especially the ceramic, record, which is extremely poor for Anatolia, and patchy for the south Balkans and Aegean region. Reliance on numismatic and documentary evidence alone for certain data is therefore greater than is perhaps desirable, but at this stage, unavoidable.[1]

---

[1] There is a substantial older literature relevant to the East Roman area, which still provides useful material: E. Ashtor, "Nouvelles réflexions sur la thèse de Pirenne", *Schweizer Zeitschrift für Geschichte* 20 (1970), pp. 601-07; P.E. Hübinger ed., *Bedeutung und Rolle des Islam beim Übergang vom Altertum zum Mittelalter*, Wege der Forschung, 202 (Darmstadt, 1968); R.S. Lopez, "The role of trade in the readjustment of Byzantium in the seventh century", *Dumbarton Oaks Papers* 13 (1959), pp. 67-85; "Silk industry in the Byzantine empire", *Speculum* 20 (1945), pp. 1-42; "The dollar of the Middle Ages", *Journal of Economic History* 11 (1951), pp. 209-34; "East and West in the early Middle Ages: economic relations", *Relazioni del X Congresso Internazionale di Scienze Storici* 3 (Florence, 1955), pp. 113-62; A.R. Lewis, *Naval power and trade in the Mediterranean A.D. 500-1100* (Princeton, 1951); H. Adelson, *Light-weight solidi and Byzantine trade during the sixth and seventh centuries* (New York, 1957); Ph. Grierson, "Commerce in the Dark Ages", *Transactions of the Royal Historical Society* 9, 5th ser. (1959), pp. 123-40; H. Antoniadis-Bibicou, *Recherches sur les douanes à Byzance, l' "octava", le "kommerkion": et les commerciaires* (Paris, 1963); D. Claude, *Der Handel im westlichen Mittelmeer während des Frühmittelalters*, Untersuchungen zu Handel und Verkehr der vor- und frühgeschichtlichen Zeit in Mittel- und Nordeuropa 2 (Göttingen, 1985). More recently: M.F. Hendy, *Studies in the Byzantine monetary economy, c. 300-1450* (Cambridge, 1985), esp. pp. 561-69; the essays in R. Hodges and W. Bowden eds., *The sixth century: production, distribution and demand* (Leiden-Boston-Köln, 1998); and P. Reynolds, *Trade in the western Mediterranean A.D. 400-700: the ceramic evidence*, BAR International Series 604 (Oxford, 1995). Further literature, especially in respect of ceramic evidence, will be mentioned below.

The context is well-known in its general lines, even if there remain
substantial areas where this gap in the archaeological picture, quite
apart from a lack of appropriate documentary evidence, hinders any
fuller appreciation at the present time. By the 660s, the East Roman
empire had lost its wealthiest provinces—in particular Egypt, the
source of the grain which had both fed Constantinople and other
major coastal cities as well as contributed to the supply of the East
Roman army, and Syria/Palestine, a source of considerable fiscal
income as well as of finished luxury products. It was left with that
part of Asia Minor behind the Taurus-Anti-Taurus ranges, very
roughly in a line running from the western end of the Cilician plain
up to Trebizond on the Black Sea coast. Its power in the Balkans
had been reduced to disconnected littoral strips along the Adriatic
coastline, around western Greece and the Peloponnese, the coastal
plains of the Argolid and Attica, Euboia, the coastal region running
north through Thessaloniki and around to the southern Thracian
plain. North of this region the Black Sea coast up to the mouth of
the Danube was held until the 680s (the arrival of the Turkic Bulgars),
and thereafter for much of the eighth and ninth centuries as far as
Varna or Anchialus (Gulf of Burgas), with a more-or-less limited
control of the inland regions of Thrace below the Stara Zagora,
depending chiefly on the presence of imperial troops or the willingness of the local population—Slav or non-Slav—to accept imperial
authority. Little or no control was exercised over the central and
western inner Balkan regions. The Empire retained its control in the
Aegean islands, although they were constantly threatened, and occasionally occupied, from the 650s by the nascent Muslim maritime
power, and Cyprus (divided as a condominium by treaty in 685); it
continued to hold still considerable Italian territories, albeit fragmented and under permanent threat from local Lombard rulers (but
including Rome and Sicily as well as the islands of Sardinia and
Corsica); and the North African provinces remained under increasingly precarious Constantinopolitan authority until the fall of Carthage in the early 690s. While the evidence concerning them is slender
indeed, it is clear that they retained importance for Constantinople
both economically and politically until their final loss in the 690s.[2]

This was a massively reduced and impoverished state when com-

  [2] See J.F. Haldon, *Byzantium in the seventh century: the transformation of a culture*, 2nd
ed. (Cambridge, 1997), pp. 63-75 for further literature. On North Africa: M. Brett,
"The Arab conquest and the rise of Islam in North Africa", *Cambridge History of*

pared with the Empire of the early seventh century, whatever its
fiscal and political-military problems might then have been, and it
is clear, and generally agreed, that the state's fiscal resources as well
as its control over its remaining territories must have suffered as a
result, although the degree remains uncertain. One estimate suggests
a reduction in tax revenue of as much as 75%, given that Egypt
alone has been estimated to have supplied something like a third of
the state's revenues from the prefectures of Oriens and Illyricum
combined.[3] Be that as it may, the central government was faced with
a fiscal and political crisis probably greater than any which had
afflicted the Roman state hitherto. The solutions it adopted to deal
with the problems—which affected every aspect of East Roman
administrative and social life—evolved for the most part in a piecemeal manner, by fits and starts, as the problems, and their implications for first one sector and then another of the state's operations
became apparent. Fiscal, military, judicial structures were all radically
implicated, as were relations between landlords and tenants, and
town and country. The long-term results of these changes over the
remainder of the seventh and eighth, and well into the ninth century,
were to produce a very different, yet still recognisably Roman, state
administrative apparatus, rooted in a transformed society and culture.

It hardly needs to be stressed that all this had important, in parts
dramatic implications for the production, distribution and consumption
of social wealth. Quite apart from the narrower concerns of market
exchange and the use of money, or the production and distribution

---

Africa II (Cambridge, 1978), pp. 503-13; and C. Morrisson and W. Seibt, "Sceaux
de commerciaires byzantins du VIIe siècle trouvés à Carthage", *Revue Numismatique*
24 (1982), pp. 222-41. Corsica seems to have been lost to the Lombards during
the later seventh century. For residual East Roman power in Malta, Sardinia and
the Balearics well into the eighth century: A. Boscolo, *La Sardegna bizantina e alto-
giudicale* (Sassari, 1978); E. Eickhoff, *Seekrieg und Seepolitik zwischen Islam und Abendland*
(Berlin, 1966), pp. 38ff.; T.S. Brown, "Byzantine Malta. A discussion of the sources",
in A.L. Luttrell ed., *Medieval Malta. Studies on Malta before the Knights* (London, 1975),
pp. 71-87. A naval expedition of some importance involving vessels from the Sicilian fleet as well as others was in action in 760 in the Tyrrhenian sea, for example:
see Eickhoff, *Seekrieg und Seepolitik*, p. 224; V. von Falkenhausen, *Untersuchungen über
die byzantinische Herrschaft in Süditalien vom 9. bis ins 11. Jahrhundert*, Schriften zur
Geistesgeschichte des östlichen Europa 1 (Wiesbaden, 1967), p. 4. On the situation
in the western Mediterranean and the Byzantine role there, see also E. Manzano,
"Byzantium and al-Andalus in the ninth century", in L. Brubaker ed., *Byzantium in
the ninth century: dead or alive?* (Aldershot, 1998), pp. 215-27.
   [3] See A.H.M. Jones, *The later Roman empire 284-602: a social and administrative survey* (Oxford 1964), pp. 462-64; Hendy, *Studies*, pp. 164ff.

of luxury goods, the redistribution of agrarian production by the state through its fiscal apparatus was directly affected, while movements of population disrupted established patterns of consumption and production of foodstuffs, hence also shifts in patterns of demand and the distribution of goods which were associated therewith. Changes in the nature and function of urban centres meant at the same time changes in fiscal, military and ecclesiastical administration, so that it would be reasonable to say that the whole fabric of East Roman state and society were affected in one way or another by the events of the seventh century, with all the consequences for the ways in which systems of exchange and production worked which this entailed. In the following, I will try to give some idea of the directions and emphases of those changes.

It should be stated at the outset that the situation described above did not last throughout the whole of the period with which we are concerned. By the 730s and 740s the military situation on the eastern front was becoming more stable. The regular deep penetration of imperial territory by hostile forces which characterised Muslim strategy from the 650s, involving the death or deportation of population and destruction of buildings, livestock and crops, became less frequent as a workable defensive strategy evolved. New fiscal and military administrative structures were evolving which enabled the state to maximise the extraction of resources and capitalise on the productive potential of the provincial population. New hierarchies of urban centres were developing which reflected the needs of both the state, in terms of its fiscal, military and administrative requirements, and the Church, in terms of ecclesiastical administration and ideological authority, while at the same time reflecting a more stable relationship between such centres and rural production. And by the 820s and 830s, these developments were further enhanced by an internal political and economic stability which enabled the widespread re-introduction of a bronze coinage and the re-monetisation of exchange relationships throughout the Empire's territories. Although the pace in the southern Balkan region was initially slower—since the military recovery of much lost territory was a pre-requisite—the process of urbanisation and monetisation was, if anything, much more rapid here, although this becomes apparent only after our period, especially in the tenth and eleventh centuries.[4]

---

[4] A. Harvey, *Economic expansion in the Byzantine Empire 900-1200* (Cambridge, 1989), pp. 85-89, 207-43 provides a useful survey of the relevant documentary evidence.

Some of the more obvious changes which affected production and distribution can be summarised as follows. First, there occurred what I would term a "ruralisation" of society, partly promoted by the fact that cities were already losing their role in the state fiscal system by the later sixth century. Together with the devastation, abandonment, shrinkage or displacement of many cities in Asia Minor as a result of invasions and raids, especially from the 640s but also during the period of the Persian wars (602-626), the state transferred its fiscal attention to the village community, which became the main unit of assessment by the later seventh century.[5] This process had already begun much earlier in the Balkans, of course, and it has recently been argued that the pattern of state involvement in re-structuring urban and defensive centres there, beginning in the fifth century and continuing through the sixth and into the seventh century, served as a model for similar state-led changes in Asia Minor, not simply in terms of the types of site that were selected, but also of the techniques and styles of building and fortification. The defensive properties of "urban" sites, their direct relevance to military, administrative or ecclesiastical needs, and so on, now played the key role in whether a "city" survived or not.[6]

At the same time, the pre-eminent position taken by Constantinople has long been recognised to have had far-reaching consequences for

---

[5] See the list and discussion in W. Brandes, *Die Städte Kleinasiens im 7. und 8. Jahrhundert* (Berlin 1990), pp. 120-24.

[6] See A. Dunn, "The transformation from *polis* to *kastron* in the Balkans (III-VII cc.): general and regional perspectives", *Byzantine and Modern Greek Studies* 18 (1994), pp. 60-80; "Stages in the transition from the late Antique to the middle Byzantine urban centre in S. Macedonia and S. Thrace", in Αφιέρωμα στον *N.G.L. Hammond* (Thessaloniki, 1997), pp. 137-50; "From *polis* to *kastron* in southern Macedonia: Amphipolis, Khrysoupolis, and the Strymon delta", *Castrum 5. Archéologie des espaces agraires méditerranéens au Moyen Age* (1999), pp. 399-413. Dunn provides a good survey of the relevant Balkan archaeological material in this respect, as well as the recent secondary literature. See also A. Dunn, "Heraclius' 'Reconstruction of cities' and their sixth-century Balkan antecedents", *Acta XIII Congressus Internationalis Archaeologiae Christianae* II (= Vjesnik za arheologiju I historiju Dalmatinsku, Supl. vol. 87-89) (Città del Vaticano-Split, 1998), pp. 795-806. For these changes, and the shifts in vocabulary which accompanied them, see J.F. Haldon, "The idea of the town in the Byzantine empire", in G.P. Brogiolo and B. Ward-Perkins eds., *The idea and ideal of the town between late Antiquity and the early Middle Ages* The Transformation of the Roman World 4 (Leiden/Boston/Köln, 1999), pp. 1-24; W. Brandes, "Byzantine Towns in the Seventh and Eighth Century – Different Sources, Different Histories?" *The idea and ideal of the town between late Antiquity and the early Middle Ages.*, pp. 25-57; W. Brandes and J.F. Haldon, "Towns, Tax and Transformation: state, cities and their hinterlands in the East Roman world, c. 500-800", in N. Christie and N. Gauthier eds.,*Towns and their hinterlands in late Antiquity and the early middle ages*, (Leiden-Boston-Köln, 1999).

the pattern of exchange and movement of goods in the Aegean and east Mediterranean basin.[7] The social elite was also transformed. An elite of mixed provenance—members of the older establishment and "new men" selected by the emperors on a more obviously "merito-cratic" basis—began to evolve, but which, in the context of the dras-tic shifts which were taking place, appears at first—and until well into the later eighth and ninth centuries—to have been heavily depend-ent upon personal imperial patronage for their posts and influence.[8] This in turn had effects on patterns of demand as well as upon the production and distribution of resources, for the events of the sev-enth century produced what can be seen as a re-assertion of cen-tral state power over late Roman tendencies to decentralisation. Social status and advancement (including the self-identity of the elite) were intimately bound into the imperial system and personal asociation with the ruler, and these arrangements had important implications for the economic life of the Empire: the continued power and attrac-tion of the imperial establishment at Constantinople, with its court and hierarchical system of precedence, as well as the highly cen-tralised fiscal administrative structure, consumed the whole attention of the Byzantine elite, until the later tenth and elevcenth century hindering the evolution of a more highly-localised aristocracy which might otherwise have invested in the economy and society of its own localities and towns, rather than in the imperial system.[9]

State-influenced patterns

In any consideration of patterns of production and distribution in the East Roman world the role of the state must figure prominently. Just as in the period before the Muslim conquests, so thereafter the needs of the state in terms of supplying and housing its armies, pay-ing and maintaining its administrative apparatus, and maintaining

---

[7] See, for example, C. Mango, "The development of Constantinople as an urban centre", *Seventeenth International Byzantine Congress. Major papers* (New York, 1986), pp. 118-36.

[8] See Haldon, *Byzantium in the seventh century*, pp. 153-72, 395-99.

[9] For the development of these relationships, see M. Angold, "The Shaping of the Medieval Byzantine 'City'", *Byzantinische Forschungen* 10 (1985), pp. 1-37 for dis-cussion of the growth of provincial elites; and Harvey, *Economic expansion*, pp. 200-203, 207ff.

the imperial household tended to dominate, so that from a certain point of view the history of the East Roman political formation in the medieval period can be treated as the history of the tensions and contradictions in the relationship between the vested interests of the state, as embodied in these institutional arrangements, and those of the rest of the population. In practice, this meant, of course, between the state and any social elite which might be in a position to challenge the state for the control of resources. In itself, this is common to all political formations of this type, and is thus not unusual. What is important in this instance is the fact that such contradictions were temporarily resolved by the events of the seventh century permitting, as noted already, a more monolithic political structure to operate relatively unchallenged, at least until the tenth century.[10] Indeed, the ability of the state in the seventh and eighth centuries to implement a relatively full control over its tax-base directly determined the way in which the middle and late Byzantine aristocracy evolved. Similarly, the civil wars and the fiscal crisis of the central government in the later tenth and eleventh century especially, the corresponding shifts in both the mode of recruitment and source of manpower for the army, as well as changes in provincial and central civil and fiscal administration, can all be connected to the nature of the state's relationship with its fiscal base.[11]

The role of the government in the extraction and redistribution of resources is especially clear in terms of tax, and in two aspects: the raising of produce locally, throughout the provinces, with which to feed, clothe, arm and equip the army; and in the issue and circulation of coin, the basic mechanism through which the state converted agricultural produce into liquid fiscal resources. Grain, vegetables, clothing and so on were raised in kind, either as a portion (or occasionally the whole of) the regular land tax, or in the

---

[10] See the discussion and comparative analysis in J.F. Haldon, *The state and the tributary mode of production* (London, 1993); also "La estructura de las relaciones de producción tributarias: Estado y sociedad en Bisanzio y el Islam primitivo", *Hispania* 58.3 (1998), pp. 841-80.

[11] See my remarks in "The army and the economy: the allocation and redistribution of surplus wealth", *Mediterranean History Review* 7.2 (1992), pp. 133-53. A particular problem arose for the government during the tenth century and afterwards, because the central government was often represented in the provinces by leading officials who were also members of the very social elite which was able to confont and challenge the state's demands, thus prejudicing the interests of the centre in the extraction of fiscal resources.

form of extraordinary levies in particular goods—the system familiar from the late Roman period, in fact. Coin, on the other hand—
at least until the middle of the ninth century and after—was issued
chiefly to oil the wheels of the state machinery, and wealth was
appropriated and consumed through a redistributive fiscal mechanism: the state issued gold in the form of salaries and largesse to its
bureaucracy and armies, who exchanged a substantial portion thereof
for goods and services in maintaining themselves. The state could
thus collect much of the coin it put into circulation through tax, the
more so since fiscal policy generally demanded tax in gold and offered
change in bronze.[12] During the second half of the seventh and through
much of the eighth century, this system was constrained by circumstances, so that soldiers were supplied and taxes raised chiefly—
but never exclusively—in kind. But there always remained strong
regional as well as chronological variations: areas in which urban or
rural markets existed and were secure from hostile attack, such as
the metropolitan regions around Constantinople, were generally supplied not only with gold but also with bronze coinage, for example.
In one sense, therefore, the constraints on a generalised system of
monetary exchange had simply become much more pronounced,
since such constraints had always operated in remoter localities, or
areas where the activities of the state did not promote such monetised activity, as in Anatolia after the cutting back of the state postal
and transport service in the 530s, for example; and they continued
to operate thereafter.[13]

The gravity of the situation is demonstrated by the interesting,
and temporary (i.e. from c. 640 to c. 730) transformation in the role
of the officials called *kommerkiarioi*, the earlier *comites commerciorum*.
Originally subordinates of the *comitiva sacrarum largitionum*, they were

---

[12] Hendy, *Studies*, pp. 602ff., 662ff.; M.F. Hendy, "Economy and State in Late
Rome and early Byzantium: an Introduction", in M.F. Hendry, *The Economy, Fiscal
Administration and Coinage of Byzantium* I (London, 1989). Athough one can modify
the point according to the historical context (for example, pointing out that the role
and significance of commercial exchange and cash-crops increased very considerably during the period after the tenth century), it remains valid for the whole
Byzantine period up to the thirteenth century. For a critique of Hendy's strongly
"statist" approach, see the remarks of C. Morrisson, *Journal Numismatique* 6e sér., 33
(1991) 307-10.
[13] Hendy, *Studies*, pp. 294-305; J.F. Haldon, "*Synônê*: Reconsidering a Problematic
Term of Middle Byzantine Fiscal Administration", *Byzantine and Modern Greek Studies* 18
(1994), pp. 116-53 (repr. in J.F. Haldon, *State, Army and Society in Byzantium: Approaches
to Military, Social and Administrative History, 6th-12th Centuries* no. VIII (London, 1995)).

by the middle of the sixth century under the Praetorian prefecture. Until the early years of the seventh century their chief role lay in supervising the production and sale of silk, which was a state monopoly;[14] but it has plausibly been argued that they were, in fact, responsible both for key aspects of supplying troops with equipment and provisions, as well as being associated with the levying and storing of fiscal income in kind as well. The *kommerkiarioi* and their *apothêkai*, now represented on their lead seals, embellished with the imperial portrait and indictional dating, thus represented a pre-existing institution associated with state-run luxury production and commerce which, as a result of the fiscal and administrative crisis which engulfed the Empire in the middle years of the seventh century was given the essential task of supplying the army, an arrangement that operated well into the eighth century, until certain reforms and changes were introduced c. 730 by Leo III (717-741).[15]

These organisational arrangements appear to have experienced an important administrative change in or just before the year 730/731: henceforth, the great majority of seals no longer bear the name of one or more *kommerkiarioi*; instead, they are ascribed to the *basilika kommerkia* (the imperial *kommerkia*) of a province or group of provinces

---

[14] See N. Oikonomides, "Silk Trade and Production in Byzantium from the Sixth to the Ninth Century: the Seals of the Kommerkiarioi", *Dumbarton Oaks Papers* 40 (1986), pp. 33-53. Oikonomidès' suggestion that in the seventh and eighth centuries they were still principally occupied with the production and sale of silk has been challenged, chiefly on the basis of the climatic conditions of Asia Minor which permit the breeding of silk worms in only a small number of areas; although the political and military situation was also unfavourable: see Haldon, *Byzantium in the Seventh Century*, pp. 232ff.; the response of N. Oikonomides, "Le marchand byzantin des provinces (IXe-XIe s.)", *Mercati e mercanti nell'alto medioevo: L'area euroasiatica e l'area mediterranea*, Settimane di studio del Centro italiano di studi sull'alto Medioevo 40 (Spoleto, 1993), pp. 638ff., and further evidence against his view in A. Muthesius, "From Seed to Samite: Aspects of Byzantine Silk Production" *Textile History* 20.2 (1989), pp. 135-49; the climatologically-grounded discussion in G. Jacobi, *Die Wirtschaftsgeographie der Seide* (Berlin, 1932), pp. 51-53; and D. Jacoby, "Silk in Western Byzantium before the Fourth Crusade", *Byzantinische Zeitschrift* 84/85 (1991/1992), pp. 452-500, see p. 454 n. 7.

[15] See Hendy, *Studies*, pp. 619ff., and most recently Brandes and Haldon, "Towns, Tax and Transformation: state, cities and their hinterlands in the East Roman world, c. 500-800"; A. Dunn, "The Kommerkiarios, the Apotheke, the Dromos, the Vardarios, and the West", *Byzantine and Modern Greek Studies* 17 (1993), pp. 3-24; Haldon, *Byzantium in the seventh century*, pp. 232-44. In fact, some of these changes are pre-figured in the administrative evolution of the central finance system in the later sixth and early seventh century; but the dramatic shifts described here were certainly the product of the situation resulting from, first, the Persian wars (c. 603-627) and then the Islamic conquests.

(or *thema*, a military-administrative district).[16] The latest known seal
to bear the term apothêkê is dated to the year 728/729.[17] The exact
nature of the change is impossible to determine, given the lack of
evidence. It seems to have involved a gradual reduction in the importance of individual *kommerkiarioi*, however: instead of seals of a limited number of high-ranking *genikoi kommerkiarioi* associated with *apothêkai*
and often holding a series of consecutive appointments, there are
from the 730s instead a number of seals of *kommerkiarioi* with no
indictional dating and no imperial portrait, of named officials who
vary in rank, and who are associated with no specific region and
with no apothêkê.[18] The exceptions to this combined the position of
head of the imperial silk workshop with that of *genikos kommerkiarios*
or *kommerkiarios*, reflecting a specific position in respect of the general supervision of imperial silk production at Constantinople; although
such seals cease after 786. The seals of the *basilika kommerkia* carried
both an indictional date and the imperial portrait. They continue to
be issued until the 830s—the last known seal with an imperial portrait and an indiction is dated to 832/833. Some seals with no portrait but with an indiction date to the years up to 840/41 at the
latest. At the same time, seals of general or imperial *kommerkiarioi*
attached to specific *themata* or, more usually, specific ports or entrepôts, are produced, a connection which underlines the association of
such officials with trade and exchange activities with lands outside
the Empire. From the later eighth century, there is sound evidence
for the levying of a duty on trade, referred to as the *kommerkion*, and
there is no doubt that *kommerkiarioi* were associated with its collection.[19]

---

[16] See G. Zacos and A. Veglery, *Byzantine Lead Seals* I.1-3 (Basel, 1972), table 33
and comments; and discussion in Oikonomidès, "Silk Trade and Production", pp.
41-42.

[17] Cf. Zacos and Veglery, *Byzantine Lead Seals* I, table 16 (p. 161); and Hendy,
Studies, p. 660, n. 469.

[18] The evidence is discussed in Oikonomidès, "Silk Trade and Production", pp.
50-1.

[19] N. Oikonomidès, *A Collection of Dated Byzantine Lead Seals* (Washington D.C.,
1986), p. 50f. and "Silk Trade and Production", pp. 41-42, 48-49, 51ff. See *Theophanis
Chronographia*, ed. C. de Boor, 2 vols. (Leipzig, 1883, 1885), pp. 469-70 (*The Chronicle
of Theophanes Confessor*, trans. C. Mango and R. Scott (Oxford, 1997), p. 645):
Constantine VI reduced the *kommerkion* of 100 lbs in gold levied on the fair at
Ephesos; p. 475 (Mango-Scott, p. 653): Eirene reduces the *kommerkia* levied at Abydos
and Hieron; p. 487 (Mango-Scott, p. 668): Nicephorus I borrows from the Constantinopolitan shipowners while still levying the "usual custom dues".

The survival of the state depended upon the continued functioning of a fiscal administration which could extract sufficient resources to maintain itself and the imperial armies. Any attempt to work out what the percentage burden for the producing population actually amounted to must confront a number of methodological problems, and is likely to founder for lack of adequate statistical evidence. But that the burden was heavy, and that it swallowed up most of the surplus generated by the rural population every year is very probable: certainly, when in the later eighth and early ninth century we again have some evidence about tax rates, it seems clear that once they had acquitted their basic land tax, peasant producers had little extra to give in the event of the imposition of an extraordinary levy, for military purposes, for example.[20] Documents dating from the tenth to twelfth centuries suggest that the basic land-tax amounted to some 4.5%-5%, or 1/24, of the value of the land, the calculation of value being based on the average "normal" sale price, while rents represented usually double this amount. The percentage of the annual crop which the former represented varied, of course, but it seems that about 10%-12% would be a reasonable average, although it may have been higher at times and in particular regions; while it should be borne in mind that the absolute burden was very considerably increased both by the rent extracted by landlords; and by the addition of a number of regular supplementary impositions, and the extraordinary levies (which were often raised on a yearly basis, particularly in regions where the armies were active).[21] Whether through the use of coinage or through consumption at local level, a vast amount of the agrarian wealth produced within the Empire was consumed directly by the state, chiefly by the army.

The activities of the state in the process of extracting and redistributing wealth can be summarised, thus far, as follows. First, we have state extraction of agrarian resources, skills and labour power, with the consequent redistribution of those resources. This redistributive

---

[20] Haldon, "*Synônê*", esp. pp. 140-42; "The army and the economy", *passim*.

[21] For calculations of basic land taxes, see E. Schilbach, *Byzantinische Metrologie*, Handbuch die Altertumswissenschaft XII.4 (= Byzantinisches Handbuch IV, Munich, 1970), pp. 248-63; N. Oikonomidès, "Terres du fisc et revenu de la terre aux Xᵉ-XIᵉ siècles", in V. Kravari, J. Lefort and C. Morrisson (eds.), *Hommes et richesses dans l'empire byzantin* II: *VIIIᵉ-XVᵉ siècle* (Paris, 1991), pp. 321-37; and C. Morrisson, "Monnaie et finances dans l'empire byzantin Xᵉ-XIVᵉ siècle", in *Hommes et richesses* II, pp. 291-315, at p. 295.

process could occur locally, either through the imposition on the producers of the transportation of the goods to state depots, or through the direct consumption of the resources by state officials and the military at the point of collection/production. Thus in the period up to the 530s, for example, the imperial postal and heavy trans-port service, with its network of way-stations, stables and stud-farms, hostelries and ancillary services (farriers, leather-workers etc.) repre-sented a direct consumer of fiscal resources throughout the regions where it was established; and even though Justinian appears to have considerably curtailed its activities and extent, it certainly continued to exist throughout the Byzantine period.[22] Similarly, units of sol-diers en route to a military base or a campaign were provisioned by direct levies of foodstuffs on the districts through which they passed, and the goods and services consumed were then written off against that year's or the following year's tax-demands (in theory—the system generally worked to the disadvantage of the producers).[23] It could also occur trans-regionally, through the conversion of those resources into cash (gold coin), its collection through regular fiscal assessments at the local and provincial level, and its forwarding to Constantinople. The state might assist the process, insofar as it regu-larly established "artifical" markets through which the produce in question could be purchased for coin, which coin could then be col-lected through the fiscal system. The presence of state officials and the army, who were paid in gold, represented the most obvious way in which this could be attained, and there is good evidence not only that this happened as a matter of course, but also that it could have significant distorting effects on the price structure of the local mar-kets it affected. The use of the system of *coemptio* or compulsory pur-

---

[22] See Hendy, *Studies*, pp. 603-13, and pp. 294-96 for Justinian's curtailment; see Procopius, *Historia Arcana*, xxx. 5-7 (*Procopii Caesariensis Opera Omnia*, ed. J. Haury, 3 vols. (Leipzig, 1905-1913); revised ed. with corr. and addns. G. Wirth, 4 vols. (Leipzig, 1962-1964)); *Ioannis Laurentii Lydi De magistratibus populi Romani libri tres*, iii. 61, ed. R. Wünsch (Leipzig, 1903). It is clear from the middle Byzantine evidence that the *dromos* (the Greek term for the *cursus* [*publicus*]) was a major element in the state's operations. Originally under the authority of the Praetorian Prefects, by the 760s, and probably by the middle of the seventh century, it was an independent department under its logothete, a high-ranking officer for whom numerous seals survive. See V. Laurent, *Le Corpus des sceaux de l'empire byzantin* II: *l'administration cen-trale* (Paris 1981), pp. 195-243; N. Oikonomidès, *Les listes de préséance byzantines des IXᵉ-Xᵉ siècles* (Paris, 1972), pp. 311-12; Hendy, *Studies*, p. 608 and n. 238.

[23] *Iustiniani Novellae*, *Nov.* cxxx, and cf. *Nov.* cxxviii (a. 545), esp. §1-3 (*Corpus Juris Civilis* III) eds. R. Schöll and W. Kroll (Berlin, 1928).

chase was an alternative means of introducing cash through an artifically imposed price structure on provincial populations and redistributing locally-produced goods, and it survived, under a different name, into the middle Byzantine period. Both Procopius and Agathias comment that the system of *coemptio* was regularly abused, to the disadvantage of peasants and landowners both, and there is likewise evidence from the later period that similar structural problems accompanied its continued existence.[24]

Secondly, as well as taking, the state also gave, in an inverted version of the relationship decribed above, directed both internally and externally. The production of silk appears, at least until the middle of the ninth century, to have been more-or-less dominated by the needs of the imperial government, and high-quality silks, and the special dyes that were employed in their preparation, were an important resource, both in the Empire's diplomatic effort (silken cloths and finished items were highly prized outside Byzantium, especially in the West), as well as fiscally, serving as an alternative form of payment to middling and senior officers of the civil and military establishment. While there always seems to have been a considerable element of private enterprise in silk production and weaving, the imperial government also seems always to have exercised a strong supervisory role, controlling both the internal and foreign market especially in the higher-quality materials and the rarer dyes (various hues of "imperial" purple).[25] But this distribution network was limited: from Constantinople via ambassadors to foreign potentates, and via the imperial household to senior Constantinopolitan officials and provincial military officers. Silk could also be used as payment for goods or services from outside the Empire: in 768/769, for

---

[24] Procopius, *Historia Arcana*, xxiii. 11-14; *Agathiae Myrinaei Historiarum libri V*, iv. 22, ed. R. Keydell (Berlin, 1967). See E. Stein, *Histoire du Bas-Empire* II: *de la disparition de l'empire d'Occident à la mort de justinien (476-565)* (Paris-Bruxelles-Amsterdam, 1949, repr. Amsterdam, 1968), p. 440; Haldon, "Synônê", pp. 118-22.

[25] See N. Oikonomidès, "Silk trade and production", repeated in an abridged form in "Commerce et production de la soie à Byzance", in J. Lefort and C. Morrisson (eds.), *Hommes et richesses dans l'empire byzantin*, I: *IVe-VIIe siècle* (Paris 1989), pp. 187-92; A. Muthesius, "Silken diplomacy", in S. Franklin and J. Shepard eds., *Byzantine Diplomacy*, (Aldershot, 1992), pp. 235-48; R. Cormack, "But is it Art?", *Byzantine Diplomacy.*, pp. 218-36 for silk in diplomatic exchange. For a longer-term analysis of Byzantine silk production, see D. Jacoby, "Silk in western Byzantium before the Fourth Crusade". For officials paid in silk, see Oikonomidès, "Silk trade and production"; and J.F. Haldon ed., English trans. and commentary, *Constantine Porphyrogenitus, Three Treatises on Imperial Military Expeditions*, [C] 250-260, 501-511 (Vienna, 1990).

example, Constantine V bought the freedom of 2,500 inhabitants of the Aegean islands of Imbros, Tenedos and Samothrake, who had been seized by Slav raiders, with silken vestments.[26] Precious silks figure later, in the eleventh and twelfth centuries, in the wills of magnates or as part of endowments to monastic houses; but it is clear that this still represents a wide-ranging but relatively limited pattern of distribution. By this time, of course, commercial silk production, based especially in Greece around, for example, Thebes, had expanded and become integrated into a much more widely based market for cloths of all varieties extending across the whole east Mediterranean basin and across to Italy and beyond.[27] Similar considerations apply to other luxury articles, such as illuminated books, for example, although here the rate of production and quantities involved were exceedingly limited compared with that of, say, silk.[28]

All these forms of redistribution are essentially one-sided, of course: the state gave, as imperial largesse or diplomatic gift; and it took, and even where it paid for what it took (as with *coemptio*), it paid at depressed prices. It would be reasonable to suppose that, for the later seventh and eighth centuries at least, the state dominated the production and distribution of agricultural goods (beyond the level of producers' own consumption), and probably of luxury products such as silk. Thereafter, as economic and political stability promoted stable markets and increased monetisation of exchange at the level of day-to-day needs, as urban centres began to attract such activities, and as local elites began to evolve greater purchasing power and more complex demands for goods of all kinds, the proportion of the Empire's productive capacity integrated into market exchange relationships independent of the state's interests and activities will have increased.

Much discussion has been devoted to the question of the economic recovery of the Empire during the early years of the ninth century, and in particular the question of the extent to which the government understood the relationship between a growing market-

---

[26] See *Nicephorus, Patriarch of Constantinople. Short History*, p. 162 (§86), text, transl. and commentary by C. Mango (CFHB, ser. Washingtoniensis 13 = Dumbarton Oaks Texts 10, Washington D.C., 1990).

[27] See Jacoby, " Silk in western Byzantium before the Fourth Crusade", pp. 460ff.

[28] See the remarks of L. Brubaker, "Material culture and the myth of Byzantium, 750-950", in G. Arnaldi and G. Cavallo eds., *Europa medievale e mondo Bizantino: contatti effettivi e possibilità di studi comparati* (Rome, 1997), pp. 33-41, at pp. 40-41.

led demand for a small denomination coinage of account through which day-to-day low-level transactions could be facilitated, velocity of circulation, and rate of production of such coinage.[29] To provide an answer to this set of questions is, of course, far beyond the scope of this contribution. But it will perhaps be appropriate at this point to comment briefly on the functioning of that most significant of state-controlled means of redistribution of social wealth, its coinage.

I have already noted the three-sided redistributive mechanism which was operated through the issue of gold, by which state officials and above all the army were paid in gold, purchased their foodstuffs and other requirements in exchange for a portion of this gold, which was then collected by the government through taxation. It is obvious immediately that such a system can only operate efficiently if a plurimetallic system exists, that is, if a coinage of account—in this case, bronze—is available through which day-to-day exchanges can be carried out, change given, and so on. Such a coinage must, if it is to function at all, have a stable rate of exchange with the pre-cious metal coinage; where this broke down, price inflation followed by hoarding was usually the case and, where state fiscal require-ments were concerned, a fairly rapid move from the extraction of fiscal revenues in cash to one in which actual produce was collected, with all the consequences for the distribution of goods and personnel which that entailed. Such was the case in the fourth and early fifth centuries, and in the later seventh and much of the eighth century.

The government always faced two problems: first, to estimate how much gold coinage should be produced to maintain the cycle of redistribution; second, to know how much bronze coinage was required to facilitate this cycle at the lower level. In the first case, there are several historical examples showing the effects of a shortage of gold: the case reported by Procopius and John Lydus, noted already, where the closure of the way-stations on many of the routes operated by the *cursus publicus* deprived local producers of a ready market for

---

[29] It is in fact generally agreed that the bronze coinage did indeed have an intrin-sic value at times, although the extent to which this was recognised in respect of its exchange-value when measured against goods, as opposed to its value as a coinage of account, is debated: see J.-P. Callu, "Analyses mètalliques et inflation: l'Orient romain de 295 à 361/368", in *Hommes et richesses* I, pp. 223-37; W. Hahn, *Moneta imperii Byzantini*, III: *von Heraclius bis Leo III./Alleinregierung (610-720)*, Denkschriften der Österreichischen Akademie der Wissenschaften 148 (Vienna, 1981), pp. 39-41.

their goods, and thus of the gold with which to pay their taxes; the case noted in the fifth century by Theodoret of Cyrrhus, where a shortage of gold (reason unclear) forced the rural population to borrow gold from the local garrisons in order to pay their taxes; a similar situation as that described by Lydus and Procopius affected the rural population of the provinces during the 760s, when the Emperor Constantine V seems deliberately to have restricted the circulation of gold but demanded tax payments in coin, thus forcing the producers to sell their crops at artificially deflated prices; and there are other examples from the following centuries.[30]

In the second case, the inflationary effects of the over-issue of bronze are demonstrated by the great inflation of the fifth century, eventually culminating in the major reforms of Anastasius and then Justinian; while the lack of supplies of bronze in the seventh and eighth centuries appears to be closely associated with the transformation of urban centres and insecurity of the internal market. But in this case, the issue is a little more complex. For there is, on the one hand, an almost complete absence of bronze coins from all excavated sites in Asia Minor and the Balkans after the early 660s, with the exception of Constantinople and its immediate environs and one or two other sites, where the presence of such coins has been reasonably associated with specific and dateable military events.[31] On the other hand, the evidence also suggests a deliberate curtailment of coin production from about 658 or soon thereafter, a curtailment which has been associated with the probable internal restructuring of tax collecting mechanisms (and by definition, therefore, with the ways in which the army was paid and supplied),[32] and which would

---

[30] For Procopius and Lydus, see above n. 22; Theodoret, *Ep.* 37 ed. Y. Azéma, *Théodoret de Cyr, Correspondance*, Sources chrétiennes xl (Paris, 1955); for Constantine V see Theophanes, *Chronographia*, p. 443 (Mango-Scott, p. 611), and *Nicephorus, Short History* (Mango), p. 160 (§85). Further examples in Hendy, *Studies*, pp. 297-99.

[31] See P. Grierson, "Coinage and Money in the Byzantine Empire, 498-c. 1090", *Moneta e scambi nell'alto Medioevo*, Settimane di studio del Centro italiano di studi sull'alto Medioevo 8 (Spoleto, 1960), pp. 411-53, see p. 436, with table 2; P. Grierson, *Catalogue of the Byzantine Coins in the Dumbarton Oaks Collection and in the Whittemore Collection, II: Phocas to Theodosius III, 602-717*, vol. 1 (Washington D.C., 1968), p. 6f.; summarised in Hendy, *Studies*, pp. 496-9; 640f.; see also Brandes, *Die Städte Kleinasiens*, esp. pp. 145f.; Haldon, *Byzantium in the seventh century*, pp. 226-27. For recent excavation results which demonstrating the same pattern: M. Galani-Krikou, "Θήβα 6ος – 15ος αιώνας. Η νομισματική μαρτυρία απο το Πολιτιστικό Κέντρο", *Symmeikta* 12 (1998), pp. 141-70, esp. pp. 152ff.

[32] Haldon, *Byzantium in the seventh century*, pp. 226-27, 232-44 with earlier litera-

suggest once more that the government was concerned almost exclusively with the fiscal functions of the coinage, ignoring its involvement in market exchange.[33] This contrasts very markedly with the relatively constant rate of production and gold-content of the precious-metal coinage through from the middle of the seventh to the ninth century and beyond.[34]

Yet this purely fiscal interest, and the three-sided model on which it is founded (i.e. state ⇒ bureaucracy and army ⇒ producers [and back to the state]), can be challenged, even if we accept that the state's fiscal interests did predominate (certainly until the reforms of the later eleventh and early twelfth centuries, where the gold coinage was concerned). For there is also to be considered the reactive effect upon this relationship of the inevitable attraction of coins to markets, which serves to complicate the simple triangular relationship by adding a fourth point, as it were, above the triangle, creating in effect a three-dimensional metaphor of the dialectic between the state and its needs, the producing population, and the movement of wealth by means of market-exchange.[35] That the government, having cut back the production and distribution of bronze to the provinces after the 650s, was aware that a medium of exchange of this type was nevertheless necessary to urban markets, is evident from the fact of continued production of appropriate quantities of bronze—as far as the limited archaeological and documentary record can tell us—for Constantinople itself. This hypothesis seems the more likely when

ture; M. Phillips and A. Goodwin, "A seventh-century Syrian hoard of Byzantine and imitative copper coins", *The Numismatic Chronicle* 157 (1997), pp. 61-87, esp. 75ff.

[33] It should be noted in this connection that the history of the Byzantine coinage during this period is complex, involving considerable variations in the weight and style of the bronze issues, with several changes introduced by successive rulers, the (re-)introduction of a silver coinage linking the gold and bronze denominations under Leo III (which adversely affected the production of fractional gold denominations), and substantial reforms and stabilisation of the bronze under Leo IV and, later, Michael II and Theophilos. See Hendy, *Studies*, pp. 498-503 with sources.

[34] The purity of the gold *nomisma* was in fact reduced during the second half of the seventh century and only slowly restored by the early ninth century; but this fluctuation was, compared with that in the form and quantity of the bronze coinage, insignificant. See the detailed survey of the evidence in C. Morrisson, "La monnaie d'or byzantine à Constantinople: purification et modes d'altérations (491-1354)", in Cl. Brenot, J.-N. Barrandon, J.-P. Callu, J. Poirier, R. Halleux and C. Morrisson eds., *L'or monnayé*, I: *purification et altérations de Rome à Byzance*, Cahiers Ernest Babelon 2 (Paris, 1985), pp. 113-87, esp. pp. 123-27.

[35] See, for example, the important article by M. Corbier, "Dévaluations, infaltion et circulation monétaire au IIIe siècle", in *Hommes et richesses* I, pp. 195-211, who modifies the "state fiscality" model in this respect for the Roman world.

we then consider the dramatic increase in the issue of bronze coins during the reigns of Michael II (821-829) and his successor Theophilos (829-842), the establishment of at least one, and probably two new mints for bronze (Thessaloniki and Cherson in the Crimea), and the increase in weight of the standard bronze *follis*.[36]

Indeed, the initial minor increase in bronze coin production, associated with a slightly larger coin under Michael II in the 820s, was followed by a six-fold increase in the issue of a fully reformed and still larger coin type, and this can be associated in turn with the (admittedly sporadic) re-appearance of such coins from urban archaeological contexts from the Balkans and from Asia Minor at about the same time (and increasing in quantity thereafter). This surely suggests a clear recognition of a market-led demand for bronze (increased market activity), and the connection between that and the state's fiscal requirements.[37] Yet it is also the case that, archaeologically, most excavated sites show this upturn in finds of bronze only from the later years of the ninth and the tenth century, so that there remain some difficulties in tying increases in coin emission to the market response.[38] Nevertheless, these changes can be understood in the context of the stabilisation of the Empire's internal situation in general and the beginnings of a recovery of lost territories, especially in the southern Balkans; an increased demand for fiscal resources on the part of the state, coupled with reforms in fiscal administration making this possible; and the (assumed) increased monetisation of fiscal income, already a feature of the second half of the eighth century, but now assumed to represent once more a return to the norms of the Justinianic period.

The degree of monetisation of the economy as a whole is difficult to calculate, of course, since we would need to know the gross yearly

---

[36] See esp. D.M. Metcalf, "How extensive was the issue of Folles during the years 775-820?", *Byzantion* 37 (1967), pp. 270-310; with the comments of Grierson, *Catalogue*, III: *Leo III to Nicephorus III, 717-1081*, vol. 1, pp. 94-97, 406-408, 412-15; D.M. Metcalf, "The reformed Folles of Theophilus: their styles and localization", *American Numismatic Society Museum Notes* 14 (1968), pp. 121-53; D.M. Metcalf, The Folles of Michael II and and of Theophilus before his reform", *Hamburger Beiträge zur Numismatik* 21 (1967), pp. 21-34. For the new mints, Hendy, *Studies*, pp. 424-25.

[37] Grierson, *Catalogue*, III.1, pp. 70-71; D.M. Metcalf, "Corinth in the ninth century: the numismatic evidence", *Hesperia* 42 (1973), pp. 180-251.

[38] For summaries of the evidence, see Harvey, *Economic expansion*, pp. 86-88; M. Angold, "The shaping of the medieval Byzantine 'city'", *Byzantinische Forschungen* 10 (1985), pp. 1-37, at 7-8.

product of the economic region concerned and the amount of coin in circulation at a given moment. Nevertheless, a crude estimate can be attempted, following the model proposed for the Roman empire between the second and fourth centuries by Hopkins, who suggested that if one takes approximately 80% of the gross annual product as deriving from agrarian production and 20% from petty commodity and artisanal production, then some 20% of agrarian production (i.e. 16% of the total) might have been commercialised, and up to 75% of the remaining 20% (i.e. 15% of the total) was similarly exchanged through monetary activity. Morrisson argues that this is probably too high, at least for the Byzantine context of the ninth century, and on analogy with recent pre- or proto-industrial economies suggests a more reasonable total of perhaps 20% of the total product as monetised.[39] But it seems reasonable to conclude that the Byzantine monetary system, while it had always been central to the state's fiscal activities and the extraction/distribution of surplus produce, began from the middle years of the ninth century to play a greater role in the private, commercial sphere from which the effective lack of a bronze coinage of account had excluded it during the period from the 660s to the 820s, with the exception of one or two major urban centres including, of course, Constantinople.

Non-state activity: the ceramic evidence

Yet it is easy to over-emphasise the state's role. The political elite of the Empire, both at Constantinople and in the provinces, had demands which could only be met by the import of luxury commodities and by the movement of products such as wine, olive oil, fish, meat on the hoof, and spices across sometimes considerable distances. The ecclesiastical establishment, with bishops spread across the Empire, generated similar demands. Naturally, such demands might not always be met, and might almost never be met in the most isolated regions, although this certainly represents one way through which both gold and bronze coins might reach regions distant from the capital or the army. The movement of livestock, in

---

[39] K. Hopkins, "Taxes and trade in the Roman empire (200 B.C.-A.D. 400)", *Journal of Roman Studies* 70 (1980), pp. 101-25; Morrisson, "Monnaie et finances dans l'empire byzantin X^c-XIV^c siècle", pp. 294-95.

particular sheep, from the grazing lands of central Anatolia to be sold in Constantinople, both to state purchasers and to private households, has been invoked as one probable route through which coin might reach the interior of the region without the army or fiscal system being involved, but the amounts are uncertain, and were probably always relatively insignificant.[40]

Local trade and commerce and long-distance trade had flourished in the period before the Islamic conquests, even if, as is now generally agreed, much of that commerce depended upon the movement of goods in bulk associated, for example, with the annual *annona* in grain from either North Africa or from Egypt.[41] In the period after the Arab conquest of Egypt, the government had as a matter of urgency to locate new sources of grain, and this seems to have come chiefly from the Thracian and Anatolian hinterlands of Constantinople, regions which continued to provide the greater part of the city's supply in grains, vegetables and meat until the end of the Empire.[42] The shipping of grain to Constantinople from the western coastal plains of Anatolia, in particular from Bithynia, and from Paphlagonia, along the Black Sea coastal plain, may well have had similar results. Here, the evidence of ceramics should provide some answers, although in the present state of our knowledge it is still too soon to draw any definite conclusions. The relationship between the import of grain by the government and its accompaniment by the arrival of other goods (whether privately or publicly arranged) may be reflected in the results of excavations at Constantinople, where a sudden and dramatic upturn in the amount of African imported wares dateable very approximately to the period between c. 655 and 670 may be linked with the import of grain. At the same time, there is some

---

[40] Hendy, *Studies*, pp. 565ff.

[41] For a neat summary, see C.J. Wickham, review of A. Giardina, ed., *Società romana e impero tardoantico, III. Le merci. Gli insediamenti* (Rome-Bari, 1986), *Journal of Roman Studies* 78 (1988), pp. 183-93. On the ships, cargoes and commerce associated with the *annona*, see the survey of M. McCormick, "Bateaux de vie, bateaux de mort. Maladie, commerce, transports annonaires et le passage économique du Bas-Empire au moyen âge", *Morfologie sociali e culturali in Europa fra tarda Antichità e alto Medioevo*, Settimane di studio del Centro italiano di studi sull'alto Medioevo 45 (Spoleto, 1998), pp. 35-118.

[42] J.L. Teall, "The Grain Supply of the Byzantine Empire", *Dumbarton Oaks Papers* 13 (1959), pp. 87-139; R.-J. Lilie, *Die byzantinische Reaktion auf die Ausbreitung der Araber*, Miscellanea Byzantina Monacensia 22 (Munich, 1976), pp. 201-27; Hendy, *Studies*, pp. 44-54, 561-64.

evidence that the imposition on the populations of Calabria, Sicily, Africa and Sardinia by Constans II, during his stay in Sicily (between 663 and his assassination at Syracuse in 668), of various "afflictions", which involved some of the former being absent on voyages (*nauticationes*) and separated from their families, may have involved the movement of grain, probably to Constantinople.[43] Given the difficulties which the government in the East must have faced after the loss of the Egyptian grain supplies, this is very probably a reference to an extraordinary levy of grain to be shipped to the capital. The appearance of such a concentration of African wares at this time may be seen—possibly—as an example of how state-commandeered shipping could promote other forms of trade and movement of goods.

The role of Sicily in this respect remains vague. It had always been an exporter of grain, both to Rome as well as other regions of Italy;[44] and its importance is emphasised by the fact that Justinian's novel 104 (issued in 537) placed the island under a *praetor* responsible directly to Constantinople (just as Egypt remained under a *praefectus Augustalis*, within the praetorian prefecture of the East but responsible directly to the emperor at Constantinople).[45] During the second half of the seventh century its population (along with that of Calabria and adjacent regions) was re-assessed in respect of their tax payments, and this seems on at least one occasion to have been connected with levies in grain. In 681, the Emperor Constantine IV issued a series of *iussiones* pertaining to these regions, in which the rate of assessment of the *coemptum frumenti* was reduced.[46] The reference is significant first because the *coemptio* or *coemptum* in this text is clearly levied at a regular rate, and secondly because it is clearly levied in corn (*frumentum*). And whereas it is singled out as a regular annual imposition (along with the *annonacapita*), other imperial demands are referred to simply as *alia diversa* which the Church of

---

[43] For the pottery: J.W. Hayes, *Excavations at Saraçhane in Istanbul*, 2: *The Pottery* (Princeton, 1992), pp. 7, 100-107; the action of Constans is described in the *Liber pontificalis*, ed. Th. Mommsen, *Monumenta Germaniae Historica, Gesta pontificum romanorum* (Berlin, 1898), p. 187.10-14 (*Vita Vitaliani*). The passage has also been noted and discussed by McCormick, "Bateaux de vie, bateaux de mort", pp. 78f.

[44] Jones, *The later Roman empire*, pp. 710-11; Stein, *Histoire du Bas-Empire*, ii, p. 424.

[45] *Iustiniani Novellae, Corpus Iuris Civilis*, III (Berlin, 1928) 104: *de praetore Siciliae*.

[46] *Liber Pontificalis*, I, 366.9-10, ed. L. Duchesne, 2 vols. (Paris, 1884-1892); see also F. Dölger, *Regesten der Kaiserurkunden des oströmischen Reiches 565-1453*, Corpus der griechischen Urkunden des Mittelalters und der neueren Zeit, Reihe A, Abt. I, i-iv (Munich-Berlin 1924-1965) [2nd ed. ed. P. Wirth (Munich, 1977)], ii, no. 250).

Rome paid each year. I have suggested elsewhere that by this time
the term *coemptio* (Gr. synonê) was coming to refer to that part of
the land tax levied in kind (referred to variously as the *annona* or,
in Egypt and possibly elsewhere also, the *embolê*), and this may suggest that corn was levied—as formerly in Egypt—for transport either
to the capital or to the army elsewhere in the Empire. The *Liber
Pontificalis* records that between 662 and 668 Constans II ordered a
tax-census for the provinces of Sicily, Calabria, Sardinia and Africa,
which coincides, of course, with his presence in Italy and Sicily, and
this should have involved also the question of Sicilian grain for the
field army and court which accompanied the emperor.[47] Although
it has been suggested that Sicily cannot have been a very secure
source of grain for Constantinople after the loss of Egypt, and particularly after the rise of Arab sea-power in the 650s,[48] the government does seem to have placed some emphasis on retaining a fairly
close control over its resources: the administration of the papal pat-
rimonial lands was taken over by imperial officials in the mid-720s,
a move intended to ensure that the fiscal reforms ordered a year or
two earlier would be carried out, and which meant a considerably-
increased fiscal income for the imperial government in Constantinople
(possibly involving grain);[49] and Sicily clearly figured as a source of
grain both for Thessaloniki at the end of the sixth and beginning
of the seventh century, as well as for other eastern cities at a slightly
later date.[50] Just as importantly, the appearance of a *stratêgos*, or gen-
eralissimo for the island at a comparatively early date, c. 700, sug-

---

[47] *Liber Pontificalis*, I, 344.2-4 (cf. Dölger, *Regesten*, no. 234). Further discussion:
Haldon, *"Synônê"*, esp. pp. 134ff. Note that the system of compulsory purchase –
coemptio in the traditional sense – had already been employed on occasion to provide grain from Sicily for Rome in the last years of the sixth century: Gregory I,
Epistulae, I, 2.ix (115), MGH (*Ep.*), I, II.
[48] Lilie, *Die byzantinische Reaktion auf die Ausbreitung der Araber*, p. 203.
[49] Theophanis, pp. 404, 410 (Mango-Scott, pp. 558, 568). A census had been
carried out; and imperial fiscal officials replaced papally-appointed *rectores*. See
J. Herrin, *The Formation of Christendom*, (Princeton, 1987), pp. 349-50; A. Guillou,
"Transformation des structures socio-économiques dans le monde byzantin du VIᵉ
au VIIIᵉ siècle", *Zbornik Radova Vizantoloshkog Instituta* 19 (1980), pp. 71-78, see 74ff.
Theophanes' account is confused, and it remains unclear as to which measures were
carried out when. For a summary of the arguments and the sources for, as well as
the date of, all these events, see A. Guillou, *Régionalisme et indépendance dans l'empire
byzantin au VIIᵉ siècle: l'exemple de l'Exarchat et de la Pentapole d'Italie* (Rome, 1969), pp.
218ff.; T.S. Brown, *Gentlemen and Officers Imperial Administration and Aristocratic Power in
Byzantine Italy, A.D. 554-800* (Rome, 1984), pp. 69, 156, 180.
[50] See the evidence collected in Teall, "Grain supply", pp. 137-38.

gests that Sicily figured fairly prominently in imperial military priorities. Indeed, more seals and references in texts of military commanders for Sicily for the eighth and ninth centuries are known than for any other military province of the Empire, which is suggestive of the economic as much as of the military strategic value of the island.[51]

As is well known, North African imports dominated the central and western Mediterranean, in addition to being strongly represented throughout the eastern Mediterranean region, including the southern Aegean, until the late fifth and early sixth century. There then set in a decline in regional North African ceramic production, a reduction in the variety and sometimes the quality of forms and types, especially of amphorae, and a corresponding increase of eastern exports to the West. The incidence of African imports to the East Mediterranean, for example, as reflected in both fine wares (most particularly in African Red Slip) and amphorae, declines sharply from about 480-490 on, recovering only partly after the Byzantine reconquest of the area in the 530s and its partial incorporation into an East Mediterranean-centred commercial network (if "commercial" is right—"exchange network" might be more appropriate, given the important role played by the state in this context). Italian imports of African wares fall off even more dramatically, given the geographical proximity of this market, and this has been connected with both a possible re-distribution of wealth and control of resources which followed the Vandal settlement and, more importantly, the cessation of the *annona*, which had represented a considerable burden on the African economy, but one which had also—through the state-subsidised shipping amd transportation which it required—acted to cushion the costs to the private sector of exporting independently along the same routes. This may not necessarily explain the market for fine wares, of course, but it goes part of the way to explaining why, when the governmment of the western Empire turned to other sources of grain, rather than pay for Vandal supplies, both the market possibilities and the internal distribution of resources may have been affected in North Africa. There is a further complication, in that, while the general decline of North African imports is fairly apparent

---

[51] See the evidence summarised in F. Winkelmann, *Byzantinische Rang- und Ämterstruktur im 8. und 9. Jahrhundert*, Berliner Byzantinistische Arbeiten 53 (Berlin, 1985), pp. 84-90.

from the 450s on, tempting one to connect it directly with the Vandal presence and all that that entailed, it has been shown that the reduction in the importation of African fine wares to the southern Aegean can certainly be dated already before 425 (as an approximation).[52]

This does not seem to reflect any decline in the market potential of the eastern Mediterranean region and the Aegean as a whole. On the contrary, the incidence of Phocaean slip-coated wares increases in proportion as that of African wares decreases; while over the same period the importance of imports from the Middle East, especially Syria and Cilicia, increases. Complicating the matter is the fact that North African fine wares continue to appear in quantity on major urban sites throughout the sixth century, even if on a smaller scale than before, but no longer on many of the southern Aegean regional or provincial sites where it had previously been found. And while North African coarse wares seem to have been able to recover their position to a certain extent at major centres, local Aegean wares now dominated both the hinterland and competed with the western imports. They are also themselves exported, being found on sites in Syria, Palestine and Asia Minor, precisely those areas from which exports were drawn to match the decline in North African imports at an increasing rate over the fifth century. An Aegean-Middle eastern exchange zone clearly existed which overlapped and to a degree undercut the exchange with North Africa, which may be suggestive of both shifts in profitability and costs for both the exporters and the importers of North African goods.[53]

But North African amphorae continued to hold an important position in the archaeological record in the southern Aegean area—indeed, at Perissa on Thera only North African types, including Aegean imitative wares, were found, to the exclusion of those asso-

---

[52] See in particular the survey articles of C. Panella, "Gli scambi nel Mediterraneo Occidentale dal IV al VII secolo dal punto di vista di alcune 'merci'", in *Hommes et richesses* I, pp. 129-41; C. Panella, "Merci e scambi nel mediterraneo tardoantico", *Storia di Roma* 3.ii (Turin, 1993), pp. 613-97; C. Abadie-Reynal, "Céramique et commerce dans le bassin égéen du IVe au VIIe siècle", *Hommes et richesses I*, pp. 143-59. For further discussion of the material dealt with in this section, see also the contributions collected in V. Déroche and J.-M. Spieser eds., *Recherches sur la céramique byzantine* (= Bulletin de Corrrespondance Hellénique, suppl. 18) (Paris, 1989).

[53] The different exchange zones are nicely described in Panella, "Merci e scambi", pp. 663-67. See also P. Reynolds, *Trade in the western Mediterranean A.D. 400-700: the ceramic evidence*, BAR International Series 604 (Oxford, 1995), pp. 34-35, 118-121; Abadie-Reynal, "Céramique et commerce", pp. 155-57; J.W. Hayes, *Late Roman pottery* (London, 1972), p. 418; Hayes, *Excavations at Saraçhane*, pp. 5-8.

ciated with the Syrian/Palestinian littoral;[54] and while there existed also a direct line of imports to Constantinople and some other major cities, the northern Aegean region and much of Greece demonstrates a highly localised exchange-pattern with very little evidence, except in some coastal centres, of imports from further afield. Local wares seem to hold their own well, so that although African imports are by no means negligible (and at certain sites, such as Argos, for example, and others especially in southern Greece, are found in quantity), they never dominate to the extent that is the case in the southern region. The underlying reasons for this resistance to imports, if that is what it is (and it occurs elsewhere, too), may be found in a more or less autarkic and highly localised peasant economy, in which the market potential for imports was limited (and in return for which the region may have had little to offer in any case) by the fact that the potential imports could be produced more readily locally. Thus, in the later fifth and sixth centuries, two types of fine wares predominate, North African and Phocaean, but they do not share the same pattern of distribution.

The routes taken by amphorae and fine wares are different, of course, partly explicable through the different interests of exports for profit and state-backed transportation (for goods associated with the *annona*, for example), and partly also through the resistance (or unprofitability for the exporters) to imports offered by some regional economic sub-systems. Amphorae from both Palestine and North Syria are found in quantity in the Peloponnese and in Constantinople from the middle of the sixth century, for example, complemented by amphorae from western Asia Minor, presumably representing imports of olive oil and wine. But we do not yet know enough about these sub-systems to say more than this at the present.[55]

From the late sixth and early seventh century, new fine wares begin to predominate locally—thus the glazed white ware of Constantinople, for example, which—in its multiplicity of functional forms—

---

[54] See E. Geroussi, "Annual reports on excavations at Perissa on Thera", *Archaiologikon Deltion* 45-49 (1990-1994).

[55] See the useful distribution maps for the different coarse and fine wares and their patterns of movement in Panella, "Merci e scambi", figs. 5(b), 6-8. See also W. Hautumm, *Studien zu Amphoren der spätrömischen und frühbyzantinischen Zeit* (Bonn, 1981), pp. 58-77; Abadie-Reynal, "Céramique et commerce", pp. 157-59; and J.P. Sodini, "La contribution de l'archéologie à la connaissance du monde byzantin (IVe-VIIe siècles)", *Dumbarton Oaks Papers* 47 (1993), pp. 139-84, at 174-77; Reynolds, *Trade in the western Mediterranean, loc. cit.*; Panella, "Merci e scambi", pp. 664-66.

becomes the dominant local fine ware until the period of Latin domination in the thirteenth century. While the production of lead-glazed
wares can be traced back at least to the fifth century in the central
Balkans and Thracian region, it is only at this point, with the increasing localisation of fine-ware production which has been alluded to,
that it begins to dominate, albeit in a highly localised pattern.[56] The
ceramic picture is thus one of a number of overlapping networks of
local production and export/import, with longer-distance movement
of both fine and coarse wares: northern and southern Aegean networks, for example, the former less open to the longer-distance movement of pottery, but with specific foci at sites which served as centres
for local redistribution of wares, such as Constantinople and Argos,
to which both fine and semi-fine wares from North Africa on the
one hand, and amphorae from Syria/Palestine, on the other, were
directed. Constantinopolitan glazed wares also reached Carthage during the first half of the seventh century, illustrating that the connection between the capital and this distant provincial centre was
not a one-way relationship.[57] From the first half of the seventh century the northern region begins also to show the impact of the white
glazed ware localised at Constantinople, which shares the field with
later Phocaean red slip wares; while evidence from the southern/central Aegean shows that locally-produced amphorae types illustrates an
Aegean-based export network, presumably for olive oil, possibly for
wine also. This type (Late Roman 3) and its later sub-types produced
locally appears from the sixth through into the eighth century,
with a distribution extending to Chios, Crete, Cyprus, Constantinople

---

[56] Hayes, *Excavations at Saraçhane*, pp. 12-34; J.-M. Spieser, "La céramique byzantine médiévale", in *Hommes et richesses*, pp. 249-60, see 250; Panella, "Merci e scambi",
p. 658. For useful orientation: V. François, *Bibliographie analytique sur la céramique
byzantine à glaçure. Un nouvel outil de travail*, Varia Anatolica, 9 (Paris, 1997). See also
G.D.R. Sanders, *Byzantine glazed pottery at Corinth to c. 1125* (Ph.D. University of
Birmingham, 1995); and the collection in V. Déroche and J.-M. Spieser, eds.,
Recherches sur la céramique byzantine. Bulletin de correspondance Hellénique, suppl.
XVIII (Paris, 1989). Glazed tiles were produced at or near Constantinople, and the
same style of tile produced using local materials at Preslav in the later ninth century: see R.B. Mason and M. Mundell Mango, "Glazed 'tiles of Nicomedia' in
Bithynia, Constantinople, and elsewhere", in G. Dagron and C. Mango, eds.,
Constantinople and its Hinterland. SPBS Publications 3 (Aldershot, 1995), pp. 313-31;
and D. Papanikola-Bakirtzis, F. Mavrikiou and Ch. Bakirtzis, *Byzantine glazed pottery
in the Benaki Museum* (Athens, 1999), pp. 17-18 for a slightly different interpretation
of this evidence.

[57] J.W. Hayes, "Problèmes de la céramique des VIIe-IXe siècles à Salamine et à
Chypre", *Salamine de Chypre, histoire et archéologie: État des recherches*, Colloques internationaux du CNRS, no. 578 (Paris, 1980), pp. 375-87, at 378f.; *Saraçhane*, pp. 12ff.

and the western Asia Minor coast; the related Late Roman 2, which disappears by the end of the seventh century, is found over a similar area and as far afield as the southern Black Sea coast and Carthage.[58]

It is this highly regionalised pattern which appears to dominate thereafter, although it does not mean that the movement of goods or wares ceased—quite the contrary. This has been relatively well, although by no means fully-documented for Constantinople.[59] Evidence for the disruption of local ceramic production in the Peloponnese, and the appearance of hand-formed pots on certain sites—Olympia, Argos, Isthmia, for example—has suggested to some the arrival of Slav immigrants during the later sixth and seventh centuries and the cessation or radical reduction of the production of the previous Late Roman types of pottery. But it has recently been pointed out that both hand-formed and wheel-turned wares were produced at the same time and at the same sites, suggesting in fact that the indigenous population, isolated from major supplies from outside their localities, produced both, the former for cooking and basic domestic uses.[60] Inland, particularly in Asia Minor, where it has long been recognised that local production predominated throughout the Late Roman period anyway, there is little doubt that the pattern of production will have remained more or less the same at the most general level, although considerable dislocation of both centres of

[58] See Panella, "Merci e scambi", pp. 663f.; Sodini, "La contribution de l'archéologie", pp. 175-76; C.L. Striker, "Work at Kalenderhane Camii in Istanbul", *Dumbarton Oaks Papers* 29 (1975), pp. 306-18, see 316; A.H.S. Megaw, "Excavations on a castle site at Paphos", *Dumbarton Oaks Papers* 26 (1972), pp. 323-43, at 328, 340; Hautumm, *Studien*, figs. 62ff.; F.H. Van Doorninck, "Reused amphorae at Yassi Ada and Serçe Limani", *Bulletin de Correspondance Hellénique*, Suppl. XVIII (1989), pp. 248-49 (figs. 1, 8); N. Atik, *Die Keramik aus dem Südthermen von Perge* (= *Istanbuler Mitteilungen*, Beiheft 40) (Tübingen, 1995), p. 199.

[59] Hayes, *Excavations at Saraçhane*, 2, p. 7. For possible connections between Constantinople and Islamic Bostra, for example, see F. Sogliani, "Le testimonianze ceramiche tardoantiche e medievali a Bosra (Siria). Per un primo contributo alla conoscenza delle tipologie", *Ravenna, Costantinopoli, Vicino Oriente*, XLI Corso di Cultura sull'Arte Ravennate e Bizantina (Ravenna, 1994), pp. 433-62, at 442f.

[60] For the traditional view see, for example, T.E. Gregory and P.N. Kardoulias, "Geographical and surface surveys in the Byzantine fortress at Isthmia, 1985-1986", *Hesperia* 59 (1990), pp. 467-512; Sp. Vryonis, "The Slavic pottery (jars) from Olympia, Greece", in Sp. Vryonis ed., *Byzantine Studies. Essays on the Slavic world and the eleventh century* (New Rochelle, NY, 1992), pp. 114-42; P. Aupert, "Les Slaves à Argos", *Bulletin de Correspondance Hellénique* 113 (1989), pp. 417-19. This has been cogently challenged by H. Anagnostakes, N. Poulou-Papadimitriou, "Η πρωτοβυζαντινή Μεσσήνη (5ος-7ος αιώνας) και προβλήματα της χειροποιήτης κεραμικής στην Πελοπόννησο", *Symmeikta* 11 (1997), pp. 229-322, esp. pp. 252-91.

production and of ceramic types, whether coarse, fine or semi-fine
wares, must have occurred in the conditions prevailing during the
second half of the seventh century, even in the areas nearest to
Constantinople—we simply have, at the moment, no real analysis of
the regional ceramic types to inform us. Very little ARS or Phocaean
ware appears to have reached Amorion, for example, although routes
across Anatolia from Constantinople were regularly travelled by both
military and non-military personnel.[61] At other inland centres, such
as Ankara, as well as at less important sites on the coast such as
Anemourion, where local wares can be clearly identified, highly-
regionalised production predominated after the middle of the seventh century, with very little evidence for any inter-regional movement;
while in more distant regions which had been tied in with a wider
late Roman network, such as Cherson in the Crimea, the ceramic
evidence shows a very marked decline in non-locally-produced wares
after the middle of the seventh century (although Constaninopolitan
wares have been identified).[62] Some evidence of the movement of
fine wares from western Asia Minor into the Aegean continues to
occur up to the later seventh century—on Chios, for example, where
Phocaean RS has been found in contexts after c. 650, or on Thera
and Cyprus, where clay lamps or amphorae of the type LRA 13
are found up to about the middle of the seventh century, tailing off
thereafter (the contexts are not always securely dateable), replaced
by local imitations of the earlier types.[63] The proportion of imports
to Cyprus, for example, appears to diminish fairly rapidly after about

---

[61] Although local conditions were obviously crucial in such cases: at Amorion,
for example, large quantities of Sagalassos ware, produced from the second to the
mid-sixth century, were found, demonstrating that where a specific market existed,
and where the distances involved were not too great (Sagalassos, in Pisidia, is about
150 miles south of Amorion) goods in bulk were transported. See S. Mitchell,
E. Owens and M. Waelkens, "Ariassos and Sagalassos 1988", *Anatolian Studies* 39
(1989), pp. 63-77, see esp. pp. 74-77; and C.S. Lightfoot, "Amorium excavations
1994: the seventh preliminary report", *Anatolian Studies* 45 (1995), pp. 105-38, at
p. 122 (Claudia Wagner, "Pottery").
[62] See R.M. Harrison, "Amorion 1991", *Anatolian Studies* 42 (1992), pp. 207ff., at
216. For Anemourion, see the summary report in J. Russell, "Anemurium: the
changing face of a Roman city", *Archaeology* 33.5 (1980), pp. 31-40; and esp.
C. Williams, "A Byzantine well-deposit from Anemourium (Rough Cilicia)", *Anatolian
Studies* 27 (1977), pp. 175-90. The ceramic profile here is of the dominance of
Phocaean and related wares, with an admixture of Palestinian wares, until the 650s,
followed by a period of local production and the appearance of some glazed wares,
although not from Constantinople. For Cherson: A.I. Romancuk, 'Torgovlya Cher-
sonnesa v VII-XII vv.', *Byzantinobulgarica* 7 (1981) 319-31.
[63] For example, J. Boardman, "Pottery", in M. Balance, *et al.* eds., *Excavation in
Chios 1952-1955: Byzantine Emporio* (Athens, 1989), pp. 88-121, see pp. 92f., 106;

650, with increasing evidence of an extremely close exchange relationship with Constantinople: some 15% of the amphorae from
Saranda Kolones and Salamis appear to be imports, or re-exports,
from the capital; ceramic evidence from the excavations at Pseira
on Crete shows similarly a concentration of locally-produced wares,
with little evidence for imports, which were mostly of Aegean origin. Similarly at Sparta the predominant types from the later seventh to ninth centuries were locally-produced wares, evidence for
which was also found at the Saraçhane site, suggesting some exchange
of produce from the Peloponnese to the capital during this period.[64]
Late Roman forms continued to be produced without interruption
well into the seventh century, and often well after 650, with production centres located across the Aegean from Boeotia to Samos
and across to Crete and Cyprus.[65] The dramatic effects of warfare
on local ceramic production can be inferred from the destruction of
a kiln and associated features at what seems to have been a farmstead site near Thermes on Samos, dated to about 670, a result presumably of a visit by Arab sea-raiders.[66]

At the interface between state-directed and private activity it might
be expected that some archaeological evidence would support the
notion that goods moved via private means accompanied state-directed
transportation, and that ceramic evidence for this might be forthcoming from, say, archaeological contexts of the later seventh and
eighth centuries from those regions or regional centres through which

E. Prokopiou, "Αμαθούντα· ανατολική νεκρόπολη. Τάφο οστεοφυλάκιο του 7ου μ.Χ. αι",
Reports of the Department of Antiquities of Cyprus (1995), pp. 264-67; and the annual
reports on the excavations at Perissa on Thera by E. Geroussi, in Αρχαιολογικόν
Δελτίον, 46ff. (1990ff.).

[64] See A.H.S. Megaw, "A Byzantine castle site at Saranda Kolones, Paphos",
Reports of the Department of Antiquities, Cyprus (1970-1971), p. 131; Hayes, "Problèmes
de la céramique des VIIe-IXe siècles à Salamine et à Chypre"; N. Poulou-Papadimitriou,
"La monastère byzantin à Pseira, Crète: la céramique", *Akten des XII. Internationaledn
Kongresses für christliche Archäologie* 2 (Bonn, 1991), pp. 1123-25; G.D.R. Sanders,
"Excavations at Sparta: the Roman stoa, '88-'91. Preliminary reprort I", *Annual of
the British School of Archaeology at Athens* 88 (1993), pp. 251-86; G. Waywell and
J. Wilkes, "Excavations at the ancient theatre of Sparta, 1992-4: preliminary report",
Annual of the British School of Archaeology at Athens 90 (1995), pp. 435-61.

[65] See A.H.S. Megaw and R.E. Jones, "Byzantine and allied pottery: a contribution by chemical analysis to problems of origin and distribution", *Annual of the
British School of Archaeology at Athens* 78 (1983), pp. 235-63, at pp. 246-47; H.W.
Catling, "An early Byzantine pottery factory at Dhiorios in Cyprus", *Levant* 4 (1972),
pp. 1-82 (although it should be noted that the dating and stratification is problematic at this site).

[66] E. Geroussi, "Παλαιοχριστιανική κεραμική απο τη Σάμο", *Αρχαιολογικόν Δελτίον*
47-48 (1992-1993), pp. 251-68.

grains were taken to Constantinople—as we have seen, chiefly north-western Anatolia and the south-western Pontic littoral (Paphlagonia). The appearance of a concentration of African wares at Constantinople may possibly be associated with the shipping of grain to the city in the 650s and 660s. But this is hardly firm evidence for such a connection, and so while it must remain a possibility that similar movements of goods flowed from these nearer provinces to the capital, it is not yet clearly archaeologically attested. Whether or not the incidence of stamped or moulded polychrome glazed white wares from Constantinople at sites around the Black Sea coast or with access to the Aegean, and from contexts dating to the middle or later ninth century onwards, reflects this sort of relationship is at present difficult to say.[67]

The extent to which the condition of roads affected either the movement of goods overland by the state, or through private commerce, is very difficult to determine. Laws in the *Codex Theodosianus* dating to the later fourth and early fifth century note the poor condition of many roads.[68] The western sections of the Via Egnatia, the major route from Constantinople to the Adriatic coast, were according to one report, barely passable in the middle of the fifth century.[69] There appears also to have been an increasing reliance upon beasts of burden for the movement of goods and people, rather than on wheeled vehicles drawn by draught-animals; and this may in turn have had effects upon the ways in which goods, whether in bulk or

---

[67] See *The Great Palace of the Byzantine Emperors*. The University of St Andrews 1935-1938 (London, 1947), p. 46—a first report on the excavations carried out in Istanbul on behalf of the Walker Trust; Hayes, *Excavations at Saraçhane*, pp. 12, 19; Sanders, *Byzantine Glazed Pottery at Corinth*, pp. 232-33, 259-60; R. Waagé, "The Roman and Byzantine pottery", *Hesperia* 2 (1933), pp. 279-328, at 321-22—for Athens, Agora excavations; Ch. Bakirtzis and D. Papanikola-Bakirtzis, "De la céramique en glaçure byzantine à Thessalonique", *Byzantinobulgarica* 7 (1981), pp. 421-36, at 422—various Greek sites; A.L. Jacobson, *Keramika e karamičhesko prizvodstvo srednevekovoy Tavriki* (Leningrad, 1979), pp. 83-93; I. Barnea, "La céramique byzantine de Dobroudja, X^c-XII^c siècles", in Déroche and Spieser, eds., *Recherches sur la céramique byzantine*, pp. 75, 139; J. Čhimbuleva, "Vases à glaçure en argile blanche de Nessèbre (IX^c-XII^c s.)", in *Nessèbre* II (Sofia, 1980), pp. 202-53, at 214-28.

[68] On the state of roads in the later fourth and fifth centuries, see *Cth.* xv. 3, 4 (A.D. 412), remarking upon "the immense ruin of the highways" throughout the prefecture of Oriens (*Theodosiani libri xvi cum constitutionibus Sirmondianis*, eds. Th. Mommsen, P. Meyer *et al.* (Berlin, 1905)).

[69] Via Egnatia: Malchus of Philadelphia, *Fragments*, §18, eds. C. and Th. Müller, *Fragmenta Historicorum Graecorum*, 5 vols. (Paris, 1874-1885), p. 127. Parts of the Via Egnatia were almost impassable in wet weather, according to Procopius, *Buildings*, IV, viii. 5.

not, were transported. Large, heavy amphorae, easily stacked and carried on ships or carts, were less easily managed on mules or donkeys.[70] Ninth- and tenth-century evidence shows that wine or oil could be carried, in considerable quantitites, in large leathern skins of 50 liter capacity slung on mules, for example; other goods—grain, dried fruits, for example—were transported in panniers slung in pairs, two pair per animal. It is entirely possible that the disappearance of imported amphorae from certain parts of the Roman world reflects not just changes in patterns of exchange and export/import of goods, but changes in the mode of their transportation. The picture thus becomes even more complicated than may appear at first sight.[71]

Trade and commerce: the structure of demand

The evidence for trade and commerce in general may be examined at two levels: the movement over long-distances of luxury commodities, such as spices, precious stones and, for example, papyrus (although the latter was certainly state-led and seems to have been paid for in gold coin);[72] and the movement of goods to local markets, or from region to region, within the Empire. "Local" trade can also include cross-frontier exchanges over short distances, of course, although the evidence for this is even sparser.

It is clear that the state intervened with a fairly heavy hand in the movement of goods both within and across the imperial frontiers. In respect of external trade—imports and exports—the state could play as heavy-handed a role as it did in the internal redistribution of wealth through the fiscal apparatus. The clauses of the Byzantine-Bulgar treaty of 715-718, renewed with minor changes in 812/813, nicely illustrate the nature of state control: not only was trade permitted by each side on condition that certain political arrangements

---

[70] R.W. Bulliet, *The camel and the wheel* (Cambridge, Mass. 1975).

[71] Haldon, ed., *Constantine Porphyrogenitus, Three Treatises on Imperial Military Expeditions,* [C] 142-44; for the capacities involved see, E. Schilbach, *Byzantinische Metrologie,* pp. 112-13.

[72] The import of papyrus faltered in the 690s, when the Caliph Abd al-Malik ordained that the sheets should be marked with Koranic texts before their export. Justinian II objected, but without effect. See H.A.R. Gibb, "Arab – Byzantine relations under the Umayyad Caliphate", *Dumbarton Oaks Papers* 12 (1958), pp. 219-33, at 231-32.

were respected (such as the return of deserters and traitors on demand
of their own government/ruler); licences were issued to those merchants permitted to cross the border, and any trader without such
a pass was liable to have his goods confiscated. While the stipula-
tions reflect the mutual suspicion of erstwhile enemies, similar treaties
were renewed on several occasions thoughout the eighth and ninth
centuries.[73] Trade across the frontier certainly flourished, both on
the eastern front and in the Balkans, but the government tried hard
to control anything it thought of relevance to its own concerns. The
export of weapons and gold was forbidden, under penalty of death,
for example; and although it must be the case that control was by
no means absolute, evidence for fairly strict controls at key *emporia*
and frontier trading centres is abundant, including at Abydos, at the
entrance to the Hellespont, which served to control and tax maritime traffic, and at towns such as Thessaloniki.[74] The government
needed to import ores of varying sorts, including iron ore, and the
discovery of Byzantine gold coins at a Bulgarian mining centre suggests that this was paid for in coin rather than in finished products,
although nothing is known about the amount or frequency of this
trade.[75] Long-distance trade eastwards was certainly affected by the
Islamic conquests, as is shown by the expansion of the northern
route East, either around the western coast of the Black Sea and
thence across South Russia and the Caspian route eastwards, or by

---

[73] Theophanes, *Chronographia*, p. 497 and n. (Mango-Scott, p. 681); J. Ferluga,
Untersuchungen zur byzantinischen Provinzverwaltung VI-XIII Jahrhundert (Amsterdam, 1992),
pp. 159-82, at 163f. [orig. publ. as J. Ferluga, "Der byzantinische Handel auf der
Balkanhalbinsel vom VII. bis zum Anfang des XIII. Jahrhunderts", *Papers Presented
at the Vth International Congress of South-East European Research Studies, Belgrade 1984*
(Skopje, 1988), pp. 31-52]; J. Ferluga, "Mercati e mercanti fra Mar Nero e Adriatico:
il commercio nei Balcani dal VII al'XI secolo", *Mercati e mercanti nell'alto medioevo:
L'area euroasiatica e l'area mediterranea*, Settimane di studio del Centro italiano di studi
sull'alto Medioevo 40 (Spoleto, 1993), pp. 443-89, at 458-60; N. Oikonomidès,
"Tribute or Trade? The Byzantine-Bulgarian Treaty of 716, *Studies on the Slavo-
Byzantine and West-European Middle Ages. In memoriam Ivan Dujcev*, Studia Slavico-
Byzantina et Mediaevalia Europensia 1 (Sofia, 1988), pp. 29-31.
[74] N. Oikonomidès, "Le kommerkion d'Abydos, Thessalonique et le commerce
Bulgare au IXe siècle", in *Hommes et richesses* II, pp. 241-48.
[75] S. Vryonis, "The question of the Byzantine mines", *Speculum* 37 (1962), pp.
1-17, at p. 14; and in general on mining J.C. Edmondson, "Mining in the later
Roman empire and beyond", *Journal of Roman Studies* 79 (1989), pp. 84-102. For
the relevant legislation and further discussion: Hendy, *Studies*, pp. 257-60. For the
late ninth-century legislation governing precious metals: J. Koder ed., *Das Eparchenbuch
Leons des Weisen*, CFHB 33 (Vienna, 1991), §§2.4-2.6, 2.8. For the various local trade
networks from the later eighth and ninth centuries, see Ferluga, "Mercati e mercanti fra Mar Nero e Adriatico", pp. 455-57.

sea from Constantinople to Cherson or Trebizond, and thence onto the eastern route. The dramatic rise in political importance of the Khazar Khanate from the middle years of the seventh century, which thenceforth dominated the western steppe until the mid-ninth century, at precisely the point when the southerly routes through the Caliphate once more began to flourish, demonstrates the shift in emphasis.[76] At the same time, there is some relatively solid evidence from written sources that the commercial role of some of the major southern Black Sea ports—Trebizond, Amastris, Heraklea, Sinope, in particular—was flourishing over the same period, which would add some substance to the overall picture.[77] Yet even during the eighth century various luxury goods, such as spices, seem to have reached Constantinople by sea, regardless of the political-military situation.[78] And by the middle of the ninth century, cross-border trade from North Syria and Mesopotamia into the Byzantine provinces and sometimes as far as Constantinople seems to be well-established, although it is impossible to say how early this evolved, or even whether it was ever entirely interrupted, which seems to me very probable.[79]

Internal commerce is rather more difficult to gauge.[80] The role of the imperial *kommerkiarioi* and their storehouses, or *apothêkai*, is, in this respect, especially problematic. As noted already, they have been closely associated with the movement of goods required by the state,

---

[76] D.M. Dunlop, *The history of the Jewish Khazars* (Princeton, 1954), esp. pp. 224-39; see also N. Pigulevskaya, *Byzanz auf dem Wegen nach Indien* (Berlin, 1969), pp. 155ff.; E. Patlagean, "Byzance et les marchés du grand commerce: vers 830 – vers 1030. Entre Pirenne et Polanyi", *Mercati e mercanti nell'alto Medioevo*, pp. 587-629.

[77] Very little archaeological evidence is available in this respect, although work at Amastris in particular is beginning to provide a fuller picture here. See J. Crow and S. Hill, "The Byzantine fortifications of Amastris in Paphlagonia", *Anatolian Studies* 45 (1995), pp. 251-65, esp. p. 258 on the defences of the harbour facility. The written sources are mostly hagiographical: see the survey in D.Z. de Ferranti Abrahamse, *Hagiographic sources for Byzantine cities 500-900 A.D.* (Ann Arbor, 1967), pp. 277, 302-03, 304ff., 315ff.

[78] Gibb, "Arab – Byzantine relations under the Umayyad Caliphate", p. 231.

[79] J.F. Haldon and H. Kennedy, "The Arab-Byzantine Frontier in the Eighth and Ninth Centuries: Military Organisation and Society in the Borderlands", *Zbornik Radova Vizantoloshkog Instituta* 19 (1980), pp. 107 (with n. 107), 109; Patlagean, "Byzance et les marchés du grand commerce".

[80] I have not dealt with the production of precious metal objects – gold- and silverware – other than coin, chiefly because this seems to have represented a tiny portion of the overall pattern of production and demand after the 630s, and even before this can be regarded as very specific and idiosyncratic. See in particular D. Feissel, "Le Préfet de Constantinople, les poids étalons et l'estampillage de l'argenterie au VIe et au VIIe siècle", *Revue numismatique* 28 (1986), pp. 119-42.

and in association with fiscal demands, at least for the most part
and until the first half of the eighth century, after which the equivalent institution of the imperial *koomerkia* seems to continue similar
functions until the first half of the ninth century. But seals for such
officials associated with ports along the Black Sea coast—Heraklea,
Ionopolis, Kerasous, Trebizond, Sinope and others—suggest more
than this, and that trade of some sort, regulated and controlled, certainly, existed, presumably between the ports in question and their
hinterlands, and Constantinople; although that grain ships travelled
from the southern Black Sea coast to Cherson in the middle years
of the seventh century suggests a wider network, and certainly sup-
ports the other evidence for the probable movement of grain from
the Paphlagonian coastal region to Constantinople after the loss of
Egypt.[81] Port-to-port trade on a small scale, and longer-distance
commerce from the Black Sea and the Aegean islands and coastal
zones to Constantinople should probably be assumed to have continued with only minimal disruption, although the dominance of
Constantinople as a gross importer should be borne in mind. The
literary evidence suggests that coastal cities such as Attaleia, Smyrna,
Ephesos and Trebizond continued to serve as local market centres
and entrepôts for commerce, however much their physical shape was
changed (usually in terms of massive reduction in area and concentration in an acropolis or similar fortified centre), and the archaeological evidence, where it is available, does not contradict this picture.[82]

Apart from coastal cities possessing port facilities and markets, an
important opportunity for trade was offered by the numerous yearly
fairs, *panêgyreis*, held on particular saints' days in many towns. Trebizond,
Ephesos, Sinope, Euchaita, Chonai, Myra, Thessaloniki, Nikomedeia,
all held a yearly market, and since this is a tradition which goes
well back into the late Roman period, it is highly likely that where

---

[81] For grain ships delivering to Cherson, see *Vita S. Martini Papae* (P. Peeters,
"Une vie grecque du pape S. Martin I", *Analecta Bollandiana* 51 (1933), pp. 225-62),
p. 261. For a sample of the seals: Zacos and Veglery, *Byzantine Lead Seals*, I, no.
180 (Paphlagonia and Ionopolis, a. 692/693), no. 164 (Lazica and Kerasous, a.
689/690), no. 178 (Lazica, Kerasous, Trebizond, a. 691/693), no. 179 (Lazica,
Kerasous, Trebizond, a. 692/693), no. 250 (Kerasous, a. 735/736), no. 2765 (seal
of the general kommerkiarios of the coast of Pontos, a. 727/728), no. 2894 (Sinope
and the Pontos, a. 832/833 or 847/848); see also N.P. Lihachev, "Datirovannye
Vizantiiskie pechati", *Izvestiya Roskiiskoi Akademii Istorii Materialnoi Kul'turi* 3 (1924),
pp. 152-224, no. 9 (Herakleia, a. 734/735), no. 10 (Kerasous, a. 738/739), no. 3
(seal of the general kommerkiarios of the *apothêkê* of Honorias, Paphlagonia, the
coast of Pontos and Trebizond, a. 721/722[?]).
[82] Brandes, *Die Städte Kleinasiens*, pp. 124-31 ("Städte mit relativer Kontinuität").

conditions allowed they continued through the seventh, eighth and into the ninth centuries, the more so since many continue to be celebrated today (or, in Turkey, until 1921). There are a number of literary references to such fairs, and to the fact that they take place once a year, suggestive of the limited nature of the commercial activity carried on outside anything other than highly localised trade: a particularly clear example comes from a ninth- or tenth-century hagiography, in which a peasant farmer in Paphlagonia travels to the yearly market of his district with his cart laden with products which he wishes to exchange, "some by sale and some by barter", states the text.[83]

Merchants and traders occasionally appear in literary sources after the early years of the seventh century—in 715, for example, a mutinous army on the north-western coast of Asia Minor attempted to use merchant vessels to transport itself to Constantinople, but was unable to seize enough for the whole force (probably a few thousands at the most).[84] But most merchants will have operated along the coastal routes and by sea. Even before the disruption of the seventh century inland commerce was restricted either to luxury goods (moving by caravan over vast distances) or to the very highly-localised exchange of agrarian produce, or goods which could be carried on the back of the imperial *annona*. Only the state could afford anything else. But there were clearly important regional variations: the numismatic and textual evidence for Sicily, for example, shows that the island did not suffer to the same extent as the Balkans and Asia Minor from a dearth of coinage in the later seventh and eighth centuries, that commerce seems to have been fairly flourishing, and that it continued to serve as an important stepping-off point for travellers eastwards throughout this period.[85] Yet inland conditions are perhaps indicated in the *Life* of Theodore of Sykeon, whose mother ran

---

[83] For late Roman antecedents: Jones, *The later Roman Empire*, pp. 855-56; Sp. Vryonis, "The Panêgyris of the Byzantine saint: a study in the nature of a medieval institution, its origins and fate", in S. Hackel ed., *The Byzantine Saint* (London, 1981), pp. 196-228; Sp. Vryonis, *The Decline of Medieval Hellenism in Asia Minor and the Process of Islamization from the Eleventh through the Fifteenth Century* (Berkeley-Los Angeles-London, 1971), pp. 39ff. For the peasant: H. Delehaye ed., *Synaxarium ecclesiae Constantinopolitanae e codice Sirmondiano nunc Berolinensi adiectis synaxariis selectis*, Propylaeum ad Acta Sanctorum Novembris (Brussels, 1902), p. 721.24-25 ("De Metrio agricola . . .").

[84] Theophanes, *Chronographia*, pp. 385-86 (Mango-Scott, p. 536).

[85] The evidence is collected and discussed in C. Morrisson, "La Sicile byzantine: une lueur dans les siècles obscurs", *Quaderni ticinesi di numismatica e antichità classiche* 27 (1998), pp. 307-34. See also above.

an inn on a major East-West thoroughfare in the region of Ankyra in the 580s and after, and in which merchants occur hardly at all—the customers of the inn and others who passed through the village were chiefly imperial officials and soldiers.[86] That traders did operate inland is evident from occasional references in texts: for example, in 782 an Arab raiding force was bottled up by Byzantine troops in Bithynia, but was able to negotiate itself out of difficulties (by the seizure of the two Byzantine emissaries sent by the empress Eirene). Interestingly, the deal included access to markets where the Arab soldiers could buy provisions.[87] But the general situation is probably reflected in the fact that Byzantine troops mustered for the yearly campaigning season in Anatolia had to bring several days' provisions with them, and were thereafter supplied by the provincial authorities through compulsory purchase and extraordinary levies. Provisions were deposited at key locations, in granaries or storehouses according to a ninth-century Arabic report, from which they were collected by the army and loaded onto pack-animals, carts and the soldiers themselves as they passed through. The same Arab source notes (and in marked contrast to the situation in the Islamic world): "there is no market in the Roman camp. Each soldier is obliged to bring from his own resources the biscuit, oil, wine and cheese that he will need", a point confirmed by numerous references in Byzantine sources.[88]

---

[86] For the expense and problems of land-transport, see Jones, *The Later Roman Empire*, pp. 841-44; Haldon and Kennedy, "The Arab-Byzantine Frontier in the Eighth and Ninth Centuries" pp. 79-116, at pp. 87-88; W. Harris, "Between archaic and modern: some current problems in the history of the Roman economy", *The inscribed economy. Production and distribution in the Roman empire in the light of the 'instrumentum domesticum'*, Journal of Roman Archaeology, Suppl. Ser. VI (Ann Arbor, 1993), pp. 11-29, at 27-28. The *Life* of Theodore of Sykeon: A. Festugière ed., *Vie de Théodore de Sykéon*, 2 vols., Subsidia Hagiographica 48 (Brussels, 1970) (extracts transl. in: E. Dawes and N.H.Baynes, *Three Byzantine Saints* (Oxford 1948), pp. 88-192).

[87] For the Arab expedition of 782, see E.W. Brooks, "Byzantine and Arabs in the time of the early Abbasids, 1", *English Historical Review* 15 (1900), pp. 737-39.

[88] See Abû'l-Kâsim 'Ubayd Allâh b. 'Abd Allâh b. Khurradadhbîh, Kitâb at-Masâlik wa'l-Mamâlik, in *Bibliotheca Geographorum Araborum* VI, ed. M.-J. de Goeje (Leiden 1870ff. [R. Blachère, 1938ff.]), pp. 76-85, at pp. 83, 85; and for supplying armies in general, J.F. Haldon, *Warfare, state and society in the Byzantine world, 565-1204* (London, 1999), pp. 143-76, where sources and further literature are given.

Some conclusions: ideology and the market

In respect of fiscal demands we have already seen the dominant character of the state's intervention. But we should also emphasise that the ways in which fiscal resources were assessed, collected and distributed generated a particular set of administrative-bureaucratic procedures, so that a whole institutional-managerial apparatus evolved, socially and ideologically legitimated and realised in the imperial system of precedence. The close relationship between fiscal apparatus and military organisation, especially in respect of the fiscal mechanisms through which troops and state officials in general could be supported, is the dominant feature.[89] And it left little room at the level of production and distribution of wealth for outwardly-directed commercial activity or enterprise. Even when the state farmed fiscal contracts, the opportunities for private entrepreneurial activity were limited, not just by state intervention, but by social convention: what one did with newly-acquired wealth was not invest in independent commercial enterprise, or even in land, but rather in the state apparatus.[90] Titles, imperial sinecures or actual offices, and court positions were first on the list of priorities. And although land and the rent accruing from landed property (in addition to the ideologically positive realisation of self-sufficiency, *autarkeia*) were important considerations, it is clear that imperial titles and pensions were just as fundamental to the economic position of the power elite. Investment in commerce was, at least until the eleventh century and after, and as in the Roman empire, entirely marginalised.[91] There is every

---

[89] See in particular J.F. Haldon, "Military Service, Military Lands, and the Status of Soldiers: Current Problems and Interpretations", *Dumbarton Oaks Papers* 47 (1993), pp. 1-67, esp. pp. 11ff.

[90] How the tax- and contract-farmers of the seventh and eighth centuries – especially the *kommerkiaroi* – employed their wealth is impossible to say, although it is clear from their titulature and *curricula vitae*, as far as they can be reconstructed from the sigillographic record, that advancement within the imperial service must have been absolutely crucial to their status and social position. See F. Winkelmann, *Byzantinische Rang- und Ämterstruktur im 8. und 9. Jahrhundert*, Berliner Byzantinistische Arbeiten 53 (Berlin, 1985), pp. 135-37; and Haldon, *Byzantium in the seventh century*, pp. 233ff. with references.

[91] The strength of the notion of self-sufficiency, the history of which goes back to the ancient world, is evident in the attitudes of the dominant elite, Hendy, *Studies*, pp. 567-69; and the discussion in P. Magdalino, "Honour among Romaioi: the framework of social values in the world of Digenes Akrites and Kekaumenos", *Byzantine and Modern Greek Studies* 13 (1989), pp. 183-218.

reason to think that there existed a flourishing and successful merchant class in the Byzantine empire during much of the ninth, tenth and eleventh centuries, and it is reasonable to suppose that there were plenty of merchants and traders before that time (note the trading arrangements with the Bulgars, referred to already), but little is known about them until the later eleventh and twelfth centuries.[92]

This brings us to a further, structural, element. Wealth was extracted predominantly from agricultural production, appropriated as rent paid in a variety of forms to private landlords (including the state, the Church and monasteries), and as tax by the state. It was redistributed both through local market exchange and through the disbursements of the central government to the army, bureaucracy and holders of state titles and pensions. While the social elite, both great magnates and smaller-scale landlords or local gentry, derived status both from positions and titles in the imperial system as well as from the possession of land, it should be emphasised that the former was indispensable—landed wealth alone was not enough, and large amounts of landed wealth would invariably be transmitted through membership of the imperial system.[93] The wealth which the members of this elite could expect to derive from trade and commerce, both during the earlier period of its evolution as well as in the tenth and eleventh centuries was, in comparison with that derived through rents and state positions, negligible.[94] The result was that, while merchants were an active and important element in urban economies by the eleventh century, playing an important role in the distribution of locally-pro-

---

[92] See Harvey, *Economic Expansion in the Byzantine Empire*, pp. 235-36 on fairs and markets; also A. Laiou, "Händler und Kaufleute auf dem Jahrmarkt", in G. Prinzing and D. Simon eds., *Fest und Alltag in Byzanz* (Munich, 1990), pp. 53-70 (notes at pp. 189-74) (repr. in *eadem, Gender, Society and Economic Life in Byzantium*, XI); M.F. Hendy, " 'Byzantium, 1081-1204': the economy revisited, twenty years on", in M.F. Hendy, *The Economy, Fiscal Administration and Coinage of Byzantium* III, (London, 1989), pp. 22-23; for the Balkans, see esp. the important surveys of J. Ferluga, "Der byzantinische Handel auf der Balkanhalbinsel"; also J. Ferluga, "Der byzantinische Handel nach Norden im 9. und 10. Jahrhundert", in K. Düwel, H. Jankuhn, H. Siems and D. Timpe eds., *Untersuchungen zu Handel und Verkehr der vor- und frühgeschichtlichen Zeit in Mittel- und Nordeuropa*, IV (Göttingen, 1987), pp. 616-42 (also repr. in Ferluga, *Untersuchungen zur byzantinischen Provinzverwaltung VI-XIII Jahrhundert* (Amsterdam, 1992), pp. 131-57).

[93] On the rise of the local "gentry" and their relationship to the expanding urban and rural economy in the eleventh century and after, see esp. M. Angold, "Archons and Dynasts: local aristocracies and the cities of the later Byzantine empire", in M. Angold, ed., *The Byzantine Aristocracy, IX to XIII Centuries* (Oxford, 1984), pp. 236-53.

[94] See the remarks of Harvey, *Economic Expansion in the Byzantine Empire*, pp. 226ff.

duced commodities, they appear still to have occupied a relatively subordinate position in the process of wealth redistribution as a whole. Particularly important is the fact that they played no role *in ideological terms* in the maintenance of the Empire and in the social order as it was understood.[95] The social elite had only a limited interest in their activities, as suppliers of luxury items on the one hand, and as a means of selling off the surpluses from their own estates in local towns or regular fairs, or the capital, on the other. And even here, the evidence makes it clear that it was more often than not the landlords' own agents who did the selling and buying, rather than independent middlemen.[96] In other words, it was the structure of the state and its functional requirements, in conjunction with the relationship between the state centre and the dominant social-economic elite, which rendered commerce marginal, certainly in ideological terms, but to a degree also in practical economic terms. The degree to which these points apply specifically to the situation between the middle of the seventh and the middle of the ninth century is, of course, open to debate. But given the particularly prominent position of the imperial government in the economy and society of the Empire at this time, and therefore on the horizon of elite aspirations, it seems unlikely to have been very different.

Of course, this aspect of Byzantine social values should not be seen as monolithic; on the contrary, the very existence of merchants,

[95] In the tenth century, for example, descriptions of the political economy of the Empire entirely ignored the role of trade: see, for example, the *Tactica* (xi.11) of the Emperor Leo VI, ed. R. Vári, *Leonis imperatoris tactica* I [proem., const. i-xi], II [const. xii-xiii, xiv, 1-38], Sylloge Tacticorum Graecorum III (Budapest, 1917-1922), (also in : *Patrologia Graeca* 107, cols. 672-1120). Even in the sixth century commerce was ranked 6th in importance, before wholesalers, and after the priesthood, the law, councils, the state fiscal system and technicians, according to the opening chapters of a treatise on strategy: *Anonymi Peri strategias*, ed. and trans. G.T. Dennis, "The Anonymous Byzantine Treatise on Strategy" in *Three Byzantine Military treatises*. Text, translation and notes, *CFHB* 25 (= Dumbarton Oaks Texts 9 (Washington D.C., 1985), pp. 1-136, see §2 (p. 12). For later Roman attitudes to commerce and banking, see Hendy, *Studies*, pp. 242ff.; and the general survey in A. Giardina, "Modi di scambio e valori sociali nel mondo bizantino (IV-XII secolo)", in *Mercati e mercanti nell'alto medioevo: L'area euroasiatica e l'area mediterranea*, Settimane di studio del Centro italiano di studi sull'alto Medioevo 40 (Spoleto, 1993), pp. 523-84.

[96] See N. Svoronos, "Remarques sur les structures économoques de l'empire byzantin au XIe siècle", *Travaux et Mémoires* 6 (1976), pp. 49-67, esp. pp. 65ff.; Harvey, *Économic Expansion in the Byzantine Empire*, pp. 238-41 and Hendy, *Studies*, p. 567 discuss the direct disposal by major producers of agricultural surpluses of their produce, and the exclusion of middlemen. See also the discussion of M. Angold, "Archons and Dynasts", p. 240.

the willingness of local elites during the eleventh century and after to engage very actively in, for example, the production and marketing of silk, shows that there existed levels and nuances within society as a whole, and that these nuances can probably be related to the social geography of the Empire as much as to the structuring of social-economic identities. It also suggests that the evolution of such views over several centuries, reflecting the growth of new social-economic relations, was more complex than is usually assumed.[97]

It is very difficult, in dealing with the period from the seventh to the ninth century, to escape the conclusion that the role of the state was absolutely dominant, not only in respect of the extraction, movement and distribution of wealth, but also in terms of shaping demand. This applied, indeed, at three different levels: institutionally, through the ways in which the fiscal system was structured; geographically, through the ways in which the habitat and social values of the social elite were structured; and ideologically, through the ways in which the very existence of the East Roman imperial system determined attitudes to exchange and production. By the same token, however, it must be said that the sort of evidence we would require to modify or challenge this model is simply not yet available: detailed ceramic profiles of major inhabited sites, careful analyses of the connections as reflected in the ceramic record (and in other archaeologically attestable materials) between population centres, neither are available, except on a very small basis for very limited areas of Greece; and even here, the picture is still extremely indistinct. It is highly likely, in fact, that the all-powerful role of the state and its apparatuses will have to be modified in various ways, particularly once we are in a position to say more about patterns of consumption of local elites in the provinces. Yet it is also clear that it was only in the middle of the ninth century and afterwards that urban life and a fully monetised social economy begin to recover, so that this very statist picture is probably not entirely wrong. The next twenty or thirty years will, it is to be hoped, make it possible to see how far it is correct.

---

[97] See in particular Jacoby, "Silk in western Byzantium before the Fourth Crusade", who adduces good evidence from the tenth century and after that the presumed anti-commercialism of the social elite did not hinder investment absolutely, and that it has been substantially exaggerated by too uncritical a reliance on the literary sources, especially letters which, in their nature, are highly ideological.

PRODUCTION, EXCHANGE AND REGIONAL TRADE IN THE ISLAMIC EAST MEDITERRANEAN: OLD STRUCTURES, NEW SYSTEMS?

Alan Walmsley*

1. *Reconfigurations in the Early Islamic east*

When, in the seventh century, the diocese of *Oriens* was redefined as *Bilâd al-Shâm* by the Islamic conquest of Syria-Palestine, the east Mediterranean provinces of the early Byzantine (or, to others, Late Roman) empire were reconfigured to accommodate a profoundly new politico-military environment. In general terms the permanent physical detachment of Syria-Palestine from Byzantine control brought about a significant change in the status and orientation of the region. The geographical and cultural outlook of its people, already subjected to powerful agents of change in the half century before the Islamic conquest, were further modified by the establishment of a new Muslim administration. Previously a distant region on the eastern frontier of a Mediterranean empire, Bilâd al-Shâm was transformed into the geo-political heartland of a new Islamic empire. Between 660 and 750 Damascus formally served as the capital of this Empire, one that, by the early eight century, spread from Spain to India. With the establishment of the 'Abbâsid caliphate in al-'Irâq (750) and the foundation of a new imperial capital at Baghdâd shortly after, the importance of Bilâd al-Shâm was clearly diminished. However the region's strategic location within the Islamic empire, and growing interaction with the Byzantine empire to the north, ensured continuing social, economic and military roles for Bilâd al-Shâm in the later eighth and ninth centuries.

Although it is now generally agreed that the imposition of Islamic hegemony left the existing social and cultural environment of Bilâd

* ARC Australian Research Fellow, Department of Classics and Ancient History, University of Western Australia. I am grateful to the many friends and colleagues who have sent me offprints and references, and without whose help this study would be even more incomplete.

al-Shâm essentially intact, it remains more difficult to assess levels
of disruption, if any, to production systems and trade networks, or
the extent to which these developed in new directions under Islamic
administration during the course of the eighth century. Arguably,
economic structures were already in a fragile state at the time of the
Islamic conquest, due to political and military upheaval in the last
decades of Byzantine rule. Some attempt is made to clarify these
issues in this chapter, predominantly from an archaeological perspective, although we are far from reaching any definitive statement.

Sources

Perhaps some comment on the range and quality of the source material, both written and archaeological, is necessary at the outset.
Written sources for the eighth century are limited in number and
scope.[1] In particular they pay scant attention to economic issues
except taxation, and were mostly composed well after the events they
purport to describe. Fortunately with archaeology the range of data
is comparatively good, and includes excavated architecture, coins,
pottery and other classes of material culture. A major drawback,
however, is the inadequate reporting of archaeological discoveries,
especially for the period under consideration. Early Islamic levels,
often incidental to the main objectives of many projects, are usually
reported only in brief (if at all) and the archaeological context of
the material, both architecture and material culture, is frequently
poor.[2] All too often the "Muslim" or "Arab" deposits are clumped
together irrespective of age, and no progression in the archaeological
data can be discerned. As a result, a number of major and important sites, although rich in Islamic occupation, offer little useful
information on socio-economic conditions between the seventh and
ninth centuries. Nevertheless the last two decades in particular have
seen a tightening of research focus on the Early Islamic period, not-

---

[1] See B. Lewis, "Sources for the Economic History of the Middle East", in
B. Spuler ed., *Wirtschaftsgeschichte des vorderen orients in Islamischer Zeit* (Leiden, 1977),
pp. 1-17 for a useful survey of the relevant written sources.

[2] R. Schick, "Palestine in the Early Islamic Period: Luxuriant Legacy", *Near Eastern
Archaeology* 61 (1998), pp. 74-108 presents a concise and informative historical review
of Early Islamic archaeology in Israel and Jordan. Depressing is the numerous mentions of sites with significant yet unpublished Islamic strata, for instance Jerusalem,
'Abdah, Khirbat al-Mafjar (except for architecture) and Udhruh.

ably in Jordan and Syria, involving the systematic, often problem-oriented, reconnaissance of regions and the survey and excavation of sites such as Aylah, ʿAmmân Citadel, Jarash, Pella (Fihl/Tabaqat Fahl), Baysân and, in northern Syria particularly, Déhès, al-Raqqah and the Balîkh valley (fig. 1).[3] Based upon the results of surveys and excavations such as these it has become possible to construct a quite detailed, if at times patchy, profile of economic activity in Early Islamic Bilâd al-Shâm, in which production and trade served a central function especially in the eighth century.

The historical environment

a. *Seventh century dislocations*

The seventh century stands as a defining moment in the history of the Middle East, and it was a particularly turbulent period for Oriens/Bilâd al-Shâm. In the first three decades of the century, Oriens was subjected to a succession of potentially disastrous calamities.[4] In 602 the emperor Maurice Tiberias was overthrown by Phocas

---

[3] These sites are referenced below. For recent interpretative analyses see, for instance, H.I. MacAdam, "Settlements and Settlement Patterns in Northern and Central Transjordania, *ca* 550-*ca* 750", in G.R.D. King and A. Cameron eds., *The Byzantine and Early Islamic Near East 2. Land Use and Settlement Patterns* (Princeton, 1994), pp. 49-93; Schick, "Palestine in the Early Islamic Period"; D. Whitcomb, "Islam and the Socio-Cultural Transition of Palestine – Early Islamic Period (638-1099 C.E.)", in T.E. Levy ed., *The Archaeology of Society in the Holy Land* (London, 1995), pp. 488-501; also the rigorous review by C. Foss, "The Near Eastern Countryside in Late Antiquity: A Review Article", *Journal of Roman Archaeology Supplementary Series* 14 (1995), pp. 213-34; and C. Foss, "Syria in Transition, A.D. 550-750: An Archaeological Approach", *Dumbarton Oaks Papers* 51 (1997), pp. 189-269; and more generally A. Cameron, *The Mediterranean World in Late Antiquity A.D. 395-600* (London, 1993). Place names pose a considerable problem, as many sites can have up to four or five names. In this study commonly accepted names have been used for well known localities such as Damascus or Jerusalem, archaeological names have been used for major sites (hence Pella instead of Early Islamic Fihl, modern Tabaqat Fahl), or the Early Islamic name has been used (e.g. Aylah, modern al-ʿAqabah in Jordan).

[4] For historical studies of this period, each with its own approach, see F.M. Donner, *The Early Islamic Conquests* (Princeton, NJ, 1981); M. Gil, *A History of Palestine* (Cambridge, 1992); J. Haldon, *Byzantium in the Seventh Century. The Transformation of a Culture* (Cambridge, 1990); W. Kaegi, *Byzantium and the Early Islamic Conquests* (Cambridge NY, 1992); H. Kennedy, *The Prophet and the Age of the Caliphates: The Islamic Near East from the Sixth to the Eleventh Century* (London, 1986); I. Shahid, *Byzantium and the Arabs in the Sixth Century*, vol. 1 part 1: *Political and Military History* (Washington DC, 1995), and papers in A. Cameron ed., *The Byzantine and Early Islamic Near East 3. States, Resources and Armies*, Studies in Late Antiquity and Early Islam 1 (Princeton, NJ, 1995).

in a bloody usurpation of imperial rule; from 608 to 610 the revolt
of the Heraclii spread from North Africa through Oriens towards
Constantinople; shortly after Syria-Palestine was subjected to invasion and occupation by the Sassanid Persians until 628; then, as the
coup de grâce, the region underwent total military conquest by the
burgeoning Islamic caliphate (633-40). Furthermore during this time,
in 638-39, much of the region was visited by the plague, perhaps
twice. While any one of these events could have resulted in severe
and potentially permanent disruption to prevailing economic structures, surely the combined shock—usurpation, invasion and endemic
disease—should have been enough to deliver a fatal blow? Yet the
evidence, historical and archaeological, would indicate otherwise.
Excavations of numerous urban and rural sites with early seventh
century occupation have failed to produce any specific evidence attrib-
utable to these potentially disastrous events. The village of Rihab,
located east of Jarash, presents an interesting example. Two churches
were built (or refurbished) during the middle years of the Sassanid
occupation and, more tellingly, two further churches were erected
in 635 right in the midst of the Muslim campaigns.[5] Seemingly, neither the Sassanid nor Islamic conquest precipitated a social crisis in
much of Syria-Palestine, and local community structures were essentially
unchallenged by the greater historical events happening around them.

Nevertheless, there is a clear argument for a short-term dislocation. The Sassanid invasion in particular resulted in major damage
to the urban infrastructure of a few major towns, specifically Antioch
and at Jerusalem where Constantine's great *Martyrium* church was
plundered.[6] There was also significant economic loss, represented,

---

[5] Plague: M.N. Dols, "Plague in Early Islamic History", *Journal of the American
Oriental Society* 94 (1974), pp. 371-83. Rihab: M. Piccirillo, *The Mosaics of Jordan*
(Amman, 1993); and more generally A. Shboul and A.G. Walmsley, "Identity and
Self-Image in Syria-Palestine in the Transition from Byzantine to Early Islamic
Rule: Arab Christians and Muslims", *Mediterranean Archaeology* 11 (1998) pp. 255-87,
esp. pp. 284-86. For additional evidence for seventh century continuities, see below.

[6] The extent of damage in Jerusalem is disputed, although claims that the monumental *Nea* church of Justinian was destroyed must be rejected on written and
archaeological grounds. Damage to the Martyrium, which may have been burnt,
must have been repaired by the time of the Islamic conquest, as this church with
its golden dome attracted the admiration of the Muslims. The comparatively low
level of urban destruction over much of the diocese of Oriens can be contrasted
with the apparent devastation wrought on Anatolia (for which see C. Foss, "The
Persians in Asia Minor and the End of Antiquity", *English Historical Review* 90 (1975),
pp. 721-47).

for instance, by the concealment of coin hoards at the start of the seventh century. The burial of numerous and sizeable hoards in both precious and base metal points to growing social anxiety after the Sassanid sack of Antioch, and the non-recovery of these hoards further reveals that the Sassanid conquest of all Syria-Palestine (610-614) resulted in economic dislocation and personal loss on a reasonable scale.[7] In general it would be misleading to underestimate the extent of socio-economic disruption caused by the political and military events of the early seventh century, but in the long run town and country survived surprisingly well the rigours of these three decades of upheaval. The character of the subsequent economic recovery, and the means and processes by which it was attained, are central to this study, with the growth of agricultural and industrial production and the forging of trade routes contributing significantly to the revival.

b. *The impact of the Umayyad caliphate (661-750)*

Social and political events in the later seventh and the first half of the eighth century set Bilâd al-Shâm firmly in the centre of a vast and continually growing empire, a position that could have only favoured economic growth.[8] The most significant political event was the ascendancy of Mu'âwiyah, governor of Bilâd al-Shâm, to the caliphate and the resultant transfer of the capital of an ever expanding

---

[7] Hoards that can be attributed to the Sassanid invasion include: D.T. Ariel, "A Hoard of Byzantine Folles from Qazrin", *Atiqot* 29 (1996), pp. 69-76; D.C. Baramki, "A Hoard of Byzantine coins", *Quarterly of the Department of Antiquities in Palestine* 8 (1938), pp. 81-85; G.M. Fitzgerald, *A Sixth Century Monastery at Beth-Shan* (Philadelphia, 1939); C. Lambert, "A Hoard of Byzantine Coins", *Quarterly of the Department of Antiquities in Palestine* 1 (1932), pp. 55-68; S.J. Mansfield, "Coin Hoards 1995: Near East, 68. Unknown (Near East), 1993 or before", *The Numismatic Chronicle* 155 (1995), pp. 354-58. Others can be plausibly attributed to the advance of the Muslim armies in the 630s (e.g. G.E. Bates, "A Byzantine Hoard from CoeleSyria", *American Numismatic Society Museum Notes* 14 (1968), pp. 67-109). These appear to be fewer in number, perhaps indicating a less disturbed time and/or greater recovery of buried wealth. Another rise in the concealment of hoards is discernible, possibly, during the power struggles over the caliphate in the 680s (see, as examples, W.E. Metcalf, "Three Seventh-century Byzantine Gold Hoards", *American Numismatic Society Museum Notes* 25 (1980), pp. 87-108; C. Morrisson, "Le Trésor Byzantin de Nikertai", *Revue Belge de Numismatique et de Sigillographie* 118 (1972), pp. 29-91).

[8] For the political history of the period see, as a selection, P.K. Hitti, *History of the Arabs* (London, 1970), pp. 189-223; Kennedy, *The Prophet and the Age of the Caliphates*, pp. 82-123; M.A. Shaban, *Islamic History, a New Interpretation*, vol. 1: *A.D. 600-750 (A.H. 132)* (Cambridge, 1971); L.V. Vaglieri, "The Patriarchal and Umayyad Caliphates", *The Cambridge History of Islam*, vol. 1: *The Rise and Domination of the Arabs* (Cambridge, 1970), pp. 57-103.

Islamic empire to Damascus by 661. Over the next ninety years
(661-750), the Umayyad caliphate he founded was underpinned by
the economic and military resources of Bilâd al-Shâm, even though
the decentralised nature of the Umayyad administration meant that
only a small percentage of tax revenues were actually remitted to
the central treasury in Damascus. A sizeable proportion of the gold and
silver coin, olive oil and wheat collected as tax was retained and distributed at the provincial level, primarily to pay for the army and
the local administration. Two alternative sources kept the central
finances of the early Umayyad caliphate afloat: the booty and tribute
resulting from the continuing wars of conquest, and major agricultural
developments in the newly occupied lands.

In many ways the 680s marked the beginning of a new age of
peace and prosperity in Bilâd al-Shâm. In socio-economic terms the
most profound changes were initiated by the vigorous reform agenda
of the Caliph 'Abd al-Malik (r. 685-705), which included a major
overhaul of administrative and fiscal structures after 50 years of flat
economic performance. Specifically the implementation of a unified
monetary system and the refurbishment of roads boosted trade in
Bilâd al-Shâm and throughout the Empire. The caliphates of 'Abd
al-Malik and his sons al-Walîd (705-15) and Sulayman (715-17) were
characterised by the channelling of considerable surplus wealth into
large and numerous building projects, mostly state programmes but
private initiatives as well. New towns were founded, for instance al-
Ramlah on the coastal plain of Palestine, and major centres embellished with impressive imperial structures notably the Dome of the
Rock and al-Aqsa mosque in Jerusalem, and the Great Mosque of
Damascus.[9] Under the later Umayyads, particularly Hishâm (724-
43), commerce was further encouraged by the construction of new
urban market places, and rural agricultural development programmes
were accelerated to compensate for declining returns from military
campaigns and inadequate tax receipts from the provinces.

As this paper sets out to show, the strongly pro-development activities of the Umayyads brought demonstrable economic benefits to a
wide section of society in Bilâd al-Shâm, noticeably from the time
of 'Abd al-Malik. The presence of wealthy urban elites, the main-

---

[9] For a convenient and comprehensive review of religious and secular buildings
of the Umayyad period in Bilâd al-Shâm see: K.A.C. Creswell revised by J.W.
Allen, *A Short Account of Early Muslim Architecture* (London, 1989), pp. 18-226.

tenance of an army, improved intra- and inter-regional communications and major capital works programmes in towns and the countryside directly and indirectly stimulated many other areas of economic activity. The archaeological and written evidence argues for a considerable growth in production and trade during the first decades of the eighth century, especially the expansion of urban-based manufacturing activities and the development of rural industries.

c. *The ʿAbbâsid challenge*

Although many of the Umayyad economic improvements were to outlive the dynasty, the spectacular gains of the early eighth century were threatened by events in the second half, primarily the successful ʿAbbâsid rebellion (748-50) and the geographical shift of the ruling household to al-ʿIrâq, ultimately Baghdâd.[10] However the suddenness of the geo-political change, and its economic impact, should not be unduly emphasised. The later Umayyads spent long periods outside of Damascus and the last Caliph, Marwân II (744-50), went further by transferring the imperial capital to the Jazîrah (north-west Mesopotamia). Many governmental structures remained intact after the ʿAbbâsid take over and were possibly strengthened in line with the centralising policies of the ʿAbbâsids and to counter pro-Umayyad movements in parts of Bilâd al-Shâm, which sometimes spilled over into ineffectual rebellion. Even after the establishment of Baghdâd by al-Mansûr (754-75), Bilâd al-Shâm retained a strategically crucial position between al-ʿIrâq and the increasingly important province of Egypt. Furthermore the growing sanctity of Jerusalem (early Islamic Iliyâ) and other holy places greatly enhanced the standing of Palestine (Filastîn) during the ʿAbbâsid period.[11]

For the last two decades of our period the ʿAbbâsid caliphate was racked by civil war. Although the conflict was fought outside of Syria,

---

[10] See especially the following for the political history of the ʿAbbâsid dynasty: Hitti, *History of the Arabs*, pp. 288-331; Kennedy, *The Prophet and the Age of the Caliphates*, pp. 124-57; M.A. Shaban, *Islamic History, a New Interpretation*, vol. 2: *A.D. 750-1055 (A.H. 132-448)* (Cambridge, 1976).

[11] The development of Jerusalem (*Bayt al-Maqdis*, or simply *al-Quds* "the Holy") as a sacred city in early Islam accelerated after the end of the Umayyad dynasty, for which see A. Elad, *Medieval Jerusalem and Islamic Worship. Holy Places, Ceremonies, Pilgrimage* (Leiden, 1995); S.D. Goitein, "The Sanctity of Jerusalem and Palestine in Early Islam", *Studies in Islamic History and Institutions* (Leiden, 1966), pp. 135-48; F.E. Peters, *Jerusalem: the Holy City in the Eyes of Chroniclers, Visitors, Pilgrims, and Prophets from the Days of Abraham to the Beginnings of Modern Times* (Princeton, NJ, 1985).

and was followed by an impressive 'Abbâsid revival, it resulted in permanent changes to social and military structures in the Islamic world and a significant break with the past. Most notably traditional Muslim elites were politically and economically disenfranchised, losing their salary entitlements ('atâ') established at the time of the Islamic conquest, and the imposition of strong central government abruptly ended the administrative (especially fiscal) independence of provinces.[12] The proceeds of these gains were channelled into a slave army, further undermining the standing of traditional elites. Hence just as 680 and the reforms of 'Abd al-Malik represent a relevant date to begin this study, so 830 presents an ideal date with which to end it.

2. *Towns, ports and roads: the infrastructure of trade*

An unbroken socio-economic role for towns

The persistent Persian threat of invasion to the towns of Roman and Byzantine Syria-Palestine, which on more than one occasion had become a reality, had taught the ruling urban elites that piecemeal resistance was futile. Much more was to be gained by negotiating with the conquering forces to preserve, by surrender, the existing urban fabric. Accordingly, the Sassanid occupation of 611-628 proceeded with only occasional disruption to urban life, although Antioch and Jerusalem both suffered. However, with Jerusalem the damage was seemingly confined to the town's imperial church monuments: Constantine's *Martyrium* and Justinian's *Nea*. By comparison the Islamic conquest of 633-40 was overwhelmingly non-destructive, even in the few cases where towns were taken by military action (notably Caesarea/Qaysâriyah in Palestine).[13] Most towns readily capitulated

---

[12] The strong centralising policies of the 'Abbâsid caliph al-Ma'mûn (813-833) is reflected, for instance, in his major reforms of the coinage—the first since 'Abd al-Malik—in the 820s. It followed a protracted period of instability resulting from a dispute over succession to the caliphate with his brother al-Amîn (809-813); see T. El-Hibri, "Coinage Reform under the 'Abbasid Caliph al-Ma'mun", *Journal of the Economic and Social History of the Orient* 36 (1993), pp. 58-83.

[13] See the major corrective to earlier views of a destructive conquest of Qaysâriyah in K.G. Holum, "Archaeological Evidence for the Fall of Byzantine Caesarea", *Bulletin of the American Schools of Oriental Research* 286 (1992), pp. 73-85. Even in the few cases where towns repudiated their original agreements with the Muslim generals, for instance Tabariyah, 'Asqalân and Antioch, agreements were renegotiated and mil-

to the Muslim armies by treaty (*sulh*), which ensured personal, civic and religious rights upon payment of poll and land taxes. Consequently the urban structure of Bilâd al-Shâm was largely unscathed by the Sassanid and Islamic conquests.

The immediate and considerable concern of the early Caliphate with the continuing urban health of Bilâd al-Shâm can be seen, along with other policy decisions, in the institution of a new provincial structure. Bilâd al-Shâm was divided into four, later five, military provinces, the *ajnâd*, in which towns retained administrative responsibilities (mostly taxation) for the surrounding district (*kûrah*).[14] Along with maintaining a major administrative role, towns remained the cultural and economic foci of their districts, with many continuing to host large annual fairs. These not only enhanced commercial life but also brought intellectual benefits to both urban populations and the rural hinterland. Certain towns were also granted the responsibility of issuing copper coin (the *fals*, pl. *fulûs*) during the monetary reforms of 'Abd al-Malik in the 690s (only Damascus issued coin in precious metals).[15] The appearance of an officially sanctioned copper

itary retribution avoided: see: Al-Baladhuri, *The Origins of the Islamic State*, trans. P.K. Hitti (Beirut, 1966 [1916]) pp. 179 (Tabariyah), 219 ('Asalân), 227 (Antioch).

[14] For the structure and towns of the *ajnâd* in south Bilâd al-Shâm see: A.G. Walmsley, *The Administrative Structure and Urban Geography of the Jund of Filastin and the Jund of al-Urdunn: the cities and districts of Palestine and east Jordan during the early Islamic, 'Abbasid and early Fatimid periods* (Ph.D. thesis, University of Sydney, 1987). While I. Shahid sees a Byzantine "proto-*thema*" origin for the *ajnâd* (I. Shahid, "The Jund System in Bilad al-Sham: Its Origin", in M.A. Bakhit and M. Asfour eds., *Proceedings of the Fourth International Conference on the History of Bilad al-Sham. Bilad al-Sham during the Byzantine Period*, English Section, Vol. 2 (Amman, 1986), pp. 45-52; I. Shahid, "Heraclius and the Theme System: New Light from the Arabic", *Byzantion* 57 (1987), pp. 391-406; I. Shahid, "Heraclius and the Theme System: Further Observations", *Byzantion* 59 (1989), pp. 209-43), J. Haldon and the current author have independently argued that the *ajnâd* were an outcome of the Islamic conquest of al-Shâm (J. Haldon, "Seventh-Century Continuities: the *Ajnad* and the 'Thematic Myth'", in A. Cameron ed., *The Byzantine and Early Islamic Near East 3. State, Resources and Armies*, Studies in Late Antiquity and Early Islam 1 (Princeton, 1995), pp. 379-423; Walmsley, *The Administrative Structure and Urban Geography of the Jund of Filastin and the Jund of al-Urdunn*), which is in line with W. Kaegi's thinking on the subject, that is, no major changes to governmental institutions under Heraclius (see: W. Kaegi, "Two Studies in the Continuity of Late Roman and Byzantine Military Institutions", *Byzantinische Forschungen* 8 (1982), pp. 87-113).

[15] Annual fairs in major centres attained an "international" stature in the Byzantine period, for instance that at Ghazzah (Gaza) in southern Palestine, which was attended by Pre-Islamic traders from Makkah. These continued unabated after the Islamic conquest. In the later seventh century Jerusalem hosted a fair attended by "a huge crowd from almost every country and many nationalities", according to Arcuf the Pilgrim who visited in c. 679-688 (J. Wilkinson, *Jerusalem Pilgrims Before the Crusades*

coinage seemingly replaced informal minting in the decades between c. 660 and 692. While all provincial capitals were authorised to issue fulûs, it is unclear why only some of the district centres were given minting responsibilities, but the pattern would seem to reflect a level of administrative, commercial and perhaps urban seniority. The wide circulation of this coinage in eighth century Bilâd al-Shâm, and the discovery in site finds and hoards of coins minted in other regions of the Islamic world, is a valuable indicator of trade networks (see further below).

Markets: the sûq and khân

Markets for the manufacture and exchange of goods constitute a defining feature of the Early Islamic town in Bilâd al-Shâm. The appearance in the Middle East of the "medieval" *sûq*, a covered market street joining mosque, bath (*hammâm*) and warehouse (*khân*), has been the focus of much interest in Islamic scholarship.[16] Particular attention has been paid to describing the process by which the broad, open thoroughfares of the Classical cities in the East were transformed into the "medieval sûq". In the pioneering studies of Jean Sauvaget on Lâdhikiyah, Damascus and especially Aleppo (Halab) in Syria, this process was seen as an entirely Islamic phenomenon and, in some way, represented the cultural reassertion by the "Oriental" east over an ordered, Hellenized urban environment.[17] In the per-

---

(Warminster, 1977), p. 95). On early Islamic numismatics and the reforms of 'Abd al-Malik see especially M.L. Bates, "The Arab-Byzantine Bronze Coinage of Syria: An Innovation by 'Abd al-Malik", *A Colloquium in Memory of George Carpenter Miles (1904-1975)* (New York, 1976), pp. 16-27; M.L. Bates, "History, Geography and Numismatics in the First Century of Islamic Coinage", *Revue Suisse de Numismatique* 65 (1986), pp. 231-62; M.L. Bates, "Byzantine Coinage and its Imitations, Arab Coinage and its Imitations: Arab-Byzantine Coinage", *ARAM* 6 (1994), pp. 381-403; P. Grierson, "The Monetary Reforms of 'Abd al-Malik. Their Metrological Basis and their Financial Repercussions", *Journal of the Economic and Social History of the Orient* 3 (1960), pp. 241-64.

[16] For these buildings within their sociological setting see E. Sims, "Trade and Travel: Markets and Caravanserais", in G. Michell ed., *Architecture of the Islamic World. Its History and Social Meaning* (London, 1978), pp. 97-111.

[17] See the classic studies by J. Sauvaget, "Esquisse d'une histoire de la ville de Damas", *Revue des Études Islamiques* 8 (1934 [1937]), pp. 422-80; J. Sauvaget, *Alep* (Paris, 1941); also E. Wirth, "Zum Problem des Bazars (sûq, çarsi). Versuch einer Begriffsbestimmung und Theorie des traditionellen Wirtschaftszentrums der orientalisch-islamischen Stadt", *Der Islam* 51/52 (1974/1975), pp. 203-60, 206-46, N. Al Sayyad, *Cities and Caliphs: on the Genesis of Arab Muslim Urbanism* (New York,

haps most influential of his studies, that on Aleppo, Sauvaget ascribed the "fall" from the Graeco-Roman urban ideal to the socio-political disorder that characterised the tenth and eleventh centuries.[18] As Sauvaget was dealing with still functioning towns, he relied upon historical rather than archaeological evidence to date the formation of the Syrian sûq. However by drawing on an alternative source of evidence, archaeology, Kennedy concluded that the process of sûq formation began considerably earlier, principally from the mid sixth century and onwards, and was well advanced by the early seventh century (that is, at the time of the Islamic conquest).[19] To Kennedy the process remained the same—the invasion of public space and the "decline of the classical city"—but it was initiated long before the arrival of Islam and was indicative of a political, economic and demographic collapse of towns that weakened Bilâd al-Shâm in the lead up to the Islamic conquest.

New archaeological work conducted since the publication between 1985 and 1992 of Kennedy's now oft-cited papers reveals that the whole issue of urban change, particularly the form and status of markets, in Late Antique-Early Islamic Bilâd al-Shâm is considerably more complicated than the essentially single, linear and irreversible process described by Sauvaget and Kennedy.[20] What is very clear (and illustrated in this section) is that no one "universal" trend can be recognised between the seventh and early ninth centuries, except for an overall expansion of the commercial role of many towns. In some instances, this expansion was achieved by commandeering central space in existing towns to produce an enclosed, sûq-like

---

1991) for a general treatment, especially pp. 18-33 and 90-107 for Damascus and Aleppo; and N. Elisséeff, "Dimashk", *Encyclopaedia of Islam, New Ed.* 2 (Leiden, 1965), pp. 277-91 for Damascus.

[18] Sauvaget, *Alep*; see also the analysis by R.S. Humphreys, *Islamic History. A Framework for Inquiry* (Princeton, 1991), pp. 234-38.

[19] H. Kennedy, "The Last Century of Byzantine Syria: A Reinterpretation", *Byzantinische Forschungen* 10 (1985), pp. 141-84; H. Kennedy, "From *Polis* to *Madina*: Urban Change in Late Antique and Early Islamic Syria", *Past & Present* 106 (1985), pp. 3-27; H. Kennedy, "Antioch: from Byzantium to Islam and back again", in J. Rich ed., *The City in Late Antiquity* (London, 1992), pp. 181-98 at pp. 192-93, drawing together archaeological results from Antioch, Jarash, Apamea, Busrâ and other sites.

[20] See: R. Foote, "Commerce, Industry and Orthogonal Planning: mutually compatible terms in settlements of Bilâd al-Š⁻ᵐ during the Umayyad period", *Mediterranean Archaeology* 12 (1999) for a major st   growing evidence for a continuing tradition of ordered urban planning in Early Islamic Bilâd al-Shâm and the considerable expansion of commercial and industrial activities in towns under the Umayyads.

structure (eg. Palmyra, see below). However, there is considerable
new evidence for the simultaneous construction of broad, shop-lined
thoroughfares in both new and existing towns, resulting in an urban
vista reminiscent of the eastern "Classical City".

a. *Market streets and the "sûq" question*
The evidence for new and expanded markets within existing towns
in Early Islamic Bilâd al-Shâm is widespread, especially for the eighth
century. However, the way markets were accommodated within the
prevailing urban plan varied, from the conversion and modification
of existing space to the construction of completely new market centres, with varieties in-between. New and remodelled structures could
be present in a single town. For the purposes of this study, a few
examples from better dated and reported sites will suffice. Evidence
for the remodelling of existing space can be found at Palmyra, Baysân,
Jarash, Bayt Râs and Pella, whereas instances of more substantial
rebuilding programs are known from Arsûf, Baysân again, Tabariyah
and, following a devastating earthquake, also Pella (fig. 1). Archaeologically it can be demonstrated that the commercial development
of these sites was particularly intense during the later seventh and
eighth centuries.

In Palmyra, the central course of the main colonnaded street north
west of the tetrapylon was infilled with a long line of shops to produce a market centre very reminiscent of a sûq.[21] Excavations exposed
45 shop units extending 180 m and divided into two sections, without the western end of the sûq being reached. At least four phases
in construction can be identified, with shops 10-17 forming the original nucleus of the eastern wing (pl. 1). However the excavators
concluded that the whole sûq was erected over a relatively short
time in either the late seventh or early eighth century.[22] The new
line of shops opened northwards onto a lane, roughly the width of
the earlier north footpath of the street. At the same time, the original
shops on the north side of the street were reutilized. The development

---

[21] K. As'ad and F.M. Stepniowski, "The Umayyad Suq in Palmyra", *Damaszener
Mitteilungen* 4 (1989), pp. 205-23.

[22] The archaeological evidence, as far as it is presented, does not support a late
seventh century date for this construction, which seems too early. Rather the development of nearby sites, especially Rusâfah, Qasr al-Hayr al-Gharbî and Qasr
al-Hayr al-Sharqî, would suggest a date in the reign of the Caliph Hishâm (724-43),
which is in general agreement with the evidence from the excavations.

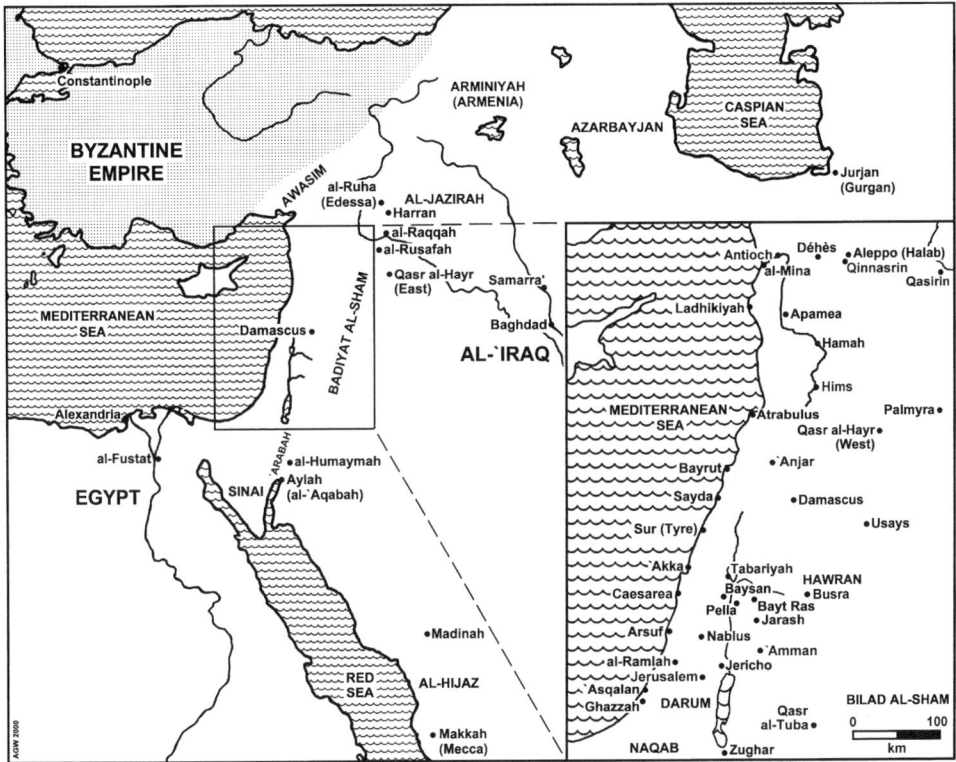

Fig. 1. Bilâd al-Shâm and the central Islamic lands in the second half of the eighth century.

Pl. 1. Portico and doorways into a row of shops in the heart of the Umayyad sûq of Palmyra.

resulted in a large commercial complex composed of an axial walk-way some seven metres wide and flanked on either side by a near-continuous line of around 100 shops. The complex continued to be occupied into the ʿAbbâsid period, although the nature of this occu-pation (commercial or domestic) is uncertain. While the Palmyra sûq may seem to represent a clear case of encroachment on a "classical" urban infrastructure, it could have been intended as an improve-ment to this stretch of the colonnaded street. Here the south facade of the street was little more than a continuous wall, and the line of new shops over the street may have been meant to overcome the inconvenience and inefficiency of having a single line of shops.

At Baysân, Jarash and Bayt Râs a similar picture of urban modi-fication can be demonstrated, although on a less comprehensive scale than at Palmyra. Shops and possibly small manufacturing units, indicated by the presence of small ovens,[23] were built over the central thoroughfare at Baysân, progressively narrowing a major access route to a narrow lane. Based on a literal reading of the numismatic evidence, the excavators date the start of this process to the late fifth or early sixth century, but this seems to reflect the urban adaptation of a pagan edifice under early Christianity. Elsewhere they ascribe an early seventh century date, which seems more likely for the commercial development of the town centre, with construc-tion increasing in intensity during the Umayyad period.[24] The trend is very much the same at Jarash (although more poorly recorded), with the area from the Oval Piazza to the South Tetrapylon Piazza developing into a busy and congested commercial town centre, appar-ently to the detriment of outer suburbs.[25] Concentrated into an area

---

[23] Small ovens, or *tabûns*, are often interpreted as indicative of domestic occupa-tion, but equally they could have been used in an industrial context, such as smelt-ing small crucibles of copper or glass. There is evidence for such a link in the ʿAbbâsid complex at Pella.

[24] G. Foerster and Y. Tsafrir, "City Center (North); Excavations of the Hebrew University Expedition", *Excavations and Surveys in Israel 11: The Bet Sheʿan Excavation Project (1989-1991)* (Jerusalem, 1993), pp. 3-32 at pp. 18-19, 22-23. For an early seventh-century date for a rapid increase in the urban infilling of towns see: A.G. Walmsley, "Byzantine Palestine and Arabia: Urban Prosperity in Late Antiquity", in N.J. Christie and S.T. Loseby eds., *Towns in Transition: Urban Evolution in Late Antiquity and the Early Middle Ages* (Aldershot, 1996), pp. 126-58 at pp. 144-45.

[25] Walmsley, "Byzantine Palestine and Arabia", with references; for an original analysis of settlement in Late Antique and Early Islamic Jarash (although not with-out its problems) see A. Zeyadeh, *An Archaeological Assessment of Six Cities in al-Urdun: From the Fourth Century to the Mid-Eighth Century A.D.* (M.A. thesis, Yarmouk University, Jordan, 1988), pp. 83-118, who correctly emphasises the commercial nature of occu-pation in the area of the two piazzas and south cardo.

almost 300 m in length and covering the space of the two piazzas were shops, light industrial installations and domestic residences.[26] In the south-west quadrant of the South Tetrapylon a large new building was erected, extending partly over the piazza. The building's plan, rectangular with corner towers and porticoes, indicates that it served a public function, perhaps administrative but possibly also commercial as a khân. Shops and light industry were also uncovered along the cardo north of the South Tetrapylon, extending over roughly another 150 m. Continuity of use in the eighth century of a market at Bayt Râs can also be demonstrated.[27] Originally constructed in the Roman period as part of a tiered marketplace, by c. 600 the sûq (as termed by the excavator) consisted of nine vaults in a line, all but one of which were rebuilds of the fourth or fifth century. In the seventh or early part of the eighth century, an arcade was constructed in front of the vaults, expanding the area of the market and creating an enclosed space. Further refurbishment of the area was undertaken in the ninth to tenth century, when it continued as a market.

The promotion of town-based commerce in the eighth century through the construction of new market centres within existing urban centres can be demonstrated at three major sites: Baysân, Arsûf and Tabariyah. At Baysân, first reports ascribed the building of a new commercial street for the town to the Byzantine period, but the recent discovery of a Kufic inscription now firmly dates this major urban project to the reign of the Umayyad Caliph Hishâm.[28] An

---

[26] C.S. Fisher, "Roman Buildings V. Buildings Partly Excavated. D. The 'Forum'", in C.H. Kraeling ed., *Gerasa, City of the Decapolis* (New Haven, 1938), pp. 153-58; L. Harding, "Recent Work on the Jerash Forum", *Palestine Exploration Quarterly* 81 (1949), pp. 12-20; C.H. Kraeling, "Roman Buildings III. The South Tetrapylon", in *Gerasa, City of the Decapolis*, pp. 103-15; also Zeyadeh, "An Archaeological Assessment of Six Cities in al-Urdun", pp. 96-103; A. Zeyadeh, "Urban Transformations in the Decapolis Cities of Jordan", *ARAM* 4 (1992), pp. 101-15 at pp. 104-106.

[27] C.J. Lenzen and E.A. Knauf, "Beit Ras/Capitolias. A Preliminary Evaluation of the Archaeological and Textual Evidence", *Syria* 64 (1987), pp. 21-46; C.J. Lenzen, "From Public to Private Space: Changes in the Urban Plan of Bayt Ras/Capitolias", in K. ʿAmr, F. Zayadine and M. Zaghloul eds., *Studies in the History and Archaeology of Jordan*, vol. 5 (Amman, 1995), pp. 235-39.

[28] For the earlier Byzantine dating see Foerster and Tsafrir, "City Center (North)", pp. 25-32; for the redating to Hishâm refer to Y. Tsafrir and G. Foerster, "Urbanism at Scythopolis-Bet Shean in the Fourth to Seventh Centuries", *Dumbarton Oaks Papers* 51 (1997), pp. 85-146 at pp. 123, 138-40. The "Byzantine Commercial Street" of Baysân stands as another example of attributing, without justification, the refur-

earlier ("Roman") pool and colonnade were covered over by the construction of more than 20 shops, approached by a covered walkway lined on the street side with piers and columns supporting arches (fig. 2). The inscription, composed of mosaic, once adorned the entry gate to the market, and displayed the order of Hishâm to the governor of the province of al-Urdunn (Jordan) to undertake the construction of the market, presumably from provincial funds. While, as Foote notes, Hishâm instructed the building of sûqs throughout the Islamic empire, the Baysân example is the first firm evidence for the application of this policy although Baysân is not specifically mentioned in this context. A similar major redevelopment, resulting in the creation of a new market street, can be observed at the coastal town of Arsûf.[29] Relatively narrow (2.5 m) and long (65 m+), the open street was flanked on both sides by a series of single and double-roomed shops and courtyards, delineated along the street by shallow entrance bays. According to the excavators the Arsûf sûq was a development of 'Abd al-Malik, although the pottery recovered from the earliest stratum appears 'Abbâsid in date. Perhaps this sûq can also be attributed to Hishâm, or even later (early 'Abbâsid?). The street had an extended life, probably until the Crusades, with eight superimposed street levels being identified. A similar profile can be suggested for the small area of shops and street excavated at Tabariyah.[30] This town, newly appointed as capital of al-Urdunn, expanded considerably after the Islamic conquest, spreading over previously unoccupied fields and a cemetery south of the walled Byzantine town in the eighth and ninth centuries. The line of the Roman period cardo was continued from the South Gate, and the new street provided with shops. Shops were also a feature within the confines of the Byzantine town, and in due course (the date is unclear from the reports) these impinged on the paving of the Roman-Byzantine street.

The excavations at Baysân, Palmyra, Arsûf and Tabariyah demonstrate conclusively that the provision of linear and ordered market

---

bishment of towns to the Justinianic period, whereas there were equally favourable conditions in the later sixth, much of the seventh and certainly the first half of the eighth centuries.

[29] I. Roll and E. Ayalon, "The Market Street at Apollonia-Arsuf", *Bulletin of the American Schools of Oriental Research* 267 (1987), pp. 61-76.

[30] G. Foerster, "Tiberias. Excavations South of the City", in E. Stern ed., *New Encyclopaedia of Archaeological Excavations in the Holy Land* 4 (Jerusalem, 1993), pp. 1470-73.

Fig. 2. Preliminary reconstruction of the Umayyad marketplace at Baysân (from Y. Tsafrir and G. Foerster, 'From Scythopolis to Baysân – changing concepts of Urbanism', in G.R.D. King and A. Cameron eds., *The Byzantine and Early Islamic Near East 2. Land Use and Settlement Patterns* (Princeton, 1994), pp. 95-115, fig. 16).

streets was a common feature of towns in Early Islamic Bilâd al-Shâm. There was no monodirectional process of irreversible urban decay following the Islamic conquest. Indeed quite the opposite appears true—an urban revival in may areas after the upsets of the early seventh century—and we can only speculate about street refurbishment in other major towns especially Damascus. Once this point is understood the gridded and shop-lined streets of the new Islamic settlements of the seventh and eighth centuries do not appear unusual or, indeed, atypical for the period. 'Ayn al-Jarr ('Anjar in Lebanon), Aylah (al-'Aqabah) and seemingly al-Ramlah, all new foundations,[31] were divided into quadrants by intersecting, shop-lined streets with tetrapylon-style monuments at the main crossroads.[32] As one Arabic source remarked the foundation of al-Ramlah by Sulayman, governor of Filastîn and later caliph, "ruined" neighbouring Ludd,[33] and an economic cause for this decline can be easily identified. Sulayman would have made every attempt to ensure the long-term viability of his new foundation, including the intentional relocation of commercial activity to al-Ramlah by the construction of markets. The denial to Ludd of any significant involvement in the rapidly growing market economy of the early eighth century resulted in stagnation and ensured its demise.

b. *Khâns*

The prevalence of shop-lined streets in the Early Islamic towns, new and old, of Bilâd al-Shâm highlight the absolutely central role of the market economy in the later seventh and eighth centuries. The identification of a second institution, specifically a large enclosed and

---

[31] Or rather new, enclosed suburbs of existing towns. Byzantine period settlements were located next to 'Anjar and Aylah (and had the same name), while al-Ramlah was, to all intents and purposes, an offshoot of Ludd (Lod) on the coast of Palestine. A similar case has been made for a northern suburb being added to Tabariyah in the Early Islamic period; see: T.P. Harrison, "The Early Umayyad Settlement at Tabariyah: A Case of Yet Another *Misr*?", *Journal of Near Eastern Studies* 51 (1992), pp. 51-59. Likewise Hishâm built a new settlement next to the large and walled Byzantine site of Rusâfah, and it was given the appropriate name of *Rusâfah Hishâm*.

[32] 'Anjar: Creswell rev. Allen, *A Short Account of Early Muslim Architecture* pp. 122-24; Aylah and al-Ramlah: D. Whitcomb, "The Misr of Ayla: New Evidence for the Early Islamic City", in K. 'Amr, F. Zayadine and M. Zaghloul eds., *Studies in the History and Archaeology of Jordan*, vol. 5 (Amman, 1995), pp. 277-88; Whitcomb, "Islam and the Socio-Cultural Transition of Palestine", pp. 488-501, at pp. 491-92.

[33] Al-Ya'qûbî, *Kitâb al-Buldân*, Bibliotheca Geographicorum Arabicorum vol. 7 (Leiden, 1892) pp. 116/328.9-10, 14-15.

courted compound for trade and storage (generally called, in an urban context, a khân), also reveals the importance of commerce in the Early Islamic period. These storehouses, dedicated to light manufacturing and exchange, became a feature of towns in Bilâd al-Shâm in middle Islamic times, but their identification in the first centuries of Islam is still in its infancy.[34]

The presence of a khân at Jarash has already been alluded to, and this possibility is supported by a similar development in the urban centre of Pella, Early Islamic Fihl. In the late seventh or, more plausibly, early eighth century a new commercial centre was constructed next to the cathedral church, involving a comprehensive remodelling of space and, more significantly, a major change in civic function for the area. A paved open court on the north side of the church was converted into a large enclosed market place by the construction of perimeter rooms, porticoes and porches on two levels, very close in layout to a khân.[35] As in the case of later khâns animals, notably but not exclusively camels, and their keepers stayed on the ground floor,[36] while the rooms on the upper storey prob-

---

[34] Khâns in Islam: Sims, "Trade and Travel: Markets and Caravanserais", pp. 97-111 at pp. 100-101.

[35] R.H. Smith and L.P. Day, *Pella of the Decapolis Volume 2. Final Report on the College of Wooster Excavations in Area IX, the Civic Complex, 1979-1985* (Wooster, 1989), pp. 60-71, 90-92. However they date the erection of the complex to sometime between 614 and 635, and see it as serving an ecclesiastical rather than commercial function. See Zeyadeh, "An Archaeological Assessment of Six Cities in al-Urdun", pp. 59-61; and A.G. Walmsley, "The Social and Economic Regime at Fihl (Pella) and Neighbouring Centres, Between the 7th and 9th Centuries", in P. Canivet and J.-P. Rey-Coquais eds., *La Syrie de Byzance à l'Islam VIIe-VIIIe siècles: actes du colloque international* (Damascus, 1992), pp. 249-61 for the alternate view presented here. I am, however, now less inclined to directly link the creation of a new monumental entrance and staircase to the cathedral atrium from the west with the formation of the market to the north (see A.G. Walmsley, "Coin Frequencies in Sixth and Seventh Century Palestine and Arabia: Social and Economic Implications", *Journal of the Economic and Social History of the Orient* 42.3 (1999) pp. 326-50). Rather the expanded urban role of the zone north of the church in the late seventh or early eighth century could well explain, at least in part, the decreasing importance and eventual blocking of the western atrium entrance.

[36] The structure, destroyed in a single massive earthquake or two successive quakes in the mid-eighth century, contained the skeletons of seven camels, two humans, four cows, a horse and its foal. For the use of camels as pack animals in the Early Islamic period see C.J. Kraemer, *Excavations at Nessana 3. Non-Literary Papyri* (Princeton, 1958), pp. 209-11, Document 74, which is a requisition dated to c. 685 for two camels and their drovers to work the Qaysâriyah-Baysân road. The presence of cows does not necessarily preclude a primarily commercial role for the building, especially as it was mid winter when the final earthquake struck.

ably housed humans and valuable goods. The discovery of a small blacksmith's shop, reminiscent of the one found at the south tetrapylon of Jarash, indicates that light industry was also practised on the ground floor of the enclosure. Hence Fihl's new market centre performed both a commercial and an industrial function, and saw the loss of open urban space to production and trade serving at least local needs but perhaps a wider market (see further below).

Following the comprehensive destruction of Fihl by tectonic action in the mid-eighth century, considerable effort was channelled into rebuilding a replacement commercial centre for the town, the main feature of which was two large khân-like enclosures (fig. 3). Excavations in the eastern enclosure have revealed a gated entranceway, central courtyard flanked by rooms, an external staircase for access to a second level, and a large installation consisting of a series of industrial fireplaces. A considerable amount of glass was recovered during the excavations in refuse from the building, strongly indicating that the fireplace installation was created for the large scale production of glass vessels.[37]

Caravanserais

There is convincing evidence that the Marwânid Umayyads, especially Hishâm and al-Walîd II (743-44), took a particular interest in building caravanserais, the rural corollary of the khân, in countryside Bilâd al-Shâm. While the growth in caravanserai (and khân) numbers probably began with the extension of trade networks earlier in the eighth century, the size and number of constructs under Hishâm and al-Walîd II would suggest a deliberate policy to stimulate commerce and trade through infrastructure development. Particularly relevant are the massive, free standing caravanserais constructed at strategic locations on the main trade routes, most notably just north of Jericho (Arîhâ), at Qasr al-Hayr East and West, and Kharanah, 65 km ESE of 'Ammân.

---

[37] A.G. Walmsley, "Architecture and Artefacts from Abbasid Fihl: Implications for the Cultural History of Jordan", in M.A. Bakhit and R. Schick eds., *Proceedings of the Fifth International Conference on the History of Bilad al-Sham. Bilad al-Sham during the Abbasid Period*, English and French Section (Amman, 1991), pp. 135-59; Walmsley, "The Social and Economic Regime at Fihl (Pella) and Neighbouring Centres" pp. 249-61; glass: M. O'Hea, "The Glass Industry of the Decapolis", *ARAM* 4 *The Decapolis* (1992), pp. 253-64.

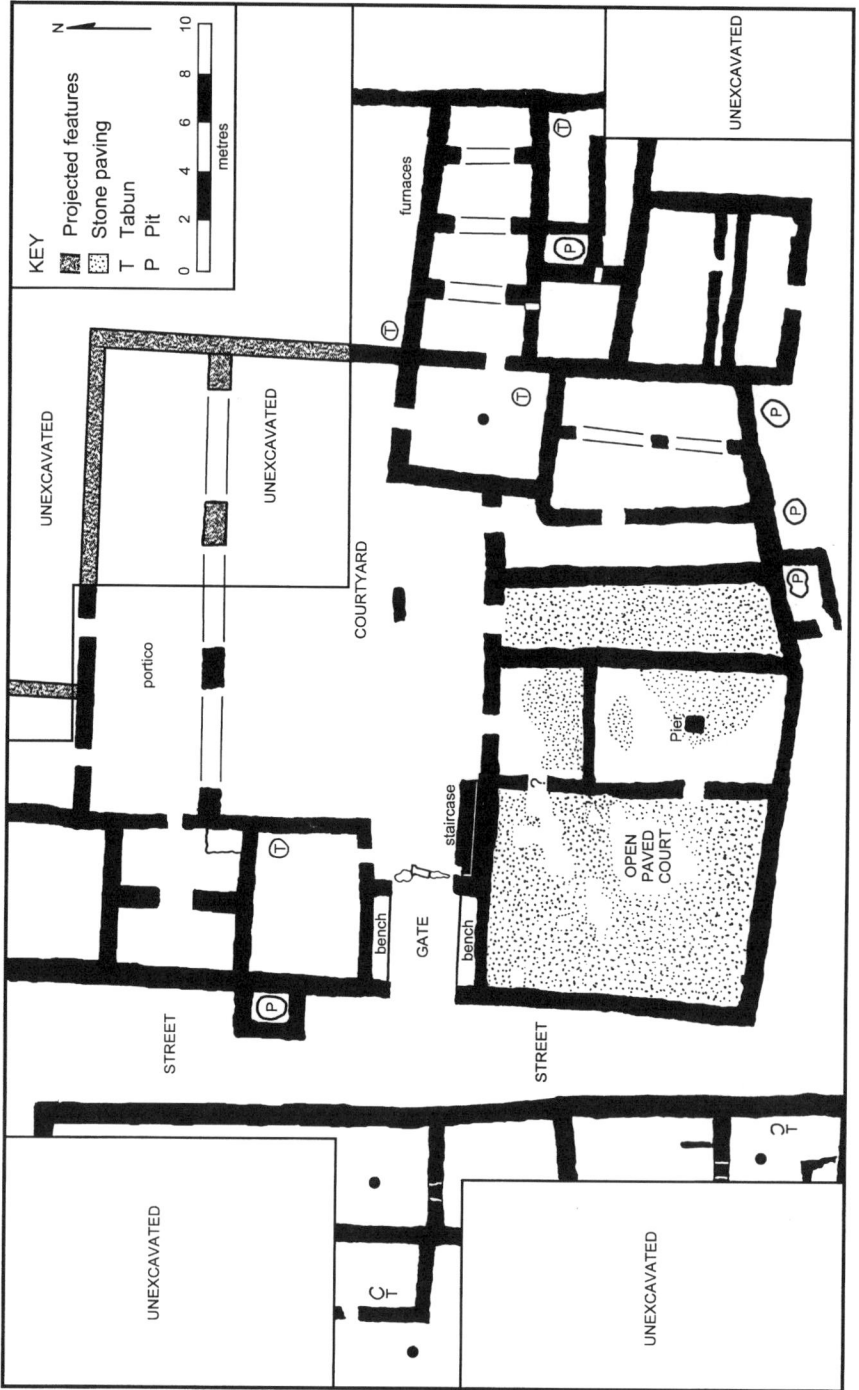

Fig. 3. Plan of the excavations at the 'Abbāsid town centre of Fiḥl (mid-eighth to early tenth centuries).

The caravanserai at Jericho is located immediately north of Umayyad Khirbat al-Mafjar ("Hisham's Palace"), and although clearly an integral part of this palatial complex it has attracted little attention.[38] Set within a perimeter wall of approximately 73 (N-S) by 58 (E-W) m, the caravanserai was built of stone and brick, but today is poorly preserved with most walls reduced to only a few courses (pl. 2). The northern excavated half consists of a large central courtyard flanked by elongated rooms built in symmetrically planned blocks. Each room had only one doorway, which opened out onto the courtyard. Located in the courtyard were a deep stone lined cistern fed by a drain via a settling tank and, in the north-west corner, a broad staircase. Later walls were built over the courtyard, and surface pottery indicated continued occupation until at least the later ninth century. More impressive due to its better state of survival is the caravanserai at Qasr al-Hayr East.[39] Sitting on crossroads between Syria and al-'Irâq, the caravanserai formed an integral part of a large rural development in the *bâdiyah* (steppe lands) east of the cultivation. Other elements of the development included a large residential compound (the *madînah*, or "city"), a seven square km agricultural enclosure and a bath. An inscription reliably attributes the construction of this complex to the caliphate of Hishâm. The caravanserai, an irregular structure measuring approximately 67 by 72 m, boasts a fine towered enclosure wall with a single, wide gateway facing west. Inside the layout shares many features with Jericho. Around a porticoed courtyard, with its drain fed cistern and two staircases, stood banks of deep, high-roofed rooms and, in the north-east and south-east corners, small living quarters identifiable by the room layout and latrines set into the external wall. At Qasr al-Hayr West, where Hishâm also built, the caravanserai is smaller, and features a porticoed central court, staircase and flanking long rooms.[40] An inscription dates the structure to 109 H. (727).

---

[38] Khirbat al-Mafjar, one of the justifiably better known Umayyad sites in Bilâd al-Shâm, was built on the northern outskirts of Jericho, an imperial domain, by al-Walid II (743-44) during the caliphate of his predecessor Hishâm; see: Creswell rev. Allen, *A Short Account of Early Muslim Architecture*, pp. 179-200; R.W. Hamilton, *Khirbat al Mafjar* (Oxford, 1959); R.W. Hamilton, *Walid and His Friends. An Umayyad Tragedy*, Oxford Studies in Islamic Art vol. 6 (Oxford, 1988).

[39] Creswell rev. Allen, *A Short Account of Early Muslim Architecture*, pp. 149-64; O. Grabar, *City in the Desert: Qasr al Hayr East*, Harvard Middle East Monographs vols. 23 & 24 (Cambridge, Mass., 1978).

[40] As at Qasr al-Hayr East the caravanserai is part of a much larger development,

Pl. 2. The caravanserai of Jericho (Arîhâ). General view of the surviving structure – to the left and foreground: storerooms/shops; right background: (unexcavated) section of courtyard.

Caravanserais were also built as independent structures at strategic points on major roads to encourage travel and trade, for instance the "fort" at Khan al-Tuggar on the main route between Tabariyah and al-Ramlah (for the route see below). Actually an Early Islamic caravanserai next to springs, the courtyard building measured 71 by 63 m and featured towered walls and a gateway on the east side.[41] Probably serving a similar function were the many and varied Umayyad buildings in the bâdiyah of Bilâd al-Shâm, collectively known as the *qusûr* ("castles").[42] While built to serve more than one purpose, the qusûr were often conveniently located on established routes to the Arabian Peninsula and would have also facilitated travel, intentionally or not, through providing convenient stopping places in an inhospitable environment. The well-preserved walled building at Kharanah, while military in appearance, functioned primarily as a caravanserai. Probably built under al-Walîd I, it is almost square at 36.5 by 35.45 m, with impressive towered walls and a gateway facing south. Inside numerous rooms were arranged around a small courtyard on two levels. On the ground floor, either side of the entrance passageway, two expansive halls were constructed, almost certainly stables. The Caliph al-Walîd II also appears to have paid considerable attention to improving the routes to the Hijâz, commencing large buildings at al-Mshattâ, al-Tûba and Bâyir. Of these, the unfinished double enclosure at Tûba looks the most likely to be a caravanserai, especially as the complex did not include any imperial features such as a reception hall or lavish decoration (in contrast with, say, Mshattâ). Additionally Tûba's double-compound layout

---

for which see Creswell rev. Allen, *A Short Account of Early Muslim Architecture*, pp. 135-46; D. Schlumberger, "Les Fouilles de Qasr el Heir el Gharbi (1936-38). Rapport Préliminaire", *Syria* 20 (1939), pp. 195-238, 324-73.

[41] Z. Gal, "Khan et-Tuggar. A New Look at a 'Western Survey' Entry", *Palestine Exploration Quarterly* 117 (1985), pp. 69-75.

[42] For qusûr as commercial structures see especially: G. Bisheh, "Qasr Mshash and Qasr 'Ayn al-Sil: Two Umayyad Sites in Jordan", in M.A. Bakhit and R. Schick eds., *Proceedings of the Third Symposium, the Fourth International Conference on the History of Bilad al-Sham. Bilad al-Sham during the Umayyad Period*, English Section, Vol. 2 (Amman, 1989), pp. 81-103; Creswell rev. Allen, *A Short Account of Early Muslim Architecture*; G.R.D. King, "The Distribution of Sites and Routes in the Jordanian and Syrian deserts in the Early Islamic Period", *Seminar for Arabian Studies* 17 (1987), pp. 91-105; G.R.D. King, "The Umayyad Qusur and Related Settlements in Jordan", in *Proceedings of the Third Symposium, the Fourth International Conference on the History of Bilad al-Sham*, English Section, Vol. 2, pp. 71-80. It is most important not to view the qusûr in isolation, social or geographical.

is reminiscent of the khân-like 'Abbâsid period centre of Fihl, although the plan of the former is clearly more symmetrical.[43]

The prominence given to urban shopping complexes, khâns for the production, storage and exchange of goods, and caravanserais to facilitate the movement of people and goods strongly indicates that commerce and the market economy experienced a strong resurgence in Bilâd al-Shâm under the Marwânid Umayyads. The caliphs, especially Hishâm and al-Walîd II, seem to have intentionally built up the infrastructure of trade with the clear purpose of encouraging the movement and exchange of goods. In the following ninth and tenth centuries, after the relocation of the imperial capital to al-ʿIrâq, towns came to depend increasingly on production and trade for their continued viability, once state patronage of projects ceased and government administration became centralised in the major centres.[44]

Seaports and coastal towns (Fig. 1)

Written sources only briefly allude to the development of the coastal towns of Bilâd al-Shâm, especially 'Akkâ, Sûr, 'Asqalân and Atrâbulus (Tripoli in Lebanon), in the first decades after the Islamic conquest and, subsequently, under the Umayyads.[45] The sources give the impression that the sole concern of the early caliphs with the coastal towns was military and strategic, as the Mediterranean coast represented a new frontier zone created by the ongoing conflict with the Byzantines. Little interest, it would seem, was shown in the commercial expansion of harbours until the later ninth century with the advent of Ahmad ibn Tûlûn, the semi-autonomous 'Abbâsid governor of Egypt (868-884).

It is undeniable that the Islamic military provinces of Bilâd al-Shâm, the *ajnâd*, were specifically configured to provide the necessary financial and human resources to defend the coast against Byzantine

---

[43] Kharanah: S.K. Urice, *Qasr Kharana in the Transjordan* (Durham, N.C., 1987); Tuba: Creswell rev. Allen, *A Short Account of Early Muslim Architecture*, pp. 201-11.

[44] Walmsley, *The Administrative Structure and Urban Geography of the Jund of Filastin and the Jund of al-Urdunn*; A.G. Walmsley, "Fatimid, Ayyubid and Mamluk Jordan and the Crusader Interlude", in R. Adams, P. Bienkowski and B. MacDonald eds., *The Archaeology of Jordan* (Sheffield, 2000); Whitcomb, "Islam and the Socio-Cultural Transition of Palestine".

[45] For a straightforward reading of the written sources see: A. Elad (Elʿad), "The Coastal Cities of Palestine during the Early Middle Ages", in L.I. Levine ed., *Jerusalem Cathedra*, vol. 2 (Jerusalem, 1982), pp. 146-67.

raids and attempted occupation. While a mostly military function does not of necessity preclude involvement in commerce and trade, there is little evidence to assess levels of activity in the eighth century. Regretfully the comprehensive archaeological investigation of the seaports of Early Islamic Bilâd al-Shâm has barely begun, although recent excavations at Qaysâriyah, Arsûf and 'Asqalân do indicate a more detailed and complicated socio-economic role for seaports than simply military posts. However earlier work at al-Mina and Seleucea, the two ports of Antioch on the north coast of Bilâd al-Shâm, indicates that a severe reduction in size and function occurred on the north Mediterranean coast during the seventh and eighth centuries.

The compelling evidence from Arsûf, namely the market street, has already been described. The presence of a commercial avenue in Arsûf, one of the lesser important maritime towns of Early Islamic Palestine, indicates that normal urban structures were maintained and even improved in the eighth-early ninth century. Consequently, the coastal centres should be seen as more than just fortified garrisons in the Umayyad and early 'Abbâsid periods. Caesarea to the north of Arsûf, although more greatly affected by a change in circumstances,[46] similarly retained many urban features after the Islamic conquest, with evidence for more than a modicum of trade and production. Large scale excavations of the harbour and the land site of Caesarea have produced a vast body of data on the Early Islamic town, but unfortunately no real consensus has been reached on either the geographical extent or urban character of the later seventh to ninth century settlement.[47] Of major note is the remarkable but commendable "about face" by archaeologists of the Joint Expedition to Caesarea Maritima on the nature and urban impact of the Islamic

---

[46] Most notable was the demotion of Caesarea from the chief metropolis of Palaestina to a district centre of the Jund Filastîn, of which al-Ramlah was the new capital from the early eighth century. Also the conquest of the town was the most protracted in all Palestine, for it was not taken until c. 641 following a long siege, which gave the ruling elite plenty of opportunity to leave by sea.

[47] See the various reports in A. Raban and K.G. Holum eds., *Caesarea Maritima: a Retrospective after Two Millennia* (Leiden, 1996); R.L. Vann ed., *Caesarea Papers: Straton's Tower, Herod's Harbour, and Roman and Byzantine Caesarea* (Ann Arbor, 1992) and the illuminating survey, now a little dated, by K.G. Holum and R.L. Hohlfelder, *King Herod's Dream: Caesarea on the Sea* (New York, 1988). Numerous missions have worked at Caesarea, among which was a large tourism project that cleared a huge section along the sea front. Regrettably, publication and especially analysis has not kept up with the field programme.

conquest. Early reports spoke of a "destruction complete and irre-
trievable", and thereafter "among [the] ruins a few survivors attempted
to clear enough space among the rubble to make life possible". Later
in time "Umayyad settlers ... [were] attracted by the wealth of building material available in the ruined city. They kept the port open
for the shipment of their products".[48] Three significant points can
be gleaned from the early report. Firstly, the excavators believed the
Byzantine town was devastated by the Islamic conquest as evidenced,
they believed, by a heavy destruction layer, and most of its population evicted. Secondly, Umayyad occupation represents the arrival
of new settlers, but the quality of settlement was considerably inferior
("industrial"). Nevertheless (and lastly), the port was still used by the
Umayyad settlers "for the shipment of their products". With hind-
sight it has now become very easy to criticise the simplistic interpretations offered by archaeologists working on major urban sites in
the late 1970s (nearly all of whom came form a Classical or Biblical
background with no professional knowledge of early Islam), but unusually the correction to the Caesarea sequence came from archaeologists working within the Joint Expedition, notably Kenneth Holum
and especially Chérie Lenzen.[49] Discarded are the early seventh century destructions; in their place has emerged a more historically
agreeable image of no significant disruptions to urban life at the time
of the Islamic conquest. Understandably Islamic Caesarea (Qaysâriyah)
was smaller than its Late Antique predecessor in keeping with its

---

[48] L.E. Toombs, "The Stratigraphy of Caesarea Maritima", in R. Moorey and
P. Parr eds., *Archaeology in the Levant* (Warminster, 1978), pp. 223-232; see also R.C.
Wiemken and K.G. Holum, "The Joint Expedition to Caesarea Maritima. Eighth
Season 1979", *Bulletin of the American Schools of Oriental Research* 224 (1981), pp. 27-
52, who speak of a destruction layer resulting from a "Muslim sack" of the city.
[49] Holum and Hohlfelder, *King Herod's Dream*, which contains a still overly dramatic interpretation of early seventh century changes, for instance "the victorious
Muslims very likely craved revenge and therefore unleashed special fury against
Caesarea" – a jaundiced view at odds with just about all reliable literary and archaeological evidence. Considerably more balanced is a later paper by Holum,
"Archaeological Evidence for the Fall of Byzantine Caesarea" which expressly rejects
a Sassanid and Muslim destruction of Caesarea and offers changes in the socio-
economic fabric of the town after the conquest as reasons for its contraction.
Unfortunately the first comment was in a popular book; the second interpretation
only appeared in a learned journal. Holum (in note 2 of the paper) acknowledges
the importance and considerable contribution of a doctoral thesis by C. Lenzen,
Byzantine/Islamic Occupation at Caesarea Maritima as Evidenced through the Pottery (Ph.D.
thesis, Drew University, 1983), an essential work which laid the groundwork for the
more reasoned consideration of Late Antique and Early Islamic Caesarea.

reduced political and economic status, but even so the extent of its geographical contraction is disputable.[50] As Lenzen demonstrated as early as 1983, the stratigraphy and pottery from Caesarea shows a clear continuity of occupation from the Byzantine to Fâtimid periods, with evidence for urban reconstruction under 'Abd al-Malik. After the Islamic conquest the town's orientation turned towards the sea at the expense of the Byzantine street grid, a sure indication that the harbour continued to play a significant role in the life of Qay-sâriyah. Located next to the harbour was a major public facility, comprising a paved court in front of vaults (cf. Bayt Râs), prob-ably a market dating to the Byzantine period. A polygonal building was added in the Umayyad period, and the complex retained this new configuration until the tenth century. At some point the Early Islamic settlement was walled, perhaps more than once as the walls identified as Islamic, which enclose an area equivalent to the Crusader settlement, represent the fortified central town (fortified nucleus?) of Tûlûnid and Fâtimid times and hence, perhaps, not the full extent of the Umayyad and early 'Abbâsid town.[51]

While Caesarea seemingly experienced a cognisable diminution in status and size after the Islamic conquest—but even then was amply populated and equipped—other ports on the east Mediterranean lit-toral of Palestine and Lebanon were not as severely effected. After, it would appear, only a short period of adjustment a line of coastal sites led by 'Asqalân, 'Akkâ, Sûr and Atrâbulus grew into maritime centres of some note. Realising the importance of the coastal sites

---

[50] Quite possibly the absolute settlement size of Byzantine Caesarea has been exaggerated, as almost certainly not all of the land within the circumference wall was built up, while equally Islamic Qaysâriyah could have been underestimated, as suburbs may have existed outside of the Tûlûnid and 'Abbâsid town wall. In any case, the value of such comparisons, based on ill-defined absolutes, is highly suspect.

[51] Lenzen, *Byzantine/Islamic Occupation at Caesarea Maritima as Evidenced through the Pottery*, pp. 120-94, 423-15; L.I. Levine and E. Netzer, *Excavations at Caesarea Maritima 1975, 1976, 1979 – final report*, Qedem vol. 21 (Jerusalem, 1986), pp. 64-65, 184-86, where the reorientation of the town towards the sea is quite marked; also Holum and Hohlfelder, *King Herod's Dream*, pp. 208-11; Holum, "Archaeological Evidence for the Fall of Byzantine Caesarea". For the continued functioning of the harbour in the ninth century see Raban and Holum eds., *Caesarea Maritima*, pp. 664-66. In the tenth century a ship from Egypt put in at Qaysâriyah due to inclement weather, which suggests that the harbour still afforded a level of protection worth seeking (S. Goitein, *A Mediterranean Society: The Jewish Communities of the Arab World as Portrayed in the Documents of the Cairo Geniza. Volume 1: Economic Foundations*, (Berkeley, 1967), p. 321).

the Umayyads, especially Mu'âwiyah (first as governor of Bilâd al-
Shâm and then caliph), 'Abd al-Malik and Hishâm, developed their
urban infrastructure and settled migrants from other regions. The
stationing of the Umayyad navy and its workshops in 'Akkâ and,
later, Sûr would have brought particular benefits to these towns. The
extent of depopulation of the coastal towns seemingly varied from
place to place, as one source talks of "many Greeks" remaining in
Sûr.[52] The settlement of new migrants in the coastal towns may have
been desirable partly to replace people who had left and partly to
counterbalance to the number of "Greeks" that remained. The importance of this strategy was reinforced following rebellions and the temporary occupation by the Byzantines of a number of major coastal
towns, including 'Asqalân and Atrâbulus. On another occasion a
"Greek patrician (re?)settled in Atrâbulus during the caliphate of
'Abd al-Malik, but revolted two years later and after killing the governor fled (back?) to Byzantium". Later he was captured travelling
with many ships to a "Muslim coast town", and executed.[53] Interestingly
his movements sound very much like those of a trader between
Byzantium and the Muslim coast of al-Shâm.

Antioch, the urban "basket case" of the Late Antique East, similarly shows modest continuity in the Early Islamic period, especially
in its commercial heart. Antioch's well documented decline began
in the century before the Islamic conquest, when the town suffered
from a series of calamitous events including earthquakes, fire, plague
and conquest.[54] Hence its significance, like its size, was much reduced
by the time of the Islamic conquest. Under Islamic hegemony (the
town was retaken by the Byzantines in 969), Antioch was assigned
a minor political and military role, yet excavations along the main

---

[52] Al-Baladhuri, *The Origins of the Islamic State*, p. 180. "Hishâm ibn al-Laith from
our *sheikhs* who said, 'When we took up our abode in Tyre and the littoral, there
were Arab troops and many Greeks already there. Later, people from other regions
came and settled with us, and that was the case with all the sea-coast of Syria.'"
See also p. 196, where Muslims are settled in conquered towns to prevent revolt.
Also to be taken into account is the state of the coastal towns before the Islamic
conquest; Kennedy ("The Last Century of Byzantine Syria" pp. 147-48, 156, 168-
69, 180-82) argues for a significant reduction in urban life and prosperity at the
end of the sixth century. If so, the extent of any improvement in the seventh and
especially eighth century is even more significant.
[53] Al-Baladhuri, *The Origins of the Islamic State*, p. 195.
[54] See especially: Kennedy, "The Last Century of Byzantine Syria"; Kennedy,
"Antioch: from Byzantium to Islam and back again"; Foss, "Syria in Transition,
A.D. 550-750" at pp. 190-97.

colonnaded street revealed a significant level of urban continuity until about 800. Thereafter the urban area of Antioch contracted considerably. "After the disasters of the second half of the sixth century" Kennedy writes, "Antioch survived and thrived. It is true that it was much smaller than the classical city at its zenith . . . There is also evidence that, while the Early Islamic period was one of modest rebuilding along the main streets, the ninth and especially tenth centuries represented the nadir of the city's fortunes".[55] The very fragmentary nature of the archaeological evidence from Antioch makes it impossible to understand the economic background to this urban history, but it is no coincidence that the decline of the town coincided with the powerful ascendancy of Aleppo into the new political and commercial hub of north Syria.

Excavations at al-Mina, the natural harbour of Antioch some 20 km downstream at the mouth of the Orontes, and Seleucea, Antioch's second (but artificial) harbour to the north, present a less positive view of economic continuity.[56] Seleucea, the principal port of Antioch in Classical times, underwent a "gradual and peaceful" decline in the latter half of the sixth century, becoming "effectively depopulated before the Arab conquests". Similarly, the perceived absence of seventh and eighth century material at al-Mina was taken to mean the port was abandoned, and only reoccupied with the expansion of land trade to the east in the mid-ninth century. By the tenth century, the site had regained importance and the presence of imported glazed ceramics reveals extensive trade with Mesopotamia. However considering the age of the excavations, the limited area opened up, the scanty nature of the relevant deposits, and the brevity of the reports, the seventh and eighth century hiatus is certainly not proven. A more plausible scenario for al-Mina is the continued utilisation of the Byzantine structures until the mid-ninth century, at which time the economic revival of the north Mediterranean coast promoted a substantial rebuilding of the port.

The significance of maritime trade to the economy of Early Islamic Bilâd al-Shâm is graphically demonstrated by the foundation of a new seaside settlement at Aylah (al-'Aqabah) at the head of the Gulf of 'Aqabah on the Red Sea. Built adjacent to the Roman-Byzantine

---

[55] Kennedy, "Antioch: from Byzantium to Islam and back again", p. 195.
[56] Al-Mina: A. Lane, *Medieval Finds at Al Mina in North Syria* (Oxford, 1938); Seleucea: Kennedy, "The Last Century of Byzantine Syria", pp. 154-55.

township on empty land between the town and the coastline, Aylah rapidly became an active party in the Red Sea and Indian Ocean trade.[57] Commerce was also encouraged by the passage of the annual Pilgrims' Caravan from Egypt to the Hijâz. According to the site's excavator, Donald Whitcomb, Aylah could have been founded as early as the caliphate of 'Uthman (644-656). However this early date has not been generally accepted, and the architectural traditions and pro-expansion economic policies of the Marwânid period suggests that the early eighth century is a much more plausible date for Aylah's foundation. The new town was rectangular in plan, and delineated by hefty circuit walls measuring 170 by 140 m (fig. 4). The walls were symmetrical, with towers and a centrally located gateway in each wall. The gates were joined by axial streets lined with shops, and at the intersection of the streets stood a tetrapylon, as at 'Anjar. By the early 'Abbâsid period (750-850) Aylah was a prosperous port. Excavations at different locations within and out-side of the walls have shown that during this century many existing buildings were refurbished and new structures built. Notably Aylah's congregational mosque was enlarged, forcing a western deflection of the north-south axial street, and a new beach side sûq constructed along the outside face of the town's south wall. In addition the neigh-bouring Roman-Byzantine town continued to be occupied and refur-bished throughout the early 'Abbâsid period. Not until the tenth century was the earlier town substantially deserted, which coincides with the widespread use of church *spolia* within walled Aylah.

The port of Aylah is an early manifestation of the major role of Indian Ocean trade in the economy of the Middle Islamic world. The town flourished in the eighth and ninth centuries, but there-after suffered a series of major setbacks. Particularly damaging was the political fragmentation of Bilâd al-Shâm from the tenth cen-tury, a series of natural calamities, and the increasing domination of the Indian Ocean trade by al-'Irâq and Egypt. The construction of large and wealthy imperial cities in al-'Irâq, notably Baghdâd, the

---

[57] For 'Abbâsid Aylah see especially: D.S. Whitcomb, *Ayla: Art and History in the Islamic port of Aqaba* (Chicago, 1994); Whitcomb, "The Misr of Ayla"; D.S. Whitcomb, "A Street and the Beach at Ayla: the Fall Season of Excavations at 'Aqaba, 1992", *Annual of the Department of Antiquities of Jordan* 39 (1995), pp. 499-507; and for Indian Ocean trade generally see: K.N. Chaudhuri, *Asia before Europe: Economy and Civilisation in the Indian Ocean from the Rise of Islam to 1750* (Cambridge, 1990); G.F. Hourani, *Ancient Seafaring in the Indian Ocean in Ancient and Early Medieval Times* (Beirut, 1963).

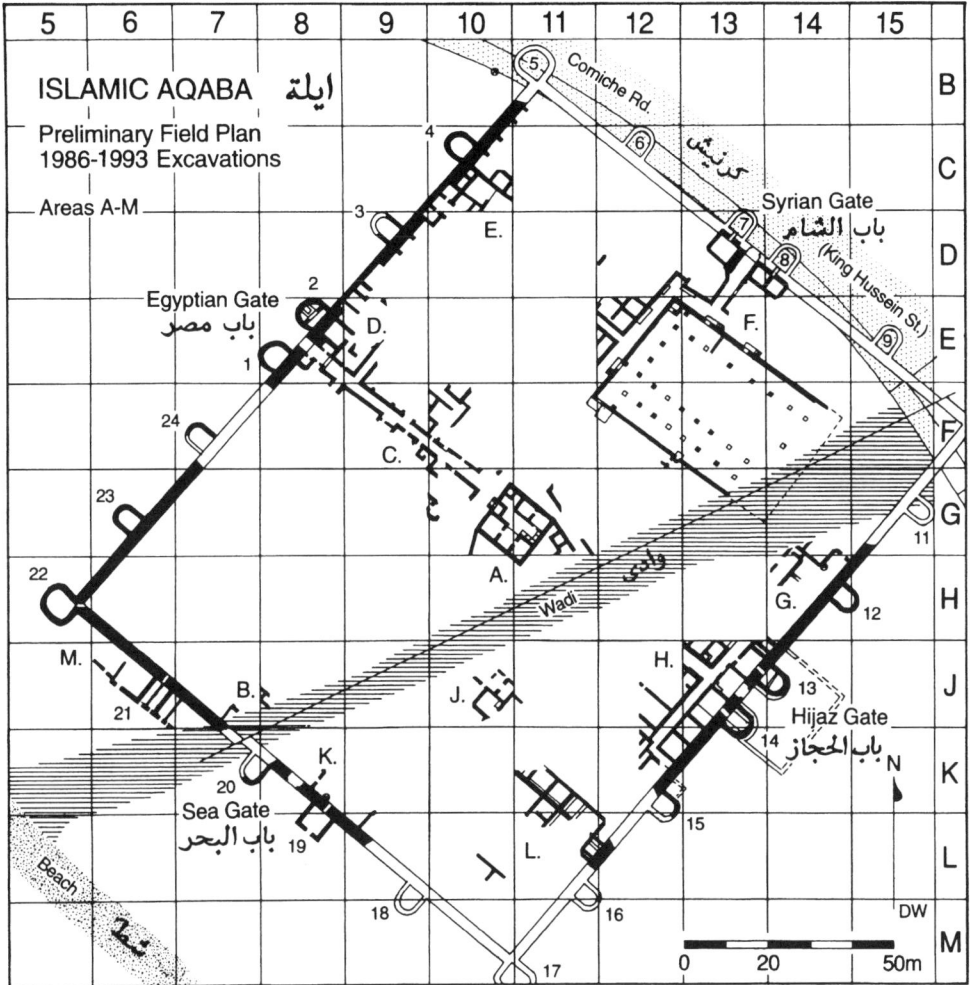

Fig. 4. Plan of Early Islamic Aylah (from D.S. Whitcomb, *Ayla: art and history in the Islamic port of Aqaba* (Chicago, 1994), p. 11).

regularisation of routes along the Euphrates valley to the Mediterranean, and the forging of direct sea routes through the Arabian Gulf to China and East Africa under Hârûn al-Rashîd (786-809) created a vibrant long distance trade network without geographical or commercial precedent. In the next century, and especially with the rise of the Fâtimids in Egypt (from 969), Cairo took a pivotal role in combining the Red Sea-Indian Ocean trade route with renewed contacts across the Mediterranean Sea, the latter initiated by fledgling maritime states on the Italian peninsula.[58] The greatly changed political and economic environment brought about by these changes marginalised tenth century Aylah, and its diminished status is reflected in the much reduced size of the settlement and the poorer quality of its architecture.

Considerably more difficult to assess, due to the scarcity of data, is the social and economic health of the Mediterranean ports in the eighth century, and especially the role of sea trade in their economies. Unlike at ʿAqabah, later occupation at some of the major coastal sites has largely obscured or destroyed the evidence for Umayyad and early ʿAbbâsid settlement, for instance at ʿAsqalân. Caesarea, dependent on an artificial harbour, can not be thought of as having a typical settlement history for the coast. However, the available archaeological and literary evidence would indicate that the ports of southern Bilâd al-Shâm did enjoy modest prosperity. Any disruption at the time of the Islamic conquest was followed by a gradual recovery, in part due to their military role but also the persistence of commercial exchange with Egypt as seen, for instance, in the recovery of Egyptian amphorae from a mid-eighth century context at Pella (see below). This positive reading of the evidence finds support in the urban histories of other towns on the Mediterranean littoral, from major centres, particularly Antioch and al-Ramlah, to smaller

---

[58] A treatment of trade expansion in the Indian Ocean lies geographically and mostly chronologically outside of this paper, and has been well summarised from an archaeological perspective in R. Hodges and D. Whitehouse, *Mohammed, Charlemagne & the Origins of Europe* (London, 1989). Hodges and Whitehouse place particular emphasis on establishing the date of direct contact with south China as revealed by the excavations at the trading port of Sîrâf on the Iranian coast of the Arabian Gulf. For a numismatic perspective on Sîrâf, particularly during its heyday in the tenth century, see N.M. Lowick, "Trade Patterns on the Persian Gulf in the Light of Recent Coin Evidence", in D.K. Kouymjian ed., *Near Eastern Numismatics, Iconography, Epigraphy and History. Studies in Honor of George C. Miles* (Beirut, 1974), pp. 319-333.

sites such as Tell Qaymun (Yoqne'am) and Tell Michal.[59] If, as it is suggested here, the Mediterranean ports did post modest gains in the eighth century, then the well documented improvements made by the Tûlûnid (late ninth century) and Fâtimid rulers of Egypt would have been contingent upon, and facilitated by, the considerable groundwork laid down in Umayyad and 'Abbâsid times.

Urban links: the intra- and inter-regional road network

The elevation of Mu'âwiyah to the caliphate in 660 and the promotion of Damascus, his adopted city, as the capital of the expanding Islamic state placed this town at the centre of an extensive road network. The network was maintained by the *Dîwân al-Barîd*, the Department of Posts and Intelligence, a major ministry in the Umayyad and 'Abbâsid governments (its budget was only exceeded by expenditure on the Holy Cities and the defence of the frontier).[60] The *Barîd* used the network to transmit orders and all types of information between central government, provincial capitals and district towns. However, the roads not only served the bureaucratic needs of a growing imperial administration. By offering greater security, they also encouraged trade including the movement of luxury items to satisfy the growing requirements of the Muslim elite. Additionally the roads facilitated the transport of construction materials for new building projects in the capital, the provincial centres and places in between.

In contrast to the obvious importance of the road network to government in the Early Islamic period, only minimal archaeological and epigraphical research has been conducted into its precise structure and role in Umayyad and 'Abbâsid times. The major source of information remains a select group of Arabic geographical works

---

[59] Yoqne'am: A. Ben-Tor, M. Avissar and Y. Portugali, *Yoqne'am I. The Late Periods* (Jerusalem, 1996). Ramlah: highlighted by ninth century Islamic sources, Al-Baladhuri, *The Origins of the Islamic State*, pp. 143-144; Ibn Khurradadhbih, *Kitâb al-Masâlik wa'l-Mamâlik*, Bibliotheca Geographicorum Arabicorum vol. 6 (Leiden, 1889), pp. 78-79, 117; al-Ya'qûbî, *Kitâb al-Buldân*, pp. 116, 328; Qudâmah, *Kitâb al-Kharâj*, Bibliotheca Geographicorum Arabicorum vol. 6 (Leiden, 1889), pp. 219, 228; selected archaeological works: M. Rosen-Ayalon and A. Eitan, *Ramla Excavations. Finds from the VIIIth Century C.E.* (Jerusalem, 1969); M. Sharon, "*Waqf* inscription from Ramla c. 300/912-13", *Bulletin of the School of Oriental and African Studies* 60 (1997), pp. 100-108; Whitcomb "The Misr of Ayla", pp. 281-83.

[60] Briefly see: Hitti, *History of the Arabs*, 322-25, with map; D. Sourdel, "Barid", *Encyclopaedia of Islam, New Ed.*, vol. 1 (Leiden, 1960), pp. 1045-46.

dating to the ninth and tenth century, but these provide only a basic skeleton of major routes. Mostly the geographers described the road system as it functioned in the early 'Abbâsid caliphate, and only occasionally were features of the Umayyad structure described. Further details about selected routes belonging to the Umayyad road system have been preserved in the occasional epigraphic source, specifically milestones. Taken together the sources communicate the existence of three primary highways supplemented by numerous secondary routes, and reveal a road network firmly focused on the major towns of Bilâd al-Shâm.

a. *The great Post Road* (Ṭarîq al-Barîd)

The great "Post Road" was the major highway of Bilâd al-Shâm, transversing the region from north-east to south-west. Although the focus of the road changed with the overthrow of the Umayyads and the transfer of the Islamic capital from Damascus to al-'Irâq, the importance of this interregional highway was undiminished in the second half of the eighth century.

From Damascus the post road crossed the provinces of al-Urdunn and Filastîn, passing through their capitals of Tabariyah and al-Ramlah respectively, before following the Mediterranean coast to reach Egypt and its capital of al-Fustât. The way station at Khan al-Tuggar, built between Tabariyah and al-Lajjûn (Legio, a former Roman legionary camp) in the Esdraelon Plain (the *Marj ibn 'Amir*), would have been one of many that dotted the post road. Twelve stations are indicated between Tabariyah and al-Ramlah, with an average distance between each of nearly ten km. Northwards from Damascus the road passed through Hims and Qinnasrîn, both capitals of provinces with the same names, before continuing to al-Raqqah, capital of the Jazîrah (north-west Mesopotamia), and then al-'Irâq. In the 'Abbâsid period, following the foundation of Baghdâd, the post road through Bilâd al-Shâm remained important, as it linked the new Islamic capital and al-Raqqah to al-Fustât, one of the major regional capitals of the Empire. The written sources mostly refer to this structure, when the road also passed through Aleppo, which took shape during the second quarter of the eighth century.

b. *The coastal route*

The major Mediterranean coast road of Classical times that linked Antioch with Alexandria, the two great cities of the Hellenistic east, was replicated in part during the Early Islamic period although its standing, which waned with the falling fortunes of both centres, was secondary to the *Tarîq al-Barîd*. Nevertheless the government administrator and geographer Ibn Khurdâdhbih (d. 913) paid particular attention to this route.[61] His interest can be attributed to the speedy promotion of al-Raqqah, strategically located on the Euphrates River in the Jazîrah, by the early 'Abbâsid caliphs. In 771-72, the Caliph al-Mansûr (d. 775) began a new suburb for the town named al-Râfiqa (the "companion"), while Hârûn al-Rashîd (d. 809), who resided in al-Raqqah between 796 and 808, further enlarged it by constructing ten square kilometres of palaces.[62] By the early ninth century only Baghdâd was larger than al-Raqqah/Râfiqa, and like Baghdâd the influx of state funding created an economic powerhouse of centralised production, consumption and commerce, the benefits of which radiated throughout the region (see further below).

Returning to the coast road, beginning in al-Raqqah the road headed westwards to the Mediterranean coast, passing through Aleppo on the way. Thereafter the route followed the coast down to Atrâbulus, Bayrût, Saydâ (Sidon), Sûr (Tyre) 'Akkâ, Qaysâriyah, Arsûf, 'Asqalân and Ghazzah. The route was especially significant as it linked each of the major coastal ports with its neighbour, and served not only administrative and military functions but also supported commercial exchange.

c. *Roads from Damascus to Makkah*

From the earliest days, the road from Damascus to Makkah was critical to the Islamic State for it connected Madinah, home of the Orthodox caliphs (until 656), with Damascus, capital of Bilâd al-Shâm. The prominence of the route was enhanced by the religious role it served. Each year Muslim faithful would travel from Damascus and Jerusalem via 'Ammân to the Hijâz on the pilgrimage (*Hajj*), which is obligatory for all adult Muslims of sound health and sufficient

---

[61] Ibn Khurradadhbih, *al-Masâlik*, pp. 97-98, 71. For the fading fortunes of Antioch see above, while for Alexandria see the recent and valuable study by A.L. Udovitch, "Medieval Alexandria: Some Evidence from the Cairo Genizah Documents", *Alexandria and Alexandrianism*, J. Paul Getty Museum (Malibu, Ca, 1996), pp. 273-84.

[62] Creswell rev. Allen, *A Short Account of Early Muslim Architecture*, 243-48, 270-75; M. Meinecke, "Raqqa on the Euphrates: Recent Excavations at the Residence of Harun er-Rashid", *The Near East in Antiquity* 2 (1991), pp. 17-32; M. Meinecke, "al-Rakka", *Encyclopaedia of Islam, New Ed.*, vol. 8 (Leiden, 1995), pp. 410-14.

means. Thus the *Darb al-Hajj* served both a religious and an administrative function. Under the Umayyads, with Damascus as the capital of the Islamic empire, the road took on a major administrative
role, with three alternate routes to the Hijâz south of ʿAmmân.[63] Its
commercial functions are, however, unrecorded, but considering the
great wealth that flowed to Makkah and Madinah in the form of
generous state pensions the route probably carried large amounts of
basic and luxury goods. This trade must, in part, have been a major
factor behind the considerable prosperity witnessed in the ʿAmmân
district (the Balqâʾ) during the Early Islamic period, especially the
eighth century.[64]

d. *Regional routes*

Trade and the presence of local markets would apparently explain
the inclusion of some regional roads, but not others, of Bilâd al-
Shâm in the geographical sources. The roads emanating from Zughar,
located south of the Dead Sea, is an interesting and informative
example. Zughar, Byzantine Zoara, was a busy market town and
renowned for its dates and indigo.[65] From Aylah a road headed
northwards along the desolate Wâdî ʿArabah (a journey of about 4
days, with conveniently placed water sources on the way), and after

---

[63] Qurʾân 2.196, 3.97. For an analysis of the route, see A. Musil, *The Northern
Hegaz. A Topographical Itinerary*, Oriental Explorations and Studies vol. 1 (New York,
1926); A. Musil, *Arabia Deserta*, Oriental Explorations and Studies vol. 2 (New York,
1927); G.R.D. King, "The Distribution of Sites and Routes in the Jordanian and
Syrian deserts in the Early Islamic Period", *Seminar for Arabian Studies* 17 (1987), pp.
91-105 for the three routes south of ʿAmmân.

[64] The archaeological evidence, from isolated monuments and farmsteads to large
urban centres, is prolific. See, for a small sample, Creswell rev. Allen, *A Short Account
of Early Muslim Architecture* (the *qusûr*); King, "The Umayyad Qusur and Related
Settlements in Jordan"; MacAdam, "Settlements and Settlement Patterns in Northern
and Central Transjordania, *ca* 550-*ca* 750"; A. Northedge, *Studies on Roman and Islamic
ʿAmman. The Excavations of Mrs C-M Bennett and Other Investigations* (Oxford, 1992);
M. Piccirillo, "The Activity of the Mosaicists of the Diocese of Madaba at the time
of Bishop Sergius in the Second Half of the Sixth Century A.D.", in K. ʿAmr,
F. Zayadine and M. Zaghloul eds., *Studies in the History and Archaeology of Jordan*, vol. 5
(Amman, 1995), pp. 391-98; R. Schick, "Palestine in the Early Islamic Period".

[65] The markets and the cultivation of dates and indigo are mentioned by the tenth
century geographers, but clearly these activities are much earlier in date; in the Madaba
Mosaic Zughar is depicted as a walled settlement with date palms. See the descriptions in Ibn Hawqal, *Configuration de la Terre (Kitab Surat al-Ard)*, trans. J.H. Kramers
and G. Wiet (Paris/Beyrouth, 1964); al-Muqaddasî (al-Maqdisî), *The Best Divisions
for the Knowledge of the Regions (Ahsan al-Taqasim fi Maʿrifat al-Aqalim)*, trans. B. Collins
and M. al-Tai (Reading, 1994), p. 161, who describes Zughar as "little Basra".

reaching Zughar separated into three main branches. Two climbed out of the Jordan Rift Valley, one north-westwards towards Habrâ (Hebron) and Jerusalem, the other north-eastwards to 'Ammân and Damascus. The third stayed in the valley and passed along the western shore of the Dead Sea to Jericho (equipped with a khân, above) and Nâbulus. A fourth route, also to the eastern Highlands, struck south-eastwards to Adhruh and the Pilgrims' road. The three northern routes linked Jerusalem, Nâbulus and Damascus with the commodity markets of Aylah and Zughar, and accordingly would have fulfilled a primarily commercial function.

Although other regional routes were seemingly more diverse in their function, they nevertheless would have promoted commodity trading and the movement of merchants. The elevation of Jerusalem as a political and religious centre offers a clear example. The first Umayyad caliph, al-Mu'âwiyah, perhaps intended to make Jerusalem his capital; certainly he was crowned there. The construction of the Dome of the Rock and the al-'Aqsâ mosque (first phase) by 'Abd al-Malik on the former site of the Jewish temple (the *Haram al-Sharîf*) was accompanied by an upgrade to roads from Damascus and Ludd, Filastîn's capital before al-Ramlah. Milestones were erected in 705 to commemorate work at 'Afîq (the pass into the Jordan Valley east of Lake Tiberias), on the Jericho-Jerusalem road and the al-Ramlah-Jerusalem road. Under al-Walîd I a massive palatial complex was erected south of the Haram. Throughout the Early Islamic period (and, of course, until this day) individuals travelled to Jerusalem to pray at its holy places, especially on the Haram. Prospective pilgrims, both local and from outside Bilâd al-Shâm, could prepare themselves for the *hajj* while residing there. The result was a vibrant and cosmopolitan town with, undoubtedly, markets and a demand for traded goods to match.[66]

---

[66] On the status of Jerusalem, see A. Elad, *Medieval Jerusalem and Islamic Worship. Holy Places, Ceremonies, Pilgrimage* (Leiden, 1995); on the monuments Creswell rev. Allen, *A Short Account of Early Muslim Architecture*, pp. 18-42, 73-82, and Elad *Medieval Jerusalem and Islamic Worship*; on the milestones, recently: A. Elad, "The Southern Golan in the Early Muslim Period. The Significance of Two Newly Discovered Milestones of 'Abd al-Malik", *Der Islam* 76 (1999), pp. 33-88.

The urban environment and road networks: an impetus to trade

The archaeological and written sources demonstrate conclusively that an infrastructure conducive to trade—large, well organised and numerous towns and an efficient communications network—existed throughout Bilâd al-Shâm from the later seventh and into the eighth century. During this period, the region was part of an extensive Islamic empire possessing a common currency and language. Policy decisions by the ruling elite actively promoted the market economy, as demonstrated by the construction of new shop-lined streets, the expansion of existing markets, and the construction of khâns and caravanserais. Neither was the upkeep of seaports neglected. At least a modest level of activity can be argued for the harbours and coastal towns of the Mediterranean, although only for the Red Sea port of Aylah does the eighth century appear vibrant and expansionary with trade as the primary catalyst.

In practical terms, the movement of merchants with their merchandise between towns and regions was greatly assisted by the presence of a developed road network. A good example of merchants travelling along established routes is preserved in the geographical work of Ibn Khurdâdhbih. Although the use of the state-maintained Barîd network was generally restricted to official business, Ibn Khurdâdhbih recounts how the post-road route through Bilâd al-Shâm was used by multilingual Slav merchants while journeying to the Far East from North Africa.[67] After leaving al-Fustât the merchants followed the route to al-Ramlah and Damascus before continuing to al-ʿIrâq. The post road and subsidiary routes clearly offered a convenient travel network for the merchants. Not only did it directly link the major market towns of the Empire; the network also offered a safer and more economical way between the main centres of population.

The infrastructure of commerce and exchange was a standard feature of the urban character of eighth century Bilâd al-Shâm. The archaeological evidence would strongly indicate that many towns were equipped with markets, and these were economically linked by an elaborate road network. Major highways connected Bilâd al-Shâm with Egypt and al-ʿIrâq, greatly facilitating the potential for trade. As these roads, in part, served an official function, their upkeep and security was ensured by the Islamic State. It can be argued that

---

[67] Ibn Khurradadhbih, *al-Masâlik*, pp. 154-55.

the continuing urban viability of a town in Bilâd al-Shâm after the mid-eighth century had much to do with the strength of its market economy, enhanced in some centres (e.g. Jerusalem, Hebron) by the growth of religious pilgrimage. Another crucial and related factor was a veritable explosion in urban-based manufacturing industries and developments in the rural economy, issues to which we can now turn.

3. *Towns, the rural hinterland and the production of tradable goods: the objects of trade*

Urban industry

The economies of many towns in Early Islamic Bilâd al-Shâm became increasingly focused on the manufacture of tradable commodities, especially in the eighth century. Often the impact of this industrialisation on the urban environment was considerable, especially in smaller towns. Industrial complexes, large and small in scale, were commonly inserted into the existing infrastructure, often at the expense of public space (footpaths, streets and plazas) and by commandeering defunct civic monuments (from the compounds of pagan temples to bathhouses). Most of these new industries were primarily localised in their outlook and, almost exclusively, only utilised the limited range of primary materials procurable in the immediate district. However, with the main centres, such as al-Raqqah, the separation of domestic and industrial activities was ensured by the construction of independent manufacturing quarters, which placed potentially dangerous and often polluting industries outside and upwind of the town. The archaeological evidence for industry, which predominantly comes from a greater concentration of excavations in south Bilâd al-Shâm, obviously favours those enterprises that left tangible and legible remains, for example pottery manufacture, glass working, fabric and metal working.

Excavations at Baysân have uncovered particularly explicit evidence of an influx of industrial activities into the heart of the Classical town.[68] Prevalent were installations for the production of pottery.

---

[68] See the earlier discussion on "Market Streets and the *Sûq* Question" (above), and R. Bar-Nathan and G. Mazor, "City Center (South) and Tel Iztabba Area; Excavations of the Antiquities Authority Expedition", *Excavations and Surveys in Israel*

Preparation areas, a storeroom and ten updraft kilns were uncovered within and in front of the defunct Roman theatre. A network of pipes and channels provided water to the factory, which produced a large range of domestic vessels and lamps. Two kilns were found with their contents intact, and great quantities of wasters, lamp moulds and unbaked pottery were recovered. This was not the only potting installation in Baysân. A large building and additional kilns were found within the compound of the former "Byzantine agora", kilns were also found inside the amphitheatre to the south, and elsewhere. Ceramic production was also practised at Jarash on a commercial scale.[69] For instance major potting complexes dating to the Umayyad period were excavated in and around the deserted North Theatre and in the forecourt of the Temple of Artemis. Later, in the 'Abbâsid period (ninth century), three kilns producing cooking pots, moulded lamps, "cut ware" bowls and red painted bowls and cups were inserted into an abandoned Umayyad period house on the western arm of the south decumanus. Earlier in date, and intended to produce a very different product, were the kilns of an industrial complex excavated at Aylah.[70] Wasters recovered around the kilns

---

11: The Bet She'an Excavation Project (1989-1991) (Jerusalem, 1993), pp. 33-51; G. Foerster and Y. Tsafrir, "City Center (North)"; Y. Tsafrir and G. Foerster, "From Scythopolis to Baysân – changing concepts of Urbanism", in G.R.D. King and A. Cameron eds., *The Byzantine and Early Islamic Near East 2. Land Use and Settlement Patterns* (Princeton, 1994), pp. 95-115; Tsafrir and Foerster, "Urbanism at Scythopolis-Bet Shean in the Fourth to Seventh Centuries".

[69] See especially W. Ball, J. Bowsher, I. Kehrberg, A. Walmsley and P. Watson, "The North Decumanus and North Tetrapylon at Jerash: An Archaeological and Architectural Report", in F. Zayadine ed., *Jerash Archaeological Project 1, 1981-1983* (Amman, 1986), pp. 351-409; M. Gawlikowski, "A Residential Area by the South Decumanus", in *Jerash Archaeological Project 1, 1981-1983*, pp. 107-136; M. Gawlikowski, "Céramiques byzantines et omayyades de Jerash", in H. Meyza and J. Mlynarczyk eds., *Hellenistic and Roman Pottery in the Eastern Mediterranean – Advances in Scientific Studies. Acts of the II Nieborów pottery workshop* (Nieborów, 1995), pp. 83-86; M. Gawlikowski, "Arab Lamp-makers in Jarash: Christian and Muslim", in K. 'Amr, F. Zayadine and M. Zaghloul eds., *Studies in the History and Archaeology of Jordan*, vol. 5 (Amman, 1995), pp. 669-72; R. Pierobon, "Gerasa 1: Report of the Italian Archaeological Expedition to Jerash, Campaigns 1977-1981. Sanctuary of Artemis: Soundings in the Temple-Terrace, 1978-1980", *Mesopotamia* 18-19 (1983-1984), pp. 85-111; R. Pierobon, "The Italian Activity Within the Jerash Archaeological Project, 1982-83. Archaeological Research in the Sanctuary of Artemis. 2: the Area of the Kilns", in *Jerash Archaeological Project 1, 1981-83*, pp. 185-87; J. Schaefer and R.K. Falkner, "An Umayyad Potters' Complex in the North Theatre, Jerash", *Jerash Archaeological Project 1, 1981-83*, pp. 411-35.

[70] A. Melkawi, K. 'Amr and D.S. Whitcomb, "The Excavation of Two Seventh Century Pottery Kilns at Aqaba", *Annual of the Department of Antiquities of Jordan* 38 (1994), pp. 447-68. The seventh century date is curious; associated ceramics suggest no earlier than the mid-eighth.

included cooking pots, casseroles and water juglets, but the major product were amphorae (the significance of these is discussed further below). Direct evidence for potters' workshops has also been found at al-Ramlah, Tabariyah, and Caesarea. The Caesarea kilns, of 'Abbâsid-Tûlûnid date, produced lamps and decorated cream ware bowls, cups and "flasks" (water bottles).[71] Not surprisingly al-Raqqah was host to a large ceramics industry.[72]

Glass blowing, utilising the copious sand deposits along the east Mediterranean shore, was also practised at industrial levels. Crucibles, slag and ingots are the clearest evidence for glass making, and some or all of these elements have been reported from al-Raqqah, Caesarea, Baysân, Tiberias, Jarash and Pella (Fihl). The Pella workshop, of 'Abbâsid date, was located in the post-earthquake khân, and is represented by a row of furnaces in the central court and glass waste.[73] Although glass ingots had to be brought c. 70 km inland from the coast, the attraction of Pella was its fuel, presumably the hot-burning refuse from olive pressing. Elegant and technically very proficient free blown beakers, either plain or with "nipped" decoration, footed bowls, pinched bowls and a variety of flasks were the products of the Pella glassblowers.

The growing industrialisation of town centres is manifest in the construction of new installations devoted to the manufacture of other commodities, although the evidence is less comprehensive. At Baysân, the intact domed hall of the eastern bath was converted into a major industrial complex in the Umayyad period. The hall was subdivided into four rooms, each with six pools and a plastered workspace, around a central court. Channels and drains feed water into and out of the pools. The installation was probably devoted to the preparation of flax for linen production, a commodity for which Baysân was renowned, and survived until destroyed in the earthquake(s) of the mid eighth century.[74] At Caesarea the discovery of iron slag,

---

[71] Holum and Hohlfelder, *King Herod's Dream*, pp. 231-41.

[72] Volumes of kiln ash gave the manufacturing site the name Tell 'Aswad ("black mound"); see: Meinecke, "Raqqa on the Euphrates", p. 30; Meinecke, "al-Rakka", p. 412.

[73] O'Hea, "The Glass Industry of the Decapolis"; M. O'Hea, "Glass from Areas XXXIV and XXIX (Hellenistic-Abbasid). Abbasid Glass from Area XXIX", in A.G. Walmsley, P.G. Macumber, P.C ͠ ᵈwards, S. Bourke and P.M. Watson, "The Eleventh and Twelfth Seasons of E   ᵤions at Pella (Tabaqat Fahl) 1989-1990", *Annual of the Department of Antiquities of Jordan* 37 (1993), pp. 165-240, at pp. 222-27.

[74] Bar-Nathan and Mazor, "City Center (South) and Tel Iztabba Area; Excavations of the Antiquities Authority Expedition", pp. 37-38.

copper waste pieces, charcoal and ashes suggest the presence of metalworks devoted to iron tool and copper vessel production. Black-smiths' shops were also identified at Pella and Jarash. A workshop, possibly for dyeing, was excavated at Tabariyah, and a series of indus-trial ovens dated to the second half of the eighth century were uncovered in the south baths at Busrâ.[75]

We can be sure that these incidences of industrial activity in the Early Islamic towns of Bilâd al-Shâm were not unusual. The glass-works at Pella and the ceramic workshops of Jarash and Baysân, for instance, are only examples of a more widely based and active man-ufacturing economy. However, the greater presence of these activ-ities in town centres becomes marked in the eighth and ninth centuries. Does this trend reflect a generally more industrialised society, or a greater reliance of some towns on manufacturing industries, or is it simply a very visible element in their urban decline? The answer is probably a combination of all three possibilities, weighted according to the circumstances. The presence of an imperial household in Damascus and, later, al-Raqqah along with local elites in the provin-cial and district towns of Bilâd al-Shâm would have created a significantly greater demand for manufactured items, from luxury to the everyday. In major centres such as Raqqah and, presumably, Damascus demand was met by isolated industrial quarters. For other towns, the strong demand for consumables offered something of an economic haven in the face of growing urban contraction, as seems to be the case with eighth and particularly ninth century Baysân, Pella and Jarash. Vacant space in these towns was taken up by work-shops producing fabrics, pottery and glass. While the occupation of old temple compounds and defunct bathhouses is to be expected, unusual is the setting up of a potters' workshop in a domestic area of west Jarash (presumably by the house owners) in the ninth cen-tury. The once monumental heart of the Classical town had seem-ingly become undesirable by this time (due to earthquakes or failure of the water supply?), and was given up in favour of its predom-

---

[75] Caesarea: Holum and Hohlfelder, *King Herod's Dream*, p. 211; Pella and Jarash: see A.G. Walmsley, "Land, Resources and Industry in Early Islamic Jordan (Seventh-Eleventh century). Current Research and Future Directions", *Studies in the History and Archaeology of Jordan* 6 (1997), pp. 345-51; Tabariyah dye works: Foerster, "Tiberias. Excavations South of the City", p. 1473; Busrâ workshop: S. Berthier, "Sondage dans le Secteur des Thermes Sud a Busra (Syrie) 1985", *Berytus* 33 (1985), pp. 5-45.

inantly domestic eastern half. Interestingly the final demise of Jarash as a centre of note (it is ignored by the tenth century Arabic geographers) coincides with the closing of these kilns, an event brought about, it can be argued, by a significant change in consumer taste for household ceramics.[76] Economic and political changes had challenged Jarash's commercial base, which had become narrowly focused on manufacturing industries and administrative responsibilities.

Rural settlement and production

a. *Exploitation and the processing of mineral resources*

The products of mining and smelting industries, especially iron, copper and gold, were in strong demand in Early Islamic Bilâd al-Shâm. The archaeological evidence, although limited, indicates that these industries were officially organised and promoted by the Umayyad and early 'Abbâsid administration. The clearest evidence comes from a major reassessment by U. Avner and J. Magness of previously unrelated archaeological discoveries in the southern 'Arabah and al-Naqab.[77]

Avner and Magness' study has identified a heightened level of activity in the exploitation and smelting of mineral ores in southern al-Naqab and the 'Arabah, a geographical region seen as part of Aylah's hinterland. Copper was mined at a number of locations, with one mine having galleries and halls over three km long. Near the mines were several smelting camps, easily identified by expanses of slag waste from the smelting process. Acacia was the preferred wood for the charcoal used in smelting the copper ore. Evidence for gold production and a stone quarry was also found. Associated with the mining and smelting activities were six villages, built in a distinctly similar style. The essentially uniform structural characteristics and fixed room dimensions suggests these villages were created at the direction of a single body, most probably the State at a provincial level. Each village had an industrial core to its economy: copper smelting, pottery firing, and shell working for jewellery and furniture

---

[76] Discussed in A.G. Walmsley, "Turning East. The Appearance of Islamic Cream Wares in Jordan – the End of Antiquity?", in E. Villeneuve and P.M. Watson eds., *La céramique byzantine et proto-islamique en Syrie-Jordanie (IVᵉ-VIIIᵉ siècles)* (Beyrouth, 1999), in press.

[77] U. Avner and J. Magness, "Early Islamic Settlement in the Southern Negev", *Bulletin of the American Schools of Oriental Research* 310 (1998), pp. 39-57.

inlays. The villages lay near main routes through the area to Egypt and Palestine, providing reciprocal benefits to settler and traveller.[78] On the northern route to Zughar (see above) a fortress was built at the oasis of Ghadhyan (Yotvata), and supported by the establishment of a major agricultural estate (below). Excavations at the fort recovered a gold *dinar* from the caliphate of al-Mahdî (775-785), a clear indication of the considerable regional significance of this area, and the roads that passed through it, in the eighth century.

The evidence from the Aylah hinterland is impressive but surely not exceptional for eighth century Bilâd al-Shâm, and the countryside around many towns would have equally been host to a wide range of mining and industrial activities. Yet the Aylah example is particularly significant because it clearly shows that mineral exploitation in the Early Islamic period was a highly organised and capital intensive industry. The impression gained is of a state-controlled industry, bringing wider benefits to rural areas through settlement programs, agricultural development and support for communication routes.

b. *An "agricultural revolution"?*

The agricultural regime of Bilâd al-Shâm experienced fundamental change in the seventh and eighth centuries. Perhaps during the Sassanid occupation, but certainly following the Islamic conquest, many new crops were introduced (notably sugar cane, rice, cotton, bananas, indigo and citrus fruits) and established crops improved (dates, grapes and figs for instance). The introduction and cultivation of these new crops, many of which came from the tropical east, has been dubbed the "Medieval Green Revolution".[79] The evidence indicates that this rural "revolution" initiated considerable economic and (possibly) social change in the countryside. There is no question that the agricultural economy similarly underwent considerable expansion in Early Islamic Bilâd al-Shâm, especially but not exclusively under the Marwânid Umayyads. The archaeological evidence

---

[78] In the Early Islamic period Aylah and its hinterland fell under the jurisdiction of Egypt, because the al-Fustât-Hijâz land route, including the pilgrim's road, passed through Aylah.

[79] A.M. Watson, "A Medieval Green Revolution: New Crops and Farming Techniques in the Early Islamic World", in A.L. Udovitch ed., *The Islamic Middle East, 700-1900. Studies in Economic and Social History* (New Jersey, 1981); A.M. Watson, *Agricultural Innovation in the Early Islamic World: The Diffusion of Crops and Farming Techniques, 700-1000* (Cambridge, 1983).

for eighth century rural expansion includes epigraphic sources, the results of regional surveys, some excavation data, and the presence of large state-owned farm estates in environmentally marginal zones.

The area most likely to benefit from the introduction of new crops was the Jordan Valley, as climatically it was most suited to the introduction of tropical crops. A deep rift valley, it is pleasantly warm in winter and hot in summer, and north of the Dead Sea well supplied with water. Geographical sources leave little doubt that sugar cane, rice, indigo, bananas were widely cultivated by the tenth century, but probably the widespread adoption of these crops took place in the early eighth century. Archaeological evidence in support of this view includes a large estate north of Tabariyah, a new agricultural development at Jericho and the establishment of new villages engaged in sugar production on the valley floor.[80] The settlement sequence at Tell Abu Qa'dan, a sugar village, is particularly informative. Constructed of mudbrick, the village was first established in the eighth century and continuously occupied for around 800 years. Pottery evidence for sugar production is overwhelming in later levels, although it is more difficult to identify for the earlier periods. It may be no coincidence that the expansion of agricultural activity in the Jordan Valley was matched by a change in land use in the adjoining hills, for instance around Pella.[81] Although probably not the sole reason, the introduction of labour intensive agriculture in the valley may be partly responsible for the implementation of less intensive exploitation strategies in the Pella foothills. Farmsteads were deserted and a highly developed viniculture replaced by other agricultural activities, perhaps a mixture of aboriculture, spring cropping in the small valleys and animal herding on the hill flanks. The

---

[80] Tabariyah and Jericho estates: Creswell rev. Allen, *A Short Account of Early Muslim Architecture*, pp. 93-95; O. Grabar, J. Perrot, B. Ravani and M. Rosen, "Sondages à Khirbet el-Minyeh", *Israel Exploration Journal* 10 (1960), pp. 226-43; G.R.D. King, "Settlement Patterns in Islamic Jordan: the Umayyads and their Use of the Land", in S. Tell, G. Bisheh, F. Zayadine, K. 'Amr and M. Zaghloul eds., *Studies in the History and Archaeology of Jordan*, vol. 4 (Amman, 1992), pp. 369-75, dated to the reigns of al-Walid I and Hishâm respectively; villages: H.J. Franken and J. Kalsbeek, *Potters of a Medieval Village in the Jordan Valley*, vol. 3 (Amsterdam/Oxford, 1975); J. Kareem, *Evidence of the Umayyad occupation in the Jordan Valley as seen in the Jisr Sheikh Hussein region* (MA thesis, Yarmouk University, 1987); D.S. Whitcomb, "The Islamic Period as Seen from Selected Sites", in B. MacDonald ed., *The Southern Ghors and Northeast 'Arabah Archaeological Survey*, vol. 5 (Sheffield, 1992), pp. 113-18.

[81] P.M. Watson and M. O'Hea, "Pella Hinterland Survey 1994: Preliminary Report", *Levant* 28 (1996), pp. 63-76, at p. 74.

demand for labour, and the potential greater earnings from specialised "cash crops" on the Jordan Valley floor, drew away the farm
workers from the Pella hills.

A similar process may account, in part, for the steady depopulation of the limestone hills (the Bélus Massif) between Antioch and
Aleppo in north Syria. Modern exploration of the deserted villages
(the so-called "dead cities") that visually dominate this bleak hill zone
has sought to explain why these architecturally impressive settlements,
characterised by huge stone churches and houses, came to be abandoned after the Islamic conquest. In a pioneering and justly famous
study by G. Tchalenko the abandonment of the villages, which he
perceived as happening suddenly, was attributed to an economic
cause.[82] In very simple terms, Tchalenko explained the apparent
prosperity of the Bélus Massif on cash-cropping monoculture, and
specifically the intensive cultivation of olive trees for oil production.
However, he argued, the Islamic conquest ruptured crucial trade
links with the Mediterranean world, causing a sudden and permanent collapse of the olive oil industry and economic destitution in
the villages.

Work that is more recent has raised serious doubts on both
Tchalenko's explanation for economic collapse in the region and his
chronology of decline. In an influential study, Hugh Kennedy has
cogently argued that the rural decline began much earlier, around
the middle of the sixth century. The failure of the olive monoculture was caused by the collapse of local, not export, markets (especially Antioch) following periodic visitations of the plague, earthquakes
and occupation by the Sassanids. Failed farms were consolidated into
larger agricultural estates, perhaps owned by the monasteries, which
were devoted to mixed farming, rather than monoculture. However
work at one of the villages, Déhès, by a French team led by J.-P.
Sodini and G. Tate has produced a rather different economic model.
Instead of specialised monoculture, most villages practised a broadly
based economy of animal husbandry and mixed agriculture, including (but not exclusively) olive cultivation. The vast majority of village buildings functioned as utilitarian domestic units on two levels,
with the ground floor devoted to stabling animals and agrarian activities and living quarters concentrated on the first floor. While con-

---

[82] G. Tchalenko, *Villages antiques de la Syria du Nord. Le Massif du Bélus a l'Epoque
Romaine*, vols. 1-3 (Paris, 1953-58).

struction activity seemingly peaked in the early sixth century, archaeological and architectural evidence additionally and importantly showed that many buildings were continuously occupied well into Islamic times. Houses were periodically refurbished (although to a variable standard), and often subdivided, an activity often seen as reflecting population growth but equally may reflect complex inheritance matters. Indisputable evidence for population decline on a large, and ever increasing, scale does not appear until the early ninth century. Even then, abandonment of the villages did not take place until the following tenth century, probably in response to the destructive Byzantine-Muslim conflicts that embroiled the region. Interestingly the ninth century depopulation coincided with the growth of al-Raqqah (above) and Aleppo, and the need for settlers in the fortified borderlands with Byzantium (the *Thughûr*). The greater security offered by towns in troubled times, the rise of new economic opportunities in Aleppo and especially al-Raqqah, a huge source of employment, and the demand for settlers in the border *Thughûr* would have offered a much needed opportunity to the increasingly impoverished villagers in the nearby hill zones.[83]

It should come as no surprise that the Raqqah hinterland was densely occupied with district centres and agricultural villages in the Early Islamic period. Particularly detailed evidence has been produced by survey work and excavations in the Balîkh Valley, a northern tributary of the Euphrates River in the Jazîrah.[84] Two important sites stood at either end of the Balîkh in the Early Islamic period: Harrân near its headwaters in the north and al-Raqqah to

---

[83] Sixth century decline: Kennedy, "The Last Century of Byzantine Syria", at pp. 157-62; Déhès: J.-P. Sodini, G. Tate, B. Bavant, S. Bavant, J.-L. Biscop and D. Orssaud, "Déhès (Syrie du Nord). Campagnes I-III (1976-1978), Recherches sur l'Habitat Rural", *Syria* 57 (1980), pp. 1-304; G. Tate, *Les campagnes de la Syrie du Nord du IIe au VIIe siècle*, I (Paris, 1992), esp. pp. 275-350; see also Foss, "The Near Eastern Countryside in Late Antiquity", at pp. 213-23, and Foss, "Syria in Transition, A.D. 550-750", at pp. 197-204. Thughûr: P. von Sivers, "Taxes and Trade in the 'Abbasid Thughur, 750-962/133-351", *Journal of the Economic and Social History of the Orient* 25 (1982), pp. 71-99.

[84] K. Bartl, "The Balih Valley, Northern Syria, During the Islamic Period. Remarks Concerning the Historical Topography", *Berytus* 41 (1993-4), pp. 29-38; K. Bartl, *Frühislamische Besiedlung im Balîh-Tal/Nordsyrien* (Berlin, 1994); C.-P. Haase, "Madînat al-Fâr/Hisn Maslama — First Archaeological Soundings at the Site and the History of an Umayyad Domain in Abbasid Times", in M.A. Bakhit and R. Schick eds. *Proceedings of the Fifth International Conference on the History of Bilad al-Sham. Bilad al-Sham during the Abbasid Period*, English and French Section (Amman, 1991), pp. 206-25.

the south near the junction with the Euphrates. A major road joined the two urban centres, and linked important east-west routes (as has already been seen for al-Raqqah). Between Harrân and al-Raqqah were five settlements (not all positively identified), including an Umayyad foundation Hisn Maslamah, built by one of the sons of 'Abd al-Malik while provincial governor (709-719). Constructed as a fort, water was brought from the Balîkh by canal, which also irrigated adjacent agricultural lands belonging to Maslamah. Suburbs grew up outside the original walled settlement, and excavations suggest occupation peaked at the site in the 'Abbâsid period. Written sources confirm the dense settlement of the Balîkh in the eighth and ninth centuries, describing the valley as filled with irrigated estates, villages and agricultural farmlands.

Other agricultural development projects were undertaken in the Euphrates area. Prominent was the *Nahr Maslamah*, also dug under Maslamah ibn 'Abd al-Malik, a massive irrigation project near Neocaesarea (Qâsirîn, modern Dibsi Faraj) to water fields on the south bank of the Euphrates. Thereafter Maslamah, who had extensive rural holdings, held these lands and villages as a fief, and they were passed on to his descendants until confiscated by the 'Abbâsids after the 750 revolution. Not surprisingly extensive excavations at Qâsirîn have uncovered major occupational levels dating to the Umayyad and 'Abbâsid periods, ending at the time of a severe earthquake in 859.[85] By way of contrast the Jazîrah plain, at least parts of its grain-growing northern reaches, appears to have suffered from a population loss and deteriorating socio-economic conditions over the same period.[86] Again, the attraction of the new Islamic cities (al-Raqqah, Baghdâd, and Mawsil) and rural development projects may have accounted, in part, for the demographic decline.

The rural landownings of Maslamah were not exceptional, for the

---

[85] Canal: Al-Baladhuri, *The Origins of the Islamic State*, p. 232; T.J. Wilkinson, "The Physical Environment of Dibsi Faraj; A Preliminary Study", an appendix to R.P. Harper, "Excavations at Dibsi Faraj, Northern Syria, 1972-1974: a Preliminary Note on the Site and its Monuments", *Dumbarton Oaks Papers* 29 (1975), pp. 319-38, at pp. 334-38; Qâsirîn: Harper, "Excavations at Dibsi Faraj"; see also O. Grabar, "Umayyad 'Palace' and the 'Abbasid 'Revolution'", *Studia Islamica* 18 (1962), pp. 5-18; O. Grabar, *The Formation of Islamic Art* (New Haven, 1973), pp. 34-35.

[86] The premise is based on survey data (although with some literary support), so some caution must be exercised. See: T.J. Wilkinson and D.J. Tucker, *Settlement Development in the North Jazira, Iraq. A Study of the Archaeological Landscape* (Baghdad, 1995), pp. 69-77.

ownership of agricultural estates by the Arab ruling elite was popular and geographically widespread in Umayyad Bilâd al-Shâm. As with Maslamah's estates, many of these properties were seized by the 'Abbâsid ruling family and preserved as an operating entity. Well known since the seminal studies of Sauvaget and Grabar are the usually expansive agricultural estates associated with the "desert castles" (qusûr) of the Jordanian and Syrian steppe lands, the bâdiyah, although not all were completely new foundations.[87] In some instances the qusûr represent embellishments and improvements, often substantial, to existing rural properties confiscated at the time of the Islamic conquest or subsequently purchased. The provision of water on a major scale was a crucial part of each establishment as evidenced by the dams, aqueducts, canals, reservoirs, sluices, wells and cisterns identified near many qusûr. As well as supplying the buildings, the water was directed to field systems, usually enclosed, where agriculture and possibly animal breeding took place. An interesting example is Qasr al-Hayr al-Gharbî ("west"), built by Hishâm in 727 to the north-east of Damascus. Water to a palace, bathhouse and khân was conducted through a subterranean canal from a dam of likely Roman-period construction located 16 km to the south. A garden was enclosed by walls measuring 1050 by 442 m, and was supplied with water from a 2.75 m thick barrage that, by spanning the valley floor, channelled the winter rains into the agricultural enclosure.[88] On many of the qusûr, the cultivation of olive trees was a favoured activity. One of Hishâm's establishments was named al-Zaytûnah (from zaytûn, "olive"), a probable reference to one or other of the Qasr al-Hayr sites, presumably because of its extensive olive plantation.

In addition to the estates owned by the caliph and his family, other members of the Arab ruling elite could, and often did, own rural properties. These were commonly obtained as grants from the caliphs in the years after the Islamic conquest, but could be purchased. However in the early period, immediately after the conquest, the

---

[87] J. Sauvaget, "Les Ruines Omeyyades du Djebel Seis", *Syria* 20 (1939), pp. 239-56; J. Sauvaget, "Chateaux Umayyades de Syrie. Contribution a l'Etude de la Colonisation Arabe aux Ier et IIe Siècles de l'Hégire", *Revue des Etudes Islamiques* 35 (1967), pp. 1-49; Grabar, "Umayyad 'Palace' and the 'Abbasid 'Revolution'"; Grabar, *The Formation of Islamic Art*, esp. p. 32.

[88] Creswell rev. Allen, *A Short Account of Early Muslim Architecture*, pp. 135-42; D. Schlumberger, "Les Fouilles de Qasr el Heir el Gharbi (1936-38). Rapport Préliminaire", *Syria* 20 (1939), pp. 195-238, 324-73.

acquisition of estates by Muslims was considered degrading and regressive. They could benefit from the taxes, but should not own the land, as they would be liable to pay the land tax, the *kharâj*, rather than extracting it. Opinions quickly changed, encouraged by the circulation of *hadîth* (sayings of the Prophet Muhammad) in favour of farming and land ownership. One tradition in particular praised the Muslim who oversaw the economic development of unproductive land. By the eighth century the acquisition of rural properties had become a popular way of investing money, due to the profitability and security they offered. Often estates were granted a special tax status, which benefited both landowner (who paid less tax) and caliph (who received the tax directly). Revealing is the history of a family of settlers in the Jibâl district of western Iran who traded in perfumes and sheep and invested the proceeds in estates. Their increasingly wealthy descendants promoted the local town by building fortifications and attracting a population, and subsequently became highly influential in the 'Abbâsid court under Hârûn al-Rashîd. Here we see trade could serve as a source of wealth, but absolute richness and an esteemed social position was obtained by owning land. In the opinion of many religious scholars of the time, agriculture was clearly preferable to trade, due to its greater usefulness.[89]

The acquisition of estates in conquered areas by the elite (some of whom came from Pre-Islamic land owning families) began in earnest under the Caliph 'Uthmân (644-656), for his predecessor, 'Umar, did not approve of the practice. A favoured area for obtaining estates was the *Dârûm* region, an area of steppe lands in southern Palestine positioned east of 'Asqalân. It was here that the "Conqueror of Palestine", 'Amr ibn al-'Âs, owned an estate called 'Ajlân which served as a place of retreat during political upheavals.[90] Also used to political advantage was the village-estate of 'Ali ibn 'Abd Allah ibn al-'Abbâs known as Humaymah, located further to the east on the other side of the Wâdî 'Arabah. Purchased in 687/8, the site was embellished with a mosque and *qasr*, and became a focal

---

[89] A. Elad, "Two Identical Inscriptions from the Jund Filastin from the Reign of the 'Abbasid Caliph, al-Muqtadir", *Journal of the Economic and Social History of the Orient* 35 (1992), pp. 301-60; M.J. Kister, "Land property and *Jihâd*", *Journal of the Economic and Social History of the Orient* 34 (1991), pp. 270-311.

[90] See the references above, also M. Lecker, "The Estates of 'Amr b. al-'As in Palestine: Notes on a New Negev Arabic Inscription", *Bulletin of the School of Oriental and African Studies* 52 (1989), pp. 24-37.

point of the 'Abbâsid revolt against the Umayyads. Considerable investment, indicative of a state project, was made in developing agricultural farms near the oases of the southern 'Arabah near Aylah. At Ghadhyan, underground canals (*qanats*, tunnels reached by vertical shafts to the surface) with a total length of 10 km brought water to about 300 ha. of fields. The farm at Evrona was also supplied by qanats, with again about 300 hectares of new fields cleared from rocky and previously uncultivated land. An excavated farmhouse produced date pips, olive and peach stones, almonds, carob seeds, and wheat and barley. The qanats were a new innovation at both sites (suggesting their introduction into Palestine with the Islamic conquest), as they cut through earlier open canal systems dating from Nabataean through to Byzantine times.[91]

The Umayyad estates in Palestine were commonly confiscated by the 'Abbâsid caliphs and new ones were acquired by purchase. In the early tenth century, estates located in Palestine were still owned by the caliph and court members, in spite of the political uncertainty of the period. Archaeological evidence also demonstrates that, contrary to common opinion, at least some of the bâdiyah estates in Jordan and Syria continued after the rise of the 'Abbâsid caliphate, for instance al-Muwaqqar near 'Ammân and Qasr al-Hayr al-Sharqî.[92] Although perhaps maintained as state properties by the early 'Abbâsids, their continued occupation also suggests that they may have been reasonably self-supporting and were not entirely dependent on cash grants from the government.

4. *Commodities and the nature of trade: old structures, new systems?*

From the wide range of indicators presented above, it would seem as though very favourable conditions existed in Early Islamic Bilâd al-Shâm for the widespread movement of goods, both internally and

---

[91] Humaymah: recently R. Foote and J.P. Oleson, "Humeima Excavation Project, 1995-96", *Fondation Max Van Berchem Bulletin* 10 (1996), pp. 1-4; J.P. Oleson, K. 'Amr, R. Foote and R. Schick, "Preliminary Report on the Humayma Excavation Project, 1993", *Annual of the Department of Antiquities of Jordan* 39 (1995), pp. 317-54; 'Arabah: Avner and Magness, "Early Islamic Settlement in the Southern Negev".

[92] Muwaqqar: M. Najjar, "Abbasid Pottery from el-Muwaqqar", *Annual of the Department of Antiquities of Jordan* 33 (1989), pp. 305-22; Qasr al-Hayr: Grabar, *City in the Desert.*

with neighbouring regions. The political, cultural and economic primacy of towns persisted strongly after the Islamic conquest due to the presence of powerful urban-based elites and the establishment of a successful and unified system of government, the new Islamic caliphate. The existence of a developing market economy and its successful consolidation in the first half of the eighth century is indicated by many improvements to the urban environment, notably the construction of markets, and the maintenance of an extensive communications network by the government. A growing demand for commodities, especially after the establishment of the Umayyad caliphate in Damascus, is revealed in the strong performance of urban and rural industries. Unfortunately, trying to comprehensively map the nature and extent of the resultant exchange is very difficult, due to the sparse and patchy evidence available. There is some written material, but this mostly dates to after the eighth century, and a little more archaeological data. Of the latter certain categories of ceramics and coins are particularly informative, and will constitute the bulk of the archaeological evidence considered here. However, these conventional indicators of exchange have greater limitations in the Early Islamic period. Quite significant changes occurred in the way goods were shipped in the eighth and ninth centuries, and copper coinage essentially ceased to be produced and was replaced by fractional silver. In addition, the establishment of banking structures, such as letters of credit, would have reduced the circulation of precious coin.[93] Therefore, the absence of major trade indicators in the archaeological record may not reflect the demise of commerce, but the fact it was being conducted in a different, and less visible, way.

Written sources

The brief glimpses afforded by written sources indicate that commodity exchange over long distances was taking place by the mid-

---

[93] New shipping methods, the economic role of fractional silver, and banking structures appear well developed in the documents of the Cairo Geniza, for which see: S. Goitein, *A Mediterranean Society*, Vol. 1: *Economic Foundations*. Their evolution in the eighth and ninth centuries, during a time of considerable political and cultural unity, can be argued, and is indicated by the virtual irrelevance of copper currency by the ninth century and the effective disappearance of amphora from the archaeological record at roughly the same time. While facilitating trade within the Islamic world, these structures may have not helped in, and could have acted as a disincentive to, building commercial ties with regions outside of the Islamic polity.

ninth century, but that this trade was restricted in both geographical extent and the types of items exchanged. The justly famous account of the multilingual Jewish merchants known as the Radhanites (Râdhâniyah) in the geography of Ibn Khurdâdhbih (d. 913) is as remarkable as it is exceptional, probably, for the age.[94] From Spain and Italy the merchants brought slaves, eunuchs, furs, specialist cloth and swords, travelling by sea and land over a variety of routes as far as southern Arabia, India and China. On the return journey, they carried aromatics and spices, especially those required for the making of medicines. All of these commodities, being perishable, would leave no clear evidence in the archaeological record.

The Radhanites were, seemingly, a "unique" class of traders, in that they successfully transversed a number of major geographical and political spheres. Perhaps more typical is a second mid-ninth century source in which a vast range of merchandise is listed as entering 'Irâq. The source reveals that the major orientation of inter-regional trade in this century was with the eastern Muslim provinces and, beyond them, India and China. Commercial ties with countries to the west were much less extensive. Egypt and North Africa provided some specialist commodities, but outside of the Muslim world, the only direct ties were with Armenia, Azarbayjân and the territory of the Khazars. From these districts came slaves, body armour, furs, saddles, carpets and wool, and only indirectly an opening to trade with Byzantium.[95]

The 830s and 840s were characterised by a major expansion of commercial activity in the Islamic world, and quite possibly this growth was accompanied by significant changes to the existing trade networks. New commercial opportunities arose with the creation of huge urban markets in al-'Irâq and the Jazîrah, and resulted in the formation of enlarged and increasingly direct trade links with non-Muslim territories, especially China and Russia (see below for an

---

[94] From the considerable literature see, usefully: M. Gil, "The Radhanite Merchants and the Land of Radhan", *Journal of the Economic and Social History of the Orient* 17 (1974), pp. 299-328; R.S. Lopez and I.W. Raymond, *Medieval Trade in the Mediterranean World: Illustrative Documents* (New York, 1955), and generally C. Cahen, "Commercial Relations Between the Near East and Western Europe from the VIIth to the XIth Century", in K.I. Semaan ed., *Islam and the Medieval West: Aspects of Intercultural Relations* (Albany, 1980), pp. 1-25. Gil argues two important points: firstly that the Radanites were natives of 'Iraq, not European Jews, and secondly their visits to *Firanja* referred to Frankish Italy, not France proper.
[95] Lopez and Raymond, *Medieval Trade in the Mediterranean World*, pp. 27-29.

archaeological view). The 840s also marked the beginning of a major shift in economic fundamentals on the Muslim-Byzantine frontier in northern Bilâd al-Shâm.[96] Under the Umayyads and early 'Abbâsids the frontier was a zone of near-continuous conflict where the ideologically driven and often vigorously pursued struggle with Byzantium was acted out. Very limited written evidence exists for direct trade on any scale between the competing powers in the eighth century, and the border town markets mentioned in the sources would have served mostly local needs. A lessening of hostilities from the mid-ninth century and the expansion of trade on the Euphrates route between the Arabian Gulf and the Mediterranean Sea via Baghdâd and al-Raqqah, would have created a situation more conducive to trade. The ninth century redevelopment of al-Mina, Antioch's natural harbour (above), coincided with the commercial revival of the Euphrates route.

In general terms the extent to which written sources accurately describe the situation before the mid-ninth century is very difficult to assess. Exchange systems would have developed to meet the expansion in trade during the 830s and 840s, making them structurally different from those in force during the previous century. To understand, however imperfectly, the nature and extent of exchange in the eighth century, before the ninth century changes, we need to turn to archaeological sources.

Archaeological sources

The many difficulties associated with Early Islamic archaeology outlined at the start of this chapter (negligently excavated, interpreted and reported sites) are particularly obstructive to a consideration of economic issues, especially trade. Furthermore, many major centres, notably Damascus and coastal localities, are inadequately investigated, especially from an archaeological perspective. In many cases, these towns have experienced unbroken occupation until today, a major impediment to archaeological investigation. Nevertheless, questions on the nature and extent of eighth century trade in Bilâd al-

---

[96] J.F. Haldon and H. Kennedy, "The Arab-Byzantine Frontier in the Eighth and Ninth Centuries: Military Organisation and Society in the Borderlands", *Recueil des travaux de l'Institut d'études Byzantines* 19 (1980), pp. 79-116, esp. pp. 107-11; also Sivers, "Taxes and Trade in the 'Abbasid Thughur".

Shâm are not beyond consideration, although the material allows for little more than a deliberation on what exchange could have happened. The archaeological information is, largely, still too limited to argue from an absence of evidence.

The most valuable sources for identifying intra- and inter-regional trade networks in Early Islamic Bilâd al-Shâm are ceramics and coins, as these have been found in sufficient quantity and are usually reported in reasonable detail. While a study of these material groups can establish the existence of local and long distance contact and exchange, the exact nature of that interchange can not always be established. Furthermore, the evidence for commerce in the eighth and ninth centuries has to be treated on its own terms, and comparisons with trade systems of earlier periods (especially the Roman empire) can be invalid. For instance, a shift from ceramic containers to materials such as animal skins and wickerwork baskets, as revealed in the Cairo Geniza, significantly reduces the reliability of archaeological data as a faithful record of exchange. Clearly one category, pottery, leaves a very clear message in the archaeological record; the other, being perishable, is next to invisible. Changing methods of transportation, especially a growing reliance on sea borne trade, from the later eighth century apparently had an obvious and significant impact on the way commodities were transported, particularly consumables and fragile goods.

a. *Ceramics and trade*

Pottery, an enduring, visible and comprehensible record of human activity, was widely manufactured and commonly traded in Early Islamic Bilâd al-Shâm. Tableware, cooking vessels, storage jars and mixing bowls were produced in the kilns of Baysân, Jarash and many other as yet unidentified locations and distributed to local and regional markets. Fabric types and forms show considerable continuity from late sixth and early seventh-century Byzantine types.[97] Unlike the

---

[97] For a detailed summary see: J.-P. Sodini and E. Villeneuve, "Le Passage de la Céramique Byzantine à la Céramique Omeyyade", in, *La Syrie de Byzance à l'Islam VIIe-VIIIe siècles*, pp. 195-218. That the Islamic Conquest did not sever existing commercial links with Egypt, North Africa, Cyprus and Byzantine Asia Minor has been adequately demonstrated by the unbroken import of fine Red Slip tableware into south Bilâd al-Shâm in the seventh century. Examples have been found as far inland as Busrâ (Bostra), Jarash, 'Ammân and Umm al-Rasâs. Rather, the fall in imports that occurred during this century was determined by declining production initiated by changes in local tastes in different parts of the Mediterranean world;

Byzantine period, however, the demand for household pottery—notably fine wares—in the eighth century was almost solely satisfied by local production (although nearly all coarse wares and many varieties of fine wares were locally produced in earlier centuries, and this shift was gradual and should not be exaggerated). In general terms, the excavation of domestic levels datable to the eighth century typically produces a limited number of fabrics and shapes, and only a few exotic varieties. The heightened demand on local producers probably accounts for the considerable expansion of pottery workshops in eighth century Jarash and Baysân, as described earlier, and presumably many other localities. In a different league, however, were the large jars (amphorae) used for shipping major consumables, especially olive and sesame oil, wine and fish sauce (*garum*). These continue to be common in the seventh and eighth centuries, when they were transported for their contents over great distances.

Of primary interest is the ceramic evidence for localised trade networks, of which there is a reasonable amount. In southern Bilâd al-Shâm two pottery types are particularly informative, as they are distinctive and, hence, easily identified and usually reported. The first type has traditionally been called "Fine Byzantine Ware", although it is now known that this pottery, while originating in the mid-sixth century, was very popular in Palestine and Jordan between the seventh and ninth centuries. The second type is a distinctive pale cream to pink ware, sometimes with an off-white slip, which was decorated freely and liberally with a diagnostic regime of painted geometric designs in a deep red to purplish-red paint. Chronologically the origin of this Red Painted Ware is later, probably the second quarter of the eighth century, and it continued strongly into the ninth century.

"Fine Byzantine Ware" (perhaps better called Palestinian Fine Table

---

see: C. Wickham, "Trade and Exchange, 550-750: the view from the West", in L. Conrad ed., *Late Antiquity and Early Islam* 4 (Princeton, in press). This process was largely complete by the beginning of our period (680), although Egyptian Red Slip "A" and "C" was still arriving at Pella and Tiberias until at least the middle of the eighth century (for which see D. Stacey, "Umayyad and Egyptian Red-slip 'A' Ware from Tiberias", *Bulletin of the Anglo-Israel Archaeological Society* 8 (1988-9), pp. 21-33; P.M. Watson, "Change in Foreign and Regional Economic Links with Pella in the Seventh Century A.D.: The Ceramic Evidence", in *La Syrie de Byzance à l'Islam VIIe-VIIIe siècles*, pp. 233-48; P.M. Watson, "Ceramic Evidence for Egyptian Links with Northern Jordan in the 6th-8th Centuries A.D.", in S. Bourke and J.-P. Descoeudres eds., *Trade, Contact, and the Movement of Peoples in the Eastern Mediterranean. Studies in Honour of J. Basil Hennessy*, Mediterranean Archaeology Supplement 3 (Sydney, 1995), pp. 303-20).

Ware, so hereafter PFTW) is a major class of Late Antique and Early Islamic pottery, superior in form and manufacture to the Red Slip wares popular in the Late Antique East.[98] The clay was finely levigated and ultra-thinly thrown on a fast wheel to produce extremely elegant cups, bowls, jars and jugs. The firing was very controlled, and produced a mellow light orange to brown coloured fabric. J. Magness believes the ware was inspired by metallic prototypes. Decoration of the outside surfaces involved knife burnishing, an orderly wavy line impressed below the rim on sixth and seventh centuries cups, and incised "nicks" on jars and jugs. The first cup varieties also had a distinctive ring base, formed by the removal of surplus clay with a paring knife. PFTW reached its technological excellence in the eighth and ninth centuries, when high-walled cups of varying sizes were produced with exceptionally thin walls. New shapes, especially dishes and plates, also appeared by the eighth century to take the place of the increasingly unavailable, or undesirable, Red Slip wares.[99] However, the jars and jugs ceased to be produced around this time, and by the early ninth century these forms had been replaced by completely new types in a fine cream ware. The fabric and shape of these new cream ware varieties were inspired by a ceramic tradition originating outside Bilâd al-Shâm (see further below).

PFTW was extensively distributed in Palestine and Jordan, with find sites centring on the north and central Jordan Valley, the Jordanian mountain range (particularly in the north), the Palestinian hills and south in the Naqab (Negev). Magness plausibly suggests that the Jerusalem area was the production centre for PFTW, although

---

[98] The ware type has not been studied sufficiently, but see: M. Gichon, "Fine Byzantine Wares from the South of Israel", *Palestine Exploration Quarterly* 106 (1974), pp. 119-39; J. Magness, *Jerusalem Ceramic Chronology, circa 200-800 C.E.* (Sheffield, 1993) pp. 166-71; A.G. Walmsley, "Tradition, Innovation, and Imitation in the Material Culture of Islamic Jordan: the First Four Centuries", in K. 'Amr, F. Zaya-dine and M. Zaghloul eds., *Studies in the History and Archaeology of Jordan*, vol. 5 (Amman, 1995), pp. 657-68 for a start.

[99] Co-incidentally the production of a major series of plates with bichrome and sometimes stamped decoration, known as "Jarash Bowls", ceased in the middle to late seventh century (see: A. Uscatescu, "Jarash Bowls and other related local wares from the Spanish Excavations at the *Macellum* of Gerasa (Jarash)", *Annual of the Department of Antiquities of Jordan* 39 (1995), pp. 365-408; A. Uscatescu, *La Cerámica del Macellum de Gerasa (Yaras, Jordania)* (Madrid, 1996); P.M. Watson, "Jerash Bowls: Study of a Provincial Group of Byzantine Decorated Fine Ware", in F. Zayadine ed., *Jerash Archaeological Project 2 (1984-1988)* (Paris, 1989), pp. 223-53).

no workshops have been located. From Jerusalem, appreciable quantities of PFTW were moved north and south for a distance of up
to 120 km. Distribution was particularly marked to the north-east
and south-west of Jerusalem along the well travelled and, from the
beginning of the seventh century, the increasingly important state-
run route between Egypt and Damascus. The production and distribution of PFTW offers a revealing glimpse into cultural and
economic developments in south Bilâd al-Shâm in the Late Antique-
Early Islamic period. There is evidence for clear continuity at the
time of the Islamic conquest, conspicuous market adjustments and
technological improvements in the seventh and eighth century, and
growing competition from new structures in the early ninth century.

Red Painted Ware (hereafter RPW) was another major household
ware in south Bilâd al-Shâm from the eighth century onwards.[100]
The fabric was well levigated with small limestone, calcite and chert
inclusions, and was well fired to produce a hard ceramic coloured
pale buff-pink to brick red. On darker bodied vessels, a cream slip
was initially applied to provide a contrasting background for the
paint. The appearance of the ware is well dated to the early eighth
century and, by the middle of the century, jars and jugs in this ware
were reasonably common, for instance in the earthquake destruction
level at Pella (fig. 5). Painted decoration on jars and jugs consisted
of straight and wavy lines, loops, spirals, sprigs, slashed stars and an
"arcade" pattern. Around the middle of the eighth century new forms
were introduced, notably table bowls, cups and plates. The bowls,
probably used for serving food, are technically and artistically excellent examples of the potters' art. Known as "palace ware", these bowls
had bevelled rim, straight sides and a flat base. They were slipped
and elaborately decorated with linear and floral motifs, apparently
based on geometric mosaic patterns. The cups were decorated with
wavy lines, plain festoons hanging from the rim, and sprigs, however the style of decoration and fabric is dissimilar to the other red
painted bowls and jars. Kilns producing the cups were excavated at
Jarash, but the production centre for the "palace ware" bowls and

---

[100] The following two paragraphs are based on the BA Honours dissertation
of K. King, *Early Islamic Ceramics: Red Painted Ware of the 8th and 9th centuries A.D.,
with Particular Reference to the Site of Pella in Jordan* (BA (Honours) thesis, University
of Sydney, 1990). See also Walmsley, "Tradition, Innovation, and Imitation in the
material Culture of Islamic Jordan", p. 661.

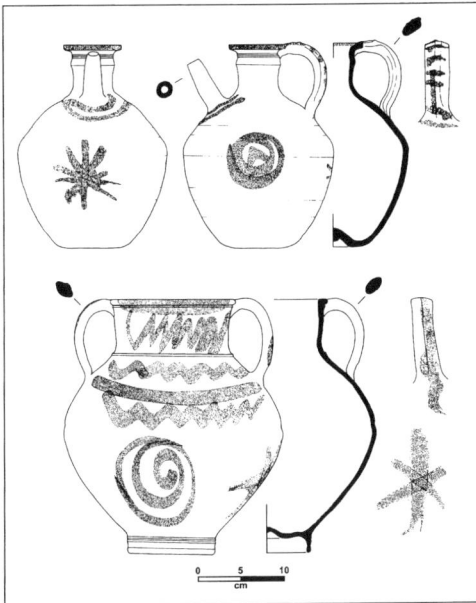

Fig. 5. Cultural innovation and artistic creativity under the Marwânid Umayyads:
Red Painted Ware from a mid-eighth century context at Pella in Jordan.

jars is unknown. Their common occurrence around 'Ammân, especially at Rujm al-Kursi, suggests the workshop or shops were located in this area.[101]

The distribution of RPW was regionally broad. Sites with reported finds of RPW are clustered east of the Jordan River, but its discovery is rare south of the Wâdî Mûjib (this tends to discount an origin in Nabataean painted pottery). West of the Jordan RPW has been found extending into the Palestinian hills, mostly between Jerusalem and Nazareth but rarely in the Naqab or on the Mediterranean Coast. Notable is the extension of find sites into the Hawrân, including Busrâ, al-Risha and Usays, an indication of commodity transfer for over 150 km along the north-east bâdiyah routes in the eighth and ninth centuries. RPW represents another example of

---

[101] Jarash: M. Gawlikowski, "A Residential Area by the South Decumanus", *Jerash Archaeological Project 1, 1981-1983*, dated to the ninth century; Rujm al-Kursi: A.-J. Amr, "Umayyad Painted Pottery Bowls from Rujm al-Kursi, Jordan", *Berytus* 34 (1986), pp. 145-59, with an imprecise Umayyad date. Evidence from Pella and Jarash suggest a predominantly early 'Abbâsid attribution for "palace ware" bowls.

major innovation in the material culture of the eighth century. A range of quite fine household wares was produced in a new and vigorous ceramic style that seems to appear abruptly and without local precedence. Within a generation RPW was a regular household item and was traded widely in the region, up to 150 km away from the point of production.

As two high quality and well-reported examples of Early Islamic ceramics, PFTW and RPW suggest that trade structures in eighth century Bilâd al-Shâm were built upon a series of overlapping regional networks, each involving the centralised production and distribution of goods. The spread of pottery indicates that these networks could operate smoothly up to 100 km away from the commodity source, but reached a physical limit at around 150 km. The dissimilarity of the ceramics from south Jordan, especially Aylah, and northern Bilâd al-Shâm, notably Déhès and Qâsirîn (Dibsi Faraj), reinforce the impression of active and regionally distinctive distribution networks.[102] Few imported house wares penetrated this essentially local supply system, unlike the two previous centuries, especially the sixth, when a broader range of ceramics included varieties from Mediterranean locations. Nevertheless, the falling off in supply of externally sourced domestic pottery, especially tableware, was countered with a substantial rise in locally produced pottery types. These were not inferior substitutes, but decoratively innovative and technologically advanced replacements. They further reveal the considerable economic and cultural vitality of eighth century Bilâd al-Shâm.

Wider in their distribution, geographically and chronologically, were amphorae and amphora-like jars, as these were widely traded for their contents (chiefly vegetable oils, date purée, wine and fish paste) in the east Mediterranean. Unlike other classes of pottery,

---

[102] Aylah: D. Whitcomb, "Evidence of the Umayyad Period from the Aqaba Excavations", in M.A. Bakhit and R. Schick eds., *Proceedings of the Third Symposium, the Fourth International Conference on the History of Bilad al-Sham. Bilad al-Sham during the Umayyad Period*, English Section, Vol. 2 (Amman, 1989), pp. 164-84; Déhès: D. Orssaud, "Le Passage de la Céramique Byzantine à la Céramique Islamique", in *La Syrie de Byzance à l'Islam VIIe-VIIIe siècles*, pp. 219-28; Sodini, Tate, Bavant, Bavant, Biscop and Orssaud, "Déhès (Syrie du Nord). Campagnes I-III (1976-1978)"; Qâsirîn: R.P. Harper, "Athis – Neocaesarea – Qasrin – Dibsi Faraj", in J.C. Margueron ed., *Le Moyen Euphrate. Zone de contacts et d'échanges* (Strasbourg, 1980), pp. 327-48; and generally on the regional diversity of Umayyad wares: Sodini and Villeneuve, "Le Passage de la Céramique Byzantine à la Céramique Omeyyade", in *La Syrie de Byzance à l'Islam VIIe-VIIIe siècles*, particularly pp. 211-12.

amphorae are numerically and typologically better represented in the archaeological record of the seventh century than the eighth, which could reflect the decreasing use of amphorae in medium and long distance trade. However, as already noted, it is probably misleading to simply view this change as evidence for a decline in commodity trade after the Islamic conquest. For instance, the evidence from Pella indicates quite clearly that patterns of amphora exchange were not appreciably disrupted by the Islamic conquest, with major amphora types of Palestinian (Gaza), Egyptian and Cypriot origin continuing strongly into the mid to late seventh century.[103] In the eighth century, when other evidence would indicate a rapid increase in economic activity, the range of imported amphorae at Pella was much less. Specimens recovered from the mid-eighth century earth-quake destruction are largely restricted to one variety originating in the Egyptian delta, although as this type of amphora occurs in good numbers the trade in its contents (date purée?) must have been reason-ably substantial.[104] Like the Red Slip wares, the absence of other amphora varieties at Pella (and elsewhere) resulted from an end to their production, but this does not discount a continuing trade in their contents in the eighth century using different containers, most notably skins for wine. Nevertheless changing agricultural practises may also account for a drop in the amphora trade. The promotion of agricultural activity by the Muslim elite (as described above) prob-ably resulted in a substantial increase and diversification of crop pro-duction. In particular many of the bâdiyah estates of the Umayyad period seem to have focused on olive cultivation and viniculture, especially as grapevines and olive trees, once established, could tol-erate the poor, dry soils. Hence the production of these essentials, the principal commodities traded in amphorae, became sufficiently diversified in the eighth century that demand was increasingly met at the local level to the cost of inter-regional trade.

Accordingly, changes in distribution and frequency patterns of

---

[103] P.M. Watson, "Change in Foreign and Regional Economic Links with Pella in the Seventh Century A.D.: The Ceramic Evidence", in *La Syrie de Byzance à l'Islam VIIe-VIIIe siècles*, pp. 239-40, 245; Watson, "Ceramic Evidence for Egyptian Links with Northern Jordan in the 6th-8th Centuries A.D.", pp. 315-17, 319-20.

[104] The Australian excavations at Pella have recovered twelve examples, seven of which are complete specimens. See: Watson, "Ceramic Evidence for Egyptian Links with Northern Jordan in the 6th-8th Centuries A.D.", in *Trade, Contact, and the Move-ment of Peoples in the Eastern Mediterranean*, pp. 319-20.

amphorae between the seventh and eighth centuries probably resulted from a combination of unrelated factors. Most importantly, these changes did not herald the end of inter-regional trade, as the many eighth-century Egyptian amphorae at Pella show that trade continued in some commodities at least. Informative is the presence of industrial amphora kilns at Aylah, which probably operated well into the eighth century. The excavators convincingly argue that amphora production at Aylah far exceeded local requirements, and the discovery of Aylah amphorae at seventh to ninth century sites in south Arabia and Ethiopia would indicate they were used to repack the agricultural produce of southern Bilâd al-Shâm (for example the celebrated almonds of Maâb) for shipment by boat on the Red Sea.[105] A major destination for this produce would have been the towns of the Hijâz, where the growth of a large and suddenly wealthy elite would have created an unprecedented demand for products such as oil, wine, grain, dried fruits and nuts. The Aylah amphorae attest to not only long distance trade, but also the common use of other, less visible, containers to move produce within Bilâd al-Shâm. Clearly, the agricultural products had to be brought to the port for reshipment, yet the absence of numerous discarded containers in the archaeological record would suggest perishable materials were used. The general preference for camels as pack animals in Early Islamic Bilâd al-Shâm would have also favoured the use of non-ceramic and easily transportable packaging, for instance skins, sacks and straw baskets.[106] While later in date, the Cairo Geniza is replete with these type of containers being use to transport both liquids and solid articles. The abandonment of amphorae as containers was a progres-

---

[105] Melkawi, 'Amr and Whitcomb, "The Excavation of Two Seventh Century Pottery Kilns at Aqaba".

[106] The standard use of pack camels is revealed in a requisition of c. 685 to work the Caesarea-Baysân road discovered at Nessana (see: Kraemer, *Excavations at Nessana 3. Non-Literary Papyri*, pp. 209-11, Document 74). The document says, in part, "make sure that you have ready two camels and two labourers who are to perform compulsory service from Caesarea to Scythopolis. Keep in mind also that he (an unnamed senior official) wants good camels, and workmen who have pack-saddles and straps." Note that the camel drivers themselves were to provide pack, not riding, saddles and straps to secure the loads between Caesarea and Scythopolis/Baysân. Carts, probably never popular in the rough terrain of Bilâd al-Shâm, were very rare in Early Islamic times. The Pilgrim Arcuf, who travelled in Palestine sometime between 679 and 688, reported that the pine wood burnt in Jerusalem was "transported on camels, since there are very few wagons or even carts to be found in Judaea" (J. Wilkinson, *Jerusalem Pilgrims Before the Crusades* (Warminster, 1977), p. 106).

sive process, and one that probably began in earnest in the seventh century. As with Red Slip wares, amphora production persisted in Egypt longer than other regions, perhaps as late as the eleventh century. Unlike Bilâd al-Shâm, long distance transport in Egypt was almost exclusively by water (viz. the Nile), which sustained the use of amphora as a medium of transport.

b. *Ceramics, cultural reorientation and the potential for exchange*
At the end of the eighth or the start of the ninth century, a revolution took place in the ceramic repertoire of Bilâd al-Shâm. Until this time, Early Islamic pottery had barely deviated from prevailing Late Roman/Late Antique ceramic traditions, and even new ceramic types including Palestinian Fine Table Ware and Red Painted Ware were produced utilising existing potting technologies. The changes of the late eighth-early ninth century were the first significant break with the past following the Islamic conquest. They required the acceptance of new and exotic styles of pottery and the mastery of new and technologically challenging techniques by local artisans. For the consumer, a significant change in taste was involved. Both form and decoration were strikingly different to existing styles, yet tellingly the new types were rapidly adopted, often to the detriment of "traditional" producers including the potters of Jarash.

The first new type of ceramic was a utilitarian domestic ware, consisting of jars, jugs, flasks and bowls in a soft, aerated, off-white to pale yellow or very light brown ware, and known as Islamic Cream Ware (ICW).[107] The jars and jugs in particular were thinly thrown on a fast wheel, sometimes reaching almost "eggshell" thinness, a process made possible by the use of high-grade clay. Additionally the lower body was often pared (trimmed) which left a flat disk base. Shapes were regularly angular, and were undoubtedly inspired by contemporary metalwork in silver. Decoration involved a combination of clay techniques: incision, applied knobs and bands, shallow ribbing, indentations and grooves. Painted decoration was not applied

---

[107] For Cream Wares in Bilâd al-Shâm see: J. Magness, "The Chronology of Capernaum in the Early Islamic period", *Journal of the American Oriental Society* 117 (1997), pp. 481-86; Walmsley, "Turning East. The Appearance of Islamic Cream Wares in Jordan – the End of Antiquity?"; D. Whitcomb, "Khirbat al-Mafjar Reconsidered: The Ceramic Evidence", *Bulletin of the American Schools of Oriental Research* 271 (1988), pp. 51-67.

as a rule. For south Bilâd al-Shâm, ICW represented a major departure in prevailing ceramic traditions, with the inspiration for the shapes, decoration and fabric treatment originating in the fine wares of early ʿAbbâsid ʿIrâq and common at ninth century Sâmarrâ. A second innovation in the ceramic repertoire of Bilâd al-Shâm was the introduction of various types of glazed pottery, especially splashed polychrome, thick turquoise and "Coptic glazed" varieties. While earlier eighth century dates have been proposed for Coptic glazed ware in Egypt, where the type originated, contexts in Bilâd al-Shâm have been consistently later eighth century and thereafter.[108]

The social and economic impact of ICW and the glazed wares, externally inspired but quickly and expertly replicated by local potters, was considerable. Found throughout Bilâd al-Shâm, the widespread adoption of these cross-regional and definitively "Islamic" ceramics reveal a growth in productive contact with Egypt, al-Jazîrah and al-ʿIrâq. The revolutionary nature of the change was reflected in the demise of two long established local pottery wares, PFTW and Jarash White Painted Ware (JWPW).[109] The distinctive jars, jugs and juglets from Jarash, characterised by a dark reddish body and linear white painted decoration, were manufactured until the early ninth century when, as evidence from Pella shows, ICW vessels performing the same function shunted them off the market. Technically both PFTW and JWPW peaked just before their demise, as demonstrated by the exceptionally delicate PFTW cups, which suggests cultural and not technological factors behind their decline. This substitution of well established local ceramic traditions with exotic styles indicates a ready acceptance of new cultural attitudes from outside Bilâd al-Shâm by the second generation after the overthrow of the locally based Umayyad dynasty. To them it would have been obvious that

---

[108] G.T. Scanlon, "Slip-Painted Early Lead-Glazed Wares from Fustat: a dilemma of nomenclature", in R.-P. Gayraud ed., *Colloque International d'Archéologie Islamique*, Textes Arabes et Études Islamiques vol. 36 (Cairo, 1998), pp. 21-53; D. Whitcomb, "Coptic Glazed Ceramics from the Excavations at Aqaba, Jordan", *Journal of the American Research Centre in Egypt* 26 (1989), pp. 167-82; D. Whitcomb, "Glazed Ceramics of the Abbasid Period from the Aqaba Excavations", *Transactions of the Oriental Ceramic Society* (1990-1), pp. 43-65.

[109] The ready acceptance of ICW forms may also reflect a more extensive change in tastes, as the jars, jugs and juglets in PFTW, JWPW and ICW all seem to copy metal originals. JWPW probably replicated copper vessels with silver trace inlay (represented by white wavy lines), ICW copied silver work and PFTW, according to Magness, imitated gold originals. If so, the adoption of the ICW shapes at the expense of the "old" PFTW and JWPW varieties also reflects considerable changes in style and preference in metalwork over the eighth and ninth centuries.

the heart of the Islamic world had shifted east to al-'Irâq, the home of the 'Abbâsid court. The absorption of Bilâd al-Shâm into a strong and unified Islamic empire not only opened their region to new and universally preferred cultural values, but also would have presented new economic opportunities for both producer and merchant.

c. *Prestige items and trade*

A significant feature in the material culture repertoire of Early Islamic Bilâd al-Shâm, especially in the eighth century, is the frequent appearance of high quality stone and metal objects in the archaeological record, even from quite mundane domestic contexts. The political and economic unity of the Islamic world in the eighth century facilitated the movement of these items over considerable distances. Perhaps, as demonstrated by the Radhanite traders, the post roads of the Empire offered merchants a convenient and comparatively safe transport network while, at the same time, the rise of a new and wealthy elite in the principal cities increased demand.

Copper vessels serving a variety of domestic purposes have been recovered in respectable numbers at a number of Early Islamic sites, including Pella, Jarash, 'Ammân, Fidayn (Mafraq), Umm al-Walîd and Usays. Of particular note is the magnificently decorated brazier from Fidayn in north Jordan and a superb dish with an intricate fenestrated ring-base from Pella. Both objects exhibit a close affinity with Coptic art of the period and are, in all likelihood, Egyptian imports. Notably the arcade setting for the fervent "romp" scenes on the Fidayn brazier is a very popular Coptic composition, not only in metal but textiles, book illuminations, murals, wood and stone.[110]

Steatite was another popular import, almost certainly from the mines and workshops of south Arabia and the Hijâz. Plain and finely engraved flat-based bowls for serving and cooking food are a regular discovery, with examples from Usays, Pella and Aylah for instance. Other items made from steatite, especially lamps, incense burners and small containers, were also favoured imports. While not really

---

[110] Mafraq: G. Philip, "Art and Technology", in P. Bienkowski ed., *The Art of Jordan: Treasures from an Ancient Land* (Liverpool, 1991), pp. 86-108, at p. 98, pl. 118; Pella: A. McNicoll, R.H. Smith and B. Hennessy eds., *Pella in Jordan 1. An Interim Report on the Joint University of Sydney and The College of Wooster Excavations at Pella 1979-1981* (Canberra, 1982), p. 140, pl. 59a; Coptic art: A. Badawy, *Coptic Art and Archaeology: The Art of the Christian Egyptians from the Late Antique to the Middle Ages* (Cambridge, Mass., 1978), pp. 321-23, figs. 5.1-2; J. Strzygowski, *Koptische Kunst* (Vienna, 1904), pp. 253-62.

a superior luxury item, the flat based steatite serving bowls, appeal-
ingly decorated with intricate geometric and floral designs, gained
sufficient popularity that an imitative form in pottery soon appeared
to meet demand at the lower end of the market.

These few examples only hint at the broad range of perishable
commodities that would have been brought into Bilâd al-Shâm.
However, the discovery of carbonised silk clothing with two charred
skeletons of earthquake victims at Pella confirms the widespread distribution of prestige goods in the region under the Umayyads.

d. *Coins and trade*

An arguably more valuable indicator of commerce and exchange in
Early Islamic Bilâd al-Shâm is the distribution and circulation of
coin, both base and precious. The numismatic evidence divides into
two distinct categories: coin hoards and site finds. Most hoards consist of precious coin, usually gold *solidi* and silver *drachms* in the seventh century and gold *dînârs* and silver *dirhams* in the eighth, although
copper hoards do exist from the seventh century when base coin
still retained some commercial value. A number of large hoards in
all three metals reveal the extent and nature of commercial contact,
direct and indirect, between Bilâd al-Shâm, the rest of the Islamic
world, Byzantium and, after the eighth century, Eastern Europe. Site
finds, by way of contrast, are predominantly copper, usually Byzantine
folles and pre-reform Umayyad coinage in the seventh century and
Islamic *fulûs* thereafter. Hoards, formed by the intentional collection
and concealment of money, and site finds, casual losses usually but
not exclusively of low-value, are obviously very different in character, yet both categories preserve a valuable snapshot of the direction
and strength of medium and long distance commercial contacts.

Although post-conquest seventh century hoards are relatively uncommon, the few published examples demonstrate conclusively that
Byzantine gold *solidi* and copper *folles* circulated widely in Bilâd al-
Shâm into the last decades of the century. A hoard found at Palmyra
contained 27 gold coins dating from 607 to 649-50, Nablus 29 coins
from 607 to 668, Baysân 27 coins from 625 to 685, Damascus 50
coins from 583 to 685, Nikertai 534 coins from 590 to 681, and
Daphne (near Antakya) 65 coins from 583 to 681 plus one imitation.[111] Of these the large Nikertai hoard, found near Apamea in

---

[111] See C. Morrisson, "La Monnaie en Syrie Byzantine", in J.-M. Dentzer and

Syria, is the most illuminating.[112] The spread of issues, which ranges from Maurice and especially Phocas to Constantine IV, is essentially constant without any appreciable interruption caused by the Islamic conquest. From a total of 516 *solidi* and 18 *semisses*, 345 coins or 64.6% belong to the 50 years 590 to 640 (69 per decade), and 188 or 35.2% to the following 40 years (47 per decade). In the post-conquest period 159 or 29.8% were issues of Constans II, and a further 27 or 5.1% early issues of Constantine IV. More than the other seventh century gold hoards, the size and range of the Nikertai hoard leaves little doubt that Byzantine gold coinage was extensively imported into Bilâd al-Shâm and circulated freely, seemingly as official currency, into the early 680s.

The evidence from the copper coinage, both hoards and excavation finds, is not entirely consistent with the supply patterns of precious coin, notably after the 650s.[113] As with the gold coins, however, the Islamic conquest did not interrupt supply of Byzantine coppers to Bilâd al-Shâm, and large numbers of official Constans II issues continued to arrive in the 640s and 650s. However very few entered Bilâd al-Shâm after 658, and the Constans II *folles* of class 9-11 and coppers of Constantine IV, while not completely absent, are comparatively scarce when compared with figures from Cyprus and Anatolia. The large hoard from the Hamâh area in Syria demonstrates this pattern clearly, as do chance finds from a number of excavations in the region.[114] The Hamâh hoard, which must have been concealed in the 670s, also shows that production of local imitations (73 out of 298 coins) of late Heraclius and earlier Constans II

W. Orthmann eds., *Archeologie et histoire de la Syrie 2. La Syrie de l'époque Achéménide à l'avènement de l'Islam* (Saarbrücken, 1989), pp. 191-204 at pp. 198-99 (with references), who lists five hoards of precious (gold) coin containing only official Byzantine issues of Constans II (641-668) and Constantine IV (668-685), and eight "mixed" hoards, seven of which are copper, containing both official and imitation Byzantine issues. Several of the gold hoards were probably concealed during the bloody succession dispute to the caliphate that divided al-Shâm in the mid-680s. Hence, the absence of coins after 685 in hoards or as casual finds may not necessarily reflect an end to supply from Byzantium at that time. Most of the post 685 gold coins would have still been current when, only a few years later, the first dinars were produced and the circulating Byzantine issues melted down.

[112] Morrisson, "Le Trésor Byzantin de Nikertai".

[113] For a comprehensive study of both classes of information see: M. Phillips and T. Goodwin, "A Seventh-Century Syrian Hoard of Byzantine and Imitative Copper Coins", *Numismatic Chronicle* 157 (1997), pp. 61-87.

[114] Phillips and Goodwin suggest that "the flow of coins ceased because the Byzantines decided unilaterally to stop it", although they concede there are other

types overlapped with the continued import of regular coin from Byzantium. These and other irregular issues spanned the gap between the end of Byzantine supply after 658 and 'Abd al-Malik's official copper series beginning in 692. The wide distribution of both regular Byzantine coin and local imitations in country Bilâd al-Shâm, especially the north,[115] reveals the ongoing importance of the monetary economy after the Islamic conquest. The role of base coin was further enhanced, with considerable economic benefits, by the reforms of 'Abd al-Malik at the end of the seventh century.

Table 1. Coins from Jarash: Mints and Totals

Jund al-Urdunn			Jund Filastîn			Jund Dimashq		
mint	*pre-reform*	*post-reform*	*mint*	*pre-reform*	*post-reform*	*mint*	*pre-reform*	*post-reform*
Tabariyah	-	37	al-Ramlah	-	9	Dimashq	3 (2)	24
al-Urdunn¶	-	18	Filastîn§	-	2	'Ammân	- (1)	3
Baysân	43# (4)	1	Ludd	-	1	Busrâ	-	1
Jarash	3 (5)	3	Iliyâ	-	3	TOTAL	3 (3)	28
'Akkâ	-	3	Yubnâ	-	1			
TOTAL	46 (9)	62	'Asqalân	-	2	Al-Jazîrah		
			Bayt Jibrîn	-	2	al-Ruhâ	-	12
						TOTAL	0	12
			TOTAL	0	20			

Notes

¶ Minted in the capital, Tabariyah.

Four specimens were overstruck with Arabic legends: one with the First and Second Shahadah, two with *tayyib* ("good") and one with "Baysân"; see A.R. Bellinger, *Coins from Jerash, 1928-1934*, Numismatic Notes and Monographs no. 81 (New York, 1938) p. 121 nos. 506-509, p. 122 no. 514 respectively. Very possibly Bellinger attributes the pre-reform issues from Jarash to Baysân, so this figure is probably too high and the Jarash figure too low; cf. the Spanish totals (in brackets).

§ Minted in the capital, al-Ramlah.

( ) Bracketed entries are from the Spanish excavations of the Macellum, and are shown separately as no post-reform totals were available.

possible explanations (Phillips and Goodwin, "A Seventh-Century Syrian Hoard of Byzantine and Imitative Copper Coins", pp. 81-83). They argue that the vast majority of the coppers were sent to Bilâd al-Shâm because of political, not commercial, reasons. The item traded, so to speak, were the coins themselves.

[115] For example at Déhès, see: C. Morrisson, "Déhès. Campagnes I-III (1976-1978), Recherches sur l'Habitat Rural: Les monnaies", *Syria* 57 (1980), pp. 267-87.

The recovery of pre-reform (Arab-Byzantine) fulûs from excavations allows some attempt at documenting the extent, both in distance and volume, of trade within Bilâd al-Shâm, as many of the pre-reform coins can be attributed to a particular mint. Few sites, however, have been sufficiently explored or published to produce enough coins for a valid study, but one of the exceptions is Jarash in Jordan. Coins from the Yale Excavations of 1928-1934 and the Jarash Archaeological Project 1991-1993 are sufficiently numerous to reveal some interesting economic trends (table 1).[116] Very noticeable from the pre-reform totals was the confined economic outlook of Jarash in the later seventh century. The pre-reform coins almost exclusively came from mints located in Jarash's own province, the Jund al-Urdunn (55 out of 61 fulûs, fig. 6-a, showing percentages). Coins from major neighbouring centres, particularly Busrâ, Damascus and 'Ammân,

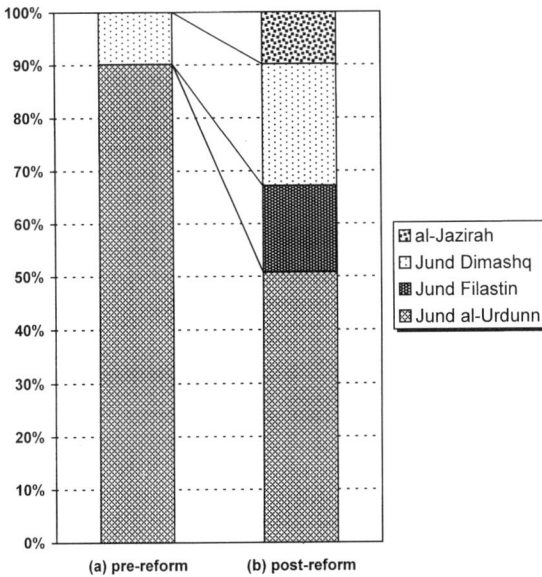

Fig. 6. Origin by province of pre-reform (a) and post-reform (b) Early Islamic coins found at Jarash (see table 1).

[116] Yale: A.R. Bellinger, *Coins from Jerash, 1928-1934* (New York, 1938); JAP: T. Marot, *Las Monedas del Macellum de Gerasa (Yaras, Jordania)* (Madrid, 1998), for the coins from the Spanish mission, except the post-reform Islamic varieties. The rest of the coins from the Jarash Archaeological Project are currently unpublished, but are being prepared by the author and Julian Bowsher.

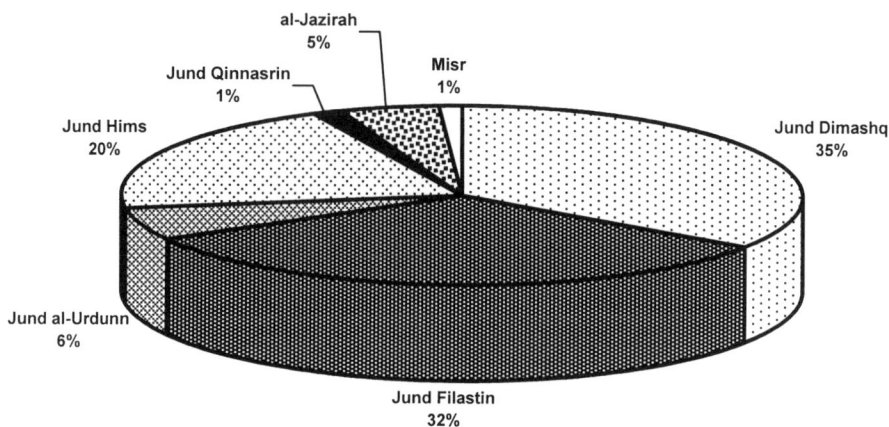

Fig. 7. Origin by province of post-reform Islamic coins from Jericho (see table 2).

are uncommon and issues from mints in Filastîn completely absent. While volumes for the different pre-reform types are difficult to establish the figures do suggest that Jarash's commercial hinterland was very limited and did not extend to any appreciable extent outside of its own province.

In the first half of the eighth century, Jarash's economic reach expanded considerably according to the coin data (table 1), even if the majority of coins still came from within al-Urdunn (62 out of 107, fig. 6-b). When compared with the pre-reform totals, the post-reform fulûs from mints located outside al-Urdunn constitute a much larger percentage of the total (46%, compared with 10% of the pre-reform total). The range of mints is also wider: 17 specimens from 5 mints in Filastîn, and 28 specimens from the Jund Dimashq, mostly Damascus itself. The expansion of trade links in the first half of the eighth century, as revealed by the coins, would have encouraged economic activity at Jarash, although the continuing scarcity of 'Ammân coins is indicative of limited commercial relations between these neighbouring towns. The economic orientation of Early Islamic Jarash was, rather, to the west and especially with Baysân, Tabariyah, al-Ramlah and the coastal towns of Filastîn, and northwards to the imperial capital of Damascus. A similar pattern is apparent at Pella, although coin totals are fewer.[117] A respectable number of mints are represented in the Pella post-reform finds, with specimens from Filastîn, Dimashq and Egypt in addition to the home products of al-Urdunn.

Evidence for an expansion of economic and commercial contacts in the eighth century is mirrored by other numismatic evidence. Hoards and site finds of precious and base coin dating to the first half of the eighth century reveal that coin could move great distances within the confines of the Islamic empire, but much less so outside it. The most illuminating example of Islamic monetary universality under the Marwânid Umayyads is the remarkable Silver Hoard of Damascus, concealed at the end of the Umayyad period probably during the siege of the city by the 'Abbâsid forces.[118] The hoard comprised 1309 Sassanid drachms, the earliest dated 543 (Khusru I), 128 Arab-Sassanid dirhams, one Khuwarizmian dirham, and 2377 Umayyad dirhams the last dated 749-50. The hoard was probably compiled in the East as it included surprisingly large numbers of Sassanid and Arab-Sassanid silvers but no Byzantine silver hexagrams, many of which were produced and circulated from 621 until the end of the century. Revealing is the great number of dirham mints represented in the hoard and their geographical spread, although almost three-quarters were dirhams from Wâsit in southern 'Irâq (1748 of 2377 coins, or 73.5%). Another 8.8% (208 coins) were minted in Damascus.[119] However the remaining 17.7% came from a wide range of mints: in the far west al-Andalus (Spain, 38 specimens) and Ifrîqiyah (modern Tunisia, 66 specimens), in the far east Kirmân (21 specimens) and Harât (7 specimens) and, to the north, Armîniyah (Armenia, 2 specimens)—that is, almost the full extent of the Umayyad empire. While the absolute numbers of dirhams may be small, their presence is significance as regional mints often operated erratically and at much less volume than Wâsit and Damascus.

---

[117] A.G. Walmsley, "The Islamic Coins", in R.A.G. Carson, K.A. Sheedy and A.G. Walmsley, *Pella in Jordan 7: The Coins from the Excavations, 1979-1990*, Mediterranean Archaeology Supplementary Series (Sydney, forthcoming 2000).

[118] M.A. al-Ush, *The Silver Hoard of Damascus* (Damascus, 1972).

[119] Of these 62 were struck in 131 H. (749-50). This, and the absence of hexagrams, would suggest that the hoard arrived in Damascus only a short time before it was concealed.

As already established by the Jarash and Pella material, post-reform base coin circulated more widely in Bilâd al-Shâm than its pre-reform counterpart, although it must be remembered it had more time to achieve this and was produced in greater numbers.[120] Another interesting example is presented by the coins from an excavation at Jericho, which in the Early Islamic period was included in the Jund Dimashq. The excavations produced stray finds and two hoards, with specimens from a range of mints (table 2, fig. 7).[121]

Table 2. Post-Reform Coins from Jericho: Mints and Totals

Jund Dimashq		*Jund Hims*	
Dimashq	29	Hims	17
Jund Filastîn		*Jund Qinnasrîn*	
al-Ramlah	23	Halab	1
Ludd	3		
Iliyâ	1	*al-Jazîrah*	
		al-Ruhâ	4
Jund al-Urdunn			
Tabariyah	4	*Misr*	
al-Urdunn	1	Iskandariyah	1

The Jund Dimashq and the Jund Filastîn provided almost an equal number of coins. The prevalence of coins from Filastîn should not come as a surprise. Jericho lay on the eastern border of Filastîn, and was strategically located midpoint on the Jerusalem-'Ammân road, near the Jordan River crossing. The large number of coins from Dimashq can be attributed to Jericho's placement in that province, yet even so the number is high considering the distance the coins had to travel. The scarcity of coins from al-Urdunn, which abutted Jericho to the north, is unexpected, especially when a much greater number of coins came from the more distant Jund Hims. The coins suggest Jericho's principal trade axes easily reached north-eastwards as far as Damascus and even beyond,[122] and westwards to Jerusalem

---

[120] Imitation and Arab-Byzantine types were also removed from circulation on a large scale at the time of 'Abd al-Malik's reform and either restruck or melted down. See, for a hoard of restruck fulûs, S. Qedar, "A Hoard of Monetary Reform Fulus", *Israel Numismatic Journal* (1984-85), pp. 65-75.

[121] G.C. Miles, "Catalogue of Islamic coins", in J.B. Pritchard ed., *The Excavations at Herodian Jericho, 1951* (New Haven, 1951), pp. 29-41.

[122] As at Jarash and Pella, there were an inexplicably significant number of coppers from al-Ruhâ (Urfa, Edessa) in the Jazîrah, located some 665 kms to the north-east of Jericho. As table 1 earlier showed, at Jarash there are no recognisable coins from the intervening provinces of Hims and Qinnasrîn, making the al-Ruhâ issues even more unexpected. This suggests their introduction into al-Urdunn and Filastîn

and Ramlah on the Mediterranean littoral. By way of contrast, the route northwards up the Jordan Valley to Tabariyah was commercially insignificant.

The few ninth and tenth century hoards of precious coin recovered in Bilâd al-Shâm reveal the continuing unified nature of the monetary system in the Islamic world, even though political unity was lost with the progressive disintegration of the 'Abbâsid caliphate. For instance, no less than ten Islamic dynasties are represented in a major hoard of 376 dinars found at al-Ramlah.[123] Although the coins date from between 761 and 979, about half were Hamdanid and Bûyid issues produced in northern 'Irâq and Iran over a reasonably short fifteen-year period. The geographical spread of mints is equally impressive, ranging from al-Muhammadiyah (in Algeria) to Armîniyah in the east. A hoard of 90 silver pieces from Tel Isdûd (Âzdûd) north of Gaza similarly reflects the extent of the monetary economy in the Islamic world of the tenth century.[124] Six dynasties and numerous mints are represented, with the majority from the Filastîn mint (al-Ramlah). While very much a locally compiled hoard, coins from Baghdâd, Arrajân (in Fârs) and even Constantinople (a miliaresion of Basil I and Constantine) were current in Filastîn for inclusion in the hoard.

One of the most remarkable and far-reaching initiatives in Early Islamic trade was the forging of profitable trade routes into Eastern Europe, beginning in the late eighth to early ninth century. Literary sources and numismatic evidence equally reveal that between the early ninth and early eleventh centuries Muslim merchants actively bartered with Rûs ("Russian") traders, exchanging dirhams and dinars for furs and slaves. As the written sources refer to the mid-ninth century and later, the most valuable and reliable evidence for the start and development of trade between the Islamic world and Eastern Europe are the numerous dirham hoards recovered in Russia and the Baltic.[125] Two major conclusions can be drawn from these hoards.

---

was not accidental, and probably represent low value military pay carried by troops returning from the Byzantine border region.

[123] S. Levy and H.W. Mitchell, "A Hoard of Gold Dinars from Ramlah", *Israel Numismatic Journal* 3 (1965-66), pp. 37-66.

[124] J.L. Bacharach, "A Hoard of ` ʿm Dirhams from Tel Ashdod", *Atiqot* 14 (1980), pp. 83-92.

[125] See the detailed studies in T.S. Noonan, "Ninth-Century Dirham Hoards from European Russia: a Preliminary Analysis", in M.A.S. Blackburn and D.M. Metcalf eds., *Viking-Age Coinage in the Northern Lands: the Sixth Oxford Symposium on Coinage and*

Firstly, the make up of the hoards indicates that the dirhams were directly imported from current stock in the Islamic empire. Their compositions are compatible with hoards of the same date recovered within the Islamic empire, yet are quite different from hoards found in Transoxiana. As is to be expected many mints were represented in the Eastern European hoards, although most coins were 'Irâqi or North African products. Secondly, the dirham hoards from the Caucasus reveal that Islamic trade with Russia was initially conducted over a westerly Caucasus or Caspian route, and not over any eastern route through central Asia. Hoard dates suggest that a western route to Eastern Europe was established in the 770s-780s, with the volume of exchange reaching significant proportions in the early ninth century.

The mechanisms by which trade first took place between Muslim and Rûs merchants can be identified through an analysis of the composition and chronology of early ninth century dirham hoards from the Caucasus.[126] Although written sources of the mid-ninth century and later only describe a sea route across the Caspian, the hoard evidence convincingly shows that trade with European Russia was, at first, conducted over a land route through the Caucasus. The appearance of dirham hoards in the Caucasus coincides with the appearance of the first hoards in Eastern Europe, and it is difficult to avoid the conclusion that these two events were linked in some manner. Furthermore, hoards from both regions were similar in their composition, to the extent they shared one important difference with other hoards concealed in the Middle East at about the same time. Unlike the Middle East hoards, the newest dirham (or failing that one of the most recent) in the hoards from the Caucasus and Eastern European was the product of a south-Caucasian mint, often Armîniyah. Clearly, these newly minted dirhams could have only been added to

---

Monetary History, BAR International Series 122 (Oxford, 1981), pp. 47-117; T.S. Noonan, "The Regional Composition of Ninth-Century Dirham Hoards from European Russia", *Numismatic Chronicle* 144 (1984), pp. 153-65; T.S. Noonan, "Why Dirhams First Reached Russia: the Role of Arab-Khazar Relations in the Development of the Earliest Islamic Trade with Eastern Europe", *Archivum Eurasiae Medii Aevi* 4 (1984), pp. 151-282; also the analysis in Hodges and Whitehouse, *Mohammed, Charlemagne & the Origins of Europe*, pp. 111-26. Although continuing long after the period under consideration in this study, Muslim trade with European Russia commenced in the late eighth century and grew strongly in the early ninth. Its development represents an important turning point in the orientation and structure of Islamic trade, and so requires some treatment here.

[126] See especially Noonan, "Why Dirhams First Reached Russia".

an existing trade collection while the hoard was in transit through the southern Caucasus.

Critical in the formation of a secure trade route through the Caucasus at the end of the eighth century was the dramatic improvement in Muslim-Khazar relations. For over a century the Khazars and the Muslims had competed for domination over the Caucasus, reaching a peak in the early eighth century with the appointment of Maslamah b. 'Abd al-Malik (builder of Hisn Maslamah, see above). His aggressive confrontation with the Khazars for control over the northern Caucasus brought an equally aggressive response, but neither side could force a resolution to the conflict. By the mid-eighth century it was apparent to both sides any further escalation of the conflict would be costly, and following the rise of the 'Abbâsids a new policy of rapprochement was implemented by the Caliph al-Mansûr. 'Abbâsid priorities were directed elsewhere, notably towards the escalating war with Byzantium and suppressing internal revolts while, at the same time, the Khazars faced growing pressure from Byzantium. With both parties disheartened and distracted, the second half of the eighth century was characterised by a gradual de-escalation of the conflict and a reciprocal growth of trade through the Caucasus. The new era in Muslim-Khazar relations which resulted corresponded, accidentally or otherwise, with the meteoric expansion of the 'Abbâsid economy of which the Eastern European trade formed a part.

The export of dirhams to Eastern Europe and the Baltic continued in large numbers until the early eleventh century, yet the presence of hoards in the Caucasus datable to the 860s and 870s declines significantly before they disappear altogether. The falling number of hoards would argue for an end to any significant trade over the Caucasus routes, and this conclusion is supported by the written sources dating from the second half of the ninth century and after. In the earliest of these works, the geography of Ibn Khurdâdhbih,[127] Rûs merchants cross the Caspian Sea from the Khazar-held Volga delta to the port of Jurjân on the south-eastern coast. From Jurjân, the Rûs merchants were able to reach Baghdâd and other market centres in the Islamic realm. By the end of the century Muslim-Rûs trade was largely confined to the new maritime route, along which thousands of dirhams travelled into Russia and, by way of Viking contacts along the Volga, further afield to Scandinavia.

---

[127] Ibn Khurradadhbih, *al-Masâlik*, pp. 115, 153.

By way of contrast base coinage, although reformed under the
'Abbâsid caliph al-Ma'mûn (813-33), became progressively insignificant
for commercial transactions in the ninth century. By the century's
end the face value of fulûs had lost any meaning due to the disintegration of the 'Abbâsid caliphate as a political and economic force.
The effective demise of an empire wide unit of small change also
sees an end to a very illuminating source of information on exchange
in the Early Islamic world.

5. *The eighth century: defining moment or passing phase?*

The Eastern Mediterranean littoral in the seventh century was subjected to a series of politico-military shocks with long term consequences to the region's economic systems. The overthrow of Maurice,
the revolt of the Heraclii, and the Sassanid invasion were swiftly followed by the profoundly significant Islamic conquest of 622-640.
Twenty years later Damascus, located in the geographic centre of
Bilâd al-Sham, became the capital of a rapidly expanding empire.
In every case, however, these events did not result in sudden and
catastrophic change to existing economic systems, even if coin hoards
suggest short-term disruptions did occur. Production and exchange
at the local and regional level was already in considerable flux at
the start of the seventh century, before the troubles set in. The following decades introduced additional challenges, but the archaeological record, from local ceramic production to coin supply and
circulation, indicates that the economy was able to adapt with only
the occasional failure to the new socio-political environment.

The rate of development to existing economic structures and trade
systems quickened in the late seventh century, and particularly with
the accession to the caliphate of the active 'Abd al-Malik in 685.
The evidence for a period of major and permanent change, which
is considerable, is found across a range of historical, archaeological,
and numismatic sources. Clearly significant were the monetary reforms, by which a common and officially sanctioned currency was
created for the whole empire. Other major initiatives included administrative reforms, particularly the adoption of Arabic as the language of government, and a program of massive urban and rural
renewal especially improvements to the commercial infrastructure of
towns. The promotion of new urban centres and their elites, notably

Damascus, and the obligatory distribution of wealth to the Muslim hierarchy of Bilâd al-Shâm and the Hijâz resulted in a substantial re-orientation of trading systems. Overall, these changes greatly favoured economic growth particularly in the first half of the eighth century. However, some centres were disadvantaged, for instance Ludd by the foundation of al-Ramlah as the new capital of Filastîn, and Baysân by the elevation of Tabariyah to provincial capital. The numismatic evidence reveals a general broadening of trade follow-ing the reforms, yet the ceramics indicate that commerce within Bilâd al-Shâm was conducted through a series of overlapping net-works rather than by way of one large common system. The struc-ture of Early Islamic government may partly account for this arrangement. Under the Umayyads and early 'Abbâsids the admin-istrative and tax structures were regionally, not centrally, based. Most tax, which included goods in kind notably wheat and oil, was dis-tributed at the provincial level and only relatively small amounts were remitted to central treasury. Long distance exchange, to the extent it relied upon imperial structures, would not have been encour-aged by this system of decentralised administration.

In economic terms, the 'Abbâsid revolution and the subsequent foundation of Baghdâd resulted in major transformations to the trade systems of the Islamic empire. Baghdâd and the other 'Abbâsid founda-tions in al-'Irâq created an enormous demand for consumer goods arguably not seen since Rome in its heyday. Social and political changes also encouraged the growth of a merchant economy, espe-cially in the ninth century. The centralisation of government by the 'Abbâsid administration and the reciprocal disempowering of regional elites fostered trade links over increasingly greater distances. By the end of the eighth century merchants, Muslim and non-Muslim, were travelling long distances by land and water to destinations beyond the Islamic realm to acquire desirable commodities for the profitable markets of an increasingly sophisticated and culturally unified Islamic society.

OVERVIEW:
PRODUCTION, DISTRIBUTION AND DEMAND, II

Chris Wickham

In the conclusion to our companion volume, I described the sixth century as "the last of the Roman centuries".[1] The eighth century takes us fully into the post-Roman world; attempts to prove the contrary have never succeeded. But this poses a new set of problems. In the sixth century, most of the lands of the former Roman empire maintained a certain homogeneity owing to the survival of at least some Roman institutions, whether political, religious or even economic. It was necessary to separate out some elements of divergent development in northern and southern Europe, but it was also possible to give an overview of the whole: the sixth century was a period of economic involution, of regionalisation, from Denmark to Syria, even if the speed of this development was very different from place to place. By the eighth century, however, the regionalisation of economies was so complete that in some cases little linked them at all. The eighth-century economy looks very different from the standpoint of each major area. In the North Sea economic zone, we find active exchange, new trade routes and ports of trade, the beginnings of the new economic world of the central middle ages and beyond. In the western Mediterranean, we find relative stagnation, as the final collapse around 700 of the late Roman international exchange system, focused on North Africa, makes clear how localised the next levels of exchange had by now become. In the eastern Mediterranean, by contrast, two coherent state systems, one weaker (Byzantium), one stronger (the Caliphate), maintained or underwrote relatively large-scale exchange networks that had often changed relatively little— indeed in some provinces, notably Egypt, hardly at all—from the late Roman period.[2] It is impossible to encompass such difference

---

[1] C. Wickham, "Overview: production, distribution and demand", in R. Hodges and W. Bowden eds., *The sixth century* (Leiden, 1998), pp. 279-92, at p. 279. I am grateful in this conclusion for the critical comments of the other authors of this book, and of the other members of ESF TRW Group 3.

[2] See, for the first two zones, the basic surveys of D. Claude, largely based on

in a single analysis, and in this overview I shall not attempt to do so. After having discussed these three patterns separately, however, I will discuss what structural elements they do have in common.

The economy of the early middle ages has always been a difficult test for supporters of continuity. The ESF programme on the "Transformation of the Roman World", of which this volume is a product, explicitly set out to transcend the often facile catastrophism of earlier generations of scholars, and rightly so. But economic historians know that the economy of the twelfth century, say, has barely a single point in common with that of the fifth, except at the level of the regular heartbeat of subsistence agriculture; this difference might be the product of Transformation, rather than catastrophe, but it was a pretty big transformation nonetheless. Nearly every economic indicator in the sixth century pointed downwards, as we saw in our previous volume: demography, the quantity of interregional exchange, even (probably) the intensity of agrarian exploitation. By the eleventh century, however, every one pointed upwards, and some of them had done so for some time. We are thus entitled to ask such questions as: when can the low-point between these two tendencies actually be located? why did this inversion of tendency occur, what was its prime cause? and to what extent was there a real discontinuity between two economic realities, one Roman, the other medieval? We chose to side-step these questions in the sixth-century volume precisely because we concluded that that period was still on the Roman side of any divide; they cannot be side-stepped in a volume on the eighth century. But, in a highly localised economic environment, it must be recognised that the answers to each question could well be different from place to place. Given such an environment, we certainly could not accept that one of the three economic zones just sketched out is the norm (or, a Core), the others atypical (or, Peripheries). It may indeed be, for that matter, that even to say that there were only three such zones is an oversimplification. But in a synthetic conclusion, some simplification is inescapable, and I will stick with these three for the moment.

---

literary and documentary sources, "Der Handel im westlichen Mittelmeer während des Frühmittelalters" and "Aspekte des Binnenhandels im Merovingerreich auf Grund der Schriftquellen", in *Untersuchungen zu Handel und Verkehr der vor- und frühgeschichtlichen Zeit in Mittel- und Nordeuropa* (Göttingen, 1985), vols. 2, and 3 pp. 9-99. For the second two, the indispensible archaeological starting point is C. Panella, "Merci e scambi nel Mediterraneo tardoantico", in A. Carandini *et al.* eds., *Storia di Roma* 3.2 (Turin, 1993), pp. 613-97, focussed on the period up to 700.

1. *The North*

In the North Sea world, the economic superpower was Francia. The active eighth-century international exchange that was the underpinning of the prosperity of the *emporia* of the coasts of the North—Hamwic, London, Ipswich, York, Quentovic, Dorestad, Ribe, and Hedeby and Birka in the Baltic, to name only the best-known—was, above all, exchange to and from the Frankish lands, and is measured by the quantity and distribution of Frankish goods in England and Denmark, far more than by the quantity of exports between England and Denmark themselves (even though these are documented too, as Ulf Näsman notes for glass products). Francia was, of course, far larger and far more institutionally coherent than either England or Denmark, even if one could consider these latter two as in any sense single units. The long eighth century was a period of state-building in both, for sure; but it also saw the only prolonged period of full Frankish unity ever, almost unbroken for 120 years (720-840), under four generations of Carolingians, which gave a powerful impetus to Frankish economic hegemony, as well as, of course, territorial expansion. It is not surprising, in fact, that it is precisely this period that was the high-point of the *emporia*, which indeed in several cases failed outright in the decades of political crisis that followed, as Näsman and Adriaan Verhulst have stressed in this book.

We must begin with the reality of this long-distance exchange activity, for it has long been one of the best-known markers of the vitality of our period, ever more clearly defined by the steady publication of more and more of the great *emporia* excavations, Birka and then Hedeby beginning in the first half of this century, Dorestad, Ribe and Hamwic in more recent decades, and Ipswich and London soon (we hope) to come.[3] But it is equally important to stress that this exchange is only one part of the economic reality of the eighth century. What emerges above all from our articles on the North, Ulf Näsman, John Moreland, Adriaan Verhulst, Stéphane Lebecq and Ian Wood, is the importance of production. The point is pretty obvious in itself: one cannot understand exchanges of goods unless one understands how and where they were produced. But it is fair

---

[3] For surveys, see R. Hodges, *Dark age economics* (London, 1982); H. Clarke and B. Ambrosiani, *Towns in the Viking age* 2nd ed. (London, 1995); for Hamwic, see below, note 9.

to say that the relations of production have in recent years been less
fully studied than exchange, outside the well-trodden arena of the
manorial system at least. It also emerges that a focus on production
allows one to be less dazzled by the great years of Charlemagne
than has sometimes been the case.

Here, we need to begin with agriculture, the overwhelmingly dominant economic sector in our period. Lebecq surveys monastic agricultural production in his article for this volume. The high-point of
this has traditionally been seen as the ninth century, because of the
wealth of evidence produced by the polyptychs of the period. Lebecq
points out that the formation of monastic estates goes back to the
seventh century, and that certain crucial indicators of the development
of agrarian production, such as mills and wine-presses, and agrarian
specialisms such as salt-making, can be found right from the start.
It is true that the sharpening of landlordly control over production
is most clearly evidenced by the development of the bipartite manor
(the *régime domanial classique*), involving the generalisation of the obligation of large-scale labour-services on demesnes to the peasantry
of many north Frankish estates, and that this development seems to
have been fastest in the late eighth century—for demesnes are not
very well-documented at all before 750, whereas they are already of
major importance in many monastic estates in the Seine-Rhine area
by the early ninth century. Furthermore, this increase in control was
a feature of the Carolingian heartland above all (as well as parts of
northern Italy), and has often been seen as a spin-off of the development of Carolingian political power.[4] Lebecq, however, implies a
different origin, in the more gradual structural integration of scattered monastic estates, which had been going on for a century, and
in the steady expansion of the possibilities for selling produce in the
markets of northern Francia and then, by extension, in the *emporia*

---

[4] For recent manorial bibliography, which is extensive, see in particular the articles collected in A. Verhulst, *Rural and urban aspects of early medieval northwest Europe*
(Aldershot, 1992); J.-P. Devroey, *Etudes sur le grand domaine carolingien* (Aldershot, 1993);
W. Rösener ed., *Strukturen der Grundherrschaft im frühen Mittelalter* (Göttingen, 1989);
and P. Toubert, "Le part du grand domaine dans le décollage économique de
l'Occident (VIIIe-Xe siècles)", *Flaran* 10 (1988), pp. 53-86. Only the last pays attention to parallel Italian developments. For the manor before 750, see M.J. Tits-
Dieuaide, "Grands domaines, grandes et petites exploitations en Gaule mérovingienne",
in A. Verhulst ed., *Le grand domaine aux époques mérovingienne et carolingienne* (Gent, 1985),
pp. 23-50, which takes a minimalist approach; I would be even more minimalist
than her, as I shall argue elsewhere.

on the coast. This fits the relatively recent interpretation of the manorial system as a feature of an open, expanding economy, as in the
work of Pierre Toubert and Jean-Pierre Devroey, rather than an
older view which saw it as the exemplar of agrarian self-sufficiency
in a world without exchange. The underlying point these historians
are making is that the intensification of the exploitation of peasant
producers, and of the control of their productive activities, which is
represented by the manorial system, is hard to explain unless it corresponds to an increase in demand; it is thus given a context and
motive by earlier signs of expansion, such as the development of the
efficiency of the transformation of agrarian produce (as with mills
and wine-presses), a probable slow demographic increase, and, above
all, the increase in evidence for commerce.[5]

This interpretation is convincing. It also, in its emphasis on demand,
focuses our attention on who had the wealth to buy. I will return
to some of the implications of this issue in a moment, but one answer
lies, of course, in the enormous concentrations of wealth that monastic estate networks themselves represented already in 700 and indeed
well before. These networks were enormous both in the total hectare-
age of these estate-complexes and in their wide geographical spread,
and it is indeed likely that one of the impetuses to the expansion of
agrarian exchange was the simple necessity to move goods from
peripheral estates to the central places of their proprietors, as Lebecq
stresses. Furthermore, these movements were not restricted to monastic estates. We know that some seventh- and eighth-century aristocratic and episcopal estate-networks were just as large and widely
dispersed: indeed, such aristocratic networks lay at the origin of most
monastic estates.[6] In an important argument, Wood shows that they
could even be dispersed across political frontiers, which further aided
the extension of Frankish exchange activity on an international level.
Royal lands were more extensive still, of course. The major lay and
ecclesiastical figures of eighth-century Frankish political society dwarfed

---

[5] Land clearance, however, may be less important an element in agrarian expansion in our period than has sometimes been thought. See, for example, L. Bourgeois,
Territoires, reseaux et habitats, Thèse de doctorat, Université de Paris-I, 1995, pp. 389-
404, for an effective counter to earlier views that the pre-Carolingian Paris region
was largely forest.

[6] There is no recent synthesis of this topic from an economic point of view, but
see the important social analysis, with references, of R. Le Jan, *Famille et pouvoir
dans le monde franc (VIIe-Xe siècle)* (Paris, 1995), esp. pp. 71ff., 122ff., 387ff.

any other landowners in the Latin world in their wealth and the geographical spread of their holdings; the only owners to match them were a handful of public powers in southern Europe such as the pope and the king of the Lombards. Such concentrations of wealth were the underpinnings, that is to say, for the particular vitality of northern European exchange in our period; monastic estates are the best documented ones, but were not necessarily atypical in the patterns of their exploitation.

These concentrations of agrarian wealth were matched in our century by active artisanal production. This can be seen most clearly in ceramic patterns. The classic Merovingian ceramic tradition of black carinated fine pottery (*vases biconiques*, *Knickwandtöpfen*), which was produced in every major kiln site in northern Francia, died out around 700; it was replaced as a fine ware by rather more centralised productions, such as Badorf ware and the other Vorgebirge wares from the Cologne area, or Tating ware from (among others) the otherwise more utilitarian Mayen kilns, or the wares from La Londe near Rouen, which dominated the valleys of the Rhine and at least the lower Seine, including the coastal *emporia*, and indeed the *emporia* of England and Denmark. In the eighth century, even more than in the sixth, these were probably the most elaborate production networks for ceramics north of Syria-Palestine and Egypt.[7] We cannot compare this sort of evidence of geographical scale with that which we have for other artisanal media, such as metal or glass, but it must at least be said that there is a lot of evidence for metalworking in prosperous inland centres like Huy, Maastricht and

---

[7] Cf. Wickham, "Overview", p. 282 for the sixth century. For Egypt, see below, note 38. For a good brief survey of the Carolingian Rhineland networks, see R. Hodges, *The Hamwih pottery*, CBA Research Reports 37 (London, 1981), pp. 62-68, 83-84; for updates see the articles of A. Verhoeven, W.A. Van Es and W.J.H. Verwers, in D. Piton ed., *La céramique du Vème au Xème siècle dans l'Europe du Nord-Ouest* (Arras, 1993), pp. 209-15, 227-36; and U. Gross, "Die Töpferware der Franken", in *Die Franken. Wegbereiter Europas* (Mannheim, 1996), pp. 581-93, which is also the best overview of earlier Merovingian wares. The coarser Mayen wares and their Parisian analogues always had a wider circulation: see M. Redknap, "Medieval pottery production at Mayen", in D.R.M. Gaimster *et al.*, *Zur Keramik des Mittelalters und der beginnenden Neuzeit im Rheinland*, BAR International Series 440 (Oxford, 1988), pp. 3-37 and pers. comm.; M. Petit in *L'Ile de France de Clovis à Hugues Capet du Vᵉ siècle au Xᵉ siècle* (Paris, 1993), pp. 248-51, 274-75. For La Londe, see N. Roy, "Un atelier de poterie du haut moyen âge en foret de la Londe, près de Rouen (Seine-Maritime)", in Piton, *La céramique*, pp. 341-53.

Cologne, as well as in the *emporia*.[8] The implication of this archae-ological evidence, as also of more casual literary evidence for arti-sanal productions, is that their basic distribution areas were each of the great river valleys, the Rhine, Meuse, Scheldt, Seine, Loire, as is clear from Verhulst's article. These distribution patterns were, that is to say, geographically determined; they cannot easily be mapped onto the networks of distribution of agricultural goods, which depended on often chance collections of property-owning—although those, too, certainly (and unsurprisingly) privileged river communications where possible. But it seems that the distribution range of artisanal pro-duction at least matched the geographical scale of agricultural wealth, which fits the fact that rich landowners were the major likely pur-chasers of non-utilitarian goods; it is worth reiterating that northern Francia had both unusually rich landowners and unusually widely available artisanal productions in the eighth century.

This stress on the wealth of the Frankish élites gives a further context to one of Verhulst's major conclusions: that internal exchange, focused on former Roman cities, was more important in the long run for Francia than the external exchange focused on the *emporia*. The cities of the Rhine and Meuse had pre-existed Dorestad, and would be major centres long after Dorestad had vanished, because they responded to the real regional exchange needs of the Frankish élites. The economic activity of these cities had already resumed in the seventh century; they developed in the eighth, for the most part, but they only declined slightly, if at all, in the difficult Viking decades, and would revive again in the tenth century and later. These cities were at the centre of the active regional and international exchange of the central middle ages; the patterns of that exchange thus have their roots in the seventh century or, indeed, the late sixth. These continuities, too, match the general continuities in north Frankish élite landowning.

One can thus counterpose, first, a stable network of regional and interregional exchange in northern Francia, based on the wealth of agrarian élites and divided, roughly, by river valley; and, second, a

---

[8] See in general Verhulst in this volume. For Cologne, see S. Schütte, "Continuity problems and authority structures in Cologne", in G. Ausenda ed., *After empire* (Woodbridge, 1995), pp. 163-75; M. Gechter and S. Schütte, "Zwischen St. Alban und Judenviertel in Köln", *Rheinische Heimatpflege* 35 (1998), pp. 37-56.

level of international exchange, which was focused on the *emporia* at
the mouths of those rivers, and which—the point has often been
made, and it remains a convincing one—was rather more explicitly
linked to the political and economic needs of the kings of the high
Carolingian period. This opposition has its counterpart in the patterns on the other shores of the North Sea, too. In both England
and Denmark, *emporia* have been associated with kings (Hamwic with
the kings of Wessex, London with Mercia, Ipswich with East Anglia,
Ribe with the emerging kingdom of Denmark, and so on), and can
be argued to have acted as funnels for the channelling of relatively
rare prestige goods to a restricted group of people around the kings,
as Ulf Näsman and John Moreland (the latter with a critical stance
to the issue, it must be noted) make clear in this book, and as
Richard Hodges argued before them. There is even more contrast
than in Francia, however, between the economic vitality of a Hamwic
or a Ribe and the rather more restricted exchange networks of the
inland areas of most of England and Denmark, including even
Hamwic's hinterland, as it at present seems—and this notwithstanding the very wide range of crafts documented inside the latter town.[9]
This contrast has sometimes puzzled archaeologists, and does indeed
indicate that more work is needed before we can know who actually bought Hamwic's products, but seen from a Frankish perspective it is perhaps less surprising as an overall picture: everything we
know about Anglo-Saxon and Danish aristocracies (or Anglo-Saxon
churches) in our century makes it clear that they had not yet achieved
anything remotely resembling the levels of wealth or economic dominance, and thus potential demand, of those of Francia. Independent
regional economies would in most cases be far simpler as a result;
although they would of course exist—Näsman and Moreland set
them out in this book for Denmark and England, and the patterns
of exchange of, for example, metalwork or glass have already been
extensively analysed for sixth- to eighth-century England—they would
be far more embedded in social relations, such as gift exchange (see

---

[9] A.D. Morton, *Excavations at Hamwic I*, CBA Research Report 84 (London, 1992);
P. Andrews, *Excavations at Hamwic 2*, CBA Research Report 109 (London, 1997),
e.g. p. 254; D. Hinton, *The gold, silver and other non-ferrous alloy objects from Hamwic*
(Southampton, 1996), e.g. p. 100. See further Moreland's second article in this volume. Hamwic obviously depended on its hinterland for food and raw materials,
but its finished products have not been found outside the town, offering a contrast
to the hinterland of Ipswich.

Moreland's first article in this book), or the dendritic (ruler-focused) networks analysed in most detail by Hodges.[10] Most *emporia* were even less organically linked to these regional economies than they were in Francia. As in Francia, it was tenth-century, more than eighth-century, urbanism that was linked to regional exchange, and that would last into the future.

Three other points may be worth making before we leave this brief survey of the North. The first is that it homogenises some sharp regional differences. Verhulst stressed that even the Meuse and the Rhine, relatively near neighbours, have different histories, with curves of rising and falling prosperity that do not fully match. The Seine was certainly different again. (Unfortunately, we cannot extend our observations southward in Francia, for the wide lands between Paris and the Mediterranean coast, themselves both areas of solid recent research, have as yet been studied too patchily for generalisations to be made.) Why different parts of northern Francia had different trajectories we cannot yet say; but the fact needs recognition, for it has parallels elsewhere. In Denmark and England, regional difference is clearer still: in both cases, one can distinguish between a zone where urban and rural exchange was slowly becoming more integrated and hierarchical (respectively, southern Jutland and eastern England between the Thames and the Tees) and other areas where artisanal activity tended to be relatively simple and localised. In eastern England, this is evidenced by the capillary distribution of a mass-produced pottery, Ipswich ware, in East Anglia, and similar patterns in the east Midlands and east Yorkshire for the distribution even of handmade wares, as well as a relatively dense concentration of so-called "prolific" sites like Flixborough, as Moreland makes clear in his second article; in my view, none of these patterns have significant parallels in the rest of the country. Similar ceramic networks have been proposed for south Jutland, which Näsman contrasts with the north and the islands of Denmark. Again, exactly why these differences developed cannot easily be said at present. It can scarcely be doubted that one reason is proximity to Francia, given that in each case we are dealing with coastal areas—although other coastal areas were less developed. Another reason may be that kingship and the con-

---

[10] R. Hodges, *Primitive and peasant markets* (Oxford, 1988), pp. 17-25, 34-61, following Carol Smith. For metalwork and glass, see C.J. Arnold, *An archaeology of the early Anglo-Saxon kingdoms*, 2nd ed. (London, 1997), pp. 101-48.

centration of wealth were more developed in these areas. This may well work for Denmark, although it has to be said that it works less well in England: we know too little about East Anglian kingship to be sure of its role there, but the hegemonic kingdom in the eighth century was of course Mercia, whose heartland does not seem to show up any developed exchange system at all. (Kent is a particularly strange anomaly: closest to Francia, recipient of rich Frankish goods from the fifth century onwards, relatively well-organised, with clear documentation of urbanism and rich landowning in eighth-century Canterbury, it ought to have generated a capillary exchange system on a par with East Anglia, but none has as yet been detected.)[11] We are, that is to say, only at the beginnings of our understanding of these regional differences, which is comprehensible, given the fact that a generation ago they were invisible. But they add to the overall tenor of the arguments of the authors of northern articles in this book: that regional production and exchange was the most important reality of our period, notwithstanding the vitality of international commerce.

A second point is a problem: who, exactly, bought the goods that were increasingly available in markets and fairs on the rivers and coasts of the North Sea zone? It is usually easy to answer this question when we deal with artisanal products, which are, after all, generally found on the sites occupied by their buyers (or recipients)—although, as we have seen, Hamwic's clientele has not yet been fully delineated. The problem comes with grain: if every monastic estate sold its surplus, who was there around who had the resources to buy it, but not the land to produce it himself? Certainly not aristocrats or kings, who may have been doing the same; there was anyway a limit to the amount of bread that even the most voracious mead-hall could consume. Nor is there any point in speculating that

---

[11] See, still, J.G. Hurst, "The pottery", in D.M. Wilson ed., *The archaeology of Anglo-Saxon England* (Cambridge, 1976), pp. 283-348, at pp. 299-311; Hodges, *Hamwih pottery*, pp. 52-61; I am grateful to Helena Hamerow and Paul Blinkhorn for discussions. See also D. Williams and A. Vince, "The characterisation and interpretation of early to mid Saxon granitic tempered pottery in England", *Medieval archaeology* 41 (1997), pp. 214-20; R.J. Silvester, "The addition of more-or-less undifferentiated dots to a distribution map? The Fenland Project in retrospect", in J. Gardiner ed., *Flatlands and wetlands*, East Anglian archaeology 50 (1993), pp. 24-39, at pp. 27-28. For Flixborough, see C.P. Loveluck, "A high-status Anglo-Saxon settlement at Flixborough, Lincs.", *Antiquity* 72 (1998), pp. 146-61. For Canterbury, see N.P. Brooks, *The early history of the church of Canterbury* (Leicester, 1984), pp. 22-30. See further Moreland's second article in this volume.

grain might have been exported overseas, for the same problems would arise. Any answer here is hypothetical, but a few observations can be made. One market for grain was obviously towns (and perhaps, by extension, the prosperous but ecologically marginal Frisian coast), although even the most optimistic analyst of the Carolingian economy would probably not argue that this was a major motor of the exchange system. Another may have been the army: Carolingian armies were not standing, but the campaigning season (often preharvest, one must remember, therefore in the most difficult months for supplies) involved larger numbers of men than any equivalent gathering anywhere in the West, for up to three months of the year. They were supposed to bring their own supplies, and indeed presumably did, for no public military commissariat is recorded on this scale in our period. But where did they get them? Logically, either from their own lands, or from the marketed surplus of non-combatants, who included some (though not, of course, all) monasteries. Either way, the intensification in agrarian production of the eighth century and early ninth may here have had a purpose.[12] A final observation is that wine, rather than grain, was more likely the agrarian market leader. The middle Seine to middle Rhine region is the furthest north that grapes can be grown in quantity, but wine is regularly referred to in literary sources as available in the lands to the north of this, both in Francia and in the nations beyond. This latter, at least, was inevitably the product of exchange, whether it was bought, or brought in rent to northern landowners, or the object of gift-exchange and international diplomacy. Vineyards in this northern area—unlike in southern Europe—are always specified with care in early medieval sources, and are also always subject to specific, often more intensive, agrarian régimes. They were always profitable, that is to say; and they may have become still more profitable when the major Carolingian political centre stabilised at Aachen, well to the north of the vine zone. The sale of wine may have substantially fuelled the eighth-century development of northern exchange, conceivably more than anything else.[13]

---

[12] See A. Boretius ed., *MGH Capitularia I* (Hanover, 1883), nn. 32 c. 64, 74 c. 8, 75, 77 c. 10, 171 (pp. 89, 167-71, 349-52); cf. F.L. Ganshof, *Frankish institutions under Charlemagne* (Providence, 1968), p. 67 ·ith a slightly different interpretation. I am grateful to Tim Reuter for discuss· .ıd references here. My comments in the text on grain apply equally to meat.

[13] Examples of vineyards specified with some care include, from our period, J.M. Pardessus ed., *Diplomata, chartae, epistolae, leges ad res Gallo-Francicas spectantia* (Paris,

The third and final point I want to make concerning the North returns to the question of the moment of change: the moment when the downturn in exchange at the end of the Roman world reversed itself in this area. It seems to me clear, from the articles in this book and from analogous work, that the shift occurred well before the eighth century. In the North, the systemic crisis came in the fifth and early sixth; in Francia, a slow reconstruction of networks of settlement and exchange seems to be under way by 550, and in England it must have begun by 600, even if at a much lower level. The point was made in our sixth-century volume, and it seems even clearer now. I argued then that one powerful reason for this was the wealth and coherence of the early Merovingian political and social system; the concentration of power represented by the Carolingian rulers and their major supporters was of course at least as great, despite certain major structural changes such as the end of the land tax. How eighth-century production, distribution and demand compared with that of the eleventh and twelfth centuries, an object of sharp debate,[14] cannot be dealt with here, but the two periods were certainly on the same side of the line: the Viking-period downturn (if indeed there was one), and the discontinuity in the routes of long-distance exchange represented by the end of the *emporia*, did not disturb a generally upwards trajectory, towards steadily greater medium-distance exchange and agrarian/artisanal specialisation, which would be features of the rest of the middle ages and indeed later.

2. *The western Mediterranean*

The first point to make about this zone, consisting of Spain, Mediterranean Gaul, Italy and North Africa, is that it resists easy synthesis in our period. It is regrettable that *force majeure* removed several of the contributors to this book in this section, for even local syntheses are hard to come by (although they do exist for Italy). The reason for this, too, is probably their difficulty. The continuing sev-

---

1843-49), nn. 350, 514, 586. See Devroey, *Etudes*, n. XI, pp. 577-81, and, very generically, R. Dion, *Histoire de la vigne et du vin en France des origines au XIXe siècle* (Paris, 1959), pp. 171-87.

[14] See for example the discussion in *Flaran* 10 (1988), pp. 182-94. For one regional analysis, see now Adriaan Verhulst's *summa* for Flanders, *The rise of cities in north-west Europe* (Cambridge, 1999).

enth-century presence of African Red Slip and amphorae on coastal sites, in particular (though not only) in substantial entrepôts such as Marseille, Rome and Naples, has attracted the attention of recent research, to the detriment of studies of eighth-century patterns. It must be added that after these diagnostic wares have gone, local wares are simply harder to date, as (among others) the south French C.A.T.H.M.A. collective have noted,[15] especially since the second half of the seventh century, by coincidence, also marks the end of furnished burials in Italy and Spain, which are another good dating tool. Nor is there a significant quantity of documentary material to make up for these archaeological difficulties, except in parts of Italy. I will begin, here, with thumbnail sketches of the situation in some of the western Mediterranean regions in the eighth century, in greater detail than was necessary for the North, before attempting to generalise. I will leave out North Africa, however, where research has barely begun to confront the regional situation after the end of its major Roman exports.

Let us begin with southern France, illuminated in this book by Simon Loseby's article on the decline of Marseille. Loseby makes it quite clear that the decline in international exchange in the western Mediterranean is a seventh-century phenomenon, and that soon after the start of the long eighth century, around 680, it had gone, taking with it all the evidence we have for the prosperity of Marseille. Loseby must be right to propose that the Rhône corridor itself was relatively unused in the eighth century; the alternative Alpine routes for the transport of luxuries would be made easier by the Frankish conquest of Lombard Italy in 773-4. But the period was not simply a nadir for international transactions; the eighth century also emerges from all recent urban excavations as the low point in recorded activity—to Marseille we can add Lyon and Geneva in the middle Rhône valley, where continuity of occupation is clear across our period, but rebuilding only begins again in the ninth.[16] This latter pattern may point to a steady weakening of regional exchange networks; such an

---

[15] C.A.T.H.M.A., "Importations des céramiques communes méditerranéennes dans le Midi de la Gaule (V^e-VIIe s.)", in *A cerâmica medieval no Mediterrâneo ocidental* (Mertola, 1991), pp. 27-47, at pp. 43-44.

[16] F. Villedieu, *Lyon St.-Jean. Les fouilles de l'avenue Adolphe Max* (Lyon, 1990), pp. 51-52, 114-16; C. Arlaud *et al.*, *Lyon St.-Jean. Les fouilles de l'îlot Tramassac* (Lyon, 1994), pp. 43-49; C. Bonnet, *Les fouilles de l'ancien groupe épiscopal de Genève* (Geneva, 1993), pp. 66-70.

interpretation would be supported by recent work on south French ceramics, from which we can see that, although there seems to be a continuing regional traffic in utilitarian *céramique kaolinitique*, finer wares by now have only microregional distributions, such as the painted ware of the small area around Lunel in the Hérault. The clearest rural study I have seen for southern France in our period, for Dassargues near Lunel, pinpoints the eighth century, once again, as the low point for exchange, with no ceramics found at all except *kaolinitiques*; the ninth century saw more diversification, however.[17]

The indicators for this region are univocal, then, in their pin-pointing of an eighth-century crisis. Why it took place is, however, less easy to say. The end of international commerce is on a different economic plane from the microregionality of local exchange just referred to. But why was the latter so weak? The south of France suffered war in the early eighth century; the combined effect of Charles Martel and the Spanish Arabs cannot have helped regional vitality. But at least some examples of large landowning did continue to structure parts of the region, as isolated wills make clear (Abbo in upper Provence and beyond in the 730s, Braiding in Nîmes in the 810s—as also the lands of the church of Marseille in the polyptych of the same decade; Leibulf in Arles in the 820s). Nor can we necessarily postulate urban or rural depopulation: Lyon and Dassargues tell us about relative economic inactivity, but in the framework of a continuity of habitat.[18] Something evidently switched off in the eighth-century Midi, but it is not yet clear what.

In Italy, there is a wider range of evidence, although it is equally evident that regional difference was acute. For the purposes of this quick review, I will only develop two instances of this, counterpos-

---

[17] See C.A.T.H.M.A., "Céramiques languedociennes du haut moyen âge (VI-XIe s.)", *Archéologie du Midi médiéval* 11 (1993), pp. 111-228, pp. 218-22 for *céramique kaolinitique*, 213-15 for Lunel. For an update on both, see C.A.T.H.M.A., "Céramiques languedociennes du haut moyen âge (VIIe-XIe s.)", in *La céramique médiévale en Méditerranée* (Aix-en-Provence, 1997), pp. 103-10. For Dassargues, see B. Garnier *et al.*, "De la ferme au village", *Archéologie du Midi médiéval* 13 (1995), pp. 1-78, at pp. 19-21, 46.

[18] See above, notes 16, 17; another example is A. Parodi *et al.*, "La Vaunage du IIIe siècle au milieu du XIIe siècle", *Archéologie du Midi médiéval* 5 (1987), pp. 3-59, e.g. pp. 8-9. For the documents, see, respectively, P. Geary, *Aristocracy in Provence* (Stuttgart, 1985); C. Vic and J. Vaissete, *Histoire générale du Languedoc* 2 (Toulouse, 1875), preuves, n. 22; B. Guérard, *Cartulaire de l'abbaye de Saint-Victor de Marseille* (Paris, 1857), pp. 613-56; J.H. Albanès, *Gallia Christiana novissima* 3 (Valence, 1901), nn. 195-96.

ing the Lombard kingdom of northern Italy and Tuscany on the one side and the papal territory of modern Lazio on the other. In this book we have Alessia Rovelli's numismatic guide to the intricacy of exchange in each zone; I will fill her analyses out with reference to other sorts of evidence.

The first point to make is that the Lombard kingdom shows a general trajectory of activity that parallels the south of France. The Po valley had never imported many African goods, and in the early seventh century had its own fine pottery, notably the stamped and shiny *ceramica longobarda* and some local glazed wares. Around 650, however, these cease to be found, and only localised common and coarse wares can be identified in the valley for the rest of the early middle ages. Much the same is true of Tuscany, although here the localised ceramic traditions continued to use higher quality fabrics, and these began to improve again in the mid-ninth century. Only on the Tuscan coast did some interregional exchange survive, with, for example, Campanian semi-fine wares identified in eighth- and ninth-century Pisa.[19] The early ninth century in northern Italy would see the rise of Venice, which might be interpreted as the natural successor to Marseille as an *emporium/*port of trade for eastern Mediterranean goods coming into the Frankish world; but, once again, the eighth century appears as a gap. The Po itself is attested in the eighth century as a shipping route, but it is significant that the major good referred to as an object of commercial exchange along it was salt—even in the Neolithic, salt must have been brought from the salt-marshes of the delta into the fertile north Italian hinterland, and if this is what ships were mostly carrying in our century then it indicates, not exchange, but the lack of it.[20]

The evidence from the Lombard kingdom points then, once again, to a fairly restricted role for exchange. But we do have more evidence than this from Italy than from southern France. For a start,

---

[19] G.P. Brogiolo and S. Gelichi, "La ceramica comune in Italia settentrionale tra IV e VII secolo", in L. Saguì ed., *Ceramica in Italia* (Florence, 1998), pp. 209-26; G.P. Brogiolo and S. Gelichi, "Ceramiche, tecnologia ed organizzazione della produzione nell'Italia settentrionale tra VI e X secolo", and R. Francovich and M. Valenti, "La ceramica d'uso comune in Toscana tra V-X secolo", in *La céramique médiévale*, pp. 139-45, 129-37; S. Bruni ed., *Pisa Piazza Dante* (Pisa, 1993), pp. 413-14.

[20] See the references in C. Wickham, *Early medieval Italy* (London, 1981), pp. 88-91, a survey with a slightly more upbeat tone, and the more detailed analysis of R. Balzaretti, "Cities, *emporia* and the monasteries", in N. Christie and S.T. Loseby eds., *Towns in transition* (Aldershot, 1996), pp. 213-34.

we have the coinage, as Rovelli shows, a bimetallic gold and silver system, pegged to Byzantine weights and fineness, which allowed for a certain complexity of exchange levels, lasting until the drastic and perhaps economically negative introduction of the silver *denarius* by the Franks in the 780s. Secondly, we have considerable evidence for urbanism in Italy, more indeed than in any part of Francia, thanks to excavations in a dozen cities, with eighth-century levels found in Milan, Verona, Brescia, Venice, Pisa, and several others. There has been an extensive debate about the nature of early medieval urbanism in Italy, which would be inappropriate to summarise here, but archaeologists and documentary historians tend now to concur on certain common grounds for understanding the survival of cities: they by now largely consisted of wooden buildings, perhaps on stone foundations, usually respecting classical squared street-plans, but allowing for considerable gaps between relative concentrations of settlement. Cities did nonetheless maintain a network of monumental stone and brick buildings, mostly churches, but including some public buildings and, at least sometimes, two-storeyed buildings for urban aristocrats. Although poor, they were evidently genuine demographic as well as political centres, and it must therefore be assumed that they were the focus of local artisanal production and both artisanal and agricultural exchange for their own territories, even if by now (or as yet) rarely outside them. Economic relationships, that is to say, can be supposed to have been relatively dense on the level of the diocese, although not necessarily beyond; this would fit both the survival of localised ceramics of reasonable quality, even when larger-scale productions or imports had ended, and our charter evidence, which tells us about the existence of urban trades and the beginnings of a rural land market. This pattern would also fit what we know of the Lombard aristocracy, which was urban-based but not generally hugely rich. Overall, we could propose that demand was urban, but not in this period sufficiently great or specialised to allow for the generation of new artisanal productions in large quantities, unlike in northern Francia, more rural though the latter undoubtedly was.[21]

Where there is more disagreement is over the date of the begin-

---

[21] The most up to date survey of cities is G.P. Brogiolo and S. Gelichi, *La città nell'alto medioevo italiano* (Bari, 1998). For the aristocracy, C. Wickham, "Aristocratic power in eighth-century Lombard Italy", in A.C. Murray ed., *After Rome's fall* (Toronto, 1998), pp. 153-70.

nings of the inversion of the slow downward trend of seventh-century exchange. I implied above that it was not until after 800 that one can see some increase in exchange complexity. It is important to recognise, though, that other people, such as Paolo Delogu, Gianpietro Brogiolo and Sauro Gelichi, put the date earlier. For Delogu, the critical date is 680, when a peace treaty between Lombards and Byzantines allowed the stabilisation and then development of exchange networks—hence, among other things, the numismatic complexity discussed by Rovelli. For Brogiolo and Gelichi, the mid-eighth century is perhaps a better moment, for it is from around then that we can identify a wave of prestige church buildings, with a resultant concentration and expansion of artisanal employment, which continued without a break thereafter.[22] Taking the framework of the Lombard kingdom as a whole, then, one must recognise that the patterns of production, distribution and demand are sufficiently complex that one cannot look for a single point at which economic indicators began to change. But the eighth century was clearly a period of relative localisation, of relative simplicity, in exchange; in this, Italy was very unlike northern Europe.

Rome was both similar to this and different. Here we are helped by the remarkable wealth of the Crypta Balbi excavation in the heart of the city, which gives us the best evidence in Italy for the period from the seventh century to the tenth, both in its quantity and in its continuity. It is clear as a result that Rome was largely dependent on North African imports of both fine wares and amphorae, up to the end of their production around 700; this picture is confirmed, at least as regards amphorae, from excavations at Ostia, and fits the close links between the papacy and other parts of the eastern Empire (including, up to the 690s, Africa) that is visible in the written sources from the seventh century. After 700, these links ended, as the Crypta shows; Rome, which had never developed a local fine pottery industry, had to make do with common wares, even if good quality ones, for at least half a century. But a complex coinage system continued until around 730, as Rovelli makes clear, and so did other artisanal activity. Rome was still by far the largest city in the West, after all,

---

[22] P. Delogu, "La fine del mondo antico e l'inizio del medioevo", in R. Francovich and G. Noyé eds., *La storia dell'alto medioevo italiano (VI-X secolo) alla luce dell'archeologia* (Florence, 1994), pp. 7-29, at pp. 17-23; Brogiolo and Gelichi, *La città*, pp. 43, 108, 159-60.

with a population of perhaps 25,000, and its internal demand must have been sufficient to sustain unusually high levels of exchange. This gives a context for the local development of Forum ware, a heavy-glazed fine ware, around the middle of the century, probably on Constantinopolitan models. This ceramic type, by far the most elaborate produced anywhere in the western Mediterranean in the eighth century, developed steadily: by the late ninth century it was being exported and imitated in central Italy and along the Tyrrhenian coast, as far as Provence.[23] Rome thus had an early eighth-century low-point, along the lines of the experience of northern Italy, and its exchange networks became more local as a result, something that is also reflected in what we know of papal landowning, which became focused above all on Lazio in the second third of the century. All the same, Rome's international links, like those of the rest of Byzantine Italy, had continued far longer than those in the Lombard North, and the city's productive revival had begun by the late eighth century, far earlier than anywhere else in the peninsula. Even Rome's low point was not a moment of inactivity; church-building and thus artisanal patronage continued throughout the early middle ages without a break, as Robert Coates-Stephens has shown, thus making possible the remarkable flowering of elaborately-decorated churches and (as we see in recent excavations) urban housing surviving from the century after 770, the density of which has little parallel anywhere in the Latin West in the same period.[24] In Rome, the early eighth-century involution in production and distribution stabilised at a rather higher level than anywhere else in the western Mediterranean; this testifies to the continuing economic infrastructure entailed by the continuing existence of a substantial urban population, as well as to the

---

[23] For the Crypta, see the articles of L. Saguì and M. Ricci in Saguì, *Ceramica in Italia*, pp. 305-30, 351-82 (and B. Ciarrocchi *et al.*, pp. 383-420, at pp. 390-91, for the Ostia parallel) for the seventh century; for the eighth, M.T. Cipriano *et al.*, "La documentazione ceramica dell'Italia centro-meridionale nell'alto medioevo", in *A cerâmica*, pp. 99-122; L. Saguì *et al.*, "Nuovi dati ceramologici per la storia economica di Roma tra VII e VIII secolo", in *La céramique médiévale*, pp. 35-48, at pp. 42-46; L. Paroli and D. Romei in L. Paroli ed., *La ceramica invetriata tardoantica e altomedievale in Italia* (Florence, 1992), pp. 43-53, 351-93, for Forum ware and its context.

[24] R. Coates-Stephens, "Dark age architecture in Rome", *Papers of the British School at Rome* 65 (1997), pp. 177-232; see further R. Krautheimer, *Rome: Profile of a city 312-1308* (Princeton, 1980), pp. 89-142; B. Ward-Perkins, *From classical antiquity to the middle ages* (Oxford, 1984), pp. 61-65. For urban housing, see R. Santangeli Valenzani, "Edilizia residenziale e aristocrazia urbana a Roma nell'altomedioevo", in S. Gelichi ed., *I Congresso nazionale di archeologia medievale* (Florence, 1997), pp. 64-70.

collective wealth of the city aristocracy, and, above all, of the popes.

There is not space to continue this characterisation of Italian regions. It is worth noting, though, that the Roman picture of relative continuity of more localised production and exchange in the eighth century is matched in other Byzantine cities of the South, notably Naples.[25] Unlike in Marseille, the final demise of the late Roman exchange system did not lead to the end of archaeologically-attested activity in these centres; here, the urban survival that is a feature of Italy as a whole involved considerable artisanal activity. This may be because continuing political links with the eastern Empire carried with them some exchange activity (as would certainly be true, after all, for the ninth century, as the Campanian cities and Venice both show); it may also be that urban élites remained relatively rich in the South, though this we cannot test, for the documentary record is absent. Conversely, however, as in Rome, if there is a low point in exchange for these cities, it remains the eighth century.

Spain, at least in parts, presents a bleaker picture. Of course, the eighth century was once again a difficult period for Spanish political history, with the destruction of the Visigothic kingdom in 711, followed by more than a generation of instability, only partially reversed under the Umayyads at the end of the century, whose geographical remit was as yet relatively restricted. But in archaeological terms, Spain presents similar long-term trends to France and Italy: the sixth and seventh centuries already show a steady regionalisation of production and exchange, and in the eighth century this only intensified. Here, the African-focused exchange systems had never got much farther than the Mediterranean coast and the Guadalquivir valley, and were already in fast decline at the start of the seventh century. Inland, the fine-ware systems of *terra sigillata hispánica tardía* were becoming more regionalised and losing their fineness already in the sixth century. Everywhere in Spain that has been seriously studied shows a network of localised exchange systems, with very little linkage between them, already before the Arab conquests.[26]

---

[25] P. Arthur, "Early medieval amphorae, the duchy of Naples and the food supply of Rome", *Papers of the British School at Rome* 61 (1993), pp. 231-44; P. Arthur ed., *Il complesso archeologico di Carminiello ai Mannesi, Napoli* (Lecce, 1994), pp. 219-20; P. Arthur and H. Patterson, "Ceramics and early medieval central and southern Italy", in Francovich and Noyé, *La storia*, pp. 409-41, at. p. 421.

[26] See as a survey S. Gutiérrez Lloret, "Eastern Spain in the sixth century in the light of archaeology", in Hodges and Bowden, *The sixth century*, pp. 161-84; for

Once this has been said, however, one must make distinctions. These local systems were not all alike in the eighth century. With some schematism, we might distinguish between three types. In the first, there was a radical destructuring of exchange and of all settlement hierarchy, with a reversion to slow-wheel and hand-made pottery, indicating a breakdown of markets and a notable deprofessionalisation of the local artisanal tradition, in ways that resemble post-Roman Britain rather than the Mediterranean. One example of this is the region of Murcia-Alicante (Tudmīr in the eighth century), object of the most sophisticated early medieval regional study yet available for Spain, by Sonia Gutiérrez, an area, furthermore, of unusual urban discontinuity; another is the region around Motril south of Granada. Both of these were coastal regions somewhat cut off from major eighth-century power centres; their destructuration may be a feature of further up the coast as well, in parts of Catalonia.[27] In other areas, as a second type, we find a situation more similar to much of southern France, with an array of very local but still good-quality "common" wares in a late Roman provincial tradition: much of the inland plateau, the Meseta, is like this, for example.[28] Finally, in a few instances of a third type, local ceramics of a somewhat higher quality can be found, with at least semi-fine wares surviving through the eighth century: the recent Morería excavations at Mérida are one example, the Cercadilla site at Córdoba is another (though there the levels seem to begin around 780); Montefrío near Granada may be a third. All three of these sites belong to the network of southern cities that lay at the core of early Umayyad power. In each case, too, the later development of new, more "Islamic", glazed finewares was already under way by the later ninth century,

---

inland *terra sigillata*, L. Caballero, "Cerámicas de "epoca visigoda y postvisigoda" de las provincias de Cáceres, Madrid y Segovia", *Boletín de arqueología medieval* 3 (1989), pp. 75-107, whom I thank for useful discussions and bibliography.

[27] S. Gutiérrez Lloret, *La cora de Tudmīr de la Antigüedad tardía al mundo islámico* (Madrid, 1996); A. Gomez Becerra, "El poblamiento altomedieval en la costa de Granada", *Studia historica. Historia medieval* 13 (1995), pp. 59-92; a Catalan example is the highly localised ceramics recently analysed for the eighth-century type-site of El Bovalar in M.A. Cau *et al.*, "Algunas consideraciones sobre cerámicas de cocina de los siglos IV al VIII", *Quaderns científics i tècnics* 9 (1997), pp. 7-36, at pp. 14-15. Another instance is probably the (less geographically marginal) upper Guadalquivir valley, for which see J.C. Castillo Armenteros, *La Campiña de Jaén en época emiral (s. VIII-X)* (Jaén, 1998).

[28] Pers. comm. Lauro Olmo and Manuel Retuerce.

as it also was in the type-site for early Spanish glaze, Pechina near Almería—by contrast, the areas characterised by the first and second types began to import or imitate glazes rather later, if at all.[29]

This typology is a fairly rough one, and it is as yet unclear whether some zones fit into the first or the second category, for example. But it does seem possible to distinguish at least the blurred outlines of three alternative local developments in eighth-century Spain: a set of microregions with a major breakdown in settlement hierarchy, productive hierarchy, and thus (presumably) social differentiation; a set of microregions where considerable localisation and simplification had taken place, at the expense (probably) of urban continuity, but in a framework of a continuity of the basic patterns of rural society; and a set of city territories where more articulated hierarchies persisted. If the second has apparent parallels in southern France, the third has more parallels in Italy. This overall level of localisation, however, is rather greater than that found in most of Italy in our period; and the destructuration in the first set has few parallels in the Mediterranean at all. It is striking that such a localised economy seems to have begun to develop while the last Visigothic kings were vigorously legislating in Toledo; small wonder that their legal rhetoric sometimes sounds rather shrill.

How can we generalise from this dauntingly diverse set of western Mediterranean examples? One point that must be repeated is that the eighth century looks particularly localised in this area because it is the first century in which the international network of African exports can no longer be found on sites. But it is also the case that, even setting aside African fine wares and amphorae, the eighth century is a period of increased localisation of regional productions: indeed, this localisation was presumably already a major context for

---

[29] For the Morería, pers. comm. Santiago Feijoo; for Cercadilla, M. del C. Fuertes Santos and M. González Virseda, "Avance al estudio tipológico de la cerámica medieval del yacimiento de Cercadilla, Córdoba", in *IV Congreso de arqueología medieval espanola. Actas* 3 (Alicante, 1993), pp. 771-78 – cf. for a critical framing, and later references, P.C. Scales, "Cordoba under the Umayyads", in G. De Boe and F. Verhaeghe eds., *Urbanism in medieval Europe* 1 (Zellik, 1997), pp. 175-82, a reference I owe to Ann Christys; for Montefrío, E. Motos Guirao, "La cerámica altomedieval de «El Castillon»", in A. Malpica Cuello ed., *La cerámica altomedieval en el sur de al-Andalus* (Granada, 1993), pp. 209-37; for Pechina, F. Castillo Galdeano and R. Martínez Madrid, "Producciones cerámicas en Baŷŷāna", in *La cerámica altomedieval*, pp. 67-116 – cf. M. Acién Almansa *et al.*, "Excavación de un barrio artesanal de Baŷŷāna", *Archéologie islamique* 1 (1990), pp. 147-68.

the fact that African exports became steadily less widely available in the seventh century, even on coasts, and eventually ceased. This development had already begun in the sixth century; in the eighth, it was as complete as it would ever be. But of course the completeness of the breakdown of regional and local exchange patterns would vary very considerably from place to place—there was space, indeed, for a huge array of variations between Alicante and Rome. I have been implying that one basic cause of such differentiation was the scale of landowning, and thus the concentration of wealth, in each microregion. This cannot be demonstrated in more than a minority of cases, but it does fit, for example, northern Italy, and arguably also the Meseta,[30] even if not, perhaps, southern France. More work on regional analyses, however, is needed before we can get much further; furthermore, the varying articulations between urbanism, ceramic systems, landowning patterns, and the economic structure of the state need to be explored in rather more detail than they have been hitherto. I will return to the problem at the end of the conclusion. But the existence of such regional differences can, at least, scarcely be doubted: this is an important first step.

The final point to be made here is a question that must remain open: why, given this often microscopic level of localisation, the same century recurs so regularly as the nadir for exchange. It may be that this regularity is often misleading: circa 700 is the externally-imposed date when African wares disappear, and an eventual reversal of the localisation of exchange occurs across a much less regular time-span—already before 800 in some places (Rome), and not until 950 or later in others. Anyway, as already noted, the whole of the eighth century is seen by many Italian scholars as at least a practice-ground for future developments. But it is nonetheless notable that the eighth century is a period of relative inactivity everywhere in the western Mediterranean; there is nowhere that remotely matches the internally generated exchange of the Rhineland in the same period. At least we can say that the dialectic between political, proprietorial, and commercial expansion that was a feature of eighth-century development in northern Francia was absent further south. Why this was, will, however, have to await future research.

---

[30] I derive this tentative conclusion from the geographical distributions documented in the slate archive of Diego Álvaro (province of Ávila), for which see I. Velázquez Soriano, *La pizarras visigodas* (Murcia, 1988).

3. *The eastern Mediterranean*

In this third sector, it is less necessary to provide regional synthesis, for John Haldon and Alan Walmsley's articles do just that. One should add that they break new ground, for no syntheses of the Byzantine lands and of Syria-Palestine of comparable scope existed for our period before them. The two present instructive contrasts, however. Both Byzantium and the Arab Caliphate can be seen as lineal heirs of the eastern Roman empire, using much of the basic Roman public infrastructure, especially the tax system; but they developed this infrastructure in steadily divergent ways, and their material prosperity was in our period very different.

The reasons for this contrast can easily be set out. It was of course Byzantium that experienced the most direct development from the eastern Empire; it kept the capital, at Constantinople, and the central governmental bureaucracy, and a dense network of Roman cultural patterns, social practices and attitudes to legitimacy. But the Arab conquest had deprived it of two thirds of its territory and perhaps three quarters of its revenue, even though continued military danger required Byzantium to keep up spending on its major outlay, the army. The emperors were forced back on some of their poorest territories, the Anatolian plateau and parts of the limestone lands of Greece, and even these were under regular threat for a century and a half. Only the Aegean and Marmara coasts were zones of genuine agrarian prosperity, together with two more distant territories, Sicily and the Crimea, both of which remained under Byzantine control throughout the eighth century. Under these circumstances, as Haldon describes, something had to give, and this was the provincial aristocracies and the exchange networks they had generated: production and distribution were dominated in our period by fiscal needs, and commercial demand came a distant second. Out of the regions analysed here, by far the clearest example of a fiscally-driven economy in our period is the Byzantine empire: the only other region of the former Roman world with analogous structures was Egypt, not discussed in this volume. Only in a few places were there active exchange systems at a more local level, notably Constantinople and its Marmara hinterland, where relatively high levels of urban demand, from a city substantially larger than Rome (in the debates about Constantinopolitan size in this period, 40,000 is presented as a pessimistic estimate), allowed for the development of an elaborate ceramics industry, available over a substantial region, as well as, probably, some continuing local agrarian specialisations.[31] These patterns have not yet been matched in the hinterlands of other surviving cities like Thessaloniki and Izmir, however; the Izmir region, indeed, saw the abrupt end of its major ceramic export, Phocaean Red Slip, already in the late seventh century.

The Arab lands were considerably more buoyant. They were anyway richer: Syria, Palestine and Egypt all had prosperous agricultural specialisations and wide-ranging artisanal traditions. It has also been forcefully argued, by Hugh Kennedy and others, that the Umayyad fiscal system was rather more decentralised than the Roman system had been (and than the Byzantine one still was).[32] Tax revenues, which from Egypt in particular were huge, largely stayed in the provinces they had been drawn from; the long-distance, state-backed transportation of agricultural products (Egyptian grain, Palestinian wine, and so on) that had underpinned much Mediterranean prosperity up to the seventh century in the East (as also up to the fifth century in the West) largely ceased. The active exchange that Walmsley describes was thus rather more separated from the needs of the state than was the case in Byzantium, or than had been the case in the sixth century. The tax system of course made some people extremely rich, notably the Caliph in Damascus and his entourage, but also, extending more widely, all the Arabs registered on the military lists (*dīwāns*), who were settled in most Syrian and Palestinian cities, especially local capitals like Aleppo and Tiberias/Tabariya and al-Ramla. This will have helped the maintenance of demand, as much as or more than the distribution of large landowning, which had never been as extensive in the East as in the West, and may well have lessened after the Arab conquest (apart, that is to say, from the vast lands of the Umayyads themselves). But it is clear from the strikingly prosperous urban archaeology of Syria and Palestine, clearly summarised here by Walmsley, that in these areas a local commercial infrastructure, and demand for artisanal goods, was maintained, with little change

---

[31] For Constantinople's population, see the contrasting arguments of C. Mango, *Le développement urbain de Constantinople (IVᵉ-VIIᵉ siècles)* (Paris, 1990), pp. 54-55, and P. Magdalino, *Constantinople médiévale* (Paris, 1996), pp. 17-18. For urban exchange networks, see J.W. Hayes, *Excavations at Saraçhane in Istanbul* 2 (Princeton, 1992), e.g. pp. 15-18, 53-57.

[32] The fullest version of this argument is in H. Kennedy, "The financing of the military in the early Islamic state", in A. Cameron ed., *The Byzantine and early Islamic Near East* 3 (Princeton, 1995), pp. 361-78.

in level from the Roman period. There is argument in the recent literature about whether the prosperity of the Umayyad period really did match that of the fifth and early sixth centuries, which tend generally to be recognised as a peak of economic activity in all the eastern Roman provinces.[33] But it would be hard to dispute that, in the eighth century, nowhere in Europe could match the levels of capillary artisanal production already found in a dozen and more cities of the Levant, and a considerable number of rural sites as well. Levels of demand evidently remained high. One can legitimately suppose a survival of rich urban élites that was greater in Syria and Palestine (and Egypt) than in any other part of the former Roman empire, outside a handful of great political/demographic foci such as Constantinople and Rome. This anyway fits the maintenance of urban building activity into the eighth century in every city of the area that has been studied, except Antioch and Apamea in northern Syria.[34] In many cases, as Walmsley shows, this also continued well past 749-50—the traditional date for Syrian decline, thanks to at least one major earthquake and the 'Abbāsid move to Iraq.

In one respect, however, the Syrian-Palestinian experience matches that of Byzantium, and indeed that of Latin Europe: in the breakdown of large-scale interregional exchange. Red Slip finewares from Phocaea, Cyprus and even Africa could be found all over the Levant in, say, 600; conversely, Palestinian wine amphorae and north Syrian (probably) oil amphorae could be found over much of the rest of the Mediterranean. In inland Palestine and Syria, the main coastal amphora types (LRA 1, 4, 5) had much less of a distribution—they were clearly designed for export, that is to say, and in Jerusalem or the Decapolis more local amphorae tend to be found.[35] But the network of long-distance exchange spread inland as far as the desert,

---

[33] A contrary view in, for example, P.-L. Gatier, "Villages du Proche-Orient protobyzantin (4ème-7ème s.)", in G.R.D. King and A. Cameron eds., *The Byzantine and early Islamic Near East* 2 (Princeton, 1994), pp. 17-48. Earlier, catastrophist, views of the Umayyad period are not worth citing, for they were based on inadequate ceramic knowledge; a late and extremist version of that paradigm is C. Dauphin, *La Palestine byzantine*, BAR International Series 726 (Oxford, 1998), pp. 351-72, 518-25.

[34] See for a survey C. Foss, "Syria in transition, A.D. 550-750: an archaeological approach", *Dumbarton Oaks papers* 51 (1997), pp. 189-269, at pp. 190-226.

[35] J. Magness, *Jerusalem ceramic chronology, circa 200-800 C.E.* (Sheffield, 1993), pp. 160-61, 181-83; P. Watson, "Change in foreign and regional economic links with Pella in the 7th century A.D.: the ceramic evidence", in P. Canivet and J.-P. Rey-Coquais eds., *La Syrie de Byzance à l'Islam, VIIe-VIIIe siècles* (Damascus, 1992), pp. 233-48, at pp. 238-39.

as Red Slip distributions show. In our century, this pattern had gone, and, instead, we find relatively localised ceramic systems, in the middle Euphrates valley, in the Decapolis, in the Balqa', around Jerusalem, or around 'Aqaba, with much less interconnection. This has some similarities with the local economies of the western Mediterranean. It could be proposed that, with the shift in the Umayyad period away from fiscal centralisation, these relatively local exchange systems represented the geographical scale of the concentrations of private wealth that did survive; it is significant that interregional ceramics reappeared with the recentralisation of the 'Abbāsid fiscal system. Although, of course, this relatively local geographical scale did not lessen the notable complexity and sophistication of all kinds of artisanal production—Umayyad élites may have been more regionalised, but they were not poorer—nonetheless, the eighth century again appears as a moment when wider relationships were at a low point. Areas which had traditionally been particularly orientated to export must surely have gone into decline. This is what Tchalenko argued for northern Syria, and some of his main points still stand despite twenty years of well-aimed critique;[36] another area that would have been particularly exposed was the specialist wine-growing area around Gaza (here, unfortunately but unsurprisingly, archaeology has been less active). The best equipped microregions for continued prosperity would have been those with less involvement with long-distance exchange, as presumably in the Decapolis. In the long run, the eighth century was not the economic low point for Syria and Palestine; unlike any other region studied in this book, they were on the ancient side of the ancient-medieval divide. (Exactly when the economic divide actually was, and what it meant at all in this region, remains obscure and contested, however.) But the Levant in our century nonetheless has some formal parallels with all the other regions of the Mediterranean: here, too, the eighth century was the first century that post-dated the end of the long-distance maritime exchange systems that had been perfected in the late Roman world.

---

[36] G. Tchalenko, *Villages antiques de la Syrie du Nord* I (Paris, 1953), esp. pp. 422-38; the major critique is in G. Tate, *Les campagnes de la Syrie du Nord du IIe au VIIe siècle* 1 (Paris, 1992), esp. pp. 335-50.

4. *Conclusion*

Unlike many of my friends and colleagues, I have never been a fan of Henri Pirenne; but it has to be recognised that some of the patterns discussed in this book were, at least partially, foreseen by him three-quarters of a century ago. Pirenne's stress on the "closing of the Mediterranean" was based on an analysis of luxury commodities, which was successfully contested on an empirical level already in the 1950s, and which anyway made no economic sense even at the time, for luxuries are by definition marginal to economic systems when seen as a whole. Furthermore, he supposed that the North Sea economic revival postdated the year 1000, a position that recent research largely undermines; and, of course, Pirenne wanted to argue for an economic dominance of the Seine-Rhine area that had already become complete in the central middle ages, in a destiny which underpinned and justified the economic, political and cultural hegemonies of the late nineteenth century—a Grand Narrative that can no longer convince, and that anyway could only work at all if twelfth- and thirteenth-century Italy was set aside. All the same, it is striking that the archaeology of the last few decades invites us to reinstate one of the major planks of Pirenne's theory, the substantial cutback in Mediterranean-wide exchange around 700, and this time to give it greater analytical weight, for the end of Red Slip exchange is a guide to the fate of bulk artisanal production and distribution (textiles, iron, wood), and the end of Mediterranean-wide amphora distributions is a guide to the fate of the long-distance transportation of foodstuffs—these two being truer markers of exchange systems than are luxuries.

It is therefore not surprising that Simon Loseby began with Pirenne in this volume, for Marseille was a crucial element in the latter's argument, as the link between the Mediterranean and the Frankish heartland: the breaking of that link can still be described much as Pirenne proposed. We cannot any longer attribute this break to the Arabs, as Richard Hodges and David Whitehouse already saw fifteen years ago in the first, and most influential, "return to Pirenne" among the archaeologists.[37] All the same, the close relationship between

---

[37] R. Hodges and D. Whitehouse, *Mohammed, Charlemagne and the origins of Europe* (London, 1983); note now the French translation, *Mahomet, Charlemagne et les origines*

long-distance exchange and the fiscal coherence of the late Roman
state does at least mean that the Arabs belong with the Vandals as
the most effective forces that undermined the pan-Mediterranean
political and thus, eventually, economic system. In the western
Mediterranean, the seventh century was already a period of localisation, and the Arabs had little effect on the decline of Marseille;
in the East, though, they broke the fiscal link between Carthage,
Alexandria and Antioch on the one hand and Constantinople on
the other, and this had a notable effect on the localisation of exchange
systems, producing, for that matter, different forms of crisis in each
of these four great centres, even if not in their hinterlands.

That said, we still have to go further to explain the differences
between our three major economic zones. In particular, we must
avoid the sort of rhetoric of catastrophe that sometimes gets attached
to the western Mediterranean in our period, not only because it
tends to be more effective as rhetoric than as real analysis, but also
because it is a serious obstacle to an understanding of how the
localised economies of that zone would revive in the next centuries
to such an extent that Italy had become largely hegemonic over the
international exchange of both the other two zones by 1200. It is
perhaps best to see the economic patterns of all three zones as the
product of sets of local variables, which themselves were fairly regular
across Europe and the Mediterranean. Let us conclude with an
attempt to do so.

One of these variables, and the most important, was the concentration of agrarian wealth. It can be argued that one of the ground-
rules of pre-capitalist agriculture is that peasants tend to dominate
the patterns of production, and that aristocrats dominate the patterns and intensity of exchange (including that of all artisanal products except at the most simple village level). In a society with more
rich people, there is more exchange, and if these rich people have
interregional links there is more interregional exchange. It is useful
to distinguish between the scale of private landowning and the scale
and coherence of fiscal systems (i.e. between rent and tax) when
looking at concentrations of wealth, for rent and tax do not always
go to the same people; furthermore, most fiscal systems operate on
a rather larger geographical scale than most landowning. It is also

---

de l'Europe (Paris, 1996), updated and with errors corrected; see further Panella,
"Merci e scambi", pp. 679-80.

useful to investigate the extent of urbanism in any given society, because cities could be collective concentrations of wealth, acting as centres of demand that integrated their territories, even if individual urban landowners were not particularly rich. Cities are the best, but not the only, guide to systemic coherence, that led to other forms of interdependence, some of which deserve recognition as independent variables: most notably the extent of local regional specialisations. These specialisations might be in artisanal products, or else in agricultural products—wine, oil, grain, timber, sheep, salt, and so on. These were almost never monocultures in the ancient or medieval worlds, for peasantries almost always had a subsistence base as well, but they could be specialisations at least in the surplus that peasants transferred to landlords or the state. One of the main markers of a coherent and articulated exchange system is indeed the extent to which different sets of producers are reliant on each other, whether intraregionally or, eventually, interregionally, for their basic needs, as with the late Roman dominance of (among others) Africa and Phocaea over fine pottery, or the thirteenth-century dominance of (among others) England and the Iberian peninsula over wool production. We must ask who needed these specialised products, and how badly. In times of economic decline, the degree to which regions had previously become dependent on interregional systems is a relevant variable as well.

With these variables in mind, let us look at our three zones again. The North shows the widest geographical scale of exchange in the eighth century; this much is clear. It has to be recognised that Badorf ware, say, was a relatively simple ceramic product, and would have looked rustic, hardly "fine" at all, if set beside Fine Byzantine (or Palestinian Fine Table) ware, Constantinopolitan Glazed White ware, or indeed Forum ware. But it was available over a much wider regional and interregional territory than any of these in our period, quite densely in the middle and lower Rhineland and much of the Low Countries (itself a substantial geographical area), and then to a lesser degree across the North Sea zone as a whole. This range was linked above all to the scale of aristocratic (and ecclesiastical, and royal) landowning, which in this area seems to be the most significant of the set of variables just characterised. Of the others, the fiscal system barely existed as an independent economic structure under the Carolingians. (I mentioned the army earlier as a source of demand, and its link to Carolingian public power is obvious, but its supply lines seem to have been private.) Nor did urbanism, although there certainly were some active urban centres, as Verhulst shows in this book. Northern Europe is also relatively ecologically homogeneous; the only important agrarian export was as yet wine, for major timber or pastoral specialisations still lay in the future; there were few examples of real interregional interdependence (although there were some: Frisia had to buy timber and possibly grain from the Franks, for example). The network of really rich aristocrats, bishops, abbots, and kings was thus the main network that underpinned the active exchange up and down the rivers of the north Frankish lands. And, as a collectivity of wealth and prestige, it dominated further afield too, in England and Denmark (themselves containing rather simpler political and economic systems), and beyond, into regions not studied in this book, the rest of Scandinavia and the west Slav lands: the density of exchange was obviously less outside the Frankish political frontier, but, taken as a whole, it was a far wider and more elaborate exchange network than anything known in the eighth-century Mediterranean, except at the narrowest luxury level.

The eastern Mediterranean shows a different sort of structure for exchange: more geographically restricted, but denser. The interregional exchange of the Roman empire had by now gone, a couple of generations after the breach of the east Roman fiscal system by the Persian and Arab conquests. It was replaced by a network of more limited exchange areas, which had for the most part formerly coexisted with Mediterranean fiscal-supported exchange, but were now all that was left. Two of these were substantial, the region around Constantinople and the Nile valley, the latter of which had always been a relatively independent and homogeneous region, and remained so, even continuing Red Slip pottery production, several centuries after it had vanished elsewhere.[38] In Syria and Palestine, however, and still more in the non-metropolitan Byzantine lands, the main exchange areas were rather smaller, groups of city territories at most and sometimes less. Nonetheless, the sophistication of production and the complexity of exchange often remained extremely

---

[38] The best recent account is D.M. Bailey, *Excavations at El-Ashmunein* 5 (London, 1998), esp. pp. 8-58, with earlier bibliography; see, among the latter, esp. G. Pierrat, "Essai de classification de la céramique de Tôd de la fin du VIIe siècle au début du XIIIe siècle ap. J.-C.", *Cahiers de la céramique égyptienne* 2 (1991), pp. 145-204. See further C. Vogt, "Les céramiques omeyyades et abbassides d'Istabl'Antar-Fostat", in *La céramique médiévale*, pp. 243-60.

high, particularly in the Arab lands. Here, more variables were at play than in the North. The geographical scale of landowning, never as great as in parts of the West, remained restricted to relatively small regions or city territories. In some parts of the East, notably in the non-metropolitan Byzantine lands, the wealth of individual landowning families or institutions may well have decreased, and the aggregation of such families in cities certainly lessened as Byzantine urbanism declined. In Syria and Palestine, however, cities tended to survive at something close to Roman levels of activity until 750 or indeed later, and private landowning presumably did as well. In Byzantium, the slack was taken up by the state; the documentation for exchange activities privileges fiscal logistics and state patronage, much more than it does in Umayyad Syria and Palestine apart from the great caliphal building projects (which were, nonetheless, numerous). Byzantine archaeology is relatively underdeveloped, but it has to be said that the ceramic record, very localised except around the great demand focus of Constantinople, does not show that fiscal activity maintained artisanal production at a particularly high level. All the same, if it were not for the state, some of the more provincial parts of Byzantium might have undergone the systemic meltdown found in parts of Spain, as the hand-made pottery found in Greece implies. It must finally be noted in this tracking of variables that the eastern Mediterranean is much more ecologically differentiated than northern Europe, allowing for—sometimes forcing—regional specialisations in wine, olive oil, stock-rearing, or irrigated market gardening. The overall regionalisation of the eighth century may be the ultimate cause of actual land abandonments, where marginal lands had been developed for the exchange needs of earlier centuries, as in the limestone hills of northern Syria or the Negev hinterland of Gaza. Even when this did not occur, the sharp differences between plateaux and plains will either have encouraged continued interregional exchange or caused brusque local reorientations of productive emphasis. I am being unspecific here, for we do not have the evidence for it as yet, least of all in the case of the most obvious example, the borders of the high and extreme inland plateau of Anatolia. The issue will be an interesting one to test in the future.

In the western Mediterranean, we find a situation more like Byzantium, but without the state. Private landowning wealth was more restricted, as it seems, than in northern Francia; urbanism declined; there is little trace of regional specialisation. We must draw

distinctions here too, for in Italy urban continuity, even if at a
restricted material level, can be posited for much of the peninsula,
whereas in France or Spain the evidence for this is, as it seems,
more discontinuous. This relative concentration of wealth in cities
in Italy, added to a well-documented continued domination by those
cities over their territories, allowed for the maintenance of a network of small-scale integrated nuclei of exchange that could develop
quite fast, and did after 1000 or so. The first to do it, Rome, actually began in our period; but Rome was unusually large, and others
would follow only later. In the western Mediterranean, then, as in
the North, the scale of landed wealth was the most important
variable with, here, the strength or weakness of urbanism as a contributory factor. It is worth recalling that this zone was famous in
the late empire for the huge wealth of its (senatorial) élites, who
owned in some cases across the entire western Mediterranean basin.
The fragmentation of the zone between several different post-Roman
successor states must have been a major cause of the decline of these
élites, and thus of the exchange dependent on them. It is, furthermore, likely that the western Mediterranean as a whole was more
dependent for its late Roman prosperity on the fiscal links between
its northern and southern shores than either of the other two zones
had been, thus causing generalised economic crisis in parts of Italy,
and, most radically, in Mediterranean Spain and North Africa, when
that fiscal coherence broke down. Revival, when it came, had to
begin from very small units indeed.

*   *   *

The eighth century is an interesting period, precisely because it is
so fragmented. Despite the existence of three very large political systems, the Frankish, Byzantine and Arab empires, in economic terms
it was polycentric, without many foci that were dominant over wide
peripheries at all—perhaps only one, the Frankish heartland, and
that had relatively little influence in the South. We have to look at
regional economic realities first, with interregional relations a distant
second. In recent years, thanks mostly to archaeology, it has become
possible to do this, and we will steadily get ever clearer a picture of
such regions. But it is worth finishing by pointing out that it is these
regional realities that also mark the future. The reversal of the economic involution that marked the sixth century could only take place

when each region stabilised as an inward-looking unit; that is to say, when it ceased to attempt to maintain the external links of a past age, and developed internally instead, with new external relationships evolving out of that, rather than being imposed from the outside. This was happening in the North by 600; in the western Mediterranean, where the Roman infrastructure had lasted longer, the eighth century was the earliest it occurred, and the date was often later. Only in the eastern Mediterranean did the firm survival of states and fiscal systems make the parameters for these changes more complex; but 800 is as good a date as any for the start of Byzantine economic revival too. In the eighth century, with the triumph of these localised economies, we can see the regional roots of the renewed prosperity of the eleventh and twelfth centuries. It is instructive to realise that much of the economy of the Italian mercantile cities of that era, notwithstanding their extensive use of antique imagery as a legitimating device, had more recent roots than did that of the Rhineland or the Hansa. But, as already implied, it is important to remember that even the most extreme examples of economic localisation in the early middle ages were almost never terminal.

INDEX